DUE

THE RUSSIAN PUSH TOWARD JAPAN

THE RUSSIAN PUSH
TOWARD JAPAN

Russo-Japanese Relations, 1697·1875

BY *GEORGE ALEXANDER LENSEN*

PROFESSOR OF HISTORY
THE FLORIDA STATE UNIVERSITY

1971

OCTAGON BOOKS
New York

Reprinted 1971
by special arrangement with George Alexander Lensen

OCTAGON BOOKS
A Division of Farrar, Straus & Giroux, Inc.
19 Union Square West
New York, N. Y. 10003

Library of Congress Catalog Card Number: 75-120640

ISBN-0-374-94936-0

Printed in U.S.A. by
NOBLE OFFSET PRINTERS, INC.
NEW YORK 3, N. Y.

TO

HUGH BORTON

WHOSE WISDOM AND PATIENCE

HAVE BEEN A FOUNTAIN

OF INSPIRATION

PREFACE AND ACKNOWLEDGMENTS

THE history of the Far East in the twentieth century has been conditioned to a considerable degree by the struggle of Russia and Japan for the mastery of Northeast Asia. This Russo-Japanese struggle has often caused bitter rivalry and warfare between the two powers, but from time to time attempts have also been made to eliminate this hostility by a merger of military resources and to advance Russian and Japanese ambitions in the Far East by mutual aid. In our own day studies of the Russo-Japanese War, of the fishery disputes, the Siberian intervention, the frontier clashes of the 1930's, and of the political and territorial differences in the years since World War II, have left the impression of an "historical enmity" between Russia and Japan. Yet in the years between 1905 and 1917 the two countries allied their efforts, and there were men in Japan who wished to do so again on the very eve of the Soviet Union's entry into the Pacific phase of the Second World War. As late as June, 1945—only two months before Russia plunged into the Far Eastern holocaust—a former prime minister of Japan and one-time ambassador to Moscow told the Soviet ambassador that "if the Soviet Army and the Japanese Navy were to join forces, Japan and the Soviet Union together would become the strongest powers in the world."

The Japanese attitude toward Russia today cannot be understood solely in terms of political and economic ideology. It has been shaped by centuries of intercourse between Russians and Japanese, dating back to 1697, the year of the first recorded encounter of a Japanese castaway and a Russian explorer. What were some of the lasting "first impressions" made by the Japanese and the Russians on each other? What was the nature of Russian pressure on Japan? Did a flourishing trade with Russia materialize after the opening of Japan or were Russian pleas for trade merely a cloak for more sinister designs? By whom was Russian policy toward Japan determined and how consistent was this policy over the years? Questions such as these suggested the need for a detailed narrative of early Russo-Japanese relations prior to a survey of dealings in the modern period.

Russo-Japanese relations fall quite naturally into two major historical parts, with 1875, the year in which Russia obtained the cession of southern Sakhalin in exchange for Russian claims to the northern

Kuril Islands, as the breaking point. The relations from 1697 to 1875, with which this volume deals, form a logical unit, revolving primarily around two Russian objectives: the establishment of commercial and diplomatic relations with Japan and the delineation of a Russo-Japanese frontier. After 1875 considerations of a different nature fix the attention, and Russo-Japanese relations, with their extension to the Asiatic mainland, become a more integral part of Far Eastern international relations as a whole. (I plan to deal with the period from 1875 to the present in a second volume.) Yet Japan's loss of her empire and the interruption of her normal commercial and diplomatic relations with Russia at the end of World War II seem to have turned the clock of Russo-Japanese relations back to the years before 1875.

The story of the Russian push toward Japan is one of high adventure, created by the ambitions and initiative of individuals. It should be of interest not only to the specialist, acquainted with Japanese and Russian, but to the general reader of historical literature. I have thought it advisable, therefore, to convert Russian and Japanese ranks and titles into their nearest English language equivalent, shunning such transliterations as *probirnykh del master, kapitan 2-go ranga*, and "Ise-no-kami" in favor of "pharmaceutist," "commander," and "Lord of Ise." In this way the general reader should not be overburdened by relatively unimportant terminology and additional footnotes; as for the specialist, I trust he will have no difficulty in reconverting the ranks and titles to the original, if he so desires, and will not be hampered in the correct pronunciation of Japanese names by the absence of diacritical marks. Similarly I have tried to give greater simplicity and order to the narrative by converting both Russian and Japanese dates to the Gregorian calendar now in general use in the West. In the transliteration of Russian words and names I have followed the system used by the Library of Congress, as one most readily permitting reconversion to the original spelling. I have deviated from this rule in the case of such generally accepted forms as "St. Petersburg" and have dropped the apostrophe indicating a soft sound from the names of persons and ships. There were many persons of foreign birth or foreign descent in the Russian service. Generally I have given their names as they were spelled in Russian. Patronymics have been relegated to the Index. In order to reduce the size of this book, footnote citations have been trimmed as much as possible. Full data may be found in the bibliography.

I acknowledge with deep appreciation the inspiration and support given me over the years by teachers and friends at Columbia University, especially Professors Hugh Borton, L. Carrington Goodrich, Ryusaku Tsunoda, and Sir George Sansom; the encouragement given to me in my research here at the Florida State University by my colleagues, notably Professors Weymouth T. Jordan, Charles S. Davis, and Werner A. Baum; and the sponsorship of my sojourn in Japan by the President and faculty of Hokkaido University. I am greatly indebted to the kind and constant assistance of helpful librarians at the East Asiatic and Butler Libraries of Columbia University, the Slavonic division of the New York Public Library, the Japanese and Russian collections of the Library of Congress, the Municipal Library of Hakodate, the National Diet Library and Toyo Bunko in Japan, and the Florida State University. I acknowledge also the stimulating and efficient support of Miss R. Miriam Brokaw, Managing Editor of the Princeton University Press, the helpful suggestions of the anonymous readers consulted by the Press, and the valuable advice of Mr. Serge V. Glad, Historian of the Association of Russian Imperial Naval Officers in America, concerning the most suitable translation of Russian naval terms and ranks and the acquisition of some of the illustrative material.

I am profoundly grateful to the United States Educational (Fulbright) Commission in Japan, the Social Science Research Council, the Penrose Fund of the American Philosophical Society, and the Research Council of the Florida State University for financial assistance in the writing of this book. Publication itself was made possible by the generous help of the Ford Foundation and the Subcommittee on Grants of the Joint Committee on Slavic Studies of the American Council of Learned Societies and the Social Science Research Council. Needless to say, the ideas, conclusions, and possible errors in this book are solely my own responsibility.

Permission to quote copyrighted material is gratefully acknowledged to publishers as follows: Oxford University Press, *Select Documents on Japanese Foreign Policy 1853-1868* by W. G. Beasley (London, 1955); Grove Press, *The Japanese Discovery of Europe. Honda Toshiaki and other Discoverers 1720-1798* by Donald Keene (New York, 1954); Fleming H. Revell Co., *A History of Christianity in Japan* by Otis Cary (New York, 1909); American Baptist Publication Society (Judson Press), *Christianity in Modern Japan* by Ernest W. Clement (Philadelphia, 1905). The University of Florida Press has graciously permitted reuse of material covered by me in *Russia's Japan Expedition of 1852 to 1855* (Gainesville, 1955). I am grateful to the American Press for permission to use the map of "Russian Activity in Alaska," an AP Newsfeature dated June 17, 1958.

G.A.L.

Tallahassee, Florida
February 1959

CONTENTS

ILLUSTRATIONS

(Following page 208)

xiii

MAPS

CHAPTER ONE · THE SETTING

JAPAN CLOSES THE DOOR

IN 1542 or thereabouts—the date is not quite certain—the winds of fate carried the first Europeans to the shores of Japan. Three Portuguese on a Chinese junk were swept by a typhoon across the East China Sea to Tanegashima, an island south of Kyushu. There they were kindly received by the Japanese, whose hospitality was exceeded only by admiration for the arquebuses which the Portuguese carried. For years thereafter firearms were known in Japan as *tanegashima*. The safe return of the three Portuguese to the coast of China with gifts from the Japanese swelled the ambitions of their countrymen, who in their imagination pictured the islands of Japan as "silver islands" and the people of Japan as raw material for the Christian Church; before long a wave of Portuguese traders and priests inundated Japan. Like their predecessors they were received well, and the Japanese appeared eager for cultural as well as commercial intercourse. But these were days when trade was overshadowed by piracy, and Christian love by bigotry—days when swashbuckling buccaneers manned the frontiers of Western civilization, and "Southern Barbarians" was not an inappropriate term for those who visited Japan. The association of firearms with Tanegashima eventually faded, but foreigners, Christianity, and firearms remained identified in the public mind as "each and equal members of a trinity of terrors."[1]

At mid-sixteenth century Japan was still waist-deep in the morass of civil war into which she had sunk toward the end of the fifteenth century. She was still in the period labeled by historians "Sengoku": The Country at War. Her emperors were powerless and destitute—one lay unburied for forty days, while another sold poems to sustain himself. The military dictators of the Ashikaga clan, who since 1338 had dominated court and country, had lost their grip, and local chiefs vied with each other for supremacy, while famines and epidemics decimated the population. To those who remembered the past, the layers of Japanese society gave the appearance of having been turned over with a gigantic plow. The old aristocracy had all but sunk out of sight, while men of low birth and high ability had been thrust to

[1] William Elliot Griffis, *The Mikado's Empire*, I, 248.

3

the surface. Untrammeled by tradition, these men accepted new ideas and methods if only they promised success. Despite the ravage of civil war Japan remained intellectually alert. The foreigners with their new weapons, their promises of wealth, and their new religion were welcome.

For nine decades after the arrival of the first Portuguese—throughout Japan's "Christian Century"—Jesuit, Franciscan, Dominican, and Augustinian missionaries propagated the "tried and tested true Catholic doctrine" with less hindrance from the Japanese than from their own limited knowledge of the Japanese language. Converts numbered in the hundreds of thousands. Buddhism envisaged a lengthy chain of rebirths after death; the new faith promised paradise upon death. At the same time the new faith did not appear excessively different. Indeed it seemed at first merely another sect of Buddhism, for not only did the Jesuit fathers pattern themselves in dress and manners after Zen priests—the intellectual and social elite of the Buddhist clergy—but there was a resemblance in the outward trappings of Catholicism and Buddhism. As one historian has observed:

The very idols of Buddha served, after a little alteration with the chisel, for images of Christ. The Buddhist saints were easily transformed into the Twelve Apostles. The Cross took the place of the *torii*. It was emblazoned on the helmets and banners of warriors, and embroidered on their breasts. The Japanese soldiers went forth to battle like Christian crusaders. In the roadside shrine Kuanon, the Goddess of Mercy, made way for the Virgin, the mother of God. Buddhism was beaten with its own weapons. Its own artillery was turned against it. Nearly all the Christian churches were native temples, sprinkled and purified. The same bells, whose boom had so often quivered the air announcing the orisons and matins of paganism, was again blessed and sprinkled, and called the same hearers to mass and confession; the same lavatory that fronted the temple served for holy-water or baptismal font; the same censer that swung before Amida could be refilled to waft Christian incense; the new convert could use unchanged his old beads, bells, candles, incense, and all the paraphernalia of his old faith in celebration of the new.[2]

The "spiritualism" of the East is often exalted at the expense of the "materialism" of the West. Yet it is the materialism of the West which has struck the greatest rapport in the Far East. The Japanese have invariably shown more interest in the material and institutional products of foreign civilizations than in the underlying philosophical

[2] *Ibid.*, I, 252; Charles R. Boxer, *The Christian Century in Japan*, 78, 320-321; P. Emil Naberfeld, *Grundriss der Japanischen Geschichte*, 97.

theories. Buddhism was introduced into Japan originally more for political and material than for religious reasons. Christianity likewise was welcomed less for its own sake than as a vehicle of commerce, military strength, and political utility. When Oda Nobunaga actively supported Christianity, while razing Buddhist strongholds to the ground, he did so as a tactical rather than spiritual move, making use of Christianity as a counterweight to the influence of Buddhism. When local lords extended their welcome to the missionaries, they extended it in fact to the traders; they craved arquebuses more than Holy Scriptures. This association of firearms and other Western products with Christianity was both the strength and weakness of the Church. It made possible the introduction of Christianity to Japan; yet it resulted also in its expulsion.

By the seventeenth century Japan emerged from the period of civil war unified by the genius of three warriors: Oda Nobunaga, Toyotomi Hideyoshi, and Tokugawa Ieyasu. Once again, and more effectively than ever, Japan was to be ruled by a military central government. But her leaders, still insecure and suspicious, guarded against conspiracy from any quarter.

Christianity was not confined to the poor and weak. When Japanese forces overran Korea in the 1590's in a bid for mastery of the Far East, Christian officers and troops formed one of the spearheads. These officers, as well as Christian leaders elsewhere, were a potential menace to the Japanese polity. By its very nature Christianity was politically subversive, infringing on the demands of the totalitarian state. Nor did the missionaries simply withhold from Caesar what was not Caesar's; they encroached on Caesar's domain and sought to guide the political consciences of their flock. Increasingly the resemblance between Christianity and Buddhism faded. Confident of their foothold in Japan, the fathers unveiled the less seemly attributes of seventeenth century Catholicism: fanatical intolerance, the Inquisition, conversion by the sword, and political intrigue.

The Japanese were disappointed in the returns of foreign trade and feared lest the potentially hostile feudal lords on the outskirts of the empire unduly strengthen their power by the acquisition of Western firearms. They were aware of the political machinations of the Catholic fathers and listened with interest to the advice of English and Dutch Protestants who eagerly reported how their kings dealt with Papists. They were shocked by the flagrant European traffic in Japanese slaves who in poverty-stricken Japan cost so little that even the Negro and Malay servants of the Portuguese speculated in them. They were disgusted with the endless murderous brawls among the low foreign adventurers who resorted at the Japanese sea ports— murderous brawls which cast suspicion on the sincerity of Christian professions. When eventually a serious rebellion, replete with Christian banners and slogans, confronted the leaders of Japan, it appeared to them only desirable to bring down the curtain on intercourse with the Christian world.

In Japan, as in England, the persecution of Catholicism was essentially political, but not without romantic overtones. Like Henry VIII, Toyotomi Hideyoshi found one consort insufficient. He had been married six times and had a harem, which a procurer sought to round out for him by the addition of some Christian girls. The procurer was turned down so contemptuously that Toyotomi was enraged. In the middle of the night he directed five questions to the startled Jesuits: Why did they force the Japanese to become Christians? Why did they make their followers destroy the temples? Why did they persecute the Buddhist priests? Why did they violate Japanese customs by eating meat? Who had given the Portuguese permission to buy Japanese and carry them as slaves to India? When the fathers failed to counter these semi-rhetorical questions to his satisfaction, Toyotomi ordered the following morning (July 25, 1587) that they leave the country within twenty days.[3]

The fathers did not respect Toyotomi's commands, nor the commands of his successors, and went on with their preaching. When the Japanese authorities would bodily place them on a ship and deport them, they would merely return in disguise. In desperation the Japanese resorted to stronger measures, first against the native converts, then against the foreign missionaries. The threat of torture and execution did not deter the fathers. With renewed determination, indeed with hope and spiritual longing, they chose the path to martyrdom, bolstered as they faced torture by the exhortations of a special manual which circulated among the faithful:

Hope and confidence should occupy your mind, since at that moment God shall tender a special help. And if possible utter anything which would benefit the soul of the bystanders. Say, for instance, "There is no way besides the religion of Christ which can save you in the future life. I am now going to sacrifice my life as a testimony to the truth of this

---

[3] Otis Cary, *A History of Christianity in Japan*, I, 105-106.

religion. There is no joy greater than this, because this is the way to infinite bliss."[4]

At first the Japanese authorities seemed reluctant to deal as rudely with the foreigners as with their own countrymen. Even when death was adjudged the penalty, the fathers were treated as men of honor and distinction in that they were offered the privilege of disembowelling themselves. But with time the fate of foreign and Christian martyrs rushed together in the same torrent of blood, and burning alive became the standard form of punishment for missionaries and converts alike. This ghastly business was performed with greater ingenuity than in Europe, where contemporary martyrs were fastened tight to the pole, with faggots at the base. In Japan the faggots ringed the stake at a radius of several feet while the victim was attached only by the wrist, free to amuse the morbid crowd as he jumped about in ludicrous agony.

No less ingenuity was displayed by Japanese inquisitors as they sought to sway the faith of the Christian converts by torture. Among the mildest of their grisly methods was the so-called water torture. The martyr was hung upside down and revolved slowly with his head in a bucket of water filled to a level above his nostrils. In another version of the water torture he would be tied down on a board—the left hand free to signal recantation—with his head hanging down, while the inquisitors continued to pour an incessant stream of water on his face as he desperately gasped for air. Other victims would be taken to sulphur springs, where boiling water was slowly poured into incisions made in their flesh. Still the believers clung to their faith and measures became increasingly gruesome until by 1632 hanging in the pit had displaced most other forms of ultimate punishment. Tightly bound around the body as high as the breast, with the forehead lightly slashed to give some vent for the blood, and with one hand as usual left free to indicate recantation, the victims were hung head downwards from a gallows into a pit filled with excreta and other filth. Most of the martyrs expired after a day or two, but some lived for more than a week.

Anti-Christian in expression, the drive to eliminate foreign thought and influence extended eventually to merchants as well, and led to a series of decrees which all but terminated Japan's intercourse with the West. The last and most comprehensive of these was the edict of June 1636. Addressed to the joint governors of Nagasaki by the

4 Boxer, 354.

four great councilors of the empire, it prohibited the departure of any Japanese vessel for a foreign country and forbade on pain of death any Japanese to go abroad or, if abroad, to return. It provided for the deportation of any foreign offspring and its foster parents and called for the continued ferreting out of Christian missionaries and native converts, offering two hundred to three hundred pieces of silver for information leading to the discovery of a Jesuit, while threatening with arrest any foreigner who aided the priests.[5]

In 1624 the English had left Japan of their own volition. The following year the Spaniards were expelled. Now with the edict of 1636 the door of Japan was almost closed. Then came the Christian rebellion of 1637 and the Portuguese seemed implicated. In 1638 they too were expelled. The door was shut.

The "Christian Century" failed to leave a positive imprint on the face of Japanese history. Barren were the fruits of Christian endeavor and suffering. All that Japan had inherited from nearly a hundred years of contact with the West were firearms, smoking tobacco, sponge cake, foreign words, venereal disease, and "the permanent addition to that catalogue of terrors which priest and magistrate in Asiatic countries ever hold as weapons to overawe the herd."[6] No one in Japan was to look back to the "Christian Century" with sentiment. Its memory formed a hurdle to the resumption of relations with the West. Portuguese vessels which arrived in 1639 were turned back with a copy of the prohibition of 1638. When the traders of Macao persisted further and in 1640 dispatched a mission to confer with the Japanese, the latter calmly beheaded the four envoys and fifty-seven of their companions and burned their vessel. Only thirteen men of low rank were spared to take back word of Japan's determination to be left alone. Near the places where the Portuguese heads lay exposed, tablets were erected to announce the error of their ways. One proclaimed:

So long as the sun warms the earth, let no Christian be so bold as to come to Japan; and let all know that if the King of Spain, or the Christians' God, or the great God of all violate this command, he shall pay for it with his head.[7]

5 *Ibid.*, 353, 439-440.
6 Griffis, I, 258-259.
7 Cary, *History*, I, 231 footnote; Richard Hildreth, *Japan as It Was and Is*, I, 192.

DESHIMA

Japan had closed her door. Yet there was a barred cell-like window through which glimpses of the world could be espied. This window was Deshima, a fan-shaped little island, artificially constructed off Nagasaki in 1641, on which the Dutch, who had followed to Japan in the 1580's, were suffered to retain a precarious foothold throughout the seclusion period. Shrewd traders that they were, the Dutch had deflected the wrath of the inquisitors to their Catholic competitors, had hidden, if not denied, their own Christianity, and had proffered their services to the Japanese with humility. As Maurice of Nassau had written in a letter presented to Tokugawa Ieyasu in 1612:

. . . And the intentions of the Spanish and Portuguese are difficult to understand because they are hidden deep in the minds of the Padres who reveal nothing, and this is a matter that you should consider very carefully. And the intention of the Padres is to convert all Japan to their faith by degrees, and as they hate other religions there is sure to be a struggle between the sects and a great disturbance in the country. And then the Padres hope to turn matters to their own advantage.

Now the Dutch who came to your country will do whatever you may please to require of them, and consider it a pleasure to do so. And so they will continue to do in the future. . . .[8]

The Japanese saw the advantage of a window upon Europe through which they could receive whatever foreign goods they might desire and, more important, through which they could keep abreast of European designs. Every year the Dutch had to submit a report about the latest world happenings. Yet for all their usefulness, the Dutch were treated without honor or respect, indeed at times like the most dangerous of criminals. Their strange existence on Deshima blends with the mistrust and fear of Christianity in a historical backdrop which throws into greater relief the thoughts and deeds of the leading actors on the stage of Russo-Japanese relations.

Deshima measured only eighty-two common paces in width and two hundred and thirty-six in main length, yet it housed a number of buildings in which the Dutch lived—wooden two-storied cottages, the lower floors of which were used for storage of goods—as well as special fireproof warehouses, a kitchen, buildings for the transaction of sales, for the accommodation of gubernatorial deputies, for fire apparatus, laundry, Japanese guards, interpreters, and so forth.

[8] A. L. Sadler, *The Maker of Modern Japan*, 235.

When Dutch ships paid their annual visit to the harbor and their crews hung about on Deshima for two or three months, the island seemed to be bulging at the seams, but upon their departure only the factor and several companions remained to keep a lonely vigil.

They were completely isolated from Japan. A high, roof-covered, deal-board fence topped by a double row of pikes hemmed in the island, while thirteen large posts erected in the water clearly marked the line beyond which no Japanese must trespass. The two strong gates which faced the water on the north were never opened except when Dutch ships were laden or unladen under strict supervision. A small stone bridge joined the island with Nagasaki, but on the city side there was a guardhouse and normally the end of the road. Even the fire holes for fetching water were nailed shut and the gutters which ran into the sea had purposely been made crooked so as to forestall any communication with the outside.

A heavy guard protected Japan from the handful of Dutch. In the 1690's it consisted of a regular gate guard of five men plus servants, supported by two ship guards, two spy guards, a servant of the presiding governor, and a servant of the deputy-governor, not to mention six night watchmen and a harbor guard, when no foreign ships were in port. When ships arrived the guards were proportionately increased in number and rank. Meanwhile the Dutch found it necessary to post guards of their own to guard against the guards. At all times a meticulous hourly record was kept in a journal by the gate guard of everyone and everything that passed through the gate, sworn searchers seeing to it that nothing slipped through without special permission from the governor or chief officer of the street.[9]

There were occasions when the Dutch were permitted to cross the bridge to Japan, but they were guarded closely and remained effectively isolated, being allowed to do little more than thank the Japanese for their many favors. During the annual pilgrimage of the resident of the Dutch East India Company to the capital, he and his retinue were treated like prisoners. "We are not suffer'd to speak to any body, not even without special leave to the domesticks and servants of the Inns we lodge at," one European recalled. "As soon as we come to an Inn, we are without delay carried up stairs, if possible, or into the back apartments, which have no other view but into the yard, which for a still greater security, and to prevent any

[9] Engelbert Kaempfer, *The History of Japan*, II, 174-184.

thoughts of an escape, is immediately shut and nail'd up."[10] He noted that such a yearly journey of homage to the Japanese ruler was required not only of the Dutch but also of native lords and vassals. Nor were measures taken by the government at the Deshima guard post basically different from the measures taken commonly toward its own people at the numerous guard gates along the highways of the country. Deshima was a reflection of the model police state which the Tokugawa Shogunate had imposed upon Japan.

The Shogunate, as its Japanese name "Bakufu" or "Tent Government" indicates, was a military dictatorship. The Emperor continued as legal sovereign in the ancient capital of Kyoto, while actual power was exercised by the Tokugawa Shogun or Generalissimo and his advisers from newly founded Edo, the Tokyo or "Eastern Capital" of today. Foreigners talked of the spiritual and secular rulers of Japan, but as often as not during the Seclusion Period failed to distinguish between the two and referred to the Shogun as Emperor, a confusion encouraged by officials of the Shogun as they disguised his subordinate status by referring to him as "Taikun" (tycoon) or Great Lord.

The political structure of Tokugawa Japan was centralized feudalism. The Tokugawa family with its various branches and immediate vassals owned between a quarter and a fifth of the country's agricultural land and from it derived its revenue. The remainder of the land was in the hands of daimyo or lords, who, though they exercised a considerable degree of local autonomy, were vassals of the Shogun, and of the daimyo's own followers or samurai, the knights of Japan. Socially and economically the Tokugawa masters had stratified the population of the country into four classes: warriors, farmers, artisans, and merchants. The ruling elite, amounting with its families to about one-sixteenth of the population, was a hereditary class of fighters, forbidden to pursue any other vocation. Yet with the unification and seclusion of Japan the Shogunate thought it dangerous to foster the martial spirit of its vassals and the ruling class of Japan became increasingly parasitic—forbidden to work, forbidden to fight. The paradox of Tokugawa policy which exhorted the military to live according to the obligations of *Bushido* or the "Way of the Warrior," yet at the same time enforced peace and order, is best illustrated by the fate of the famous forty-seven *ronin* (masterless samurai). Their lord, humiliated by the Master of Ceremonies, wounded him, and

[10] *Ibid.*, II, 191-192.

was forced to disembowel himself for drawing the sword in the Shogun's palace. The obligations of *Bushido* demanded revenge and, after years of cunning and patience, forty-seven of his former samurai cut off the head of the Master of Ceremonies. Theirs was a noble act in the light of Bushido, but a country at peace could not tolerate vendettas, and so, after considerable deliberation, the forty-seven *ronin* were ordered to commit suicide, becoming at the same time national heroes, no less celebrated in democratic Japan today.

In a police state security becomes an obsession. Tokugawa Japan was a police state par excellence. The domains of the feudal lords were so reshuffled as to place the most reliable vassals in strategic positions throughout the country, one guarding against another. Responsibility was always shared: in the sphere of administration where decisions were reached by councils and where officials operated in pairs constantly watching each other, or on the level of daily existence where every five households were grouped together as a *go-nin-gumi* answerable for the crimes of any of its members. The national seclusion of Japan was but one aspect of a more general policy of security through isolation. The imperial court was isolated so that no feudal lords could approach the Emperor except with the permission of the Shogun. The Shogunate itself was isolated, above the reaches of the people. And most important of all, the feudal lords were partially isolated from their own domains and families. By the ingenious system of "Alternate Residence" every lord and vassal of importance had to spend a stipulated period of time in the new capital, maintaining there a residence corresponding to his position. The expense of maintaining such a residence year round, not to mention the trip to the capital and back with a suitable retinue, diminished the economic power of the feudal lord. At the same time his periodic absences weakened his hold on his own domain. And when he returned to his territories his family had to remain in the capital as hostages. Along the various highways leading to and from Edo, barrier gates protected the safety of the Shogunate by guarding against the smuggling out of hostages or smuggling in of firearms. The barrier at Hakone, for example, specialized in the examination of women traveling westward. It was manned by twenty officials assisted by female inspectors, who examined the bodies and hair of women voyagers. Those who sought to avoid the barrier by choosing a detour faced death by crucifixion. A notice-board erected at Hakone in 1711 instructed all travelers as follows:

All persons passing through this gate must remove their head-coverings (straw hats and "zukin"). The doors of palanquins must be opened on entering. Women travellers must be strictly examined in relation to their passports, and those riding in carrying chairs must be taken to the lodge of the barrier guards for examination. Passports are required for the wounded persons, dead bodies or other suspicious burdens.

Court Officials and Daimyo need not be inspected if they have previously given notice of their arrival, but if anything seems suspicious, any person, whatever his rank is subject to inspection.

These rules shall be strictly obeyed.

1711, 5th month.   MAGISTRATE OF THE SHOGUN.[11]

The Tokugawa system which thus carefully enveloped Japan in a net of government control, and discouraged initiative and unconformity by the severity of its punishments, succeeded in perpetuating itself for over two and a half centuries. Its greatest contribution was to bring to the people of Japan the blessings of prolonged peace. Yet its economic and ideological foundations were unsound; in a sense the Tokugawa system contained in itself the seeds of its own destruction. The power of the Shogunate and its vassals was based on an economy of agriculture. Rice was the measure of wealth, the means of payment for the services of the samurai. But the institution of "Alternate Residence," though it indisputably provided political protection, so stimulated commerce as to foster the development of a money economy and the concomitant rise to influence of merchants and financiers, as well as the growth of an essentially anti-feudal urban culture in the capital itself, which by the eighteenth century had become the largest city in the world. Meanwhile the Shogunate's attempt to deflect the energies of the warriors from military to intellectual pursuits stimulated the study of Japanese history and the ultimate realization that the Shogun was an usurper of imperial prerogatives. The efforts of foreigners to reopen Japan were to meet with increasing receptiveness as more and more Japanese became dissatisfied with the conditions of the day and began to consider foreign trade and foreign methods as a possible means of rejuvenating Japan.[12]

Among the various schools of learning, which flourished in Tokugawa Japan the most interesting in this connection was the "Rangaku" or "School of Dutch Learning," which eventually in-

---

[11] Neil Skene Smith, *Materials on Japanese Social and Economic History*, 57.

[12] Eijiro Honjo, *A Social and Economic History of Japan*, 291; see also G. B. Sansom, *Japan*, chapters XXI-XXIII.

cluded under the same name English, French, and Russian studies. With the prohibition of Christianity a ban had been imposed not only on Christian literature but on all Western knowledge. As the fear of European subversion gradually subsided this ban was modified to apply to religious writings only. After 1720, Japanese scholars were able to devote themselves to the study of Dutch language, medicine, natural science, mathematics, astronomy, and military science. The restrictions on the Dutch were relaxed enough to permit them to assist the Japanese scholars in their endeavors. Such men as Engelbert Kämpfer and Philipp Franz von Siebold (German doctors in the Dutch service), Isaac Titsingh, Karl Thunberg and J. L. C. Pompe van Merdervoort contributed not only to the Western knowledge of Japan but also to Japanese knowledge of the West. Japan had closed her door, but Deshima served as a window through which the Japanese could peer at the world outside.[13]

RUSSIA PUSHES EAST

The country which first and most persistently sought to reopen Japan was Russia, whose explorers in their eastward drive at one time spanned the continents of Europe, Asia, and America. The place of origin of the Russian people is not certain, but there is general agreement that the early Russians entered Russia from the west. They pushed northward and eastward into European Russia and continued pushing eastward, past the Ural mountains, until the tremendous plain that stretches from the Baltic and Black Seas to the Pacific Ocean was in their hands. The movement of Russians into Siberia antedates even the establishment of the Romanov dynasty (1613). Cossacks began pushing into western Siberia during the reign of Ivan the Terrible (1533-1584) and before. The attachment of the peasants to the soil at the time of Boris Godunov (1598-1605) and additional hardships during the "Time of Troubles" (1604-1613) which followed, with the appearance of a pretender to the throne, and the death of Boris Godunov, accelerated the eastward migration of Russians who sought to escape the privation, bondage, and political disorder of their mother country. Some of the Russians settled in the familiar regions of western Siberia; others continued to push farther east, exploring and subjugating new territories and peoples. Even when they reached the Pacific shores they did not stop, but, taking

[13] Donald Keene, *The Japanese Discovery of Europe*, 5-38.

to the sea, pressed on to the east until by the turn of the nineteenth century the Northern Pacific threatened to become a Russian lake.[14]

Propelled primarily by the wealth of peltry in the east, the continental expansion of Russia was given direction at once by the natural barrier of mountains, deserts, and inland seas which frames the Eurasian plain on the South and by the great rivers whose tributaries run parallel to this barrier. Led by individuals, it was controlled by the government; for the government was the chief fur trader. Fur was exacted from the natives as tribute and from the traders and trappers as tax. More fur was obtained by purchase, the government having first call on the best peltry of its countrymen. At the same time the government retained for itself a monopoly on the sale of black foxes and sables to China. By the sixteenth and seventeenth centuries fur had became Russia's most important single item in foreign and domestic commerce, Russian furs being prominent in the markets of both Europe and China, and in essence the whole problem of the administration of Siberia revolved around the taking and giving of fur tribute.[15]

The stimulus which fur gave to the eastward push of Russia is of particular interest because this "golden fleece" was a common denominator of Russian and American expansion. Fur led the Russians to the American continent, as it was to lead Americans across their own continent to the Pacific shores and beyond. In both cases the trade with China was an added incentive.[16] But constructive as the thirst for wealth may have been ultimately from a national point of view in terms of exploration, conquest, and colonization, it fostered not only the subjugation of native peoples, but graft, corruption, cruelty, and even open warfare among rival tribute collectors—a fact confirmed by the number of Siberian officials sentenced to hang by the Russian government. Historians agree concerning the vicious nature of the early pioneer day officials. F. A. Golder writes after careful study:

[14] Prince A. Lobanov-Rostovsky, *Russia and Asia*, 1-10; N. V. Kiuner, *Snosheniia Rossii s Dal'nim Vostokom na protiazhenii tsarstvovaniia Doma Romanovykh*, 2; S. Znamenskii, *V poiskakh Iaponii*, 5.

[15] Lobanov-Rostovsky, 2; Robert J. Kerner, *The Urge to the Sea*, 84-85; F. A. Golder, *Russian Expansion on the Pacific*, 18.

[16] Another somewhat more fanciful common denominator of Russian and American expansion might be found in heliotaxis and heliotropism. Sixteenth-century American explorers regarded their urge westward as a lure to follow the sun. Funaoka Seigo develops the theory that the Russians in their expansion eastward were similarly driven by the basic human need for sunshine. (Hugh Borton, *Japan's Modern Century*, 3; Funaoka Seigo, *Japan im Sternbild Ostasiens*, I, 160-161.)

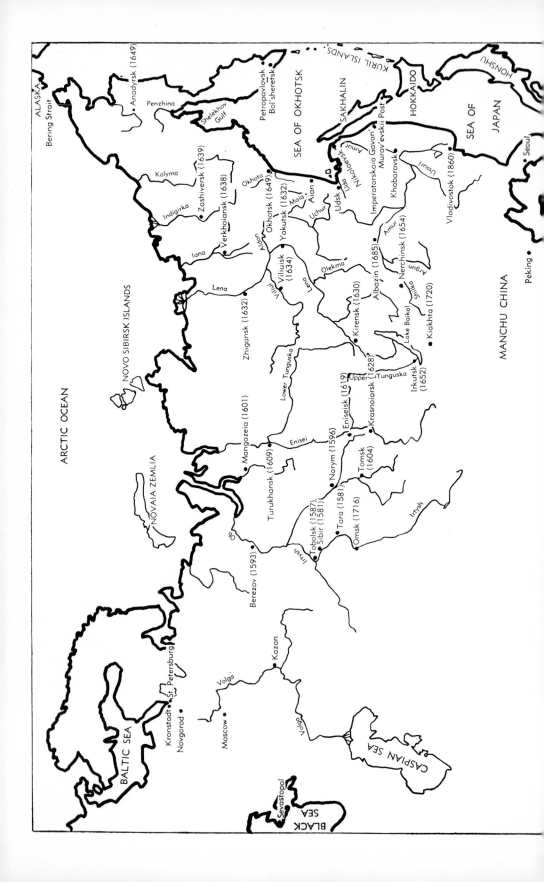

Were it not for the fact that the evidence on this point is uncontradictory one could hardly believe that these men were as low and as depraved as the contemporary literature pictures them. They were without the fear of God and without the feelings of shame. They traded, gambled, mortgaged, and sold their wives and daughters as if they were chattel. The traffic in women was carried on publicly and from the proceeds of the sale the government received ten per cent as it did from the sale of ordinary merchandise. Other forms of vice were even less concealed. Although aware of this demoralizing state of affairs, the government was not in a position to put an end to it because it could not depend on the soldiers, who often mutinied and killed their officers, robbed whom they should protect, and then fled across the Chinese border and from there carried on their depredations. If caught and brought back two or three were punished by having their noses cut off and the remainder were reinstated in service.[17]

Part of the difficulty was due to the fact that the government in Moscow was slow to realize the importance of the Siberian territories. But even the establishment of a separate Department of Siberian Affairs in Moscow in 1637 and the reorganization of Siberia in 1708 by Peter the Great on western European standards could not overcome the lack of honest administrators. Nor did the appointment of a special customs officer (*golova*) as a check on the chief officer of the province (*voevoda*) inhibit the exactions of the latter, and of his family and friends.

The chief officer continued to shortstop the best furs, to misappropriate part of his subordinates' salaries, and to beat and otherwise mistreat the natives. There was little recourse against these depredations during the chief officer's period of service, for he himself was chief justice of the province, and could readily dispose of any complaints. This does not mean that the government was unaware of the official's misconduct. On the contrary, measures were taken repeatedly to prevent the chief officer from bringing back to Russia either directly or through others more than the amount of furs and money allowed him by law. The customs officers on the Siberian frontier were instructed by Moscow to surprise the returning chief officer of the province and his party, and to look for smuggled furs "in the wagons, trunks, baskets, clothes, beds, pillows, wine barrels, boxes, in the baked bread . . . to search men and women without fear of any one . . . examine their persons, their trousers, and note especially

[17] Golder, *Russian Expansion*, 19-20, note 8.

whether the women have skins sewed in their petticoats . . . look sharp that they do not get away with any furs."[18]

The art of administering the eastern territories thus boiled down to the discovery of the degree to which the natives could be taxed, short of inciting them to rebellion or to flight across the Chinese border. The policy of the Russian government was moderate and the tribute light, the exactions of the local officials illegal and excessive. They held the natives responsible not only for their own tribute, but the tribute of those who had fled or died; and, in competition with other tribute collectors, they forced the natives to pay their own share more than once. When the natives promised to comply, the officials took hostages; when the natives refused to pay, the tribute collectors killed the men and divided their women and children among their followers. One can readily understand that for many natives the tribute became insufferable and they sought recourse and revenge in waylaying and killing their oppressors.[19]

Neither the government in Moscow nor its Siberian representatives can be said to have initiated or planned the push east. Plunder and loot sufficed to draw adventurers and freebooters of every sort to the regions beyond the restraining arm of government. Cossacks, who unlike their settled countrymen formed a kind of military republic on the outskirts of the Russian realm and who in their warfare with the Tartars had come to adopt their marauding ways, scattered across the Asian continent, unconscious of their role as *avant coureurs* of Russian civilization.[20] Eventually the Russian government, seeking to secure Moscow from the onslaught of Asian raiders by pushing back the frontier and reinforcing it with a chain of forts[21] in what might be described as a quest for peace through expansion and colonization, made use of the Cossack communities, organizing them into special hosts, whose military frontier settlements served at once as a source of produce and as cavalry-striking power.[22]

Spearheaded by such men as Ermak Timofeevich, colorful river pirate and Don Cossack leader, whose conquest of the Tartar city

---

[18] *Ibid.*, 20-21, note 12.

[19] *Ibid.*, 18-24.

[20] Shanghai Mercury, *The Story of Russia and the Far East* (hereafter cited as *Story*), 5-7; Kiuner, 2.

[21] The Russian fort was known as an *ostrog.* A rectangular wooden stockade, walled in by a second stockade and a moat, it contained a number of buildings, including usually living quarters, a granary, a customhouse, and church. (Raymond H. Fisher, *The Russian Fur Trade*, 35.)

[22] Lobanov-Rostovsky, 35-37.

Sibir and of the Tobolsk region in the early 1580's won him not only imperial pardon for his crimes but favor and wealth, Russian adventurers penetrated farther east. In 1587 they founded Tobolsk, in 1596 Narym, in 1619 Eniseisk, in 1632 Yakutsk. By 1649 they reached the Pacific coast at the shores of the Sea of Okhotsk.[23] At times the rigors of the Siberian climate tempted some to seek a more southerly route, but fierce opposition on the part of Asian tribes gave added meaning to the cry of "Eastward Ho!" Once the Pacific barrier had been reached the wanderers probed south again.[24]

In 1644 Vasilii Poiarkov penetrated to the Amur River with a party of freebooters, hunters, and Cossacks. The success of his expedition and the optimism of his report about the riches of the Amur region and the weakness of the local tribes triggered other expeditions to this area.[25] Thus Erofei Khabarov led a force to the Amur River in 1650 and 1651. In part Poiarkov's report proved true. There was considerable wealth in the form of tribute and plunder, and the natives were weak. But Poiarkov had not foreseen that the natives could call for military support on the neighboring Manchus, who by now ruled China. And so the excesses of Khabarov set off a generation of warfare between Russian and Manchu forces, and postponed Russian enjoyment of the resources of the Amur region for two centuries.[26]

[23] V. A. Samoilov, *Semen Dezhnev i ego vremia*, map between pages 104 and 105; A. V. Efimov, *Iz istorii velikikh russkikh geograficheskikh otkrytii v Severnom Ledovitom i Tikhom Okeanakh*, 56; L. S. Berg, *Ocherki po istorii russkikh geograficheskikh otkrytii*, 84; A. V. Efimov, *Iz istorii russkikh ekspeditsii na Tikhom Okeane*, 49. In those days western Europeans were familiar only with the southern part of the Pacific Ocean; they had little knowledge of the part north of the Japanese main island of Honshu and of California. The Russian explorers who first reached the eastern shores did not realize that they had found the Pacific; indeed they did not know of its existence. Instead they referred to the ocean as Lamskoe More (after *Lama*, the native word for sea). Some reserved this designation only for the northwestern part of the Sea of Okhotsk, calling the northeastern section Penzhinskoe More; the sea at the eastern shore of Kamchatka was known as Bobrovoe More (Beaver Sea) and near the mouth of the Anadyr River as Anadyrskoe More. (Znamenskii, 8.)

[24] *Story*, 11-12. According to some historians Semen Dezhnev and a party of Cossacks sailed across to the American continent at mid-century. Regarding the controversy connected with this voyage, see Raymond H. Fisher, "Semen Dezhnev and Professor Golder," 281-292.

[25] Poiarkov may have brought back word of Sakhalin Island (Golder, 256), but there seems to be no evidence that he actually set foot on the island, as stated by some writers.

[26] E. G. Ravenstein, *The Russians on the Amur*, 25. Poiarkov left a legend that the Russians lived on human flesh, shooting down the natives to be roasted at Russian campfires. Though Poiarkov was tried for murder by his own government, "to all Asiatics, the Red Hairs were cannibals." (Harry Emerson Wildes, "Russia Meets the Japanese," 55.) "We cannot deny to Poyarkof the merit of having been the first to explore the course of the Amur," Ravenstein wrote. "At the same time his treacherous

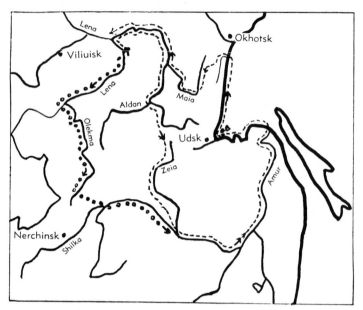

The Expeditions of Poiarkov and Khabarov

The Russian government did not desire hostilities with the Manchu empire and sought to curb the outrages of the Cossacks by calling Khabarov to Moscow and leaving Onufrii Stepanov in his stead.[27] But the activities of the Russians along the Amur River remained a thorn in the flesh of the Manchus and in the spring of 1655 the latter launched a large-scale attack on Fort Kumarsk, the main Russian position. Repulsed by the Russians with heavy losses, the Manchus resorted to a scorched earth policy, vacating the shores of the Amur River and destroying all settlements. This threw the Russians onto their own meager resources. But though it deprived them of convenient booty, it did not discourage their inroads. Attempts by Stepanov to turn the Cossacks to the pursuit of agriculture and peace came to naught, for the Cossacks, accustomed neither to work nor discipline, stepped up their forays against the Manchus and engulfed

and cruel behaviour towards the natives, who had received him with open arms, makes him suffer greatly in our estimation; whilst his want of foresight, in entering an unknown region, in the middle of winter, without a sufficient supply of provisions, proves him to have been a man scarcely fit for the command of an expedition of this kind." (Ravenstein, 13.)

[27] So self-confident had some of the Russians become, that in 1670 the military commander of Nerchinsk instructed the Cossack Ignatii Milovanov to demand at Peking that the great Manchu emperor K'ang Hsi become a vassal of the Russian tsar. (Michel N. Pavlovsky, *Chinese-Russian Relations*, 127-144.)

the Amur region in anarchy. Eventually, in 1658, Stepanov himself led five hundred Cossacks on a raid into Manchuria. They were engaged by a superior Manchu force and Stepanov and over half of his men were killed.

By 1661 the Russians had abandoned the whole of the Amur, yet twenty years later, thanks ironically to the efforts of such men as the Polish exile to Siberia Nikifor Chernigovsky, Russia seemed more firmly established than ever in this region, and in 1684 the territory was made into the separate province of Albazin, with a special coat of arms and seal for the city of Albazin. But the Manchus and Chinese had other plans for the Amur region, and in 1685 the foremost Russian stronghold at Albazin was laid waste by a powerful Manchu army. The generosity of the victorious Manchus in permitting the Russian commander and his men and the inhabitants of Albazin to depart freely for Nerchinsk was not appreciated by the Russians, and when the Manchus withdrew to Aigun, a city on the right bank of the Amur River, the Russians hastened to reestablish Albazin and other Amur settlements. The Manchus did not wax enthusiastic over Russian persistence and dispatched an overwhelming army to expel the intruders again. But before the inevitable decision was reached on the battlefield, representatives of the two governments, meeting on Russian initiative, concluded in 1689 the Treaty of Nerchinsk, demarking the Russo-Chinese frontier. Negotiating from a position of strength—with the Russian negotiators practically at their mercy—the Manchus made China's first treaty with the West no less than an "equal" one. Indeed it favored China, leaving the Amur region in Manchu hands.[28] Once more the expansionist drive of Russia was deflected eastward.

The obstacles which the Russian landsmen had to overcome as they ventured into the Pacific were tremendous. The northwestern

[28] Admiral G. I. Nevelskoi, *Podvigi russkikh morskikh ofitserov na krainem vostoke Rossii*, 27-37; Gaston Cahen, *Some Early Russo-Chinese Relations*, 14-16; Ravenstein, 38-44; Aitchen K. Wu, *China and the Soviet Union*, 56. A translation of the main body of the Treaty of Nerchinsk may be found in Victor A. Yakhontoff, *Russia and the Soviet Union in the Far East*, 351-352. According to Ravenstein (p. 62) there was an intriguing difference in the preambles of the Russian and Chinese texts. Russian: "The Plenipotentiaries, in order to remove all cause of discontent between the two empires, to conclude a permanent peace, and to settle the frontiers, agree, in their conference at Nerchinsk, to the following articles." Chinese: "In order to suppress the insolence of certain scoundrels, who cross the frontier to hunt, plunder, and kill, and who give rise to much trouble and disturbance; to determine clearly and distinctly the boundaries between the empires of China and Russia; and lastly, to re-establish peace and good understanding for the future, the following articles are, by mutual consent, agreed upon."

shores of the Sea of Okhotsk whence they set out were dotted with cliffs that broke steeply through the surface of the water. The western coast of Kamchatka was lower and its lagoons, behind the tongues of the river mouths, offered shelter, but entrance into these rivers was as difficult as into the rivers of the Okhotsk shore. The dangers lurking along the coastal sandbanks and surfs of the Sea of Okhotsk were accentuated by the tide fluctuations of the rivers. They were further multiplied, particularly in the north, by frequent fogs in late spring, by numerous storms in summer, and by ice—in broad strips along the shore and in roving masses at sea—in winter. As the Russians pushed out to sea, compass-less, in primitive little flat-bottom boats with oars and straight deerskin sails that could be hoisted in favorable wind only, and even in deerskin-covered, birch-frame river boats, they resembled more the Vikings of the ninth and tenth centuries than their own western European contemporaries. But danger merely lured the hardy adventurers on; the anger of the elements and the resistance of the natives played second fiddle to the promise of easy wealth held forth by the eastern regions. In a combination of private plunder and imperial expansion, the government and its none too obedient subjects joined hands in pushing back the Russian frontier to the shores of America and Japan.[29]

TIDINGS OF JAPAN

The west Europeans had approached India, China, Japan, and the Spice Islands from the south, by way of Africa. Some sought a Northwest Passage through the barrier of the American continent. The Russians set out from the opposite direction in search of a Northeast Passage. In this, the voyages and experiences of the western Europeans were of little help. As the Russians put out to sea in their frail little crafts, they ventured into the unknown.

News about Japan reached Russia relatively late. Not until the seventeenth century do we find mention of Japan in Russian sources. The little information which the Russians first had probably came from the Dutch who had retained a foothold in Japan and who were welcome guests and teachers at the Russian capital in the middle and particularly late seventeenth century. It was the government-inspired translation into Russian of a Dutch work, the *Atlas* of the Flemish

[29] Znamenskii, 9-12; William Coxe, *Account of the Russian Discoveries between Asia and America*, 10-13.

geographer Gerhardus Mercator in 1637 which formed the basis for
a number of subsequent Russian manuscripts that made mention of
Japan. One of these described Japan as a country of three major
islands—the largest of which it called "Iapan"—and of many smaller
islands, a country commercially advanced and abounding in gold,
pearls, precious stones, and other riches. But it placed Japan most
vaguely in the waters between America and China. The first Russian
maps of Siberia, compiled in the second half of the seventeenth century, gave no indication of Japan. Nevertheless more and more data
about Japan was gradually being accumulated in Russia.

Not all foreign reports about Japan were useful. Western European
misconceptions about the disposition of northern Japan and about
the existence of fabulous gold and silver islands east of northern
Japan did more to delay than to hasten Russian discovery of Japan.
The contradictory stories which European travelers brought back
from Japan about Hokkaido—then still called Ezo and Matsumae—
which they described as a body of land situated to the north of the
Japanese main island and inhabited by a non-Japanese people (the
Ainu), were so confused that European cartographers were unable
to record its position correctly or uniformly. Some portrayed Hokkaido as a huge separate island, others as a continuation of the Japanese main island. Some joined it to the Asian continent, others joined
it to the American continent. Actual exploration of the northern
territories by the Dutch seamen Maerten Gerritsen Vries and
Hendrick Cornelisz Schaep—the first and until the end of the eighteenth century only western European explorers of this region—
merely compounded the confusion. Blinded by fog, Vries crossed over
from Hokkaido to Sakhalin without noting the strait that separates
them and thus regarded Sakhalin as a continuation of Hokkaido. One
of the Kuril Islands (Etorofu) he named Staaten Eyland; another
one (Kunashiri) he mistook for part of Hokkaido, and still another
one (Uruppu) for the shore of America, naming it Compagnies Land,
"proving" thereby at once the tremendous expanse of Hokkaido and
the proximity of America to Japan. Stories picked up by Cossack
explorers along the Pacific coast failed to clarify the situation, and
the general overextension of Hokkaido to the North backed by the
observations of Vries misled the Russians into regarding the two
bodies of land, Hokkaido and Sakhalin, as one and the same.[30]

[30] Znamenskii, 17-26; Golder, *Russian Expansion*, 117-131; Berg, 98; Lawrence C.
Wroth, *The Early Cartography of the Pacific*, 220. For an account of the development of

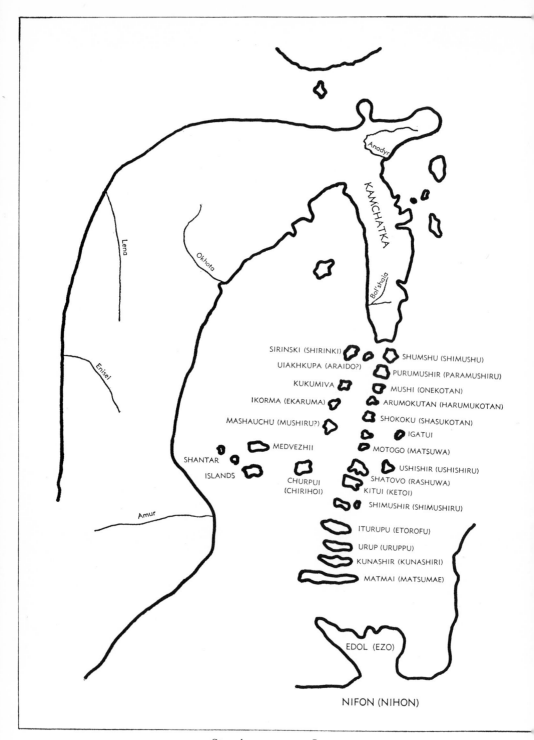

Stepping-stones to Japan

In 1678 Nikolai Spafarii, upon his return from China as Russian envoy, submitted a set of lengthy notes to the Department of Foreign Affairs. He had been instructed to collect information about the countries adjacent to China, and his report on Japan, although inaccurate, was the first serious attempt to relate the geographical position of Japan to the Russian far east. Writing on the basis of information gleaned from western European books, from the Jesuits in Peking, from Chinese books translated by these Jesuits, as well as the accounts brought back from the Amur River by Vasilii Poiarkov and fellow Cossacks a generation earlier, Spafarii reported that the large island of Japan stretched southward from a point vis-à-vis the mouth of the Amur River down the China coast at a distance of some two days travel from shore. Though Spafarii spoke elsewhere of an island opposite the Amur Estuary and of other islands far at sea, his northwesterly projection of Japan was no doubt the product of his consolidation of Hokkaido and Sakhalin; at the same time Spafarii's findings helped to perpetuate this misconception.

The maps of Siberia and adjacent regions, compiled by Semen Remezov at the turn of the eighteenth century, though diverse in their description of the Japanese Islands and Sakhalin, also supported Spafarii's view of the proximity of Japan to the Amur Estuary. The Koreans, to the south of the Amur, were reported to be trading with the Japanese. To establish commercial relations with Japan it seemed necessary only to cross the Amur and to participate in the Korean-Japanese trade or else to proceed directly to seemingly nearby Japan itself from the mouth of the Amur, where it was said large vessels could be built. But the Treaty of Nerchinsk barred the Russians from the Amur River and it appeared that Japan would have to be approached from points near the mouths of the Uda, Ulia, or Okhota rivers, when word was received that in its northern parts, which Remezov had left uncharted, Japan might extend to the Russian mainland in yet another region—in the vicinity of newly discovered Kamchatka.

The news of the alleged proximity of Japan to Kamchatka was brought to Moscow in about 1700 by Volodimer Atlasov, the famous explorer of Kamchatka. Having noticed that the implements of the inhabitants of the peninsula were not exclusively primitive, but in

---

Japanese geographical knowledge concerning Hokkaido, see Suematsu Yasukazu, *Kinsei ni okeru hokuho mondai no shinten*, 65-97.

part of a higher technique, Atlasov had inquired as to their origin and had learned that they were brought to the continent by strangers from islands at sea. As Atlasov followed the direction in which the natives pointed, he observed "what appeared to be islands" on the horizon opposite the first Kuril River. The closest one of these was probably Araido-to, the northernmost of the Kuril Islands, whose peak, Oyakoba Yama, rises to over seven and a half thousand feet. The natives received from these islands china and crockery, cotton fabrics, striped and colorful nankeens, and clothing. But the natives could not identify the "magnificent people" who inhabited the islands, nor could they tell anything about their country. The foreign goods were recognized eventually as Japanese and the conclusion was drawn that the strangers who came from the neighboring island were Japanese; it was not realized that the goods were brought instead by middlemen—the inhabitants of the southern Kuril Islands.[31]

The illusion of the proximity of Japan—though Atlasov himself did not know of Japan by that name if he knew of it at all—was given added speciousness by the discovery of an actual live Japanese, Dembei, a merchant's clerk from Osaka. Dembei was the forerunner of a whole series of Japanese castaways, thrown periodically on the shores of Russian activity. On the eve of her seclusion, Japan had begun to expand into southeast Asia and her countrymen had made their way to the Philippines, Annam, Siam, and Java, establishing flourishing colonies there. But her voluntary isolation had compelled Japan not only to restrict her territorial expansion, but to scuttle her naval efforts, and to discontinue the construction of big seagoing vessels. Meanwhile the rapid growth of internal trade, spurred by the demands of "Alternate Residence," resulted in the large-scale

[31] Znamenskii, 22-37; A. Sgibnev, "Popytki russkikh k zavedeniiu torgovykh snoshenii s Iaponieiu," 38, footnote; Golder, 98. The origin of the term "Kuril" is controversial. It was believed at first that the Cossacks so named the Kuril Islands after their smouldering volcanic mounds—*kurit'sa* being the Russian equivalent of "to smoke." (Sgibnev, 38.) But the term was applied to the peoples of Southern Kamchatka and to Southern Kamchatka itself (Kuril'skaia Zemlia) before it was applied to the Kuril Islands. (Golder, *Russian Expansion*, 109.) A more plausible explanation, therefore, is that the term was borrowed by the Cossacks from the Kamchadals, who refer to the inhabitants of Southern Kamchatka as "Kuzhi" ("those who live to the south" or "local ones"), the Cossacks taking the Kamchadal "zh" for an "r." The Kuril Islands, Sakhalin, and Northern Japan were still inhabited by the Ainu. The northernmost Kuril Islands and southern Kamchatka were populated by a mixture of Ainu and Kamchadals—the Koriaks living in the north and west of Kamchatka, the Kamchadals along the Kamchatka river and its tributaries. The Gilyaks called the Ainu "Kugi"; the Ainu themselves called their islands "Kuri-misi" ("People's Land"), again terms similar to "Kuril." (Znamenskii, 35-36; Golder, *Russian Expansion*, 109-110.)

development of water transportation along the coasts of Japan. The hundreds of vessels which now dotted the shores and navigable rivers were stunted in size and seaworthiness by law. An unexpected storm— and many a vessel and crew were doomed. Japanese literature abounds in the tales and fables of castaways who after years of absence returned to their homeland. Usually, however, they were never heard from again. Only those whose ships were laden with staples had any hope of survival. Dembei had sailed in the winter of 1695 in a fleet of thirty transports laden with rice, sake, powdered sugar, damasks, nankeens, cottons, sandalwood, and iron from Osaka to Edo, when his vessel had been separated from the others by a typhoon and had been driven eastward into the open sea. Forced to cut down mast and sails to keep the vessel upright, he and some dozen shipmates were helplessly tossed about the ocean for twenty-eight weeks. Fortunately their cargo included ample foodstuffs and, once the storm abated, they salvaged a floating tree from the sea and, erecting a makeshift mast with new sails, shaped out of damask, succeeded finally in reaching Kamchatka, where they sighted a river and proceeded upstream. But Kamchatka offered little sanctuary to the weary Japanese. They were set upon by some two hundred arrowshooting, ax-swinging natives and, though they escaped extermination by a hasty surrender of their cargo, they found themselves prisoners on foreign soil.[32]

Two of the Japanese had died at sea. Two others perished— murdered by the natives, as Dembei is quoted in one place, or poisoned by the pungent diet of rotten fish and roots on which their captors thrived, as Dembei is quoted elsewhere. Ten of the survivors remained in the region of capture until carried away by vessels of undetermined nationality. Only Dembei, his hand wounded by an arrow, was taken inland to Kamchatka River to become eventually the first Japanese ever to visit European Russia.[33]

[32] Martin Ramming, *Reisen schiffbrüchiger Japaner im XVIII. Jahrhundert*, 1-4; N. N. Ogloblin, "Pervyi Iaponets v Rossii 1701-1705 gg.," 11-24; Harima Narayoshi, "Rokoku ni okeru Nihongo gakko no enkaku," 45; Znamenskii, 37. See also Iurii Zhukov, *Russkie i Iaponiia*, 8; Keene, 58; Wildes, "Russia Meets the Japanese," 55-61; Efimov, *Iz istorii russkikh ekspeditsii*, 68; Efimov, *Iz istorii velikikh*, 84; Philipp Johann von Strahlenberg, *Das Nord- und Östliche Theil von Europa und Asia*, 437-438.

[33] Ogloblin, 14, 20; Zhukov, 9-10; Znamenskii, 37-38; Hiraoka Masahide, *Nichi-Ro kosho shiwa*, 3. Zhukov asserts that the other two Japanese were taken there also. (Zhukov, 9-10.) Dembei and his shipmates were probably not the first Japanese to have been driven to the shores of Kamchatka. Some Japanese writing found by Lukas Morozko on the peninsula in 1696 is considered to be of earlier origin. (Wilhelm Barthold, *Die geographische und historische Erforschung des Orientes mit besonderer Berücksich-*

Atlasov did not know Dembei for a Japanese. Nonetheless their meeting in 1697 was the first recorded encounter between a Russian and a Japanese, and may be considered the beginning point of Russo-Japanese relations. Informed at Fort Anadyrsk on the Icha River of a stranger, allegedly a Russian, held captive by the Kamchadals at Nane River, Atlasov had him fetched.[34] But though he recognized at once that Dembei, the stranger, was not Russian, he failed to discern his true nationality. In general appearance Dembei seemed to resemble a Greek; he was of lean build and had a sparse beard and black hair. Questioning him at first through an interpreter in the Koriak language, some of which Dembei had learned in the two years of his captivity, and later, after Dembei had remained with him awhile, in Russian, Atlasov concluded finally that Dembei was an Indian from the state of Uzakinsk. It is likely that Atlasov had never heard of Japan. India, on the other hand, was renowned in Russia for its riches even in folksongs, and Dembei talked much of the wealth of his country. Furthermore Edo, the name of Japan's capital, sounded like "Endo" in Osaka dialect, and India suggested itself to Atlasov. The state of Uzakinsk similarly was probably a corruption of the name of Dembei's native city Osaka, which he no doubt gave as his place of origin. But Indian or Japanese, the value of Dembei as a firsthand source of information about foreign lands was obvious, and Atlasov decided to take him along to Yakutsk. Five days' journey out of Fort Anadyrsk the feet of Dembei, who was not accustomed to skiing, swelled up to such an extent that he had to return to the fort and await transportation by carriage. When he reached Yakutsk he found that the chief officer had decided to deliver him to higher authorities and, provided with materials for clothing, allowance for footwear and nourishment, and one ruble spending money, Dembei continued on to Moscow with an escort of Cossacks. News of Dembei's discovery aroused much interest in the capital, interest mixed with concern for his well-being when it was learned that the Cossacks transported also public funds, and orders were issued exhorting the Cossacks to maximum speed and care.

In the closing days of 1701 or at the beginning of 1702 Dembei

---

tigung der russischen Arbeiten, 123; V. V. Bartold, *Materialy dlia istorii fakulteta vostochnykh iazykov,* 1.

[34] Dembei stated in Russia that it had been he who had sought out Atlasov upon the arrival of the Russians in Kamchatka, having been impressed by Russian cleanliness, and anxious lest he be left to starve. (Ogloblin, 21; Zhukov, 10.)

reached Moscow. Here he was correctly identified as Japanese. Nobody could be found who spoke his language, but the members of the Department of Siberian Affairs who interviewed him were better versed in geography than Atlasov, and they had at hand a German account of Japan with pictures of Japanese scenes and objects which Dembei, who by now had broadened his Russian vocabulary, readily identified as Japanese.[35]

Emperor Peter the Great, who had an ardent interest in foreign countries, received Dembei in an extended audience at Preobrazhenskoe Selo near Moscow on January 19, 1702. The same day he decreed that Dembei be instructed in Russian and, having learned Russian, be assigned several young people to teach them both spoken and written Japanese. He stated that it was to be left up to Dembei whether or not he was to be christened, and that Dembei was to be consoled with the promise of eventual repatriation. In April 1702 Dembei was transferred from the Department of Siberian Affairs to the Department of Artillery, there to begin his studies. It is not clear how successful he proved either as student or teacher. In 1705 Peter inquired whether Dembei had actually been taught Russian and in turn had taught Japanese, how many students he had instructed, and whether he was still teaching, but no answer has been handed down. Nevertheless it appears that the same year a Japanese language school was established in St. Petersburg with Dembei as instructor. In 1710 Dembei petitioned for permission to return to Japan, but Peter refused to release him notwithstanding earlier assurances that he could go back upon the completion of his teaching duties. As if to emphasize the finality of his decision Peter went back on yet another promise and ordered Dembei christened; henceforth Dembei was known as Gavriil (Gabriel).[36]

Peter had returned from Europe in 1698. Though he had heard of Japan before his celebrated voyage abroad—in 1688 he had written to Andrei Vinius, secretary of the Department of Siberian Affairs, about the Christian persecutions in Japan—it is likely that in Holland he had acquired additional information about the Dutch in Japan, particularly as he was on close terms with Nikolai Vitsen,

[35] Ogloblin, 13-14; Ramming, *Reisen*, 8; Bartold, *Materialy*, 1; Znamenskii, 37-40.
[36] Ogloblin, 12, 16-18; Znamenskii, 43-44; S. I. Novakovskii, *Iaponiia i Rossiia*, 10-11; Zhukov, 13. Golder, *Russian Expansion*, 101, note 3; Letter from Chief of Artillery Department Efim Zybin to General-in-chief of Artillery Ia. V. Brius, 464. The actual establishment of the school is questioned by Barthold on the ground that he has found no mention of it in contemporary records. (Barthold, *Geographische*, 124.)

mayor of Amsterdam, who had made a careful study of Vries's expedition to Japan and had himself recorded information concerning Japan on a map dedicated to Peter. Dembei now provided new data of importance. Not all his statements were accurate; not all were correctly understood. But this does not detract from their significance; on the contrary, some of the misinformation was especially exciting. Dembei described Japan as a civilized country with walled cities and sturdy buildings, rich in gold and silver, and with internal commerce well developed, a country whose prosperous people worshipped images like those of China and who, though they lived at peace with their neighbors, had firearms.

Dembei reported that the Japanese did not go abroad, that their vessels were limited in size and design to the needs of coastal trade. But he added that Germans (in actuality the Dutch) came to Nagasaki and there and only there resided and traded with the Japanese. He did not elaborate on his government's seclusion policy. To do so in a foreign land would have been impolitic. Yet the omission left the Russians without reason for not seeking out Japan and failed to warn them (or to corroborate warnings that they may have received from others) against the dangers that awaited their mariners at the shores of Japan. Consequential was also a misunderstanding which gave the impression that Japan was part of the Eurasian continent. Dembei did not know that "Kitai" was the Russian name for China. When asked about "Kitai," he apparently mistook it for Akita, a place on the northwestern coast of the Japanese main island and declared emphatically that he had gone there by sea *and by land*. In the absence of data about the northern limits of Japan, the Russians were thus led to conclude erroneously that Japan was joined to Korea by a land bridge under Chinese suzerainty. This prospect must have intrigued Peter for to the economic significance of Dembei's testimony concerning Japan's wealth and foreign trade there was added strategic meaning: if Japan with her firearms bordered on China—perhaps as Spafarii had reported vis-à-vis the Amur River—the Russians, who in spite of withdrawal had retained their interest in the Amur region, might someday find themselves face to face with a new rival on the continent.[37]

[37] Znamenskii, 30; Efimov, *Iz istorii velikikh,* 74, 85; Ogloblin, 21-24.

CHAPTER TWO · IN QUEST OF JAPAN

BY DOGSLED AND BIDARKA

THE discovery of Dembei was a guidepost that routed Russia's search for Japan via Kamchatka. An imperial ukase of 1702 commanded both the subjugation of dissident tribes on Kamchatka and the collection of information about Japan with a view to establishing commercial relations with the latter. The one hundred men whom it ordered to Kamchatka were not adequate to the task, however; more manpower was required to secure Russia's hold on the peninsula. But the imperial wish was not forgotten and in 1710 Dorofei Traurnikht, the chief officer of Yakutsk, referred to the ukase in his instructions to Cossack Vasilii Sevastianov, who set out for Kamchatka to make inquiries about the Japanese and other "wealthy peoples" in the Pacific Ocean and about the establishment of trade with them; and when in 1711 mutineers sought to justify the slaying of some superiors, they argued that one of them had failed to provide the emperor with the information demanded by the ukase.

Meanwhile, in 1704, the Kamchatkan tradesman Vasilii Kolesov had been ordered by the authorities in Yakutsk to explore the limits of Kamchatka and to investigate whether there existed islands nearby and if so to whom they belonged. Two years later, in 1706, one of Kolesov's subordinates, Mikhail Nasedkin, determined the peninsular character of Kamchatka and sighted the first Kuril Islands. But though Nasedkin and his detachment of fifty men took their dog sleds to the very tip of Kamchatka, they halted for lack of ships. Yakutsk authorities were to order the construction of the necessary ships, but by the time these orders arrived, the crossing of the first islands had been negotiated.

The impetus that suddenly carried Cossacks and government servants across the waters to nearby islands was not bravery but fear of retribution. Driven to revolt by the hardships of service and the exactions of the officialdom, the mutineers in 1711 murdered three of their superiors (among them the explorer Atlasov!) and for three months roamed through Kamchatka under the leadership of Danila Antsiforov and Ivan Kozyrevskii, robbing and plundering. Then, to

31

mitigate the punishment which was their due, they played up to the evident interest of Peter the Great in the Pacific area by padding their professions of remorse with pledges to subjugate the native "treacherous thieves" of the Bol'shaia River area and to add new territories to the Russian empire. At the same time they reported that they had freed four Japanese castaways from Kamchadal captivity and had learned from them, as two of the Japanese spoke some Russian (!), that their country was on an island opposite Cape Lopatka in the Pacific Ocean.[1]

True to their promise, the Cossacks and government servants made their way to Cape Lopatka, and from there on small boats and *bidarkas* crossed seven dangerous miles of strong currents and eddies to Shimushu,[2] the first Kuril Island. The natives who inhabited Shimushu were Kamchadals who had lived on southern Kamchatka until the conquest of the peninsula by the Cossacks had forced them off the continent. Now they were subjugated with ruthlessness. Then, disappointed in the flat island's lack of fur-bearing animals, the Russians pushed on to Paramushiru, the second Kuril Island, on three captured barges. But their thirst for peltry remained unquenched. The natives of this large island, pure Kurilians who had migrated hither from islands to the south and are commonly known as Ainu (from the Kurilian word "man" or "inhabitant"), were too numerous to permit the use of force; yet they rejected peaceful requests for tribute and so the Russians had to leave empty-handed. Nevertheless their visit to Paramushiru was not completely in vain. They learned from the Ainu that strangers whose land could be seen from the southern part of the island came to Paramushiru to barter nettle cloth, iron, and other commodities for beaver skins. The island of the strangers, they gathered from the Japanese castaways, was in turn near the city of "Matmai" (Matsumae) and the empire of "Apon" (Japan). Catering again to the interests of Peter, the mutineers could promise to explore Japan itself.[3]

---

[1] Znamenskii, 47-50; Novakovskii, 12. At the time Cape Lopatka was known as Kamchadal'skii Nos, that part of the Pacific Ocean as the Sea of Penzhinsk.

[2] For the sake of consistency and convenience all Kuril Islands are given by their Japanese names, as they are still listed on U.S. Navy and Army maps as well as in most atlases available in American libraries. The Russian variations of the Japanese names may readily be found in standard gazetteers, and are indicated on some of the maps in this book.

[3] A. Polonskii, "Kurily," 374-375. The advance of the Russians to the second island and consequently the authenticity of information received there is open to question. The mutineers may well have exaggerated the weight of their services in order to swing

The Kuril Archipelago, according to Golovnin. Sakhalin, as proved later, is an island.

Upon their return to the mainland in autumn 1711, the Cossacks and government servants found Kamchatka under the jurisdiction of a new commander, Vasilii Savelev. But notwithstanding their own repeated avowals of repentance, they refused to submit to his authority and would not surrender Fort Bol'sheretsk with its personnel and

the balance of justice in their favor. One of the leading figures in these exploits, Grigorii Perelomov, testified in 1712 under torture that the men had not gotten beyond the first island and that although two islands could be seen at sea, their relationship to Matsumae was not known. (Znamenskii, 51-52.)

stores of tribute. On the contrary the mutineers considered murdering Savalev and plundering the various strongholds on Kamchatka and then migrating to the islands beyond the straits. This plan was never put into effect, partly because of the loss of the leadership of Antsiforov who in the spring of 1712 was killed in combat with the natives. When the more experienced Vasilii Kolesov replaced Savelev as commander of Kamchatka, the mutineers bowed in submission.

Kolesov, who had been honored for his previous service on Kamchatka, had orders to deal severely with the mutineers. His original instructions from Yakutsk provided for the death of Antsiforov and six of the ringleaders and at least one of them, Grigorii Perelomov, was interrogated under torture. These instructions were soon superseded by orders from the governor of Siberia, Prince Matvei Gagarin, sparing the mutineers on condition that they would turn to the subjugation of hostile natives and the exploration of new lands. In accordance with these modified instructions Kozyrevskii—whose name had somehow been glossed over in the original list of condemned ringleaders, yet whose close association with Antsiforov made him of value as a potential explorer and who had ingratiated himself by informing on two of his comrades concerning more recent crimes— was let off with a fine and orders to compile a sketch of the limits of Kamchatka and the islands beyond the strait. This he did after another trip to Bol'shaia River, drawing no doubt both on his personal recollections of the voyage to the island and on information gathered from various natives and from the Japanese castaways, shipwrecked in 1710. Among the various things brought back from the expedition were twenty-two Japanese gold coins.[4]

The stories of the castaways about the wealth of the Japanese Islands beyond the Kuril Archipelago goaded Kolesov to take a more determined step in the realization of Peter's ukases, and in spring 1713 he ordered Kozyrevskii to explore the Kuril Islands and the empire of Japan. At the head of an expedition of fifty-five well-armed government servants and hunters from different Kamchatkan forts, as well as eleven tributary natives and with a Japanese castaway by the name of Sanima as guide and interpreter for the Japanese empire, Kozyrevskii visited Shimushu and Paramushiru, the first two Kuril Islands. But though he overcame fierce native resistance and sighted a third island, it was too risky to proceed farther south without native guide, compass, or sails and he returned to Kamchatka before the

---

[4] Harima, 792; Znamenskii, 52-54.

seasonal cessation of navigation. Nevertheless Kozyrevskii had added to his information sufficiently to be able to draft the first Western description of the whole Kuril Archipelago.[5] Inaccurate as this description proved in detail, it was important *in toto*, for while it made Japan more distant, it also made it more accessible because it revealed the island route from Russia to Japan. At the same time it pointed to a leak in Japanese seclusion and to the possibility of Russo-Japanese trade outside Japan, for Kozyrevskii reported that Japanese traders came to the sixth island to obtain ore in exchange for iron and cast iron kettles, lacquered eating utensils, cotton, and silk materials, as well as swords and knives. This information he had obtained indirectly from a native of Etorofu, and from Sanima.[6]

While Kozyrevskii was thus engaged in approaching Japan by way of the Kuril Archipelago, others advanced into the Pacific Ocean from the coastal regions north of the Amur Estuary. In 1714, before Kozyrevskii's report could have been received in the capital, orders went out to Nerchinsk to send two men to the limits of the Russian empire to explore lands at sea. The two duly reached the Sea of Okhotsk and turning southward journeyed landwise down the shore until they sighted an island. Inexperienced though they were in navigation, the two men safely reached that island in a small boat; but on their way back, the boat sank and the two perished, taking with them the secret of what they had seen. It is likely that their fateful journey had taken them either to the western extremity of Sakhalin or to one of the Shantar Islands, which had just been discovered successfully by Cossacks dispatched from Fort Udsk. Although it is not certain whether the two men had set out in search

[5] Znamenskii, 54-56; Golder, Russian Expansion, 111-113; Polonskii, 390. Kozyrevskii identified the sixth island as Shokki. His enumeration of the Kuril Islands, followed by other early travelers, differs from present usage in numerical designation—he counted only the major islands—and at times even in name. See map of Shestakov. Kozyrevskii reversed the order of Uruppu and Etorofu. The map compiled by Lieutenant Commander V. M. Golovin a century later included smaller islands in its count. See map. According to Golovin's count Ezo or Matsumae (Hokkaido), on which Atkis (Akkeshi) was located, is the twenty-second island. The first Japanese map of the Kuril Islands was drawn up by Sasaki Hyoye in about 1667. (Hiroteru Yamamoto, "History of the Kuriles, Shikotan, and the Habomai Islands," 461.) A picture of the relatively accurate map of the Kuril Islands by Nagakubo Sekisui (1786) may be found in the Japanese Ministry of Foreign Affairs, Public Information Bureau, *The Northern Islands*, 17.

[6] In later years Russian statesmen were to lay claim to the northern Kurils on the ground of prior discovery. Yet if Kozyrevskii, as it seems, had obtained a large part of his information from the Japanese castaways, Kozyrevskii's description does actually more to discredit than to substantiate Russian "finders-keepers" claims. Kozyrevskii reported that he had extended Russian suzerainty to the two northernmost islands.

of Japan, persistent belief in the proximity of Japan nourished the hope that the empire might be reached from where they had started. Certainly it was with this expectation that two merchant houses in St. Petersburg, when they petitioned the Senate in 1716 for permission to trade with Japan and the East Indies, unfamiliar as yet with the details of Siberian geography, routed their cargo from Arkhangelsk to the Pacific coast by way of the Northern Dvina River and the Arctic Ocean to the mouth of the Ob River, across Lake Baikal and via the rivers Selenga, Ingoda, Shilka, and Amur.[7] The Amur River was still in Chinese hands, but its overwhelming importance as an artery of communication dictated its inclusion in Russian calculations of transcontinental transportation. Arkhangelsk was the gateway to contemporary Russian trade with western Europe. The merchant houses thus proposed to become middlemen between western Europe and the Far East. Enthusiastically endorsed as the plan was by Iakov Brius, General-in-chief of Artillery, with whom the petition was filed, it fell short of realization because the eastern regions were as yet insufficiently explored. Yet it spurred the acquisition of the necessary knowledge. When lack of suitable personnel prevented the governor of Siberia from supplying Brius with data about the navigability of the Amur and information about Japan, which he had requested in support of the above petition, Brius recommended to Peter that trained geodesists be dispatched to make a scientific survey of eastern Siberia and of a water route to Japan.[8]

In 1719 Ivan Evreinov and Fedor Luzhin, geodesists with Naval Academy training in the latest western European techniques of cartography, departed for the extremities of the Russian empire ostensibly to determine whether Asia joined America, but in fact to explore the Kuril Islands and to collect detailed information about Japan. They reached Okhotsk in the summer of 1720 and repairing an old, but large, boat which they found there continued to Kamchatka by sea in September. In spring 1721 they moved the vessel from Icha River, where it had wintered, to Bol'sheretsk, and on June 2 set sail for the islands to the South and Southwest. The seafarer Konradii Moshkov who had accompanied the geodesists from Okhotsk

[7] The concept of trade between Europe and the Far East by way of the Arctic was not new. The Muscovy Company had been organized in the sixteenth century with a view to finding a Northeast Passage, and Russian seafarers voyaged at that time past Novaia Zemlia and Vaigach Island to the mouth of the Ob and Enisei.

[8] Polonskii, 389-393; Sgibnev, "Popytki," 39-40; Znamenskii, 57-60; Novakovskii, 14.

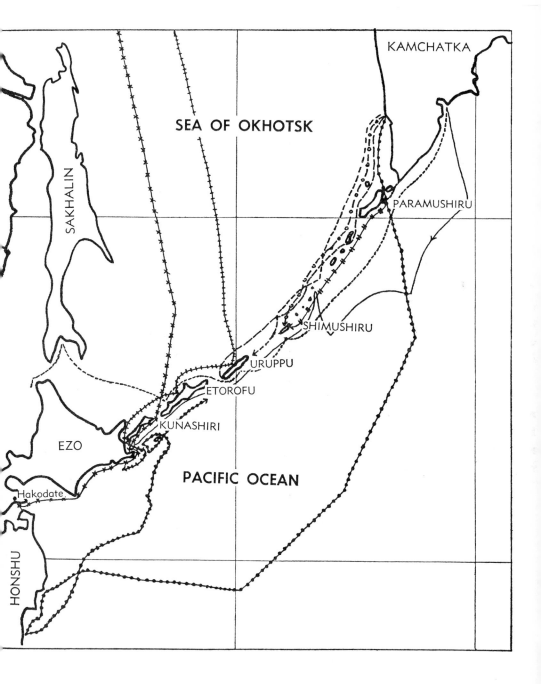

KAMCHATKA

SEA OF OKHOTSK

SAKHALIN

PARAMUSHIRU

SHIMUSHIRU

URUPPU

ETOROFU

KUNASHIRI

EZO

PACIFIC OCEAN

Hakodate

HONSHU

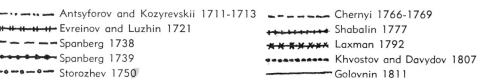

—··—··— Antsyforov and Kozyrevskii 1711-1713
╫—╫—╫—╫— Evreinov and Luzhin 1721
— — — — — Spanberg 1738
◆—◆—◆—◆— Spanberg 1739
—○—○—○— Storozhev 1750

— — — — Chernyi 1766-1769
+—+—+—+—+ Shabalin 1777
✕✕✕✕✕✕ Laxman 1792
◆·····◆ Khvostov and Davydov 1807
———————— Golovnin 1811

Early Russian Voyages
to the Kuril Islands and Japan

navigated the vessel; only one other person in the retinue of the Cossacks seems to have had nautical experience—a captive Swede by the name of Andrei Bush.

The Russians got as far as the fifth or sixth island,[9] when a storm tore their sail and forced them to cast anchor. On the third day both cables broke, and the Russians were swept into the open sea. Tossed about for a week, they were finally carried to Paramushiru Island by a change in wind. Short of food and water they let down a cannon and an anvil. When they tried to weigh this makeshift anchor the cable snapped, and once more they were at the mercy of the elements. But the wind was favorable and in spite of a torn sail they succeeded in reaching Bol'sheretsk toward the beginning of July. Here they made wooden anchors, weighted down with frying pans from the ship, and later that month safely negotiated the crossing to Okhotsk, and the geodesists returned to Europe.

In 1722 Evreinov and Luzhin were received by Peter at Kazan and made a personal report. From the beginning their mission had been cloaked in secrecy, and it is not known what they communicated, though they are said to have presented a map containing sixteen of the Kuril Islands. As it seems unlikely that the search for a route to Japan per se had motivated this secrecy, scholars speculate that Peter may have taken interest in the Kuril Islands not only as stepping stones to the Japanese empire, but may have hoped to find among them the legendary islands of gold and silver. The sixth island, which Evreinov and Luzhin may have reached, was the one from which, according to Kozyrevskii, the Japanese obtained ore. There is no reason to assume that the geodesists had learned anything new about Japan. On the other hand, they had advanced farther along the Kuril chain than any of their countrymen and thus had taken Russia yet another step closer to Japan.

The voyage of the two geodesists marked the beginning of a more scientific approach in Russian exploration. The vessel which they had reconditioned in Okhotsk was a sixty-foot-long one-master, on which the seafarer Nikifor Treska had negotiated the first maritime voyage from Okhotsk to Kamchatka in 1716. This open boat, how-

---

[9] Individual differences in numbering the islands make it impossible to determine exactly how far Evreinov and Luzhin traveled. Sgibnev writes that they got as far as the fifth island; Baer and Polonskii that they reached the sixth island (Shokki). (Sgibnev, "Popytki," 41; K. E. Baer, *Die Verdienste Peter des Grossen um die Erweiterung der geographischen Kenntnisse*, 34; Polonskii, 394. See also Stepan Krasheninnikov, *Opisanie zemli kamchatki*, 491, 786 note 4; Efimov, *Iz istorii velikikh*, 148.)

ever imperfect, was the first vessel of a new, western European construction to sail along the Kuril Archipelago, and was superior in seaworthiness to the frail little crafts heretofore in use.[10]

Situated on the Gulf of Finland, St. Petersburg, the new capital of Russia since 1713, had become the cradle of a modern fleet, which included for the first time in Russian history real sea-going ships, some two and three decks high, studded with as many as a hundred cannons. To be sure some had been constructed in too great a haste with green timber and other inadequate materials, and soon sprang leaks and rotted; others were lost at sea by inexperienced commanders and crews. But nonetheless, thanks to foreign help, in but a brief span of time a Russian navy mushroomed on the Baltic shores.

The remoteness of the eastern regions delayed the introduction of western European techniques to Pacific navigation, but the ever-present interest in furs—the desire to transport them to the markets of Europe as quickly, safely, and inexpensively as possible—was to overcome all distance. The cost of native raids on overland caravans, which between 1703 and 1715 took some two hundred Russian lives and between 1707 and 1712 completely blocked the exit of any tribute from Kamchatka, challenged the Russians to transport the furs to the Okhotsk shores by open sea. This was a task which demanded more than the mere issuance of orders by the governor of Siberia, more than the half-hearted efforts of local officials whose sober moments seemed dedicated to feathering their own nest. Consequently expert seamen and ship's carpenters (among them Moshkov and Treska) were sent out from St. Petersburg and Yakutsk. Their instructions clearly mirrored the difficulties ahead. On one hand the men were promised both worldly and spiritual rewards: wealth, promotions, and imperial favor if by the grace of Christ they would reach Kamchatka and if by Divine grace they would return in one piece; life everlasting and care of their families, if by the will of Christ they did not survive. On the other hand they were threatened with certain death if they delayed or slowed down their voyage to Kamchatka or returned without having completed their mission. Whatever the incentive, the seamen and ship's carpenters arrived in Okhotsk in 1714 to lay the keel of a Russian fleet on the Pacific.

By the summer of 1716 a sixty-foot-long one-master was completed.

[10] Sgibnev, "Popytki," 41; *Polnoe sobranie zakonov russkoi imperii*, v, no. 3266; Znamenskii, 70-72; Zhukov, 14-15; Gerhard Friedrich Müller, *Sammlung russischer Geschichte*, III, 109-110; Otomo Kisaku, *Hokumon sosho*, I, 108-112.

With Treska at the helm, it ventured to Kamchatka and back. Hazardous and slow though its one-year round trip was, it proved the feasibility of such a sea route. It was this modern vessel that Evreinov and Luzhin were to use in their exploration of the Kuril Islands.

Other seafarers were sent to the Okhotsk shores, as was also a much prized compass. But because the transportation of tribute seemed the *raison d'être* for a Pacific fleet, not many vessels were required and shipbuilding bogged down. Nevertheless seamen and carpenters continued to improve their skill and such minor voyages as those of Evreinov and Luzhin laid the foundations for the ultimate realization of naval expeditions on a much larger scale.[11]

TO THE SHORES OF JAPAN

Throughout the first quarter of the eighteenth century Peter the Great remained the major fountainhead of Russian interest in Japan. The hanging in 1721 for the gross misuse of funds of Prince Gagarin, who had displayed at least mild enthusiasm in the execution of Peter's plans of exploration, only added to the burden of initiative on the part of the government, for once the expeditions to the Kuril and Shantar Islands had disclosed that Japan was not in the immediate vicinity of the Russian shores, Gagarin's successor, Prince Cherkasskii, retained little inclination to push its discovery. Once again reports from China and Japanese castaways became the main sources of information about Japan.

The Swede Ivan-Lorents Lange, when he proceeded to Peking with the embassy of Leon Vasilevich Izmailov in 1719 as first Russian commercial agent, bore instructions to gather all the information possible about Japan and about trade with Japan. The Dutch drew their greatest profits from this trade; so would the Russians once permission was granted to navigate the Amur, "especially in view of the low costs or losses and the lack of danger involved in the travel of the Russians and the importation of their goods and the exportation of others." The intelligence that Lange brought back about Japan after being expelled from Peking in 1722 for trying to communicate with envoys from Korea in an attempt to obtain from them additional information about China and nearby lands did not clarify the question of Japan's location, but it did throw light on the conditions of trade, stating that trade was permitted to the Dutch

[11] Znamenskii, 61-69.

only, that it consisted in the exchange of tawed skins from Batavia for Japanese gold, silver, and porcelains, and that it was limited to four or five Dutch vessels a year. Lange described how the Japanese forced the Dutch to disarm and to remain within the confines of a special fortress, and how, when they were permitted to visit the city, they must first trample on a cross to give evidence that they would not propagate the Christian faith. He added that the Japanese were no more versed in military matters than the Chinese, had but a few small vessels, and relied primarily on arrows rather than firearms.[12]

Stories of Japan's wealth in gold, silver, and other things were corroborated by the mounting number of Japanese castaways in Russia. In 1708 and again in 1710 Japanese junks had been wrecked at Kamchatka. Of those Japanese who survived the first wreck, all fell into the hands of the natives but four, who were taken prisoner by the boyar Chirikov. Of the ten men who lived through the second wreck, four were killed by the natives, six taken into custody by Antsiforov.[13] Fearful lest the eventual death of Dembei put an end to Japanese language instruction, the government had ordered that in the event of such wrecks one castaway be sent to St. Petersburg. And so one of these men—apparently the same Sanima who had accompanied the expedition of Kozyrevskii—was taken to Yakutsk, christened Ivan, and sent on to the capital, where he arrived in 1714.[14] In 1729 another rice-laden junk was carried to Cape Lopatka. This time the Cossack Andrei Shtinnikov got to the Japanese before the natives did. But this was hardly cause for thanksgiving, for though Shtinnikov welcomed the castaways with professions of friendship, he craved their belongings and set upon them with the Kamchadals, killing all but two of the Japanese. As news of the robbery seeped out, local authorities vied with each other in conducting an investigation. The Japanese captives were freed and Shtinnikov thrown into jail until he agreed to split the booty with the officials. Only in 1733 did justice triumph when a new investigation was launched and both Shtinnikov and one of his earlier investigators were hanged. The two

[12] *Ibid.*, 73-75; K. Skalkovskii, *Russkaia torgovlia v Tikhom okeane*, 364; Kiuner, 9-10.
[13] Sgibnev, "Popytki" 38. According to Znamenskii four Japanese were rescued in 1710. (pp. 49-50.)
[14] Barthold and Znamenskii state that Sanima arrived in St. Petersburg in 1714; Efimov that he arrived in 1719; Zhukov in 1711. According to Sgibnev Sanima was assigned to Dembei as an assistant. Barthold on the other hand notes that there is no evidence that Sanima ever taught Japanese to any Russians. (Barthold, *Geographische*, 125; Znamenskii, 50; Efimov, *Iz istorii velikikh*, 100, and *Iz istorii russkikh*, 88; Zhukov, 13; Sgibnev, 56; Bartold, *Materialy*, IV, 4-5.)

castaways, Sozo and Gonzo, were sent to Yakutsk, to Tobolsk, to Moscow, and eventually to St. Petersburg where in 1734 they were presented to the Empress, Anna Ioannovna, who ordered that they be christened (Sozo receiving the name Kuzma Schulz, Gonzo the name Demian Pomortsev) and that they be taught Russian.[15]

In the first quarter of the eighteenth century, Edo was the most populous city in the world with possibly a million inhabitants. Osaka numbered over three hundred and fifty thousand residents. Japan as a whole harbored already some thirty million souls.[16] The Japanese castaways, from Dembei to Sozo and Gonzo, were therefore struck by the bareness of Russia's eastern regions; even the sight of eighteenth century Moscow and St. Petersburg did not eradicate the impression of emptiness. When scholars from the Academy of Sciences interviewed them in 1735, they described Japan as a country of large cities, and fascinated their hosts with stories of Japan's great wealth in precious metals, costly materials, and foodstuffs.

In June of 1736 Schulz and Pomortsev initiated Japanese language instruction at the St. Petersburg Academy of Sciences under the supervision of Andrei Bogdanov, assistant librarian of the academy.[17] But though two students (Petr Shenanykin and Andrei Fenev) were assigned to the Japanese, the secrets of their tongue remained uncommunicated. Schulz died at the age of forty-three in the very year that Japanese instruction commenced, and Pomortsev followed only three years later, in 1739, at the early age of twenty-one. Pomortsev, the more talented of the two, could not write Japanese, but he had learned a considerable amount of Russian and in collaboration with Bogdanov had compiled three Japanese primers in Russian script. The Academy of Sciences preserved the memory of the two teachers with alabaster forms made of their faces. Fenev and Shenanykin continued their studies and even undertook to teach others, but the results were to be unsatisfactory. Still, steps had been taken to train

[15] Barthold, *Geographische,* 123-130; Bartold, *Materialy,* IV, 1-5, 14-19; Harima, 792-793; Znamenskii, 80-82; Novakovskii, 18-20. Harima suggests Japanese characters for Sozo and Gonzo. Barthold renders the names as Soza and Goza.

[16] Smith, 34-35; Sansom, *Japan,* 466.

[17] Some authorities assert that Bogdanov was the son of Sanima by a Russian wife. Bartold (*Materialy,* IV, 3-4) elaborately disproves this, pointing out that Bogdanov was too old to have been born since Sanima's arrival. It is not impossible that A. Bogdanov, an artist, rather than A. I. Bogdanov, the librarian, was thus related and named in honor of the librarian. If the assertion of A. I. Bogdanov's biographers that he was born in 1707 in Siberia as the offspring of a Japanese were true, he would have had to be the son of Dembei, then the only Japanese in Russia, but Dembei was at that time already in Moscow.

interpreters for the day when the improved Russian vessels would finally penetrate to the shores of Japan.[18]

Peter the Great's interest in Japan was unquestionable. Even during his campaigns in northern Europe and the Near East he found time to listen to discussion of Russian trade in the Pacific area—with Japan, the Philippines, and America. But his death in 1725 threatened to take the wind out of the sails of Russian voyages east. Just then the Cossack Kozyrevskii, whose adventures had attracted attention a decade earlier, appeared on the scene again and with extravagant claims once more fanned up Russian interest in Japan.

Kozyrevskii had disappeared from the forefront of early explorations in 1716, when, in consequence of new mischief on his part, he was deprived of his possessions and commanded to shave his head. But the robes of the monk Ignatii, which Kozyrevskii donned, failed to confine his turbulent spirit, and he was for ever at odds with those about him. Thus in 1724 he found himself under arrest, and escaping from his guards, faced the prospect of increasingly heavy punishment, when he resorted to the stratagem that had saved his neck in 1711: he offered to show the way to Japan. In a petition to the chief officer of Yakutsk he asked to be sent to Moscow to instruct the highest authorities how and by what means Japan could be reached. This proposal was duly forwarded to the governor of Siberia and though it did not lead to Kozyrevskii's release to Moscow, it forestalled his incarceration. Captain Vitus Bering, a Dane who had entered Russian service in 1703, was then passing through Tobolsk on his way to Okhotsk with instructions in Peter's own hand to outfit an expedition to determine whether or not Asia and America joined. (As will be recalled the geodesists Evreinov and Luzhin had failed to

---

[18] Harima, 792-794; Barthold, *Geographische*, 123-130; Novakovskii, 17-20; Znamenskii, 81-82. Znamenskii reverses the order and dates of Sozo and Gonzo's deaths.

In 1745 more Japanese were wrecked off Kamchatka. Five of them (known in Russia as Melnikov, Reshetnikov, Svinin, Popov, and Chernykh) were sent to the Japanese language school in St. Petersburg, then attached to the Senate Office, but none of them had the talent of Pomortsev. In 1753 the school was transferred to Irkutsk. Fenev, Shenanykin and three of the castaways were sent there. In Irkutsk the school remained with interruptions until 1816, but still without success. No Russian student of Japanese was assigned to the first Russian expedition to Japan (1739). Fenev and Shenanykin participated in a subsequent voyage (1742), but the vessels failed to reach Japan. In 1761 the Irkutsk school was strengthened by the addition of personnel of another Japanese language school, previously in Ilimsk. In 1772 four students were made "corporals of Japanese." But when in 1792 Tugolukov, a student of the school, finally made his way to Japan with the Laxman expedition, the Japanese proved unable to understand him. (Bartold, *Materialy*, IV, 18-19; Kiuner, 13 footnote; Harima, 793-800.)

pursue this part of their instructions.) It seemed only reasonable to present Kozyrevskii to Bering, and they met in Yakutsk in 1726.[19]

Bering's mission was clear. A voyage to Japan would have exceeded the scope of his present expedition. But he promised to take the matter up upon his return to the capital. Meanwhile Kozyrevskii's talk of new lands and islands in the Pacific as well as the urgings of the Cossack Afanasii Shestakov that the natives of the nearby islands be brought more firmly under Russian sway had reached the ear of Empress Catherine I and Shestakov was ordered to explore the seas bordering the Russian far east and subjugate new lands with a view to further Russian expansion southward toward Japan. The expedition of Afanasii Shestakov, to which Kozyrevskii attached himself, was readied by 1729. It encompassed several ships: the *Gavriil* and *Fortuna*, vessels left from Bering's first expedition, and the *Vostochnyi Gavriil* and *Lev*, newly constructed. The vessels did not travel together; they had different assignments. Yet the whole venture sounds almost like a family affair: Afanasii Shestakov set out on the *Vostochnyi Gavriil*, accompanied by the *Lev*, while the *Fortuna* was commanded by his son Vasilii Shestakov and the *Gavriil* by his nephew Ivan Shestakov (who had participated in the first Bering expedition). The expedition as a whole was a failure. Afanasii Shestakov himself and many of the men with him were killed by natives near the Penzhina River, but Vasilii Shestakov succeeded in visiting some of the northern Kuril Islands[20] and one of the Shestakovs[21] in reaching Kamchatka just in time to help rescue the Japanese castaways, Sozo and Gonzo, from the clutches of Shtinnikov—and share some of the loot.[22]

Bering's experiences in the East, both on land and at sea, gave him pause to ponder Russian objectives in the Pacific region. In 1730 he submitted two memoranda to Empress Anna Ioannovna[23] in which he dwelled on the development of Siberia and the need of exploring Russia's own northeastern shores and the shores of America across the Pacific. His expedition of 1725 to 1730 had failed to solve the

---

19 Znamenskii, 55-56, 74-76; Polonskii, 396-397; Sgibnev, "Popytki," 43; Novakovskii, 16.

20 Shestakov claimed to have gone as far as the fifth island, but it is more likely that he did not go beyond the second island.

21 According to Kiuner Ivan, according to Znamenskii Vasilii.

22 Kiuner, 11-13; Efimov, *Iz istorii russkikh*, 156-159; Znamenskii, 79-82.

23 Novakovskii (p. 28) writes that Bering memorialized Catherine I, but that the plans materialized in the reign of Anna Ioannovna. This would mean that Bering presented the memoranda several years earlier, but he did not return until 1730.

question of the contiguity of America and Asia, and much remained to be checked in this area. At the same time he emphasized the desirability of establishing contacts with Russia's nearest oceanic neighbor, Japan. "It would be not without benefit," he wrote, "to explore the Okhotsk and Kamchatka water ways to the mouth of the Amur and beyond to the Japanese islands, because I hope that it will be possible to find there suitable places for trade." Bering believed that trade with Japan (direct or indirect by way of the Kurils) would be of great profit. The lack of Russian vessels in that region could be overcome by building a ship on Kamchatka. "It will be possible to draw also on the Japanese vessels which happen to be coming the other way," he suggested.[24]

Bering's memoranda thus envisaged a new and larger expedition with broader objectives. Such an expedition required a Pacific base of operations. No longer was it adequate to obtain basic materials from Yakutsk. Bering proposed the development of the Okhotsk region and in particular the transformation of the little settlement at the mouth of the Okhota River into a regular port with facilities for shipbuilding and repairs, as well as the training of students in navigation.[25]

The Empress received Bering's suggestions with favor and initiated preparations for the first successful Russian expedition to Japan. She appointed Grigorii Skorniakov-Pisarev commander of the Okhotsk region, ordering him to populate it with colonists and artisans, and to construct a port with a small wharf and to build not only several small vessels suitable for runs to Kamchatka and back with furs and with merchants and their wares but also large ships, and to set up manual blast-furnaces and to forge anchors and other necessary nautical equipment. Although Skorniakov-Pisarev was to make use of local resources, she promised him the assistance of expert carpenters and seamen from the capital and elsewhere. The seamen would be necessary because Skorniakov-Pisarev was to do more than just establish a base of operations on the mainland. He was to send tribute collectors to islands already discovered and men and supplies to Kuril Islands not yet known. If possible he was to establish commercial relations with Japan. In this connection he was advised, as

---

[24] Sgibnev, "Popytki," 43; Znamenskii, 83. For a slightly different rendering of Bering's second memorandum see Golder, *Russian Expansion*, 166-169. Chirikov modified the original statement.

[25] Golder writes that Chirikov had suggested that the boats be built at Okhotsk and not in Kamchatka.

Bering had suggested, that if more Japanese castaways were found, they be treated well and be taken back to their homeland, thereby giving cause for friendship and a pretext for free trade.

But Skorniakov-Pisarev failed to smooth the way for Bering. During the reign of Peter the Great, Skorniakov-Pisarev had distinguished himself as Director of the Naval Academy and as Chief Procurator of the Senate, but in later years he had run afoul of a court favorite and had been flogged and banished to Siberia. In exile Skorniakov-Pisarev had gone to seed. Upon his appointment as commandant of Okhotsk he had set out to the east, but stopped for almost three years at Yakutsk where he and the local chief official not only quarreled over men, equipment, and supplies for Okhotsk, but became rivals in denouncing and even arresting each other. When Skorniakov-Pisarev finally reached Okhotsk he gave himself over to plunder, turbulence and drink. Instead of laying the foundations for Bering's expedition he set up a harem and took delight in riding down the icy slopes of Okhotsk with his concubines.[26]

Meanwhile Bering's plans had been carefully examined by the Senate, the Admiralty College, and the Academy of Sciences and in the process the expedition had increased constantly until it reached gigantic proportions. Bering's proposals included related but quite different objectives, and so the Second Bering Expedition, known also as the Great Northern Expedition and the Second Kamchatkan Expedition encompassed really several expeditions. These fell into two main categories: naval expeditions of discovery sent to explore the shores of Russia, America, and Japan and scientific expeditions designed to investigate Kamchatka, the eastern regions, and lands already discovered and lands yet to be discovered by the other expeditions. Bering himself, newly raised to the rank of Captain-Commander, was in command of the total venture. Lieutenant-Commanders Martin Spanberg,[27] like Bering, a Dane, and Aleksei Chirikov, a Russian, who had served with him on his first expedition, were again appointed his assistants. Chirikov was to accompany Bering to America. Spanberg on the other hand was to proceed to Japan, assisted by Lieutenant William Walton, an Englishman who had but recently entered the Russian service, and by Ensign Aleksei Shelting, the young son of a Dutch seaman. The Second Bering Expedition

---

26 Znamenskii, 84-86; Golder, *Russian Expansion*, 169.

27 Morten Spangberg in Danish; variously spelled also Spagenburg, Spagenberg, and Supangenberugu.

was starred with scientists of note, a large number of ships, a complement of about 570 men, costly equipment and ample funds—all participants were granted double pay and two years' pay in advance. Thus the new Russian attempt to establish relations with Japan was part of what Golder has called "one of the most elaborate, thorough, and expensive expeditions ever sent out by any government at any time."[28]

Spanberg was ordered to construct three vessels, either at Okhotsk or on Kamchatka, and on these to set out in search of Japan by way of the Kuril Islands. En route he was to collect tribute from the northernmost islands, which were already part of the Russian domain. He was to describe the other Kuril Islands, treat the natives there well, and make them Russian subjects, if they themselves so desired, and even then not to demand any tribute. He was to make inquiries, and if he found that any of the islands were Japanese, was to attempt to establish friendly relations with the inhabitants. He was not to linger on the islands, but was to push on to Japan itself. There he should do his utmost to establish friendly relations with the Japanese, or at least to make them well disposed toward Russia. Should he find Japanese castaways on Kamchatka, he was to take them along as a pretext for his visit. Under no circumstances was he to seize Japanese vessels at sea to bolster his expedition, as Bering had suggested, nor to undertake any other hostile acts. He was instructed to investigate the conditions of Japan and of its ports. He was specifically warned to do so with great care, lest he be led into a Japanese trap and captured. If attacked by Japanese vessels he was to withdraw.[29]

Bering's memoranda to Empress Anna Ioannovna had been submitted in 1730. Colonists had been ordered dispatched to the Okhotsk area in preparation for the expedition in 1731, and the Senate had officially approved the expedition at the end of the following year. But such were the problems of overland communication and the difficulties involved in outfitting the large expedition that though Spanberg left St. Petersburg in spring of 1733, he did not reach

---

[28] Golder, *Russian Expansion*, 170-171; Znamenskii, 86-87. Among the scholars of the expedition there were: the historian, Professor Fedr Ivanovich Miller (Gerhard Friedrich Müller); the doctor, chemist, and botanist, Georg Gmelin; the naturalist, Wilhelm Steller, and others. (Hirabayashi Hirondo, "The Discovery of Japan from the North," 321.)

[29] Berg, 94; *Polnoe sobranie zakonov* VIII, nos. 6023, 6291; Kurt Krupinski, *Japan und Russland*, 11; Golder, *Russian Expansion*, 221-222; Znamenskii, 87-88.

Okhotsk until autumn of the following year and was not able to set sail until the summer of 1738! Part of the delay was due to constant friction—sometimes even armed clashes—among the various officials. At times such conflict was due to the coarse nature of the daredevil explorers; at times it was due to national prejudice—Spanberg's disdain for things Russian or Chirikov's resentment of Spanberg's attitude.[30]

When Spanberg reached Okhotsk in advance of Bering, who, engrossed in organizational work, had halted at Yakutsk, he found that Skorniakov-Pisarev had failed to establish the necessary quarters. He therefore set about constructing shelter and vessels at the mouth of the Okhota River. But Skorniakov-Pisarev, who arrived somewhat later, disapproved of the site and began a separate project. There followed the usual recriminations and mutual denunciations notwithstanding the fact that in choice of site they were both proven wrong by a sudden flood that washed away all their labors. Nor did Bering's arrival in Okhotsk put an end to dissention. On the contrary, Skorniakov-Pisarev ordered his subordinates to shadow members of the expedition, whom he suspected of illegal acts, all the way to Kamchatka while Bering, who had even less trust in Skorniakov-Pisarev's emissaries, denied them passage. There was jealousy and bitterness within the ranks of the expedition as well. We have already mentioned the dislike between Spanberg and Chirikov. Yet the two teamed up in denunciations of their leader, Bering!

Such waste of effort only encumbered a task already difficult. Four years after the initiation of the expedition its leader had not yet reached the Pacific shores. The government which had approved the undertaking in the belief that it could be completed in six years, therefore, began to put pressure on Bering to hasten matters along. His pay was cut in half and he was threatened with demotion. At the same time, the government realized that the delay was not solely Bering's fault, and sent special officers to Siberia to enforce local response to Bering's needs. Nevertheless it was summer 1740, before the two-masted packet boats *Sviatoi Petr* and *Sviatoi Pavel*, on which Bering and Chirikov were to sail to America, were completed.

Spanberg's somewhat smaller vessels were readied before this: in the autumn of 1737. They consisted of the newly-constructed flagship *Arkhangel Mikhail*, a one-masted brigantine sixty feet in length

---

30 *Polnoe sobranie zakonov,* VIII, 1002-1013; Znamenskii, 89; Zhukov, 22. Golder states that Spanberg reached Okhotsk early in 1735. (*Russian Expansion,* 173.)

and eighteen feet in width, captained by Spanberg himself and manned by Navigator Petrov, Pharmaceutist Gardebol, the medic Goviia and a crew of sixty-three; the newly built *Nadezhda*, a three-masted double sloop, seventy feet in length and eighteen feet in width, commanded by Lieutenant Walton and manned by Navigator Kazimirov and a crew of forty-four; and the renovated *Sviatoi Gavriil*, built for Bering's first Expedition and commanded by Ensign Shelting and manned by Naviagator's Mate Vereshchagin and a crew of forty-four. Another vessel, the *Fortuna*, had also been reconditioned, but remained in the Sea of Okhotsk, and was wrecked shortly.

On June 29, 1738 the *Arkhangel Mikhail*, *Nadezhda*, and *Sviatoi Gavriil* weighed anchor and went out to sea but encountering ice entered the security of Bol'shaia River at Bol'sheretsk on the western coast of Kamchatka for a week on July 18. Then, on July 26, swelled by the addition of several new participants—Navigator's Mate Rodichev, the geodesist Svistunov, three sailors and two interpreters—and replenished with fresh supplies, the vessels resumed their voyage. When they reached Paramushiru Island they set course to the southwest and headed down the archipelago. The sea was calm and the air felt pleasantly warm. But the usual summer fogs soon engulfed the ships and the captains lost sight of each other. On July 30 the *Sviatoi Gavriil* fell behind, on August 4, the *Nadezhda*. Spanberg sailed alone as far as Uruppu, naming and entering on a map the various islands he passed. The fog prevented an accurate count and Spanberg listed thirty-one Kuril Islands—more than actually existed in the area he had visited. Uruppu, Spanberg named Ol'khov Island. He sighted an island south of Uruppu, but did not proceed farther. The jagged, fathomless shores of the islands, the swift currents, and the countless unknown dangers ahead had become increasingly fearful as the nights of onrushing autumn shortened each day. The other vessels had fallen behind and provisions ran low. Spanberg rounded Uruppu and on August 14 at approximately latitude 45°30' N. turned back to Bol'sheretsk, where he arrived safely on the 28th of the same month. There he found Shelting, who had started back the day after they had become separated and had returned to Bol'sheretsk already on August 18. Walton, on the other hand, had proceeded farther south than Spanberg—to latitude 43°N.—and come about only on August 22, reaching Bol'sheretsk on September 4. Neither Spanberg nor Walton had sighted Hokkaido, though Spanberg reached the latitude where it was purported to lie and Walton penetrated even

to the latitude where it was in fact situated. Neither Spanberg nor
Walton had attempted to land on any of the Kuril Islands; they had
entered the islands on a map (though inaccurately) but without taking time to explore them. And yet the Russian push toward Japan
had entered a new phase. The new vessels had easily traversed waters
that the fragile crafts of earlier days could only have negotiated with
difficulty, if at all. Spanberg and Walton had seen islands that Kozyrevskii and his contemporaries had known only by hearsay.[31]

On June 1, 1739, earlier in the season than the preceding year,
Spanberg and his companions started out again, this time accompanied by a fourth vessel, the eighteen-oar sloop *Bolsheretsk* which
had been constructed during the winter out of birch wood in the
harbor in whose honor it was named. Four days later they reached
the first Kuril Island where an interpreter was taken aboard and
where, for some undetermined reason, Walton and Shelting exchanged command of their ships—Walton transferring onto the
Sviatoi Gavriil, Shelting onto the *Nadezhda.* On June 12, the Russian
vessels set course for Japan, but not by way of the Kuril Islands as
in the previous year. Instead, they steered southward into the open
sea, hoping to reach the so-called Land of Gama. When, contrary to
the assertion of the geographer Guillaume Deslisle, the apocryphal
Land of Gama failed to materialize, they altered course at latitude
42°N. and headed southwest to latitude 39°N. and thence due west.
On June 25 the *Sviatoi Gavriil,* separated from the squadron allegedly because of damages sustained in a heavy storm, but possibly
because Walton, like other subordinate commanders of his day,
wished to do some exploring on his own.[32]

On June 27, Spanberg and his companions sighted at long last
the northeastern shores of the Japanese main island at about latitude
39° N. and followed down the coast for two days, casting anchor on
the 18th at latitude 38°41′ N. off the east coast of Iwate Prefecture.
The Russians were dazzled by the luxurious vegetation of the countryside that stretched out before them, all the greener by comparison
with the barren shores of Okhotsk and Kamchatka. They were impressed also by the numerous settlements that dotted the coastline.
Two boats came within close view, and the Russians motioned them

---

31 Znamenskii, 89-92; Golder, *Russian Expansion,* 174-175, 221-222; Tabohashi Kiyoshi,
Kindai Nihon gaikoku kankei-shi, 52.

32 Znamenskii, 92-93; Berg, 98; Golder, *Russian Expansion,* 222-223; Efimov, *Iz istorii
velikikh,* 184; F. A. Golder, *Bering's Voyages,* II, 14 note 18. According to the diary of
Sven Waxell the ships were separated by fog. (Hirabayashi, 324.)

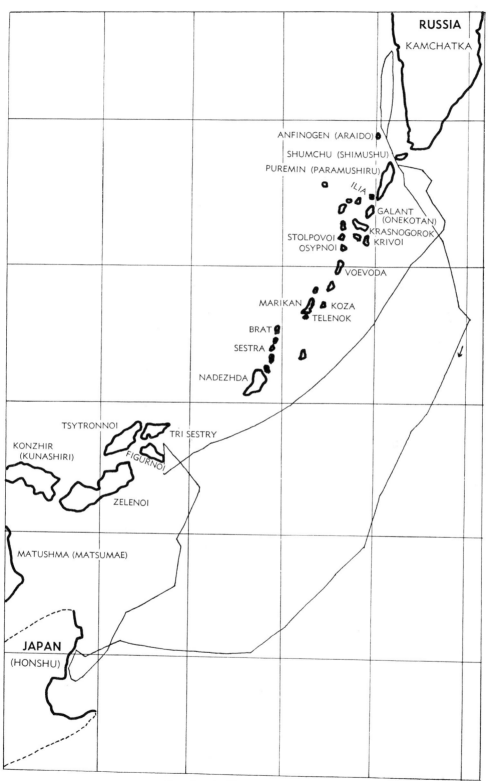

RUSSIA

KAMCHATKA

ANFINOGEN (ARAIDO)

SHUMCHU (SHIMUSHU)

PUREMIN (PARAMUSHIRU)

ILIA

GALANT
(ONEKOTAN)

KRASNOGOROK

STOLPOVOI   KRIVOI

OSYPNOI

VOEVODA

MARIKAN   KOZA

TELENOK

BRAT

SESTRA

NADEZHDA

TSYTRONNOI   TRI SESTRY

KONZHIR
(KUNASHIRI)

FIGURNOI

ZELENOI

MATUSHMA (MATSUMAE)

JAPAN
(HONSHU)

Spanberg's Voyage to Japan

to pull up. The Japanese would not come nearer, but in turn beckoned the Russians to land. This Spanberg did not dare to do, and weighing anchor sailed farther south. On July 3 he cast anchor again at approximately latitude 38°23′ N., off Aji-shima, Ojika County, in the province of Mutsu in the domain of the lord of Sendai.[33]

The Russian ships had been sighted here and there along the coast and reports poured into Sendai from everywhere. Even from aboard the ships the excitement on shore could be discerned. At one place Spanberg dispatched the *Bolsheretsk* to within less than a mile and a half of the coast. But he did not dare to effect a landing. The Japanese, on the other hand, in spite of the strictest prohibitions, seemed anxious to deal with the foreigners. Already at sea, near the tiny island Tashirohama, fisherman Kisabei had audaciously boarded one of the Russian vessels and stared at the tall strangers. Now two junks laden with foodstuffs, tobacco, and gold coins pulled alongside and began a spirited trade. Before long officials, headed by Chiba Kanshichiro, arrived from Sendai. Without fear or hostility but with the greatest politeness they approached Spanberg, who received them with due hospitality, treating them to wine and food, showing them about the ship, and handing gifts of fur to their servants. The Kurilian interpreters whom Spanberg had brought along proved valueless. Nevertheless a great many thoughts can be conveyed by gestures. To confirm his whereabouts Spanberg produced a map and a globe. The Japanese readily pointed out Japan, saying "Nippon, Nippon," reassuring Spanberg that he had indeed found the way. And though he had instructions not to disclose the approaches to Russia, Spanberg took this opportunity to point out to Chiba the proximity of Russia to Japan.[34]

Meanwhile the number of small boats that milled about the squadron had increased until some eight hundred or more Japanese on seventy-nine boats surrounded the Russians. As yet they showed no signs of hostility, but one could hardly foretell how long the interest of the onlookers would remain one of amicable curiosity, and Spanberg withdrew into the open sea and headed back north. As he passed Tashirohama Island, a settlement elder by the name of Zembei visited the flagship. Again Japanese and Russian eyed each other with mu-

33 Tokutomi Iichiro, *Kinsei Nihon kokumin-shi*, XXIII, 141-142; Znamenskii, 93-94; Berg, 98; Hirabayashi, 323.

34 Znamenskii, 93-96; Zhukov, 27; Golder, 223-224. See also D. M. Pozdneev, *Materialy po istorii severnoi Iaponii i eia otnoshenii k materiku Azii i Rossii*, II, 2:18-19; Captain James Burney, *A Chronological History of North-eastern Voyages of Discovery*, 152-153.

tual curiosity. As always, Japanese garments called for comment: "Their dress is white and fastened with a band round the body. The sleeves are wide, like those on a European dressing gown, but without gores. None were seen with trousers and all went barefoot. Their shame they either tied up or covered with a piece of silken cloth or linen."[35] When Zembei bowed his head, one of the Russians could not resist the temptation of stroking it. His hand became all greasy from the oily hairdo and everybody laughed heartily. Zembei did not take offense. He was too engrossed in making mental notes of everything. When he went back on shore he made a full report of what he had observed to the lord of Sendai.[36] Sailing north Spanberg explored the southern Kuril Islands. Then on July 5 he briefly re-approached the shores of Japan at Hokkaido near latitude 41° N. before finally resuming his homeward voyage.

While Spanberg was thus carefully probing the shores of Japan, receiving Japanese visitors here and there, yet not daring to touch land, Walton actually broke the isolation of Japan and sent his men onto Japanese soil. As will be recalled, Walton had separated from the squadron on June 25. On June 27 he came upon the southeastern shore of Honshu at about latitude 37°42′ N. and turned southward. On June 30 the *Sviatoi Gavriil* cast anchor in the open sea at about latitude 35°10′ N. near Amatsu Village in Nagasa County in the province of Awa (Chiba Prefecture) and sent ashore a boat with Kazimirov, his second navigator, a navigator's mate and six seamen to obtain fresh water.

More than a hundred Japanese boats came forth to meet the boat and surrounded it so closely that the Russians could hardly row. As the latter persisted, however, the Japanese took no measures to turn them back. On land the Russians were greeted politely and helping hands quickly filled their water barrels, possibly in the hope of ex-pediting their departure. When Navigator Kazimirov left two soldiers to guard the boat and with Navigator's Mate Vereshchagin and the remaining four sailors proceeded to town, no effort was made to harass them. On the contrary, Kazimirov was invited into Japanese houses and regaled with wine, rice, fruit, and various delicacies. These Russians—the first of their countrymen to set foot in Japan— viewed everything with fascination; they were particularly impressed

[35] Sven Waxell, *The American Expedition*, 83-84.
[36] Japanese sources cite the names and impressions of common Japanese who saw the Russians. See, for example, Motoyama Keisen, *Mamiya Rinzo tairiku kiku*, 24-25.

to see about them so much unaccustomed cleanliness and order. Returning to his boat, Kazimirov espied a two-sworded samurai and companion standing nearby, but though he was alarmed at their presence, they did not interfere.

As the Russians rowed back to their ship, they were followed by a multitude of boats. A Japanese official in costly robes came aboard the *Sviatoi Gavriil* with red wine and exchanged presents and drinks with Walton while a brisk trade developed between the sailors and the Japanese, the former selling a number of trifles, mostly old shirts and stockings for a quantity of copper coin. Nevertheless the potential danger of a boarding attack by the numerically superior Japanese, who crowded about the vessel on some one hundred boats, made it seem unwise to tarry overnight, and upon the departure of the official, Walton weighed anchor, discharging one of his cannons in salute. Unlike Spanberg he did not withdraw to the north right away, but pushed farther south, casting anchor here and there along the Japanese coast. On July 3, he stood close to shore and requested fresh water from some Japanese who had approached the vessel. The Japanese brought the water and even offered to lead the *Sviatoi Gavriil* into port. This Walton would not risk. He continued southward and the following day (July 4) at about latitude 33°28′ N. cast anchor and sent several men ashore to gather medical herbs and some tokens of Japan. On July 5, in the general vicinity of Katsuura on the east coast of Wakayama Prefecture, Walton turned back and headed homeward.

When the Russians departed, the Japanese officials turned to their reports. The Russians had been received with politeness if not friendliness. Only once, as their southward journey brought them relatively close to the Japanese capital, had an official seemed to order his countrymen not to deal with them. Elsewhere Japanese officials themselves had sought out the Russians and had interchanged civilities. At least so the Russian records state, and we have no reason to question them on this point. The Japanese reports, though they corroborate Russian data as to the number of men who landed and as to the houses they entered, studiously avoid any reference to signs of welcome. The Russians are portrayed as having entered the Japanese houses without invitation and as having helped themselves to whatever they wanted. The Japanese records could not have stated otherwise. The officials were committed to the exclusion of foreigners. A report describing the amicable reception of the intruders on land would have been no less than a confession of neglect of duty. Thus the official who visited Walton aboard ship was described as having followed the vessel out to sea without catching up with it.[37]

The story of the expedition, narrated above, was pieced together from both Japanese and Russian sources. At the time of the events neither the Japanese nor the Russians saw the whole picture. The Japanese did not know the foreigners were Russians until two coins and a card with a cross, which the Russians had left behind, were identified by the Dutch on Deshima as coins "from the Muscovia country" and an ace of clubs. At first their information was limited to such eyewitness descriptions of the strangers as that of the priest Ryumon who reported: "Their appearance resembled that of Dutchmen, with red wavy hair and caps of various kinds. Their noses were long and pointed. Their eyes were the color of sharks. The trunks of their bodies, however, were normal just like those of ordinary people."[38] From the Dutch the Japanese learned more about the Spanberg expedition.[39] The Russians knew only the latitude of the place where they had cast anchor or gone ashore. The place names have come to us from Japanese sources. Yet the Russians knew that they had been in Japan and were pleased with what they had seen. "The members of the party were loud in proclaiming their pleasure at having been able to visit the country, declaring that Japan was indeed a nation with whom friendly relations must be formed."[40]

The impact of the Spanberg expedition on Japan was not great. The first arrival of the Russians aroused little concern. Certainly it created no panic. The Shogunate decreed that the foreigners be captured if they landed, but be allowed to flee if they chose to do so. Dissatisfied that his ancestors should have treated these ships like ordinary ones, a modern Japanese historian has commented in disgust: "They had no way of knowing that these ships had been especially dispatched to investigate the conditions of Japan. Even after they learned from the Dutch that they had been Russian ships they did not urge precautions. There were a great many Shogunate officials who ignored the existence of foreign countries."[41]

[37] Znamenskii, 96-101; Pozdneev, II, 2:19-20; Golder, *Russian Expansion*, 225-226; Okamoto Ryunosuke, *Nichi-Ro kosho Hokkaido shiko*, 1:47-48; Burney, 156-157; Hirabayashi, 323; Waxell, 79; Tabohashi Kiyoshi, "Junana-hachi seki ni watareru Rokoku no Taiheiyo hatten to tai-Nichi kankei," 503-506.

[38] Hirabayashi, 327.

[39] Inobe Shigeo, *Ishin zenshi no kenkyu*, 37-38; Kono Tsunekichi, "Anei izen Matsumae-han to Rojin to no kankei," 663; Tabohashi, "Junana-hachi," 506-507.

[40] Hirabayashi, 328.   [41] Inobe, 38.

One wonders what would have happened if Spanberg and Walton had not hastened back to Russia but had taken advantage of the apparent amicability of the Japanese to attempt the establishment of friendly relations. To be sure the Shogunate was still committed to the seclusion policy and troops were in fact dispatched to forestall inroads and if possible to capture the intruders, but Japanese efforts were only half-hearted. It is unlikely that Japan would have opened her doors, but negotiations would have been of mutual edification, and Spanberg would have been in a stronger position upon his return to Russia to refute the arguments of his critics.

The homeward journey was a difficult one for the Russian vessels. Many of the crew members were ill and the flagship alone counted thirteen dead. Walton on the *Sviatoi Gavriil* returned to Bol'sheretsk on August 5, 1739.[42] The other vessels were unable to keep together. Ert on the *Bolsheretsk* reached Bol'sheretsk on August 8, Spanberg on the *Arkhangel Mikhail* on August 25, Shelting on the *Nadezhda* on September 11. From Bol'sheretsk the ships continued to Okhotsk. The *Sviatoi Gavriil* and *Bolsheretsk* arrived on September 2, the *Arkhangel Mikhail* on September 9. Shelting on the *Nadezhda* was driven back by heavy storms and did not get through till the following season. Together or not, the four vessels had found their way back from Japan. The northern route linking Russia with Japan had been traversed in both directions. The squadron had blazed the trail for later expeditions. The explorers had every reason to return with high hopes and high hearts. Whatever dreams of praise and rewards they may have cherished, however, were soon dispelled. The first Russian penetration to the very main island of Japan was capped by a dramatic anticlimax: the Russian authorities refused to believe that Spanberg and Walton had actually visited the shores of Japan!

There were a number of reasons for this strange turn of events. The findings of Spanberg and Walton ran counter to accepted beliefs. Deslisle, Strahlenberg, Kirilov, and other cartographers had recorded the apocryphal Land of Gama and Staaten Eyland, yet Spanberg and Walton had found neither. Spanberg and Walton had also failed to sight the tremendous Hokkaido of contemporary maps; nor had they located Japan where it was supposed to be. Not even Bering, their commander-in-chief, could trust their findings. The journals of Spanberg and Walton did contain technical errors. Attempts by the Admiralty College to rework their calculations and chart their course

---

[42] Golder gives the date as August 3.

on a map were unsuccessful. Skorniakov-Pisarev, with whom Spanberg and quarrelled when building and equipping the vessels and whom Bering had likened to a "mad dog" when he advised his subordinates not to associate with him, sought to discredit the expedition by informing the Senate that Spanberg and Walton had been to Korea rather than to Japan. Even the members of the expedition tried to discredit each other.

No doubt the strain of dangers and privations, life at close quarters, and the monotony of daily chores conspire to knock many a head together at sea. The Russian expeditions had considerably more than their share of dissension. The traditional veneration of foreigners in St. Petersburg was transformed to jealousy and national rivalry in the wilderness. And so Spanberg the Dane disliked Walton the Englishman and neither had much use for their Russian subordinates. In the words of Golder: "Spanberg complained that Petrof, his pilot, was a drunkard. Petrof said that Spanberg made him change the journal and cursed him in German and Russian and threatened to hang him. Walton said that Kasimerof, one of his officers, was disobedient, would not stand his watch, nor keep the journal. Kasimerof charged that Walton beat him. Walton and the priest accused Spanberg of mistreating them. The crews swore that Spanberg and Walton abused them. . . . Bering examined Spanberg's log book, finding there many errors, and Spanberg detected in Walton's enough faults to fill a sixteen page notebook."[43]

Spanberg set out for the capital to clarify matters in person. It was characteristic of the confusion that surrounded his expedition to Japan that he was not permitted to reach St. Petersburg. At Yakutsk he was halted by orders from the Admiralty College. Subsequently he was commanded by the Imperial Cabinet to resume his voyage posthaste. At Kirensk, not far beyond Yakutsk, however, new orders from the Admiralty College forced him to turn back and try to discover Japan all over again.

Unfortunately Spanberg's second expedition was less successful than the first. When he returned to Okhotsk in August 1740, he found that Bering and Chirikov required all available provisions for their own voyage to Kamchatka and North America. He had to retrace his steps to Yakutsk and there prepare supplies. Not until June of the following year (1741) did he come back to Okhotsk. By this time

[43] Golder, *Russian Expansion*, 226-227; Znamenskii, 101-105.

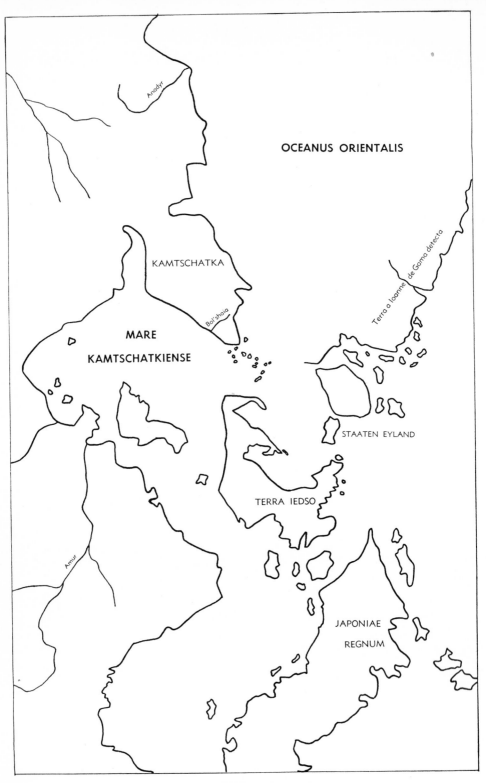

The Apocryphal Staaten Eyland
and Land of Gama

it was too late to set sail for Japan and Spanberg could go no further than Bol'sheretsk, where he waited until the summer of 1742.

In Okhotsk Spanberg's old vessels had been refurbished and a new seventy-foot-long packet boat, the *Sviatoi Ioann*, constructed in place of Walton's former vessel, the *Sviatoi Gavriil*. But the old vessels were no longer as seaworthy as before. During the passage to Bol'sheretsk the brigantine *Arkhangel Mikhail* lost her main mast and the double-sloop *Nadezhda*, which went out of the way to survey the western coast of the Sea of Okhotsk and sail among the Shantar Islands, sprung a leak. Before long even the new vessel, hastily constructed out of raw timber, was to prove unsatisfactory.

Walton was no longer with Spanberg. He had been promoted to captain and had been called to St. Petersburg, but died on the way in 1741. The *Sviatoi Ioann*, which Spanberg captained himself, was manned by seventy-eight persons, including a son of Spanberg and two interpreters, Shenanykin and Fenev, who had studied Japanese under the castaways Gonzo and Sozo. The *Arkhangel Mikhail*, Spanberg's former flagship, now commanded by Shelting was manned by forty persons, the *Nadezhda* under the command of Ptizhev by thirty-three persons, the *Bolsheretsk* under Navigator Kasin by thirteen.

On June 3, 1742 the four vessels set sail for Japan for the third time. They reached the northernmost Kuril island together, but as they continued to the southwest were separated one by one from each other by recurrent fog: first the *Arkhangel Mikhail* fell behind, then the *Nadezhda*, then the *Bolsheretsk*. Once again Spanberg had to approach the shores of Japan alone. The weather cleared up and, though the winds remained unfavorable, it was the proper time for crossing these waters. On July 3 Spanberg called together his officers to decide whether to continue the voyage. They were then at latitude 41°45′ N. and by their own calculation not far from Japan. The danger of cruising without escort, persistent unfavorable winds, and illness aboard ship inclined most of the officers towards turning back. Others disagreed, and it was finally decided to continue the search for Japan until July 17. But a week later, on July 11 at about latitude 39°35′ N. the hastily constructed *Sviatoi Ioann* sprung a large leak and without further question had to hasten homeward. When it reached the first Kuril island (July 25), it found the other three vessels at anchor. Only the *Arkhangel Mikhail* had attempted to seek out Japan, but though it had penetrated down to latitude 38°30′ N. had been no more successful than the *Sviatoi Ioann*.

From the first Kuril island the *Sviatoi Ioann* proceeded in the company of the *Arkhangel Mikhail* and *Bolsheretsk* to Kamchatka and then to Okhotsk, where the three vessels arrived on September 6. The brigantine *Nadezhda*, meanwhile, had been put once again under the command of Shelting, who sailed from the Kuril island to chart with the assistance of geodesist Gvozdev the Okhotsk coast from the Uda River down to the Amur Estuary. On August 12 at latitude 50°10′ N. Shelting came upon the eastern shore of Sakhalin Island— the first Russian explorer to do so—and turning southward pushed down to latitude 45°34′ N. But he mistook Sakhalin for Hokkaido and in the thick fog, which blanketed the ocean, not only failed to chart the shores of Sakhalin but also to notice that he had reached the strait which separates Sakhalin and Hokkaido. Fog and head winds forced him to turn back (August 28) and on September 21 he rejoined the squadron at Okhotsk.

Spanberg's second expedition thus failed to unravel the contradictions of the first. If anything, it added to the confusion. Symbolic of its failure was the tragic death of Bering, who had fathered these voyages. On his way back from North America and the Aleutian Islands in 1741, Bering's vessel, the packet boat *Sviatoi Petr*, was wrecked on the island, which now bears his name, and he and many of his crew died there. Spanberg had launched his second expedition before news of Bering's death reached him, but from the very beginning the renewed attempts to find Japan lacked the means and stimulus of the first. It remained for a special commission appointed by the Admiralty College to determine where Spanberg and Walton had actually been in 1739. After careful study the commission finally concluded in 1746 that Walton had without doubt been at the eastern shores of Japan and that Spanberg, though this seemed far less certain, had probably been there too. It is only when we examine contemporary Japanese records that we can prove that Walton and Spanberg both had definitely carried the Russian flag to the shores of Japan.[44]

[44] Golder, *Russian Expansion*, 226-230; Znamenskii, 105-107.

CHAPTER THREE · SECRET CONTACTS

KURILIAN INTERLUDE

THE so-called Bering expeditions were of geographical importance. The diverse voyages of Bering, Chirikov, Spanberg, and Walton changed the cartographical face of the northern Pacific Ocean. In this their "negative" findings were of significance. Gone was the apocryphal Land of Gama from the comprehensive Russian atlas published by the Academy of Sciences in 1745. Gone also were Staaten Eyland and Compagnies Land, and in their place there remained merely two insignificant Kuril islands. The oversized Ezo (Hokkaido) which had stretched to the very shores of the continent had shrunk; too much so in fact, for it was represented only in part by the island "Matushka." On the positive side, the northern and central Kuril Islands were portrayed quite accurately, as was the northern Pacific coast. Unfortunately this atlas of "the whole Russian empire and bordering lands" extended only as far as latitude 40° N. in the south and thus encompassed but a fragment of Japan, leaving unexploited some of Spanberg's and Walton's efforts. On the other hand, it went beyond the findings of the mariners in projecting vis-à-vis the mouth of the Amur River the northern part of Sakhalin Island under the name "Sagalien." This data had been gleaned from French maps based on the surveys of Jesuits who in the early eighteenth century had been commissioned by Emperor K'ang Hsi to chart the whole Manchu Chinese Empire. The Jesuit maps referred to the Amur River by its local name, "Sagalien-ula" (Black River) and to the island at its mouth as "Sagalien-anga-hata" (Island at the mouth of the Black River), a relationship of terms which was to be used over a century later by a Russian negotiator in the argument that China's cession to Russia of the northern bank of the Amur River (1858) embraced also the cession of strategic Sakhalin Island.[1]

The Bering expeditions had found the northern route to Japan. Walton had penetrated within easy reach of the capital. Spanberg and Walton both had met Japanese officials. These officials, however, had been minor ones, and neither Spanberg nor Walton had nego-

[1] Znamenskii, 108-110; Berg, 99. As Ravenstein points out, *sakhalin* alone means no more than "black." Local natives referred to the island as Taraika or Choka; the Japanese called it Karafuto or Oku-Ezo (p. 265).

tiated—nor indeed tried to negotiate—the establishment of diplomatic or commercial relations. Yet the desirability of trade with Japan was obvious. The dependence of Siberia on European Russia for supplies needed in the development of Kamchatka and the eastern regions was costly and time-consuming. Trade with Japan might well do more than delight aristocratic palates with exotic luxuries—it might furnish the far-flung Russian Empire with essential commodities. Herein lies at least a partial explanation of the persistent recurrence of Russian attempts to enter into dealings with the Japanese. Nevertheless for several decades after the flagging conclusion of the extravagant Bering expeditions the Russian government, which since the death of Peter the Great had provided expeditions with less stimulus than backing, left the initiative for renewed contacts with the Japanese increasingly in private hands.

The private attempts to establish commercial relations with Japan were once again routed step by step down the Kuril Islands. The academician Fedor Miller, who had been associated with the Bering expedition, had written about the importance of the Amur River as an artery of trade with China, Japan, and India (1741). Chirikov had elaborated on the strategic necessity of Russian access to the Amur, not only as a convenient route of communication with Kamchatka, but as a step without which it would not be possible for Russia to subjugate the territories and peoples to the east, and had recommended the establishment of a wharf in the mouth of the Amur (1746).[2] But though the government shared these views and in 1756 sent Councilor Bratishchev to Peking in order to secure Manchu consent, the mission failed, and Russian expansion was perforce directed once again via the Kuril Islands. Chirikov clearly recognized the strategic importance of the Kuril Archipelago to the Russian Empire, both as a gateway to the Pacific and a shield against foreign encroachment on her far eastern domains, and urged the exploitation of one of the islands as a naval base.[3] The government failed to follow this lead and it remained for local individuals on their own to extend the Russian frontier in this direction.

The first Cossack voyages to the northernmost Kuril Islands had been carried out to curry favor and forgiveness of the government, as well as rob the natives of furs. Plunder still remained a powerful

[2] Kiuner, 14; V. A. Divin, *Velikii russkii moreplavatel' A. I. Chirikov*, 209-211. Miller was not the first to think of such a route. A similar project can be found in European literature as early as 1681.

[3] Divin, 211; Sgibnev, "Popytki," 45.

incentive, but now a more respectable commercial motivation can be discerned. Not only were the populous southern Kuril Islands themselves rich in peltry, but their proximity to Japan, particularly in view of reported Japanese visits, gave rise to the hope of indirect trade with Japan by way of the Kurils.

The Ainu who inhabited the Kuril Islands (as well as southern Sakhalin and Hokkaido) were a bearded lot. The Japanese referred to them as "hairy barbarians." And hairy they were, when compared with the Oriental peoples about them. The Russians agreed that the Ainu were "shaggy." Unlike the Japanese, the Russians were bearded themselves, and more than one Russian traveler observed that these hairy natives reminded him of the peasants back home, if not of "real Muscovites." The Kuril Ainu, a proto-Caucasian people, led a primitive existence. They knew neither agriculture nor animal-husbandry. They subsisted on hunting, and gathering roots and berries. Their less primitive objects (metal utensils, swords, knives, lacquerware, and silk and cotton fabrics), they obtained from the Japanese in exchange primarily for the skins of local sea and land animals, dried fish, blubber, and eagle feathers. Not all the Ainu were in direct contact with the Japanese. The Ainu of Kunashiri Island were the ones who traded with the Japanese when they came to Kunashiri or else when they themselves traveled to Hokkaido. From them the natives of Etorofu and Uruppu obtained the Japanese products and in turn took them to the more northerly islands and even to Kamchatka, until the inroads of the Russians in the north made this too dangerous. Frequently Shasukotan Island served as trade center, attracting Ainu from the north and south for barter. So far, the Kuril Islands were neither Russian nor Japanese, though footholds had been gained at both ends of the archipelago. The Ainu were not united politically and their consequent weakness was a standing invitation to adventurers from the north and south, who soon were to advance toward each other with equal ruthlessness and disregard of native rights.

Whatever controversy the reports of Spanberg and Walton had aroused concerning their visit to the shores of Japan, did not extend to the description of the Kuril Archipelago. Their accounts of the furry wealth of these islands, multiplied by the stories of Bering's associates about the great riches of the Aleutians, precipitated a mad scramble of fortune hunters down the islands. As they set out on flimsy crafts, hastily knocked together with raw timber, wooden nails, and other inadequate substitutes, without even the most elementary knowledge of navigation, and lacking the most essential supplies, many were destined to perish. But those who survived, returned richly rewarded for their efforts and by their success encouraged others to try for the same. It was everyone for himself, the interest of officials at Okhotsk being confined to a ten per cent levy on private peltry. Only when the chaotic descents of the hunters threatened to result in the extinction of the precious furbearing animals, did the authorities step in and seek to control private enterprise. Following an inquiry of Governor Soimonov of Siberia in 1759, the fur-hunters (*promyshlenniki*) were required to secure permission to build new vessels. These now became larger and sturdier (including two-masted, cramp-iron-braced *gvozdenniki* and genuine sea-going vessels). The resulting expense forced the small capitalists, who had dominated the scene, to merge their resources with larger companies, an experience shared by the early American China traders. At the same time the Okhotsk region replaced Kamchatka as the center of shipbuilding, since the necessary permission was available at Okhotsk, and because suitable men and materials could more readily be found there.

The Aleutians and the northwestern shores of America bore the brunt of Russian penetration, because they excelled the Kuril Islands in peltry and at times were less hamstrung by government interference. Spanberg had returned from the Kurils without a single fur; Chirikov who had visited the Aleutians and America brought back many furs, including some nine hundred beaver skins. In succeeding years hunters extracted their share from the Kuril Islands, but never in such quantities as from the Aleutians. Still, fortunes were made on the Kurils, and in 1757 a merchant's clerk felt satisfied enough to erect a chapel to St. Nicholas on Shimushu Island in gratitude. The government too could expect a handsome haul if it succeeded in imposing tribute on the inhabitants of all the Kuril Islands, and the various tribute collectors were exhorted by both local and Siberian authorities to push farther south.[4]

As the Russians continued southward, they were bound sooner or later to come into contact with the northward-moving Japanese. In 1744 the Russian Novograblennyi was informed on Makanru Island by Kurilians who had been on Shimushiru that a Japanese high official from Kunashiri had asked them to inform the Russians to bring their wares to his island. Novograblennyi forwarded this re-

4 Znamenskii, 111-122.

quest to Bol'sheretsk, enclosing a map of the Kuril Archipelago prepared by himself, indicating settlements as well as species of animals.
The following year, in 1745, tribute collector Slabodchikov found
ten starving Japanese on Onekotan Island. Together with seven other
companions, who had since died of privation, they had sailed from
Matsumae toward Shimushiru when the mast of their vessel broke,
and they were tossed about helplessly for months. Finally, they were
cast ashore at Onekotan.[5] Thanks to the Russians, who fed them oil
and fat and supported them as they attempted to walk again, the Japanese survivors gradually regained their strength. From Yusancheya,
one of the castaways, Slabodchikov learned that Shimushiru was noted
for its abundance of gold and silver, that it housed factories in which
damask and velvet were produced, that to the south of Shimushiru
there were lands rich in lumber, and on Atkis (Akkeshi on Hokkaido)[6] there was a fine harbor, frequented by large Matsumae vessels
in quest of beaver and eagle feathers.

Meanwhile the exactions of Russian tribute collectors in the
northernmost Kuril Islands precipitated a mass exodus of Ainu. The
instructions of the Department of Siberian Affairs of 1731 had envisaged the levy as one beaver skin per native, but the tribute collectors,
as they extended their activities southward, recording the names of
the natives in their books, would enter the name of anyone they met,
regardless of whether they had already entered his name elsewhere.
Thus, while the necessities of the hunt carried the Ainu from island
to island, many found themselves hit by several levies of tribute
collectors. They therefore fled farther south to escape new exactions.
This the Russians would not tolerate, regarding the refugees very
much like escaped serfs, and demanded their return, meanwhile
holding responsible those who had remained for their own tribute
as well as the tribute of those who had fled. In the years 1750 to 1753
the Russian commander of Shimushu Island and several native elders
toured some sixteen islands in an attempt to persuade the fugitives
to return, but the latter would not hear of it and almost killed one
of the elders, though in most cases they agreed to pay tribute. The
farther south the Russians pushed the more reluctant they found
the natives. On tiny Ushishiru only ten natives furnished tribute; on
larger Shimushiru all categorically refused to become Russian sub-

[5] Sgibnev lists the island as the fifth island; Onekotan would be the fourth. Znamenskii gives the number of survivors as nine; he says the vessel was en route to Samur.
[6] Atkis or Akkeshi was a place on Ezo (Hokkaido). Occasionally, however, it was
mistaken by Russians as a separate island.

jects or to pay tribute. By 1761 Governor Soimonov complained that tribute was being collected from only three or four of the Kuril Islands.[7]

Soimonov's interest was not confined to the collection of tribute. He had learned from Japanese in Irkutsk that the Kuril Islands down to and including Kunashiri were independent of Japan and that control of them would facilitate the establishment of commercial relations with the latter. Hence he instructed Colonel Plenesner, commandant of the forts of Okhotsk, Anadyrsk, and Kamchatka, to investigate the islands carefully and, if possible, to bring them into the Russian Empire. At the same time, he petitioned the Senate to permit private fur-hunters to exploit the islands again in the expectation that private enterprise, as in Siberia, would hasten expansion into new territories, while lightening the load on public funds.

Plenesner did not further the exploration of the Kuril Islands. But Izvekov, who a year later became commandant of Kamchatka, did so after Chikin-Novograblennyi, Kurilian elder of the second island, requested permission to join with his fellow elder Chuprov of the first island and with the Cossack leader Chernyi to set out after the fugitives and to subjugate the Kurilians to the south.

The instructions which were drawn up for the leaders of this little expedition by the Bol'sheretsk Command in 1766 were rather far-sighted. They prohibited explicitly the abuse of the natives. Chernyi was ordered, when exhorting the Kurilians to become Russian subjects, to persuade them of the goodness of Russian conduct and treatment both by word and deed, not to extort from them anything by force, and to practice restraint when asking them to enter a tributary relationship. The instructions expressed interest in the way of life and standard of living of the Kurilians and in the type of weapons which they used, particularly whether they had firearms. The expedition was to investigate secretly whether the natives traded already with someone else and whether they owed allegiance to another power. It was to gather as much information as possible about the activities of the Japanese, if they came to these islands, and bring back samples of Japanese products obtained in exchange for the Russian and Chinese goods which they would take along, though under no circumstances in exchange for guns or ammunition. In the instructions given earlier that year it stated further: "If there be

---

[7] Polonskii, 399-400; Sgibnev, 46; Znamenskii, 122-124. These and other Russian incursions in 1756, 1758 and 1759 were reported by the Ainu to the Japanese on Hokkaido. (Kono, 665-666.)

found somewhere Japanese, cast there on a vessel or by some other way, or some other unknown peoples, they are to be brought to Bol'sheretsk, without antagonizing them in the least; furthermore, should there be anywhere those who have come to trade, to treat them kindly and politely to make inquiries at first hand."[8]

The expedition extended over a period of three years, from 1766 to 1769. From the very outset it was marked by lack of organization. The three leaders set out independent of each other and wintered on different islands: Chikin-Novograblennyi on the twelfth, Chuprov on the seventh, Chernyi on the first. In spring 1767 Chikin-Novograblennyi and Chuprov made a common effort to penetrate to Shimushiru, but there Chikin-Novograblennyi died and Chuprov retraced his steps. Chikin-Novograblennyi had been the inspiration of the expedition. Making his way back, Chuprov came upon Chernyi, who now assumed command. This was unfortunate for the Cossack leader was unsuited for the peaceful incorporation of the natives of the Kuril Islands into the Russian Empire. In fact, he began with the subjugation of his own expedition, regimenting his followers to rise to the beating of drums, to line up in military formation, and march to work, giving emphasis to his orders with liberal lashes of his whip. The native oarsmen had little chance to rest. Whenever they stopped for any length of time he made them hunt beavers, sending their wives to hunt birds, and gather sweet herbs from which wine could be distilled.

On the northern islands Chernyi found several fugitives, and ordered them to return to their old hunting grounds. As he proceeded farther south he found such a large number of fugitives that he did not dare order them back. He promised to permit them to stay where they were, in return for which they paid him tribute and joined him in his expedition southward. But when they found themselves subject to the same regimentation as the oarsmen they deserted him at the first opportunity. The opportunity came in the spring of 1768, when the expedition, after wintering on Shimushiru, tried to negotiate the crossing to Uruppu Island in a storm and was scattered in different directions. Nevertheless Chernyi made his way across safely and, pushing farther south than any of his countrymen had yet done on *bidarkas*, peacefully obtained tribute from the inhabitants of Uruppu and Etorofu. As he remained on Uruppu over the winter, stories of his tyranny spread and the islanders, on whose hunting grounds he

[8] Polonskii, 410; Sgibnev, 46-47.

had encroached, angrily cast away the tribute receipts he had given them and withdrew to Etorofu. As they did so, they begged the interpreters to ask on Kamchatka that Chernyi and men like him not be sent again, wondering at the same time whether all Russians might not be like that.

Chernyi, meanwhile, made the most of his good fortune, and immersed himself in wine and women, while fugitives and oarsmen toiled for him under the constant threat of his whip. On his way back from Uruppu he decided to immortalize his achievements by erecting in his own memory a wooden cross on one of the Chirihoi (Black Brothers) Islands, bearing the date of the event. When he reached Shimushiru, he found that the fugitives, who had accompanied him southward on the promise that they would not have to return to their home islands, refused to proceed any farther north. He gave orders to whip them into obedience, but they scattered, the men hiding among the rocks of the island, the women and children putting out to sea on a *bidarka*. The *bidarkas* of those who had hidden, Chernyi had burned together with their possessions. The women, who had not succeeded in escaping, he had whipped and tied up and, taking along six of the men, he resumed his voyage northward. For a while he continued to mistreat those under him, but as he drew closer to home he began to change his conduct. He freed the fugitives and gave them gifts, discarded drum and whips, and generally treated his subordinates civilly after having exacted from them written pledges to keep silent about his previous transgressions. Not everyone remained silent and stories of his excesses came to the ears of the authorities. Chernyi and Chuprov were called to Irkutsk to elaborate on the brief written report submitted by Chernyi but, though a special investigation concerning Chernyi's conduct was begun, he escaped human punishment by succumbing to smallpox not long after his arrival in Irkutsk.

Chernyi had accumulated a great fortune. He also left behind a journal of considerable geographical merit—the first direct description of the northern and central Kuril Islands down to Etorofu, filled with detailed information concerning the nature of the islands, large and small. He reported that several Japanese vessels, with a crew of about twenty men each, visited Akkeshi and Kunashiri Island annually to trade for two or three months. Japanese products included wine, tobacco leaves, cereals, swords, knives, axes, and kettles. But helpful as Chernyi's contribution was in familiarizing the Russians with the Kuril Islands, it was outweighed by the unfortunate impression of the Russians he had given the inhabitants of these islands. As a Russian historian notes, Chernyi demonstrated to them what Russian treatment was like in fact rather than in word. He had sown seeds of hatred that were to blossom into warfare when other Russians were to follow his trail.[9]

In spring 1770 a large number of Kurilians crossed over from Etorofu to Uruppu on one of their usual fishing trips. At Moshiho, where they went ashore with a good catch, they came upon a group of Russian hunters led by seafarer Sapozhnikov, who were wintering on the island. When the Russians spotted the natives, they demanded that they hand over their sea otters or leave hostages. Frightened, the natives began to apologize profusely and then suddenly, when the Russians seemed off guard, fled back onto their boats and paddled away. Shortly they separated into three groups. One went ashore at Chiyashikomanai, not far from where they had encountered the Russians; the other two proceeded to Monmoi and Furenai respectively. Early the next morning Russians found the first group and headed ashore. The Ainu rushed to their boats, but it was low tide and, having pulled them onto the beach the previous night, they could not launch them. They had to face the Russians where they were, prepared for the worst. Their poison arrows and short swords were no match for rifles, and when the Russians opened fire, killing their leader and two others, they took to the mountains. They made their way cross-country to Furenai, spreading word of what had happened. The Ainu were badly shaken. They had always come to Uruppu. Uruppu was considered part of Etorofu. Hence, "the coming of the Russians was an injustice from beginning to end." They did not have the power to withstand the Russians and, fearful of the consequences of another meeting, they returned to Etorofu.

The following year, in 1771, the elders of Etorofu met in council. For years their people had been crossing over to Uruppu to catch sea otters, the skins of which they sold at Matsumae. Cut off from Uruppu they would be unable to make a living. The elders decided, therefore, not to give up hunting on Uruppu, but to go there again and to deal with the Russians, should they meet them, as circumstances required. The Ainu buried their possessions in the ground and set out, leaving their homes in the care of the women and children, and a few old men. They had not been gone long when a party

---

[9] Polonskii, 412-420; Znamenskii, 125-128.

of Russians arrived, raided their homes, unearthed their possessions, and hauled away whatever seemed of value, throwing the rest into the sea.

When news of this misfortune was brought to the Ainu hunters by two of their people, it found them already outraged. The Russians of the same vessel had opened fire on them when they had tried to hunt on Uruppu Island at Waninau. Supported by other natives, particularly those from Rashowa, where Russians had gone ashore four years earlier, they resolved to exterminate the Russians on Uruppu. They equipped themselves with lances—knives mounted on long sticks—and prepared a large supply of poison arrows. Then they separated into a number of groups to seek out the enemy.

Rarely could the natives afford a frontal attack in the face of firearms. Whenever possible they would resort to treachery. At Sukomafu they received with a show of great hospitality a number of Russians who had made their way across the mountains from the eastern lagoon. They prepared a banquet in their honor, and gladly agreed to accommodate them for the night. When the Russians were asleep, they stole their weapons and at a given signal swooped down on them, spearing them to death. They had learned from the Russians that some of their comrades had gone to Makanru Island in quest of sea lions; after hiding the corpses in the grass they set out for Makanru. When they arrived they found a number of Russians who had put up a large tent. They approached them with apparent humility and offered their services. Then they settled down near them and waited for nightfall. When the Russians were asleep the Ainu once again stole their weapons and killed them before they could resist. The Ainu were elated. Back on Uruppu, they shared their joy with the other islanders and, encouraged by their success, made plans to attack the main Russian stronghold at Waninau in the eastern lagoon. Skillfully hiding in the tall grass as they sneaked up to the Russian settlement, they launched a surprise attack. Several Russians were killed at once, others were killed as they fled aboard their vessel. From the vessel the Russians began to fire back and the Ainu withdrew. Pleased with their revenge, they returned to Etorofu to tell about the dozens of Russians they had killed. The figures which they relayed to Japanese chroniclers were exaggerated. Nevertheless, Russian sources admit that when the vessel of merchant Protodiakonov, to which the hunters on Uruppu had belonged, returned to Petropavlovsk harbor in the fall of 1772 laden with two hundred and fifteen beaver skins, its crew, thanks to the efforts of the Ainu, had been reduced from thirty-nine to eighteen.

In the meantime other Russians—the party of merchant Nikonov—penetrated to the same islands. They did not suffer similar casualties because the corpses which they found on Makanru and a warning sign erected on Uruppu prompted them to proceed with caution. They did not acquire many furs, however. Sapozhnikov would not tolerate a competitive party on Uruppu and turned them away on the grounds that he had cleared the island of natives.

As one looks back at Russian penetration of the Kuril Islands in the generation after Spanberg's voyages, one is struck by the fact that, although the Russians were not yet firmly entrenched, they nevertheless acted as if the islands down to Uruppu were already part of the Russian empire. At the same time they were conscious of native resistance and the proximity of Japanese officials. When, in 1772, they decided to fit out another expedition to explore the Kuril Archipelago and the Japanese Islands, they decided to go under the guise of a fishing expedition, but on a man-of-war.[10] Russian precautions were directed against the Kurilians rather than the Japanese. The latter had received the first Russian visitors without hostility, and, in spite of the seclusion policy, there was reason to hope that renewed contacts would again be amicable. The Russian government did not know that, meanwhile, a man, with a deep personal grudge against Russia, had appeared on the shores of Japan and, posing as a Russian officer, had tried to incite the Japanese to a preventive attack on Russia. This man was Mauritius Augustus, Count of Benyovszky.

A MYSTERIOUS WARNING

In the last decade of the eighteenth century, the adventures of Mauritius Augustus Count of Benyovszky were the talk of Europe. Benyovszky[11] was a native of Verbó, Hungary (1746),[12] the son of an

---

[10] Sgibnev, "Popytki," 45-47; Okamoto, 1:48-51; *Hyakka zuihitsu*, II, 120-121; Hokkaido-cho, *Shinsen Hokkaido-shi* (hereafter cited as *Hokkaido-shi*), v, 1291-1294; Znamenskii, 128-130; Pozdneev, II, 2:20-25; Kono, 668.

[11] "Benyovszky" is the Hungarian and probably most correct spelling of the name. Sgibnev notes that "Benevskii" signed as "Baron," sometimes as "Count Moritz Anadarde Benev"; in Kamchatka he was usually known as "Beinosk" or "Beinak." (A. S. Sgibnev, "Istoricheskii ocherk glavneishikh sobytii v Kamchatke," 52.) Other variations of Benyovszky's name, with the authors by whom they are used in parentheses: Mauritius Augustus Count de Benyowsky (Captain Pasfield Oliver); Baron Moritz Aladar de-Benev (D. N. Bludov); Beniovskii (Bludov and A. A. Polovtsov); Beisposk (Ivan

Austrian cavalry general. For a while he served in some Austrian regiment and may have participated in a campaign in the Seven Years' War (1756-1763). In 1756, when visiting an uncle in Latvia, he learned that his cousins had taken possession of his estate in Hungary and returning, drove them out by armed force. For this he was tried and convicted at the court of Vienna as a rebel and disturber of the public peace, was deprived of his property, and banished from Hungary.[13] Benyovszky made his way to Poland and later on to Hamburg. There he learned navigation and undertook voyages to various places.[14] In 1767 he entered the services of the Polish Confederates against Russia, was captured by the Russians (1768), and released on his word of honor never again to take up arms against Russia. A year later, in 1769, he was captured again by the Russians, weapons in hand, and was exiled to Kazan. Taking advantage of the fact that he was permitted to live in town, presumably on parole, he conspired, with his inseparable Swedish friend and assistant Adolf Wynbladth,[15] to escape. But the skipper of the vessel on which they planned to sail to freedom notified the authorities, and in December 1769 Benyovszky and Wynbladth were exiled to distant Kamchatka. On the way to Kamchatka their galiot was overtaken by a heavy storm which exhausted the efforts of the crew. For a while, the two friends and three fellow-exile Russian officers thought of taking possession of the ship, but the season for navigating was almost over and they decided to bide their time.

Planning an uprising on Kamchatka, Benyovszky enlisted Petr Khrushchev, an audacious captain of the guard, who had participated in a revolt against Catherine the Great in 1762. Assured of the support of the officers with whom he had arrived, Benyovszky also gained the support of the various political exiles. Peter the Great had failed

Riumin); M. A. Benovskii (V. I. Shtein); mr-Chevillart (Shtein); M. A. Beniowsky and Benyowszky (Dimitrii Pozdneev); Hanbengoro (most Japanese sources); Ausu (Okamoto Ryunosuke).

12 In his memoirs Benyovszky states that he was born in 1741. Parish registers at Verbó (Verbova) reveal, however, that he was born five years later. (William Nicholson, *The Memoirs and Travels of Mauritius Augustus Count de Benyowsky*, 30.) Verbó in western Slovakia was the county seat; Benyovszky was actually born in the village of Benovo, from which his name seems derived. There one of my colleagues, Professor Victor S. Mamatey, saw a plaque in the years before World War II commemorating the birth of "General" Benyovszky.

13 V. I. Shtein, "Samozvannyi imperator madagarskii (M. A. Benovskii)," 177; A. A. Polovtsov, *Russkii Biograficheskii Slovar'*, II, 693.

14 Nicholson, 30-31; Polovtsov, II, 693.

15 Spelled also "Vinblad" and "Vinbland."

to provide for an orderly system of succession to the throne. For years after his death the imperial court was torn by the intrigues of rival factions. Guard officers were frequently implicated in such conspiracies and exiled to Kamchatka after torture and public punishment—such as flagellation with the knout, ripping of the nostrils and cutting out of the tongue. On Kamchatka they would meet other political exiles who, like Benyovszky and Wynbladth, had fought for the independence of some non-Russian minority. The life of the exiles was extremely harsh. With only a few days' provisions, a gun, ammunition, an ax, and a knife to provide for their shelter and nourishment, they were reduced to the primitive existence of the natives, bullied by every commander, official, and common Cossack. In such circumstances many exiles succumbed; but there were others who would take any risk to escape.[16]

In addition to the exiles, the conspirators acquired the invaluable experience of Navigator Churin, commander of the government galiot *Sviatoi Petr i Sviatoi Pavel*, who faced courtmartial for insubordination and unpaid debts, and of sailors, workers, and other non-exiles. To gain their allegiance and to give some resemblance of legality to the rebellion, Benyovszky and his companions fabricated the rumor that they had been exiled as adherents of Grand Duke Pavel Petrovich, whose mother, Catherine the Great, had unjustly deprived him of the throne; Benyovszky even displayed a letter which Pavel Petrovich allegedly had entrusted to him for delivery to the Roman Emperor. For those not interested in the fortunes of Pavel Petrovich, Benyovszky and Khrushchev had still another story: the old legend of islands of gold and silver in the Pacific Ocean. These islands, they said, were not far away, and they promised that after they had found them, those who did not wish to continue to Europe could go ashore again on the Kamchatkan Peninsula. The true objectives of their plan the leaders kept to themselves.

In those days the whole of Bol'sheretsk consisted of not more than thirty-five houses with a total garrison of seventy Cossacks, including minors and old men, many of them continuously away on missions. It is less surprising that the conspirators should have triumphed eventually, than that such a large plot was not discovered. As a matter of fact it was discovered. But Captain Grigorii Nilov, the commandant of Kamchatka was old and decrepit and drunk. At the same

---

[16] Znamenskii, 131-132.

time he had utter confidence in Benyovszky, who tutored his son.[17] When reports of an impending uprising persisted, his subordinates finally prevailed on him to send several soldiers to arrest Benyovszky. These the conspirators took prisoner and made preparations for a night attack. Meanwhile two seamen who had learned of the impending assault on the fort hastened to warn the commandant. But the guards were drunk and would not let them through, particularly as one of the two seamen was equally inebriated. That evening, on May 7, 1771, when the local guards were too drunk to resist, Benyovszky and some seventy followers rose in open revolt and, brutally murdering the governor who had so trusted Benyovszky, looted all government property, and forced the inhabitants of Bol'sheretsk to swear allegiance to Emperor Pavel. Then they proceeded to Chekalinsk Harbor, where they took possession of the government galiot *Sviatoi Petr i Sviatoi Pavel*, which in size resembled the *Sviatoi Mikhail* on which Spanberg had voyaged to Japan. In the past, similar sea voyages had been planned for months and even years, but the rebels could not wait. On May 11, after less than four days' preparation, they set out to sea, well-provisioned, and with a valuable load of government furs, leaving behind a memorandum, addressed to the Senate and signed by Benyovszky and seventy of his followers, protesting that Pavel Petrovich had been deprived of the throne illegally; condemning the war with Poland, the monopolization of salt and wine, and the curbing of the freedom of the deputies charged with the drawing up of new statutes. As punishment for having tried to forewarn the authorities, the two seamen and Nilov's secretary were forced not only to sign the memorandum, but to go along on the cruise, together with a Kamchadal couple who allegedly owed money to Khrushchev.[18]

Sailing down the Kuril Archipelago, the galiot reached Shimushiru in four days. Here, as the rebels took on water and firewood, baked bread, repaired the tackling, made and hoisted an English ensign, a conspiracy was exposed among the more reluctant voyagers. One of the forcibly-detained seamen and the Kamchadal couple were there-

---

[17] In his memoirs Benyovszky claims that he tutored also the governor's three daughters, the eldest of whom, Afanasiia, immediately fell in love with him and later accompanied him to Macao. This is not true. The governor, whose appointment to Bol'sheretsk was temporary, had brought along only his son; his wife and daughter stayed in Izhig. (V. I. Shtein, 182.)

[18] Polovtsov, 693-695; Shtein, 187; D. N. Bludov, "Bunt Ben'ovskago v Bol'sheretskom ostroge," 201; Znamenskii, 137-138. Most of the Russian sources refer to the galiot simply as *Sviatoi Petr*, Bludov as *Sviatoi Pavel*. Most Japanese sources more correctly talk of *Sviatoi Petr i Sviatoi Pavel*.

fore left behind on the island; the others, having willingly agreed to continue with Benyovszky, were forgiven. From Shimushiru the adventurers proceeded southward, down the east coast of Japan, farther than Walton and their countrymen had penetrated thirty-two years before. They then traversed the remainder of the northern Liu Ch'iu Islands. After a ten-day stop at Oshima they visited Formosa, where they had a skirmish with the natives, and, continuing to the China coast, entered Macao in mid-September. The voyage was a nautical feat, but not without its toll. Three of the crew died at sea, and fifteen upon landing. The provisions were spoiled, the crew ill, and, as they gorged themselves on fresh food, more died. But Benyovszky was well.

Having studied Latin, he was the only one aboard ship who could converse with the Portuguese governor and promptly claimed the galiot, with her armament and provisions, as his own. He moved into the governor's mansion and began negotiations with the English, French, and Dutch commercial companies, which sought to exploit his discoveries in their own interest. Finally, he sold out the vessel and cargo to the governor from under the feet of his partners. Beaten and despised, Benyovszky's followers had been aggrieved further by his order that no one cross himself while praying. They did not know that he had told the governor that they were Hungarian; had they made the sign of the cross from right to left in their natural Russian Orthodox fashion, they would have revealed the truth to the Portuguese. When they learned of the sale of the galiot they made efforts to resist. Wynbladth and Stepanov disclosed Benyovszky's past to their shipmates and urged them to return to Russia. To travel, as Benyovszky wanted, on a French vessel, with the French at war with the English, was to run the danger of being impressed into French service. Wynbladth through the local British representative petitioned the authorities of Macao to arrest Benyovszky as a fugitive criminal. But Benyovszky outwitted them, by telling the governor that his crew was planning a mutiny and the capture of the town, and had his followers thrown into jail until they signed a new pledge of allegiance to himself.[19]

During the winter, illness further diminished the band of *émigrés*. In the beginning of 1772 Benyovszky embarked on a French frigate

[19] A. S. Sgibnev, "Bunt Benevskago v Kamchatke v 1771 g.," 759; Bludov, 213; Polovtsov, 693-695; Znamenskii, 143-149. Polovtsov mentions Benyovszky's voyage to the Kuril Islands and "Tanao-Simu"; it makes no mention of his contacts with the Japanese off Shikoku and Kyushu.

in Canton for Ile de France (Mauritius) in the Indian Ocean, with all but Stepanov, who had refused the new pledge. From there Benyovszky and his companions rounded Africa and beat their way up to France, some returning to Russia, others accompanying him to Paris (1773). Thus Benyovszky's Russian companions, who had sailed farther on the Pacific Ocean than any Russian navigators before or after them in the eighteenth century, were also the first of their compatriots to sail almost around the world.

In France Benyovszky entered the services of the French government, which dispatched him to Madagascar, ignoring his assertions that it would be easy to establish commercial relations with the Japanese by founding settlements on such islands adjacent to Japan as Formosa, Kunashiri and Oshima. From the inhabitants of the latter he claimed to have a written permission to return. At Madagascar Benyovszky founded a colony in 1774, but the stubborn resistance of the natives, differences with the Governor of Ile de France, and the mistrust of the French government prompted him to forsake the island. He returned to Europe, reentered the Austrian service and in 1778 participated in an engagement with Prussian forces. In 1781 Benyovszky turned up in Baltimore, Maryland, where he made contacts with a rich trading house and, with its help, planned a new expedition to Madagascar. Assured of cooperation in Baltimore, and later in London, he returned to Madagascar in 1785 and, arousing the natives against his former employers, the French, proclaimed himself ruler of the island. The following year his career was cut short by a stray bullet during a French attack on his capital.[20]

Unembellished, Benyovszky's life was one of adventure. His memoirs, published simultaneously in English, French, and German, however, painted his escapades in such Münchausen-like colors that ultimately it became impossible to separate fact from fiction. At first his memoirs were accepted at face value, because little was yet known about eastern Asia and Africa, and any new account was welcome. Benyovszky's tall tales caught the imagination of writers and poets, and were capped by a five-act drama by the noted playwright Augustus von Kotzebue in which Benyovszky crowns the bloody uprising by eloping with the governor's daughter.[21] Gradually the character of Benyovszky's memoirs became apparent and editors of later editions thought it necessary to warn the reading public in the fore-

[20] Polovtsov, 693-695; Znamenskii, 131, 150-151; Tokutomi, XXIII, 173-174.
[21] *Count Benyowsky; or, The Conspiracy of Kamchatka.*

word. The *Gentleman's Magazine* commented: "Whatever advantage may result from them to navigators, as concurrent evidence of the late discoveries, it must be acknowledged that, independent of the Count's character, as drawn by his own pen, which represent him as little influenced by a regard to truth, or indeed any principle of morality whatever, his accounts savour much of the romantic embellishment and exaggeration."[22] Captain Pasfield Oliver added: "It is . . . almost useless to minutely analyse each successive step of the Hungarian Count as given in his fictitious journal." And again: "It is needless to follow this master of the art of war through all his exploits, it is sufficient to say that it was Benyowsky who did everything and surpassed everybody like Thackeray's inimitable 'Major Goliah O'Grady Gahagan, H.E.I.C.S.' with his 'tremendous adventures.' "[23]

Yet Benyovszky's memoirs were too important to be simply dismissed as fictitious, and European historians tried to sift out the grains of truth by referring to the testimony of eyewitnesses. Their attention was focused on the Kamchatka uprising, nautical data, and the attempted colonization of Madagascar. They skimmed over Benyovszky's visit to Japan. A. S. Sgibnev, in his thirty-two page account of the Kamchatka uprising, devotes one third of a page to Benyovszky's visit to Japan; in his thirty-four page historical survey of the main events on Kamchatka from 1759 to 1772, he dismisses it in two sentences; and in his thirty-six page description of early Russo-Japanese relations, he ignores it completely. V. I. Shtein sets aside two pages in his forty-two page study, "The false emperor of Madagascar," for an account of Benyovszky's visit to Japan, as reported by one of Benyovszky's reluctant companions. This neglect of Benyovszky's dealings with the Japanese by the eighteenth and nineteenth century Russian historians is significant. The record of Benyovszky's dealings with the Japanese is important more for what Russian observers have omitted than included, because the Russian ignorance of the rising Japanese mistrust of Russian actions and objectives was one of the striking characteristics of early Russo-Japanese relations and was no less conducive to trouble than the forebodings of the Japanese.

Benyovszky's own narrative is too unreliable to serve as a primary

---

22 *Gentleman's Magazine*, IX, 2:725.

23 Nicholson, 47, 31. Shtein speculates that Benyovszky's purpose in writing his fabulous memoirs was to excite the interest of greedy Englishmen, and by posing as an expert on Asia and Africa to find backing for another expedition. He did indeed obtain financial support in the United States. (Shtein, 177.)

source for his activities in Japan. Fortunately we have the more credible testimony of the Cossack Ivan Riumin, a cashiered chancery clerk who had participated in Benyovszky's voyage to Japan.[24] This is how Riumin reports Benyovszky's stay in Japanese waters:

On July 18, 1771, after a heavy storm in which the vessel almost went to the bottom of the sea, Benyovszky and his companions sighted land. Toward evening they approached it and, taking in sails, cast anchor. They observed numerous guard fires along the coast. In the morning they saw people on the beach signaling them not to come ashore but go out to sea again. Nevertheless, Benyovszky lowered the yawl and sent Wynbladth, Stepanov, and several others ashore. The Japanese, who had gathered on the beach, did not want them to land, but did nothing to stop them. When the Russians entered the Japanese houses they were hospitably offered wine and rice. Later, with Wynbladth and Stepanov in a Japanese boat, some of the Japanese paid a visit aboard the vessel. They were equally well received, given presents, and asked, by means of gestures, whether there was a suitable harbor where the vessel could lay to and take on fresh water. Obligingly the Japanese pointed to a bay in the north and the Russians departed. Soon they came upon two Japanese boats. A Japanese boarded the vessel with several followers and, upon the arrival of three more boats, had the ship towed into harbor, where a Japanese settlement and a stone wall, bordered by woodland and mountains, stretched out before the eyes of the Europeans. When they started ashore in the yawl, however, the Japanese, who lined the beach, conveyed by gestures that if they let them land both they themselves and the foreigners would lose their heads. Again and again in years to come the Japanese would show that they feared their own officials more than the foreigners. The Russians returned to the galiot; toward evening they were brought water and rice.

Two Japanese guard boats decked with paper lanterns anchored near the ship, and remained there night and day until Benyovszky's departure. When Benyovszky and a group of men tried to go ashore on July 20, guard boats blocked their way, but the Japanese themselves did not hesitate to visit the Russians. On boats from the different bays, they paddled about the galiot with their attractive womenfolk and stared at the strangers from a distance. Others, among them elders and priests, dared to climb aboard, where their spirits were heighened with vodka and presents. The Russians told the Jap-

---

[24] Ivan Riumin, *Zapiski kantseliarista Riumina o prikliucheniiakh ego s Beniovskim.*

anese that they were Dutchmen en route to Nagasaki and asked them to forward a letter addressed to the Dutch, written by Benyovszky.

On July 23,[25] the galiot prepared to leave for the coast of China. It had stayed for several days and, as the officials had reported this to their superiors, they apparently did not wish it to leave before the arrival of other officials or of new instructions. As the Russians started to weigh anchor, the Japanese hastened aboard and urged them to stay overnight. When their request fell on deaf ears, the guards on the boat near the bow, laid hands on the anchor cable. This the Russians interpreted as an attempt to capture or kill them, because the Japanese were known "idol-worshippers and Christian-haters." Benyovszky gave orders to discharge the cannons; frightened, the Japanese tumbled into their boats and rowed hastily ashore. When the Russians reached Macao they were told that the Japanese had previously destroyed two Spanish vessels and had tortured their crews to death, a third vessel barely making its escape, and consequently were assured that they had acted correctly.[26]

Thus Russian sources portray Benyovszky's stay in Japanese waters. If we turn to the pages of standard Japanese reference books, however, we find such mysterious statements as: "Hanbengoro repaired to Nagasaki, and through the Hollanders informed our country of Russia's sinister designs";[27] "Hanbengoro told of Russia's sinister designs and advised the Japanese to look after the fortifications of the northern regions";[28] and "Beniyopusukii—a naturalized citizen of Prussia—pretending to have been cast ashore at Awa and Satsuma, secretly surveyed the coast of Japan and returned home."[29] Benyovszky's name has been rendered in many ways even in the West. It is not surprising that it should have been transformed into Hanbengoro by the Japanese.[30] But to what kind of warnings about Russia's "sinister designs" do the Japanese books refer?

[25] Riumin gives the date of departure as June 12 (old style). A glance at the other dates clearly indicates, however, that this is either a misprint or a careless mistake. It should read July 12 (old style), which corresponds to July 23 (new style).

[26] Riumin, 15-22.   [27] Heki Shoichi, *Kokushi dai-nempyo*, III, 203.

[28] Tochinai Sojiro, *Yojin nihon tanken nempyo*, 63.

[29] Yashiro Kuniji, *Kokushi dai-jiten*, IV, 2365. Most Japanese sources identify Benyovszky as a Pole. The spelling of Benyovszky's country in *Kokushi dai-jiten* suggests Prussia, though ordinarily Prussia is transliterated differently. It is possible that we have here a transliteration of Polsha, the Slavic name for Poland.

[30] According to some authorities Benyovszky posed in Japan as commander in the Navy of Her Imperial Roman Majesty, the Empress of Austria. (Keene, 42.) "Hanbengoro," "Hanbengorofu," or "Wanbengoro" are natural derivatives of "von Bengoro," a Germanic version of his name. "Ausu," as he was also called by some Japanese sources, is no doubt a corruption of August or Augustus.

Japanese sources describe Benyovszky's visit as follows: In the eighth year of Meiwa (1771) Hanbengoro was driven by the wind to the shores of Awa Province (in southeastern Japan) and later to Oshima in Satsuma. He was in fact a spy, gathering information about Japan. He had run out of food and he and his men were in great distress. The daimyo of Hachisuka took pity on them and supplied them with food, fuel, and water. They sailed on with a favorable wind. Hanbengoro was so touched by the gracious conduct of the daimyo, that he left a letter addressed to the Dutch factor in Nagasaki, in which he communicated that Russia was spying on Japan. Then he sailed on to Oshima where he requested the same hospitality. Unaware of his "criminal plan to spy on that place" the Japanese gave him all possible aid. More and more overwhelmed by Japanese hospitality, he began to worry whether the letter had arrived, and told the Japanese that there were matters of utmost importance to Japan that he had to convey. They notified Lord Shimadzu, daimyo of Satsuma, and the latter sent an official. Hanbengoro handed him six letters in horizontal Western writing, as well as a map, expressed his gratitude and left.[31]

Riumin testified in his report that Benyovszky "wrote a letter of information to the Dutch in Nagasaki, and gave it to the Japanese for delivery," though he adds that "it is not known whether it was forwarded or detained by those Japanese."[32] Benyovszky's own memoirs admit the transmittal of communications. An entry under July 29 states: "In a bay on the coast of Japan . . . Mr. Wynbladth was charged with a letter, written in Dutch, containing a declaration respecting my voyages and a request for supply of provisions."[33] An entry on August 5 is more elaborate. It incorporates the text of the letter given to the Japanese to be forwarded to the Hollanders at Nagasaki:

Health to the officers-in-chief of the Factory of the Dutch East India Company.

I acquaint you, gentlemen, that, finding myself upon the coast of Japan, whither I was driven by a series of those incidents which often at sea compel the navigator to seek his safety wherever he can, I find myself in distress which cannot be described, for which reason I have thought proper to address myself to you, and to request you to send me an inter-

---

[31] Okamoto, 1:51-55.   [32] Riumin, 20.   [33] Nicholson, 305.

preter, and assistance to conduct me to your post. My ship is a corvette, with near one hundred persons on board. An answer, if you please.

I have the honour to be, gentlemen,

Your servant

Maurice August Benyowsky.

P.S. In order that you may not be prejudiced by suspicions against me, I declare to you, that having been chief to the confederacy of Poland, I had the misfortune to be made prisoner by the Russians, whose sovereign exiled me to Kamchatka, from where I have made my escape, by the exertion of courage and valour, with ninety-six companions; and in consequence thereof I am now upon the coast of Japan, in my way to return to Europe.[34]

None of these Russian statements, however, suggest a secret warning against Russia.

Turning once again to Japanese sources, we learn that in the letter transmitted at Awa, Benyovszky reported that he was a Dutchman, had formerly fought against Muscovy, had been taken prisoner, had escaped, and, on his way home, had been driven to Japan unintentionally. The kindness of the governor of Awa had preserved their lives, and he thus wished to express his gratitude through the factor.[35] Of the six "letters" left by Benyovszky at Oshima, five were merely letters of thanks for Japanese hospitality and copies and translations of them from German into Latin. As the Japanese interpreters were unable to decipher the letters, they asked the Dutch factors Daniel Armenault and Arend Willem Feijth to translate them into Dutch. Then they themselves translated them into Japanese. It is the sixth one, dated Oshima, July 20, 1771 that contains Benyovszky's warning:[36]

Caught in a storm for several days, battling the sea, we were driven to the territories of Japan for a second time. Thanks to your kindness we received your country's help. I am extremely sorry that I cannot meet you. I am expressing my fidelity in this letter. Having received orders from Russia to reconnoiter [Japanese] strongholds, I sailed this year with two galiots and one frigate from Kamchatka to the Japanese shores and cruised along them. We were supposed to assemble in one place. I have heard the notion expressed with certainty that next year raids will be made on the territories of Matsumae [Hokkaido] and on neighboring islands. We made a survey of these regions in latitude 41°38′ N. Thereupon we constructed fortifications on the so-called Kuril islands, near Kamchatka, and stored military supplies and the like. I did not in the

[34] *Ibid.*, 323; Suematsu, 117-118.

[35] Tokutomi, xxiii, 174; Okuma Shigenobu, *Kaikoku taiseishi*, 422-423.

[36] Tabohashi, 136-137; Pozdneev, ii, 2:25-33; Suematsu, 120-125.

least conceal the above from Hogoederensu[?] and wanted to report it, but the sending of this kind of letters has been really prohibited by the Russians. Since I have now carried out my fidelity to you I hope you will keep this in strictest confidence even from your friends as we are both Europeans. Speaking secretly, I hope you will send ships from your country [Japan] to ward off that harm [Russia's alleged designs on Japan].

A map of Kamchatka was enclosed![37]

Armenault deprecated Benyovszky's warning. "In spite of my intellectual backwardness," he wrote, "I assume that it contains statements having no basis, and everything in it is indigestible and difficult to investigate. The new captain left Europe only this past summer, but has heard no rumors about anything like the statements in this letter. . . ."[38] But though he promised to investigate the matter thoroughly upon his impending return to Europe, his lack of familiarity with the northern regions did not allay Japanese concern. The Shogunate tried to keep the matter secret, but news leaked out. According to Japanese historians Benyovszky's warning "created a great sensation not only in the Japanese government, but even more so among thoughtful people in general, exceeding anything that

---

[37] Kondo Morishige, *Henyo bunkai zuko*, 141-143. Kondo's translation is important because it was utilized by Japanese statesmen and historians. The original text differed somewhat. Professor Donald Keene quotes the original letter, preserved in document 40/11488 in the Rijksarchief at The Hague:

Highly Illustrious, High and Well-born Gentlemen,
Officers of the Highly Esteemed Republic of Holland

Unkind fate, which has for some time been driving me here and there on the sea, has brought me for a second time into Japanese waters. I have come ashore here in the hope I might possibly meet with your high excellencies, and thus obtain help. It has been a great misfortune for me not to have had the opportunity of speaking to you personally, for I have important information to disclose. I have deemed it necessary because of my general respect for your illustrious states to inform you in this letter of the fact that this year, in accordance with a Russian order, two galliots and a frigate from Kamchatka sailed around Japan and set down all their findings in a plan, in which an attack on Matsma [Hokkaido] and the neighboring islands lying under 41°38′ N. Lat. has been fixed for next year. For this purpose a fortress has been built on the Kuril island nearest to Kamchatka, and ammunition, artillery and a magazine have been readied.

If I could speak to you personally, I might reveal more than writing permits. Your high illustriousnesses may make such preparation as you please, but my advice, as an ardent well-wisher of your illustrious republic and co-religionist, would be that you have a cruiser ready if you can. With this I further commend myself and am as subscribed, your most obedient servant

Baron Aladar von Bengoro
Army Commander in Captivity

20 July 1771 on the island Usma.

When I went ashore I left there a map of Kamchatka which may be of use to you. (Keene, 43-44.)

[38] Okamoto, I: 51-55; Kondo, 141-143; Okuma, 419.

might have been expected." Indeed Benyovszky's warning so stimulated Japanese advocates of coastal defense that his sixth letter has been called the "first piece of national defense literature."[39]

Needless to say Russian designs on Hokkaido at that time were a figment of Benyovszky's imagination. As an American historian observes: "Far from planning aggressive moves against Japan, the Russians had all they could do to hold together their Pacific empire, which had never consisted of much more than a wretched colony in Kamchatka (where vodka was the most plentiful commodity), a handful of traders in the Kuriles and a string of tiny outposts in America, sometimes marked by such revealing names as Massacre Bay."[40] Benyovszky had executed a neat bit of personal revenge and had skillfully covered up his tracks.[41] At the same time he had once again double-crossed his Russian companions. When he sold the ship from under their feet they were bound to object, but they never learned that Benyovszky had deliberately aroused Japanese mistrust of their own countrymen. To be sure they were political and criminal exiles, even rebels. When they had fled from Siberia, they had considered approaching some foreign power to send two vessels to Kamchatka to rescue the remaining exiles and give them the opportunity to start life anew elsewhere as colonists. But they were Russians and it is unlikely that they would have willingly tolerated Benyovszky's stratagem. The Japanese believed that Benyovszky's voyage must have added considerably to Russian knowledge of the Japanese waters. Although it exceeded all previous penetrations, and a journal and chart of the cruise were taken back to Russia, they never got beyond the file on the Kamchatka uprising.[42]

The Japanese were unfamiliar with the true character of Benyovszky. They lacked the means of verifying his "disclosures." Nor did they have reason to disbelieve him in view of whatever reports they had received about Russian activities in the Kuril Islands. Modern Russian historians have failed to understand how the Japanese could ever believe that a high official, such as Benyovszky purported to be, could ever betray his mission out of mere gratitude; yet the Japanese concept of gratitude and obligation to one who has saved one's life—and well it may have seemed that the Japanese supplies did

[39] Tabohashi, 139-141; Keene, 43.   [40] Keene, 44.

[41] Not until over a century later, until after the Russo-Japanese war, did a Russian historian working with Japanese sources uncover the traces of Benyovszky's duplicity. (Pozdneev, ii, 25-33.)

[42] Znamenskii, 151.

so—is such that a confession like Benyovszky's would be conceivable. Many Japanese regarded Benyovszky as a hero and were convinced that he had indeed revealed Russian secrets out of boundless gratitude for Japanese help. In the words of one Japanese historian: "Even though his name was handed down incorrectly, he has for a long time been one of the important figures in modern Japanese foreign relations."[43]

A SECRET VOYAGE

Peter the Great had been the fountainhead of Russian interest in Japan; his initiative had aroused the ambitions of commercial enterprise. Yet, when the explorations, begun in the early eighteenth century, finally arrived at their destination, and the exact position of Japan's northernmost large island was established at the end of the Kuril Archipelago, neither government nor business showed their former interest. War with Turkey, the annexation of the Crimea and Novorossiia, military action in Poland, and the Pugachev uprising at home absorbed the attention of the government; while the steady profits from the wealth of furs on the Aleutians and on other islands off the American coast disinclined the commercial leaders to deflect even a part of their resources to the uncertain prospects of trade with Japan. The initiative thus passed into the hands of local authorities in the Russian far east, whose separation from the capital in time and space gave them ample latitude for independent action. They could not expect to "open" Japan—that would have to be done on a higher level—but they hoped to induce Japanese merchants, who frequented Hokkaido, to barter with Russian traders and to make some sort of agreement with local officials like themselves. They were increasingly troubled with the feeding of a swelling population, and trade with Japan, together with the acquisition of the arable southern Kuril Islands, held out some means of relief. Thus it was that in 1772, when Catherine the Great in the wake of Benyovszky's uprising appointed Captain Matvei Bem as the new commander of Kamchatka, Governor Bril of Irkutsk handed him instructions which encompassed the establishment of commercial relations with Japan.

Chernyi and his men, Bril pointed out, had penetrated in the late 1760's to Etorofu, but no map, only a rough draft of his log book,

43 Tabohashi, 141.

had been handed down. Called to Irkutsk to clarify various points, Chernyi had died of smallpox before testifying. In his log book he had asserted that he had heard from the Ainu that the Japanese visited the twenty-second island (Hokkaido) and that they had begun to come also to the twentieth island, remaining for about two months to exchange their manufactures and foodstuffs for beaver skins, eagle tails, fats and so forth. Bril wanted this verified. He instructed Bem to dispatch, under the guise of a fur hunting expedition, a warship to chart and explore in detail the Kuril Archipelago down to the twenty-second island and, if possible, Matsumae itself. Preferably private individuals should be induced to undertake this venture; if not, the expedition was to be sent out in secret, with an experienced navigator and one or two of Chernyi's former interpreters on board. The Japanese whom they might meet must be treated with respect and politeness; they must be questioned as to the kind of goods they needed and the type of products they could give in exchange, about price values, and the possibility of concluding a trade agreement. The Ainu were to be persuaded gently to become Russian subjects; they were to be invited aboard ship, one at a time, to see for themselves how Russians lived. Any foreigners brought back willingly from the islands or found castaway on Kamchatka, should be taken to Okhotsk at government expense and there maintained until further instructions from Irkutsk, while being taught Russian and being used as foreign language instructors for Cossack children.[44]

Bem fully reciprocated Bril's interest in the Kuril Islands. In fact, he soon advocated in one of his reports to Bril that the islands be annexed before other countries did so after hearing about them from Benyovszky, and urged that a fortress be built on Uruppu. In these plans Bem was supported indirectly by the commandant of Okhotsk, Captain Zubov, who, in the late 1770's, had repeatedly petitioned the governor of Irkutsk to let him take possession of the Kuril Islands and establish commercial relations with Japan. "The merchants are interested in profit and not in discoveries," he wrote in September 1777, "and although Spanberg and Walton have been at the shores of Japan, they were there only for reconnaissance purposes and not to establish relations." Two years later, in July 1779, he pleaded: "I could go as a merchant, without giving my expedition any official status. I would attempt to discover new islands. On the

[44] Znamenskii, 153-154. Sgibnev, "Istoricheskii otchet," 46-48.

island nearest Japan I would build stores and under the pretext also a good fortress near a convenient harbor. The garrison of that fortress could keep the Kurilians in submission. I could make this expedition in one summer. Don't tell me the harbor of Okhotsk and the vessels exist only for the purpose of bringing provisions to Kamchatka.—No, we must have discoveries! As for a ship for this voyage it is already prepared."[45] But the governor of Irkutsk listened neither to the impetuous pleadings of the commandant of Okhotsk, who was noted for his avarice and loose living, nor to the counsels of the more balanced commander of Kamchatka, for such large scale colonization would have required not only the consent of the Imperial government but financial expenditures beyond local means. This does not detract from the fact that there were local officials who sought unwittingly to give substance to Benyovszky's warning.[46]

In 1774 Bem found a merchant who agreed to outfit an expedition to Japan. The merchant, Pavel Lebedev-Lastochkin of Yakutsk, who operated on a large scale in the Aleutians, purchased the necessary supplies at Okhotsk and sent them to Kamchatka on a government transport. But the vessel sank and with it Lebedev-Lastochkin's investment. The fact that such shipwrecks were common, because of the shortage of experienced and sober navigators, did not make it any easier for Bem to persuade Lebedev-Lastochkin all over again to finance the project. Lebedev-Lastochkin finally agreed, taking into partnership the merchant Grigorii Shelikhov,[47] who in later years was to become the founder of the Russian colonies in America, but now had just arrived on the scene, and was not yet fully oriented, and several small shareholders, among them Bem himself. As compensation for their risk (in violation of Catherine the Great's manifest of 1762) Bem granted Lebedev-Lastochkin and Shelikhov a temporary monopoly of the Kuril fur industry and trade, by ordering that, until the completion of the expedition, no other Russian vessels visit the islands. None of the backers accompanied the expedition in person, however, as they could not neglect their other obligations for an undetermined period of time.

The *Sviatoi Nikolai* was purchased for the "Secret Voyage," as the expedition was being called, and duly repaired and outfitted. On Lebedev-Lastochkin's request the Siberian nobleman Ivan Anti-

---

45 Sgibnev, "Popytki," 50.   46 Pozdneev, II, 2:10; Znamenskii, 155.
47 Spelled also Shelekhov.

pin, who was versed in navigation and knew some Japanese,[48] was put in command. As assistants he was given Navigator's Apprentice Putintsev and the feeble-minded Japanese language student Ivan Ocheredin. The remainder of the crew consisted of a boatswain, three sailors, forty-five workers (among them twenty-one Kamchadals and one Aleutian), a secretary, a first-aid man, and a sober corporal of the Bol'sheretsk military command, who could be counted upon to replace anyone who became drunk. The armed vessel had enough supplies and provisions for a year's voyage.

The *Sviatoi Nikolai* was to sail directly from Petropavlovsk Harbor to Uruppu without touching at any other island. Aware that Russian activities of the past had aroused the hatred of the Ainu, Bem stressed the need for caution in his instructions to Antipin. He made the following points concerning the conduct and objectives of the Secret Voyage on the Kuril Islands: If the Ainu were not subject to any power, they should be invited to become Russian subjects, protection being offered them against their neighbors. Those who had run away should be asked to return, but if they refused to do so, they must be left in peace. On pain of death, the natives must not be mistreated. A fortress should be constructed at a suitable place, preferably on Uruppu, and the Russians must remain under arms at all times. On Uruppu two pounds of rye, barley, wheat, oats, and hemp should be sown as an experiment and inquiries made as to the mineral resources of this and other islands. Only after the Russians had securely established themselves on Uruppu, were they to push farther south, island by island. They were to chart the islands, taking note of those areas suitable for agriculture and, if available, copy native maps. After relations with the natives had been improved and order established on the Kuril Islands, part of the expedition could devote its attention to fur hunting. Antipin and Putintsev, if they found no Japanese on Etorofu, must continue on to the Japanese city of Matsumae, after having persuaded several Ainu—by whatever gifts— to accompany them, so that the arrival of the Russians, whom the Japanese did not know, would not arouse their mistrust. On meeting the Japanese, the Russians were to act courteously, kindly, and decently. They were to announce that they had been dispatched by Empress Ekaterina Alekseevna because in spite of the fact that she had known of Japan for a long time, there was as yet neither ac-

---

[48] Antipin had learned Japanese at the language school in Irkutsk prior to coming to Kamchatka. (Hayashi Kingo, *Roshiajin Nihon empo-ki*, 32.)

quaintance nor trade between the two countries as between Russia and other nations. They were to call themselves merchants, displaying the wares of Lebedev-Lastochkin and Shelikhov to convince the Japanese of their friendly intentions; their guns and ammunition meanwhile must be kept hidden. They were to find out from the Japanese what they required and what they could trade in exchange, to determine the prices, and to inquire whether the Japanese might not like, for the sake of mutual trade, to make a treaty on some island as a guide for the future; if the Japanese agreed to mutual trade and the conclusion of a treaty, a written statement was to be taken from them. In this connection Bem advised Antipin to hike the prices of Russian products while lowering the cost of Japanese ones. No alcoholic beverages were to be purchased except for one bucket to be tasted in Russia; no firearms were to be sold. Having gained the confidence of the Japanese, the Russians were to gather detailed information about the extent of the Japanese Empire, about its cities, economy, and way of life. They were to find out what foreigners came to trade with them by sea or land, whether the Japanese had any seagoing vessels of their own and if so, where did they sail? They were to obtain data on Japanese military forces, training, fortifications, and weapons and, if possible, to acquire Japanese maps.

Bem's instructions are remarkable for their thoroughness; they were detailed to the extent of ordering the voyagers to put out their fires to prevent damage on the islands. They are even more remarkable as an expression of policy of a local Russian commander. Contrary to the wishes of the central government and the Governor of Irkutsk as the granting of a commercial monopoly, the building of a fortress on Uruppu, and the subjugation of the Kuril Islands may have been, and important and understandable as the queries concerning Japanese fortifications and military potential may have been, even to a country which desired peaceful relations with its neighbor, the objectives of the Secret Voyage were such as to justify Japanese apprehension. Interestingly enough, Bem instructed Antipin to try to capture Benyovszky and commanded, in view of the rivalry between the authorities of Kamchatka and Okhotsk, that the expedition return to Kamchatka and under no circumstances to Okhotsk.[49]

On July 5, 1775, the *Sviatoi Nikolai* left Petropavlovsk Harbor and in a month reached Uruppu. Afraid to wait in the southern bay,

[49] Pavlovskii, 445-446; Sgibnev, "Popytki," 31, 47-48; Znamenskii, 156-160.

where natives had attacked Protodiakonov's vessel, the Russians continued to the northern part of the island. Here the winds drove the *Sviatoi Nikolai* to a less protected sandy bay. The Russians unloaded the ship and arranged living quarters, but they lacked timber for rollers and could not bring the vessel ashore. A storm set in shortly and the *Sviatoi Nikolai* was wrecked. The Secret Voyage was stuck on Uruppu. The Russians sighted some Ainu in the distance, but did not dare to hail them. They occupied themselves with hunting furs and, when spring came, some of the workers loaded *bidarkas* and departed for Bol'sheretsk. Before the loss of the *Sviatoi Nikolai*, in the preceding year, Lebedev-Lastochkin had sent out four *bidarkas* with provisions for the expedition. Three perished in a storm; the fourth the workers now met, and with it returned to Bol'sheretsk. When Shelikhov learned of these misfortunes he withdrew his support of the Secret Voyage; not Lebedev-Lastochkin who still hoped to recover his investment.

In 1776 Lebedev-Lastochkin sent the Irkutsk trader Dimitrii Shabalin to Uruppu with two supply-laden *bidarkas*. At the same time he requested permission from the governor of Irkutsk to rent a government vessel for the purpose of bringing the Kurilians into the Russian Empire, establishing commercial relations with Japan, and rescuing the stranded crew. The governor of Irkutsk granted this request and the brigantine *Natalia* under the command of Navigator Petuchkov was assigned to him for a period of three years. The *Natalia* was a vessel of the Okhotsk command, and thus the rival authorities of Kamchatka and Okhotsk were now both associated with the Secret Voyage. On September 21, 1777, the *Natalia* left Okhotsk. She reached Uruppu safely and there remained for the winter.

In the summer of 1778, four years after the beginning of the expedition, the Russians were ready to push beyond Uruppu. Shabalin, a quick-witted and energetic man, who had joined the expedition merely as interpreter, now became the actual leader. Leaving the *Natalia* and part of the crew at the island, Shabalin and thirty-two men, together with the language student Ocheredin and two Ainu, crossed over to Etorofu on three *bidarkas*. In the preceding year some Russian hunters had also visited Etorofu. Two had been killed by the islanders. A Matsumae official had investigated the incident and had publicly expressed regret. The Russians had taken advantage of the occasion to indicate their desire for rice, tobacco, and meat and to urge the establishment of trade. The Japanese official had explained that it was not in his power to decide this. The Russians then departed, stating as they left that they would come back again. On his return to Matsumae the Japanese official pleaded for trade, but to no avail. Now the Russians saw no Japanese. As the Ainu approached gesticulating wildly, they prepared for battle. But they held their fire as they learned that these were ceremonial gestures of welcome, and instead presented the Ainu leaders with gifts. Having proclaimed some of the natives Russian subjects, Shabalin and his men went on to Kunashiri. There they claimed more Ainu subjects and, after gathering some information of an island to the north (Sakhalin), finally penetrated to Hokkaido.[50]

Discharging their muskets, the Russians approached the eastern coast of Hokkaido at the little settlement of Notkome (Nokkamapu, east of Nemuro). The inhabitants were frightened until natives from Rashowa Island went ashore from one of the *bidarkas* and assured them that the Russians had come with peaceful intentions and only desired to confer with the Japanese, about whose visits to this region they had learned from the Ainu on Shimushiru. There was a Japanese merchant ship nearby and the opportunity for trade with Japanese merchants seemed close to hand. The Russians did not realize that, while they themselves were commercial people with a certain amount of authority delegated to them by officials in Siberia, the Japanese in charge of local operations were neither merchants nor hunters but government officials. Japanese trade with the Ainu was given on lease and was conducted under the control of officials who accompanied the merchant vessels and themselves traded in objects monopolized by the government. The Japanese inspector Kudo Seiemon informed the Russians through an interpreter that, since it was night, the Matsumae official Araida Daihachi had retired to the tribute office and all negotiations would have to be postponed until morning. But the Russians insisted that they had come from a distance and would not be able to feel at ease in a place entirely unfamiliar to them, and must see the official at once. They proceeded to the tribute office where they found the official and met briefly with him. They posted four or five guards at their temporary camp, but agreed to recall them, when the Japanese assured them that the natives had been told to conduct themselves properly and that they could sleep in perfect safety.

[50] Sgibnev, "Popytki," 48-50; Tokutomi, XXIII, 130; Znamenskii, 160-161.

The following morning the Russians conferred with Araida. They explained, through a native interpreter from Shimushiru, that Japan and Russia had for a long time been anxious to establish trade relations with each other and that therefore they had brought samples of their merchandise with them. Araida replied that he did not have the authority to act upon this matter, but promised to bring it before his lord upon returning to Matsumae; the latter would then make an appropriate report to the shogunate. He informed the Russians that no speedy reply was possible and that an answer would be brought to Etorofu in the summer of the following year. Araida then ordered their immediate departure and the Russians left Notkome. They returned to Uruppu where they rejoined Antipin and the rest of the crew. Shortly thereafter they set sail on the *Natalia* and reached Okhotsk in early September. Araida had not promised trade with Russia, but his evasive reply had been misunderstood. According to Russian sources, Araida had expressed fear to trade with the Russians without permission from his government, but had agreed with Shabalin that, until the decision of the Japanese sovereign became known, goods could be exchanged in the harbor on the northern side of Kunashiri Island. Allegedly Araida asked the Russians to come to that harbor by July 31, 1779 to confirm details of trade and procedure, and gave them letters to the Russian government in which the desire to trade with Russia was expressed. Shabalin thus arrived with joyful tidings as well as a handsome load of furs.

Lebedev-Lastochkin decided to send the brigantine back to Uruppu without delay and, having taken into partnership the merchants Popov and Mylnikov and the Okhotsk Commandant Zubov, loaded the vessel with a valuable cargo of goods and provisions. Shabalin was officially put in command of the new expedition and given letters from Lebedev-Lastochkin and Zubov to the commander of the Japanese vessel. On September 18, 1778 the *Natalia* put out to sea.[51]

Araida Daihachi, meanwhile, had returned to Matsumae and delivered to his lord a letter and gifts which the Russians had left. The next year, in 1779, Japanese officials were sent out to bring a reply to the "redheaded" foreigners, but were considerably delayed by unfavorable winds. Shabalin and Antipin wintered on Uruppu. In the summer of 1779 they proceeded with forty-five men on seven *bidarkas* to Etorofu and then to Kunashiri. When they did not find

[51] Polonskii, 455; Znamenskii, 162-163; Okamoto, 55-56; Sgibnev, "Popytki," 31-49; Pozdneev, II, 2: 33-36; Kono, 669-670; Hayashi, 54.

any Japanese there, they continued in search of them until they reached Hokkaido once more. At Notkome they waited for the Japanese delegates who sent word of their unavoidable delay and asked the Russians to remain there. This they did for a month, imposing tribute on several Ainu, then moved on to Akkeshi. In the harbor lay a Japanese vessel. As they passed it on their *bidarkas* a flag was raised on the ship, and the Russians replied with a three gun salute. When they touched shore they were met by Japanese sailors and a Japanese interpreter of Ainu and were shown where to rest. Nearby they saw a wooden commercial office, where the Japanese traders stayed. On September 6, Shabalin and Antipin conferred with the commander of the Japanese vessel. He read them a letter from the Lord of Matsumae in which the latter wrote that bad weather had prevented his officials from coming that summer, but that they could meet the Russians on Kunashiri the following year. The Russians must not visit Hokkaido again; Akkeshi was Japanese, the leaders of the local Ainu receiving Japanese goods in exchange for native products. If the Russians did need Japanese things they could obtain them through the Ainu. In the days that followed, Russians and Japanese freely visited and entertained each other and even exchanged gifts, though later the Japanese commander, afraid of his superiors, returned the boots and other presents given to him. The Russians were about to depart, when word was received that a vessel bearing two envoys from Matsumae was on its way. The envoys arrived on September 16, and, after elaborate preparations, the Russians were received. The officials informed the latter that their ruler had forbidden them to trade with the Russians and that the Lord of Matsumae had instructed them consequently to tell the Russians that they must not come again to Kunashiri and Etorofu. Should they be in need of food and wine they could send Ainu from Uruppu. If trade with Japan was their desire, they should go to Nagasaki where other nations gathered for that purpose. They returned the letter and gifts which the Russians had brought the previous year, but supplied them with provisions and firewood and accepted some bags of sugar in exchange. Thus trade in the regions nearest to Russia had been denied, but mention of Nagasaki kept alive the prospect of relations elsewhere. According to Japanese sources, mention of Nagasaki was made or meant in a somewhat less promising sense. Japanese sources render the statement like this: "... foreign trade is limited exclusively to the port of Nagasaki, and as it is not permitted at all in other places, no matter how much you would ask, permission will not be given. In the future to cross the sea and to come here will be of no use whatsoever."[52]

On October 11, 1779, the Russians returned to Uruppu and there remained for the winter. On January 19, 1780, a series of earthquakes began to shake the island. On the morning of the 29th a tidal wave, that rose some forty-two feet above the horizon, tore the *Natalia* off her two anchors and carried her about thirteen hundred and thirty feet inland, where she was left stranded as the waters receded. Unable to drag the brigantine back into the sea, Antipin and fourteen men departed for Bol'sheretsk in a *bidarka*, arriving there in September. The following year Antipin traveled to Irkutsk to report on the expedition. Shabalin with fifty-two men remained on Uruppu waiting for Lebedev-Lastochkin to send a vessel. When none arrived by the summer of 1782, Shabalin and his men loaded the remaining company property onto four *bidarkas* and headed safely back to Kamchatka.

Lebedev-Lastochkin, meanwhile, had hastened to St. Petersburg in 1779 to report in person about the apparent success of the Secret Voyage, carrying with him the ship's journal and a map of the Kuril Islands and the letters and gifts received from the Japanese. As he passed through Irkutsk, he made a report to Governor Nemchinov, who in turn sent along a letter to Prince Viazemskii in which he proposed that Commandant Zubov be dispatched to Japan and asked that Lebedev-Lastochkin, in reward for such services as the subjugation of up to fifteen hundred natives and as compensation for the great losses suffered by him, be granted a monopoly on trade and hunting in the Kuril Islands. But the intercession of the governor did not have the desired effect. Filled with ambitions in the West, the Imperial government lacked as yet the taste for imperialism in the Far East. The expense involved in the administration and defense of so many distant subjects would only outweigh the tribute obtained from them. On June 9, 1779, Catherine the Great decreed that, because of the difficulties involved in the administration of distant conquered territories, the Ainu, who had been made subjects, should be let free and not required to pay tribute, though it would be desirable to maintain friendly relations with them for the sake of

---

[52] Okamoto, 55-56; Pozdneev, II, 2:33-36; Yano Niichi, *Roshia no toho seisaku*, 134-135; Ebina Kazuo, "Kaikoku-ron no ransho," 375; *Hokkaido-shi* II, 276-277. The latter contains a Russian picture of the meeting at Akkeshi in 1779.

commercial profit; the right to trade with Japan was granted to all Russian subjects alike, monopolies having been abolished by the manifest of August 11, 1762; the orders issued by the governor of Irkutsk, restraining all merchants other than Lebedev-Lastochkin from going to the distant Kuril Islands, were to be revoked; and Zubov was to be sent out only if the governor himself thought such a trip useful.

When Lebedev-Lastochkin, upon his return to Irkutsk in 1781, learned of the fate that had befallen the *Natalia*, he petitioned the governor of Irkutsk that, as compensation for the 79,500 ruble loss which he had borne, he be assigned another government vessel for trade with the islands. Major General Klichka issued appropriate instructions, and on May 22, 1781, the galleon *Sviatoi Georgii* was put at his disposal. Lebedev-Lastochkin ordered the captain to sail to Uruppu, salvage the *Natalia*, and then proceed to the Aleutian Islands for trade. Frightened by the earthquakes the captain went directly to the Aleutians. Another attempt to remove the *Natalia* proved equally abortive and the vessel was left to rot on Uruppu. This was too much even for Lebedev-Lastochkin, and he abandoned his attempts to trade with the Kuril Islands and Japan. Captain Zubov was ordered to Irkutsk in 1781, to elaborate on his plans for establishing trade relations with Japan. He went to Irkutsk, but while waiting there was courtmartialed for violence, drunkenness, and disorderly conduct. The Kuril Islands faded into the background of Russo-Japanese relations: tribute could no longer be exacted from the natives; the earthquakes of 1780 had frightened the beavers away from the islands; and their rôle as stepping stones to trade with Japan could no longer be supported. After the tremendous losses of Lebedev-Lastochkin, private capital could no longer be prevailed upon to finance expeditions to Japan independently. Henceforth the Russian government had to sponsor or, at least, finance such ventures.[53]

53 Sporadic individual activity in the Kurils continued. In 1786, the Japanese explorer Mogami Tokunai was welcomed by three Russians when he landed on Etorofu Island. Having separated from their countrymen on Uruppu because of dissension, the Russians voluntarily accompanied Mogami to Kunashiri, and apparently remained there. (Yamamoto, 467; Minakawa Shinsaku, *Mogami Tokunai*, 48-51.) Three years earlier, in 1783, the Russians had set foot on Sakhalin. Commanded by Petr, son of a Japanese castaway (Rihachiro of Sai Village in Nambu) and a Russian wife, some seventy Russians are said to have arrived on a large vessel. Details are not known, but a quarrel evidently ensued with the natives and all the Russians allegedly were killed. The Russian vessel was carried away by the waves and was driven to the shore of Uruppu. There a native chieftain from Etorofu, who had been hunting in that region, came upon the ship and climbed aboard. All he could find was the corpse of one

The voyages of Spanberg and Walton had led the Russians, for the first time, to the shores of Japan. The contacts, which had taken place with the Japanese, had been so hasty, however, that, though the location of Japan had been discovered, its people remained unknown. The exploration of men, like Chernyi, had filled in some of Spanberg's findings. But it was the Secret Voyage which completed the exploratory quest of Japan. To be sure, the Russians had only been on Hokkaido, with its predominantly Ainu population. But Hokkaido was indisputably Japanese territory. Here the first official contacts between Russia and Japan took place; here the matter of trade with Russia was first put before the Japanese government. It was only a matter of time till negotiations were to be resumed on a larger scale.[54]

Russian, who seemed to have been stabbed to death, and a rich cargo of cloth, cotton, gold, and silver. The natives regarded the find as a gift from heaven. They carried off the welcome load; then they burned the ship. As more and more Russian vessels began to approach Uruppu on hunting voyages, the natives became concerned for fear the goods be discovered and they be blamed for the murder of the crew. Panic-stricken, they piled the loot into nine canoes and in spite of bad weather set out for a better hiding place. A sudden storm foiled their plans and the treasure was claimed again by the ocean. Not one of the more than a hundred natives, who had manned the boats, survived. When a Russian vessel arrived at Uruppu soon afterwards, the natives, who had remained behind, thoroughly frightened by now, disclosed what had happened. The Russians expressed anger at the way in which the natives had appropriated Russian property; at the same time they took advantage of the misfortune to claim that existing conditions showed a lack of administration, that there was no reason why Russia should recognize the island as under Japanese rule. Uruppu needed a responsible administration that would restrain the natives from similar misdeeds. Those who colonized the island—the Russians—were to be its rightful owners. (Okamoto, 1:56-57; Suematsu, 109.)

[54] Polonskii, 456-462; Sgibnev, "Popytki," 49-52; Znamenskii, 164-167; Okamoto, 55-56; Pozdneev, II, 2:31-36.

CHAPTER FOUR · THE OPENING WEDGE

KODAYU AND LAXMAN

IN the second half of January, or in the opening days of February 1783,[1] the Japanese transport *Shinsho Maru* was proceeding along the coast of Suruga Province with a cargo of rice from the domains of the Lord of Kii, when a sudden squall smashed her rudder. Unable to control the vessel, the crew kept her upright by downing the mast and jettisoning most of the cargo. The helpless ship was swept out to sea, and tossed about for a period of eight months. The fresh water gave out, but the crew managed to collect rain water by edging the upper deck with boards and cutting a hole in it, under which they set a container. On August 12, one of the seventeen shipmates died. Soon after on August 17, their spirits were lifted by the sight of an island. Hastily they ripped apart rice bags, sewed them into a small sail, and, using cables as rudders, drew nearer. The island seemed barren of trees and inhospitable, but the Japanese had little choice. They put firewood, rice, clothing, and other necessities into a boat and rowed ashore. On land they met some natives. In vain they tried to make themselves understood, but the natives kept pulling them at the sleeve and gesturing to them to come along. After much discussion, five of the Japanese ventured to accompany the natives. Soon they encountered two men dressed in red, who fired their muskets in the air when they saw them. These, they learned later, were Russian hunters and the place was Amchitka, one of the Aleutian Islands. Here they and their other shipmates remained for four years. Their ship was smashed against the shore and, though they managed to save most of the equipment and salvaged what timber they could, life on this northern island was harsh indeed. In a short time seven of the castaways, weakened already by privation at sea, died.

In 1787, the Japanese managed finally to leave the island and make their way to Kamchatka, either by their own efforts on a ship constructed from the wreckage of the *Shinsho Maru*, as they later claimed, or on a Russian vessel that had called at Amchitka, more likely the

[1] In the twelfth lunar month of the second year of Temmei. Most Japanese sources err in equating this with 1782; the twelfth lunar month extended from January 3 through February 1, 1783.

latter. At Nizhne-Kamchatsk the hunters, with whom they had come and from whom they had learned some Russian on the island, handed them over to the governor. The leader of the Japanese, a native of the village Minami-Wakamatsu in the domain of the Lord of Kame-yama in Izu Province, by the name of Kodayu remained in the house of the governor. The eight other castaways were put up in a boarding-house, looked after by an official, a doctor, and a soldier. But, well-treated as they were, the ravages of a famine on Kamchatka took the lives of three more castaways in 1788.[2] Earlier that year the French traveler M. de Lesseps had met the nine Japanese and recorded his impressions of them. Of Kodayu he noted: "The freedom with which he enters the house of the governor and other persons would among us be thought insolent, or at least rude. He immediately fixes himself as much at his ease as possible, and takes the first chair that offers; he asks for whatever he wants, or helps himself, if it be within his reach." Lesseps was no less impressed by Kodayu's intelligence. "He is possessed of great penetration, and apprehends with admirable readi-ness everything you are desirous to communicate. He has much curiosity, and is an accurate observer."[3] These are significant com-ments, for Kodayu jotted down whatever he saw and served as a channel of information between the Russians and Japanese.

In the summer of 1788, the six remaining castaways were taken across Kamchatka to Tigilsk, from there by sea to Okhotsk, after an arduous snow-covered overland journey, to Yakutsk, and finally to Irkutsk, where they arrived in February of 1789. Here they aroused much curiosity and were in great demand at social gatherings. Every-where they were treated with kindness and compassion; yet they dreaded the Russians' plans for making them soldiers or officials, or even for setting them up in business as merchants, and repeatedly petitioned that they be returned home. Fortunately they made the acquaintance of Eric Laxman, a Finnish-born professsor of natural science at the St. Petersburg Academy, who was just then engaged in some research in this region. Interested in Japan for years, Laxman readily took them under his wing in the hope of adding to his knowl-edge of their country.[4] In January 1791, when he started back for St. Petersburg he took along Kodayu and two of his companions—

[2] Ramming, *Reisen*, 14-17; Kamei Takataka, *Hokusa monryaku*, 8-9.
[3] Keene, 61-62; Ramming, *Reisen*, 18.
[4] Ramming notes that Professor Laxman enclosed a detailed map of Japan drawn by Kodayu in a report to the Academy in 1790 and discusses this and other maps of Kodayu. Kamei takes issue with Ramming's findings. See Ramming, *Reisen*, 21-25; Kamei, 28-32.

the other two castaways having fallen ill, one of them very seriously.[5]

In St. Petersburg Professor Laxman succeeded in arousing interest in his plan of sending an expedition to Japan under the pretext of returning the castaways. Six years earlier, in August 1785, the resumption of negotiations with the Japanese had been added to the many tasks of an expedition, under Captains Joseph Billings and Gavriil Sarychev, to the Russian possessions in northeast Asia and the northern Pacific, but it had failed to reach the shores of Japan. Then, on January 2, 1787, an imperial ukase had projected the dispatching of Russia's first round-the-world expedition under the command of Captain Mulovskii. Planned on a large scale, essentially to assert Russian rights in territories discovered by Russian seafarers, it too envisaged renewed negotiations with the Japanese, but was called off almost at the last moment, because of war with Turkey and the expected break of diplomatic relations with Sweden.[6] Catherine the Great now ordered Professor Laxman to elaborate on his proposal in writing.

Laxman drew up a memorial in which he listed in some detail the merchandise that could be sold and bought in Japan. He described the Japanese intolerance of foreigners, commenting that, in view of the good behavior of the Dutch, this intolerance had lessened considerably and, on the basis of Kodayu's testimony, was no longer a threat as in the days of Kämpfer. He noted that the standard of living and needs of the Japanese had increased, and with it the importance of their trade; that unfavorable reports of Japanese actions were purposely spread by the Dutch and English to keep the profits of trade to themselves.

For acquaintance and commercial relations with Japan no one has so much convenience as the Russian merchants, who trade on the Pacific Ocean, and what is more, our very proximity gives us the nearest right to it. No one has easier communication, no one can benefit from it more, than our merchants who for a long time already have been thinking of this acquaintance, wherefore it is extremely desirable that they might get the opportunity for the first step in this matter through the return of the remaining shipwrecked Japanese who are still in Russia. . . . If they will be taken like friends to their fatherland and will begin to praise such benefactions of ours, the spreading of such good words on the part of the good merchants who travel for local trade to Ezo and to the islands adjacent to our Kuril ones, will encourage the establishment of trade and

5 Ramming, *Reisen*, 23-25; Keene, 60-64; Sgibnev, "Popytki," 53.
6 Novakovskii, 46-47; Sgibnev, "Istoricheskii ocherk," CII, 32-33.

acquaintance with us, should the Japanese government, against all expectation, leave this without any consideration. . . .[7]

In the last part of his memorial Laxman insisted that Russian navigation of the Amur River was absolutely essential for the development of Russian trade and territories, and proposed that the Amur be secretly reconnoitered by vessels of the projected Japanese expedition. In a supplement to this memorial, Laxman made some further comments and suggestions: Both English and Dutch merchants had tried persistently to get hold of the Japanese he had brought to the capital; there was no truth to the rumor that the Amur Estuary had become overgrown with reeds and thus was no longer navigable; a settlement should be established at a suitable place on the very mouth of the Amur, the Russian Kuril Islands, or on the more southerly unoccupied islands in order to facilitate trade with the Japanese and to forestall the need of having to do in northern Japan what the Dutch must do on Deshima; the population of Russia should be increased along the Chinese frontier; the two Japanese who had adopted Christianity (Shinzo or Nikolai Petrovich Kolotygin and Shozo or Fedor Stepanovich Sitnikov) should be used as language teachers in Russia, while those about to be repatriated should still be utilized in the same capacity during the lengthy voyage.[8]

On September 24, 1791, Catherine the Great decreed that Professor Laxman's plan concerning an expedition to Japan be executed. In the ukase addressed to Lieutenant General Ivan Pil, Governor General of Irkutsk and Kolyvansk, she included the following points: (1) To use for the voyage to Japan a private vessel with a sufficient complement rented at government expense or, if Captain Billings returned in time, one of his vessels with the necessary crew, making certain that its commander be a native Russian, and if no native Russian of talent be available, then a foreigner, but not an Englishman or Dutchman; (2) to send on this vessel, at full government expense, all the Japanese except the two who had adopted the Christian faith; (3) to have one of Professor Laxman's sons, who was serving in Irkutsk and was versed in astronomy and navigation, accompany the Japanese to their fatherland, ordering him to make astronomical, physical, and geographical observations en route and in Japan, investigating also commercial conditions there; (4) in consultation with Professor Laxman to draw up clear instructions for

---

[7] Polonskii, 468-469.
[8] *Ibid.*, 470-473; Hayashi, 77; Ramming, *Reisen*, 28.

the commander of the expedition; (5) on the occasion of returning the castaways to address the Japanese government on paper, setting forth the care with which they had been treated as evidence of the Russian desire for intercourse and commercial relations with Japan, assuring it that Japanese subjects would receive assistance and kind treatment in Russian ports and territories; (6) to present to the Japanese government, as a gift in the name of Pil, up to two thousand rubles' worth of proper goods purchased at government expense; (7) to try to induce some Irkutsk merchants or their agents to accompany the expedition with their wares in order to gather some practical experience concerning the possibilities of trade with Japan; (8) not to follow Professor Laxman's plan, regarding the Amur River, lest Russian trade negotiations with China should be hindered; (9) to use the two castaways who could not return to Japan as teachers of Japanese, "which with the establishment of commercial relations with Japan will be very much needed," placing them at the public school in Irkutsk at an appropriate salary with five to six local students, who in time could also serve as translators.[9]

The Empress herself received the castaways and told them that it had been decided to send them home. Gifts were bestowed on them, Kodayu receiving a jeweled tobacco box, a Swiss watch, and a gold medal. In Irkutsk, in St. Petersburg, and during a stay in Moscow they were wined and dined and people of rank and distinction came to call on them. In January of 1792, the castaways returned to Irkutsk with Professor Laxman, who wished to direct from there the necessary preparations for the expedition to Japan. His twenty-six-year-old son, Lieutenant Adam Laxman, went at once to Okhotsk, from whence the vessel was to sail. He did not, however, play an active role until after departure from Russia.

With the assistance of Commandant Ivan Kokh of Okhotsk and the cooperation of officials elsewhere, Professor Laxman organized the expedition with a minimum of friction. His major obstacle and source of delay was the shortage of suitable personnel. As the Empress desired the employment of a Russian as commander of the vessel, Navigator Grigorii Lovtsov was named to this position, even though he lacked more advanced nautical training. For assistants he was given Navigator Olesov and Navigator's Mate Mukhoplev. Neither was particularly reliable. As Professor Laxman was to write after the

---

[9] Document No. 16985, dated September 24, 1791; Polonskii, 473-475; Novakovskii, 49-52; V. Lagus, *Erik Laksman,* 242-245.

safe return of the expedition from Japan: "The fortunate outcome of the voyage surprises me the more, because the navigators seemed to me so very suspicious, but could not be replaced by anyone. It is true that Olesov and Mukhoplev had learned something, but because of unsatisfactory conduct and their dipsomania, they had to be put under the almost completely ignorant Lovtsov, only because he is more sober, and so God piloted the ship."[10] No suitable private vessel was found in Okhotsk, nor had any of Captain Billings' vessels arrived in port. Professor Laxman, therefore, selected a government transport, the brigantine *Ekaterina*, which was duly repaired and supplied. The merchants Shelikhov and Golikov as well as V. Rokhletsov agreed to take over the commercial aspects of the expedition, and merchandise for trade as well as gifts was fetched from Moscow. The complement chosen for the *Ekaterina* numbered no more than forty: Lieutenant Laxman, Navigators Lovtsov and Olesov, Navigator's Mate Mukhoplev, Interpreter Sergeant Tugolukov (who was immediately attached to the castaways to study Japanese),[11] Interpreter Geodesist Trapeznikov, a boatswain (Sapozhnikov, who had been on Uruppu in 1770), a quartermaster, fifteen sailors, two carpenters, a blacksmith, a student medic, an artillery corporal, three soldiers, the Irkutsk merchant Dmitrii Shabalin (who was familiar with the Kuril Islands and in 1778 had visited Hokkaido), two agents of Shelikhov, of Golikov, and of Rokhletsov, with two servants, the three Japanese castaways, and the fifteen year old son of Commandant Kokh as a volunteer at his own expense.[12] Lovtsov selected the crew; other than that, as in the case of Lieutenant Laxman, his authority began only when the expedition had been readied for departure. The relative roles and rights of the young envoy and of Navigator Lovtsov during the expedition were clearly spelled out to them by Pil: "When the vessel will have been manned with a crew and persons, then Laxman too must board it and, without interfering except for needed counsels, be subject to Navigator Lovtsov's authority in sailing and dispositions, considering himself as a passenger like the Japanese and other government servants and commercial agents.

[10] Ramming, *Reisen*, 29; Polonskii, 476-478; Sgibnev, "Popytki," 53.

[11] According to Japanese sources Tugolukov had studied Japanese in his youth under the castaway Kyusuke, who had been shipwrecked in the Kyoho period (1716-1735). Trapeznikov is said to have been the son of Kyusuke, and thus half-Japanese. (Ramming, *Reisen*, 29.)

[12] Polonskii, 478; Ramming (*Reisen*, 28-29) and Sgibnev ("Popytki," 53) list Shabalin as the agent of Shelikhov and Golikov; they give the number of the crew as twenty sailors and four soldiers.

Lovtsov, on the other hand, being experienced in sailing, is entrusted with the vessel, cargo, all servants and passengers on the basis of naval regulations."[13]

On September 24, 1792, one year to the day after the ukase of Catherine the Great, the expedition put out to sea. It had orders to proceed down the Kuril Archipelago directly to the twenty-second island (Akkeshi, Hokkaido) and there to announce its arrival and purpose to a Japanese vessel and, in the absence of any such vessel, send a Russian-manned junk to the nearest Japanese city. Laxman and Lovtsov were specifically instructed to treat the inhabitants of the island amicably and to impress on crew and passengers alike that they must create a favorable impression of Russia by their conduct. Upon the return of their comrades on the junk and, if necessary—in order not to miss the seasonable time of navigation—even without their return, Lovtsov was to leave the twenty-second island and with due nautical caution sail to the very capital of Japan, recording all incidents in the journal. Pil warned that the castaways must not be offended in any way. At the shores of Japan, to prevent their escape, they must be guarded, but unobtrusively. The instructions dwelled on the delivery of the Russian state paper to the Japanese, on the investigation of trade possibilities, Japanese internal affairs, and troubles between Japanese and Ainu on the Kuril Islands. Again and again it was found necessary to caution the members of the expedition to refrain from excessive drinking, gambling, or anything else that would detract from respect of Russia.[14] In view of Japanese antagonism toward Christianity, care was to be exercised to spare Japanese sensibilities (and suspicions) in this regard also. Russian adaptability and respect for Oriental customs, characteristic of Russian policy in the Far East, were clearly expressed in the instructions: "I leave it to you to impress it strictly on the crew, that they do not sometime in accordance with custom and habit cross themselves while praying but keep their faith in their heart. To this end you must in advance take from all without exception the crosses, images, prayer-books and everything that only portrays Christianity, or bears the sign of the cross."[15]

Setting course for latitude 45° N., where Hokkaido was believed to be, the *Ekaterina* found herself at Etorofu on October 7. Continuing to the southwest, the brigantine sighted the northern coast of Kunashiri with its snowcovered sugar cone, Mount Piko, and pro-

---

[13] Polonskii, 480.   [14] *Ibid.*, 481-483.   [15] *Ibid.*, 554.

ceeding southward, arrived at the strait between Kunashiri and Hokkaido (Nemuro Kaikyo). She was prevented by bad weather from entering the strait until October 17, when she finally put into the

Japanese barracks

Nemuro

The "Ekaterina" wintered here

Japanese barracks
Russian barracks

Japanese barracks

The "Ekaterina" stopped here

EZO

(HOKKAIDO)

Akkeshi

Nemuro and Akkeshi at
the Time of Laxman

narrow strip of water, which, in later years, Lieutenant Commander Vasilii Golovnin was to name in her honor (Proliv Ekateriny), and rounding the southernmost tip of Kunashiri cast anchor. The anchorage proved unsatisfactory and the following day, on October 18, 1792, the Russians crossed to the northern shore of Hokkaido. A boat was sent out to reconnoiter the coast in search of a wintering place, and Shabalin, who knew Ainu, even managed to converse with some of the natives. The following day, on October 19, a *bidarka*, with the interpreter Tugolukov and Navigator Olesov, reached the mouth of Nishibetsu River. Here there was a Japanese tax and storage point, and, as the Russians landed, they were met by six Japanese as well as a horde of Ainu. One of the Japanese was a Matsumae merchant, who had several landing places on lease on Shikotan, Kunashiri, and Hokkaido; the remaining four were servants. The Japanese received the Russians well, particularly as one of the castaways had come along to reassure them. They entertained the Russians at dinner and then four of them—the commercial agent and three servants—plus several Ainu paid a visit aboard the Russian ship. They told the Russians about Nemuro Bay, and left two old Ainu aboard as guides. The next day, on October 20, the Russians entered Nemuro, where there was a small Japanese settlement and some miserable Ainu huts, followed shortly by the official from Nishibetsu.[16]

Laxman and his companions were cordially received on shore. He explained the purpose of his visit and expressed the intention of constructing some buildings at Nemuro and to stay for the winter. The Japanese made no objections and even offered to assist in the construction. When Laxman asked whether the natives might give him trouble, the Japanese replied that trouble from the Ainu was unlikely, but, as a precaution, they themselves would winter at Nemuro with him, though, with the exception of a few guards for their wharfs, and buildings, and so forth, they usually left for Matsumae at about this time to return again in May. From them the Russians learned the name of the governor of Matsumae and, on October 23, sent him a letter, translated into Japanese by Tugolukov and the castaways. In it Laxman and Lovtsov asked the governor to inform the Edo government of their arrival and, carefully avoiding any reference to trade, stated merely that they intended to deliver to the capital the castaways, whom they had brought, because of Catherine's "high motherly and exclusively humanitarian protection." They explained that the lateness of the season had forced them to winter in Nemuro and asked that this information be forwarded to the central government, so that, if weather or some

16 *Ibid.*, 487-488; Pozdneev, II, 2: 48; Okamoto, I: 58; Sgibnev, "Popytki," 54; Lagus, *Erik Laksman*, 256-257; Suematsu, 212-213. Years later Philipp Franz von Siebold renamed the bay of Nemuro "Laxman Bay."

other unavoidable circumstance required them to pull ashore before reaching the capital, they be permitted to do so unhindered, as "neighboring allies," and not be regarded as "antagonistic and infidel adversaries." They concluded with the request that the governor inform them when a reply from the government was received.[17]

The arrival of Laxman set in motion feverish correspondence between Nemuro, Matsumae, and Edo. Matsumae Yunosuke, eldest son of Michihiro, Lord of Matsumae, who just that year had received permission to retire, duly forwarded the Russian request to the capital. He reported that the Russians had instructions to surrender the castaways in Edo and had insisted on continuing to the capital in the course of the same year, but had been held back at Nemuro. They had agreed to wait until the fourth or fifth month of the following year. If no reply was received by then, they would go to Edo, to present their "petition" directly. "In view of these events I have sent my followers to that place," continued Matsumae. "I have ordered that until the arrival of the orders from the government they be detained. As we are dealing here with foreigners, it is difficult to calculate what intentions they nurse in their heart; I have ordered, however, as far as possible to settle everything peacefully. In view of the above reported, I take the liberty of humbly inquiring how to act in this case." The specter of a Russian visit to the capital aroused frantic defense considerations, and the government maneuvered to delay, if not halt, Laxman in the north. It approved of Matsumae Yunosuke's measures: "As the Russians have brought with them shipwrecked people, measures are to be taken that under no circumstances they sail away before a communication from Edo has arrived. It is understood that one must not deal with them rudely and admit of impoliteness. They must be treated friendly and also sent sake and rice as gifts. They will be permitted to go ashore at Akkeshi, but the Ainu as well as the people of Matsumae, insofar as they are not officials, must not talk with them."[18]

Permitted to land, treated with courtesy and freely provisioned, the Russians had reason to be satisfied at first. On October 25, they selected together with the Japanese a place near the Japanese settle-

---

17 Polonskii, 488-490; Lagus, *Erik Laksman*, 257-258.

18 Ramming, *Reisen*, 30; Pozdneev, II, 2: 49-51; Otomo, *Hokumon sosho*, VI, 14-15. According to Pozdneev, Torii, Lord of Tamba, informed Matsumae Yunosuke further that the officials Ishikawa Rokuemon (Shogen) and Murakami Daigaku were being sent to accept the castaways and that Nambu Keijiro, Tsugaru, Lord of Dewa, and the Matsumae clan had been instructed to provide guards to protect the Russians.

ment for the construction of their buildings. By November 28, two were completed, and the Russians, with the exception of the necessary guard aboard ship, moved ashore. Laxman went on small excursions collecting specimens for the academy in St. Petersburg. He also questioned the Japanese on the various subjects outlined in his instructions. Gradually, however, time began to weigh heavily on the Russians and constant inactivity sapped the health of the crew. Scurvy broke out and by spring one of the Russians and the castaway Koichi had died of the disease.

On December 23, an official arrived from Matsumae to inform the Russians that their letter had been forwarded to the capital, and to protect them from the Ainu, and otherwise be of service. He asked them many questions, particularly about geography. Since they were going to spend the winter together, he said, he wanted them to visit on friendly terms. He refused to accept gifts, which the Russians sent him the next day, but borrowed a Russian globe and atlas and copied them. In exchange he let the Russians copy a map of Ezo. On January 2, 1793, he was joined by another Matsumae official. On January 9, officials from Edo also arrived. Like the Matsumae officials before them, they asked question after question, partly to clarify Russian intentions, partly to learn more about Russia and the world outside, studiously sketching and copying everything in sight. The Russians took advantage of this to get answers to questions of their own. Frequently the Japanese and the Russians exchanged visits, though, with the arrival of officials from Edo, the Matsumae officials no longer returned the calls of the Russians. Every day Tugolukov visited the officials to improve his Japanese; they did not object, in fact welcomed him, because they had to translate the names on the Russian maps which they had copied. Tugolukov continued to probe into Japanese feelings toward Russia. One day, on February 21, he reported that he had secretly learned from the Edo officials, one of whom had served in Nagasaki for nine years, that the Japanese had been told by the Dutch a long time ago that the Russians cruelly and barbarously mistreated all foreigners, who happened to come to their country, and that the letter which they had now brought concerning the humanitarian and amicable motivation of the expedition, therefore, was received with mistrust; that they themselves had come to Nemuro in the expectation of great danger. Similarly, the ruler of Japan would view reports of the arrival of the Russians and of their desire for friendship with disbelief, until the testimonials of local officials, concerning the friendly disposition of the Russians and especially the stories of the castaways, were received. Then—they expressed the hope—Laxman's mission might conclude favorably. This would not please the Dutch, they added, for the Russians had everything the Dutch had to offer, but were closer to Japan.[19]

On March 30, the Edo officials received orders to return to Matsumae, where two high officials with a retinue of five hundred were arriving from Edo; on April 9, they departed from Nemuro. A week later, on April 17, an official arrived from Matsumae to inform the Russians that a senior official from the suite of the two high government envoys, who had arrived in Matsumae, was on his way to Nemuro, with a group of eight Edo and Matsumae officials, and a retinue of sixty.[20] On May 10, the Japanese arrived, accompanied by one hundred and fifty Ainu. Two days later, on May 12, the officials called on the Russians and invited them to come and confer at their place. That afternoon the Russians visited the Japanese. After refreshments, the senior Matsumae official read a paper, which stated that in response to the Russian letter to the governor of Matsumae, submitted by him with a report to the capital, the sovereign had dispatched two officials of the fifth rank to Matsumae. They in turn had sent him to Nemuro to tell the Russian commander to come to Matsumae by land. Neither Lovtsov nor Laxman would agree to this. Laxman pointed out that he had instructions to deliver the castaways directly by vessel only; that the long and difficult journey overland might entail delays and necessitate a second wintering at this barren location; that the climate was one to which the Russians were not accustomed, and that they would not separate. The Japanese produced every possible argument they could think of to persuade the Russians to go by land. For days they reasoned and pleaded in vain. Finally, they asked the Russians to go on a Japanese ship, which they expected shortly from Akkeshi. This too the Russians refused to do. But they agreed to wait for the Japanese vessel, so that they could go together, each on his own vessel, since the Japanese had intimated that they might lose their heads, if they lost the Russians. In the end, the officials only succeeded in delaying the Russians and, when the *Ekaterina* weighed anchor on June 15, the Japanese

---

[19] Polonskii, 492-497, 500; Lagus, *Erik Laksman,* 257; Pozdneev, II, 2: 52.

[20] Murata Choemon was the senior official. He was accompanied by two junior officials from Edo, Oda Hikobe and Inoue Tatsunosuke, as well as six officials from Matsumae. (Hiraoka, 89; Polonskii, 497-500.)

were forced to follow on sea and land. After a month-long, dangerous trip along the coast of Hokkaido, during which they touched at Akkeshi, but bypassed, because of fog, Edomo, to which they had promised to sail, the Russians arrived off Hakodate on July 15, and were towed into the harbor the following day. The Mayor of Hakodate came out to welcome them on the 15th and visited them again on the 16th. On the sixteenth the Edo official, who had left on land ahead of them, appeared and announced that his colleagues would arrive the following day. Meanwhile, he asked the Russians to decide on the number of men who would go to Matsumae and on the things to be taken along, so that the necessary preparations could be made. In the evening he sent aboard a barrel of sake for the crew. On the morning of the seventeenth another barrel was sent from the mayor of the city. The same day the Edo official came aboard again, had the vessel moved closer to shore, and invited the Russians into the city, offering them his baths. A few hours later a well-known merchant and two officials called for the Russians in two large boats. On shore the Russians were met by the festively-clad mayor and six officials and accompanied along the streets through crowds of spectators to the house over the doors of which there had been put up the sign: ROSSIISKII DOM (Russian House). Here the Russians were welcomed by the Edo official and led into chambers which opened onto a small rock garden with peach, cherry, apple, and nut trees. After their baths, they were treated to a seafood dinner and then escorted back to the shore with the same ceremony.

On July 18, the Edo and Matsumae officials arrived from Nemuro and on the nineteenth came aboard together with four other Edo officials, newly arrived from Matsumae. The Russians told them that, besides the retinue, they planned to send twelve persons to Matsumae and asked to be assigned a place where they could dry and store their provisions until their return. The following day Japanese carpenters came aboard to make boxes for the transportation of the Russian belongings and, later in the day, a warehouse was made available. The Russians were allowed to go with one of the Matsumae officials to the shore facing Hakodate and from there walk to the village of Hameda. But, when they asked the next day if they could not stroll about Hakodate, the Japanese objected apologetically that this was counter to their orders and asked the Russians to have patience until their arrival in Matsumae where there were officials of greater influence.[21]

July 24 was agreed upon as the date of departure for Matsumae. The day before, the Russians sent ashore whatever they planned to

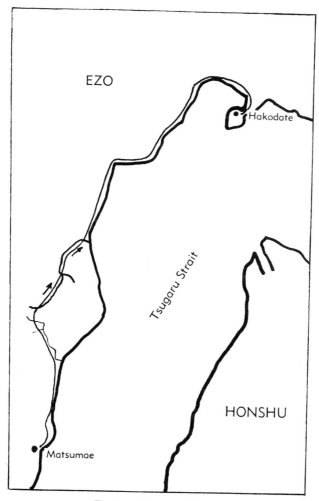

Route of Laxman from
Matsumae to Hakodate

take along and at 5 p. m. themselves landed to spend the night in a house set aside for them. On the twenty-second the Japanese had told Laxman that they did not object to a delegation of twelve, but

[21] Polonskii, 501-518; Lagus, *Erik Laksman*, 258-259.

that those, who remained behind, must go with the ship to Edomo. Laxman had objected and the *Ekaterina* was left in Hakodate for the time being. From the moment the Russians took up quarters on land they were considered and treated as guests of the Japanese government. On July 24, after breakfast, the colorful procession got under way, headed by two Matsumae officials and their followers. Laxman, Lovtsov, and Kokh rode in *norimono* (covered litters), each carried by four men, flanked by relief bearers, and by two officials to assist the visitors. Behind each *norimono* was led a saddled horse, should the Russians prefer to mount. The others—translator Tugolukov, Sergeant Trapeznikov, merchants Vlas Babikov and Ivan Palamoshnyi, and five men—rode behind, the horses led by the bridle. Every one was assisted by officials at his side. The entire retinue numbered four hundred and fifty men. Thus the Russians passed through the beautiful Hokkaido countryside, met at every village by a delegation of festively-clad elders, sitting on their heels, heads bowed. All the way to Matsumae houses had been set aside and prepared for rest and nourishment, marked as in Hakodate with the inscription ROSSIISKII DOM, and decorated with the crest of the governor of Matsumae. In this manner the procession traveled for three days. On the fourth day (July 27), at Osamasura village, the procession was relieved by another group of ceremoniously-clad officials from Matsumae and an escort of six hundred men. While the procession was being reshuffled, the Russians changed to clean dress uniforms and resumed their journey with new dignity, Laxman riding in the gubernatorial *norimono*, carried by eight men.

The Russians entered Matsumae at mid-afternoon. The streets, through which they passed, had been cleared of the populace, but countless spectators of both sexes peered from the wide-open houses along the way. Soon the procession reached a building, at the gates of which a guard of sixty men had been posted, those on the right armed with rifles, on the left with bows and arrows. Here the Russians were welcomed by two Matsumae officials, who informed them that this was their house and that they themselves were there to be of constant assistance. The spacious house, in which the Russians were accommodated in private rooms, was furnished for their convenience in Western style—even to the extent of a new wooden floor. In front of the house there was a garden and around it a low fence, which had been topped with a striped white and blue curtain, so that the city and people beyond were hidden from the Russian view.

Late that afternoon two Edo officials came to discuss the protocol of the impending meeting: they expected Laxman to conform to Japanese etiquette, to enter bootless and kneel half prostrate on the floor. Laxman replied that he could not do so, because the style of Western dress was such that the absence of footwear would be all too conspicuous, and because it was contrary to Russian custom thus to humiliate oneself before another mortal being, such bows being due to God alone. The Japanese did not persist and it was agreed that Japanese and Russians abide by their own etiquette.[22]

THE NAGASAKI PERMIT

On July 28, Laxman and his countrymen proceeded to the conference building. After the usual refreshments, six officials next in rank to the governor appeared, and one of them read a paper which acknowledged the receipt of the Russian letter and its Japanese translation concerning their arrival in Nemuro, their intention to proceed to the capital, and so forth. "One of these letters," read the official, "is written in a foreign horizontal script. There is nobody in our country who can understand it. The other letter seems to have been written in something resembling Japanese *kana*, but there are many spots in it that are completely unintelligible. The *kanji* are also difficult to understand. It is, therefore, impossible to answer the letters in detail without causing misunderstanding. As a result they are being returned."[23] They handed Laxman the paper just read, together with the documents sent by him, then led him to a special reception hall where Ishikawa Shogen and Murakami Dai-gaku, the envoys of the shogun, waited.[24] After a brief exchange of bows, Ishikawa and Murakami had Laxman shown a hundred bags of rice, which were a present from their ruler to Laxman's subordinates, and a box with three ceremonial swords for Laxman himself. Then Laxman was handed a paper from the Shogunate and asked to sign a receipt, which certified that the paper had been read and explained to him. After that both sides retired for refreshments. When the meeting was resumed in the formal hall, Laxman addressed

22 Polonskii, 523-527.

23 Tokutomi, xxv, 128; Ramming, *Reisen*, 30-31. The Japanese text has been translated here; the Russian version is somewhat briefer but similar in meaning. See Lagus, 576. There is evidence that the Japanese had understood the letters; the assertion that they were unintelligible was merely a polite pretext for withholding an answer.

24 Ishikawa Sakon Shogen Tadafusa and Murakami Daigaku Yoshinori. (Shibusawa Eiichi, *Tokugawa Yoshinobu-ko den*, I, 110; Tokutomi, xxv, 123.

the envoys: He conveyed greetings from Governor General Pil and stated that his Empress wished him to return the castaways and to speak, not only of their fate, but of everything concerning the establishment of "allied friendship and complete accord" between the two empires. The envoys listened quietly. But, when he repeated that he had been instructed to deliver the castaways to Edo, they objected, stating that they had been sent here to discuss whatever was necessary. They were willing to accept the castaways here, but, if the Russians insisted that they should be handed over at Edo, they need not return them at all. This, they explained, was due, not to lack of feeling for their countrymen, but to their fear of breaking their basic national laws. Presently, the first meeting came to an end and the Russians returned to their building. In the evening the box with Laxman's swords was delivered, with personal gifts of Japanese paper, costly cups, tobacco, lacquer trays and so forth from the Edo officials and the governor of Matsumae.[25]

On July 29, and again on July 30, two senior officials came to explain the meaning of the paper from the Shogunate. The document began with the declaration that Japan's ancient laws could never be changed. Only unarmed foreign vessels, like those of the Dutch, could visit Nagasaki. Vessels which came to any other part of Japan were subject to capture "regardless of their number." Having come to this place, without as yet having friendly relations with the Japanese, without advance notice, and on an armed vessel, the Russians ought to be detained permanently. Since they had come to repatriate Japanese castaways, had experienced great hardships, and had been unacquainted with Japanese laws, they were being excused this time and permitted to depart on condition that they did not return. Unfamiliar with Russian customs and unable to ascertain the relative position of Russia in dignity and greatness, the Japanese could take no action regarding the Russian letter beyond the acceptance of the castaways. The question of friendly relations could not be determined at Matsumae, nor must the Russians continue to Edo. "Being sufficiently informed that in accordance with the order of your chief superiors you intended originally to go from the Kuril Islands directly to the capital of Edo, we notify you, therefore, to desist from the execution of this order of your superiors and not to raise it again, so as not to make further complications for yourself." The document

25 Polonskii, 527-530; Lagus, *Erik Laksman*, 260-261; Tokutomi, xxv, 128; Okamoto, 1: 58-60; Pozdneev, ii, 2: 51-59.

sternly warned that there was no excuse for any foreign vessel to approach the Japanese capital and that such action would be fraught with the utmost danger. If the Russians refused to obey these injunctions "they will be taken prisoner and not accepting any excuses, will be dealt with according to our laws." In the future, should the Russians return the two persons who had remained behind, they must go to Nagasaki, passing other parts of Japan beyond the sight of land and stopping nowhere else. They must come on one vessel only and bring a permit, without which they would not be admitted even at Nagasaki. As to the conclusion of friendly relations and a trade agreement, the paper promised that there were officials for this purpose in Nagasaki, and requesting the Russians to consider all this thoroughly, urged them to sail home safely.[26] After the Japanese paper had been translated, the question of the acceptance of the Russian letter was raised again by the Russians. Ignoring the assertion that its acceptance would be counter to Japanese law, and brushing aside such objections to the letter, that it had not been addressed properly by name and rank, the Russians argued that, unless the Japanese did accept the letter, they could not properly understand the reason and intention of the Russian delegation. With what explanation could Laxman surrender the castaways and return without having carried out his instructions? After consulting with their superiors, the officials suggested that Laxman open the letter himself and read it to them; they would be willing to listen to it. When Laxman did not consent, they stated that perhaps, if shown the letter, they would accept it; if not, he could read it. They finally settled on this, Laxman having an extra copy of the sealed letter.[27]

The following morning, on July 31, Laxman sent gifts in Pil's name to the two senior officials. In the afternoon he met with them again, presented the letter from Pil, asked for a reply, and said that he wished to present to them the two remaining castaways. But the two senior officials merely glanced at the letter and returned it to Laxman, saying that the Russians knew already from the Shogunate paper that such documents could only be accepted for transmittal to the capital at Nagasaki. The castaways, on the other hand, they

[26] The text used here is from Polonskii, 574-576. More readable but superficial summaries may be found in Georg Heinrich von Langsdorff, *Voyages and Travels in Various Parts of the World*, 204-205 and in Captain Golownin, *Memoirs of a Captivity in Japan*, I, 15-16. For a Japanese text, differing somewhat in phraseology but not in essential meaning, see *Hokkaido-shi*, II, 331-333.

[27] Polonskii, 530-531.

were willing to accept in Matsumae. As agreed upon the previous day, Laxman then read Pil's letter. The envoys listened attentively, but at the end replied that no decision concerning this could be reached in Matsumae. They had, however, a piece of paper, bearing the seal of their ruler, and on it could write for the Russians the required permit of entry to Nagasaki, where they should go in the future to conclude a treaty. The Nagasaki Permit handed to Laxman three days later read as follows:

Permission for entrance into Nagasaki harbor is granted to one vessel of the great Russian empire; as explained already, foreign vessels are forbidden to come to places other than Nagasaki, and we repeat that the Christian faith is not tolerated in our country, so that upon arrival there be no sign of it, either in act of worship or oblation; should any agreement be reached, nothing must be done contrary to our laws as laid down in the prescript handed to you by us; it is for this purpose that we give the paper to Adam Laxman.[28]

In the evening the Japanese called for Kodayu and Isokichi at the Russian house and the following day (August 1) sent a receipt. Once the Russians surrendered the castaways they were not to see them again.

On August 1, Laxman expressed his intention of calling on the governor of Matsumae to thank him for his continued assistance and hospitality and to bring him, as the governor nearest the frontiers of the Russian Empire, gifts to further their future acquaintance. The Edo officials interfered, saying that it was unnecessary for the Russians to thank the governor of Matsumae, since neither he nor they could have any need of each other, and whatever he had done for them, he had done merely in the execution of his orders from the shogunate. Furthermore, he was still a child. What gifts they had for him, should be transmitted through one of the Matsumae officials. This the Russians did, selecting particularly desirable things, to make the best possible impression on the Japanese close to the throne. They failed, however, to get permission for their merchants to display and barter Russian wares. "You insist in vain on what we cannot do for you; it is an important matter and can be permitted only

[28] Bearing the seals of Ishikawa and Murakami, the Japanese text was addressed to Adam Laxman and Vasilii (his name was really Grigorii) Lovtsov. Noting that Christianity was Japan's "great prohibition," it forbade specifically the bringing of Christian images, utensils, and books. According to Polonskii the permit had been cut in two, one part being given to Laxman, the other part being retained by the Japanese. (*Hokkaido-shi*, II, 333-334; Polonskii, 544, 576.)

by special decree of the ruler," the officials replied, and indicated again that the slightest mistake on their part might well cost them their life.

On August 2, a Matsumae official came to thank them for the gifts to the governor. On the same day Laxman sent, as gifts to Ishikawa and Murakami, two large mirrors, a pair of pistols, glassware, and two thermometers. He took this opportunity to send them also, for transmittal, three letters from his father to Japanese scholars in the capital, together with three thermometers, and some specimens of natural history.[29] Two mirrors, glassware, and a thermometer were also sent as further gifts to the governor of Matsumae.

It was on August 4 that the last meeting of the envoys took place. The Japanese reiterated that it was not in their power to negotiate the establishment of commercial relations, but that Laxman had received a permit with which he could go to Nagasaki and there pursue the matter. Business completed, the Japanese dropped some of their formality and chatted amiably with the Russians. The same day fresh supplies were presented to the Russians.

On the morning of August 6, Laxman and his countrymen left Matsumae and, again in a procession, retraced their steps to Hakodate, where they arrived on the evening of the tenth, stopping at the house which had been set aside for them. Several days later, on August 14, Laxman was told by Tugolukov that the Japanese envoys had secretly asked him for a copy of Pil's letter. Realizing that the Japanese envoys, unable to accept the letter officially, wished to be certain of its content, and believing it important for them to have the full text, Laxman had the interpreter give them his copy, which they immediately took down and returned. On August 16, Laxman and compatriots went back aboard ship. On the morning of August 17, the *Ekaterina* weighed anchor and moved out to the roadstead, but was detained there by unfavorable winds for five days. In the early hours of August 22, the *Ekaterina* fired one cannon as signal of her departure, weighed anchor, and with sails spread headed out to sea. An hour later a worried Matsumae official caught up with the vessel to express the displeasure of his superiors at the shot. On the twenty-sixth, as they passed Shikotan Island, the Russians sighted two Japanese vessels behind them, sent out, it appeared, to see if the *Ekaterina*

---

[29] The names of these scholars are not known, but it is likely that they were Katsuragawa Hoshu and Nakagawa Junan, whose names Laxman knew from the writings of Karl Thunberg. (Ramming, *Reisen*, 32.)

was really heading for home. Taking a different course than on their way to Japan, in order to learn more about the Kuril Archipelago, the Russians passed Kunashiri on August 26 and on August 30 traversed the strait between Etorofu and Uruppu. On September 19, after a twenty-eight day journey, the *Ekaterina* arrived at the Okhotsk roadstead, just five days short of one year after having left the same harbor, and on the following day (September 20) was towed into the Okhota River.[30]

On January 24, 1794 Laxman and Lovtsov presented to Governor General Pil the journal and map of their expedition, the collected natural specimens, and the five papers received from the Japanese.[31] The Nagasaki Permit had been cut in two, one half being retained by the Japanese. The permit aroused great hopes among the Russians. It was interpreted as being a permit to trade in Nagasaki. In a lengthy report to the Empress on March 12, 1794, Pil proposed that the Laxman expedition be followed up at once by another more impressive expedition, on a new and better vessel, with an envoy extraordinary. "To appoint the commander of the second expedition from among the native Russian staff officers, a person expert in civil and political matters and a complete patriot, who may be permitted, in order to gain from the Japanese more respect for the business entrusted to him, during the performance of such function to announce himself to the Japanese one or two grades higher than his actual rank, and to supply him with funds and full instructions, in conformity with the proposals in the above-mentioned Japanese papers, as well with what is proper for the respect and dignity of the Russian empire and necessary for the profit and benefit of trade. . . ." Pil held forth on the many advantages of Russo-Japanese trade, producing, among others, the interesting argument: that . . . "at the time of some disagreement with China, after the example of the past years, Russia will receive from Japan cotton and in part silk goods, as the Japanese in the making of their manufactured things excel the Chinese, who, having learned of our relations with Japan, will be less haughty than now."[32] But Pil's proposal remained unanswered. In 1795 an-

[30] Polonskii, 531-537; Tokutomi, xxv, 136, 141; Pozdneev, II, 2: 59-60; Sgibnev, "Popytki," 55; Novakovskii, 56.

[31] (1) The paper of the Shogunate, received on July 28; (2) the paper concerning the unintelligibility of Pil's letter, received also on July 28; (3) the receipt for the castaways, dated August 1; (4) the Nagasaki Permit, received on August 3; (5) a list of supplies donated to the Russians by the Japanese government, received on August 4.

[32] Polonskii, 539-548; Sgibnev, "Popytki," 55.

other expedition to Japan under Professor Laxman himself was contemplated in high government circles, but the death of the professor in January 1796 put an end to these plans.[33] When Governor Nagel of Irkutsk reported to St. Petersburg in November 1795 that another group of Japanese castaways,[34] driven to the Aleutian Islands the preceding year, had been brought to Okhotsk and then to Irkutsk the Empress decided that they be returned to their fatherland, advantage being taken of this opportunity to obtain additional information about Japan and about trade with it.

An imperial ukase in the summer of 1796 ordered Lieutenant General Selifontov, Governor General of Irkutsk and Kolyvansk, to make arrangements for the return of the castaways to Japan, on either a government or private vessel, whichever would be more advantageous or more convenient, letting some merchants with goods go along, in accordance with the ukase of September 1791. Selifontov, who was then in St. Petersburg, asked Nagel to inquire whether any Irkutsk merchants would be willing to undertake such an expedition. Nagel reported that separate proposals were submitted to him by the Irkutsk merchant Kiselev, by a company of Irkutsk merchants, and the widow of Shelikhov, but that none of them were prepared to provide their own ship and that a government vessel would have to be used. He proposed that the expedition be accompanied not only by a merchant, but by a representative of the authorities, versed in local conditions and in domestic and foreign trade, who could enter into negotiations with the Japanese. To entrust such an important matter to a daring man and especially to a merchant would be impolitic, he argued, not just because he would not be able to represent Russia suitably, but also because he would be confined to dealing with Japanese merchants, who were known to be at the bottom of the social scale. Nagel noted furthermore that the distance of Nagasaki from Okhotsk would be a barrier to relations and that permission should be sought for trade at Nemuro, Hakodate, and even more convenient harbors. Most important of all, Nagel reported that he did not have the necessary funds for outfitting such an expedition.[35] Selifontov in turn reported to Catherine the Great

[33] Novakovskii, 66.

[34] Sgibnev puts the number of castaways at fifteen; Polonskii at sixteen.

[35] Nagel estimated that the expedition would cost up to 31,722 rubles, including the cost (8,000 rubles) of constructing a new vessel as no reliable transport was then available in Okhotsk. The Laxman expedition had come to 23,217 rubles, much less than the 36,318 rubles allotted.

from Tobolsk in February 1797, recommending Sabanak Kumnametev, a Tobolsk army captain, as head of the expedition, but the death of the Empress precluded any further action on her part. When Governor Letstseno of Irkutsk in March 1800 requested funds from the Minister of Commerce Prince Gagarin for the execution of the above plans, Emperor Paul I ruled that in view of the charter recently granted to the Russian-American Company this was not possible; henceforth only the Russian-American Company would be able to undertake such expeditions.[36]

Adam Laxman had failed to establish commercial relations with Japan. It is possible, some feel even likely, that, had he proceeded to Nagasaki, he might have been able to negotiate some sort of agreement. But Laxman felt that he had done all that lay within his authority, and wished to show the Japanese his sincerity by leaving without delay.[37] For this he has been condemned by some historians, notably P. Tikhmenev, who wrote that Laxman "did not understand at all the purpose of the government in sending him to Japan."[38] Sgibnev reasoned that Laxman failed to establish commercial relations, because the letter to the Japanese government had been sent in the name of Pil rather than of the Empress; because he had not gone to Nagasaki, and because Laxman himself was not very gifted. Novakovskii, on the other hand, contends that Laxman did better than any foreign contemporaries, who approached Japan, and that it was as yet beyond the power of Laxman or anyone else to shatter the historical seclusion policy of the Shogunate.[39] Other historians debate whether Laxman's low rank hindered or helped his mission. In essence the question of whether the Laxman expedition as a whole was a failure or a success revolves around the meaning of the Nagasaki Permit. To this day Japanese historians disagree sharply—some believe that the Nagasaki Permit was just a polite brush-off, a device to save time; others that it opened Japan to trade. Adam Laxman himself regarded the permit as the fulfillment of his assignment. Professor Laxman similarly felt that the expedition had been a success, that it had laid the foundations for friendly relations between Russia and Japan. He wrote in a letter: "My son did not have to deny his Christianity and to curse over the cross,

---

[36] Polonskii, 449-551; Sgibnev, "Popytki," 53-56; Novakovskii, 56.

[37] Keene, 66; Yano, 155.

[38] P. Tikhmenev, *Istoricheskoe obozrenie obrazovaniia Rossisskoi-Amerikanskoi Kompanii i deistvii eia do nastoiashchago vremeni*, 1: 10 footnote.

[39] Novakovskii, 57.

he did not have to subject himself to ridicule or to play the clown, as this has happened with the Dutch, but was received with deliberate respect. Who could have thought that a Russian vessel which traveled up to six weeks between Tigilsk [on the western coast of Kamchatka] and Okhotsk could cross from Hakodate harbor to Okhotsk in three weeks?"[40]

Without question the expedition was a success from a scientific point of view. It was the first Russian expedition to penetrate into the interior of Hokkaido, bringing back more accurate information about Japan's northern regions than had Kozyrevskii, Spanberg, Walton, and the other Russian explorers. The publications dealing with the Laxman expedition may be regarded as the first published original Russian accounts of Japan. Officially Catherine the Great showed herself pleased with the results of the expedition. Lieutenant Laxman was promoted to Captain, Lovtsov and the other participants received corresponding increases in rank and financial rewards. Professor Eric Laxman as the guiding light of the whole venture was made Collegiate Councilor and awarded the order of St. Vladimir, 4th class, and permission was granted to include a Japanese sword in the Laxman family coat of arms.[41]

No one can tell whether the expedition might not have proven a commercial success, if it had been followed up energetically. There is evidence[42] that in the late eighteenth century Japan had been on the verge of abandoning the seclusion policy and the prompt exploitation of the Nagasaki Permit might conceivably have led to trade between Russia and Japan. Without doubt the Japanese attitude at the time of Laxman, as expressed in the treatment of him, had been freer and more receptive than it was to be again for more than half a century. But as has been seen, the Russian government failed to push the matter. This may have been due to Catherine's personal skepticism of the commercial potentiality of the Laxman expedition and of trade with Japan in general. Kodayu quoted her as having told him: "I would like to enter upon reciprocal trade relations and if you desire the same too, we can send you as many ships as you wish. However, there is no persistent desire to trade on our part and you can act, therefore, just as you wish. Upon your return, transmit these words of mine to the Emperor." And in a

[40] Letter from Professor Laxman to N. I. Panin, dated December 11, 1793, as cited in Lagus, *Erik Laksman*, 268.
[41] Novakovskii, 58, 64; Keene, 72 note 49.
[42] See chapter VI.

letter to the Frenchman F. M. Grimm she commented on August 9, 1794: "And what kind of a story is that about the Japanese castaway! He was shipwrecked and sent back home again. And that is all there is to it. Laxman's son accompanied him and returned with knicknacks which were exhibited to us this year in the Tsarskoe Selo and for which I wouldn't give ten sous. Let anybody, who so wishes, trade there, but not I."[43] The slackening of government initiative was due to preoccupation with other problems: the spread of American and French revolutionary ideas across Europe, fear of Dutch and English commercial encroachment, and trouble in North America between Indians and Russians—so violent that it even interrupted the transactions of the Russian-American Company.[44] When the Russian government, toward the end of spring 1795, seemed ready to make use of the Nagasaki Permit, and Eric Laxman and Shelikhov were busy preparing two expeditions to Japan—a scientific one to be headed by the professor himself and a commercial one—time had practically run out. That summer death cut short Shelikhov's active life at the age of forty-eight; in January of 1796 Eric Laxman died and, later in the same year, the Empress. The demise of Catherine the Great, who, in spite of personal skepticism, had been a major force in the realization of the Russian expeditions, was a great loss to government interests in the Far East.[45]

The most lasting accomplishment of Lieutenant Adam Laxman was the sympathetic impression, which he made on the Japanese, an impression which was to outlast the hatred incurred by some of his countrymen in later years.[46] In this respect Professor Laxman was right when he asserted that his son had laid the foundations for the establishment of friendly relations between Russia and Japan.

[43] Pozdneev, II, 2: 66.
[44] *Ibid.*, II, 2: 89-90; Novakovskii, 65; Znamenskii, 179-180.
[45] Kiuner, 19; A. Adamov, *G. I. Shelikhov*, 36.
[46] Golownin, *Memoirs*, I, 105; Novakovskii, 58; Lagus, *Erik Laksman*, 263.

CHAPTER FIVE · BY WORD AND BY SWORD

OF PRIDE AND PROFIT

THE Nagasaki Permit brought back by Lieutenant Laxman had improved the chances for the establishment of commercial relations with Japan. When the central government failed to pursue the advantage gained, local individuals resumed the initiative. Thus the merchant Grigorii Shelikhov, who, in 1775, had been associated temporarily with the Secret Voyage to Japan, but, after the shipwreck of the *Sviatoi Nikolai* and other misfortunes, had withdrawn his support, transferring his activities to the Aleutian Islands and America, obtained permission from Governor General Pil to establish a settlement on Uruppu with the dual purpose of engaging in agriculture and of establishing trade with the Japanese on Hokkaido through the Ainu. The southern Kuril Islands were still important to the economy of eastern Siberia both in their own right and as a channel for trade with Japan. As one Russian historian put it:

The four islands occupied by the hairy [Ainu], held forth benefits for the Siberian region already by the fact that due to their southerly location agriculture was possible there. The rye, wheat, barley planted by Antipin as an experiment on the eighteenth island had ripened at the proper time and had given not a small crop; on the other more southerly islands grain could be raised still more conveniently. Furthermore there was on them enough wood suitable for shipbuilding. In occupying the southern islands, their retention by us from Kamchatka posed no danger. Although the population in Kamchatka was insignificant, the southern islands, especially Matsumae were not dangerous for us, being populated more weakly yet. The hairy ones, being subject to Russia, remaining in the middle between the Japanese and the Russians, would serve her as middlemen in trade, which of course could not be conducted on a large scale, but only to the extent that was necessary for the small number of those who lived in Kamchatka and Okhotsk. Fish and animals would be the major objects of exchange with the Japanese for their grain commodities.[1]

In 1795 a group of some thirty settlers and families, recruited from Siberian exiles, were sent to Uruppu under the leadership of

[1] Polonskii, 467.

the Irkutsk commoner Vasilii Zvezdochetov.[2] According to Japanese sources, the settlers got along well with the natives and acquainted them with some of the more rudimentary aspects of Russian culture; they even engaged in trade with Ainu from Akkeshi. When Japanese officials learned of this, some were outraged. They regarded the Russian penetration of Uruppu as an affront to Japan, the laws of which had been explained to Laxman, and urged that the settlers be captured or killed. Calmer advisers pointed out that if the Russians on Uruppu were merchants, as reported, there was no cause for alarm and that they could be forced to withdraw by the simple expedient of depriving them of the means of trade. This policy the shogunate adopted with success.[3] The Ainu of Akkeshi, Nemuro, and Kunashiri were forbidden to cross over to Uruppu. At the same time Japanese were sent to settle and fortify Kunashiri and Etorofu, while a post was erected on Uruppu itself, proclaiming the island Japanese territory.[4] By the beginning of the nineteenth century, Japanese measures and an overly strict regime imposed by Zvezdochetov had prompted the return of fourteen of the best settlers to Kamchatka, and before long of seven more families. Zvezdochetov and the others died on Uruppu, and with them Shelikhov's plan of trade with Japan.[5]

In 1800, Emperor Paul stated that all further attempts to establish relations with Japan be left in the hands of the Russian-American Company. Shelikhov was no longer alive, yet in a sense he remained involved, for the company was his "brainchild." When he had turned his attention to the Aleutian Islands and America in the late 1770's, quick fortunes in fur were being made there with utter recklessness. Driven by the desire to acquire as rapidly as possible the largest number of furs with the least expenditure of labor, the hunters exterminated the animals without cessation, adding to their booty by shrewd trading with the natives and by extortion and plunder. "Being themselves a wanton and desperate people, largely from among criminals exiled to Siberia," wrote Lieutenant Commander Golovnin years later, "they counted their life for nothing and thought the

---

[2] Sgibnev, "Popytki," 56; Pozdneev, II, 2: 14; Novakovskii, 67.

[3] *Hokkaido-shi*, II, 413-415.

[4] Znamenskii, 179-180; Otomo, *Hokumon sosho*, VI, 51-57. For Japanese pictures of the blue-eyed red-hairs and their dwellings on Uruppu, see *Hokkaido-shi*, V, 367-369. See also Lensen, *Report from Hokkaido*, 20; the man on the right appears to be Zvezdochetov.

[5] Novakovskii, 67; Sgibnev, "Popytki," 55.

same of the life of others, while the poor Aleutians they regarded as hardly better than cattle; consequently the fear of retribution in the afterlife, which affects sometimes also less inveterate scoundrels, could make no impression on them, while civil punishment they had no reason to fear, and therefore besides plunder, they often committed murders, taking away wives and children and inflicted all kinds of outrages on the poor inhabitants."[6] Shelikhov realized the necessity of substituting for such chaotic ravaging of the region a more temperate, well-planned, and cooperative effort of a company of merchants. In 1785, he joined hands with the brothers Ivan and Mikhail Golikov. The success of their cooperation attracted other merchants, notably Mylnikov and his companions, and resulted in the founding of the United American Company (Soedinenaia Amerikanskaia Kompaniia) in 1797. Better organized in its operations than the locust-like hunters that had plagued the islands before, the company strangled competition, but did not visibly alleviate the lot of the natives.[7] Catherine the Great had merely tolerated the company; preoccupied with Turkey and Sweden, she had refused, in 1788, to back Shelikhov's grandiose plans of colonization on the American continent and the Aleutians. Now that reports of the continued oppression of the natives by the company poured into the capital, Catherine's successor Paul I contemplated its dissolution.[8] The United American Company was saved from this fate by the intercession of the influential chief procurator of the First Department of the Senate, Nikolai Rezanov.

Rezanov had personal reasons for backing the company. He had married Shelikhov's daughter, receiving company stock as dowry.

---

[6] V. M. Golovnin, "Zapiska o sostoianii Rossiisko-Amerikanskoi Kompanii v 1818 godu," 54-92.

[7] Planning to establish a permanent Russian settlement on Kad'iak (Kodiak) to insure no less permanent profits for himself, Shelikhov began by occupying a small harbor on the southern side of the island, calling it Gavan' Trekh Sviatitelei (Three Saints Harbor). When he departed for Okhotsk in 1786 he left the merchant Samoilov in charge. Samoilov was succeeded by Evstrata Delarov in 1788, and Delarov by Aleksandr Baranov in 1790. In the twenty-seven years of his sway Baranov, according to Golovnin, not only failed to civilize the natives, but "himself grew wild and became a degree lower than a savage!" Scheming to obtain government privileges Shelikhov had softpedalled his commercial interests, claiming to be concerned primarily with winning new territory for Russia and new converts for the Orthodox Church. His request that missionaries be made available was granted, and half a score of monks, among them archmandrate Goasaf, were sent out at company expense. Once the missionaries arrived in Kad'iak, however, they were given neither the means nor the opportunity to engage in religious work, but were made to labor in the fields. (Golovnin, "Zapiska," 52-54.)

[8] Adamov, 30; Novakovskii, 69-70.

After Shelikhov's death Rezanov had become majority stockholder and chairman of the board of directors. Noted for his persuasive oratory, Rezanov succeeded not merely in saving the company from dissolution, but in obtaining for it additional privileges and imperial support. He did this so skillfully that later Paul's successor, Alexander I, members of the royal family and many other distinguished persons in the capital eagerly bought stock in his company. To be sure, there was more involved than merely Rezanov's persuasiveness. It so happened that the interests of the merchants coincided with those of the government as a whole. In the words of a Soviet historian, "the latter, not wishing to take the risk of international complications which might result from the official annexation of the American colonies to the Russian Empire, saw in the creation of a mighty monopolistic company a way to mask its own expansion along the shores of the Pacific."[9]

On July 19, 1799, the United American Company was granted a privilege for twenty years, and as a sign of imperial patronage was renamed the Russian-American Company (Rossiissko-Amerikanskaia Kompaniia). This Russian-American Company was in nature similar to the British and Dutch East India Companies. It received a monopoly on the exploitation and administration of northwestern America above latitude 55° N., of the Aleutian and Kuril Islands, and, upon further exploration, of territory further to the south unpossessed as yet by another power. The company was entitled to maintain military and naval forces, to build fortifications, occupy newly discovered territories, and trade with foreign countries. It had the exclusive privilege to concern itself with the establishment of relations with Japan. The general management of the company, now that it was under imperial patronage, was moved from Irkutsk to the capital; the main administrative center in the colonies was established at Novo-Arkhangelsk, the major port of Sitka Island.[10] In the eyes of some, the tsarist government saw in the company a tool for making the northern Pacific an "inland sea" of the Russian Empire. "This plan presupposed the further entrenchment of Russia along the west coast of North America, including California, the Hawaiian Islands, the southern part of Sakhalin and the mouth of

---

[9] S. B. Okun, *The Russian-American Company*, 24-25.

[10] Golovnin, "Zapiska," 55-80; Okun, 37-45. Golovnin gives the text of the Act of the United American Company (August 14, 1798) as well as of the imperial proclamation pertaining to the establishment of the Russian-American Company.

the Amur. These colonies, together with Kamchatka, Alaska, and the Aleutians, which already belonged to Russia, were to make that country the all-powerful master of the whole northern Pacific."[11]

The Russian-American Company faced many problems. In 1802, for example, its wooden fortress of Mikhailovsk on Sitka and a com-

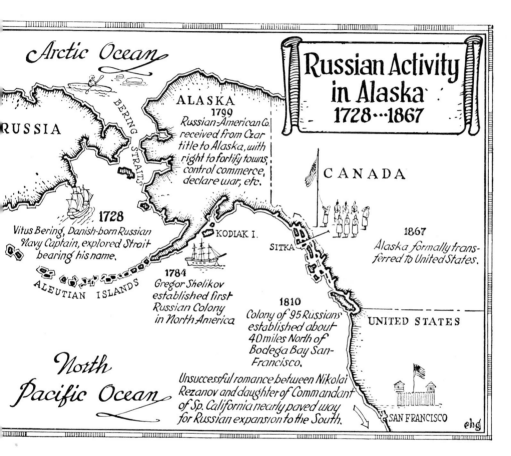

pany ship were attacked by Indians.[12] The main obstacle to the development of the Russian colonies, however, lay in the inadequacy of transportation. The cumbersome effort in which over four thousand horses were used every year to supply the eastern regions via Yakutsk and Okhotsk forced up the cost of operating to excessive

[11] Okun, 50.

[12] *Ibid.*, 54. English traders are said to have been involved in the attack. Harold McCracken believes that there is "very strong circumstantial evidence" that Americans gave "considerably more than casual encouragement" to the native attack. (*Hunters of the Stormy Sea*, 218-226.)

levels. Moreover, such bulky objects as anchors and cables could not be transported at all, and even lighter objects did not always reach their destination, for the caravans were frequently attacked and plundered. Still greater hazards had to be overcome by the poorly equipped and insufficiently manned ships as they ventured into the troublesome waters of the northern Pacific, where dangerous sailing conditions prevailed many months a year, to supply Russian outposts on the Kuril and Aleutian Islands and on the American continent. It was for this reason that Captain Adam Johann von Krusenstern, an officer in the service of the Russian-American Company, developed a plan for the more regular supply of the colonies by sea, from Kronstadt around the world by way of the Cape of Good Hope or by way of Cape Horn. At the same time, he believed, Russian trade with China could be made far more profitable if, instead of carrying furs and other products by land to Kiakhta, as was being done, they could be transported directly by sea to Canton. Krusenstern proposed that Russian vessels proceed from Kronstadt to the Aleutian Islands, Northwestern America, and Kamchatka with supplies for the colonies, there take on furs and with them sail to Canton, where they could be traded for Chinese goods needed in Russia. On the way back he envisaged stops at Manila, Batavia, and Indian ports for the purchase of additional products. Thus at one and the same time, Krusenstern calculated, the colonies could be supplied more fully and cheaply, trade with China would be increased, European Russia's yearly expenditure for Chinese and East Indian goods would be greatly reduced, and Russia would be able to furnish Far Eastern goods to Germany and other European countries at lower prices than the English, Dutch, and Swedes. Krusenstern's plan, as advocated by Rezanov, captured the imagination of both commercial and governmental leaders, among them Minister of the Navy Mordvinov and Minister of Commerce Count Rumiantsev, and, in 1802, it was agreed to send the projected round-the-world expedition as an experiment in thus supplying the colonies.[13] Emperor Alexander I decided that advantage should be taken of this expedition to send an embassy also to Japan, and a special courier was dispatched to Irkutsk to bring to the capital the Nagasaki Permit obtained by Laxman. In keeping with Pil's earlier recommendation that a new embassy to Japan be headed by a man of distinction, Rezanov, who

---

[13] Novakovskii, 71-72; Pozdneev, II, 2: 89-90.

had repeatedly advocated the resumption of negotiations with the Japanese in the belief that trade with Japan was the only rational means of supplying the colonies, was named envoy.[14] Rezanov had just lost his beloved wife and at first seemed reluctant to accept the assignment. He wrote to a friend:

You surely know already, how heavily burdened my fate is. Thus, my esteemed friend, I have lost everything. The demise of my wife, who constituted all the happiness, all the felicity of my days, has made for me my whole life desolate. . . . Estranged from everything in the world, giving myself over to my sole grief, I thought of resigning, thought, having occupied myself with the upbringing of the children, of dedicating the remainder of my days to my feelings, but here too I met with an obstacle. The Emperor graciously concerned himself with my situation, at first advised me to distract myself, finally suggested a voyage; then, having gradually led me to agreement, announced to me the wish that I take upon myself an embassy to Japan. For a long time I declined this difficult exploit; his gracious talks with me at every meeting, finally the calling of myself to him to the office and his persistent persuasions determined me to comply. . . . He gave his word to protect my orphans, while I affirmed to him, that every hour I am ready to sacrifice my life for him.[15]

To add luster to the embassy, Rezanov was made Chamberlain of His Imperial Highness and Cavalier of St. Anna First Rank, and was provided with a retinue of several officials. He was given far greater authority than Adam Laxman had had. The latter, it will be recalled, had been envoy only, with Lovtsov essentially in command of the expedition. Now Krusenstern was named commander of the vessels and director of scientific work, but Rezanov was placed in command of the expedition as a whole, so that Krusenstern's authority was limited to nautical and disciplinary measures. This was contrary to the contract originally made by the company with Krusenstern and Iurii Lisianskii, the commander of one of the vessels. Rezanov's assumption of over-all command of the expedition and of company business in America deprived these officers not merely of prestige but also of a considerable amount of money, which they had been promised in addition to their regular salary. This circumstance ignited a spark of dissatisfaction, which later almost inflamed the expedition in open mutiny. Upon completion of the mission to Japan Rezanov was to inspect the Russian possessions in

[14] Sgibnev, "Popytki," 57; Polonskii, 551-552.
[15] Letter of Rezanov to Ivan Ivanovich Dimitriev, 1331-1332.

America, load the vessels, and go to Canton for commercial negotiations with the Chinese before returning to Russia by way of the
Cape of Good Hope.[16]

The embassy to Japan was given three main tasks: (1) to demand
trade with Japan on the basis of the permit brought back by Laxman; (2) on the way back from Japan to describe as much as circumstances would permit the Kuril Islands, Sakhalin, the Amur
Estuary and the Strait of Tatary; (3) to investigate the whole eastern
border of Siberia and to take such measures as might be necessary
to carry out the mission.[17] The Russian press commented:

The expedition of Rezanov will go to Japan in order to open and establish commercial relations for Russia with these islands, where the industry and ignorance of the people are equally surprising, where some
skills have reached a degree of perfection unknown to us, but where
reason is still in the cradle. If the embassy will succeed in its intention, we
shall get from Japan some things much better than from China. Japanese tea, porcelain, lacquer, silk and cotton materials are better than
Chinese ones. The Russian American Company can obtain them in exchange for its goods. As for the Japanese with all their rudeness, they
are not such spiteful and cunning swindlers in trade, as our neighbors
the Chinese.[18]

As in the case of the Laxman expedition, the return of castaways
was to cloak the Rezanov mission in humanitarian justification, and
a group of Japanese, brought from the Aleutians in 1795, was dispatched to the capital from Irkutsk together with the Nagasaki Permit. These castaways came from the district Ojika in Mutsu Province
(Sendai). In the closing days of 1793, they had sailed from Ishi-no-
maki Harbor in the domain of Sendai on Captain Heibe's large
transport *Wakamiya Maru* with a cargo of construction materials
and rice destined for Edo, when their vessel was disabled in a sudden storm on January 2, 1794, and driven into the open sea. As
customary, the sixteen-man crew cut down the mast and jettisoned
most of the cargo to keep the vessel afloat, shaved their hair, and
supplicated Shinto and Buddhist deities with holy vows. For three
months they were carried about by shifting winds and the current of
the ocean. When they came across a shell-covered log, they consulted
the oracle regarding the distance of land, by writing several num-

16 K. Voenskii, "Russkoe posol'stvo v Iaponiiu v nachale XIX veka," 127-128; Polonskii, 552; Novakovskii, 73; Tikhmenev, 1: 102-103.
17 Sgibnev, "Popytki," 57.
18 Novakovskii, 73.

bers on a piece of paper, then made a make-shift mast from the arm of the broken rudder and spreading sail sped up their journey. Two months later, in June, 1794, they finally sighted a snow-covered, mountainous island and putting three bags of rice, the guardian deity of the ship (two paper dolls, a lock of hair of the wife of the ship owner, and two dice), and their most essential belongings into a boat, went ashore, letting the *Wakamiya Maru* run aground among the cliffs. The island on which they landed was one of the Andreianovskie Islands of the Aleutian Archipelago, somewhat to the north of the island on which Kodayu had been cast. Here they were found by Ainu and all but Captain Heibe, who died shortly after arrival, were taken to a Russian hunter, who sailed with them on their boat to a place where a Russian post was located. For a year they stayed at this spot, well-treated by the Russians. Then, on May 21, 1795, they boarded a Russian vessel, whose captain understood some Japanese, and, after touching at several other islands, reached Okhotsk. From there they were dispatched by the local authorities to Yakutsk and then—having suffered the loss of one more comrade —to Irkutsk, where they remained for eight years, burying still another countryman. In Irkutsk they were amazed to make the acquaintance of Nikolai Petrovich Kolotygin (formerly Shinzo), a shipmate of Kodayu, who was teaching Japanese to six students in the School of Navigation, and now was charged with attending to the needs of the castaways. Kolotygin, who had married a Russian wife and had a son by her, had learned to speak and write Russian well. When the castaways were sent to the capital together with the courier, who bore the Nagasaki Permit, Kolotygin accompanied them. On the way to St. Petersburg three of the Japanese fell ill and had to be left behind. Of the ten who reached the capital and were graciously received by the Emperor, only four expressed the desire to be repatriated: Gihei, Tajuro, Tsudayu and Sahei.[19]

The Russian government made no secret of the impending expedition, and news of the preparations appeared in all the journals

[19] V. Turkovskii, "Krugosvetnoe puteshestvie neskol'kikh iapontsev cherez Sibir' sto let nazad," 198-199; Ramming, *Reisen*, 50-59. Usually known by their given names only, three of the castaways had surnames as well: Okuda Gihei, Okuda Tajuro, and Doi (or Tsuchii) Tsudayu. Among those who stayed behind and became Russian subjects there was Zenroku of Ishi-no-maki, who in later years was to come within sight of his land of origin as interpreter to Lieutenant Commander Rikord. (Umemori Saburo, *Nichi-Ro kokko shiryo*, 34; Otomo, *Hokumon sosho*, VI, 88-90; Akaba Sozo, "Tsushi Kiserefu [Zenroku Ishi-no-maki], 2: 44-45.)

and newspapers. Lieutenant Commander Lisianskii and a ship-builder were sent to Hamburg, Copenhagen, and London to purchase suitable vessels. In London they acquired for twenty-five thousand pounds sterling two modern ships of the latest construction, capable of making eleven knots: the *Leandra*[20] and the *Thames*, respectively re-named *Nadezhda* (Hope) and *Neva*. This dependence on western European products and experts later aroused the anger of patriotic Russians. Golovnin wrote:

. . . about all this the foreigners knew from the newspapers, and the English took for the two vessels at least twenty-five percent more than they could have been purchased for, if one had not trumpeted so much about the great undertakings of the great company; but not only did the company consider Russian shipwrights unable to build ships, worthy of its great undertakings; it purchased at high prices in London clothing and footwear for the crews, a great quantity of supplies, the salt-meat alone from four different countries; nor was this all: it appeared to the company that in Russia there were neither physicians nor scholars and therefore it obtained from Germany at high salary Germans: physicians, an astronomer, naturalists and a writer, and thereby furnished the means for foreigners to learn the true condition of the colonies, as one of them [Langsdorff], upon return, published his journey in German, portraying vividly what the Russian American Company was.[21]

This had occurred in spite of the fact that as soon as word of the round-the-world expedition and embassy to Japan spread through St. Petersburg, Rezanov was swamped with requests from Russian scholars, linguists, doctors, officers, and officials, who wished to go along.[22]

Meanwhile the Minister of Commerce (and not the Minister of Foreign Affairs) drew up instructions for Rezanov, dealing primarily with the diplomatic aspects of his mission to Japan. A great deal of thought and research must have gone into the preparation of these instructions, because they displayed a remarkable knowledge of Japan and foresaw and considered thoroughly the various situations with which Rezanov would be confronted. Rumiantsev noted, for example, that Rezanov would be showered by the Japanese with innumerable questions and that all his answers and all conversations would be recorded verbatim. He would be asked why and from where he had come, what he had brought, where he was born, and

---

20 Voenskii, 126. Novakovskii gives the name as *Leonora*. (78)
21 Golovnin, "Zapiska," 94.
22 Voenskii, 139.

which country he represented. He would be asked about Russia—about its size, boundaries, products, form of government, military forces, enemies, allies, laws, customs, and so forth. He would be asked about himself—his character, rank, position, and about his credentials—how they are written, sealed, folded, and safeguarded. He would be asked about things which the Japanese knew already, and his replies would be recorded. He would be questioned by the officials whom he would meet at first, and later by ministers, courtiers, and other persons of note. "It is necessary, therefore," Rumiantsev warned, "that in your answers you be very careful and not only always have them in your memory, but that you also write them down in order not to trip up in your words later on." Regarding Japanese queries concerning Russia, Rumiantsev wrote:

You will reply to all these questions simply and without pretense. You will say that Russia in its size is the first country in Europe and will explain its boundaries: that the climates in the empire are different, because it occupies half the world; that Russia with her might keeps in respect and balance all Europe, China, the Turkish Empire and Persia; that her forces including infantry and cavalry number up to 700,000; that this land is governed by an autocratic sovereign, and as the Japanese respect absolute autocracy, do describe the autocratic Russian power in all its worth; you may say, by the way, that many Asiatic rulers and lords such as Siberian, Gruzian and Kalmykian, having submitted to his power now are simply among his notable subjects; that the Russian Emperor, having accepted the ancestral throne and having seen the expanse of his boundaries, marked by the glorious conquests of his ancestors, has decided to rule in tranquility and peace with the whole world and that his realm is a center of sciences, arts and laws.[23]

Rumiantsev anticipated that Rezanov would be asked whether the Russian Emperor was dependent on the Pope like other rulers of whom the Japanese knew, and instructed Rezanov to reply that the Tsar not only was in no way dependent on the Pope, but did not recognize him as a spiritual head, but dealt with him merely as with a temporal ruler of a small territory. Rezanov was to emphasize at once the limitless temporal and spiritual autocracy of the Tsar, his bravery, his humility, his thirst for knowledge about other countries, and his appreciation of the value of human life, expressed by his return of the castaways to their fatherland. Rumiantsev noted that Rezanov would gain much respect if, when approaching the person of the sovereign, he would take off his sword and give it to

23 *Ibid.*, 132-133; Novakovskii, 75.

someone, who was with him, before being told to do so; he was to stand before the ruler head uncovered. "I cannot repeat to you enough how essential it will be for you to consider the dissimilarity of their customs with ours and not to degrade theirs," admonished Rumiantsev. "Such rules prescribed Louis XIV himself, the ruler famous among monarchs for the meticulous care with which he guarded the monarchal dignity, when he outfitted an embassy to Japan.[24] In 1624 the envoys of the King of Spain, two cavaliers of the Golden Fleece, were not received, and returned only because they did not wish to conform with Japanese customs." Going on to the main purpose of the expedition—the matter of trade—the Minister of Commerce emphasized the following objectives (which showed, incidentally, how Russia had misunderstood the meaning of the Nagasaki Permit: (1) the broadening of the rights given to Laxman: to negotiate permission for more than one Russian vessel to visit Nagasaki and other harbors; (2) the establishment of trade by barter on Matsumae (Hokkaido) if the Japanese refused to admit more than one vessel to Nagasaki; (3) the bartering of Russian wares for Japanese ones through the Ainu of Uruppu, if the Japanese did not agree to direct trade on Matsumae either; (4) the gathering of information about Sakhalin—whether it belonged to China or Japan, and how it could be reached for the establishment of trade; investigation of what the Japanese knew about the Amur Estuary; what the relations were between Japan, China, and Korea; whether the Liu Ch'iu Islands belonged to Japan—and if independent, to try to reach them and establish commercial relations. Rumiantsev concluded his instructions with an explanation of the political set-up in Japan: "It is known to all, that in Japan there reigned a spiritual emperor; that one of his military commanders, having rebelled against his authority, succeeded in 1583 to promote

[24] Louis XIV had decided to send an embassy to Japan on the advice of Jean Baptiste Colbert, his well known minister and the founder of the French East India Company. In 1665 François Caron set out as envoy to Japan, but died on the way in Lisbon. The French embassy did not materialize, therefore, but the excellent instructions prepared by Caron himself, who for many years had been director of the Dutch factory on Deshima and had acquired considerable knowledge of Japan, were preserved in the French Archives. No doubt Rumiantsev consulted them. Paragraph eight of his own instructions to Rezanov, for example, was almost identical with Colbert's instructions to Caron. Colbert: *"On fera l'objection savoir si le Roy de France dépend du Pape, comme le Roy d'Espagne et d'autres. Vous répondrez qu'Il n'en dépend point: le Roy de France ne connaissant personne au dessus de Lui. . . ."* Rumiantsev: *"Sprosiat vas, ne zavisit li gosudar' rossiiskii ot papy po primeru nekotorykh im monarkhov? Vy dadite otvet, chto on ot papy nimalo ne zavisit. . . ."* (Voenskii, 134-135.)

himself to imperial dignity under the name *Kubo*, while the spiritual emperor continued his existence under the title *Dairi* and lives in splendor and esteem, but in utter insignificance, so that, having his own capital, he is forgotten and consequently you are by no means to seek access to him."[25]

In addition to his instructions, Rezanov received the imperial letter addressed to "By the Grace of God His Tenjin-Kubo Majesty, the Autocratic Potentate of the extensive Japanese Empire, Most Excellent Emperor and Sovereign," that is to the shogun, as Rumiantsev's explanation of the term "kubo" indicates,[26] magnificently written in gold on a large sheet of vellum paper, beautifully decorated, with the names of both rulers written in large letters, signed by Emperor Alexander I himself and countersigned by his chancellor, as well as translations of it in Manchu and Japanese, similarly decorated, but unsigned. The three documents were carefully placed, unfolded, in a cover of gold brocade, with gold galloon along the edges, and with four gold tassels at the ends; the case was then placed in a handsomely made redwood box, which in turn was placed in a box lined with green cloth. For showing to the Nagasaki authorities, if necessary, Rezanov received copies of these documents, printed on Dutch paper of a smaller size.[27]

In August 1803,[28] after a personal inspection of the vessels by Alexander I, Minister of Commerce Rumiantsev, Minister of the Navy Chichagov, and the commander of the expedition and Chief Plenipotentiary of the Russian-American Company, Envoy Extraordinary and Minister Plenipotentiary, Chamberlain Nikolai Rezanov, the *Nadezhda* and *Neva* left Kronstadt. Both were commercial vessels, but with the permission of the Emperor they flew the naval flag in honor of the embassy and as protection against the corsairs who were then roaming the seas.[29] The *Nadezhda*, captained by Krusenstern, had been outfitted at government expense; the *Neva*, com-

25 Voenskii, 132-136; Novakovskii, 75-77.

26 The term *kubo* or *kubo sama* originally referred to retired emperors or to emperors whose reign preceded that of the reigning sovereign. As the military dictators usurped imperial power and began to fashion their existence after that of the imperial court, however, the appellation was transferred in popular tongue to the Shogun, while the Emperor was known as *Dairi*. Divine and imperial as *Tenjin* may sound, however often "Emperor" creeps into the Russian documents, it appears clear from the instructions of Rumiantsev that the Shogun was meant.

27 Voenskii, 136.

28 Sgibnev gives the date as August 15, Novakovskii as August 19.

29 Voenskii, 140; (Oct.), 201-202.

manded by Lisianskii had been outfitted at company expense and was to proceed directly to the Russian colonies without first stopping at Japan. The *Nadezhda* carried eighty-five persons, among them Rezanov, the four castaways, and the cavaliers of the embassy: Major Ermolai Frideritsii, an expert in map-making and military science; Aulic Councilor Fedor Fosse, who was familiar with local conditions in Siberia; and Lieutenant Count Tolstoi, of the Guards of the Preobrazhensk regiment.[30] The two vessels sailed together via Copenhagen, England, Tenerife, and the St. Catherine Islands, around Cape Horn (March 15, 1804) into the Pacific to Nukuhiva (one of the Marquesas Islands) and to the Sandwich Islands (Hawaii), where their paths divided, the *Neva* going directly to the colonies, the *Nadezhda* to Kamchatka.

At Nukuhiva the friction between Krusenstern and Rezanov, caused by Rezanov's assumption of the over-all command, conflicting personalities, and possibly by national differences (Krusenstern was Estonian), flared up in a violent scene. When Krusenstern instructed Lieutenant Romberg and Dr. Espenberg to get fresh supplies from the natives in exchange for various things, Rezanov ordered the commercial agents to acquire similarly objects of ethnographic interest. Krusenstern agreed to assist them in this, but instead not only failed to assist them, but took away everything they had obtained in accordance with Rezanov's orders. Rezanov was enraged and the following day, on May 14, seeing the captain on the quarter-deck

30 Other passengers of note were: Doctor of Astronomy Johann Casper Horner, Professors of Natural History Langsdorff and Wilhelm Gottfried Tilesius (author of *Naturhistorische Früchte der ersten kaiserlich russischen unter dem Commando des Herrn v. Krusenstern vollbrachten Erdumsegelung* [St. Petersburg, 1813]), Doctor of Medicine Moritz Liband, Doctor of Medicine and Botany Brinkin, the artist Kurliandtsev, regular priest Gedeon (for the survey of the newly christened converts in America), chief commissioner of the company Fedor Shemelin, and the Company agent Korobitsyn. Officers: Lieutenant Commander Krusenstern, Lieutenant Senior Grade Makar Ratmanov, Lieutenants Fedor Romberg, Petr Golovachev, Ermolai Levenstern, Ensign Baron Faddei Billingsgauzen, Navigator Filipp Kamenshchikov, Navigator's Mate Vasilii Spolokhov, Doctor Karl Espenberg, his assistant Ivan Sidgam, Sergeant of Artillery Raevskii, and the army cadet brothers Otto and Moritz von Kotzebue, sons of the German playwright Augustus von Kotzebue, who had dramatized Benevszky's uprising on Kamchatka. Otto von Kotzebue so distinguished himself on this voyage that in 1815, on Krusenstern's recommendation, he was appointed at the early age of twenty-eight commander of Russia's second round-the-world expedition, charged with the exploration of the polar regions and of Polynesia. As regards the father, one time Russian general consul in Prussia, he was assassinated in 1819 by a German student who regarded him as a dangerous enemy of German freedom. (Novakovskii, 78-79; Königliche Akademie der Wissenschaften, *Allgemeine Deutsche Biographie*, XIII, 151-156; XVI, 772-784; XXXVIII, 298-299.)

went up to him and asked if he was not ashamed of behaving like a child and taking pleasure in not giving him the means for carrying out his assignment.

"How did you dare to tell me that I behave like a child?" Krusenstern yelled.

"Thus, Sir," replied Rezanov, "I dare it very much as your superior."

"My superior! Can this be? Do you know that I shall deal with you as you do not expect?"

"No," replied Rezanov, "I do not know; maybe you think of keeping me too on the forecastle, like Kurliandtsev? The sailors will not obey you, and I tell you that if you as much as touch me, you will be deprived of your ranks. You have forgotten the law and respect, to which my rank alone already obligates you."

Thus having spoken, Rezanov went to his cabin. A little later Krusenstern stormed into his cabin shouting, "How did you dare to say that I behave like a child, do you know what the quarter-deck is? You will see what I shall do with you."

Alarmed by Krusenstern's vehemence, Rezanov called Fosse, Titular Councilor Brykin, and the Academician Kurliandtsev to his side, ordering them to remain in his cabin and to protect him from the further insolences that seemed in the offing. Krusenstern, meanwhile, visited the other vessel and returned shouting, "Will I teach him!" Soon Lisianskii, the Commander of the *Neva*, came aboard the *Nadezhda* accompanied by Ensign Berg, called together the crew and proclaimed that Rezanov was an impostor. The insults that flowed from the mouths of the crew overwhelmed the envoy. Weakened already by illness, he fainted away. Undaunted the naval officers decided to drag him before a courtmartial on the quarter-deck, and Lieutenant Romberg came to Rezanov and informed him that the officers of both vessels were waiting for him on the quarter-deck. Lying exhausted and barely conscious Rezanov refused to go with Romberg. Krusenstern stormed into his cabin again and demanded at the top of his voice that Rezanov read the instructions, asserting that both vessels were uninformed about the command of the expedition and that he did not know what to do. Gathering his strength, Rezanov decided to go on deck with the imperial instructions to put an end to the shameless behavior of the officers. But the imperial rescript and orders, which conferred upon him the command of the expedition, failed to produce the desired effect. When he finished reading them, there was laughter and shouting: "Who signed them?" Rezanov replied proudly, "Your Emperor Alexander," but the officers remained dissatisfied and asked who had written them. "I do not know," replied Rezanov. "That's just it," shouted Lisianskii, "we want to know who wrote them, as for signing, we know that he will sign anything." And the other officers, with the exception of Lieutenant Golovachev, went up to the flabbergasted envoy and told him to go away with his ukases, that they had no commander other than Krusenstern. And Lieutenant Ratmanov cursed him most obscenely and demanded that he be locked up in his cabin. Humiliated, at the end of his strength, Rezanov sought refuge in his cabin and did not step out again, until the ship reached Petropavlovsk, even though he suffered greatly from the lack of fresh air in the tropical heat. As a result of all this Rezanov's strength was completely undermined and he suffered a nervous breakdown. Not once, however, did the ship's doctor call on him, though everyone on the vessel knew that he was ill.[31]

From the Sandwich Islands the paths of the vessels diverged. The *Neva* sailed directly to the Russian colonies, while the *Nadezhda* headed for Kamchatka, after a futile attempt at locating the legendary gold and silver islands,[32] arriving in Petropavlovsk Harbor on July 28, 1804. Rezanov decided not to continue the voyage to Japan in view of the episode at sea. He went ashore and sent a letter to the nearest representative of administrative authority on Kamchatka, Major General Koshelev, the Commandant of Nizhne-Kamchatsk, informing him that he could not undertake the voyage to Japan because of the mutiny of his officers and wished, therefore, to surrender the expedition to him. In August, Koshelev arrived with a military detachment and on Rezanov's request began a week-long investigation. With his career endangered, Krusenstern warded off the consequences of his mutinous conduct by a public apology and Rezanov agreed to continue with his embassy to Japan.[33]

[31] Voenskii (Oct.), 212-213; Novakovskii, 79-81.

[32] Krusenstern calculated that these islands lay probably in the vicinity of latitude 36° N.; there he began his search but soon discontinued it because of bad weather. He notes in his diary that Japanese maps, which he examined, showed two uninhabited islands, surrounded by underwater rocks to the east of Edo. Maps of the Genroku period (1688-1704) do include such islands. Thus mistakes on Japanese maps as well as Japanese accounts of the Bonin (Ogasawara) Islands may well have given support if not birth to stories about the gold and silver islands. (Novakovskii, 81-82.)

[33] Voenskii (Oct.), 214; Novakovskii, 83.

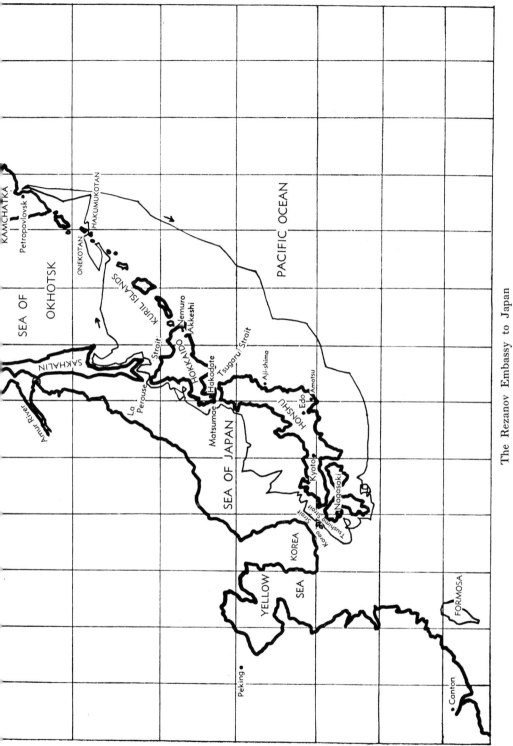

The Rezanov Embassy to Japan

Preparations were made for the voyage to Japan and on September 19, after a stay of less than two months, the *Nadezhda* quitted Kamchatka. At first the weather was favorable but on the 23rd a heavy storm overtook the vessel and for four days tossed it about. When the storm let up on September 27, the *Nadezhda* was at latitude 39°57′ N., and Krusenstern took time to discover that the various islands indicated in these waters on the maps of La Perouse and early French and Spanish maps did not exist. On October 10, Japan—Shikoku Island—was sighted at last.[34] The day before had been the anniversary of the coronation of Alexander I, and as the vessels entered the waters of Japan, Rezanov had commemorated the occasion with the following speech:

Russians:

In our voyage round the world we are at length arrived in the waters of Japan. Love of country, dignity of soul, defiance of danger, perseverance, subordination, mutual esteem, gentleness and forbearance one toward another—these are the characteristics that distinguish the Russian seaman, these are the virtues by which the Russians in general are distinguished.

You, officers of the Navy, approved conductors of the *Hope* [*Nadezhda*], well have you deserved the gratitude of your fellow citizens! You have already acquired a degree of renown of which even jealousy can never deprive you.

You, cavaliers, and associates in the embassy, my worthy companions and assistants, still remains to us the accomplishment of the brilliant objects on which we are sent, the opening to our country new sources of wealth and knowledge. And you, sailors, cherished children of the sea service, rejoice! The happy end of your diligent labors is almost attained.

Long have our hearts and minds been united in serving with zeal the excellent Monarch by whom we are deputed to these parts of the world; and may gratitude toward the beloved ruler still strengthen and animate us in the performance of our arduous task! The present is a solemn day to all the sons of Russia, but to none so solemn as to us, who are entering the Japanese dominions, who are the first to see the glorious Russian flag wave in the harbor of Nagasaki.

As representative of our great Emperor, and as the witness of your admirable performance of duty, it was no less flattering to me to share your toils and dangers than it is gratifying solemnly to assure you of the gratitude which awaits all of you in our dear native country.

[34] According to Novakovskii (84) at 32°38′35″ lat. N. at a distance of fifty-six miles; according to Langsdorff at 32°38′30″ (*Bemerkungen auf einer Reise um die Welt in den Jahren 1803 bis 1807*, I, 188) or at 32°38′33″ (*Voyages*, 212) lat. N. at a distance of thirty-six miles.

I solemnize this festival of Alexander the First's coronation in the waters of Japan, and I make it forever memorable to you in this first reward of your services. You have here the likeness of our beloved Emperor: wear it as your greatest ornament, as a testimony of the zeal and diligence in his service, through which it has been acquired. Recollect always in beholding it, that this imposes upon you still more strongly the obligation of continuing true to those duties of which your forefathers were so proud, and by which they arrived at the highest pinnacle of fame. You will learn sincerely to bless the times in which the merits of the least among his subjects, even in the remotest regions of the world, do not pass unrewarded from the throne itself.[35]

Rezanov decorated each member of the crew with a special coronation medal. At a splendid dinner the health of the Russian Emperor was toasted with wine as the thunder of Russian cannon resounded in the waters of Japan.[36]

On October 11, land was sighted for the second time but fog, rain, and wind curtained the hazards of the unknown shores and the vessel had to put out to open sea again. Time and again *kamikaze* or "divine winds" had protected Japan from foreign conquest. Two storms, one after the other, now descended on the Russians and threatened to whirl them to the bottom of the ocean. In the words of one of the voyagers:

... the raging of the elements was frightful beyond expression: all nature appeared in commotion and uproar. . . . Neither officers or crew had any respite from their labors: their utmost activity was necessary to steer the ship clear of the repeated shocks it received. Large chests of arms floated upon the deck: there was no end of the jostling and the noise: the speaking-trumpet could hardly be heard at the distance of three steps, and people were every where running backwards and forwards with lanterns. The sea, rising into mountains, seemed united with the heavens. It was impossible to trace the boundaries between the air, the clouds, and the water. One monstrous wave after another filled the ship, and seemed sinking it into the abyss: all the household utensils lay about scattered and broken: the guns at the forecastle touched the water . . . a monstrous wave dashed directly against the hinder part of the vessel, tore the gallery away from the left side, broke through the double partition into the captain's cabin, and inundated it so completely, that the water was three feet deep. Expensive books, chairs, tables, maps, presents

---

[35] Langsdorff, *Voyages*, 211-212; Langsdorff, *Bemerkungen*, I, 186-187. The English edition differs slightly in wording from the German one. Its meaning is true, however, and I have followed the standard English edition unless the difference was significant enough to demand change. A somewhat smoother but less complete version of Rezanov's speech may be found in Gertrude Atherton, "Nikolai Petrovich Rezanov," 651-652.

[36] Langsdorff, *Voyages*, 211-212; Atherton, 651-652.

designed for Japan, mathematical instruments, clothes, swam all together about the cabin, and seemed to give a foretaste of what was soon to follow. It is true, that the sailors were exhorted to take courage, and endeavour to stop the leak; but there was no one I believe who did not think within himself at the time, "It is, however, in vain!—We are notwithstanding lost!"[37]

But the storm let up and by morning the sun came out again. Damage to vessel, personal possessions, and gifts was extensive, but not as great as feared. By the evening of October 14, Japan was within sight again and on October 15, the *Nadezhda* sailed alongside Kyushu, whose prominent cape at latitude 32° 14′ 15″ N. and longitude 128° 18′ 30″ W. was named by Krusenstern in honor of Chirikov, who had visited Japan about two generations earlier. On October 16, the *Nadezhda* sailed through the Straits of Van Diemen (Osumi Kaikyo), past Satsuma and Osumi provinces, so close to shore that the houses and fields could be clearly distinguished. On October 18, she reached a wide bay, but turned back southward because of cliffs and a calm. Rounding Mageshima Island[38] the vessel resumed a northward course, sighting the Goto Islands on the 19th. On October 20, the *Nadezhda* returned to the shores of Kyushu and approached its destination: Nagasaki Harbor.

At dawn a Japanese fishing boat was noticed and the castaways hailed their countrymen and persuaded them to come aboard. From the fishermen, who ventured onto the Russian vessel and without much urging accepted brandy, they learned that news of their arrival at the shores of Japan had been flashed to Nagasaki four days earlier by signal fires at night, and that their approach to the harbor itself had been communicated by a hilltop observation post. From the fishermen Krusenstern also learned the best route for entering the harbor and by about one o'clock the *Nadezhda* was at its entrance. Soon a little boat pulled up and two Japanese officials with frank and open countenances met the Russians with apparent "great friendship and politeness." They came aboard, after first questioning the castaways in detail who the foreigners were, from where and why they had come, with how many guns the ship was armed, whether the embassy was destined solely for Japan and so forth. Turning

---

[37] Langsdorff, *Voyages*, 215.

[38] Krusenstern speaks of Meakshima Island ("Meac-sima" in the German version). By name and position this seems to be Mageshima Island. Philipp Franz von Siebold and other scholars deem Meakushima (Meakshima) to have been one of the islands of the Koshiki Archipelago. (Hani Gore, *Kuruzenshuterun Nihon kiko*, I, 155-156 note 31.)

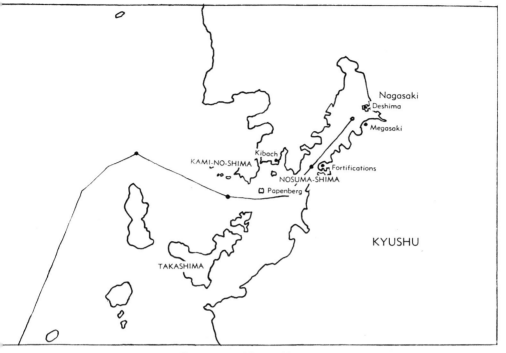

Rezanov at Nagasaki

to the Russians they asked to see the permit, and, copying it, inquired why the Russians had waited for twelve years to make use of
it, commenting that for years the Japanese had been on the look-out
for a Russian vessel, and that one of the castaways returned by Laxman was still living in Nagasaki to serve as Russian language interpreter. To make sure that these were indeed Russians who had
now arrived, the officials asked at their departure for a billet written
in Russian as proof.

In the afternoon, as the *Nadezhda* penetrated deeper into Nagasaki
bay, two other officials arrived to point out the anchorage assigned
the vessel by the governor of Nagasaki, and at about six p.m. the
Nadezhda cast anchor off Mt. Papenberg in thirty-three fathoms.
Two officials had stayed aboard until this time, and left only after
the Russians had certified in writing that they had shown them the
anchoring-place. "When we represented to them that we could only
write in the Russian language," recorded Langsdorff, "they assured
us, as before, that there were people in Nagasaki who understood
that language very well. It appeared, however, subsequently, either

141

that the idea of some of the Japanese brought here by Lieutenant Laxman being still alive in Nagasaki was merely presumed on their part, or else that these men were designedly kept out of our way during our stay there."[39]

Soon more officials came to question the Russians, as Japanese guard boats with melon-like lanterns took up positions near the vessel, and at about ten p.m. a senior official with a large retinue arrived on most colorfully illuminated boats. Past a Russian guard of honor, to the beat of drums, the dignitary and his followers were ushered into Rezanov's cabin, where all the cavaliers of the embassy and the ship's officers had been assembled. Without hesitation the leading Japanese officials and the secretary seated themselves on the sofa, their legs crossed Japanese fashion, flanked by several Japanese servants with smoking utensils and burning lanterns. Through the interpreters who knelt in a semi-circle they plied the Russians with questions. They wanted to see the original permit and were particularly interested to ascertain by what route the Russians had come—by way of the Korean Strait or the eastern coast of Japan—and in how many days they had negotiated the voyage. Anxious not to have Europeans frequent the Korean Strait, they were visibly pleased that the Russians had sailed along the eastern shore of Japan instead.[40]

The anchorage which the governor had assigned the *Nadezhda* was some four miles from the nearest land and was threateningly exposed in case of storm. Rezanov therefore requested a more protected anchoring place. The officials agreed to let the Russians enter the inner part of the bay, but on condition that they surrender in trust, until the time of their departure, all their weapons and ammunition. After some hesitation, Rezanov agreed to surrender firearms and powder, but insisted that officers and crew be permitted to retain their sidearms. At the same time he pleaded for a speedy audience with the governor. Then to his surprise, the Japanese asked whether Hendrik Doeff, the chief of the Dutch factory, and some of his subordinates might not come aboard. Rezanov agreed, and Doeff, who had all this time—for over an hour—waited in one of the boats, was called aboard.[41] As he entered the cabin, accom-

---

[39] Langsdorff, *Voyages*, 215-222; Novakovskii, 85.

[40] Ivan Fedorovich Kruzenshtern, *Puteshestvie vokrug sveta v 1803, 4, 5 i 1806 godakh*, I, 317; Langsdorff, *Voyages*, 224-225.

[41] Kruzenshtern, I, 318; according to Langsdorff, *Voyages* (231-232), the Dutch visit took place on the following day.

panied by his secretary, by the Dutch captains Musquetier and Bell-
mar, and by the traveler Baron von Pabst, he was about to salute
Rezanov, when the Japanese interpreters grabbed him by the arm
and had him salute the Japanese officials first. On the command
"Myn Heer Oberhoeft! Complement bevor de opper Banios!" Doeff
and his companions had to bow low before the chief official and thus
remain for several minutes before requesting permission to straighten
up again with the words *"kan ik wederom opstaan?"* The Japanese
chief official for his part did not deign to return the greeting. Only
after respect had similarly been paid to the other Japanese officials
could the Dutch address themselves to the Russians. The Dutch offered the Russians their services, but the latter preferred to act on
their own. Had they wished to do otherwise, it probably would
not have mattered, for the Japanese were not to permit further visits
between the Dutch and the Russians. Meanwhile the Russians were
outraged at the degrading spectacle that had unfolded before their
eyes and were determined never to submit to similar humiliation.[42]
They had heard, of course, of Japanese mistrust and of the many
precautionary measures, which the Japanese took in their dealings
with foreigners, but Rezanov was the imperial envoy of a powerful
neighboring country and the Russians expected more respect and
freedom of movement than that granted to other aliens.

The assertion of the officials that the arrival of the Russians had
long been expected seemed to justify the optimism with which
Rezanov had outlined for himself the objectives to be pursued in
the event of negotiations in the Japanese capital. He planned to
request permission for a large number of Russian vessels to frequent
a harbor in northern Japan, and there obtain the lease of a place
for the construction of warehouses. Promising a steady Russian demand for copper, camphor, and rice,[43] he would explain the nature
of Russian cargoes, get prices and samples of local products, and
seek to fix a moderate price for rice and a bearable customs duty.
Trade procedures were to be set down in writing, but merchants,
though they would obey Japanese laws, were to be free to import
and export goods of their choice and to take back whatever they
could not sell profitably. In the northern harbor Russian vessels

---

[42] Kruzenshtern, I, 312, 318; Langsdorff, *Voyages*, 231-233; Umemori, 10.

[43] The text here translated reads *psheno* which is millet. It appears likely, however,
that *psheno* is used in this case as an abbreviation of *sarachinskoe psheno* or rice.

were not to be detained at all upon arrival, and were to be supplied, like vessels wintering there, with all the necessary food at a fair price. Elsewhere vessels in distress should be accorded due help. Should trade with Japan prove unprofitable for the Russians, they should be permitted to withdraw without reflection on Russian friendship "which the Sovereign deigns to promise always and forever." As in the case of Laxman, Rezanov ordered Krusenstern to see to it that no outward sign of Christian worship be displayed.[44]

The following day, on October 21, the first secretary of the governor and several other officials arrived on flag-bedecked boats to welcome the Russians in the name of the Japanese government and to collect their powder and weapons, including sidearms. On Russian insistence Rezanov and his officers were allowed to retain their swords, as an essential part of the uniform, but no immediate decision could be reached concerning the Russian demand that a seven-man honor guard of the envoy also be permitted to retain its weapons, the Japanese objecting that not even the highest officials of their own country were allowed to carry exposed firearms. As the Russians surrendered the bulk of their weapons the officials led their vessel closer to shore. At midnight the *Nadezhda* weighed anchor and was towed to the western side of Mt. Papenberg by over sixty Japanese boats maintaining the most astonishing order of formation. The eastern side of Mt. Papenberg was more protected, but the Japanese would not permit the *Nadezhda* to proceed there as long as five Chinese junks occupied the anchorage. When the Chinese left a week later, one hundred Japanese boats towed the vessel to the eastern anchorage. But they refused to pull the *Nadezhda* into the inner harbor for repairs, as the Russians requested, not on the customary pretext that no permission had been received for this from Edo, but because allegedly a warship with such a distinguished personage as Rezanov could not stand side by side with mere Dutch merchantmen.[45] On the twenty-first the Japanese officials relieved the Russians of the original Nagasaki Permit, but, though they asked for the imperial letter as well, they were shown only a copy of it. The Japanese claimed that the handwriting and language used was one that they could not understand and that the governor himself must examine it. Rezanov told them that the letter expressed his Emperor's wish to enter into relations of friendship and trade with

[44] Polonskii, 552-554.   [45] Kruzenshtern, I, 323-327; Langsdorff, *Voyages*, 227-231.

the Japanese and that he was fully empowered to negotiate an appropriate agreement. But he refused to give them even a copy of the letter, demanding again to see the governor so that he could explain the contents in person. The following day, on October 22, Japanese officials again inquired about the contents of the imperial letter and the Russians went over the text slowly, reading and repeating each point several times to make sure that the Japanese understood it. The letter was as follows:

By the Grace of God, His Tenjin-Kubo Majesty, the Autocratic Potentate of the extensive Japanese Empire, Most Excellent Emperor and Sovereign: His Majesty the Emperor Autocrat of all of Russia wishes perfect health, long life and every felicity in reign. Having taken over the governing of the Empire, the boundaries of which My ancestors Peter I and Catherine II extended, and seeing Holland, France, England, Italy, Spain and the German land suffering from mutual war, I made it my duty to incline them by friendly insistence to universal peace. Supposing the felicity of my rule to be in tranquility and peace, I direct all My solicitude to the acquisition of the friendly disposition of all terrestrial powers in general, the rather of My neighbors. Cognizant of the dignity of the Japanese Empire, the late Empress Catherine the Great as a token of friendship in 1791 returned to the fatherland those Japanese who by mishap had suffered shipwreck and were cast by fate to the shores of My Empire and the Russian subjects then sent, having been received amicably, obtained from the Japanese Government a paper, by which permission was given to one vessel to come to Nagasaki harbor freely.

Feeling also until now such favorable disposition of Your Tenjin-Kubo Majesty and at the same time what advantages might be derived from mutual intercourse, and furthermore desiring to know the governmental structure of other parts of the world as well, I decided to send to Japan to return to your Majesty several Japanese, who hitherto, not of their own volition, by unfortunate lot, escaping death from shipwreck saved their life in my domains, and to this end, having chosen as worthy loyal subject, the Actual Chamberlain of My Court, Nikolai Rezanov, so that with due respect he could approach to Your Autocratic Person, I desire that he transmit to Your Tenjin-Kubo Majesty this letter according to the proper ceremonial with sincere respect, that he act in everything in such a way that it be pleasing to You too, and set forth to Your Tenjin-Kubo Majesty how much I try to continue and strengthen on unshaken principles the tie of My friendly disposition to You and to carry out all that, which only will be demanded from Your side, as a token of appreciation for having accepted My proposals, which consist in that Your Tenjin-Kubo Majesty permit merchant people, especially inhabitants of the Kadiak, Aleutian and Kuril islands, as [islands] neighboring unto You, to come not only to Nagasaki harbor and not only one vessel, but also

many and to other harbors with those exceptions, which will be favorable
to You. I for my part open all limits of my Empire to the friendly reception
of Your loyal subjects. On what bases to confirm mutual trade between
Our subjects; and where My trading subjects should land in Your ports—
I instructed My Envoy, the above-mentioned Actual Chamberlain Rezanov, to negotiate with a Minister of Your Tenjin-Kubo Majesty, as well
as the matter, in what way I should in the future deliver to You Your
subjects, if by unfortunate lot they are shipwrecked and save their life
on the shore of My Empire. I send with this to Your Tenjin-Kubo Majesty
as gifts a clock, made in the shape of a mechanical elephant, mirrors,
fox fur, vases of fossil ivory, muskets, pistols, and manufactures of steel
and glass. All things have been made in My manufactories. Although they
do not cost much, I desire, that they only please You and that in the
confines of My Empire there be found something that You wish.

In St. Petersburg, June 30, 1803, in the third year of My reign.
[Signed] Aleksandr. [Countersigned] Count Aleksandr Vorontsov.[46]

Having obliged the Japanese by explaining to them the meaning of
the imperial letter, the Russians complained to them that the Japanese castaways had refused to perform any work, since arriving at
the shores of their homeland. The officials had the castaways brought
before them and gave them a thorough tongue-lashing for thus casting
dishonor on Japan by their ingratitude. Impressed by this action of
the officials and by their general politeness, Rezanov, who the day
before had refused to surrender to them a copy of the imperial letter,
now voluntarily gave them one for the governor. "This appeared to
give inexpressible pleasure: the utmost satisfaction was visible in the
features of everyone," noted Langsdorff, "and what before was ceremony, seemed now converted into the confidence of friendship."The
Japanese showed their interest in trade with Russia by posing a great
many questions: "What productions Russia could and would bring
to Japan as objects of trade? Whether Russia could furnish sugar, rye,
skins, medicines, and many other articles? How many ships she

---

[46] Voenskii, 136-138; Novakovskii, 90-92. Tokutomi Iichiro cites a Japanese version of
the text, constructed by the Japanese interpreters from a Dutch translation of the
Russian original and oral explanations. It is remarkably faithful in meaning, differing
primarily in tone, the Russian gifts, for example, being designated as "tribute." Men-
tioning the permit received by Laxman, the Japanese version states: "Our gratitude
knows no bounds. To express our thanks [for the permit and Japanese hospitality] we
are sending, therefore, an ambassador to the Edo government. He humbly requests an
audience under the knee of the king of Great Japan in connection with our great desire
to gain your future good will and to open the way for trade. We have specially selected
for this purpose our trusted subject the Chamberlain Nikolai Rezanov. Since he is completely unacquainted with the laws of your country we would appreciate it if you would
expound them to him." (Tokutomi, xxv, 25, 192-195.)

could and would send annually to Japan? Whether four, five, or even more? Whence the ships would come, whether from Kamchatka or from Europe? How long the ships would be in coming? What was the best time of year for coming from Japan to Kamchatka?" The Japanese wanted to know the relative location of Kamchatka and Japan and posed other geographical questions, expressing surprise at the information that Russia had possessions in America. They examined Russian maps, and displayed considerable geographical knowledge. The Japanese were no less interested in the Russian language and asked the Russian equivalents for such common words as "good," "bad," and "good morning" and for the names of various objects and proceeded to interpolate them in their own speech. All this amazed the Europeans. As Langsdorff observed: "The inquisitiveness, the readiness at learning, and the memory of these people, surprised us exceedingly." The interpreters later asked the Russians for instruction in their language, offering in turn to teach the Russians Japanese. This was most unusual, for the Dutch were specifically forbidden to study Japanese.

On October 24, two days after the copy of the imperial letter had been sent to the governor it was returned to the Russians with the request that it be translated into Dutch, on the ground that its text, though written in Japanese script, was not understandable—not necessarily an empty pretext, because it had been worded by one of the castaway fishermen at Irkutsk. The Russians once again tried to explain the letter sentence by sentence, but with difficulty, for as Langsdorff noted, "not one among our whole party could properly be said to understand the Dutch language." Satisfactory communication remained most difficult, and misunderstandings were numerous. Nevertheless, the meaning of the letter became increasingly clearer, as did the rank and dignity of the envoy, who in the Japanese text had appeared to be but a small prince. The Japanese expressed particular surprise that the Russian Emperor should have written the letter himself, a thing never done by their sovereign. That same meeting the castaways, arrayed in Russian clothing of silk, were presented to the senior officials.[47]

On October 27, the senior official arrived again, but was received rather coldly by Rezanov who, tired of the selfsame questions, stated that he did not feel well. The Japanese communicated that a new governor had arrived in Nagasaki and that both he and his incum-

---

[47] Langsdorff, *Voyages*, 236-241.

bent colleague promised that Rezanov would soon be permitted to enter the harbor proper, adorning the irksome delay with the flattering contention that it was the exaltedness of Rezanov's position that necessitated elaborate preparations for his reception and the awaiting of special instructions from the court; had he been such an insignificant personage as Lieutenant Laxman, he would have been admitted into the harbor long ago. Yet Rezanov's half-feigned indisposition hastened a decision. That same evening the governors expressed their concern about Rezanov's health and promised that he would be moved to a better anchorage the following day. On the morning of the 28th, Japanese officials again inquired after Rezanov's health and offered the help of a Japanese doctor. Then, as mentioned earlier, the *Nadezhda* was towed from the western to the eastern side of Mt. Papenberg by a hundred little boats. The officials remained aboard the vessel during the operation, eagerly pursuing their study of geography.

At the western anchorage many Japanese, predominantly women, had rowed up to the cordon of guard boats—a guard of honor as the Japanese claimed—to have a look at the foreigners. Now that the vessel was moved eastward, closer to Nagasaki, more boats milled about the *Nadezhda*. "The number of people thus attracted to stare at us were no less entertaining to us than we to them," wrote Langsdorff. "Sometimes we saw a boat filled with children, from ten to fourteen years old, so that it seemed as if a whole school had been brought out to be treated with a sight of the Russians. In others were women, who, to judge by the richness of their clothing, must have been of high rank. There were mothers with infants at the breast, and young girls with stringed instruments; in some of the boats the people had telescopes, which were handed from one to the other; in short, old and young, married and unmarried, all came to gratify their curiosity." And on shore groups of Japanese gathered, ate picnics, and gazed at the Russians.[48]

On November 2, the Russians were informed that they would be supplied, free of charge, with provisions, but must not attempt to purchase anything else. At the same time they were told not to be alarmed at the sound of cannon fire the next day, as the Dutch ships expected to leave their anchorage and, as was their custom, would salute the imperial fortress. The Russians were not to send a boat

48 *Ibid.*, 242-249.

to one of the Dutch vessels, nor elsewhere for that matter. When the Dutch vessels duly departed from Deshima the following day, they saluted with a hundred and fifty guns each.[49] Rezanov witnessed this with displeasure and the next day, on November 4, protested to the Japanese that if mere Dutch merchantmen were allowed thus to fire gun salutes and to discharge a cannon morning and evening, it was an insult to the Russian flag that his warship had been denied this as contrary to the laws of Japan. At the same time, notwithstanding the recent prohibition, he expressed the desire to meet the commanders of the Dutch vessels, which though they had left Deshima had not yet quitted the harbor, and through them to send word to Russia of his safe arrival in Japan. He thanked the Japanese for their generosity in providing him with provisions free of cost, but said he would rather purchase them, particularly as delivery had been irregular. He waxed impatient with Japanese procrastination and voiced himself "exceedingly hurt" at being neglected. He charged that he had not been shown the friendship "which his Imperial Russian Majesty, whose representative he was, had a right to expect from the Japanese" and that neither he nor any of his countrymen would have come had they anticipated such treatment. He demanded a place on land—even an uninhabited island—where he could strengthen his failing health by exercise, and also a house on shore, where the presents for the Japanese sovereign could be laid out, and a place for the repair of the vessel.[50]

The Japanese consented to let the Russians dispatch two unsealed letters through the Dutch. When Rezanov objected that it would be improper for him to send an unsealed dispatch to his Emperor, it was agreed eventually that the letters be shown to the Governor of Nagasaki, then returned by one of the officials to be sealed by Rezanov in his presence, and once again taken to the governor and by him transmitted to the Dutch. Thus the Russians sent home word of their whereabouts.[51] As to the place on shore, the Japanese reiterated that they could not let any foreigners land without permission from the government, but then modified their stand and agreed to make

---

[49] The Japanese did not return the salute. From this the Russians concluded that they really had no cannon. Yet as the Japanese were not in the habit of acknowledging Dutch bows, it is likely that they simply did not deign to return other forms of Dutch salutation either.

[50] Langsdorff, *Voyages*, 249-253.

[51] The Russians dispatched only one letter from Nagasaki. Several German publications carried other letters purporting to have been sent by them, but these were fictitious.

an exception in the case of Rezanov, because of his illness. By November 10, a fenced-in "walk" was readied at Kibachi, on a large island. As Langsdorff described it, "it was a walk not more than twice the length of our ship, inclosed with a palisade of bamboo canes: every plant and blade of grass was torn away; the soil was perfectly levelled, and it was strewn over with sand. A small summer-house, open in front, was to serve as our shelter in case of rain. . . ."[52] Rezanov could go there whenever he pleased on condition that he give advance notice, hoisting a red flag as signal to the Japanese officer of the guard, and come with no more than nine officers, never taking ashore any common sailors and never staying over-night.

On November 20, the Dutch vessels departed and the following day the *Nadezhda* was towed to the anchorage they had vacated, directly in front of a Japanese guard post, some two miles from Nagasaki, and with a clear view of the city. Now repairs could be begun and masts, beams, and yards were taken to the walk at Kibachi. The Japanese suggested that Rezanov move aboard a Chinese junk, but when the Russians found the cabin unsuitable, they suggested that Rezanov might have a place at the very end of the city, until permission for a more satisfactory place was obtained from Edo. But though Rezanov obliged the governor by putting into writing his demand for a place on shore to repair damages incurred by the vessel in a storm and to recover from ill health, the Japanese continued to procrastinate. This irritated the Russians, and Rezanov gave vent to his feelings. He stated that much time had been lost already and that only four months remained before the vessel would have to return to Kamchatka. He feared that if they delayed any further, he would not have time to proceed to Edo and thus found it necessary to demand an immediate decision. For good measure he added the back-handed threat that, if he did not return to Europe by July, it would be assumed that some mishap had occurred, and other Russian vessels would arrive at the shores of Japan in search of him.

On December 29, at long last, Rezanov was permitted to move ashore. With his guard of honor and entourage he boarded the beautiful, large barge of Prince Hizen[53] (in preference to one of his own boats) and seated himself on a Russian chair with his credentials laid out before him on a table, while the vessel, flying the colors both of Prince Hizen and of the Russian Empire, was festively towed to

---

[52] Langsdorff, *Voyages*, 257-259.
[53] Variously called in Western sources Prince Fisi and Prince Fizen.

shore without making use of its many oars. At Megasaki a wooden house of nine apartments had been prepared, and Rezanov, Frideritsii, Fosse, Captain Fedorov, Lieutenant Koshelev, Mr. Shemelin (commissioner of the Company), Langsdorff, the guard of honor, and the four Japanese castaways took up their abode on land, the other officers and members of the crew, remaining on the *Nadezhda*. The new place—the "Russian Deshima" as Krusenstern dubbed it—was a quadrangular peninsula, enveloped by water on three sides. Along three sides of the fenced-in court, which extended some fifty paces in length and forty in breadth, the dwelling of the envoy and two magazines had been arranged. The fourth side, facing the sea, was bounded by a high double palisade of bamboo. The whole enclosure had only two doors: one leading to a small fenced-in place, the other to the water; both were provided with strong double locks and were locked and bolted every night. Thus in effect the Russians were prisoners of the Japanese or, as the Japanese liked to refer to the Dutch on Deshima, their hostages. On January 3, 1805, Rezanov was informed that permission had been received for the vessels to enter Nagasaki and the following day, on January 4, the *Nadezhda* was towed into the harbor proper, about a quarter of a mile from the landing place between Deshima and Megasaki. Yet free intercourse between the men aboard ship and their comrades on land was not permitted. The doors remained locked, until the Russians signaled with a red flag their intention to visit or leave shore. Every evening those who remained on land had to pass in review before a Japanese officer to make sure that only the number stipulated slept at Megasaki. Eventually the door leading to the small fenced-in place was left open and, as the Russians strolled there, Japanese men, women, and children, on the other side of the fence, peered at them as at animals in the zoo. On New Year's Eve the Russians could hear the Dutch celebrating gaily, while they had to pass the night, as Langsdorff phrased it "with our customary patience and philosophy, over a quiet glass of punch, to the daily music of locking up our doors."

On their arrival in Japan the Russians had found the Japanese friendly and courteous. Many brought fans to the Russians and asked them to inscribe them. At the walk first assigned to Rezanov the Japanese were always solicitous of his comfort. No sooner would he fail to come ashore then they would hasten aboard the vessel to inquire in what way they could make the place more comfortable. And though they subjected them to the measures of precaution customarily applied to foreigners, they treated them not without confidence, for they explained to the Russians how their guns were fired, showed them maps of the neighboring countryside, and many objects of interest. Gradually intercourse became more limited and less intimate, not so much due to any change in attitude on the part of the Japanese at large, as by the orders of higher officials.[54] At the place near Megasaki the Russians were completely segregated from all but a limited number of officials, who came infrequently and then only on business. Except for repairing the vessel and preparing the gifts for the Japanese sovereign, the Russians had little with which to occupy themselves. Rezanov, a good linguist, with the aid of the castaways studied Japanese and even compiled a brief Russo-Japanese manual and dictionary containing some five thousand words, later published by the Academy of Sciences. But the scientists of the expedition could not study the country except for the fish, which was sent aboard as food.

On January 28, the monotony of unoccupied waiting was interrupted dramatically, when Tajuro, one of the castaways, suddenly plunged a razor into his mouth. Some said that he had been driven to it by his conscience: allegedly he had handed to the Japanese officials a note in which he had vilified the Russians, portraying them as fanatics, who had mistreated the castaways, forcing some of them to adopt Christianity, and had claimed that the true purpose of the Russian Embassy was not to establish commercial relations, but to open the country to Christianity. Others believed that he had become exasperated at the delays. The Japanese who investigated the incident reported to the Shogunate that he had become mentally deranged as the result of acute homesickness. There is evidence that Tajuro had tried to commit suicide, not out of fear that he might not be repatriated, but on the contrary out of desperation that he would be repatriated. For, during the long delay, rumors reached the castaways that those who had been returned by Laxman had been put under arrest and that Kodayu still languished in jail, and the castaways asked Rezanov not to return them. Called to the scene by the shouts of the other castaways, Langsdorff wanted to stop Tajuro's bleeding, but the Japanese officials characteristically

---

[54] Langsdorff, *Voyages*, 258-264; Kruzenshtern, I, 331-334.

prevented him from lending a helping hand, since the governor had not yet been notified. Nor was Dr. Espenberg, who together with Krusenstern was hastily summoned ashore by Rezanov, permitted to assist the castaway. Fortunately the wound was not fatal and a Japanese physician, who arrived before long, managed to save Tajuro. Upon arrival in Japan, Rezanov had repeatedly refused to surrender the castaways without an audience, now he requested the governors to take them, but the officials no longer dared to do so without specific permission from the capital.[55]

On February 8, Rezanov sent word to the governor that his patience and forbearance "had reached the highest point." But it was early March before he received a positive reaction in the announcement that a Japanese plenipotentiary had been dispatched from the capital to meet with him. Welcome as this news was, it was dampened somewhat by the implication that negotiations in the capital were out, and, on March 24, Rezanov was specifically forbidden to go to Edo. He was told that the plenipotentiary would reach Nagasaki in ten or twelve days and that, upon the conclusion of negotiations, he must depart at once. On April 11, Superintendent Toyama Kage-michi, the plenipotentiary, arrived and three days later, on April 14, the Russians were informed of this. On the 15th, interpreters came aboard to prescribe the ceremonial to be observed during the negotiations. The Japanese demanded that Rezanov greet the plenipotentiary in Japanese fashion—with bent knees and bowed head. But this he refused to do, agreeing only to remove his shoes and ungird his sword before entering the conference hall, and there to sit on the matted floor without a chair. Finally on the morning of April 16, half a year after reaching Nagasaki Harbor, Rezanov and the cavaliers of the embassy once again boarded the barge of Prince Hizen and were ferried ashore. Ceremoniously received by several officials and a kneeling guard, the Russians were gathered into a train of Japanese officials and soldiers with Rezanov in a *norimono*, carried by eight bearers, followed on foot by Frideritsii, Fedorov, Koshelev, Langsdorff, Fosse, and a sergeant with the imperial standard. As the procession wound its way through the streets and squares of the city, the Russians were led, as if blindfolded, for buildings and people had been literally curtained from their view. Only here and there an inquisitive head, irresistibly propelled by curiosity,

[55] Ramming, *Reisen*, 61, Kruzenshtern, I, 341; Langsdorff, *Voyages*, 254, 288; Voenskii (Oct.) 229; Novakovskii, 87-88.

would pop through the drapes to stare at the foreigners.[56]

At the conference building, which the Russians entered in stocking feet, they were offered the customary Japanese pipes and tea. Then Rezanov, accompanied by Frideritsii and Koshelev, met with Toyama, Governors Hida, Lord of Bungo, and Naruse, Lord of Inaba, and Takagi Sakuemon. The first encounter was brief. The Japanese inquired why Rezanov had come, why a letter had been addressed to the Japanese sovereign in view of the fact that Laxman had been told already that this was contrary to Japanese custom and law, whether Laxman had reported this, and whether he was still alive. They stated that the permit given to Laxman provided for the arrival of a commercial vessel for further negotiations concerning the establishment of commercial relations between Japan and Russia; it did not authorize the dispatching of an embassy. Again they asked why it had taken the Russians so long to make use of the permit. Aside from these questions, which Rezanov answered, as he had answered them before to minor officials, the first meeting was taken up primarily by the exchange of formal greetings. It was the second meeting which climaxed the expedition and in one day shattered the golden hopes which had sustained the Russians all these lonely months. It was a rainy day and Rezanov had succeeded in obtaining for his retinue, as well as for himself, the privilege of proceeding to the conference place by *norimono*. Almost immediately upon his entrance, Rezanov was invited to meet with the Japanese dignitaries and, accompanied by Fosse and Fedorov, proceeded to the audience hall. Ceremoniously the Japanese read to the envoy the long-awaited reply of their government to the letter of the Russian Emperor:

Proclamation:[57]

In ancient times our country had not little relations with distant countries; but seeing their uselessness, forbade its merchants to go to foreign lands, and foreign vessels also are not easily permitted to come to our country. If, however, some vessel persists in coming, it will be driven away firmly. Only Chinese, Korean, Ryukyu, and Dutch ones can come; but these not for commercial benefits, but because they have been coming since long ago and for special reasons. Your country did not have relations with us since ancient times until now, like those countries.

[56] Kojiruien, xxviii, 549; Kruzenshtern, i, 343-345; Langsdorff, *Voyages*, 297-308; Novakovskii, 93-94.

[57] *Moshiwatashi*—proclamation; has the implication of an order or sentence rather than a letter.

In former years a vessel of yours unexpectedly brought to Matsumae survivors of ours and desired to trade. Now again you have come to Nagasaki in a friendly manner requesting the opening of trade. You have asked us about this matter already twice, and we recognize that you have a need in our country. It is impossible, however, as you request to negotiate concerning commercial relations.

Already for a long time our country has no dealings with distant countries. We do not know neighborly friendship with foreign countries, nor do we have any ties with them, their characteristics and conditions being different. This is a hereditary law for the protection of our country's frontiers. How can our government change a hereditary law merely on account of your country?

Propriety must be repaid with propriety. If we now accept gifts of your country and do not reciprocate, our country may be regarded as ignorant of propriety; if we do reciprocate, we must do likewise with other distant lands. Hence we consider it preferable to refuse. In the instance of commerce, though it may appear that adding things which your country has to those which our country lacks would be of mutual benefit, we have concluded upon detailed deliberation of this that in exchange for unvaluable foreign things we would lose useful Japanese goods. All things considered, it is not to the good of the country as a whole. Furthermore the light-minded people would cunningly compete for the goods, quarreling over prices, and interested only in profit, and thereby the manners and customs of the people would be spoiled. It being of harm in the sustaining of our subjects, we will not resort to it. Without commerce solely in fidelity to enter anew friendly relations is counter to our national prohibition, which cannot be relaxed. Thus it is our government's will not to open this place; do not come again in vain. You must sail home quickly.[58]

The reply of the Shogunate was supplemented by two notes from the governor of Nagasaki, briefer and less couched in diplomatic language. The first set forth the Japanese intent of the much misunderstood Nagasaki Permit:

On the occasion of the earlier arrival in Matsumae it was announced that it was not allowed to trade and have relations and it was forbidden to bring papers written either in Russian or in Japanese and incomprehensible to us, it being noted that reports cannot be made from Matsumae to the capital concerning foreign affairs; furthermore that it is forbidden to come to Matsumae with our people, saved on your shores, or with a request concerning a different matter, but one must come to Nagasaki,

---

[58] The reply, as given here, is based primarily on the Japanese text cited by Tokutomi (xxv, 222-223) with consideration of an almost identical, but in spots less clear, Russian version given by Polonskii (555-556). An admittedly abbreviated, somewhat toned-down version of the Japanese reply may be found in Langsdorff (*Voyages*, 311-312) and Novakovskii (95-96).

where all foreign affairs are examined, and it will be permitted or prohibited to trade. To treat of this matter one can only there, and for this a pass was given, but now you have brought an imperial letter, and hence I imagine that before you did not understand the Matsumae announcement because here the customs and language are peculiar. For this reason the injunction of our supreme council is proclaimed here again.—It has been ordered that firewood, water and provisions be given. Do not stop at anchor at the shores of Japan and depart as soon as possible from our shores.[59]

The third paper[60] was the same note over again, but phrased a little differently, whether inadvertently through the labors of another interpreter or on purpose to make certain that this time the Russians understood the full meaning of the injunction. The governor reiterated that the shores of Japan contained many cliffs and that storms were most dangerous, that the Russians therefore must not linger upon departure from Nagasaki, but go out to sea at once. He added that in the future, should Japanese be cast on the shores of Russia and wish to return, they should be handed to the Dutch, who would then convoy them to Japan by way of Batavia.

Rezanov was shocked. Less optimistic on the eve of the conference than when he had first arrived in Japan, he had still managed to retain faith in the ultimate success of his mission, a faith nourished by constant Japanese references to the expected reply from the capital. He had not foreseen such an outright rejection, in fact it seemed to him that the Japanese interpreters were shocked also. For a moment he was dumbfounded, then, his face changing, he exploded in anger: He was surprised at this Japanese insolence. Who could forbid his Emperor to write, his Emperor, who by doing so, had done greater honor to the Japanese sovereign than the latter could have expected? Both were emperors, but it was not to be decided here who was greater. Russia had no need of trade with Japan; it was a favor of the Russian Emperor toward Japan, resulting merely from the humanitarian desire to alleviate their needs. Surely they did not think of dealing with the Russians as with the Portuguese? He boasted to the officials that it would not be difficult for his Emperor to teach Japan the rules, which respect to his person required and warned that Japan should not extend her possessions beyond

---

[59] Tokutomi, xxv, 225-226; Novakovskii, 97; Polonskii, 556. There is a slight difference in the wording given by these sources. I have drawn on all of them to present the most meaningful text. See also Okamoto, 2: 13-19, and *Hokkaido-shi*, ii, 454.

[60] See Polonskii, 556-557.

the northern extremity of Matsumae Island. And as the interpreters translated his words, Rezanov made certain that they did not emasculate his scorn, adding himself, here and there, in Japanese. But in fact the letter of the Shogunate was remarkable for its diplomatic tactfulness and logic, particularly if compared with contemporary Chinese replies.[61] To the Japanese, so accustomed to restraining their emotions, the outburst of Rezanov was at once awesome and embarrassing, and Hida replied that the envoy had troubled himself exceedingly and that the meeting might perhaps be continued better another day. "With great pleasure!" Rezanov exclaimed and stamped out of the conference hall.

Negotiations were not broken off, however. Rezanov had countered the Japanese refusal to accept the Russian gifts with the refusal to accept the gifts and provisions of their government. This, the Japanese argued, would be a serious insult, which the governor and his subordinates could erase only by committing suicide and painted so pathetic a picture of mass-disembowelment, that Rezanov (who could well use the supplies) was finally persuaded to accept the provisions and gifts. When Rezanov and the plenipotentiaries held their last meeting, on April 19, a friendly atmosphere prevailed again and Rezanov seemed to have forgotten the indignities against which, two days before, he had protested so vehemently. On April 21, the Japanese accepted the castaways and issued a receipt. On April 28, Rezanov was handed a Dutch translation of the Japanese reply to the Russian state paper. The same day he was informed that the boat, which had brought him to the site near Megasaki, was ready to take him back to his ship and that he would much oblige the governor, if he would go aboard the following day. Rezanov readily agreed and, on April 29, the Russians were returned their weapons and ammunition. Japanese officials visited Rezanov to bid him farewell, expressing their regret that trade with Russia had failed to materialize, while other Japanese came to the guardhouse and, asking the envoy to autograph their fans, assured him that they would never forget the Russians.

Late in the evening of April 29, the sails were set and, early on April 30, the *Nadezhda* weighed anchor. The Japanese had forbidden the Russians to approach land again, but at the northern tip of

[61] See for example the missive from the Manchu Emperor Ch'ien Lung to King George III of Britain in A.D. 1793, as cited in A. F. Whyte, *China and Foreign Powers*, Appendix, 41.

Hokkaido dense fog forced them to interrupt their voyage. A Japanese official hastened aboard and demanded that the Russians depart at once. He threatened them with a fleet of many ships from Matsumae and, blowing up his cheeks, exploded in furious "boom booms"—a warning of things to come. The Russians assured him that, as soon as the weather improved, they would continue their voyage, and when the fog lifted the *Nadezhda* sailed away.[62]

THE AMBASSADOR'S REVENGE

From Nagasaki the *Nadezhda* proceeded up the west coast of Japan through Tsushima Strait and the Sea of Japan to Kamchatka. The Japanese had tried to dissuade the Russians from taking this route, describing it as almost impassable—narrow, full of reefs, and swept by a strong current. But Krusenstern persisted, because the western shores of Kyushu, Honshu, and Hokkaido, much of the Korean coast and of Sakhalin Island, as well as several Kuril Islands remained as yet unexplored. On the other hand, he was forced to make the promise to the Japanese not to approach their shores, except in dire emergency, and negotiated the strait without surveying either the shores of Japan or of Korea. Thick fogs, which enveloped the vessel most of the way, assisted Krusenstern in keeping the promise.[63] Only when he reached latitude 39° N. did he approach Japanese soil again, having given notice in Nagasaki that he planned to reconnoiter the strait between Honshu and Hokkaido. The *Nadezhda* entered Tsugaru (then Sangar) Strait, which proved far more narrow than contemporary maps suggested, and, on May 15, approached Matsumae City (now Fukuyama) to within three miles. Sailing out of Tsugaru Strait again, the ship continued northward, around the western shore of Hokkaido across Soya (La Perouse) Strait to Sakhalin Island. In Aniwa Bay the Russians went ashore at the Japanese settlement Kushunkotan (later called Korsakov by the Russians). Then they sailed along the eastern coast of the island up to latitude 48° N., where heavy ice forced them to discontinue their exploration, and to follow the Kuril Archipelago to Kamchatka. On June 17, 1805, they set foot on the continent again.[64]

---

[62] Novakovskii, 97-101; Polonskii, 557; Langsdorff, *Voyages*, 318; Ramming, *Reisen*, 64.

[63] Krusenstern did chart Goto, Tsushima and Oki Islands, and on May 3-5 sighted the shores of Japan between latitude 30°15′ and 33°45′.

[64] Novakovskii, 105-109; Sgibnev, "Popytki," 59-60.

At Petropavlovsk the paths of Krusenstern and the envoy diverged. In accordance with instructions from Rezanov, Krusenstern resumed his survey of the Sakhalin shores, rounding the northern part of the island and approaching the Amur Estuary. He proved that, contrary to contemporary maps, Sakhalin and Karafuto were one and the same, but, hesitant to investigate Tatar Strait too closely for fear he arouse the suspicions of the Manchus and thereby endanger Russian trade with China, if not the safety of his own vessel—he imagined the approaches of the Amur River must be guarded by a Manchu fleet— and forewarned by his instructions not to antagonize the Chinese, he retraced his steps, seconding La Perouse's misconception that the strait between Sakhalin and the mainland was not navigable. From Sakhalin, Krusenstern returned to Kamchatka and from there to Kronstadt (August 25, 1806) where the *Neva* had arrived a week earlier. Rezanov, meanwhile, in order to avoid further conflict with Krusenstern, departed for the American colonies on the Company vessel *Mariia Magdalena*. Rezanov had not regained his health—in Japan he had complained of rheumatic pains and an oppression upon the chest—and he took along Langsdorff as his personal physician.[65] In August 1805, he went ashore at Novo-Arkhangelsk (New Archangel, Sitka) on Baranov Island, the headquarters of Russian America, and busied himself with company affairs. The winter of 1805-1806 was most severe, and starvation and scurvy decimated the settlement. To replenish it with foodstuffs and to arrange for a regular source of supplies, Rezanov purchased the cargo-laden American sloop *Iunona (Juno)* and in the spring proceeded to San Francisco, there to negotiate with the Spaniards.

Rezanov was well received by the local *presidio*, Don José Darío Argüello, but though the latter agreed that commerce would be of mutual benefit, he insisted that it was illegal and that he did not have the authority to permit it. Rezanov, meanwhile, in his frequent visits to the house of the commandant, became attracted to Doña Concepción or "Concha," the commandant's beautiful sixteen-year old daughter, and asked for her hand. The parents and the Catholic clergy objected, but Doña Concepción sided with the forty-two year old widower, and together they prevailed. Rezanov was betrothed to the young woman and plans were made for a wedding upon his

[65] Novakovskii, 111; Tikhmenev, 1: 112; Langsdorff, *Voyages*, 294; Thomas C. Russell, *The Rezanov Voyage to Nueva California in 1806*, 86.

return from Europe with the necessary royal and papal sanctions. Then Rezanov worked out the preliminaries of a commercial agreement with the Spaniards and obtained the foodstuffs after which he had come. With these he returned to Novo-Arkhangelsk in May.[66]

California, not to mention Oregon and British Columbia, were much on Rezanov's mind. Even before coming to San Francisco, he had proposed, in a secret report to the directors of the Russian-American Company, the colonization of the Columbia River valley, both for its own sake and as a base for further expansion. "Should we be enabled to take the first steps in this direction," he had written from Novo-Arkhangelsk, on February 15, 1806, "I dare say that we shall be in a position to attract colonists to Columbia from various places, and that within ten years we shall grow so strong that at the first ever so slightly favorable conjuncture of political circumstances in Europe it will be possible to add the California littoral to Russian possessions."[67] But Rezanov did not forget Japan. The smart of the Japanese rebuff still rankled in him.

The failure of Rezanov's mission to Japan has been variously explained. Philipp Franz von Siebold attributed it to Rezanov's unfamiliarity with Japanese customs, etiquette, and language; the Dutch factor Doeff saw it in Rezanov's hesitation to surrender all arms immediately and in Rezanov's lack of diplomatic experience; Krusenstern, Langsdorff, and others considered Russian efforts thwarted primarily by Dutch intrigues; M. Veniukov believed Rezanov had not been persistent enough in the face of Japanese anti-foreignism; the journals *Russkii Khudozhestvennyi Listok* and *Otechestvennyia Zapiski* took Rezanov to task for inconsiderateness, impatience, and lack of tact; Bartold attributed failure to the Dutch desire to monopolize trade and to the friction between the envoy and the captain— Krusenstern, like Catherine the Great, being unimpressed by prospects of trade with Japan. Yet there is no reason to assume that, even with the cooperation of the Dutch and with more support on the part of Krusenstern, greater diplomatic skill and patience alone would have sufficed to dissuade the Shogunate from the, by now, traditional seclusion policy. Voenskii suggests that, had Rezanov come at the head of a strong naval squadron, he might have opened Japan half a century before an American show of force did so. One must not

---

[66] Atherton, 657-659; Dumas Malone, *Dictionary of American Biography*, xv, 523-524.
[67] Avrahm Yarmolinsky, "A rambling note on the 'Russian Columbus' Nikolai Petrovich Rezanov," 710; Tikhmenev, 2: 233.

forget, however, that Commodore Matthew Calbraith Perry, the American negotiator, was not acting in a political vacuum in the 1850's. The threat of force on his part was accentuated by British and French naval successes in China in the 1840's, by the pressure of a Russian fleet in Japanese waters, and the expectation of men-of-war from other countries. Actually Rezanov had not failed as miserably as he himself had assumed. Humiliated though he felt, he had been asked to do no more than to conform to the etiquette of the country and, in fact, had not been forced to do so. From the Japanese point of view, he had been permitted to abide by European customs. At their rudest, the Japanese officials had treated him with greater respect than some of his own mutinous subordinates. His diplomatic efforts had made a more favorable impression on the Japanese than on his own countrymen, so much so that Marquis Okuma Shigenobu, one time Prime Minister of Japan, expressed the view in later years that it was Rezanov who first really demonstrated to the Japanese the need of opening the country.[68]

Rezanov did not resort to force during his negotiations, yet as he left Japan he made plans to castigate the Japanese into submission. This decision was prodded by personal slight and by the feeling that his country and Emperor had been insulted. Above all, Rezanov's decision was a desperate effort to open Japan to trade, for he regarded such trade with Japan not merely as a source of additional profit for his Company and himself, but as the only satisfactory means of supplying the "breadless" Russian colonies along the Pacific. His decision to undertake hostilities against Japan seems to have matured on his way from Kamchatka to Novo-Arkhangelsk. As he sailed aboard the *Mariia Magdalena,* he associated with two young naval officers in the service of the Russian-American Company: Lieutenant Nikolai Khvostov and Ensign Gavriil Davydov. In conversation with them, he developed his plans. On July 30, 1805, he reported in a letter to Emperor Alexander I, that, having strengthened the American establishments and having built new vessels, it was now possible "to force the Japanese to open trade, which their people desires very strongly." Expressing confidence that Alexander would not disapprove, he conveyed the intention next year to set out with his "worthy collaborators" Khvostov and Davydov for the shores of Japan in order to destroy the Japanese settlement on Matsumae,

[68] Novakovskii, 100-104; Barthold, *Geographische,* 125; *Kojiruien,* XXVIII, 54.

dislodge the Japanese from Sakhalin, and spread terror along their shores, and, having deprived them of their fishery and food, to force them to enter into trade relations with Russia. With a touch of doubt, he claimed readiness to be punished as a criminal for having acted without orders, but ended on the ringing note that "my conscience will upbraid me still more, if I shall let time pass in vain and not sacrifice to Your glory."[69]

Rezanov's decision was not "anti-Japanese." He had his quarrel with those who had rebuffed him, but he thought, as he noted in the letter, that the Japanese people desired relations with Russia. As a matter of fact, he had reason to believe that this was the wish of some officials in the government itself and that strong measures on his part would enable this faction to gain the upper hand. This conviction can be traced to a conversation he had with a Megasaki official several days before his departure from Japan. The official had informed him that, in 1792, the Shogun and his advisers had sincerely planned to trade with the Russians, when the Nagasaki Permit was handed to Laxman. But as the years passed and the expected Russian vessels failed to appear, rival officials had gained influence. When Rezanov arrived, the Megasaki officials asserted, the Shogun had wished to receive him, but his advisers had insisted that imperial sanction be procured. The Emperor in turn was said to have called together over two hundred lords for advice. These failed to agree among themselves and the Emperor had had to make his own decision. Allegedly, he had declared the permission given to Laxman an insult to himself, for he had not been consulted, and made the whole question an internal political issue. Unwilling to precipitate an open break with the Emperor and reluctant to assert his dominance by force, the shogun had found it necessary to rebuff Rezanov. Rezanov thus considered military action not solely as a means of retribution and intimidation, but also as indirect support of the Shogunate in its struggle with the seemingly more anti-foreign imperial forces.[70]

---

[69] Tikhmenev, 1: 154; Novakovskii, 112-113.

[70] Voenskii (October), 234-235; Golownin, *Memoirs*, III, 279 (pages 253 to 302 are devoted to Vice-Admiral Schischkoff [Shishkov]'s "Account of the Voyages of Messrs. Chwostoff and Dawidoff"). Kurihara Ken expresses the thought that Japan can be thankful that Russia's preoccupation with Napoleon limited Rezanov's military resources to those of the Russian-American Company. (Yano, 169-170.) It is unlikely that the tsarist government should have abetted the aggressive plans of Rezanov under any circumstances, as they were counter to traditional policy toward Japan; the government was sincere in condemning and disassociating itself from the activities of Khvostov and Davydov.

Rezanov mentioned Sakhalin in his letter to Alexander I. It is possible that he had discussed the importance of the island with Krusenstern as the *Nadezhda* had reconnoitered its shores on the way back from Japan. At any rate Krusenstern, like Rezanov, envisaged the annexation of Sakhalin. Krusenstern wrote: "Control over Aniwa can be gained without any resistance and the bay can be held easily since there are no troops either in the northern part of Ezo or on Sakhalin. One small battery of twelve cannons and one small warship would suffice to beat off an attack by the Japanese, if their Emperor would get the idea of sending troops from Matsumae to chase away the strangers—which, by the way, is an impossibility."[71] Rezanov believed that a fortified Russian colony on Sakhalin Island could keep the settlement on Matsumae in constant fear and thereby force the Japanese to seek commercial relations with the Russians. At the same time, such a Russian colony would cost nothing; it could pay for itself, indeed bring in profits, through hunting. The Japanese relied heavily on coastal shipping for transportation. Rezanov proposed that company vessels seize the supply-laden barges and cut Japan's life line. This, he was convinced, would arouse so much popular dissatisfaction in Japan that the government would be forced to come to terms with Russia.[72] Rezanov recalled that in the middle of the eighteenth century his countrymen had gained a foothold on Sakhalin, but he did not know what had happened to the colonists. The Japanese meanwhile had taken possession of the island, cruelly subjugating the natives. Rezanov wished to drive the Japanese off, and to raze their establishments to the ground, proclaiming the Ainu Russian subjects instead. In the process several Japanese were to be taken prisoner and a special effort was to be made to capture one of their priests and bring back a temple with all its statues and sacred utensils. This would make it possible, once the Japanese prisoners were taken to Okhotsk, to treat them particularly well, with their priest ministering to their spiritual needs. After a year, the Japanese were to be sent back to their homeland to tell their countrymen of the good treatment they had experienced and to inspire them with confidence in the Russians![73] Startling as the psychology of such an approach may be at first glance, on occasions it was to prove effective. Certainly it is an interesting link with the modern "brainwash-

[71] Sgibnev, "Popytki," 59.
[72] Tikhmenev, 1: 154-155.
[73] Golownin, iii, 279-280.

ing" of prisoners of war. Not all prisoners were thus to be repatriated, however. According to Golovnin, Rezanov planned the exploitation of Japanese prisoners for company work in America, selecting for their settlement a tiny island in Sitka sound, to this day called Japonski (Iaponskii or Japanese) Island.[74]

At Novo-Arkhangelsk Rezanov addressed the following letter to Khvostov and Davydov on September 10, 1805:

My dear gentlemen, Nikolai Aleksandrovich and Gavrilo Ivanovich:

Your first journey to America made me acquainted with your bold, enterprising spirit; your happy return to Europe is a proof of your talents; but your second journey hither convinced me, how deeply the sentiments of true patriotism are imprinted on your generous hearts. I have also had the pleasure of making some voyages with you, which have indelibly impressed upon my mind the agreeable conviction, that an exalted spirit esteems the public good beyond every thing. The commander in chief of this country is animated with the same zeal, the same spirit, which our posterity will one day appreciate more than we do. This happy meeting together of some persons, who labour to promote one end has induced me to undertake, next year, an expedition which may perhaps open a new channel in commerce, furnish this part of the world with the necessary subsistence, and to secure them from want. For this purpose we want two armed vessels, a brig, and a tender. They may be built here, and I have already given my directions for this purpose to the governor. I must now observe to you, Gentlemen, that these first ships, for this first expedition, must have first-rate officers: as I am no seaman, I can only bear testimony to your exertions, your activity, and your success. Without attempting to penetrate deeper into this science, to which I am wholly a stranger, I can judge only by comparison, and by what I have seen, and I am convinced, that your journals fully answer my opinion. I shall not cease to have the highest respect for the great and noble actions, which in the eyes of all who love their country, place you among the most distinguished officers; I therefore now intreat you as my friends, who, are ready to sacrifice themselves to the general good, to which we so willingly devote ourselves, to be ready to take the command of the vessels in question, and to divide it between you according to your rank; for this purpose to proceed immediately to examine the drawings which the master-shipwrights will exhibit, and when you have approved of them, take upon you to superintend the building, so that they may be ready at the end of April, and we be able to sail at the beginning of May. I know that many obstacles arise, but when was a great enterprise ever accomplished without difficulties? They cannot deter us, and only add to our honor. I do not think it necessary to express myself more at length respecting this expedition, for which I shall give you, in due time, ample

[74] Novakovskii, 114.

instructions. The zeal of the workmen gives me hopes that the ships will be well built; the happy success of the undertaking is guaranteed by your experience and talents. I confess that I am impatient for the time which will call you to act; let us proceed with united endeavours, to the execution of this great enterprise, and let us shew the world that, in our happy age, a handful of bold Russians can equal those prodigious actions, to which millions of other nations attain only in a succession of Ages.

I have the honor to be, with the greatest respect,

Gentlemen,

Your devoted Servant,

Nikolai Rezanov.[75]

The purchase of the American sloop *Iunona*, on which, it will be recalled, Rezanov sailed to San Francisco in spring 1806, hastened preparations for the expedition against Japan, as only one vessel remained to be constructed. Even so, work progressed slowly, because Aleksandr Baranov, who supervised Company affairs in America, was reluctant to divert workmen from catching seal, and because he disapproved of hostilities against Japan. When Rezanov returned from California in June, the vessel was not yet completed. A month later the vessel was at last finished and named *Avos* ("Perhaps" or "It is to be hoped").

No reply—positive or negative—had as yet been received by Rezanov to his letter to Alexander I. The difficulty of ever obtaining sanction for his plans must have gradually impressed itself upon his conscience, for he began to sway in his determination. On August 2, 1806, when preparations for departure had been completed, Rezanov, who had planned to direct action against Japan personally, wrote Khvostov that he was unable to sail along, and that the tender would have to remain behind also. Rezanov did not cancel the expedition, but neither did he provide Khvostov with detailed instructions. Three days later he reassigned the tender to the expedition and, on August 6, departed himself with the vessel. On August 20, he changed his mind again and ordered Khvostov to take him to Okhotsk, so that he could hurry overland to St. Petersburg to report to the Emperor. But he reiterated his plans concerning Sakhalin and Japan. Davydov on the *Avos* was to head directly to the Kuril Islands and Sakhalin. There in Aniwa Bay or La Perouse Strait Khvostov on the *Iunona* was to rejoin him by October 9. If, for any reason, Khvostov should not reach the place of rendezvous in time, Davydov

---

[75] Golownin, III, 281-284; Novakovskii, 114-115. The references to time (beginning or end of a month) are in the old style.

was to commence hostilities on his own. Rezanov commanded that the expedition be cloaked in secrecy, all concerned being made to sign a promise not to reveal anything. Near Unalaska, one of the Aleutian Islands, the vessels separated, Davydov setting course for Uruppu Island, Rezanov and Khvostov for Okhotsk.[76]

At Okhotsk Rezanov went ashore. As he did so, he took with him the written instructions he had given Khvostov in order to elaborate on them. On October 6, as the *Iunona* lay ready for immediate departure, Rezanov sent back the instructions with the following note:

Upon your arrival at Okhotsk, I think it necessary to say something to you, respecting the instructions which have been given to you. The defect discovered in the foremast, and contrary winds, delayed our voyage. The lateness of the season therefore obliges you immediately to hasten to America. The time for your junction with the tender, in Aniwa Bay, is already past; the fishery there being ended, a happy result is not to be expected. When I consider all the circumstances I find it necessary that, disregarding all the instructions previously given, you sail to America, to increase the garrison of the harbor of Novo-Arkhangelsk. The *Avos* tender must, besides, return according to its instructions; but if the wind should allow you to put into Aniwa Bay, without losing time, endeavor to gain the natives of Sakhalin by presents and medals, and examine the situation of the Japanese settlements in that island. This alone, but particularly your return to America, will do you honor; the latter therefore must be the chief object of your exertions. You will give the same directions to the tender, in case you should meet with it. In general, you will doubtless find means to reconcile the unforeseen circumstances which may occur upon the voyage, with the interest of the company; and your talents and experience will doubtless tell you how this last direction may be best executed. On my part I regret extremely that this port does not afford means to change the mast, and that the concurrence of circumstances has induced me to change the plans.[77]

What did Rezanov want Khvostov to do? The supplementary note obscured his intentions. If Rezanov wished to cancel the expedition, why did he return the same instructions with the note? Why did he not substitute others in their stead? Would Rezanov have canceled such an expedition on the spur of the moment after having reported it already to the Emperor? It is true, the note claimed to supersede

[76] Golownin, III, 284-286; Sgibnev, "Popytki," 64; Novakovskii, 115; Atherton, 659-660.
[77] Signed Nikolai Rezanov, September 24 (October 6), 1806. No. 609; Golownin, III, 286-288; Sgibnev, "Popytki," 64. The text in the English version of Golovnin's narrative was accurate enough to be used here without modification except for the changing of place names to the forms used throughout the book.

all previous orders, but it left the way open for action on Sakhalin and in general was so filled with modifications that it was not clear at all whether Rezanov really wished to call off the whole project or merely to postpone it, if necessary. Khvostov hastened ashore to get an explanation from Rezanov, but the latter had already set out for the capital. Khvostov thought the matter over and decided that Rezanov had not intended to cancel the expedition, but merely to postpone it. He weighed the damages of the *Iunona*, the uncertainty of success, and the lateness of the season against the danger, which the unexpected delay would entail for the *Avos*, whether Davydov still expected him or had ventured to initiate hostilities on his own, and decided to carry out the original orders, his youthful appetite for glory whetted by the prospects of danger.[78]

On October 18, 1806, Khvostov reached Sakhalin Island. In Aniwa Bay he did not find the *Avos*, which had interrupted its voyage, because of bad weather and damages, and had pulled into Petropavlovsk. But he did find a Japanese vessel, riding at anchor off the small Japanese settlement at Kushunkotan. Khvostov effected a landing and, confronting a number of Japanese in their office, read them a proclamation. The Japanese could not understand it, of course, but they gathered from gestures that it was trade that the strangers demanded. Then the Russians seized four of the Japanese guards of the Matsumae clan, and carried them aboard the *Iunona*. They pillaged the warehouses taking rice, salt, sake, and other products. What they did not need they burned, setting fire to houses, vessels, and fishing nets. They even carried away the deity of a local temple.[79] At the entrance to the temple they posted a copper plate with a notice, to this effect:

1. It is unjust of the Japanese to hinder trade of the Russians on Sakhalin Island.

2. If the Japanese should change their decision and wish to trade, they can send notification thereof to Sakhalin Island or to Etorofu Island.

3. If the Japanese will persist for long in denying the just demand, the Russians will lay waste the northern part of Japan.[80]

It was the Japanese, whom Khvostov sought to intimidate; the Ainu he treated with consideration, and presented a written communication to the native chieftain:

[78] Golownin, *Memoirs*, III, 288-289; Sgibnev, "Popytki," 64.

[79] Sgibnev, "Popytki," 61-63; Novakovskii, 116; W. G. Aston, "Russian Descents into Saghalien and Itorup," 79.

[80] Novakovskii, 117; Aston, 79.

On October 12 (24), 1806 the Russian frigate *Iunona* under the command of Lieutenant Khvostov gave to the elder of the settlement on the western shore of Aniwa a medal on the Vladimir ribbon as a sign of taking the island Sakhalin and its inhabitants under the patronage of the Russian Emperor Alexander I. All other vessels, Russian or foreign, that may come in the future are to be asked to regard the elder as a Russian subject.[81]

By the end of October, Khvostov headed back for Kamchatka. Davydov was still in Petropavlovsk and they spent the winter together. On May 16, 1807, they cut their way through the ice and set out together to "liberate" the natives of the Kuril Islands from Japanese "tyranny" and acquire more loot in the process. They must have thought their actions justifiable, for they did not sneak away furtively, but dispatched a full report to the Minister of the Navy before departing. Hugging the Kuril Archipelago, one vessel on each side, Khvostov and Davydov reached Etorofu Island on May 30, and cast anchor in Naibo Bay. Two days later they landed.

Etorofu had been a Japanese colony for over a decade. It boasted a population of over a thousand Ainu, engaged mainly in salmon fishery, and a garrison of over three hundred Japanese of the Nambu and Tsugaru clans, not to mention five ladies and a sake brewer. The garrison was stationed at Shana, where a walled fortress had been erected. At Naibo, where Khvostov and Davydov first landed, there was only a small settlement.

The Russians landed in force, discharging cannons and muskets. They looted the guard house taking clothing and other property, then set fire to the Japanese settlement. Again, they sought to appease the Ainu and handed them the fish and salt they had plundered from the Japanese. When they finally withdrew to their ships, they dragged along several Japanese guards, whom they had succeeded in capturing. Among them was Nakagawa Goroji, who, having lived on Etorofu, had picked up some Russian, and had gone forth to meet the raiders in a vain attempt to negotiate with them.[82] So pleased were Khvostov and Davydov with their success that they named Naibo Bay "Dobroe Nachalo" (A good Beginning).[83]

[81] Sgibnev, "Popytki," 64; Vasilii Mikhailovich Golovnin, *Zapiski Vasiliia Mikhailovicha Golovnina v plenu u Iapontsev*, 1:102.

[82] Nakagawa by chance was to learn about smallpox vaccination in Russia. On his return to Japan this knowledge was to be of considerable benefit to his countrymen and turn the misfortune of his captivity into personal honor and renown. (Abe Masami, *Nakagawa Goroji to shuto denrai*, 23-24.)

[83] Sgibnev, "Popytki," 63-64; Novakovskii, 117-118; Inobe, 219-223; Aston, 81-82. For a map showing Russian raids in 1807, see *Hokkaido-shi*, II, 457.

On June 3, the *Iunona* and *Avos* weighed anchor. On the second day they appeared at Shana, the main stronghold. The attack on the Japanese settlement on Sakhalin Island the preceding year, had caused the Japanese to reinforce the garrison at Shana, and the Japanese who had hastened here from Naibo after the new raids brought warning of the impending threat. Guards were posted on all the neighboring headlands and watch fires were kept burning throughout the night. But the two chief officers of Shana were away, and Toda Matadae, on whom the responsibility of defense fell, hesitated to be the one to precipitate hostilities. Mamiya Rinzo, the famous Japanese explorer, who had been on the shores of Siberia, happened to be in Shana just then. He is said to have recognized the vessels as Russian men-of-war and to have urged Toda to open fire. When Toda notwithstanding the attack on Naibo, expressed the view that the intentions of the Russians might be peaceful and therefore he could not open fire, Mamiya shouted excitedly, "Quick! Quick! Shoot! We must chase them away at once!" But Toda prevailed over Mamiya and his colleagues, and sent an interpreter, accompanied by several Japanese and a number of Ainu, to meet the Russians and ask what they wanted.

Khvostov and Davydov were not inhibited by diplomatic niceties. They opened fire on the would-be negotiators, wounding the interpreter and killing one of the Ainu. Thereupon the Japanese returned fire and a general engagement ensued. The fortress was protected by several cannons of small caliber, but, due to their emplacement, they could be pointed in one direction only. The fortress was manned by over two hundred soldiers, equipped with matchlocks and bows. They did not attempt to overrun the Russian landing party, which numbered less than thirty sailors, but were satisfied with holding the Russians at bay. A relatively harmless duel followed, with the Russians firing from behind the shelter of an oil-pressing shed on the beach, and the Japanese from behind the walls of the fortress about a hundred and sixty yards away. After two hours of shooting, only one Russian and two Japanese were killed and several persons wounded. When the Russians ran out of ammunition they withdrew to their vessels. The Japanese were so relieved at the retreat of the Russians, that they did not bother to light the usual watchfires. At night, under cover of darkness, the Russians sneaked ashore again and made their way to the fortress unnoticed. When they suddenly opened fire, the Japanese were overcome by panic and took to the hills with the shout *"ware ichi"*—each one for himself! Mamiya

Rinzo, who had warned Toda not to trust the Russians was right there with the others, propelled by a Russian bullet in his buttocks. The Japanese laboriously made their way to the western shore of the island, from there to Kunashiri and eventually to Hakodate. Toda, who had fled to the hills, was no longer with them. Unable to bear the smart of the garrison's ignominious flight, he had disembowelled himself. Yet such was the bitterness of his countrymen, that one of his comrades could not resist the remark that rather than die like a dog, he should have died like a hero, facing the enemy.[84]

The Russians could not believe that the whole garrison had fled. Fearing a trap, they did not venture into the fortress until dawn. When they saw that it was really deserted, they swarmed in and hauled off its stores of rice, shoyu, and sake. Triumphantly they took the ornamental spears and halberds, which the Japanese had proudly placed at the gates of the fortress. They began drinking some of the sake, and soon the glory of victory turned into boisterous drunkenness. They burned everything—the fortress, the houses, the brewery, the Ainu huts. Traditionally the Japanese had called the Russians *"aka-hito"* or Red Men, because, as some say, their hair appeared red, or because, as others suggest, they wore red coats. So complete was the desolation, so humiliating the defeat inflicted by Khvostov and Davydov that henceforth the Russians came to be known as *"aka-oni"* or Red Devils.

When the raiders withdrew, two remained behind in a shed, asleep in a drunken stupor. They were never to awaken, for several Ainu and a Japanese, who returned after the other Russians had withdrawn, speared them to death. Their heads were cut off and salted, then sent to Hakodate together with their weapons and clothing—grisly mementos of an ambassador's revenge.[85]

On June 8, the *Iunona* and *Avos* weighed anchor and sailed to Uruppu. Not a single survivor was found here in the settlement be-

[84] The lack of courage displayed by the Japanese soldiery in the early nineteenth century was a reflection of the protracted peace with which Japan had been blessed during the Seclusion Period. It contrasted sharply with Japanese reaction to the Mongol invasions in the late thirteenth century and with Japanese militarism in the years following the opening of the country. Japanese satirists were quick to lampoon in verse and song the spineless efforts of their fleet-footed guardians. See Fukase Shunichi, "Bunka Roko jiken to rakushu."

[85] On June 6, 1807, the American merchant vessel *Eclipse* arrived in Nagasaki under Russian colors, commissioned by some official of the Russian-American Company to open trade relations with Japan. Upon advice of the Dutch factor, who hastened out to the ship and warned of Japanese anger at the Russian raids, Captain Joseph O'Kean quickly lowered the Russian flag and concealed the Muscovite supercargo. (Harry Emerson Wildes, *Aliens in the East*, 148-149.)

gun by Vasilii Zvezdochetov in 1795, only the traces of buildings and a board with the notice that, until 1803 all had gone well, but that thereafter illness and death had overtaken Zvezdochetov and some of his party, and that the remainder had decided to leave. From Uruppu Khvostov and Davydov proceeded southward again. They rounded the northwestern part of Hokkaido and, entering Tsugaru Strait from the west, sailed past Hakodate. They made no attempt to attack the city, but when they came upon a war junk, promptly opened fire. The Japanese made no attempt to fight back; they jumped into boats and rowed frantically ashore. The Russians removed whatever they wanted, then set fire to the junk. After this incident they headed back to Sakhalin and, on June 23, cast anchor in Aniwa Bay at the settlement of Rutaka, not far from Kushunkotan. The Matsumae clansmen, who had been here, had fled after the raid on Kushunko-tan, and the Russians were assured by the Ainu that no Japanese had been back since the previous year. Just for good measure, how-ever, the Russians picked out buildings which appeared to be Jap-anese, at Rutaka and elsewhere in the bay, and destroyed them. On the 27th, they came upon a deserted factory, looked it over, took several iron kettles, and set fire to the buildings. From Sakhalin, Khvostov and Davydov headed toward Hokkaido again. At Rishiri Island, near the entrance to Soya Harbor, they intercepted four Jap-anese vessels (two of the Shogunate, two of the Matsumae clan), laden with supplies for local garrisons. They appropriated the rich cargo, and destroyed the ships. In the booty there was allegedly a ten-pounder bronze cannon, captured by Toyotomi Hideyoshi from the Koreans in the closing years of the sixteenth century. By now the *Iunona* and *Avos* were loaded to the gunwales with booty, and Khvostov and Davydov were ready to leave the shores of Japan.[86] They released all but two of the prisoners they had taken on Sakhalin and Etorofu, and sent them ashore with a written declaration in broken Japanese to the following effect:

TO THE GOVERNOR OF MATSUMAE

The distance between Russia and Japan being but small, our Emperor sent his officers across the sea to request that trade between the two coun-tries might be permitted. If due inquiry had been made and a treaty of commerce concluded, all would have been well, but although our officers went repeatedly to Nagasaki they were sent away without an answer. Then things took an unpleasant turn, and our Emperor commanded us to give

[86] Inobe, 219-223; Sgibnev, "Popytki," 64-65; Novakovskii, 118-121; Aston, 82-86.

you a specimen of his power in return for your refusing to listen to his first request. If you persist in refusing his offers we will take all your northern territory away from you and if possible get an answer out of you in that way. The Red Men can always come to Sakhalin and Etorofu and chase you about.

If you comply with our wishes, we shall always be good friends with you; if not, we will come again with more ships and behave in the same way as we have done before this year.

Oroshiya [Russia].[87]

With this written declaration, Khvostov and Davydov sent ashore the oral message: that a reply should be sent to Sakhalin, Etorofu, or Uruppu. Then Khvostov and Davydov exchanged congratulatory gun salutes and started back for Okhotsk, where they arrived safely, on July 28.

Proud of having carried out Rezanov's original instructions in spite of the obstacles, which had been the alleged reason for his later indecision, Khvostov and Davydov looked forward to informing Rezanov and the government of their success. But Rezanov had never reached the capital. His return to Okhotsk from Novo-Arkhangelsk had been delayed, because Baranov, the manager, had failed to work

[87] I have cited here the version given by Aston (86), except for a slight modification in the spelling of place names. A somewhat different version appears in Okamoto's *Nichi-Ro kosho Hokkaido shiko*. Pozdneev gives the alleged original *kana* text, so poor in grammar and presentation, which Okamoto uses, together with a corrected clearer Japanese rendition. (Pozdneev, II, 2: 176-178.) These differ somewhat from the text which I have cited, but as Pozdneev notes, it is impossible to determine which of the various Japanese sources is more reliable. Still another version is given by Russian sources (Polonskii, 560):

"The neighborhood of Russia and Japan compelled one to desire friendly relations for the true well-being of the latter empire, for which purpose an embassy was sent also to Nagasaki; but its rejection, insulting to Russia, and the spreading of trade of the Japanese over the Kuril Islands and Sakhalin, as to possessions of the Russian Empire, forced this power to use at last other measures, which will show that the Russians can always inflict harm on Japanese commerce until such time, as they will be informed through the inhabitants of Uruppu or Sakhalin of the desire of trade with us. The Russians having this time inflicted such slight harm to the Japanese empire wanted only to show them thereby, that the northern territories of the latter can always be harmed by them and that further obstinacy of the Japanese government may deprive it completely of these lands."

The general meaning of the different versions is the same. They threaten the Japanese in the name of the Russian government. The version translated from Polonskii is worthy of quotation for the additional claim it lays on Russian possession of Sakhalin and the Kuril Islands. No distinction is made between the northern and southern Kuril Islands, though it is demanded that Japanese communication be sent to Sakhalin or Uruppu, not, as in the oral message cited by Aston, also to Etorofu, one of the southern islands. Japanese officials in later years stated that the Dutch, when consulted about the letter, had boosted the rank of Khvostov, adding spuriously that the Russians planned to conquer the Japanese and to send missionaries to Christianize them. (Golovnin, *Zapiski*, II, 103-104 footnote.)

on the construction of the *Avos* during Rezanov's visit to California—because he thought it better to use the men to hunt seals, and because he did not want trouble with Japan—and Rezanov had dallied to see through its completion. This delay proved fatal. Rezanov's health, which California's climate and Concha Argüello's charm had done much to improve, had been sapped again by the damp air of Sitka. He had not regained his strength, when he had set out on horseback from Okhotsk. Langsdorff, who had accompanied Rezanov to America as his personal physician, had deserted him at Sitka. Without medical advice Rezanov had pushed on through the wild wintry wastes of eastern Siberia, from sick-bed to sick-bed, until on March 13, 1807, he had finally died at Krasnoiarsk.[88]

There exist sharply different views as to the character and talents of Rezanov. Many were his critics among his own countrymen, not the least of them Captain Vasilii Mikhailovich Golovnin, a man of good and generally calm judgment, who wrote of Rezanov: "he was a quick-tempered and impetuous man, an inventive scribbler, a man of many words, having a head more able to build castles in the air than to consider and execute well-founded plans, and who lacked completely either the patience or the ability to achieve great and distant goals."[89] A contrary view was expressed by an American writer who speculated on the might-have-beens had Rezanov not died prematurely:

It was forty years before the United States was strong enough to take possession of California, and it is possible that the towering ambition of Rezanov would have acknowledged no bounds short of the Rocky Mountains . . . Rezanov's greater schemes have since become more definitely known, and no one that had studied his life and character can doubt that, had he lived ten years longer, what is now the Western section of the United States, as well as British Columbia, would be Russian territory. Perhaps a war would have been the result, perhaps not. The Russians had forty years in which to plant themselves as firmly as the Mexicans, and the British in Canada.[90]

Certainly Rezanov's death robbed Russia of one of her most ardent empire builders and deprived Khvostov and Davydov of an advocate before the imperial government.

---

[88] Atherton, 659-661; Russell, 86. Early accounts including that rendered by Mr. Russell state that Rezanov's death was precipitated by a fall from his horse. Miss Atherton challenges this. Concha Argüello, by the way, waited for Rezanov. When she was at last convinced of his death, she took holy orders, becoming California's first nun.

[89] Golovnin, "Zapiska," 86.

[90] Atherton, 660-661.

Whatever chances of gaining imperial approval Khvostov and Davydov may still have had, were ruined, upon their return, by the greed of Captain Bukharin, the commandant of Okhotsk. Stories, much adorned, of their exploits had preceded them to Okhotsk. Believing the vessels to be filled with gold and other treasures, Bukharin, who was notorious for his cruelty and autocratic use of power, arrested everyone on board the moment the ships entered port, under the convenient pretext that Khvostov and Davydov had acted without authority. As "state prisoners," Khvostov and Davydov were thrown into jail and deprived of everything down to their very clothing and shoes. While Bukharin rejoiced in the harvest of rice, sake, clothing and weapons that had come his way (worth, by his own appraisal, about 18,000 rubles), Khvostov and Davydov suffered harsh, inhuman treatment, the worse for refusing to answer questions about the expedition on the ground that their instructions had been secret. The other officers gave replies that were rather evasive, but the lower ranks were frightened into supplying the desired details. Khvostov and Davydov succeeded in smuggling out word of their predicament to Irkutsk, but it would take at least five or six months before orders for their release could be expected from St. Petersburg and, chances were, they would be dead from hunger and disease by then. Flight seemed the only road to survival. Though they were kept apart and did not even know of each other's fate, were constantly watched by guards with drawn swords, they managed to get away with the help of the inhabitants of Okhotsk and the guards themselves, who hated the commandant.

Leaving behind notes that they had drugged the guards, Khvostov and Davydov commenced their arduous journey to Yakutsk, almost six hundred miles away, on September 29. Traveling on foot, supplied by friendly hands with guns and biscuits, they actually regained some of the strength of which two months of confinement had robbed them. But not for long; emaciated by want, struggling with great hardships, they reached Yakutsk, on October 25, covered in rags and utterly exhausted. Their escape had been reported from Okhotsk, and they were detained and searched for gold. But they received permission to address a communication to Irkutsk, and Governor Treskin had them come to that city at the beginning of 1808. Thanks to the support of Treskin, the good-will of Governor General Pestel, and orders from St. Petersburg, where their letters had been received,

Khvostov and Davydov continued their journey to the capital. There Minister of Commerce Count Rumiantsev, who had supplied Rezanov with the instructions for his mission to Japan, was entrusted with an investigation of the whole affair. Rumiantsev condoned the actions of Khvostov and Davydov and, on August 21, Alexander I decreed that they not be held accountable for the raids and that their complaints about Bukharin be presented to the Admiralty for review. But the Admiralty, took a very different view of things: it acquitted Bukharin and courtmartialed Khvostov and Davydov. Meanwhile, Khvostov and Davydov had joined the campaign, in which Russia wrested Finland from Sweden, and had so distinguished themselves in battle that, notwithstanding the findings of the courtmartial, they were not punished. In all fairness to Khvostov and Davydov, one should add that they had acted less as buccaneers, out to kill and plunder, than as officers carrying out the spirit of Rezanov's orders. And the nineteenth century was a century of gun-boat diplomacy.

Their own recklessness shortly put an end to Khvostov and Davydov's adventurous careers. In reward for their exceptional prowess in the Finnish campaign they were permitted to return to St. Petersburg for a rest. On October 16, 1809, they attended a farewell party for Captain Wolf from whom they had bought the *Iunona* and who, having arrived from the United States, was about to continue to Kronstadt. The get-together was at the house of Professor von Langsdorff, who was living on Vasil'evskii Island. As they were returning in the early hours of the morning, they found the draw-bridge over the Neva River open. A ship was just passing through and in their hurry, emboldened perhaps by the inevitable farewell toasts, they tried to jump aboard the vessel and from the vessel to the other side of the river again, but in the darkness of the night, missed their footing, fell into the river, and were drowned.[91]

If the "warnings" of Benyovszky had gone unheeded, the raids of Khvostov and Davydov gave cause for real alarm. The impact of Russian aggression was tremendous. The copper plate posted on Sakhalin was taken as a declaration of war and attacks were expected

[91] Sgibnev, "Popytki," 65-66; Novakovskii, 121-123; Golovnin, *Memoirs*, III, 290-302; Pozdneev, II, 2: 233-234. According to Langsdorff, Khvostov and Davydov actually passed the bridge and called to him and Captain Wolf that they had gotten across safely, but for some reason or other must have tried to get back to them again. The death of Khvostov and Davydov is bemoaned in poetry by Anna Volkova and by A. Sh. (Shishkov?). See Gavrilo Ivanovich Davydov, *Dvukratnoe puteshestvie v Ameriku morskikh ofitserov Khvostova i Davydova*, I, xliii-xlv.

on Edo, the seat of the Shogunate itself, popular imagination identifying the Russians with the Red Devils, portrayed in Buddhist pictures of Hell. The letter to the governor of Matsumae was a warning of things to come. Feverishly the Japanese prepared to meet the Russian onslaught. As in the case of Benyovszky's "warnings," the Japanese turned to the Dutch for an explanation. The Dutch promised to delve into the true causes of the raids, but Europe's absorption in the struggle against Napoleon and the aftermath of war and peace frustrated these efforts until 1818.[92] By then another incident had elicited an explanation from the Russian authorities.

[92] Philipp Franz von Siebold, *Nippon*, I, 22-23 note 9.

CHAPTER SIX · JAPANESE REACTION

THE GREAT DEBATE

THE Japanese spoke of the sacredness and inviolability, of the unalterableness of their ancestral laws, giving the impression that the seclusion policy had remained unchanged since its inception. This was misleading, for the seclusion decrees themselves had evolved only gradually, and not so much in response to certain principles or theories as to the empirical demands of the situation. Even when isolation had become a national policy, enforcement varied, and despite the absolute power of the Tokugawa Shogunate and its totalitarian repression of criticism and dissent, there were repeated calls from within the country for the reestablishment of commercial relations with the Western world.

It must be kept in mind that Japan had embarked on her policy of seclusion without enthusiasm, that, essentially, she had been forced by outside pressure to seek security in isolation, a policy which, however justified at the time, ran counter to the natural needs of the Japanese economy and the interests of the Japanese people. The first edicts did not envisage total isolation, but excluded merely Roman Catholics and Portuguese. The dangers inherent in the unfavorable balance of trade and in the uncontrollable importation of firearms led the government to adopt increasingly sweeping measures, but by the end of the eighteenth century there was as yet no question of "unalterable" seclusion laws and the whole concept of *sakoku-shugi* ("Closed-country-ism") or isolationism developed only gradually. Even then a limited contact was kept up with the Dutch and the Chinese. There was at first no ideological basis for opposition to foreign trade; whatever restrictions were imposed on commerce with the Dutch and the Chinese were purely economic. Only by the middle of the Tokugawa period did these restrictions become part of the physiocratic framework of Confucianist philosophers, but by then they were challenged by political economists of the realist school. As early as 1720 the prohibitions against Western books and learning were modified sufficiently by Shogun Tokugawa Yoshimune to permit the study of Western medicine, geography, and military science, and, by the third quarter of the eighteenth century, a leading Japanese statesman actually attempted to circumvent the seclusion policy.[1]

This Japanese statesman was Tanuma Okitsugu, the most important minister in the administration of Shogun Tokugawa Ieharu from
1760 to 1786. A very capable and ambitious man, he had risen to a
high position from the lower stratum of the samurai class and was,
for that reason, less preoccupied with tradition and orthodoxy than
with practical considerations. One of his most noteworthy policies
was the attempt to displace the agrarian base of Japanese finances by
a commercial one, and he managed temporarily to turn the Deshima
trade into profit for Japan. When the Russians pushed down the
Kuril Islands to the very shores of Hokkaido in the 1770's, Tanuma
appraised their arrival as a great opportunity to develop foreign
trade, and gave serious consideration to entering into commercial
relations with them. His motivation was twofold: to increase the
wealth of Japan and to forestall Russian expansion. As Professor John
Whitney Hall has pointed out in his excellent study of this era, "the
Tanuma period thus offers us the prospect that Japan might have
abandoned her seclusion policy voluntarily over a half century before
she was eventually forced to do so."[2]

Tanuma's view of Russia's advance as a welcome opportunity rather
than a threat, was shared by others. Kudo Heisuke, a Sendai physician, for example, submitted to Tanuma the noted essay *Akaezo
fusetsu ko* (A Study of Red Ainu [i.e. Russian] Reports), in which
he attributed to the Russians primarily commercial designs. To be
sure, he advocated the development and colonization of Hokkaido
to forestall Russian expansion, but he laid much greater stress on
the economic benefits that would accrue from such action. Soft-
pedalling any political implications, Kudo advocated the granting of
commercial rights to Russia as a means of developing Japan's northern regions and of breaking the economically undesirable commercial
monopoly of the Dutch.[3] This position was not as radical as may
appear at first glance. In a sense it was not much more than a plea
for the legalization of a situation that already existed, since a flourishing secret trade was actually carried on in the north.[4] What Kudo
suggested was that the government cash in on the profits of this trade.

1 Ramming, *Reisen*, 67-70; John Whitney Hall, *Tanuma Okitsugu*, 83-84, 88-89;
Keene, 17.
2 Hall, 63, 90.
3 John A. Harrison, *Japan's Northern Frontier*, 17; Otomo Kisaku, *Tai-Ro kokubo no
ransho*, 1-23; *Hokkaido-shi*, II, 281-283.
4 Notwithstanding the meeting of 1779, at which the Russians were directed to Nagasaki, they and various Japanese merchants seem to have contrived to do business in the

The northern regions were still in the hands of the Lord of Matsumae, who was exempt from the usual supervision and control of the Shogunate. Matsumae clansmen had established themselves at Akkeshi in the first half of the seventeenth century, in Kiitappu (the Nemuro region) in 1701, and on Kunashiri Island in 1754, trading not only with the natives of these places, but also with Ainu, who came from Etorofu. Among the latter there were some who had hunted on Uruppu and on islands to the north; these brought word of the Russians. But the officials of the Matsumae clan were anxious to remain free from government interference and eager to keep for themselves whatever profits they might reap from the forbidden trade. They hesitated, therefore, to pass on to Edo reports that they themselves received about Russian activities on the Kuril Islands. Such news could not be kept from the ears of the Shogunate indefinitely and the "warning" of Benyovszky, reinforced by Dutch reports about the Russian study of the Japanese language, conspired to focus the attention of the government on the northern regions, but, even then, not as urgently, as might be expected in retrospect.

The Japanese population of Hokkaido was small (less than twenty-seven thousand in 1765) and was concentrated in the southwest; the number of warriors was a fraction thereof. There were some thirty thousand Ainu in the region, but their loyalty and military usefulness were uncertain. Aside from such considerations as inadequate communications, whether by land or by sea, the Matsumae clan did not have either the manpower or the finances to take sufficient defense measures of its own. It was therefore all the more reprehensible that it continued to withhold information of the Russian advances from the central government; on the other hand it appears that the latter was equally remiss in not conveying Benyovszky's "warning" to the Matsumae authorities. In the words of a modern Japanese historian, "to keep things secret was a bad habit of the time of high and low and one cannot blame solely Matsumae." The Shogunate itself did not really pay much heed to reports of the Russian advance, until private scholars became increasingly vociferous in their harangues regarding the Russian menace.[5]

---

northern regions. Needless to say, the illegality of the proceedings made secrecy necessary, and this secrecy makes it difficult to find reliable information on this subject. (Ebina, "Kaikoku-ron no ransho," 4: 375-377.)

[5] Kono, 18-33; *Hokkaido-shi*, II, 279-280. News of Russian activity was slow in reaching even the Matsumae authorities. Reports of Russian hunting on Uruppu in 1768

An inquiry concerning conditions in the north, which the government directed to Matsumae, after studying Kudo's memorial, evoked such vague and evidently evasive response that the Shogunate, in 1785, sent out a large expedition to investigate Ezo, the Kurils, and Sakhalin at first hand. Though the Matsumae officials and contractors sabotaged the efforts of the expedition, threatening to kill the Ainu, if they told of the secret relations with Russia, the investigators established that the Japanese on Hokkaido traded with Manchuria and with Russia through the Ainu, that the Russians were in possession of all the Kuril Islands north of Etorofu, and that they frequented the latter island to hunt and trade, often staying for the winter. The recommendations which grew out of this expedition, as presented to the Shogunate by Tanuma's Superintendent of Finance Matsumoto, did not support Kudo's proposal for the legalization of the secret trade; they urged its suppression on the grounds that Japanese demands could be satisfied at Nagasaki and that additional trade might once again turn the balance against Japan. Had Tanuma remained in power longer, it is conceivable that, notwithstanding this report, commercial relations with Russia might have been sanctioned eventually, but his displacement by Matsudaira Sadanobu in 1786 spelled victory for conservatism and the enforcement, with renewed vigor, of the seclusion policy.[6]

While news of the appearance of Russians in the north had not filled Tanuma and Kudo with apprehension, scholars of a more alarmist disposition soon took up their brush to agitate against the Russian menace—and, at the same time, against the Shogunate, which had neglected to take appropriate defense measures. By the end of the eighteenth century some of the advocates of national defense (which to them meant not only the construction of modern coastal fortifications and a navy, but also preventive colonization and territorial expansion) had become so outspoken, that their treatises—a whole body of defense literature—verged on what an American historian has characterized as "a condition of near hysteria."[7]

---

did not find their way to Matsumae until three years later. For a bibliographical description of Japanese studies of "the Russian problem" (ranging from geographical data to questions of national defense), see Kaikoku Hyakunen Kinen Bunka Jigyo-kai, 384-397.

[6] Hall, 100-105, 141; Ramming, *Reisen*, 18-19; Kono, 668-669; Keene, 46-48.

[7] Harrison, *Japan's Northern Frontier*, 17. For a convenient compilation of this defense literature, see Otomo, *Tai-Ro kokubo no ransho*; see also Suematsu Yasukazu, *Kinsei ni okeru hokuho mondai no shinten*.

Most prominent among the advocates of coastal defense was Hayashi (Rin) Shihei, the author of a study of Korea, Ezo, and the Liu Ch'iu islands and of *Kaikoku Heidan* (Military discussion regarding a Maritime Nation), a work completed on the eve of the arrival of the Laxman expedition. In it Hayashi voiced fear and hatred concerning the motives of Benyovszky, warned against Russian encroachment in the north, and, envisaging even the possibility of a Russian attack on Japan, developed the thesis that Japan's position as an island nation called for measures of defense unlike those of China, which still served as model for the Japanese officialdom, and, taking public issue with the shogunate's prohibition against the building of large vessels, advocated the construction of a navy. In themselves, Hayashi's views were not particularly objectionable to Tanuma's successor, Chief State Councillor Matsudaira Sadanobu, who himself became known as an ardent advocate of coastal defense. But the way in which Hayashi had taken his case to the public, rather than submitting it to the government through proper channels in the manner of Kudo, aroused the anger of the government and he was deprived of his liberty and effectively silenced.[8] Other writers, however, continued to advocate stronger defense measures. Nakai Riken, an influential historian, thought to immunize Japan from Russian encroachment by depriving Russia of the incentive of becoming an immediate neighbor; it was his proposal to make Ezo, desolate and unattractive, a buffer state. But Habuto Seiyo and most other writers on this subject argued, as had Kudo, that Japan must firmly extend her sway to Ezo before the Russians did so, and advocated preventive colonization and expansion in the northwest as measures of defense.[9] Far reaching as some of these proposals were, they were more moderate in tone than Hayashi's had been, and though they were directed primarily against Russia, it was with less animosity than admiration that their authors spoke of the Russians. Often their warnings were garbed in poetic form:

Hakodate no	Guardians of Hakodate,
Seki no fusemori	Beware!
Kokoro seyo	This is not the kind of an age,
Nami nomi yosuru	When only waves wash ashore.
Yo ni shi araneba.[10]	(Mito Rekko)

8 Keene, 48-55; Novakovskii, 59-60; Pozdneev, II, 3: 28-39.
9 Kuno, II, 228-229.
10 Pozdneev, II, 3: 54.

The arrival of the Laxman expedition at the shores of Hokkaido gave added urgency to defense deliberations; at the same time, it forced on the Shogunate an immediate reconsideration of the seclusion policy and the necessity of some sort of decision. It is significant that Matsudaira did not reject Russian overtures outright; nor did he himself in his own mind apply the seclusion laws without question. Instead, Matsudaira carefully reviewed the circumstances under which the foreigners, who, like the Russians, had come, since the closing of the country, to request trade relations, had been turned away. He concluded that the rejection of the English, in 1674, and of the Portuguese, in 1685, was not a suitable precedent for deciding the Russian request, since the Russians had no affiliation with those, whose activities had precipitated the whole seclusion policy; since they seemed to follow a different and less aggressive brand of Christianity and deserved a certain amount of gratitude for having brought back the Japanese castaways. His advisers were divided in counsel. One suggested that trade be permitted in the north; another that the castaways be accepted, but no further relations be entertained; a third that the Russians be directed to Nagasaki. It was this last advice that Matsudaira followed, after finding a parallel in the Laxman expedition and the embassy sent by the King of Cambodia in 1727, the Japanese at that time having refused the king's presents, but having granted to the expedition a permit for entering Nagasaki. The Cambodians had not followed up the permit; it so happened that Laxman did not take advantage of it either. No doubt Matsudaira was relieved, but this does not mean that the permit was no more than a face-saving rejection of Laxman. As an American scholar has pointed out, "it seems likely that had he sailed immediately to Nagasaki, an agreement might have been reached."[11]

Whatever the motivations of Matsudaira's issuance of the Nagasaki Permit may have been—whether or not he would have agreed to trade or whether he merely played for time—he awakened to the urgency of coastal defense and mapped out plans for the strengthening of seaboard regions on the ground that "an invasion of our frontiers by foreign barbarians can be expected at any moment." He stressed shogunate initiative, and the planning and supervision of national defense. Whenever local daimyo lacked funds for the maintenance of fortifications and troops, the government was to give the necessary assistance. He emphasized the importance of defenses at Shimoda,

11 Keene, 65-66.

gateway to Uraga and Shinagawa. He wanted the territories of the Nambu and Tsugaru clans, leading to the possessions of Matsumae, placed under central government control. There were an excessive number of officials in Nagasaki—why not transfer them to Nambu? Matsudaira Sadanobu stated that the guns for defenses must be of bronze. There was a bronze reservoir in Osaka. He suggested that it be replaced by one of stone, and the bronze melted and made into cannons.[12] Conscious of the dangers which lurked abroad and wishing to be reminded of them constantly, Matsudaira commissioned an artist to draw the picture of a foreign vessel, and himself inscribed this poetic warning:

Kono fune no	Not to forget
Yoru cho koto wo	Even for one moment of sleep
Yume no ma mo	That these vessels can come here,
Wasurenu wa	Is of utmost importance to the
Yo no takara narikeri[13]	world [Japan].

In 1793, the repatriated castaways Kodayu and Isokichi were interrogated by the Shogun's personal physician Katsuragawa Hoshu and by a number of other dignitaries, among them Matsudaira, in the presence of the Shogun, who deigned to peep at the proceedings from behind a bamboo curtain. Kodayu told of his reception by Catherine the Great. He recalled not only the numerous officials, who had crowded the palace halls, but also the court ladies, "white as snow," at whose sight he had become very shy, and how he had been led up to the Empress and had "licked" her hand, as she had graciously offered him the tips of her fingers. Kodayu reported about life in Siberia and in Russia. He answered countless questions about fires in St. Petersburg, about giant cannons, and about statues, clocks, camels, Christian worship, glass blowing, and several other important and unimportant matters. The interrogators drew out of Kodayu a more complete description of Russia than Japan possessed of any other country. When the castaways were asked about their attitude toward the Russians, in view of the fact that the Russians had saved their lives and had done so many things for them, the castaways admitted that they had no feeling of hostility toward the Russians. The officials wondered why the castaways had run the risk of execution in seeking repatriation, but seemed satisfied with the apologetic explanation that they had wished to come back to their families and

---

[12] Okamoto, 1: 75-83.

[13] Japanese scroll in the possession of the author; Pozdneev, II, 3: 21.

that they had not been able to adjust themselves to Russian food, climate, and language. Asked whether they had brought any message from Russia, they reported that an official had expressed the desire to take advantage of their repatriation to seek to establish commercial relations with Japan, but that he had added that Russia had no intention to impose such relations on Japan by force. Questioned about the extent of information in Russia about Japan, the castaways replied that the Russians knew "everything without exception," an assertion, which must have caused great concern. Whether it was the timeliness of these observations, or the good personal impression that Kodayu and Isokichi made, or just plain luck, they escaped the harsh treatment usually accorded to repatriates and, though they were not permitted to return to their native place, were authorized to send for their wives and live a life of relative peace and leisure on condition that they would not discuss what they had seen abroad without special permission.[14] The utter lack of hostility toward the Russians, indeed the gratitude and admiration, that permeated the testimony of the castaways was of importance in the shaping of Japanese attitude toward the Russians. Henceforth, Japanese fear of Russian encroachment was to be supplemented by respect for Russians in general and for Catherine the Great in particular.[15]

This mixture of fear and respect for Russia was voiced most forcefully by Honda Toshiaki, who had personally visited Sakhalin and the Kuril Islands. "In general, we may say that Japan is at a standstill while Russia is moving ahead," he wrote. "Because of our tendency towards ineptitude in all things, Russia has become master of standstill Japan's Kamchatka. The reason why the barbarians of islands east, south and west of Kamchatka all seem to be attracted like ants to the sweetness of the Russian system is that the Russians have made capital out of their experiences of struggle and toil during the past 1,500 years." Honda greatly admired Russian expansion and exhorted his countrymen to follow Russia's example. He advocated a new and aggressive foreign policy, with Russo-Japanese commercial relations as a cornerstone. Through this trade, to be conducted primarily on Etorofu and Kunashiri, Japan would acquire beneficial knowledge about Russia as well as profits, which could help pay for the colonization of Hokkaido, Sakhalin, and the Kuril Islands

---

[14] Ramming, *Reisen*, 32-44. According to another source, some of the castaways at least were permitted to return to their homes in Sendai. (Turkovskii, 210.)

[15] Keene, 67-68.

which he projected. Honda took issue with such defeatists as Nakai Chikuzan, who wanted Japanese activities in Ezo confined to trading posts which could readily be withdrawn in case of Russian advance without loss of face, and in 1792 submitted a definite recommendation for the settling of the island in order to contain Russian expansion, for the Russian advance, he maintained, confronted Japan with "an emergency within an emergency." Honda was convinced that in free competition between Russia and Japan for the control of the Kuril and Bonin Islands, as well as of Kamchatka, Sakhalin, the Aleutians and North America, Japan was favored by her geographical position and would emerge victorious. He even made the startling proposal that the Japanese capital be moved from Edo to Kamchatka as the center of a far-flung empire. In short, his reaction to Russian expansion was the advocacy of counter-expansion.

The development of Karafuto [Sakhalin] is an urgent matter, especially because it concerns our frontiers. As the proverb says, "Finders, keepers." What sensible person would fail to give this matter his consideration? We must not let Karafuto slip through our fingers. . . . Once great cities spring up in Karafuto and Kamchatka, the momentum will carry on to the natural development of the islands to the south, and the growing prosperity of each of these places will raise the prestige of Edo to great heights. This, in turn, will naturally result in the acquisition of the American islands, which are Japan's possession manifestly.

Above all, prompt action was of the essence. He wrote:

The Russians were informed that they might visit Nagasaki and trade there and obtained documents of authorisation before they returned home, but they have yet to visit Nagasaki. This is presumably because their plans have been upset.

Since, as I have written, the nature of their country is such that transport is most difficult, the Russians have not been able to do as much for the natives of Ezo as they wished. Now, while this remains true, is the time to take the islands back. If we plan secretly, we can make them Japanese Ezo islands, as they used to be. If these plans are put into effect, there is no doubt but that there will be two most prosperous and powerful countries in the world: Japan in the East and England in the West.[16]

There were other Japanese scholars and officials, who had toured the northern regions and returned to warn their countrymen against Russian infiltration and to advocate the preventive colonization of

16 *Ibid.*, 132-134, 148-149, 178, 223-224, 229.

Hokkaido. Foremost among them were Hirazawa Kyokuzan, Mogami Tokunai, and Kondo Morishige. The latter had dramatized Japanese claims to the northern regions, when on a visit to Etorofu, in 1798, he had removed a cross and Russian-erected posters, claiming Russian suzerainty over the island, and had put up in their stead posts with the inscription "Japanese Etorofu."[17] Not the least interesting aspect of Japanese reaction to Russia, of early Japanese agitation for defense measures against Russia, was the fact that the Russians were blissfully unaware of it, and that they did not realize that the Japanese could have any but amicable feelings toward them. Even after the raids of Khvostov and Davydov the Russians failed to be aware of the excitement and alarm, which they had aroused, and were quite unprepared for the reception that was to be accorded to Golovnin.

When Rezanov arrived in 1804, the Japanese did not turn him away immediately, as they might well have done had there been no question in their mind about continued seclusion. Nor was their delay in replying to Rezanov's demands a deliberate policy of procrastination. The Japanese hesitated for so long, because they themselves were not quite sure what measures were really most desirable, and spent much time and effort in serious deliberation. The fact that some of those, who were most alarmed at the threat of Russian expansion, proposed to meet it by commercial agreement with Russia, no doubt complicated the issue. When the *Nadezhda* had arrived at Nagasaki, the local authorities had made every preparation to repel a Russian attack, indeed, were ready to take the initiative themselves should they be slighted in any way. But the shogun, who himself is said to have favored the reception of the envoy, commanded that the Russians be treated as peacefully and hospitably as possible, and Japanese military measures were relaxed and a doctor put at Rezanov's disposal, though Russian movements continued to be highly restricted.[18]

In the capital, meanwhile, the great debate raged for months. Matsudaira Sadanobu, who was no longer in power, now favored dealing with the Russians; so did many other persons of importance. Shiba Kokan had come out in favor of trade. "Is rice not abundant and cheap and is this not a great drawback for the Samurai class?" he asked. "Is it not natural that the Russians should be allowed to

17 Pozdneev, II, 3:58-60; Kuno, II, 227-237; E. Papinot, *Historical and Geographical Dictionary of Japan*, 305-306.
18 Voenskii (October), 234-235; Novakovskii, 88-89; Langsdorff, 294.

trade in order to prepare an outlet for this surplus of grain and also to develop Ezo? And Christianity? It is so apparently dangerous, and besides it is forbidden by [Tokugawa] Ieyasu. Nobody will embrace these doctrines." "Indeed," he concluded, "Sadanobu refusing the Russians in 1792, knew the classics but not geography."[19] Others advised moderation. Aoki Okikatsu, for example, though he dreaded foreign intercourse, felt that Rezanov should not be turned down flatly, but that a promise of trade fifty years hence should be held out to him, a suggestion almost prophetic in calculation, since Japan's first treaty with a Western power was to be signed in 1854. Even the imperial court, it seems, was asked for advice and the rumblings of its opposition allegedly turned the balance of argument against Rezanov and foreshadowed the struggle for the restoration of imperial power in years to come.[20]

When the Shogunate finally decided to continue the seclusion policy unchanged, there were many outspoken protests, and the accusation was made that the treatment of Rezanov had been disgraceful.[21] Shiba Kokan noted: "Japan has shown serious lack of etiquette as though people would carelessly pull off their clothes before a correctly dressed gentleman."[22] And again: "The Russians must think that we are animals."[23] The fact that delay in the acceptance of the castaways had caused the suicide attempt of one, added fuel to the criticisms.

The ultimate Japanese decision had been reached less by reference to tradition and to unalterable laws, than by the feeling that such trade might not really be profitable and by the fear that, in any case, it might not be possible to confine dealings to trade, but that the Russians would eventually make territorial demands and seek to spread their heretical religion. Above all, the officials feared that the Russians would subvert the loyalty of the common people to the shogunate.[24] Even so, the decision was not necessarily an expression of Russophobia. Paradoxical as it may seem, Japanese suspicions of Russian designs did not displace Japanese respect and, at times, Japanese admiration for the Russians, the testimony of group after group of repatriated castaways dispelling more and more the prejudiced con-

---

[19] J. Feenstra Kuiper, "Some Notes on the Foreign Relations of Japan in the Early Napoleonic Period," 61-62.

[20] Voenskii (October), 234-235.

[21] Krusenstern, I, 346-347.

[22] Kuiper, 76.

[23] Keene, 68.

[24] Pozdneev, II, 2:115; Novakovskii, 92-93.

ception of the Russians as "barbarians." Clearly as the Japanese saw that the repatriation of the castaways was executed by the Russians not without ulterior motives, there is evidence that they felt a deep appreciation for the fine treatment accorded to their unfortunate countrymen, an appreciation that, in many instances, was kept alive down into the second half of the nineteenth century, when many Japanese expressed outspoken Russophile views. As Professor Ramming writes in reviewing the attitude of the Japanese towards Russia at the time of Rezanov's rejection: "It is noteworthy that Russia at that time enjoyed a very good reputation in Japan and was truly popular, in spite of the writings of Rin [Hayashi] Shihei, Kudo Heisuke and other authors who concerned themselves with the northern problems and warned of the new dangerous neighbor. Above all things one said to oneself, that Russia was a very large, powerful state, which had already twice sent embassies to Japan and had repatriated ship-wrecked Japanese. It was emphasized also, that like Japan it was an empire, as contrasted with the United States of America of which, precisely for this reason, one was of not very high opinion."[25]

The customary interrogation of the newly repatriated castaways corroborated the observations conveyed by Kodayu and Isokichi in 1793; it added to Japanese knowledge of Russia and yielded additional information about other remote areas, for Gihei and his companions had voyaged around the world: cast from the shores of Japan to the Aleutian Islands, and taken to Siberia and European Russia, they had been carried back to their homeland via Europe, South America, North America, and Kamchatka. Like Kodayu, they praised Russian hospitality. They had been received by Tsar Alexander I, had been shown the sights of the capital, had been taken to the theater, had been wined and dined—in short, had been treated as guests of honor. If there was any bitterness in their hearts as they trampled on Christian images as proof of their loyalty to the faith of their fathers and were repaid for their patriotism by being confined in jail, it was directed at their countrymen, who had elected to remain in Russia. In 1806 the castaways were moved to Sendai and there questioned repeatedly in great detail for over two months. Thanks to their power of observation and to the skill and thoroughness of their inquisitors, notably Otsuki Gentaku, who checked their statements against Dutch books and sought amplification and verification from Kodayu, a lengthy and valuable account of their ex-

25 Ramming, *Reisen*, 75-78.

periences in Russia, entitled *Kankai ibun* (Seagirt Tales), was compiled, an account which covered every conceivable aspect of Russian life from medicine, military science, and baking to geography, sex, and balloon ascents, and compared favorably with most contemporary European books on Japan.[26]

The attacks of Khvostov and Davydov jarred the Shogunate into action. Always eager to preserve domestic tranquility, the government had tried in years past to tone down or silence alarmist writers, but now their warnings were remembered and echoed manifold. The heretofore lukewarm interest of the Shogunate in the northern regions was suddenly moved to action. As early as 1798, the Shogunate had assumed direct responsibility for the Ezo territory; not until now, however, had it truly taken over the administration of the northern regions.[27] Troops were dispatched to strategic points on Hokkaido, reinforcements were sent to Etorofu, and hasty defense preparations were made along the northern shores of the main island. Simultaneously Japanese treatment of the Ainu was noticeably ameliorated to forestall native support of the Russians.[28] At first there was considerable confusion, and fantastic rumors of hundreds of Russian attackers, eleven or twelve feet tall, spread across the country.[29] But the government promptly clamped down on any discussion of the raids and on the whole took swift and energetic measures of defense. Where Hayashi Shihei had failed, Khvostov and Davydov succeeded in convincing the Shogunate dramatically of the need of modern weapons and techniques, and thereby actually contributed to the eventual opening of the country. Painfully aware how limited its knowledge of Russia was, in spite of the eyewitness reports of the castaways, the government ordered the Dutch to translate

---

[26] *Ibid.*, 58-66; Umemori, 34-39, 47. Several volumes long in manuscript form, the account as relayed by Umemori yet extends to over three hundred printed pages.

[27] Harrison, *Japan's Northern Frontier*, 22-24; Golovnin, *Zapiski*, II, 66; Alfons Scheinpflug, *Die Japanische Kolonisation in Hokkaido*, 39-40.

[28] Lovtsov had made a special point of Ainu dissatisfaction with Japanese rule in his report to Pil in January of 1793. Writing that the Japanese regarded the native inhabitants of the 19th, 20th, 21st and 22nd Kuril Islands as Japanese subjects, he noted that they had aroused their antagonism by demanding excessive labor and utter submission, antagonism which the Ainu conveyed to the Russians by expressive gestures as they secretly visited them at night. (Polonskii, 540.) Years later, in 1855, when renewed Russian pressure necessitated further amelioration in the treatment accorded to the Ainu, the rules of the Matsumae clan were reformed to forbid the making of Ainu women into concubines. The Ainu were permitted to use straw raincoats, basket-shaped hats, and straw sandals, and were permitted to study Japanese. It was forbidden to set fire to the houses of deceased persons, to tatoo lips and ears, and to receive bribes from foreigners. (Umemori, 27.)

[29] Aston, 84.

books on Russia into Japanese, and sent out explorers to the northern territories. Thus in 1808, Matsuda Denjiro and Mamiya Rinzo explored Sakhalin and discovered that it was an island, Tatar Strait being known to the Japanese as Rinzo Kaikyo. The following year, in 1809, Mamiya crossed over to the continent into Manchuria and penetrated as far as the Manchu-Chinese government outpost of Delen on the lower Amur, before returning to Edo and making a full report.[30]

The Shogunate meanwhile continued to deliberate on a policy toward Russia. Should peace be bought by concessions or should Japan fight in defense of the closed door, for, according to the proclamation left by Khvostov, Russia seemed determined to force the issue. After patient reflection, the government decided to resort to arms, as the majority had counseled, but even then it left room for a change in policy with a change in conditions.[31]

Many military suggestions and proposals were submitted to the Shogunate. Many plans were drafted by strategists for their own guidance. Matsudaira Sadanobu, for example, set down his "General Thoughts Concerning Coastal Defense" in a paper, which carried the notation: "this document is for my own use only and under no circumstances can be shown to anyone else." In this paper Matsudaira spoke highly of Western military planning and stressed the need of providing Edo with suitable defenses. He warned:

People who conceive of the coming of the enemy only in the same manner as before, because they have no other plans or ideas in their heads, will lose all self-control upon seeing suddenly the whole surface of the water covered with enemy vessels and will become panicky. Confused, they will forget the whole plan of action, not even thinking how much dishonor they will bring to their country. If on the other hand, the possibility of the arrival of an enemy fleet of more than a hundred vessels will be kept in mind, in the event that only ten vessels will come one will not be able to help thinking that the enemy is weak and can be overcome without any trouble. The roles of host and guest will then have changed completely and it will not be difficult to expel the latter. It is the more so if only one or two vessels of the type used by the pirates will appear. In that case we shall beat them with just the oars. I do not think, however, that we can instruct two daimyo houses to build defenses against some small robbers.

[30] Harrison, *Japan's Northern Frontier*, 27; Pozdneev, II, 3:87-95; Siebold, II, 1235; Motoyama, 63-75. A translation of Mamiya's account of his voyage to Hokkaido and of life and conditions on that island, may be found in John A. Harrison, "*Kita Yezo Zusetsu*," 93-117.
[31] Pozdneev, II, 3: 233-234.

I do not know your plans, but I think it would be extremely deplorable if it were learned in foreign countries that the entrance into our capital remains without defenses. In my humble opinion a solid and striking arming of the fortifications will serve not only to keep the enemy in check but also to maintain the prestige of our country.[32]

Specifying the type of artillery emplacements and fortifications that he thought necessary, Matsudaira criticized some of the proposals, which had been advanced by others, not only from the standpoint of military strategy, but also of honor. Thus he took exception to the proposal that hidden fortifications be constructed, camouflaged as poor houses, and that one should remain in them, wait for the enemy to land, and then suddenly make a close-quarter attack. Matsudaira stated that this was a particularly bad proposal, because, though every daimyo might in practice employ such tactics in defense of his domain, it was impossible to suggest such stratagem as a system of national defense. There might be some individual cases of valor, he admitted, but the point was that, with such a system of poor houses, the enemy would pass them by in the open sea, approach a convenient point, and from there open fire. When the hidden batteries would not reply, the Japanese would have no arguments in their defense. The defenders of a large fort might say that they did not fire because the enemy, out of cowardice, was too far away. This would be different, because it would not lower Japanese prestige. But most important, if the enemy were to come in a few dozen ships, were to enter the bay, go upstream into the interior of the country, and land openly, not like some gang of robbers, it would be impossible to fire at him from the poor houses, as they would be equipped only for a camouflaged surprise attack. If they were to open fire, the enemy would return to his ships, form a line, and engage in a real battle from his war vessels against the unfortified Japanese positions. Correct warfare did not permit, expostulated Matsudaira, that somebody interested in his own exploits would dress like a beggar or a simple soldier and, mixing with the people, would await secretly the arrival of the enemy. A good enemy, paying no heed whatsoever to some poor wretched beggars, will concentrate his force on something better and will therefore go after him, who resembles a general. If someone, scared of a person with military bearing resembling a general, were to dress like a beggar and approaching the latter were to surprise him with a death blow, he

32 Okamoto, 83-87.

would not gain anybody's approval. If a good enemy himself were to pursue a person resembling a general, paying no heed to the beggars, and were to be surprised at that time by the person who had changed his clothes, how would the latter be able to clear himself of the suspicion of having changed to avoid danger? Matsudaira observed that, because of the lasting peace in Japan, people tended to think that other countries too lived in peace, that they used their guns only to shoot birds and animals, that they were afraid of large cannons, and knew nothing of the art of gunnery. He warned that plans, made according to such fantasies, bring the most ludicrous results; in reality wars never cease in the foreign countries, and people are well versed in military matters, and know very well how far a shot will carry. Matsudaira pointed to the importance of knowing one's enemy intimately, and stressed the need of offensive power. Noting that many ships would be necessary to capture the Russian capital, he called for suitable preparation of ships and men; at the same time he envisaged the possibility of a small suicide attack.[33]

Hirayama Kozo, a samurai, who patterned his life after the exacting and frugal demands of the battlefield—rising at 4 a. m. to do his military exercises, boiling unwashed rice, and receiving no women in his house—gave vent to his outrage at the murderous forays of the Russian "barbarians" in a memorial to the government. "How dare they!" was the tenor of his approach. "Though I, Hisomu, am not a man of ability, I gnash my teeth and blush with anger, and unable to restrain myself wish to depart for the north to the sea, in advance of the large army and sacrifice my life there. . . ." Falling back on the traditional Chinese concept of fighting barbarians with barbarians, Hirayama proposed the employment of Japanese criminals in repelling the Russians, and requested permission to recruit an army of daredevil thieves, gamblers, and cutthroats. "The wild boars attack and the wolves flee," he philosophized. Hirayama pointed out how insignificant, in scope and ambition, the raids of Khvostov and Davydov were in comparison with the Mongol invasions, which Japan had weathered in the thirteenth century. A relatively small force would suffice to protect Japan, if only the initiative were wrested from the Russians. He envisaged "flying squadrons" that would attack the raiders unexpectedly the moment they set foot on land. "It is necessary to be as fast as the wind and as determined as

[33] *Ibid.*

the thunder," he exhorted, and solemnly swore that he would not live under one heaven with these robbers.[34]

Not all Japanese were equally enraged by the Russian raids. It will be recalled that quite a few had taken issue with the treatment of Rezanov and, when news of Rezanov's death reached Japan, the rumor spread that he had committed suicide because of the way he had been insulted by the Japanese;[35] others, who did not know of his death, agreed that Russia had lost face. Thus there were some, who found justification in their own feudal values for the vengeful attacks of Khvostov and Davydov, and recommended that Russian demands for trade be accepted. Arguments were advanced that trade with Russia would be beneficial in its own right and, if necessary, might be substituted for trade with China; that trade would be a cheaper and safer way of halting the Russian advance than war; and that permission to trade could be granted on condition that the Russians hand back the Ezo Islands of which they had taken possession. But the advocates of firm resistance persisted in their view, convinced that trade was but a stepping-stone for more sinister foreign designs, and that the Western powers would not rest satisfied, until they had swallowed up the whole of Japan.

This cleavage in Japanese opinion was aggravated by the reluctance of many officials to take an unequivocal stand and by the tendency to play it safe, by trying to agree with everyone. The expert advice of the Matsumae Governors Kawajiri Jingoro, Lord of Higo, and Arao Shigeaki, Lord of Tajima, as embodied in a memorandum presented to the Shogunate, in 1807, was more notable for its skillful evasion of straightforward advice than for its careful consideration of every strategic contingency. Thus the governors considered the time equally propitious for military measures or for trade. They warned that, if trade were decided upon, defense measures must not be neglected, since Russia boasted of a history of territorial expansion; at the same time they expressed the view that, dangerous as Russian proximity might be, Russian actions would not be shaped exclusively by naked power, but would be formulated in response to Japanese measures, and that utmost caution and sincerity must be used in relations with the Russians, to avoid giving the latter cause for attack. They concluded that the exclusive concentration on

[34] Pozdneev, II, 3: 234-239.
[35] D. C. Greene, "Osada's Life of Takano Nagahide," 429.

193

defense was as insufficient as the exclusive concentration on peace in insuring lasting peace, that defense measures and peace measures both led to the same goal and were equally important. When, after careful study of this document, the officials in Edo thought they perceived a leaning toward peace and trade on the part of the Matsumae governors and asked them to clarify their position Kawajiri and Arao, in a second memorandum, presented in 1808, assiduously tried to clear themselves of the implication that they were "soft" toward Russia, and wrote that trade must be permitted only after a show of Japanese force and after the receipt of a Russian apology for the raids on Japanese territory, and declared that, they themselves had taken steps to thwart further Russian aggression. But, though they remarked that it was their understanding that the Russians had been informed in Nagasaki that foreign trade was counter to national laws and though they stated that this declaration could not be taken back now, they advanced the argument that, if the Russians, from their distant regions, came to some territory bordering Matsumae, they deserved special consideration and that, if an exception to the national laws forbidding trade were made in their case, they would undoubtedly feel very grateful toward Japan. The governors foresaw the danger that one concession might lead to the demand for more concessions, but thought that trade could be limited in scope and region. After various mental gymnastics concerning the pros and cons of demanding a Russian apology, Kawajiri and Arao addressed themselves to the question of war with Russia in remarkably frank language. They stated that, brave as it sounded to maintain that the Russians were not worth fearing and should be chased away, the fact remained that such action would entail great sacrifice in Japanese lives and that insufficient study had as yet been devoted to the whole question. They warned of the severe strain that war would place on the economic resources of Japan and sketched a harrowing picture of the sufferings the people of Japan would have to endure, hinting at the possibility of an internal revolt. If, upon due deliberation, military measures were to be judged desirable, they would, of course, drive away the Russians and even carry the war to their own country, but, for the present, they felt that if the Russians were to ask for forgiveness, they should be forgiven, if they renewed their attacks they should be met with force. After a final plea for further deliberation for the sake of future generations, and, with an eye to the approbation of Heaven and of foreign countries, the governors reiterated their zealousness and concluded with the profuse apology that their outspokenness, without regard to position and rank, had been so rude that not even the death penalty would be sufficient punishment for them.

Typically, the Tokugawa statesmen were often less concerned about the foreign threat per se, than about the influence Russian raids might have on public opinion. To give in to threats would be a confession of weakness that could well have internal political repercussions. As it was, the government was not certain of the loyalty of all its subjects, fearing not only Ainu and banished criminals and political exiles, but unemployed samurai, who, unable to earn a living in peacefully secluded Japan, might deal with the Russians to the extent of betraying the secrets of their country.

The Shogunate had no ready plan of action. There was the tendency to continue to proclaim publicly that the Russians must be chased away, while realizing privately that trade relations would have to be sanctioned sooner or later. But the Russians had left word that they would come to Sakhalin and Etorofu for an answer to their demands, and the ministers found it necessary to draft a joint reply. They wrote that they could not agree to the Russian request for trade, because they had never before traded with Russia, and because they could not have commercial relations with a country that not only had attacked their territories, but threatened to renew the attacks if its demands were not heeded. They declared that, if the Russians should send many ships, they would take appropriate measures of their own and fight. If on the other hand, the Russians truly desired trade, they must first seek to make up for what they had done and return all the Japanese, who had been taken prisoner; only after that could there be any question of trade. The ministers promised to send word to Sakhalin the following year whether or not trade would be possible. They concluded that, if the Russians had no bad intentions, they must immediately leave Japanese territory and return to Russia; nothing good could come of new misunderstandings. "If further disturbances should occur," they warned, "trade will of course be completely out of the question." The letter was given to the governor of Matsumae, but not until the arrival of Golovnin was there an opportunity to transmit the letter, and by that time more effective pressure could be brought to bear on the Russians.[36]

Diverse and contradictory as the many proposals of Japanese officials and intellectuals may have been, acrimonious as the great debate often became, there was argument only about means; there was complete unanimity as to the objective: the preservation and strengthening of Japan. Sugita Gempaku might take issue with Hirayama's insistence on direct action and advocate trade with Russia, but he did so essentially because he believed that Japan, in consequence of protracted peace, would be unable to wage war successfully and concluded that the establishment of commercial relations with Russia would give Japan the necessary time and opportunity to develop the sinews of war. Whatever their position, Japanese spokesmen radiated a strong patriotism, unmatched in any other part of Asia.[37] Anxious as Kawajiri and Arao seem to have been to avoid war with Russia, they warned the shogunate that "if the country devotes herself exclusively to coastal defense, she will never be able to defend herself successfully" and expounded that "our defense will never be lasting, unless we ourselves carry out an attack on their [Russian] distant territories with our warships."[38] When Golovnin was informed later by the Japanese that they had given thought to carrying out a naval attack on Okhotsk, he laughed in their face. Unfortunately, Russian readers of Golovnin's memoirs were to remember his laughter and not the Japanese determination, in case of war, to strike directly at Russia.

THE TRAP

In the summer of 1811, the Russian sloop-of-war *Diana* approached the northern possessions of Japan. Her purpose was not to resume the fruitless negotiations of Rezanov, but merely to replenish supplies and to continue without delay its exploration of these little known waters.

The *Diana* had left Kronstadt on a round-the-world expedition in 1807, but the break between Russia and England, precipitated by Alexander I's agreement with Napoleon at Tilsit, had led to her detention at the Cape of Good Hope, even though she had English papers authorizing free sailing. One night at last, the *Diana* had

[36] Pozdneev, II, 3:241-260.
[37] Kuno, II, 232-233; Suematsu, 317.
[38] Pozdneev, II, 3:271.

succeeded in slipping out of Simon's Bay, and, late in 1809, had reached Kamchatka, remaining in adjacent waters for two winters, except for a voyage to the Russian colonies in America with desperately needed supplies. In the spring of 1811, the *Diana* had received orders to make a thorough survey of the southern Kuril Islands, the Shantar Islands, and the coast of Tatary from latitude 53° 28′ N. to Okhotsk, the reports of earlier explorers, such as Gore, LaPerouse, Gavriil Sarychev, Broughton, and Krusenstern, being as yet neither complete nor wholly accurate. On May 7, the *Diana* had started through the chopped ice of Petropavlovsk Harbor into the Bay of Avachinsk, and, on May 16, had set forth on its mission, exploring the Kuril Islands Rashowa, Ushishiru, Ketoi, Shimushiru, and two Chirpoi Islands, Makantor, and the western part of Uruppu.[39]

Lieutenant Commander Vasilii Golovnin, who captained the *Diana*, had read volume one of Krusenstern's work and knew, therefore, that the Japanese government had forbidden any Russian vessel to draw near the shores of Japan. He was acquainted also with the raids of Khvostov and, though he felt that they had been so obviously unauthorized "that the Japanese have not the least cause to believe that such an attack on them by two insignificant vessels could be made at the wish of the monarch of a great and powerful state, of the intent and might of which they must have had a clear understanding from the description of their countrymen who had lived for several years in Russia,"[40] he decided to avoid any contact with the Japanese. He even planned not to display his country's flag, when sailing past the islands under Japanese control, so as not to arouse fear or apprehension. But all his precautions notwithstanding, Golovnin suddenly found himself face to face with the Japanese.

It happened on June 29, when the *Diana* was close to the western shore of northern Etorofu. Shana Bay, which lay before the Russians, extended so deep inland as to resemble a strait, and misled Golovnin into believing that he was at another island. The map of Broughton had left this part of the coastline indefinite, and Golovnin drew nearer in order to complete the description. People, whom he saw running back and forth on shore, he supposed to be Ainu, and dispatched Ensign Fedor Mur and Assistant Navigator Vasilii Novitskii on an armed boat to question them about the island and other mat-

---

[39] Golovnin, 1:1-10; Sgibnev, "Popytki," 61. Golovnin refers to some of the islands by number. For his order of numbering, see map of the Kuril Archipelago.

[40] Golovnin, *Zapiski*, 1: 12-13.

ters of interest. As a large boat came out to meet the Russian craft, Golovnin moved the *Diana* closer to shore and himself hastened, with Ensign Vsevolod Iakushkin on an armed boat, in support of Mur and Novitskii. Meanwhile, the boat from shore had met the latter without hostility and, turning about, had escorted them to the island. When Golovnin followed ashore, he was surprised to find Mur in conversation with some Japanese.

Golovnin learned that Ainu from Rashowa, one of the Kuril Islands in the Russian domain, had come to this island the previous year, and, having been confined by the Japanese, were about to be released. Allegedly they had been driven there by bad weather, though actually, as they admitted inadvertently later on, they had come to trade with the Japanese. With the help of these Ainu, who knew a little Russian, and of a Japanese, who spoke the tongue of the Ainu, Golovnin was able to communicate with a Japanese officer, whom he saw standing on shore, surrounded by eighteen or twenty warriors in armor, carrying swords and muskets. Ishizaka Kihei, the Japanese officer, inquired why the Russians had come and whether their intentions were good or bad, adding that if trade was their purpose, they should continue down along the shore to Urbitch,[41] the main settlement. Golovnin replied that they had come in search of a safe harbor, where they could replenish their dwindling supply of fresh water and firewood, and having done this, they would depart without delay. This was not the whole story, of course, but Golovnin felt that it was impossible to disclose the true reason for their arrival. "Such a people cannot imagine, what business it is of a foreign country to send vessels for the description of alien lands from curiosity alone, without any other intention. They would have become suspicious at once."[42] By telling the Japanese that he was looking for a convenient harbor to take on needed supplies, he produced a plausible pretext for sailing along the shores of their islands and surveying them.

Golovnin assured Ishizaka that the *Diana* had come without hostile intent and backed this up with the curious, yet characteristic argument that the Japanese had nothing to fear because the *Diana* was

---

[41] Professor I. P. Magidovich, editor of Vasilii Mikhailovich Golovnin, *Sochineniia* suggests that "Urbitch" was the settlement Rubetsu on the western shore of Eto-ofu. (267, note 11.) Japanese historians, on the other hand, identify "Urbitch" as Furubetsu, a place somewhat farther west. (Hiraoka, *Nichi-Ro*, 247-248; Akaba Sozo, "Gorouin seikin no jokyo." 22:42; "Gorouin to Ishizaka Buhei," 9: 18.)

[42] Golovnin, *Zapiski*, 1: 14-16, 22.

not a merchantship, but an imperial naval vessel. Ishizaka was not convinced, however, and, referring to the raids of Khvostov and Davydov, replied that the Japanese had ample reason to fear the arrival of another Russian vessel. Golovnin countered that these attacks had not been authorized, assuring Ishizaka that, if the Emperor of such a mighty country as Russia would have desired war with Japan, he would not have confined himself to sending two little vessels, but would have sent many, and would have continued sending them until his demands would have been met. The foraging crafts had been merchantships commanded by traders and hunters and not by naval officers; their commanders had been duly punished for the wanton raids, a fact which was evidenced by the discontinuance of the raids in spite of their success. Ishizaka seemed satisfied and offered to give Golovnin a letter to the commander of Urbitch, where water, firewood, and provisions could be obtained. Meanwhile he himself gave the Russians some fresh fish, moztagon roots, and buckram in exchange for Russian gifts. As sake and French brandy flowed, their spirits rose and Golovnin even visited the Japanese tent.

Uncertain of the disposition of the Japanese, Golovnin hastened back aboard ship before dark. On shore the Ainu had warned him that the Japanese mistrusted the motives behind his arrival. Later, when the Ainu came aboard the *Diana* with the letter to Urbitch, promised by Ishizaka, they repeated that the Japanese, though the letter allegedly stated that the Russians had come with friendly intentions, expected no better from Golovnin than from Khvostov and had sent their personal possessions to the interior.[43]

On June 30, the *Diana* crossed over from Etorofu to the east coast of Uruppu with the intention of returning to Urbitch later. After three days of observations at the coast of Uruppu, the Russians sailed southward along the eastern shore of the island, increasing the fear of the Ainu Aleksei Maksimovich, who had agreed to accompany them as guide, that the regular drill and gunnery practice of the crew were a prelude to hostilities with the Japanese.

From his talks with the "Russian" Ainu, Golovnin gathered information concerning trade with the Japanese. He learned, for example, that, until the raids of Khvostov and Davydov, there had been "steady and regular" trade between the "Russian" Ainu and the

---

[43] *Ibid.*, 1: 15-20; Akaba, "Gorouin," 18: 233-235; 9: 18-22.

Japanese "such as would have been established by the public acts of two countries, and perhaps with still better order and with greater honesty." From Aleksei Golovnin heard of a safe harbor and fortified settlement on the southern shore of Kunashiri, where the necessary supplies might be obtained. He decided, therefore, to skip Urbitch and head directly to Kunashiri, especially because he wanted to explore this harbor as well as the strait, which separated Kunashiri from Hokkaido, and was practically unknown to European navigators. The discovery, in the hold, of considerable rat damage to foodstuffs at the top, made the condition of supplies underneath uncertain and a thorough examination and possible replenishment urgent.

Not until July 16, did weather permit the *Diana* to enter the strait. There it cast anchor overnight in order not to arouse undue alarm among the Japanese. Even then, large fires at the two capes reflected the apprehension of the Japanese, and on the morning of the seventeenth, as the *Diana* sailed into the harbor, two shots were fired, but fell short of their mark. A heavy fog descended on Russians and Japanese alike, and for a while the vessel was forced to lie at anchor. When the Russians continued to approach the fortress, the Japanese held their fire, even though the boat, which preceded the *Diana* to sound the depth, had come within range of their guns. The fortress, as usual, was hidden from Russian eyes by a striped curtain, interrupted in places by crudely painted embrasures of fake batteries. Only the several buildings, which stood on the hill-slope, remained exposed.

The *Diana* cast anchor about a mile and a half from the fortress, and Golovnin headed toward shore with Vasilii Srednii, the Ainu, and four oarsmen. They were within about three hundred and fifty feet from land, when the Japanese suddenly opened up with cannon fire from different parts of the fortress. Turning about, the Russians rowed for their lives, barely escaping the cannonade, which pursued them to their ship. Even, when Golovnin and those, who had hastened to his aid on armed boats, withdrew aboard the *Diana*, the Japanese batteries sustained their fire. Such an attack by the Japanese on a small boat with seven men, who had approached the shore without subterfuge, seemed dishonorable and barbaric to Golovnin but, though the thought of revenge crossed his mind, he chose to make another attempt to communicate with the Japanese and drew back from the fortress.

On the following morning, on July 18, the Russians divided a barrel into two sections and placed a glass with fresh water, some firewood, and a handful of rice in one section, and a few coins, a piece of cloth, some crystal objects, and beads in the other. This they hoped would tell the Japanese what they needed, and what they were willing to give in exchange. As if to shame the Japanese into peaceful dealings, they enclosed a sketch on which Mur had depicted the vessel as it peacefully lay in a shower of Japanese bullets. Then they placed the barrel on the water, opposite the city. No sooner had they moved away, than the Japanese got the barrel and took it to the fortress, but, though Golovnin advanced within cannon shot of the fortress the following day, there was no reply. This sorely provoked Golovnin. Nevertheless, he and his officers agreed not to resort to hostilities, unless absolutely necessary, and once again withdrew from the fortress. But supplies were needed, and Golovnin sent Rikord with an armed boat to a coastal fishing settlement. Finding the settlement deserted, the Russians helped themselves to firewood, some rice, and dried fish, but found no good water. In exchange they left some European objects. When Golovnin himself landed in the afternoon to have a look at the Japanese fishing establishment, he was happy to observe that these objects were no longer there, and concluded that, having found payment for the supplies taken, the Japanese must have understood that the Russians had come with friendly intentions.

On the morning of July 20, the Russians sighted a barrel on the water before the city. In it they found a carefully wrapped box, and in the box a Japanese letter, which they could not understand, and two pictures. Depicting the harbor and the *Diana*, the barrel, and the boat rowing up to it, one of the pictures had the Japanese batteries pointed silently inland, the other facing seaward and firing. Golovnin interpreted this to mean that the Japanese had suffered the Russians to place the barrel before the town without interference, but that they would shoot, were they to try to do so again. When the *Diana* moved to the western shore of the harbor and sent armed boats ashore for fresh water, however, the Japanese did not molest them, but merely observed their activity indirectly through a number of natives.

On July 21, when the Russians had landed once again in quest of fresh water, an Ainu approached them from the fortress and holding a cross in one hand, continued to make the sign of the cross with the other. Aleksei had not accompanied the seamen ashore and this Ainu, though he had learned to cross himself on Rashowa Island, knew only a few words of Russian. Through gestures alone, therefore, Golovnin was given to understand that the Japanese commander suggested that they confer on boats near the city, accompanied by only four or five men. To this he gladly agreed.

The Japanese, meanwhile, had placed another barrel on the water, right near a battery, and with their white fans they beckoned the Russians to come closer. This might well have been suicide, and Golovnin began to wonder already, whether he had not misunderstood the Ainu, when a boat left shore and a Japanese official and a Kurilian language interpreter approached.

The Japanese apologized for having fired, justifying their action by the fear of Russian aggression, evoked by the raids of Khvostov and Davydov. They admitted that they were now satisfied that the intentions of Golovnin were different, and professed to be delighted to hear that Russia, as Golovnin explained, was amicably disposed toward Japan. They asked what the Russians needed and how they could be of service to them. When Golovnin requested various foodstuffs, they told him to come ashore to discuss suitable compensation with their commander. This Golovnin offered to do on the following day, when the *Diana* would take up position nearer to the fortress. He was reassured meanwhile, by the secret report of the Ainu, that the good aim and rapidity of fire of Khvostov's raiders had filled the Japanese with an awesome fear of Russians and that they had been most relieved and happy to learn that it was with peaceful intentions that the Russians had come this time.

On the morning of July 22, a barrel was placed on the water once again by the Japanese. In it Golovnin found all the things, which his men had left both on land and in the barrel. Instead of removing these objects, Golovnin added coins and silken East Indian kerchiefs. He was about to return to the *Diana*, when he saw that the Japanese beckoned with white fans for him to land. Carefully he approached them, and, five hundred feet from the gates of the fortress, pulled up to shore. He had ordered his four oarsmen to keep their muskets hidden from sight, but within ready reach. Now, he told three of the oarsmen to keep the boat on the water and, letting no one touch it, watch his every movement and command, and, concealing six pistols in his pockets and bosom, stepped ashore himself, accompanied by Aleksei and the fourth seaman.

Golovnin was met by five two-sworded Japanese in silken dress and armor, and some dozen unarmed Ainu. The Japanese welcomed him most politely and asked him to wait for the commander. When he inquired why they had returned the things left by the Russians, the Japanese said they could accept nothing, until the conclusion of negotiations. Recalling that this had been the case at the time of the Laxman embassy as well, Golovnin rested satisfied. Soon, a Japanese official arrived with two attendants, one of whom carried a long spear, the other a cap. The three were fully armed, but Japanese ceremonial behavior robbed the official of military bearing in Russian eyes. "Nothing can be funnier than his walk: his eyes fixed to the ground, his arms akimbo, he barely moved his feet, while keeping his legs so far apart as if straddling a small ditch."

Golovnin and the official exchanged bows. They apologized for being such a bother to each other, and the Japanese made up a story of a boat, which he had dispatched to meet the Russians as they had entered the harbor, and declared that, had the Russians sent a boat of their own to meet it, he never would have fired on them. Golovnin in turn departed from the truth, when explaining why he had come to the Kurils. He alleged that the *Diana* had been en route from the eastern regions of Russia to St. Petersburg, when unfavorable winds had so delayed her that she had run short of fresh water and firewood; that he had met a Japanese detachment on Etorofu and received a letter pledging assistance; and that, as soon as he would receive the necessary supplies, he would sail directly to Canton, there to replenish them again. This the Japanese did not accept at face value any more than Golovnin had accepted his story, and mentioned that, according to his information, the Russians had said on Etorofu that they had come to trade. He asked Golovnin many questions—whether he was indeed the captain of the ship (this he asked several times), what his name was, what the name of the Russian Emperor was, whether he knew Rezanov, and whether there were in St. Petersburg people who knew Japanese—and wrote down the answers. Then he commanded that refreshments be brought. The Russians helped themselves to the tea, the sake, the caviar, and the other things without fear, but they were made uneasy by the fact that the men, who brought each item on a separate tray, did not withdraw again, so that shortly they were surrounded by a large number of warriors. Under the pretext of getting some French brandy from the ship, Golovnin reminded his men to be prepared for any eventuality, though he realized that the Japanese could overwhelm his little group, if they chose to do so.

When Golovnin asked when he could receive the needed supplies and requested that the official name the price, he was informed to his amazement that the official was not the commander of the fortress, as he had assumed, and that he would have to go into the fortress itself to negotiate with the latter. Golovnin agreed to do so, if the Japanese officials meanwhile would visit the *Diana*. Though one of them wished to visit the ship, this was not permitted by the commander of the fortress, who promised to come out himself soon, but then sent word that he was having dinner and would be much delayed. Golovnin would not wait, and exchanging some gifts with the Japanese, returned aboard ship, promising to visit the fortress after bringing the *Diana* closer to shore.

It was evening by the time the *Diana* cast anchor within cannon shot of the fortress, and too late to enter into negotiations. But Golovnin sent Iakushkin ashore to present the letter from Etorofu,

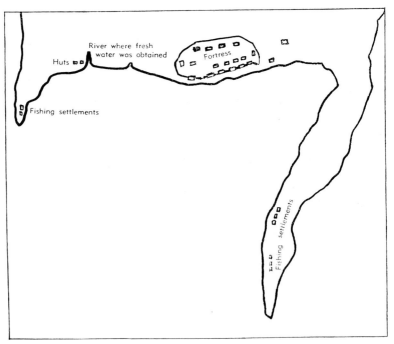

The Bay of Deceit, Southern Kunashiri

bring back fresh fish, and communicate that he would come to the fortress in the morning. Iakushkin returned with over a hundred large fish and reported that the Japanese would like Golovnin to bring along some of his officers. Suspecting the ensign of having engineered this invitation himself in the hope of being taken along, Golovnin saw nothing unusual in this request.[44]

On the morning of July 23, Golovnin went ashore with Ensign Mur, Navigator Andrei Khlebnikov, the Ainu Aleksei, and four sailors (Dmitrii Simanov,[45] Spiridon Makarov, Mikhailo Shkaev, and Grigorii Vasilev). Passing the barrel, they looked into it and saw that the Japanese had still not removed the Russian objects, but, reassured again by Laxman's experience, harbored no misgivings. They trusted the Japanese enough by now, that the sailors went unarmed and Golovnin, Mur, and Khlebnikov had only their swords and a pocket pistol, which Khlebnikov carried to signal to the *Diana* in case of fog. As a last touch of confidence, which Golovnin displayed somewhat ostentatiously in order to allay Japanese suspicions, he had the boat pulled half-way onto shore, leaving it in the guard of only one sailor and Aleksei. He took along the other three seamen, laden with chairs and with gifts for the Japanese.

For some fifteen minutes the Russians were delayed on shore by the three officials with whom they had met the previous day. Preparations for the reception had not been completed, they said. While waiting, Golovnin questioned the officials about the Matsumae coastline, then visible, and about trade relations between the main island and the Kurils. The Japanese answered his questions, but with obvious reluctance. At last the Russians were led to the fortress.

As Golovnin entered through the gate, he was shocked to find some three to four hundred heavily armed Japanese warriors and a multitude of Ainu within the enclosure. "The thought had never entered my head," he recalled, "that in such a small fortress there could be so many armed men." About thirty paces from the gate there stood a tent, to which the Russians were led. In it the Japanese commander, Nasa Masatoki, awaited them. Clad in full armor and wearing his two swords, he was seated on a chair, holding in his hands the symbolic metal staff of his position, while behind him on the floor sat weapon bearers with his spear, musket, and helmet. To

[44] Golovnin, *Zapiski*, 1: 21-42.
[45] Rikord and the English version of Golovnin give the name as Simanov; Golovnin's *Zapiski* as Simonov.

his left the second commander rested on a slightly lower chair, with his weapon bearers likewise on the floor behind him. Other two-sworded Japanese sat on the ground along the side of the tent.

As the Russians entered, the commanders rose and exchanged bows with them. Ignoring the benches prepared for them, the Russian officers seated themselves on chairs they had brought along, while the sailors occupied the benches behind them. After the inevitable tea and tobacco, the commanders posed many questions and jotted down the answers. They inquired after Rezanov and asked why Russian vessels had attacked Japanese territory. They wanted to know how many men the *Diana* carried and whether there were other ships of her size in these waters. Always ready to boost the prestige of the Russian Empire, Golovnin promptly inflated the crew to one hundred and two in number and alleged that there were very many more vessels like the *Diana* in Okhotsk, Kamchatka, and America.

While they were thus engrossed in conversation, Mur noticed that unsheathed swords were being distributed among the soldiers on the square, but Golovnin refused to share his concern. The soldiers had worn swords from the beginning; what need was there for them to unsheath them now? The second commander had left the tent a while ago. Returning, he whispered something to the commander. Nasa rose and tried to walk out of the tent, but before he got past them, the Russians stood up to say good-bye, asking about payment for supplies. Nasa sat down again and, early though it was, ordered dinner to be served. Dinner completed, he tried to leave once more, but the Russians declared that they could not wait for his return and that it was time for them to go back. Again the commander sat down. Without orders from the governor of Matsumae, he could not supply the Russians with anything, he declared, and demanded that, until the receipt of instructions from his superiors, one of the Russians remain in the fortress as hostage! Nasa said that such a reply could be expected from Matsumae in about a fortnight, but Golovnin realized that the governor of Matsumae would not make any decision without instructions from the Japanese government and that no answer could be expected before winter. He replied that he could not decide by himself to wait so long, but must confer with the officers on ship; nor would he leave a hostage. Thereupon Nasa shed his amicable countenance and putting his hand on his sword spouted forth in anger. Aleksei was too terrified to translate the lengthy harangue, but the commander's gestures and his continuous reference to Rezanov and Khvostov were explicit enough. At last Aleksei pulled himself together and explained: "The commander says that if he lets but one of us out of the fortress, his own bowels will have to be ripped open." Nasa's intentions were crystal clear.[46]

The Russians ran for the gate. Screaming, the Japanese jumped up and threw oars and pieces of wood under foot so as to trip the Russians. Mur, Aleksei, and the sailor Makarov were nabbed within the fortress. The others made it out of the gate, while bullets whisked past them. They reached the boat, but the ebb had left it hopelessly stranded on the beach, too far for them to launch it themselves. Soon they were surrounded by the Japanese. They were prisoners.

Back in the fortress, the Japanese tied the Russians so ingeniously that the pull of a long rope, held by a guard, would have broken their arms at the elbows, while a noose around the neck would have strangled them. Under heavy guard the Russians were led to another part of the island, to the shore facing Hokkaido. For over six hours they were marched, painfully bound and breathing with difficulty. At one point Golovnin fainted away and blood poured from his nose and mouth. So excruciating was the pain, if head or body were moved, that the prisoners prayed for the mercy of a speedy death.

The Japanese were not particularly distressed by the suffering of the prisoners, but neither did they gloat at their fate, except for one youth who mocked their groans in song. Had the guards wished to ease their pain, it is unlikely that they would have dared to loosen the ropes for fear the Russians commit suicide or escape, or they themselves incur the displeasure of their superiors. In general, the guards showed a certain humanitarian concern for the comfort of the prisoners, fed them with chopsticks, willingly ministered to calls of nature, and even fanned away mosquitoes and flies. When a guard, annoyed by something or other, did occasionally strike one of the Russians, his superiors would reprimand him forthwith.

At night the Russians were carried onto Japanese boats and taken to Hokkaido, where they continued their journey by boat down the coast, on foot across mountainous paths, by boat down streams and artificial waterways, on foot again. Throughout this arduous procession to Hakodate, the Japanese were filled with concern for the

[46] Golovnin, *Zapiski*, 1: 42-47; Hiraoka, *Nichi-Ro*, 248-249.

prisoners' health. They carried them over the smallest streams, not
to wet their feet, and, in one settlement, provided them with a sooth-
ing ointment for their rope-inflicted wounds. When they stopped,
Japanese villagers would come up and sit with them at length, asking
about Laxman and Rezanov and their men. They would tell of the
praise, which repatriated castaways had had for their own treatment
in Russia, voicing confidence that Golovnin and his fellow prisoners
would also be permitted to return to their country some day.
Wherever the Russians passed, crowds would gather, but their mood
was friendly and sake, candy, fruits, and other refreshments were
offered to the captives by the populace. Eager collectors of souvenirs,
many Japanese asked the Russians to draw them pictures of a Russian vessel or inscribe white fans with the Russian alphabet, numbers,
and so forth. The Russians obliged willingly, if only to have their
ropes loosened for a while. The care with which the Japanese had
preserved a fan, on which a member of the Laxman embassy had
jotted some lines of a Russian song, showed how much they treasured
such mementos.[47]

At Onno, some four and a half miles out of Hakodate, preparations
were made for a formal entry into the city. The Japanese changed
dress and put on their armor; the captives were feasted with a delecta-
ble chicken breakfast, then retied as painfully as ever. At this point
an argument broke out between the escort of Nambu clansmen, who
insisted that the captives be retied exactly as they had been when
they had taken charge of them on Kunashiri, and the government
warriors, who did not deem this necessary. The matter was finally
settled by consultation with Hakodate, and the Russians entered
the city on August 20, hands untied.

The natural setting of Hakodate is beautiful, but there was nothing
scenic about the dark, walled-in prison to which the Russians were
taken. They were freed of their ropes, but were thrown into small,
zoo-like cages, which were as uncomfortable as they were depressing.
Even the more spacious cell of Golovnin, which he occupied at
first alone, then with seaman Makarov, was demoralizing beyond
description.

On August 22, the prisoners were led before the commandant of
Hakodate, in a castle on the other side of town. One by one he
interrogated them through the interpreters of Ainu, Uehara Kumajiro

[47] Golovnin, *Zapiski,* 1:48-66; Tokutomi, xxv, 276-286.

Ermak's conquest of Siberia

Mission of the Russian Ambassador E. Ÿsbrants Ides
to China (1693)

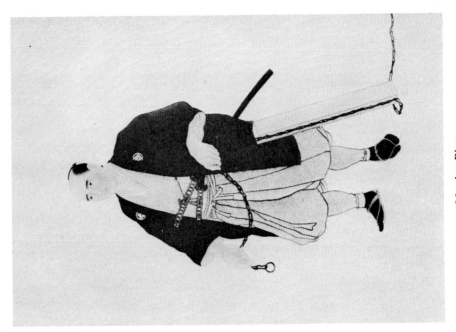

Mamiya Rinzo

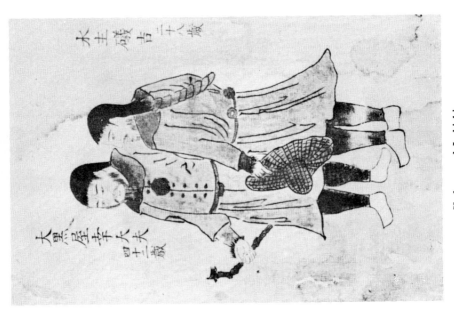

水主磯吉二十八歳

大黒屋幸太夫四十二歳

Kodayu and Isokichi

皂

レタ
金糸嵌

使節 ニコライレサノット 流令

甲ナ

スワイワタ
金緑出飾アリ

レタ
金糸嵌

天鵞
兜飾
表浅黄色也

裏猩々緋

白絹入テヤス

金皮

表猩々緋

Nikolai Rezanov

First visit of Japanese officials to the *Nadezhda*

Residence of Rezanov at Megasaki

Procession of Rezanov to the conference building

Clash of Khvostov and Davydov with the Ainu

Grigorii Shelikhov

Nikolai Rezanov

Vasilii Golovnin

Petr Rikord

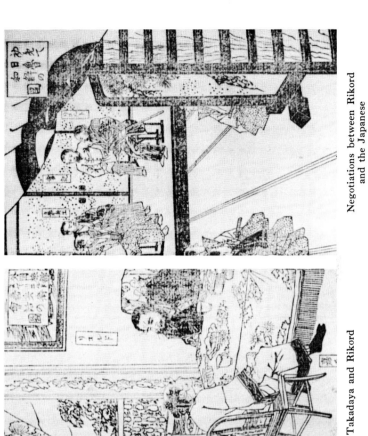

Negotiations between Rikord
and the Japanese

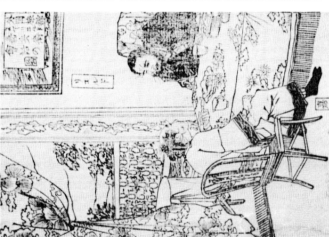

Takadaya and Rikord

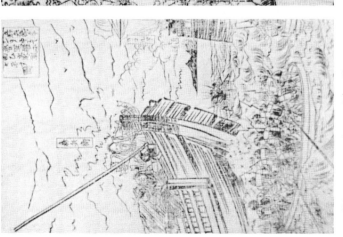

The capture of Takadaya Kahei

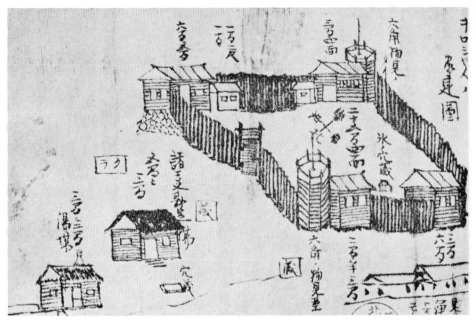

Busse's fortress on Sakhalin

Matsudaira Sadanobu's poem of warning

Aleksandr Baranov

Genadii Nevelskoi

Nikolai Muravev-Amurskii

Evfimii Putiatin

Russians in Japan

Russian sailor and Chinese
admiring Mt. Fuji

Evfímii Putiatin

More Russians in Japan

The frigate *Diana* on the Hakodate roadstead in 1854.
(Drawing by Lieutenant Aleksandr Mozhaiskii; courtesy Central Naval Museum, Leningrad)

Japanese and Russian boats before a Japanese camp near Osaka.
(Drawing by Mozhaiskii; courtesy Central Naval Museum, Leningrad)

Russian boat surrounded by Japanese near Osaka.
(Drawing by Mozhaiskii; courtesy Central Naval Museum, Leningrad)

Lieutenant Mozhaiskii sketching Shimoda Bay.
(Drawing by Mozhaiskii; courtesy Central Naval Museum, Leningrad)

The *Diana* during the earthquake at Shimoda.
(Drawing by Mozhaiskii; courtesy Central Naval Museum, Leningrad)

Shimoda Bay after the earthquake.
(Drawing by Mozhaiskii; courtesy Central Naval Museum, Leningrad)

A Japanese guard post.
(Drawing by Mozhaiskii; courtesy Central Naval Museum, Leningrad)

The Japanese plenipotentiaries: (from left to right) Tsutsui, Kawaji, Matsumoto, and Koga. Taking notes on the right: Nakamura. Kneeling before the plenipotentiaries: (Moriyama) Einosuke.
(Drawing by Mozhaiskii; courtesy Central Naval Museum, Leningrad)

А: ШАРАСМАНЬ.

Reception of the Takenouchi Mission by Alexander II

and Aleksei, his questions ranging all the way from, whether their parents were still alive and how many brothers and children they had, to the number of men a Russian officer of specified rank commanded, and why the hairdo of Golovnin differed from that of Laxman. More important, he showed the prisoners a map, copied from a Russian globe, and demanded that they indicate how they had come, and where they had been.

Several more times the commandant was to interview the Russians: on September ninth, tenth, thirteenth, and seventeenth. On the ninth, his report of the first meeting having brought a demand from Matsumae for additional facts, the commandant subjected the captives to a torrent of questions. Why had they come? Where had they been? When had they been there? How did Russian vessels navigate? Who did what aboard Russian ships? He was especially interested in learning more about the Rezanov embassy and the raids of Khvostov and Davydov, and asked about the disposition of the arms and goods carried away by the latter, all the while trying to connect the activities of Golovnin with those of Rezanov and the raiders. Jumping back and forth, reverting to the same questions, and jotting down every statement, the Japanese tried to catch any inconsistencies in the Russian testimony. But the Russians held their ground, replying truthfully to all but two major questions: they concealed a casual personal acquaintance with Khvostov and Davydov and did not disclose the geographical nature of their expedition.[48]

On September tenth, the captives were ordered to translate a letter, which Rikord had put ashore following their capture, together with trunks, bundles of clothing, and other personal belongings of theirs. Signed by all the officers aboard the *Diana* and dated July 23, 1811, the letter read as follows:

My God! Will these lines be delivered to you, and are you alive? At first it was decided, by the general consensus of all the officers remaining on the sloop, to take peaceable measures for your liberation; but that very second a cannon-ball from the fortress flew past our ears a great distance past the sloop, wherefore I decided to open fire also. What is to be done? What measures should be taken? The smallness of our cannon-balls made little impression on the city; shallow water did not permit us to put ashore a landing party, and thus, notifying you thereof, we have resorted to the last resource: to hasten to Okhotsk and return if our forces are increased there, not to leave these shores again until we have freed

[48] Golovnin, *Zapiski*, 1:66-96.

you, or have laid down our life for you, esteemed commander, and for you, esteemed friends! Should the Japanese permit you to reply, order, esteemed Vasilii Mikhailovich, as the commander: we shall do everything on the sloop; all to a single man are ready to lay down their life for you.[49]

Moved to the point of tears, the Russians were still careful not to disclose the impotence of their vessel, and they twisted the meaning of the letter as they translated it. Stating that the *Diana* had fired to defend herself rather than to inflict damage on the Japanese, they rendered the "smallness" of Russian cannon-balls, because of which little harm was done, as the "small number" of shots fired, and explained away the lack of men for a landing party, by portraying the purpose of such a landing party not as a simple assault, but as the complete surrounding of the fortress to prevent the removal of the prisoners; the need of reinforcements in Okhotsk, they interpreted as additional authority from their government, authority without which no attack on the Japanese could be executed. When the questioning shifted to other matters—international relations, conditions in Europe, and whatever came to the mind of the interrogators—the Russians replied truthfully, except, when it came to Russia's military and naval power; then they exaggerated liberally, multiplying the number of fortresses and troops in Siberia, and studding the harbors of the Okhotsk shore, Kamchatka, and North America with Russian vessels. They admitted that they had heard enough about the Laxman and Rezanov expeditions to know that the Japanese prohibited Russian vessels from coming to trade, but pleaded that they could not have imagined that such interdiction applied to ships in need or distress—even uncivilized barbarians helped those.

On September 13, the captives were questioned concerning another letter, which they had been asked to translate the previous day. Its text was embarrassing:

On October 12/24, 1806, the Russian frigate *Iunona*, under the command of Navy Lieutenant Khvostov, bestowed on the chieftain of the settlement on the western shore of Aniwa Bay a silver medal on a Vladimir ribbon as a token of taking Sakhalin Island and its inhabitants under the most gracious protection of the Russian Emperor Alexander the First. We ask every vessel which comes, Russian as well as foreign, to regard this chieftain as a Russian subject.

Russian Navy Lieutenant Khvostov

Affixed: family seal and picture of Russian naval and national flags.[50]

[49] *Ibid.*, 1:97-98.
[50] *Ibid.*, 1:99-103.

The Russians had succeeded in modifying the meaning of the note left by their shipmates, but how could they ever persuade the Japanese, who placed so much emphasis on propriety, that a person of as low a rank as Khvostov could have dared on his own, without authority from the government, to incorporate into the Russian domain a people, dependent on a foreign power, and to distribute among it medals portraying his emperor? Would the Japanese not take this letter as proof that the Russian government had instigated the raids of Khvostov and Davydov, and that Golovnin and his men were spies, sent to reconnoiter their coastal fortifications? Desperately the Russians argued that, had their government planned to annex territory, it would have done so at once on a larger scale. The Japanese nodded their heads and laughed. Not very convincingly the Russians explained that "frigate" applied to a merchant vessel, that "Vladimir ribbon" simply meant a striped ribbon, and that silver medals were of little value, Khvostov probably having bought them someplace or having taken them from his subordinates. Hopelessly they argued that the naval flag which had been drawn at the bottom of Khvostov's declaration side by side with the national flag did not identify the *Iunona* as a man-of-war, but that Khvostov had merely wished to acquaint the Japanese with both types of Russian flags, and that his actual display of the naval flag had been equally meaningless, since it had occurred without authorization. Nor was Golovnin successful in convincing the Japanese that the little wooden boards bearing the name of the *Diana*, the year 1811, and his own name, which he himself had posted on Etorofu and Kunashiri, and which the Japanese now put before him, had been left for no more sinister purpose than the tracing of his route in the event of shipwreck.[51]

The visit to the castle on September 17, terminated the round of questioning in Hakodate, but there was little that the prisoners could glean about their future. Harsh as their confinement was, they were treated relatively well, and the interminable string of visitors that called on them at the prison included not only such men as Uehara Kumajiro and Doctor Togo, who were compiling a Russo-Japanese dictionary, but amicable autograph hunters of all sorts. Even during their questioning they were treated with civility; speaking quietly and gently, almost always with a smile, the interrogators addressed them as if chatting with good acquaintances. What concerned the prisoners most, was the way in which they had become

[51] *Ibid.*, 1:103-107.

enmeshed in a net of circumstantial evidence. They were especially distressed to learn that, when Aleksei and his fellow Ainu had been captured by the Japanese, they had tried to protect themselves and to gain the favor of the Japanese by concealing the fact that they had come to trade with the islanders, making up a story that an official on Kamchatka had forced them to set out and reconnoiter Japanese settlements and strongholds in preparation for an attack on the shores of Japan by seven Russian vessels from Petropavlovsk the following year, a baseless fabrication, but highly damaging, because of two coincidences: "the following year" approximated the time of the *Diana's* arrival, and the Russians themselves, when they had tried to impress the Japanese with the naval might of their country, had put the number of warships in Petropavlovsk at "seven." It was evident also that the testimony of repatriated castaways, who were familiar with the weakness of Russia's military position in the Far East, could shatter Golovnin's contention that Russia would have initiated hostilities on a far grander scale had she intended to attack Japan, and there was the danger that Aleksei, who had made up the above story, would improvise further to ingratiate himself with his captors. The Japanese rejected Golovnin's argument that it was permissible for him to have helped himself to the desperately needed firewood and water, since there was no one in the settlement with whom he could have negotiated, and since he had left more than equitable payment, remarking dryly that according to the laws of Japan a man must starve to death rather than take a single grain of rice without permission of the owner. In desperation Golovnin handed to one of the innocent autograph hunters a "song," hoping that, like the inscriptions of Laxman's day, it would be put before the eyes of later Russian visitors. Signed by himself, the "song" read:

> If ever there will be Russians here who are not prisoners but are armed, they must know that seven of their compatriots were captured by the Japanese by deceit and cunning, were put into this jail, and kept as prisoners without any reason. The unfortunate ones ask their countrymen to take proper vengeance on this perfidious people.[52]

On October 8, all the officials except the commander of the fortress called at the prison and, through the cell bars, wished the captives a safe journey and good fortune. Then the Russians were roped around the waist and escorted to Matsumae, where they arrived four days

[52] *Ibid.*, 1:90.

later, and were promptly incarcerated in two cages, in a dark shed, inside the walled castle grounds. The shed measured some twenty-five paces in length, fifteen paces in width, and about fourteen feet in height. Three of its sides were windowless walls, the fourth a grating of heavy squared beams with a door and a small gate. Similar beams formed the cages in the center of the shed. One measured six paces in width and six in length, and was about ten feet in height; it was occupied by the three officers. Another measured six paces in width, eight in length and ten feet in height; it housed the sailors and Aleksei. The cages were provided with heavy gates, so low in height that the prisoners had to crawl through them, and these, like the gates of the shed, were now securely locked. Above the cage gates, there was a small opening for food. In the rear of each cell, there was a little closet with primitive provisions for the necessities of nature, which not even Japanese laws tried to restrict. The sides of the two cages facing each other had been boarded, so that while the Japanese could constantly watch all of the prisoners, the inmates of the different cages could not see each other. The cages, shed, and wooden enclosure were elaborate and new, designed, it appeared, for more or less permanent occupancy, and, watched constantly by guards outside the shed and by others, who entered every half hour and peered at them through the beams of the cages at close range, the Russians saw no chance for escape.

On October 14, the Russians were brought before Arao Shigeaki, Lord of Tajima, the governor of Matsumae. Amicably, he asked them questions, running the gamut from the Rezanov expedition to differences in burial service for rich and poor in Russia, then startled them by inquiring where they would like to live: in Matsumae, in Edo, somewhere else in Japan, or back in Russia. When they insisted that they wished to return to their fatherland or else die, the smile faded from Arao's face and he began to assure them earnestly that the Japanese had a heart like other people and that, if it could be established that the raids of Khvostov and Davydov had indeed been unauthorized, they would be permitted to return to Russia; meanwhile they must not grieve, but take care of themselves, and feel free to request whatever clothing or special food they required. There was comfort in the obvious sincerity of Arao's utterance, and yet had their capture not been the result of deceit? The prisoners could not help suspect that the Japanese consoled them merely to keep them from attempting suicide, expecting that, with time, they would become resigned to staying in Japan, where their Western learning was eagerly sought.

Until mid-November the prisoners were taken to the governor's castle almost every other day and questioned from morning until evening. What was the dress of the Russian Emperor? What kind of birds were there in St. Petersburg? Did the Russians like the Dutch? What salary did they get? How many times a day did Russians go to church? At what age did Russian women first give birth? When could they no longer do so? Not all the questions were equally haphazard, however. The Japanese showed great interest in the illustrations of a French book on physics and sought important information regarding Russia's economic and military power, interspersing pertinent questions in the midst of trivia, as if by accident. But there was nothing casual in the Japanese request that Mur sketch a map of St. Petersburg and indicate the exact location of military and naval garrisons, furnishing data on their size, training, and so forth.

Arao had told the prisoners to put their plea for repatriation on paper, and had furnished them with the necessary writing materials and interpreters. For almost a month they labored on the document, slowed down by the problems of syntax and vocabulary in the translation of the Russian draft into Japanese by way of Kurilian. When it was finished at last and provided, as Arao had suggested, with a covering letter to himself, stating that the document offered proof of their innocence and petitioning that he communicate with his government concerning their repatriation, Arao received the prisoners again and in a long speech declared that he believed their assurances of innocence and, though he did not have the authority to release them, would at least remove their ropes and improve their living conditions. He promised to support their plea for liberation and, as was his habit, asked them not to despair, but to pray to God and calmly await the decision of the Japanese ruler.

To the apparent satisfaction of everyone the prisoners were unbound, and as they were led out of the audience hall, guards, workers, and onlookers, whom they did not even know, rushed up to congratulate them. Even before this, the Russians had been treated relatively well. Two Japanese, once captured by Khvostov and taken to Kamchatka for a winter, tried to cook to their taste; benches had been provided so that the Russians need not sleep on the floor, and the toilets had been rebuilt Western-style. But as they were led back to their shed now, they could hardly believe their eyes. The front grating of the cages had been removed; the adjoining hall-like corridor had been furnished with new matted flooring; a teapot stood over the fire. The ugly shed seemed almost liveable. No sooner had they returned, than officials arrived with their children and, chatting pleasantly, congratulated them. When their dinner was brought, it was served on new dishes and individual trays; the food was better, the sake supply more liberal—everything was done to make the Russians feel more like guests than like prisoners. For the first time they slept in peace.

The departure of the official who was to take the Russian document to Edo was delayed, however. A second signature attesting the accuracy of its translation was ostensibly necessary, and a young man, about twenty-five years of age, was brought to the Russians for language instruction. At once the old suspicion that the Japanese planned to keep them in Japan as experts in Western culture reasserted itself, a suspicion fed by the rumor that a Dutchman, who had agreed never to leave the country, was engaged in astronomical observations and cartography in the capital; a suspicion not entirely farfetched, for in the early seventeenth century the Englishman Will Adams had been retained in such a way by the Japanese. The Russians accused the Japanese of scheming to detain them permanently: "If we were sure that the Japanese truly intended to return us to Russia, we would teach them day and night till the very time of our departure everything we know, but now, seeing the deceit, we do not want to." Upon further deliberation the Russians consented to teach the young man, so that Uehara would be assisted by a second interpreter, but when the Japanese sent an additional student, they refused categorically, repeating that they would rather die than stay in Japan; under no circumstances would they become teachers. They had agreed to instruct a second interpreter, now the Japanese sent a boy; soon there would be a whole school. "But this will never be: we will not turn to teaching; we are few and unarmed; you may kill us, but we do not want to teach."

The second interpreter, Murakami Teisuke, proved a very talented student. Unlike Uehara, who was dull and slow of learning, he picked up Russian with great facility. He brought along a box full of dictionaries and reports, prepared by castaways, who had been in Russia, and corrected and expanded a word list of his own, recording all new words in the Cyrillic alphabet. Murakami did not confine himself to linguistics, but the captives willingly answered most of his many questions concerning Russia, eager of the opportunity to paint a glowing picture of their country; when Murakami touched on matters which they did not care to divulge, they sidestepped them easily by replying that they had spent their life at sea, and their knowledge of conditions in Russia was therefore limited. They readily explained Russian words, but they refused to give English, French, or Dutch equivalents for fear the Japanese would rely on the Dutch to verify their translations. They told Murakami that the British had intercepted a letter of the secretary of the Batavia Council to the Dutch government, in which the Dutchman claimed the credit for having inclined the Japanese against Russia, and took the opportunity to tell a few stories of their own about the Dutch.

At the beginning of the new year, a delegation of officials, among them the former commander of Kunashiri and the official who had given the Russians a letter on Etorofu, departed for Edo. In addition to the documents, they carried with them samples of the Russians' belongings as well as portraits, sketched by Murakami, on which, in the words of Golovnin, "except for our long beards, there was nothing . . . that resembled anyone of us." Among the Russian belongings there were books, and in one of them the Japanese discovered a slip of red paper. As fate would have it, it was a tag from some Japanese goods, which Khvostov had plundered on Etorofu, and had been given by someone to Golovnin, who used it as a bookmark. Golovnin told the Japanese that the slip of paper was Chinese and that he did not remember where he had obtained it, but the discovery disconcerted him very much, for should the true nature of the tag be learned in the capital, he would be linked with Khvostov beyond redemption.

The more Russian Murakami learned, the more questions he could ask, and the prisoners were called upon to go over documents of the Laxman and Rezanov expeditions and books in different languages, concerning the world beyond Japan, among them an account of Benyovszky's uprising, a narrative of the Russian and English attack on Holland in 1799, and a geography of the Russian Empire; the latter with its description of Russia in the Dark Ages intrigued Murakami especially. On the ground that the governor of Matsumae did not want to be outdone by the governor of Nagasaki, who was well informed on the subject, Murakami requested amplification of the Christian ritual, which Japanese castaways had described. With interest the prisoners examined the maps which the castaways, repatriated by Rezanov, had sketched of all the lands and seas they had seen; faulty in scale, they were still surprisingly skillful in conception. When the prisoners were tired of being interrogated, they would begin asking questions of their own. At once the Japanese would become less communicative, refusing to disclose even their ruler's name or title.

By mid-February Russian patience was near the end. A promise of better quarters had failed to materialize and Murakami admitted that no decision had been reached in Edo concerning their case. In desperation Golovnin and Khlebnikov proposed to their countrymen that they attempt to escape. They could make their way to shore, take possession of a vessel, and sail to Kamchatka or the coast of Tatary. Since Japanese boats had often been driven to Russian territory, chances were that they, with their expert knowledge of navigation, could make their way back safely; at worst, it would be better to die at sea than to expire in Japanese captivity. Mur and the sailors Simanov and Vasilev objected, but the others began storing up the necessary supplies; they managed to hide a little cereal at meal time, secretly dried it at night, and stowed it away in small bags. The question arose whether it would be safe to initiate the Ainu Aleksei into the secret. After some hesitation it was decided, that his knowledge of edible roots and grasses and his familiarity with local waters, might prove valuable and, though Aleksei grew pale with fright when told of the plan to escape, he quickly pulled himself together and agreed to go along. By mid-March, when Murakami reported that no one in the capital believed the story of the captives and hinted at the existence of yet another incriminating letter of Khvostov, Mur and the two sailors also agreed to join the flight. Gradually the guards relaxed their vigilance, and the prisoners prepared to escape through a small gate, by which the toilets were cleaned, planning to pry it open with a sharp knife that Simanov had managed to conceal, when Mur unexpectedly demurred once again. His decision to stay behind forced the other captives to delay until the coming of warm weather, when, as the interpreters had promised, they would be taken on small excursions, during which an opportunity for sudden flight might present itself, without the danger of Mur thwarting their plans. It produced a rift between Mur and his countrymen; at the same time it marked a startling change in his attitude toward the Japanese. Shying away from his own comrades, Mur adopted Japanese manners and forms of salutation, addressing the officials as if they were his official superiors. The son of a German in the Russian service, Mur began to disclaim being Russian, hoping, it seems, to enter Japanese employment as an interpreter some day.

In April, the captives were transferred to a relatively comfortable house within the fortress grounds, and were invited to live with the Japanese as with their own countrymen and brothers, but news that the shogunate had decided to repel all Western attempts at negotiation, as well as the unlikelihood of sufficient Russian naval pressure to effect their release in the near future, sustained their determination to escape. By now, the guards paid little attention to them—read books, played cards in the guard house, or actually fell asleep. Only the fear that Mur might sound the alarm prevented the captives from sneaking away at night. Patiently they added to their secret store of supplies and even made a little compass.

During the night of May 5 to May 6, the Russians stole two knives from the kitchen, bored a tunnel under the wall, and, leaving behind Mur and Aleksei, slipped into the open. Silently they headed toward the mountains, intent on making their way to a coastal settlement, where they could take possession of a suitable vessel.[53]

For four days the fugitives clung to the cover of the mountains, pushing north across untrodden slopes, mountain ridges, and frozen rivers, braving unknown dangers and the chill of icy winds, their progress hampered excruciatingly by fear of discovery and an injured knee, which Golovnin had incurred, when crawling through the narrow passage under the wall. Concerned with the way their flight across the mountains was sapping them of the strength they needed to defend themselves against the wild animals of Hokkaido or to take possession of a vessel and navigate it to freedom, the Russians at last turned westward and at night ventured into the open, armed with wooden lances.

Their flight into the mountains had necessitated a great deal of zigzagging, and, as they stepped out onto the seashore, the Russians were no more than sixteen miles from where they had started. Con-

53 *Ibid.*, 1:107-201.

tinuing northward, they stole past several Japanese villages with good, but disappointingly small boats, before withdrawing to the mountains again, where they hid during the day, and sewed two sails from their shirts, making rigging out of ropes of twisted scraps of cotton. They continued their flight for several days, pushing north along the coast at night, retreating to the cover of the mountains before dawn.

At one place the fugitives spotted a suitable vessel riding at anchor, but it put out to sea before they could execute an attack; another ship, which would have been satisfactory, was guarded too carefully. At last they found several unattended boats that seemed just right— one of them fully equipped—but to their exasperation they lacked the strength to push them into the water. This, and the increasing risk of discovery as the result of the strikingly large footprints which their Siberian-type boots, sewn by Simanov, had left at least at one place, and of repeated encounters with barking dogs, prompted the fugitives to make a drastic change in plans. They had heard of a small uninhabited wooded island, some twenty-five or thirty miles from shore. If they could make their way there—and for this they only needed small boats, which they could have launched without difficulty—they could replenish their strength on the island at leisure and at the proper time make a surprise attack on one of the many vessels, which passed there, and on it return to Russia. But the change in plans had come too late. The Russians were in the midst of deliberation in their mountainous hiding place, when suddenly they found themselves surrounded by a ring of Japanese soldiers. After eight days at large, they were prisoners again.

The march to Matsumae was relatively short; the following day, on May 15, the Russians were back in the city. Along the way they saw the tell-tale footprints, which they had left during their flight, and noticed that the Japanese had marked them with stakes. So closely had the Japanese followed in their tracks, that they could have descended upon them earlier, but they had bided their time, whether, as Golovnin believed, for fear of losing too many of their own men or, more likely, because they were concerned with recapturing all of the prisoners unharmed.

Brought before the governor, Golovnin proclaimed himself solely responsible for the escape and challenged the Japanese to kill him, if they wished, but to let his men go unpunished. Dryly Arao remarked that the Japanese would kill him without a request on his part, if they desired to do so; if not, all his pleas would be in vain. Arao denied that it was the intention of his countrymen to detain the captives permanently. He asked how they had planned and executed their escape, seeking to establish whether any Japanese had been implicated. He asserted that their venture had been foolishly hopeless, but could not resist asking, what they would have said of the Japanese, had they succeeded after all, and inquired whether they were aware of the fact, that he and many other officials would have had to disembowel themselves, had they not been recaptured.

Arao spoke without rancor. Had they been Japanese, they would have been subject to severe punishment; but they were foreigners; they had broken out of confinement not in order to harm the Japanese, but to return to their fatherland; his good opinion of them remained unchanged.

Arao's personal feelings did not extend to the captives' accommodations. When they were led off to prison in the late afternoon, they found themselves incarcerated in three small cages inside a dark shed, bounded by wooden and earthen walls. The gate of the shed was boarded completely and, when it closed, there was total darkness, except when guards with lanterns entered for a check. Theirs was a normal Japanese prison, inhabited already by a sociable Japanese occupant in a fourth cage, but they were treated better than their Japanese mate and better, in fact, than criminals in many parts of Europe at that time. They suffered no physical abuse, and were cheered by gestures of compassion on the part of some of the guards, and by repeated assurances that, with time, their lot would improve and that chances for their repatriation were still good. What pained them most, was the collaboration of Mur with the Japanese. When Arao renewed his interrogation of Golovnin, he showed himself informed concerning the connection between Rezanov and Khvostov; he proved to be in possession of considerable information (and misinformation) about the voyage of the *Diana*, the aims of Golovnin, and the policies of Russia. All this he had learned from Mur who, like Aleksei, now lived apart from the other prisoners. Desperately, Golovnin tried to undermine Japanese trust in Mur, afraid that Mur alone might make his way back to Russia and deliberately distort the story of their captivity. It was with some relief, that the prisoners observed that, use Mur as the Japanese did, they were not attracted by his efforts, and retained their respect for Golovnin.

On May 16, Arao asked the fugitives whether they pleaded guilty or not. Their first reaction was to shift blame for their escape onto the shoulders of the Japanese, who had lured them into the fortress, but when they saw that this line of argument merely antagonized the Japanese and, when the governor advised them that it would be to their advantage to plead guilty, they did so, Golovnin and Khlebnikov shouldering responsibility as officers.[54]

In mid-July Arao was succeeded as governor of Matsumae by Ogasawara, a giant by Japanese standards, but an affable personality, imbued with the wisdom of venerable age. He had the prisoners moved back to the house, where they had stayed upon their first arrival in Matsumae, with an adjoining, but separate, room with its own entrance, added for Mur and Aleksei. The prisoners received their books as well as writing materials. Golovnin and Khlebnikov whiled away time teaching their subordinates how to read and write, and compiled a Japanese vocabulary in Cyrillic letters. Golovnin also kept a secret diary, surreptitiously recording his experiences and thoughts on tiny scraps of paper in a melange of Russian, French and English words, abbreviated and interspersed with different signs, understandable only to himself. Treated well, the prisoners offered their jailors gifts of clothing and other tokens of appreciation.

The captives were constantly called upon to translate documents of importance. On July 14, their first meeting with Ogasawara, they were shown a Russian paper, with a French translation attached, in which the Japanese were threatened with military action, if they persisted in their refusal to trade with Russia; addressed to the governor of Matsumae, but bearing no signature, the paper had evidently been left by Khvostov. On September 18, Golovnin and Mur were ordered to translate two Russian papers, just delivered from Kunashiri. Dated as recently as September 9, they turned out to be letters from Rikord; one addressed to the commander of Kunashiri, the other to Golovnin himself. In the former, Rikord identified himself and reported that he was returning with a number of Japanese castaways, among them the Matsumae merchant "Leonzaimo" (Nakagawa Goroji, who had been kidnapped by Khvostov);[55] he assured the commander that Russian intentions toward Japan were peaceful, and demanded whether the commander himself would

[54] *Ibid.,* 2:1-47.

[55] Nakagawa Goroji told the Russians that his name was Ryozaemon, hence "Leonzaimo."

release the captives and, if not, how soon a reply could be expected from the Japanese government; he warned that he would not leave, until he had received such a reply, and requested permission to get fresh water on shore. In the letter to Golovnin, Rikord announced his arrival at Kunashiri and told of the communication to the commander; anxious to know whether Golovnin was still alive, he asked that, if Golovnin was unable to reply in writing, he tear the letter at the line containing the word "alive" and return it with the Japanese, whom he had sent ashore.

Golovnin was not permitted to reply and neither he nor Mur had the opportunity to mark the letter, as suggested by Rikord, and return it to their anxious countryman. Once again the *Diana* was at the shores of Japan, but, unless they could get word to Rikord that they were still alive, what chance did Golovnin and his fellow prisoners have of liberation?[56]

[56] Golovnin, *Zapiski*, 2:48-73.

CHAPTER SEVEN · WISE COUNSELS

A FRIENDLY GO-BETWEEN

T HE capture of Golovnin struck the *Diana* like a bolt out of the blue sky. Through their telescopes, the officers and men left on board had followed his reception on shore with satisfaction, and, when he and those who accompanied him, disappeared into the fortress, had turned to their preparations for the festive reception of the Japanese officials aboard ship. They could hardly believe their eyes, as gunfire and screams suddenly filled the air, and they saw the Japanese rush out of the fortress, take possession of the Russian boat, and drag away the sailor and Ainu tending it.

For a moment Lieutenant Commander Petr Rikord, the senior officer aboard ship, was stunned. Then, weighing anchor, he moved in menacingly toward the shore. The Japanese batteries opened fire and the *Diana* reciprocated with some one hundred and seventy rounds, but shallow water prevented the vessel from drawing close enough to do any significant damage to the thick earthen wall and the Japanese works beyond. Only fifty-one in number, the Russians could not attempt an assault landing without inviting Japanese capture or destruction of their vessel. There was little they could do but return to Okhotsk for reinforcements. They wrote Golovnin a letter, explaining this, put it in a barrel and dropped the barrel overboard. The Japanese seemed willing to exchange messages, for in the morning they too put a barrel in the water. But when the Russians set out in a boat to retrieve it, they discovered that it was merely bait for another trap: a rope had been attached to the barrel and almost imperceptibly the Japanese were pulling it toward shore. The Russians returned to the *Diana* and, on July 26, having landed clothing, linen, books, razors, and other personal belongings of the captives at a deserted village of the promontory, quitted Gizo (Senpekotan) Bay, renamed by them for posterity Zaliv Izmeny—The Bay of Deceit.

At Okhotsk Rikord conferred with the port commandant, Captain Manitskii, a mutual friend of Rikord and Golovnin since their days of service with the British navy, then set out for St. Petersburg to make a personal report to the Minister of the Navy. When he reached Irkutsk, Governor Nikolai Treskin informed him that, on

word from Manitskii, he had already written to the government requesting authorization for an expedition to liberate Golovnin.
Rikord, therefore, did not continue to the capital, but remained
in Irkutsk. The plans for an elaborate expedition, which he worked
out together with Treskin and submitted to Ivan Pestel, Governor
General of Siberia, however, failed to meet imperial approval, since
Russia was just then absorbed in a life-and-death struggle with
Napoleon Bonaparte—it was in September of 1812 that Moscow
erupted in flames, and the French did not begin their ignominious
retreat until October 19. Instead, Rikord was ordered merely to
resume the interrupted surveys, stopping by at Kunashiri to inquire
after the fate of the captives.[1]

Accompanied by Nakagawa Goroji, who had been brought to
him in Irkutsk, Rikord hurried back to Okhotsk by carriage and
reindeer. On August 3, he put out to sea on the *Diana* with the
transport brig *Zotik*. The *Diana*'s complement had been reinforced
by one petty officer and ten men;[2] on board also were Nakagawa and
six recent castaways, whom Rikord hoped to exchange for his captive
shipmates. The victim of Khvostov's transgressions, Nakagawa lost
no opportunity to thwart Russian efforts. While still in Russia, he
had made several attempts to escape and on two occasions had
managed to destroy maps and documents relating to Japan. Rikord
had obtained a paper from the governor of Irkutsk, in which the
latter reviewed the circumstances of Golovnin's voyage and capture.
The paper declared that Japanese castaways, shipwrecked off Kamchatka, were being repatriated as proof of the friendliness of Russian intentions toward Japan, and expressed the hope that Golovnin
and his fellow-captives, having done no harm to anyone, would be
released in exchange. At the same time it warned that, if the Russian
prisoners were not returned at this time, either because permission
had not been received from the Japanese government or for other
reasons, Russian men-of-war would come again the following year
to demand their release. When Rikord asked Nakagawa, who understood some Russian, to draft a short letter in Japanese on the basis

---

[1] Petr Ivanovich Rikord, *Zapiski Flota Kapitana Rikorda o plavanii ego k iaponskim
beregam*, 1-13. An English translation of this may be found in Golownin, *Memoirs*, II,
227-356. I have consulted this translation, but have found it inaccurate and incomplete
in places; my text is based on the original Russian version, as republished in 1875 by
the widow of Rikord.

[2] The *Zotik* was commanded by Lieutenant Filatov, formerly of the *Diana*; another
shipmate, Lieutenant Iakushkin, had left Rikord to take command of the Okhotsk
transport *Pavel*.

of this paper to the commander of Kunashiri, Nakagawa produced a sheet so thoroughly covered with writing that Rikord suspected that Nakagawa had added something of his own. Challenged, Nakagawa admitted that he had really written three notes: one about the proposed exchange of prisoners, one concerning the shipwreck of the castaways, and one about his own misfortunes. When Rikord asked that Nakagawa provide him with copies of these notes, Nakagawa dutifully copied the first. Taking a knife, he then cut off the lines he had added on his own, and, with a look of defiance, put the paper in his mouth and literally swallowed his own words. The prospect of having to depend on such a man in negotiations with the Japanese was discouraging.[3]

On September 9, the Russians were back in the Bay of Deceit. A new battery of fourteen guns had been erected; striped curtains hid most of the buildings from sight; all boats had been pulled up on shore; an unnatural silence had ominously settled over the countryside. Casting anchor some two miles from shore, Rikord sent the castaway Emokichi with the letter to the commander of the island. When Emokichi failed to return, Rikord sent the castaway Chugoro ashore. At first his note was not accepted by the Japanese, but on a second try commander Ota Hikosuke received Rikord's communication and invited Rikord to a conference in town. This Rikord could not risk; neither would Ota venture aboard the *Diana*. Reluctantly, Rikord found it necessary to rely on Nakagawa, and, on September 16, sent him ashore to negotiate with the commander. If prevented from returning, he was to send back through the castaway, who accompanied him, one of the three notes, which Rikord handed him: "Lieutenant Commander Golovnin and the others are on Kunashiri"; "Lieutenant Commander Golovnin and the others have been taken to Matsumae City, Nagasaki, Edo"; "Lieutenant Commander Golovnin and the others have been killed." Returning in person, Nakagawa announced curtly: "Lieutenant Commander Golovnin and the others have been killed." But Rikord did not trust Nakagawa sufficiently to open hostilities without further evidence, and he sent Nakagawa ashore again to obtain written confirmation. This time Nakagawa did not return.

---

[3] Neither Golovnin nor Rikord give the text of Rikord's letter. A Japanese version is cited by Segawa (158-159). Ironically, it is possible that Nakagawa might have been released shortly after capture—as were some of his countrymen—had he not boosted his usefulness in Russian eyes by falsely representing himself as an official of some importance. (Abe, 25-31)

On September 18, the Russians captured a Japanese boat, but its passengers, diving overboard, managed to escape, except three—two Japanese and one Ainu—from whom Rikord failed to extract anything intelligible. More fortunate was the interception the following day of the *Kanze Maru*, a much larger Japanese ship, since they captured not only many members of the crew, but Takadaya Kahei, the captain himself.[4]

Takadaya Kahei was a man of wealth, prestige, and influence. A native of Awaji Province in south-central Japan, he had been active for years in commerce and navigation in different regions of the Japanese Empire, but especially in the north, where he had contributed to the extension of Japanese administration to the Kuril Islands. Since the beginning of the nineteenth century, he had established himself in Hakodate, and he had been on his way from Etorofu to this city with a cargo of dried fish as well as official dispatches (which he managed to throw overboard), when the *Kanze Maru* was intercepted.

On board the *Diana*, Takadaya replied straightforwardly to Rikord's halting questions in broken Japanese, but his assertion, upon seeing the text of Nakagawa's note to the commander of Kunashiri, that Lieutenant Commander Mur and five Russians were in the city of Matsumae, was bewildering. Was Takadaya telling the truth or was he contradicting Nakagawa merely to save his own life? What had happened to Golovnin? Was it possible that Takadaya should have heard of Mur and not of Golovnin?[5]

The men of the *Diana* clamored for revenge, especially since some of them claimed to recognize in Takadaya an official, whom they had seen on Kunashiri the year before. But as long as there was a change that Takadaya's assertion, that some of the captives were still alive, was true, Rikord could not endanger their safety by rash action, and he decided to withdraw to Kamchatka, taking along Takadaya, whose rich silken apparel, sword, and general bearing testified that he was of considerably higher status and education than any Japanese, who had hitherto visited Russia. Takadaya him-

---

[4] Rikord, *Zapiski*, 13-27; Segawa, 159-165; Tokutomi, XXIV, 291-292. Russian sources refer to Takadaya as Takatai-Kakhi.

[5] In point of fact, it is quite possible that Takadaya had never heard of Golovnin by name, or at least not in a way resembling its Russian pronunciation. Shogunate officials referred to Golovnin as "Owarin," and Japanese documents rendered his name also "Kabitan Koroin" (not visibly separated in Japanese) and "Koroin." (Segawa, 169.)

self made no objections, and only tried to dissuade Rikord from detaining four of his seamen in place of the four scurvy-ridden castaways, whom he had put ashore, arguing in vain that they were "stupid" and "extremely afraid of the Russians." Soon curiosity conquered fear, however, and the four attendants and their master seemed fairly at home on board the Russian man-of-war.[6]

Takadaya's shipmates were anxious to have a closer look at the strangers. One of Takadaya's passengers was a woman.[7] Invited into Rikord's cabin, she was delighted to find another female, the young wife of the junior doctor. The two ladies—the first Russians and Japanese of their sex to meet—discussed no weighty matters of state, but compared make-up, tried on each other's fineries, and embraced and kissed each other. To the Japanese woman the white complexion of the foreigner seemed most attractive, but the Russians were no less impressed by her own appearance—her lengthy brownish face, her sparkling dark eyes, small mouth, and black-lacquered teeth, her daintily painted eyebrows, pleasant speech, and lavish dress. At Takadaya's request, the crew of the *Kanze Maru* was given a chance to explore the Russian warship. Amazed, the Japanese seamen wandered about the deck of the *Diana*, their curiosity whetted with vodka. They examined the mechanism of the running rigging, admired the way in which Russian sailors scampered out upon the yards or up to the mast-head, and bartered some of their belongings for buttons, kerchiefs, and other Russian trifles.

Meanwhile Rikord had shown Takadaya a copy of the letter written by Nakagawa, and had asked him to prepare another to the Japanese authorities, informing them, among other things, that he planned to take Takadaya to Kamchatka, but would return with him the following year.[8] The letter was sent ashore with Takadaya's

[6] Rikord, *Zapiski*, 27-33; Tokutomi, XXIV, 291-294; Watanabe Shujiro, *Nichi-Ro kosho Takadaya Kahei*, 27-34.

[7] Segawa disputes the implication made by Rikord that the Japanese woman was Takadaya's mistress. He notes that Takadaya had a mistress in Hakodate whom he took sightseeing often as well as another mistress in later years, as well as a number of girl friends, but doubts that he would have taken a mistress on this voyage. Segawa identifies the woman as the wife of Kakueimon, a Japanese official serving on Etorofu. Whether Kakueimon himself was on the vessel is not clear. Rikord notes that there were sixty Japanese aboard the *Kanze Maru*, but Segawa limits the number to forty-six, counting Takadaya. Of these, nine drowned when they jumped into the sea to escape the Russians. Five, including Takadaya, were taken aboard the *Diana*. Among the thirty-two others, whose names are known, Kakueimon is not listed. If he was aboard, he must have been one of those who drowned. (Segawa, 178; Rikord, *Zapiski*, 28.)

[8] For the text of these letters see Segawa, 170-173.

female companion, but no reply was received. Nor did the sociability of Takadaya's men, who departed in an amicable spirit, extend to the samurai on shore; and once, when a Russian boat had approached the land, and now, when the vessels hoisted sails, the shore batteries opened fire. But the ships were safely out of range, and the Russians only laughed at the Japanese salvos, as they headed out to sea. Even Takadaya felt constrained to laugh and commented, "Kunashiri is a bad place for the Russians; Nagasaki is better."[9]

On October 15, the *Diana* and *Zotik* returned to Petropavlovsk Harbor, having named the strait between Matsuwa and Raikoke Island, in memory of their captive commander. Throughout the stormy twenty-two day crossing, Takadaya stayed close to Rikord, who managed eventually to extract from him the news that Golovnin was still alive. He was flattered to be allowed to share Rikord's cabin. Upon arrival in Petropavlovsk, he was not confined in the way his own countrymen had confined Golovnin, but was permitted to remain with Rikord and was treated by everyone with sympathy and kindness. Takadaya reacted with enthusiasm. He plunged into the study of Russian and, before the winter had ended, he and Rikord, who knew a little Japanese, were able to communicate quite intelligibly. When Rikord bemoaned the misunderstandings that had arisen between their countries, Takadaya exclaimed: "I perceive in my misfortune Providence, which has chosen me for its instrument. Without important reasons for going to Kunashiri Bay, I entered there by chance, not having been in it for more than five years, and thereby caused you to desist from your determined intention of attacking the settlement; consequently I became the savior of the lives of several tens of Russians and several hundreds of Japanese. This thought animates me. . . ." Takadaya reported that when Rezanov had arrived in Nagasaki all the inhabitants of Japan had rejoiced at rumors that commercial relations would be established with Russia and that there had been great displeasure when the Japanese government had rebuffed the ambassador. He himself still favored trade between the two countries. Again and again he expressed the desire to act as go-between in the *rapprochement* of the two nations. Upon his return to Japan he would describe the land of his captors as it had never been described before by a Japanese; he would assure his countrymen that the Russians had never harbored hostile intentions

[9] Rikord, *Zapiski*, 28-37.

against Japan. To be sure, the military strength and fortifications of Petropavlovsk did not escape his attention and he recorded every detail in his diary, but he flattered himself that these were purely defensive—to protect Russia against Japanese retaliation for the raids of Khvostov. As the ultimate gesture of his goodwill and sincerity, Takadaya offered his life as pledge that the Russian captives in Japan would be freed if negotiations were entered upon in Nagasaki.

It must not be assumed that Takadaya acted merely out of gratitude for being treated better than he had feared; nor was he motivated primarily by concern for his own liberation. There is no evidence that he had become enamored of the Russian way of life and hoped to propagate it in Japan. On the contrary, he devoted much effort to explain the ways of his countrymen to the Russians in as favorable a light as possible. His willingness to aid the Russians stemmed from the conviction that war between the two countries must be avoided in the interest of Japan. He insisted that Japanese recourse to arms had been purely defensive and that the Japanese would free the captives, if the governor of Irkutsk would certify in writing that the Russian government had not participated in the aggression of Khvostov. As an enterprising businessman, active in the northern regions of Japan, he must have been attracted also by the opportunities, which trade with Russia held out both for Japan as a whole and for himself. But there can be no doubt about his desire to return to Japan. Japanese historians have never questioned Takadaya's loyalty, but have praised his conduct as creditable and honorable, and have suggested that he had been inspired by the loyalty of the forty-seven *ronin*, the greatest of national heroes.

It was a long and harsh winter. Two of Takadaya's attendants, Kichizo and Bunji, died of beri-beri and asthma and a third, Kinzo was sick. Affected by the death of his countrymen, Takadaya began to brood. He complained of weak health and claimed that the scurvy festering in his feet would kill him. Though it was primarily homesickness that ailed Takadaya, Rikord realized that the liberation of Golovnin and possibly the establishment of commercial relations with Japan hinged on his safe return, and he decided to take Takadaya back to Japan as soon as weather permitted. In spring the letter from the governor of Irkutsk to the governor of Matsumae, which Takadaya had suggested, arrived, and, on May 18, 1813, Rikord cut his way through the ice and put out to sea. The *Diana* sailed alone, the *Zotik* having been wrecked at the coast of Kamchatka the preceding year.

Toward the middle of June, 1813, the *Diana* cast anchor in the Bay of Deceit. Takadaya thought of going ashore to negotiate with local officials concerning the release of the captives, but for fear that his star captive be detained, Rikord dispatched Heizo and Kinzo in his stead. When Takadaya refused to promise that his subordinates would return Rikord could not control his irritation. "Tell the commander of Kunashiri from me," he instructed the two Japanese, "that if he will detain you on shore and will not send me any news about the fate of the Russian captives, I shall have to consider this a hostile act, and will take your commander with me to Okhotsk, from where this very summer several warships will come to demand by force the release of the Russian captives. I await an answer within three days." Takadaya was greatly offended. Stiffly he observed: "Commander of the imperial vessel, you counsel rashly; your message to the commander of Kunashiri through my sailors contains much, yet according to our laws little. In vain you threaten to carry me away to Okhotsk. If the commandant should decide to detain my two sailors on land, not two nor even two thousand sailors can take my place. At the same time I warn you that it will not be in your power to take me away to Okhotsk; but of this later. Now tell me whether you have really decided to let my sailors ashore under these conditions?" When Rikord replied that he could not do otherwise, Takadaya withheld from Heizo and Kinzo the written message he had intended to send ashore and gave them new and detailed oral instructions. Then he took out his religious image and, after a while of silent prayer, asked one of his men to deliver it to his wife, entrusting to him likewise his long sword for transmission to his only son and heir. Finally Takadaya and his men exchanged drinks. Then Heizo and Kinzo were taken ashore in a boat, and set out for the settlement.

Rikord had followed Takadaya's words attentively. He had been cheered by the favorable light in which Takadaya had reviewed his treatment at the hands of the Russians. But Takadaya's curt and challenging remarks, the abandonment of his most prized possessions, and the manner of his parting with his subordinates alarmed him. He had no illusions about the return of the two seamen. He could of course prevent Takadaya from returning to Japan, but could he prevent him from laying hands on himself? After much reflection Rikord came to the conclusion that it was safer to risk the loss of Takadaya as hostage by releasing him than by detaining him, and informed him that he was free to go ashore anytime, adding that he was relying on his magnanimity; if he did not return, it would cost him his own life.

"I understand," Takadaya replied "You cannot go back to Okhotsk without a written certificate concerning the fate of all Russian captives; nor can I suffer the slightest stain on my honor, other than at the cost of my life. I thank you for your confidence, but even before, I did not intend to go ashore on the same day with my sailors; this, by our custom would not befit me; but tomorrow in the morning, if it is all right with you, order that I be taken ashore early."

"No need to give orders," retorted Rikord, "I will convey you myself."

"And so we are friends again!" exclaimed Takadaya joyfully. Then he confessed that he had been wounded by Rikord's irate message to the commander of Kunashiri. The threat of warships had not concerned him, but the threat of his being taken back to Okhotsk had implied that he was being likened to the deceiver Nakagawa. "Our national honor does not permit a man of my rank to be a prisoner in a foreign country, yet such you wished to make of me, when you announced your intention of carrying me away with you to Okhotsk." To Kamchatka, he had accompanied the Russians of his own will. "As you were stronger, I was in your hands, but my life was always in my own power. After all this I disclose to you the secret of my intentions: seeing you unshakable in your undertaking, I had firmly resolved to commit suicide. As proof of its execution, I cut off a tuft of hair on my head, [he showed a bald spot,] and laid it into the box of my religious image. This, according to our laws, signified that he who sends his own hair has taken his life honorably, that is to say has ripped open his bowels. The hair is then buried with the same ceremonial which would be observed in case of the corpse itself. As you call me friend, I will hide nothing from you: so great was my wrath, that I even wanted to kill you and your senior officer, and then have the consolation of announcing this to your crew!"[10]

[10] Segawa, 186-217; Rikord, *Zapiski*, 37-47. Rikord does not mention Takadaya's desire to go ashore. He writes that the two Japanese were sent ashore on Takadaya's suggestion.

A cold shiver ran down Rikord's spine. To think that he had shared his cabin with Takadaya! He could not resist wondering why Takadaya, if he did seek revenge, had not planned to destroy the whole ship by igniting the powder magazine. "And blow everybody up?" Takadaya retorted. "No, my friend, that I knew, but what bravery is there in that? To my way of thinking, to take revenge in such underhand manner is characteristic for small, timid souls; you don't imagine that I, who respect you as a brave commander, would have killed you in your sleep? I thought it superfluous to expound on this, but as you consider it great to take revenge by blowing up the ship, you probably thought that I intended to kill you stealthily. No! I would have set about the task with a formal challenge." Rikord understood that these were no idle boasts, that Takadaya, for all his friendliness, was first of all Japanese, determined to safeguard the honor of his country. Rikord had always respected Takadaya. This new display of bravery and sincerity endeared Takadaya in his esteem more than ever.

When Rikord and Takadaya went ashore, they were met by Heizo and Kinzo, who reported that the commander of Kunashiri had received them well, though he had not allowed them to retain any Russian objects, which they now brought back, wrapped in a bundle. Rikord was permitted to take on water at the rivulet, on condition that his men would not cross to the other side, facing the settlement. He was informed that three dignitaries—two of whom Takadaya recognized by name as good friends—had hastened there following the appearance of Russian ships and that the commander of Kunashiri was eager to meet with Takadaya. When Rikord was handed a box with papers, Takadaya took it from him and three times raised it above his head in respect. "Everything is favorable for us! I say *us*, because according to my feelings I am half-Russian," he commented, and added, "It will be very good, if you will permit me to take this box back to the commander; tomorrow without delay I shall return it to you: this our ceremonial demands." For a second, doubt flashed through Rikord's mind, but he brushed it aside, took out a handkerchief, cut it in two and handing one of the halves to Takadaya, said, "He who is my friend will bring me the other half of my handkerchief in a day or two, not later than in three." Takadaya promised to return the very next morning and vowed that death alone could prevent him from coming.

The Japanese had expected the Russians to return, and a letter signed by Takahashi Sampei and Kojimoto Hyogoro, examiners of the governor of Matsumae, had been sent to Matsumae. Reviewing Russian actions, it stated that the captives would be released, if an official explanation of the Khvostov incident were received. This was the letter which had been delivered to Rikord, and Takadaya carried it with him to the Kunashiri office, where he met with the Matsumae officials Masuda Kingoro and Ota Hikosuke, reporting to them his amazing experiences, and advocating peace between Russia and Japan. The officials carefully recorded everything and sent a special messenger to Matsumae.[11]

True to his promise, Takadaya returned the following day with the happy tidings that the Russian captives were alive and, except for Khlebnikov, who had been ill for some time, in good health. In reply to the commander of Kunashiri, who had forwarded the papers from Matsumae, Rikord sent a note in which he acknowledged their receipt, reiterated his government's innocence in Khvostov's raids and, on Takadaya's suggestion, offered to sail to Hakodate, if two Japanese could accompany him to facilitate contact with shore.[12] When Takadaya returned once again, he reported that Rikord's proposal, like the letter he had sent upon arrival at Kunashiri, had been forwarded to Matsumae, where they were translated with the aid of the captives. Hereafter Takadaya moved freely back and forth between ship and shore, supplying the Russians with information and food. He maintained that his own abduction had been fully justified in view of Nakagawa's assertion that Golovnin and his fellow-captives had been slain. In this connection, he reported that Nakagawa had not wittingly deceived Rikord, but had himself been misinformed by the commander, who tried to goad the Russians into an attack in order to avenge himself for the humiliating raids of Khvostov. Without doubt Russian determination and fire power would have resulted in the frightful slaughter of his troops; but the entire garrison, some three hundred men strong, had cut tufts of their hair in a vow to fight to the death, their grim anticipation lightened by plans to poison all the liquor, for which, in the past, the victorious seamen had shown a strong passion.

On August 1, Takadaya brought a note in Golovnin's handwriting,

[11] Rikord, *Zapiski*, 47-53; Segawa, 223-227; Akaba Sozo, "Takahashi Sampei no Kunashiri toko," 11: 9-10.

[12] For a Japanese version of the letter, see Segawa, 232-233.

which the Japanese authorities had sent to the various places, where they thought the Russians might come. Dated May 22, 1813, and signed jointly by Golovnin and Mur, it stated simply but eloquently: "We all, officers as well as sailors and the Kurilian Aleksei, are alive and are staying in Matsumae." This note and the fact that the authorities did not restrict Takadaya, as they had earlier repatriates, and even smuggled him a letter from his son, the touching contents of which he shared with the Russians, were cause for mutual elation, and when he left ship that day the sailors saluted him with a rousing "Ura!"[13]

On August 7, Takahashi Sampei, who was next in rank to the governor of Matsumae and who, it will be recalled, had signed the letter transmitted to Rikord, arrived on the governor's own official vessel, the *Choshu Maru*, accompanied by the censor Ibara Ryohei, by Uehara Kumajiro, eight followers, the Russian sailor Simanov, and Aleksei. But though he now took charge of dealings with Rikord, Takahashi decided upon consultation with Masuda Kingoro, Ota Hikosuke, and Takadaya, to leave the negotiations themselves in the hands of the latter.

On August 8, Takadaya brought Simanov aboard the *Diana*.[14] Boundless was the joy of reunion; sweet the confirmation that the other captives were alive. While the sailors besieged their shipmate with questions, Takadaya, in Rikord's cabin, read a message from Takahashi, in which the official declared that his dispatch by the governor of Matsumae in response to Rikord's letter was an expression of respect for Rikord's high position as commandant of Kamchatka. He had come to convey the conditions under which the prisoners would be freed. He sympathized with the hardships which events of the previous year and the return voyage to Kunashiri had entailed, and promised that Simanov, whom he had brought along, could visit the vessel daily, provided he slept on shore. Expressing regret that the laws of Japan did not permit him to confer with Rikord directly, he stated that Takadaya had been appointed negotiator and begged that the Russians trust him. The conditions, which had to be met before the release of the captives, were: (1) the presentation of an official

13 Golovnin, *Zapiski*, 2: 96; Rikord, *Zapiski*, 54-62.
14 Segawa, 231; Akaba, "Takahashi," 11: 11-12; 12: 18-19; Rikord, *Zapiski*, 62. Japanese dates do not match here. Segawa differs by some three weeks, giving the date of the meeting, for example, as the twenty-first day of the sixth lunar month which would have been July 19th.

certificate, testifying that the actions of Khvostov had been without the authorization or knowledge of the Russian government; (2) the return of the armor, arrows, muskets, cannons, and other paraphernalia of war plundered by Khvostov, for fear they might be regarded in the future as trophies wrested from Japan, or, should they have been removed to faraway places, presentation of a certificate, stating that no such objects could be found in Okhotsk. Takahashi wrote that it was the opinion of the Japanese government that Takadaya had accompanied Rikord voluntarily; the official Japanese paper did not take cognizance of his capture. He expressed the hope that Rikord would find it possible that very year to bring the required certificates from Okhotsk to Hakodate, where he and Kojimoto Hyogoro would accept them in person with due ceremonial, and assuring him of his cooperation in seeking the release of the captives, wished the *Diana* good speed.[15]

Important as the communication was, it sorely vexed Rikord's patience. At the first opportunity he excused himself and stepped into another cabin to talk to the released sailor in private. No sooner was Simanov alone with Rikord, than he tore open the seam of his collar and took out a carefully folded letter from Golovnin. Feverishly Rikord began to read:

Dearest Friend P. I.:

It seems that the Japanese are beginning to understand the whole truth of our affair, and are becoming convinced in the peace loving intentions of our government, as well as in the fact that the actions of Khvostov had been unauthorized, without the knowledge of the authorities and to the great displeasure of the Sovereign; but they need for this the formal assurance from the commander of some province and region of ours with the state seal affixed. There is hope that, having assured themselves of the friendly disposition of Russia toward them, they will enter into commercial relations with us, as they now have begun to understand the knavish actions of the Dutch: we told them of the letter intercepted by the English in which the Dutch translators brag that they have succeeded in Nagasaki to embroil Rezanov with the Japanese. But when you enter into dealings with the Japanese, be careful, and do not negotiate other than on boats, beyond gunshot from shore. When doing so, be not disappointed by the slowness of the Japanese in decisions and replies; we know that in their country their own unimportant matters, which in Europe would be terminated in a day or two, drag out for a month and more. In general I advise you not to lose sight of four main things: to be careful, to be patient, to observe courtesy and to be frank.

[15] Rikord, *Zapiski*, 63-67.

On the wisdom of your actions depends not only our liberation, but also considerable benefit for the fatherland; I hope that our present misfortune may return to Russia that advantage which it lost because of the mad temper and recklessness of one man; but if, contrary to expectation, events will take a different turn, gather my opinion on this subject as correctly, detailedly, and thoroughly as possible from the sailor sent, and convey it to the government; circumstances did not permit to burden the bearer with papers, and therefore it is impossible for me myself to write to the minister. But know, where the honor of the Sovereign and well-being of the fatherland demand it, I do not value my life a kopeck, and therefore you too must not spare me in such a case: it is all the same whether one dies now or ten or twenty years later; it is likewise all the same, in my opinion, whether one be killed in battle or by a villainous hand, whether one drowns in the sea or peacefully dies in bed: death is death though its forms be different. I ask you my dear friend, to write for me to my brothers and friends; maybe providence has ordained that I shall see them again, maybe—not; tell them that in the latter case they do not grieve and do not pity me, and that I wish them health and happiness. Further I beg you for Heaven's sake, do not permit anyone to write to us and do not send anything, that we be not tormented with translations and questions, but write me yourself about your decision a very small letter. I ask you to give the sailor, who has been sent, five hundred rubles from the estate left by me. My sincere respects to our comrades, the officers, my salute to the crew; I greatly appreciate and thank you all for the great pains which you have taken for our liberation. Farewell, dear friend, P. I., and all of you, dear friends! Perhaps this is my last letter to you; be healthy, in peace, and happy. Your devoted

Vasilii Golovnin

April 10 [22], 1813. In the city of Hakodate, in a Japanese prison.[16]

In the evening Takadaya and Simanov were taken back ashore. Successful as Simanov had been in delivering the secret letter, he had failed to make the intended oral amplifications concerning the place where, if necessary, an attack should be launched, for, however carefully Golovnin had coached him, Simanov was not very bright and was so shaken with the joy of seeing his shipmates and with fear for the fate of his fellow captives, that nothing of value could be gotten from him. But Rikord was not distressed, despite Golovnin's admonitions against Japanese duplicity, and was convinced that, in Takadaya, he had a man on whose "noble chest" he could lean "like on solid rock." Through Takadaya he sent a reply to Takahashi in which he wrote that, weather permitting, the *Diana* would leave for Okhotsk the following day to return the same year

[16] *Ibid.*, 68-69; Golovnin, *Zapiski*, 2: 93-94. Judging from the remark that Simanov be given money from his estate, Golovnin seems to have assumed that Simanov was being released completely.

to Hakodate with all the certificates and explanations demanded by the Japanese government. He was unfamiliar with the entrance to Hakodate Bay, and asked, therefore, that the Japanese furnish him with a pilot at Edomo, of which he had a description by Broughton. Finally, he expressed appreciation for Takahashi's friendly disposition and especially for making possible the meeting with the captive sailor. Through Takadaya Rikord also forwarded letters to Golovnin and Mur, congratulating them on their impending liberation and hinting in the letter to Golovnin that his secret message had been received. When Takadaya and Simanov came aboard again the following day to bid farewell to their friends, Takadaya refused not only to accept any gifts, but insisted that his own belongings remain on ship, partly to avoid excessive questioning, partly as a token of his confidence that they would meet again in Hakodate.

As planned, the *Diana* departed on August 10,[17] and after a safe and pleasant journey of fifteen days cast anchor in Okhotsk Harbor. Rikord duly reported the Japanese demands, and soon received a friendly letter of explanation from the governor of Irkutsk to the governor of Matsumae and the required certificate from the commandant of Okhotsk. He was also assigned the services of a "Russian" interpreter: Fedr Stepanovich Kiselev, the former castaway Zenroku.

In Japan, meanwhile, Takahashi returned to Matsumae and reported to Governor Hattori Sadakatsu, Lord of Bungo. Consulting with Shikano Sadayasu, Hattori ordered Takahashi to take charge of military and other preparations for the Russian visit to Hakodate and named Kinzo and Heizo, the attendants of Takadaya, as pilots for the *Diana*, Heizo being sent to meet the vessel at Edomo. More important, Governor Hattori called Golovnin and his fellow-captives before him, treated them to dinner, and releasing them from confinement in Matsumae, sent them with an escort to Hakodate, where they anxiously awaited the return of Rikord.[18]

On August 23, the *Diana* set out on her third visit to Japan. Due

[17] The Russian text gives the date of departure as July 9 (21). This is a misprint. As the English version testifies, he left on July 29 (August 10). Between August 10 and September 22, Rikord's reckoning becomes inaccurate. He claims that the trip lasted fifteen days. This would return the *Diana* to Okhotsk Harbor on August 24 or 25, depending on whether the day of departure is counted. He then asserts that the vessel remained in Okhotsk for eighteen days. This would mean that the vessel departed from Okhotsk between September 10 and 12. Yet Rikord specifically dates the *Diana*'s departure as August 23. He notes that the vessel voyaged twenty days before sighting Volcano Island (Edomo Bay). This would be, counting from August 23, September 11 or 12, rather than September 22, as specified. The dates given by me in the text, therefore, are those specifically identified by Rikord.

[18] Segawa, 232-236; Rikord, *Zapiski*, 69-72; Golovnin, *Zapiski*, 2: 99-100.

to the lateness of the season, it was a hazardous journey, and the vessel was prevented by storms from entering Edomo Bay, until the morning of October 4, after losing a sailor in the heavy seas. On a native boat with thirteen Ainu oarsmen, Heizo[19] came out to announce that he had been assigned to pilot the vessel to Hakodate. While the *Diana* lay to in Edomo Harbor, replenishing supplies, Rikord inquired, why it was that a common sailor had replaced Takadaya as guide, but a handwritten note from Golovnin, recommending Heizo as a trustworthy pilot and promising that Takadaya would join the vessel outside Hakodate, allayed his suspicions, and indeed, when the *Diana* neared Hakodate Bay on the evening of October 9, a beaming Takadaya climbed aboard, accompanied by the chief port official. While the vessel cast anchor for the night just outside the bay, at Yamase-tomari (Back-of-the-mountain Harbor),[20] where Japanese vessels usually stopped when an easterly wind prevented their entry into Hakodate Harbor, Rikord and Takadaya exchanged news, their conversation facilitated for once by the presence of an interpreter. From Takadaya, the Russians learned that the captives had been moved to Hakodate and that the governor of Matsumae himself had come there to effect their release. Takadaya, in turn, was brought up to date about events in Europe, especially about the defeat of Napoleon. When he finally returned ashore, a Japanese guard boat remained at anchor near the Russians, while guard fires illuminated the shore.[21]

In the morning, Takadaya directed the *Diana* to a favorable anchorage, less than a cannon shot from the city. A guard boat was placed at the side of the Russian warship, and the Russians were not to venture about in boats any more than the townspeople of Hakodate were to visit the vessel. But the novelty of a foreign man-of-war was irresistible, and curious men and women flocked alongside on rowboats of every sort, disregarding the shouts and commands of the Japanese guards, until at last the latter with their iron sticks literally beat the sight-seers back to a respectable distance. Only Japanese on official business were permitted to pull up to the Russian ship.

19 Rikord referred to Heizo as Lezo.

20 Segawa thus gives the place name in Japanese characters; Rikord gives it as "Imasi-Tomuri"; Golovnin as "Yamasee-Tomuree."

21 Rikord, *Zapiski*, 73-79; Golovnin, *Zapiski*, 2: 118-119; Segawa, 237-238; Nakamura Zentaro, *Chishima Karafuto shinryaku-shi*, 88-89.

On the morning of October 11, Takadaya appeared with a change of clothing, and asked Rikord for permission to go to his old cabin to don ceremonial garb, as he had been appointed official negotiator. When Takadaya changed, Rikord followed his example, and received him in full dress uniform and sword. Speaking through interpreter Kiselev, Takadaya informed Rikord that he would negotiate with him not in the name of the governor, but of the two officials next in rank above him. These, he said, had requested the paper from the commandant of Okhotsk. Rikord had hoped to convey his correspondence to the local authorities in person, but, to save time, he agreed. All the officers, in full dress, were called together in the cabin and the Okhotsk commandant's letter, enveloped in blue cloth, was entrusted to Takadaya with due ceremony. When Rikord declared that he had yet another official letter, addressed by the governor of Irkutsk to the governor of Matsumae, Takadaya begged that it be given to him also, but this Rikord refused to do, insisting that he could surrender it only to the governor himself or, at the very least, to the two officials to whom Takadaya was responsible. Rikord doubted that the two officials, at the sight of whom, according to Takadaya, the populace fell to their knees, would deign to negotiate on the *Diana*. He decided, therefore, that the meeting take place on land, reassured by the thought that his credentials made him an official envoy, who in the event of trouble, could count on the full backing of his government. His only concern was that his bearing and actions reflect sufficient dignity and determination to revive Japanese respect for the calling of a Russian envoy.

Golovnin had been informed of the approach of his vessel the very first night. As the *Diana* entered port, Japanese after Japanese visited him to chat excitedly of her many sails and skillful maneuvering against the wind. Soon the required letter from Fleet Captain Manitskii, the commandant of Okhotsk, was laid before him for translation. It was Manitskii who had previously testified that the raids of Khvostov had been unauthorized, that, indeed, they had aroused the displeasure of the Russian government. Arguing that the Russian ruler had always been sympathetic toward Japan, Manitskii urged the Japanese to show their good disposition by releasing the captives immediately, hinting not too subtly that further delay might prove harmful to Japanese commerce and fishing, since renewed visits of Russian men-of-war would continue to upset the seaboard population. Golovnin was pleased with the reception of the letter. The Japanese expressed confidence that it met the demands of the government and began to congratulate the captives with their imminent release, but when the latter learned that Rikord was to come ashore personally to convey the letter from the governor of Irkutsk to the governor of Matsumae, they were immediately afraid of another trap.

After a lengthy discussion of the ceremonial protocol to be observed at the meeting on shore, the Japanese permitted the Russian guard-of-honor to carry muskets, while the Russians agreed to change from boots to shoes on entering the Japanese building. On October 14,[22] Rikord set out for shore with a retinue of two officers, ten sailors, and the interpreter Kiselev. The latter, it will be recalled, was a native Japanese, and Rikord would not have exposed him to possible seizure, had he not begged to go along. "What should I fear?" he had protested, "if you are captured, everyone will be captured; they will not seize me alone; I am not a Japanese, and I ask you to take me ashore, so that I can fulfill my duty as interpreter." At the stern of the *Diana* the Russian naval flag had been hoisted between Japanese flags, while a white flag of truce fluttered from the bow. The Russians rode ashore on the governor's own barge, rowed by sixteen oarsmen, eminent merchants, who had taken this means of getting a closer look at them. Hundreds of little boats crowded with curious spectators, followed them.

Rows of Japanese lined the landing place, and, informed by Takadaya that the Japanese officials were expecting them, the Russians marched to the conference building in procession: at the head, a noncommissioned officer with the white flag, then the armed guard-of-honor, a petty officer with the naval flag, Rikord, and finally, the two officers. When they reached the building, the guard-of-honor and the colors took up position at the entrance and presented arms, while Rikord and the two officers stepped inside.

22 A discrepancy of two days appears in the narratives of Rikord and Golovnin (Segawa following Golovnin) between October 11 and October 19. Rikord asserts that discussions preparatory to his landing extended to October 12 and 13 and that he went ashore on the 14th. Golovnin states that Rikord landed on the 12th. Subsequently Rikord's account lags two days behind that of Golovnin, until on October 19, both agree again. Whereas Golovnin specifically dates events, Rikord often writes "the following day," "on the third day," etc. This is confusing not only to the reader, but must have tripped up Rikord himself, for adding his references to "the following day" and the like, one comes to the 19th, which he specifically dates, two days short. I have chosen, therefore, to rely on the dating of Golovnin for the period between October 11 and October 19.

The silence was overwhelming. Two-sworded officials in ceremonial garb filled the room like so many statues. Even the two officials next in rank to the governor, seated side by side, appeared motionless. Having changed from boots to shoes in the entrance hall, Rikord strode up to them and bowed. They inclined their heads. He bowed to the officials on the right and left, then walked to the chairs, placed as agreed beforehand, and sat down. Not a word had been spoken. Rikord was the first to break the silence. He considered himself to be in the house of friends, he said through Kiselev. The two chief officials smiled, and the elder (whom the Russians knew from Kunashiri) said something to a Japanese, who had hastened to his side. The Japanese returned to his place, made a deep bow toward Rikord and to Rikord's amazement addressed him in Russian. Murakami Teisuke (for it was he, who now interpreted the words of the Japanese commander) stated that for years the Russians had caused great disturbances at the shores of Japan, but that now everything would have a happy ending, as the explanation of the commandant of Okhotsk had been most satisfactory. Rikord remarked pointedly that "happy ending" must mean the release of the captives, and expressed Russian pleasure. When he had transmitted the letter, encased in a red box, from the governor of Irkutsk, and presented them gifts, the Japanese replied that it would take them a few days to examine the letter and draft a reply, and asking Rikord to stay for refreshments, rose, bowed, and left the room, their gifts being carried after them. "Now, thank God, I congratulate you on the quick and happy ending," beamed Murakami; "Captain Golovnin and the others will soon come to you aboard ship; we have a special prudent law that you may not meet them now, but they are well." Takadaya and several academicians came up to congratulate the Russians. Tea and sweetmeats were served, and Rikord and his companions were entertained at length before they started back aboard ship, accompanied by Takadaya. It was a beautiful day and the throng of onlookers delighted in the colorful display of flags run up on the *Diana*, as the barge pushed off from shore. The Russians, who had vowed, in the event of treachery, to lay down their lives before surrendering their flag were relieved and filled with gratitude for Takadaya's assistance.[23]

Throughout the conference Golovnin had served as a mine of

[23] Rikord, *Zapiski*, 79-94; Golovnin, *Zapiski*, 2: 119-121. Rikord had instructed Lieutenant Filatov, who had remained in command of the *Diana*, to hoist the flags without the usual accompaniment of gun salutes, so much disliked by the Japanese.

information for the Japanese, but he was unable to identify Kiselev, who had aroused their curiosity, suggesting that he must be an inhabitant of Irkutsk, who had learned Japanese from the castaways there. The Japanese and Manchu translations, which accompanied the letter from the governor of Irkutsk, were not fully intelligible, and the captives were called upon to collaborate with Adachi Sannai, Murakami Teisuke, and Uehara Kumajiro in a retranslation of the Russian text. At the same time they were permitted to communicate with Rikord, both indirectly, through Takadaya, and directly in writing. They received newspapers and journals, detailing Napoleon's withdrawal from Moscow, and letters from friends and relatives. But so bothersome was Japanese insistence that everything written must be copied and translated, that Golovnin chose not to unseal the letters and confined his messages to only a few words. More was conveyed through Takadaya, but the latter was not informed enough to satiate the captives' hunger for news from the fatherland; nor would he converse with them in Russian for fear of offending the official interpreters.

Finally, on October 19,[24] a meeting between Rikord and Golovnin was arranged, so that the latter, all too familiar by now with the strictness of Japanese laws and customs, could explain the situation: (1) the Japanese could not accept the presents from the governor of Irkutsk to the governor of Matsumae, because Japanese law made it impossible for them to reciprocate accordingly; they harbored no enmity toward Russia, and begged that the return of the gifts not be regarded as an insult; (2) the letter of the commandant of Okhotsk constituted a full and satisfactory reply; the governor's communication, therefore, would refer to it alone; (3) the governor of Matsumae could not reply to the governor of Irkutsk inasmuch as the matter would be settled on the basis of the letter of the commandant of Okhotsk and because the governor of Irkutsk had been unacquainted, at the time of writing, with a great many circumstances relating to Khvostov's actions and with the intentions of the Japanese government to reach an amicable solution; (4) Rikord should prepare a statement, addressed to the two officials, next in rank to the governor of Matsumae, to the effect that the governor of Irkutsk had no knowledge of the unauthorized papers left by Khvostov or of the desire of the Japanese government to get in touch with Russia, when

24 October 17, according to Golovnin (2: 127).

he had composed his letter to the governor of Matsumae; (5) Rikord should certify that he had fully understood the Russian translation of the communication of the governor of Matsumae, which he would be shown at the meeting with Golovnin, and promise to submit it to his government upon return to Russia.

As Golovnin and Rikord met face to face in the conference build-ing,[25] in the presence of Savelev, Kiselev, and a number of Japanese officials and interpreters, there was for a while neither connection nor order to the questions and answers which shot back and forth between them, they were so carried away with excitement. Golovnin had shaven for the occasion and wore a silken jacket and trousers with his triangular hat and saber. But the friends were unconscious of the incongruity of his garb, oblivious of everything around them. Gradu-ally they took hold of themselves, and having brought each other up to date on developments since their separation, carefully weighed the steps that lay ahead of them. Golovnin conveyed to Rikord the wishes of the Japanese, while Rikord related the instructions he had received from the civil governor of Irkutsk. The latter included the desirability of an agreement regarding the boundaries between Rus-sia and Japan and of the establishment of friendly relations. But the season was already far advanced; time was running out. To raise the boundary question would mean spending the winter in Hakodate and this, as Golovnin pointed out, would be tantamount to becom-ing voluntary prisoners of the Japanese—hardly a position of strength from which to negotiate a frontier settlement favorable to Russia. After reading a translation of the declaration of the governor of Matsumae, therefore, Rikord confined himself to writing the explana-tory notes which the Japanese demanded, before returning to the *Diana*.

In the evening Takadaya and his son Ryokichi, who had just arrived in Hakodate, were entertained aboard ship. Takadaya re-quested that the crew receive extra wine in celebration and distrib-uted gifts of clothing, but he himself refused to accept costly presents, which the Japanese government would only have confiscated. Taka-daya took a few items for luck and requested a samovar and silver

---

[25] According to Rikord, he and Golovnin met outside the building. As the governor's barge on which he rode ashore approached the wharf, Rikord spotted his friend, who stood amidst a crowd of Japanese near the doors of the house in his strange attire. Casting aside ceremony and prudence, he jumped ashore and rushed toward Golov-nin. . . .

tableware so that in years to come he could entertain his Japanese friends in Russian fashion in memory of Russian hospitality.

On October 18, Golovnin, Mur, and Khlebnikov were festively received by the governor of Matsumae, who read to them two papers: the decision of his government to release them on the ground that the raids of Khvostov, in retaliation for which they had been captured, had been proved unauthorized, and a declaration of his own, in which he expressed pleasure at their liberation, but reminded them to impress it on their countrymen that Japanese laws forbade foreign trade and required foreign vessels to be driven away. The sincerity of the governor's satisfaction at their release was mirrored in the words and gifts of Japanese well-wishers who called on them after their return from the castle, and for five days the high priest of the city offered prayers for their safe return to Russia.[26]

On October 19, Rikord went ashore with Savelev, Kiselev, and a number of sailors to accept their countrymen. Ordinarily, the silken trousers and waistcoats of flowery design in which Golovnin and Mur appeared with their regulation hats and naval swords would have given rise to great merriment, but now, as the comrades-in-arms faced each other, they scarcely noticed these external trappings. Grateful that Providence had reunited them at last, tears welled unashamedly from their eyes. When the Russians had regained their composure, the Japanese brought forth a translation of the declaration of the governor of Matsumae and the note from Taka-hashi and Kojimoto, containing the usual reminder that Japan was determined to use force, if necessary, to remain in seclusion, plus the explanation that Christianity was Japan's "great prohibition." The officials returned the gifts of the governor of Irkutsk and showed a list of supplies with which they would provision the *Diana*. At last the captives were formally surrendered, and, after a round of refreshments, the Russians started back on the governor's barge, accompanied by Takadaya and surrounded by countless well-wishers. The hurrahs with which the jubilant crew received their beloved captain and shipmates, after a separation of two years and three months, were mingled with tears, and the freed prisoners poured out their prayers of thanks before the ship's image of St. Nicholas, patron saint of Russia. Rikord sent back on the governor's barge a Japanese castaway,

26 Golovnin, *Zapiski*, 2: 121-135; Rikord, *Zapiski*, 96-101; Segawa, 248-253; *Hokkaido-shi*, 11, 478-488.

whom he had brought along from Okhotsk. The Japanese had been shipwrecked at Kamchatka in 1811, but had been injured and could not be repatriated earlier. Russian doctors had found it necessary to amputate one of his legs, and he now hobbled about on a wooden leg much to the amazement of his countrymen.

The Japanese brought aboard all the possessions the Russians had had at the moment of capture, down to the last piece of a small mirror that had been broken accidentally. Hundreds of Japanese boats plied back and forth, loading the *Diana* with fresh water, firewood, and foodstuffs. The Russians had not requested these supplies, did not need them, and said so. But the Japanese insisted that they had been ordered to provision the released prisoners for the long voyage to Kamchatka, and soon the *Diana* was laden with a thousand large radishes, fifty bags of barley, thirty bags of salt and other edibles. The guards no longer hindered their countrymen from going aboard the vessel and many of the Japanese gave the Russians a helping hand in transferring the supplies. So smoothly and vigorously did the Russians and the Japanese, who not long ago had regarded each other as enemies, work together, that in Rikord's eyes, "it seemed that the persons who differed limitlessly in their way of thinking, upbringing, and country of birth, separated from each other by fully half the globe, formed then one and the same people." Moved by kindness, cooperation, gaiety, and jokes, Russians and Japanese treated each other to vodka and sake, and, though there was little time for anything but work, "the whole day in general came to be honored as a great holiday on which the feelings of friendship of two neighboring peoples were expressed."

To officials, who came aboard to congratulate him, Rikord transmitted a letter of gratitude from the governor of Irkutsk. But, when he expressed the desire to call on the governor of Matsumae to thank him personally for the release of Golovnin, the Japanese objected. Thus, Rikord was never to see the governor, though the governor had seen him, for, when Golovnin and Rikord had met in the building on shore, he had furtively peeped at them from behind a screen. The Japanese examined with awe the personal signature of the Russian Emperor, which they had asked to see and made a guided tour of the ship. By evening so many visitors crowded aboard that it was difficult to move about on deck, and Japanese guards had to limit the number of callers. The officials refused to accept any bulky gifts, but left late that evening with strips of thin red cloth suitable for making a tobacco pouch, with pieces of glass from a lustre, unframed portraits of Russian heroes of the campaign of 1812, atlases, maps, books, and other presents small enough to be concealed in the sleeves of their kimono.

On October 22, Japanese boats towed the *Diana* out of the inner harbor. Takadaya, the senior interpreter, and other officials, whom the Russians had befriended, accompanied the vessel to the very mouth of the spacious bay. "Taisho ura! Taisho ura!" the Russians shouted in farewell, and as Takadaya and his men threw up their arms and responded with a thunderous "Ura Diana!" Golovnin headed homeward at last.

It was not an easy crossing. For six long hours a violent hurricane threatened to undo all their valiant efforts and end everything in disaster. But the *Diana* weathered this too and on November 15, 1813, as snow fell from the sky, sailed safely into Petropavlovsk Harbor. On December 14, 1813, Golovnin continued to St. Petersburg, traveling by dogsled, by reindeer, on horseback, and finally by carriage. He reached the capital on the evening of August 3, 1814, seven years to the day and hour after having left there.

Alexander I was pleased. Golovnin and Rikord were promoted in rank, and they and their subordinates were honored with pensions, decorations, and the usual rewards for outstanding service; last, but not least, it was decreed that the memoirs of their adventures be published at the expense of the government.[27]

A GILDED CAGE

The captivity of Golovnin was a milestone in Russo-Japanese relations, as Okuma Shigenobu, the noted Japanese statesman, was to point out in later years, and, unimportant as the events surrounding it might appear, they were really filled with significance. Had Golovnin died in Japanese hands, whatever the cause, Russo-Japanese relations would have taken a turn for the worse, and an aggressive Russia would have been provided with an excuse, indeed an invitation, for hostile measures. His amicable release, on the other hand, improved relations between the two nations.

The web of circumstantial evidence had been such that the Russian captives could not have extricated themselves without difficulty.

27 Golovnin, *Zapiski*, 2:135-147; *Hokkaido-shi*, 488-489; Rikord, *Zapiski*, 103-105; Segawa, 260.

Under the circumstances much had depended on the disposition of the Japanese. Had the interrogators or interpreters wished to ruin the prisoners, they could have done so easily. Instead, some of them did their best to help the Russians. For example, there had been in Golovnin's pocket a note, which he had written for the Japanese before his captivity. In it he had chided the Japanese in rather insulting language for having opened fire on unarmed persons, noting that no Russian officer could take hostile action without the wishes of the Emperor. When Murakami translated the draft, he took advantage of its illegibility in spots to skip completely those remarks, which might have given offense to his superiors, and translated only the part, which substantiated the captives' argument that they had harbored no hostile intentions and that the raids of Khvostov had been unauthorized. When Murakami left for the capital, he ran the risk of disembowelment by writing to the captives about the prospects of their release. Nor was Murakami an isolated example. Other interpreters and officials had gone out of their way to lighten the burden of the captives. It was evident that, angered as the Japanese had been by the raids of Khvostov and Davydov, and though they held Golovnin a captive, they were not inherently xenophobic.[28]

There were of course some exceptions, notably Mamiya Rinzo, the famous explorer, land-surveyor, and astronomer, whose patriotism had been aggravated by a Russian bullet in the buttocks at the time of the Khvostov attack on Etorofu, and Nakagawa, who had been spirited away by the same raiders, but most Japanese, especially the common people, showed sympathy if not goodwill toward the Russians. Golovnin was cheered by this attitude, and despite his captivity, developed a certain respect and liking for the Japanese. Tiresome as Japanese questions were, they served as a means for Golovnin to force significant information about Russia into Japan. At the same time the endless visits of Japanese scholars gave him the opportunity to learn much about Japan. From the point of view of greater knowledge and better understanding between Russia and Japan, Golovnin's dismal prison proved to be a gilded cage.

Mamiya Rinzo inquired about Russian methods of land-surveying and astronomical observation; in exchange he shared knowledge of his own. In his explorations, he had voyaged beyond the Kuril Islands to Sakhalin, even to Manchuria and the Amur River and had been

---

[28] Golovnin, *Zapiski*, 2:53, 67-73.

the first to discover that Sakhalin was an island rather than a peninsula; how much he revealed to Golovnin is not clear, but the latter does acknowledge the receipt of "much very interesting information, which is not useless for our government to know."[29] The academician Adachi Sannai, who worked on the translation of a textbook in arithmetic brought back from Russia by Kodayu in 1793, sought further enlightenment in mathematics from the captives, while the young Dutch-language interpreter Baba Sajuro advanced his knowledge of Russian by obtaining the French equivalents of Russian words and arriving at their Japanese meaning by way of a French-Dutch lexicon, and Uehara Kumajiro was able to add a supplement of Russian words to his survey of the Ainu language. Golovnin helped Baba revise a Russo-Japanese dictionary compiled in earlier years, and assisted him in the translation of a work on vaccination brought back by Nakagawa; at the same time he himself toiled for months on the composition of a Russian grammar and exercises in the form of translations of French-Dutch dialogues.[30] Once the Russians were satisfied that the Japanese really planned to release them, they became cooperative teachers of physics, astronomy, and so forth. To be sure their deliberate exaggeration of Russian might in the Far East detracted from the accuracy of Japanese knowledge, but this very inaccuracy perpetuated Japanese respect for Russian power, when such respect was no longer reasonable from a Western point of view.

Golovnin's own observations were profound. As one Russian historian has remarked, Golovnin and Krusenstern may be regarded as the fathers of Russian Japanology.[31] Golovnin's writings were the most significant Russian firsthand portrayal of the Japanese available until the opening of Japan, if not indeed, until the beginning of the twentieth century. In later years, they were crowded aside by misleading accounts, which doted on the quaintness of the Japanese, but, with the onslaught of the Russo-Japanese War, authors were to remember Golovnin's penetrating observations and to regret that his remarks had not been taken more seriously.[32] Some of Golovnin's comments had been woven into the body of his narrative; the most

---

[29] *Ibid.*, 1: 182-187.

[30] *Ibid.*, 2: 80-82. See also, Lensen, *Report from Hokkaido*, 28-45.

[31] Novakovskii, 125. In the wake of Golovnin's captivity there appeared in Russia a number of essays on Japan. See Novakovskii, 145.

[32] See, for example, M. Bogdanovich, *Ocherk iz proshlago i nastoiashchago Iaponii* and N. Shebuev, *Iaponskie vechera*, 203.

important ones, however, had appeared originally as Part III of his memoirs, in a separate description of the Japanese Empire and its people, systematically constructed around nine topics: (1) the geographical location, expanse, and climate of Japan, (2) the origin of the Japanese people, (3) national character, education, and language, (4) religious faith and ceremonies, (5) the governmental system, (6) laws and customs, (7) natural products, industry, and trade, (8) population and armed forces, (9) Japanese dependencies and colonies. It is characteristic, perhaps, that in our own day this third part, which describes the Japanese favorably, has been excluded from a new anthology of Golovnin's writings.[33]

The early Christian missionaries had spoken highly of the Japanese. "These are the best people so far discovered, and it seems to me that among unbelievers no people can be found to excel them," Francis Xavier had reported in the middle of the sixteenth century.[34] But the expulsion and ferocious persecution of Christians, Western progress and pride in the achievements of the industrial revolution, and possibly Dutch slander[35] had conspired to lower the Japanese in European esteem. Weighing the data obtained from different informants, Golovnin succeeded in extracting many truths about Japan, and, in his writings, we find a key, if not a prediction, of the speed with which the Japanese were to assimilate Western techniques in years to come. Taking issue with the contemporary European view that the Japanese were cunning, treacherous, ungrateful, vengeful, abominable, and dangerous, Golovnin described them instead as patient, modest, and courteous, and marvelled "with what patience, calm, and kindness they treated us and heard out our arguments, and often reproaches and even abuse itself, although, one must confess, their cause was more just than ours."[36] In the politeness with which the Japanese treated each other, Golovnin found evidence of their true enlightenment. They settled their differences in calm and modest fashion, in a tongue which differentiated expressions by degree of politeness, depending on the respective social status of the speakers. The same restraint and good taste governed Japanese negotiations with the Russians, and Golovnin and Rikord, whose

[33] Magidovich (ed.), Golovnin, *Sochineniia*.

[34] G. B. Sansom, *The Western World and Japan*, 115.

[35] The Dutch sought to discredit Westerners in the eyes of the Japanese to retain their monopoly on trade. It is possible that some of their unfavorable portrayals of the Japanese had been similarly motivated.

[36] Golovnin, *Zapiski*, 3: 52.

narrative was added to the memoirs of the former, testified to the diplomatic tact of the Japanese communications. The etiquette-conscious Japanese could not understand how errors of spelling and grammar could creep into Russian documents, and claimed that "no Japanese official would sign a paper, incorrectly written, as such matters may be read after a hundred years and more, and thereby will be judged those, who have written them." Remarked Golovnin: "Let the reader himself figure out who is right, and whether the Japanese deserve being called an unenlightened people."[37]

The level of Japanese education greatly impressed Golovnin. "As regards public instruction in Japan, if one compares as a mass one whole people with another, it is my opinion, that the Japanese are the most educated people in the entire world. There does not exist a person in Japan, who could not read or write, and did not know the laws of his fatherland. . . ." Golovnin admitted that Europe was ahead of Japan in science and art, in the sense that the best scientists and artists of Europe were ahead of the best minds of Japan, but contended that if a comparison were made not of the select few but of the broad masses, "the Japanese have a better understanding of things than the lower class of people in Europe."

Golovnin lauded the concern of the Japanese government for its subjects; he portrayed the people as a nation of shopkeepers and compared them to the English in their desire for order, cleanliness, labeling, and pricing of every article. He made the important observation that the government's prohibition against foreign trade was not an expression of popular will, and speculated that it actually may have been the very eagerness of the populace to trade with other nations, that induced the government to cling to the old restrictions for fear that the people would be corrupted by foreign ways. He reported that the merchant class was numerous and wealthy and that, scorned as traders might be in theory, they were influential in prac-tice—gold speaking louder than rank—even in feudal Japan.

The Japanese had their vices, foremost among them, according to Golovnin, was overindulgence in sex and alcohol, but he remarked that Japanese women were very attractive and that there was less drunkenness in Japan than in Europe. Golovnin reported that the Japanese were vengeful in the sense that revenge had once been part of their code of honor, but he commented that it was no longer a

[37] *Ibid.*, 3: 20-22; 2: 116-117 footnotes; Rikord, *Zapiski*, 66.

dominant factor in their way of life and asked, where there was a place without its own foolishness. "It is equally stupid or absurd, whether one knifes oneself or shoots oneself for a careless word, uttered unintentionally."

Golovnin described the Japanese as sensible and astute, honest, and hospitable. He recalled that Spanberg and Walton had been well received, and that neither Laxman nor Rezanov had had reason to complain about Japanese treatment, except for their refusal to permit the exploration of their settlements and to engage in trade. Golovnin considered Japanese fear of European nations justified, and though he tried to convince the Japanese that European progress had been the result of the free interaction of the talents and inventions of different nations, he appreciated their response that international relations led to destruction as well as to progress. There was truth and farsightedness in the Japanese view that the policy of isolation, whatever its shortcomings, had brought to the people of Japan the blessings of prolonged peace, while the resumption of relations with Europe on the part of Japan and China would entail an increase in war and bloodshed. But sympathize though Golovnin did with the Japanese theory that it was better to live in a small and poor but peaceful community, than in a large and rich city which was torn by constant strife, he felt that peace had sapped Japan of vital military strength, that the Japanese lacked daring, fearlessness, bravery, and manliness. Unlike other observers, however, he did not deduce from this a lack of potential prowess, but warned that "one cannot say of the Japanese, that they are cowards by nature." He explained that "if they are timorous, this is because of the peaceloving nature of their government, because of the long tranquillity in which the whole people, having no war, rejoices, or to put it better, because of the unaccustomedness to bloodshed." He warned that this pacifism was not ground for complacency. In Europe soldiers were regarded as the dregs of society and were expected to show respect when addressing gentlemen, but in Japan the samurai commanded the esteem of the common people and merchants alike. For the moment Japan was militarily unprepared. It had no navy, only drawings and models of European vessels, but he predicted:

If the Japanese government should desire to have a navy, it would be quite easy to establish it after the European pattern, and to bring it to possible perfection. The Japanese only have to invite to their country two or three good shipwrights and several naval officers: they have excellent harbors for the establishment of naval ports, all the necessary materials for building and arming the vessels, a great many skillful carpenters and very alert, brave sailors; and the people in general are extremely quick of apprehension and imitative. Japanese seamen, put on a European footing, could in short time match their fleet with the best in Europe.

Golovnin portrayed the Japanese as fiery patriots, conscious not only of the harm that foreign actions had brought in years past, but confident of their own superiority, a feeling purposely fostered by mythical stories of their country's unique origin and of the role and continuity of their imperial dynasty. The Japanese populace was kept uninformed about other countries, but officials and scholars studied modern European history, and, through the Dutch and the Chinese, followed with particular concern Russian activities in America and British activities in India. They were willing to accept Russian assurances that the raids of Khvostov and Davydov had been unauthorized, but they were by no means convinced that Russian intentions would remain peaceful, for not all rulers were alike—one loved peace, another one war. Repeatedly they quoted a prophecy of olden days: "The time will be, when a people will come from the north, and conquer Japan."

Golovnin reported that the Japanese lagged behind Europe in literature, architecture, sculpture, engraving, music, and poetry, and considered them mere infants in military science and navigation, but he insisted, at the same time, that their capabilities were tremendous. What clearer testimony can there be of Golovnin's insight into the Japanese character than this remarkable—almost prophetic—observation?

The Japanese Government wished that the nation confine itself to its own enlightenment, and make use only of inventions of its own mind; it forbids it to adopt the inventions of other peoples, lest foreign customs steal in together with foreign sciences and arts. Their neighbors must thank Providence, that it had imbued Japanese lawgivers with such a thought, and must try not to give them cause to cast aside their policy and take up that of Europe. If there will rule over this populous, intelligent, dexterous, imitative, and patient nation, which is capable of everything, a sovereign like our great Peter, he will enable Japan, with the resources and treasures which she has in her bosom, in a short number of years to lord over the whole Pacific Ocean. And what would happen then to the maritime regions in the east of Asia and the west of America, so distant from those countries which must defend them? And were it to come about, that the Japanese should take it into their head to introduce

European civilization into their country, and were to follow our policy, the Chinese too would then find themselves forced to do the same. In such a case, these two strong nations could give a very different look to European affairs. No matter how firmly the aversion to everything foreign is rooted in the government of the Japanese and the Chinese, nonetheless such a turn in their system must not be regarded infeasible: they are people, and there is nothing permanent in human affairs. What they might not want to do of their own will, they might be forced to do by necessity: for example, often repeated attacks by neighboring nations would of course force the Japanese to weigh means by which it would be possible to prevent a handful of foreigners from troubling the populous nation; this would give an inducement for the introduction of warships after the European pattern, from these vessels there would come into being fleets, and there it is probable, that the success of that measure would induce them to adopt also our other enlightened methods for the extermination of mankind, and finally all European inventions would gradually come into use in Japan, even without a special genius, such as was our Peter, but by the force and concurrence of circumstances, and as for teachers, many would come from all of Europe, if only the Japanese wish to invite them. And therefore, it seems to me, one must not, so to speak, provoke this just and honest people. If, however, contrary to expectation, some pressing reasons will force one to act otherwise, one should use all means and efforts to act with determination, that is to say so as to finish completely the matter in several years. I do not say that the Japanese and Chinese could liken themselves unto Europeans and become dangerous in our times, but this is something that is possible, and may happen sooner or later.[38]

The meaning of Golovnin's observations has been obscured in our own day for political reasons. Anxious to arouse the Russian people against the Japanese, Soviet writers and editors have emasculated Golovnin's observations so as to prove Japanese hatefulness.[39] Yet in doing so, they have done a great injustice to a true Russian hero. Golovnin's greatness (as that of Takadaya) lies not in having been captured and released, but in having weathered his experiences without hatred, in having been able to understand and forgive the actions of his captors and to give justice where justice is due.

In one respect only does the Golovnin affair leave a sour taste in one's mouth, namely in the defection of Ensign Mur. At the time it was a unique incident in the history of Russo-Japanese relations, neither Takadaya nor Golovnin having permitted their sympathies to lead them onto the road of treason and the castaways, who had

[38] Golovnin, *Zapiski*, 3: 12-20, 32-36, 45-46, 52-54, 66, 93-108.
[39] See, for example, Iurii Zhukov, *Russkie i Iaponiia*.

elected to stay in Russia, having done so under quite different circumstances, aware of the ill reception accorded by their government to repatriates in years past. Today Mur's defection is of interest not only as an isolated transgression of a Russian captive in the early nineteenth century, but as an early example of the experiences of Russians, Japanese, Americans, and others, who, in the years of World War II and the Korean conflict, courted the favor of their captors, "collaborated with the enemy," renounced their country, and when they were finally repatriated, suffered mental anguish beyond endurance. It is a vivid illustration of the fact that, as Golovnin put it, "of all possible vices not one lies so heavily on the heart, as the repudiation of one's fatherland."

Mur was a very talented young officer with a good hand. Great admirers of calligraphy, the Japanese regarded the neatness of his writing as evidence of superior education. Mur sketched well and the Japanese had him draw a great deal. They never commanded, but requested, and quite generally cultivated his cooperation. When he fell ill in September of 1812, when Russian hopes for ultimate liberation were at an ebb, the Japanese, decent as they had been in their treatment of all the prisoners, extended special consideration to Mur. He was permitted to step out of his cage, warm himself at the fire, and go up to the cages of his comrades; now and then he was handed a pipe through the bars and permitted to take a puff. No doubt this amiable treatment affected Mur's disposition toward the Japanese. But it was probably in Mur's background that we find the germs of his ambitions. The experiences of the captives had been varied and exotic, but devoid of the sex element in high adventure. Mur was handsome and stately in appearance. His fellow countrymen teased him about turning the head of some important Japanese lady and securing her help. To one toying with the thought of making a career as an interpreter or official by staying in Japan, such jests could have been more than suggestive. Had not his father done something similar? A German, he had entered the Russian service and taken a Russian wife. Why not enter the Japanese service, where Mur's knowledge would assure him of a bright future, and marry a Japanese beauty?

Mur began to inform on his comrades, to order them about, and to intimidate them in an attempt to court the favor of his prospective employers. The Japanese used Mur, as all nations use collaborators, but patriotic and rank-conscious to the extreme, they retained greater respect for Golovnin, and did not seem eager to recruit Mur's services on a permanent basis nor, contrary to Golovnin's fears, to send him back to Germany by way of the Dutch. When Rikord first returned to Japan, Mur was shaken by the possibility of repatriation, and tried to reestablish amicable relations with his comrades. But eventually, he turned against them again, the more viciously since he felt rejected by both sides. When the *Diana* returned again in October of 1813, and he saw that there was no chance of his remaining in Japan, Mur became acutely depressed. In desperation he tried to sabotage the negotiations, urging the Japanese not to accept the letter of the commandant of Okhotsk, because of its threat of Russian action along the shores of Japan. But the Japanese, who had rejected various "exposés" of Russian sinister designs on his part, replied that the letter was reasonable and that they were very much aware of the fact that, in case of war, the Russians could indeed work great damage on the shores of Japan. With no more success, Mur sought to persuade the Japanese that the paper from the governor of Irkutsk was insolent and Russian gifts unworthy.[40]

Mur refused to attend the momentous meeting between Golovnin and Rikord on October 17, but he could not avoid appearing before the governor of Matsumae the following day. He seemed deeply distressed, when the governor read to the captives the papers of their release and wished them well, uttering again and again that he was unworthy of such grace. Back aboard the *Diana*, he was greatly depressed; he did not wish to associate with the officers, dressed shabbily, and withdrew broodingly now to the crew-side of the deck, now to his own cabin. For days he would not eat at all, then gorge himself, as if to invite some deadly illness.

Lieutenant Rudakov, who had served on the *Diana* and was an old friend of Mur, was now commandant of Petropavlovsk Harbor. When the vessel returned to Kamchatka, therefore, it was arranged for Mur to stay with Rudakov and his young wife in the hope that feminine chatter would distract him. But Mur would disappear to the bath or some other lonely spot and weep bitterly. Mrs. Rudakov became frightened and Mur was moved to the house of a priest. If a woman could not console him, perhaps a priest would. But Mur's conscience could not be calmed and he was plunged into an abyss of depression reminiscent of the sufferings of the castaway Tajuro on the eve of his repatriation. He refused money that was due him, would not buy decent clothing, and walked about dressed in an old

---

[40] Golovnin, *Zapiski*, 1: 113, 132-135, 163; 2: 33-34, 45-46, 61-63, 77-78, 88-92, 123-124.

Kamchadal garment of deer skin. Finally, he sent Golovnin a report in which he described his trespasses and called himself a traitor. It was a pathetic document, quite incoherent and confused. Golovnin replied at once that in the light of circumstances Mur's conduct had not been as reprehensible as all that, and that he was young and would have ample opportunity to redeem himself. He called on Mur frequently and together with Rikord tried to allay his remorse. Their efforts appeared beneficial, and Mur seemed to regain some of his old composure. He asked for permission to move to some native Kamchadal settlement, where he would not be reminded of his guilt by Russian faces. Believing that several weeks of such isolation might be helpful, his superiors agreed, and Mur prepared elatedly for his departure. He was permitted to go hunting, though his gun was carried by one of the servants assigned to guard against any suicide attempt on his part. Mur's apparent good humor undermined the vigilance of the attendants, and on December 4, 1812, when he was temporarily left alone with his gun, he put a quick end to his suffering. The tombstone erected by the officers of the *Diana* in his memory is a monument of the compassionate understanding and forgiveness of Golovnin.

Here lies the body of
Ensign
FEDOR FEDOROVICH MUR
who in the flower of his years
died in Petropavlovsk Harbor
on November 22 [December 4], 1813

In Japan
he was abandoned
by the Guardian Angel who had accompanied
him on the road of this life.
Despair
made him lose his way.
His errors were expiated
by bitter repentance,
and
death
calmed his unhappiness.
Tender hearts!
honor his memory
with a tear.[41]

41 Golownin, II, 223, Golovnin, *Zapiski*, 2:127-146.

CHAPTER EIGHT · RENEWED PRESSURE

ANOTHER PRIVATE EFFORT

RUSSIAN assurances that Khvostov and Davydov had acted without authority had cleared the atmosphere to the extent that Golovnin and his fellow captives were released. But the Japanese government did not budge from its determination to remain outside the stream of world affairs; on the contrary, it seemed more anxious than ever to avoid further entanglements.[1] Golovnin and the other captives had been ordered to help translate into Russian the replies of the Shogunate to Laxman and Rezanov and to present these to their own government, so that there could be no room for doubt about the policy of Japan.[2]

When Golovnin returned to Russia, however, he reported to Governor Treskin of Irkutsk, that he had succeeded in learning secretly that, prior to the raids of Khvostov and Davydov, Japanese merchants had traded with Russian Ainu despite all the prohibitions. In those days the northern regions, including Etorofu, Kunashiri, and Sakhalin, had been controlled not by the central government, but by the Lord of Matsumae, who had tolerated trade with neighboring peoples as being of benefit to his own subjects. In a bay between Nemuro and Akkeshi there had stood a warehouse filled with beaver and fox skins, eagle feathers, old clothing, and glass beads of Russian origin. These had been brought to the Japanese by Ainu from the Russian domains. The Japanese had wanted more European goods, but these the Ainu had been unable to supply, afraid to demand them from the Russians, who had forbidden them to go to the Japanese. But the inability of the Matsumae clan to deal with the attacks of Khvostov and Davydov effectively, had led to the assimilation of the Matsumae domains by the central government and now the presence of Shogunate officials had put a halt to the secret trade. Upon arrival in Irkutsk, Golovnin elaborated on his observations:

(1) In general the Japanese government and the whole nation regard the Russian empire as a state that is powerful, martial, and always dreadful for Japan.

(2) In disposition toward Russia, the Japanese government has split

[1] Siebold, I, 23.   [2] Golovnin, *Zapiski*, II, 112.

into two factions. One of them seeks to avert danger by having no relations whatsoever with Russia: while the other on the contrary sees all the security for the Japanese empire in commercial relations with Russia.

(3) The first letter of the governor of Irkutsk to the governor of Matsumae and the letter from the commandant of Okhotsk to the two commanders next in rank to the governor concerning the fact that the pillages of Khvostov had been unauthorized, convinced the Japanese not only of the peaceloving disposition of our government toward them, but also that the actions of the former envoy Rezanov had been completely contrary to the will of the emperor, and as a result the party favorably disposed toward Russia has increased in strength.

(4) That although the papers of the Japanese government, with which Golovnin had been returned, resolutely forbade, under one known condition, Russian vessels to come to the shores of Japan, this followed before the receipt by the supreme Japanese government both of the first letter of the governor of Irkutsk to the governor of Matsumae as well as especially of his other letter to the governor of Matsumae, thanking him for the release of the Russian prisoners and among other things inviting the determination of the frontiers and relations between the two empires.

(5) Inasmuch as the governor of Matsumae does not have the right to answer on his own such an important subject, while the lateness of the season did not permit to await with the sloop *Diana* in Hakodate a reply from the higher Japanese government, the governor himself instructed through the interpreter most favorably disposed toward Golovnin whither and when to come for a reply. In consequence thereof Golovnin and Rikord wrote a letter to the two officials next in rank to the governor, that a Russian vessel would come the very next summer to Etorofu for a reply to the second letter of the governor of Irkutsk.[3]

The Japanese had stated repeatedly that trade with Russia could not be permitted, that any relations, whatsoever, were out of the question. Yet the Japanese have a penchant for polite vagueness and the apparent promise of a reply to the governor's second letter gave hope for a change of heart. While preparations were being made to send a ship to Etorofu, therefore, Treskin addressed a memorandum to Governor General Pestel, in which he noted that Russia must be ready to follow up without delay any possible Japanese concessions to trade. He recommended that the *Diana* or, if she was no longer seaworthy, another reliable vessel be kept in readi-

---

[3] Polonskii, 563-566. The original numbering has been modified here. Polonskii does not list a number "3"; number "3" here is equivalent to his number "4", etc. It is not clear from the Russian text whether "a" Russian vessel or "the" Russian vessel (i.e. the *Diana*) was meant. According to Segawa (232), Golovnin and Rikord promised to send a small unarmed vessel.

ness in Petropavlovsk Harbor. The officers and crew of the *Diana* were to be detained in Okhotsk, until the receipt of the expected Japanese reply. If the Japanese agreed to enter into relations with Russia, negotiations ought to be conducted not in Nagasaki, but in Hakodate, which was free from Dutch and other foreign intrigue and close enough so that communications between it and Petropavlovsk or Okhotsk might be exchanged twice within one season. Hakodate also would be the most suitable place for the exchange of the type of goods that Russo-Japanese trade would entail—fish, whale-oil, mammoth bones and peltry from Siberia and America, and barley and salt from Japan. At the same time storage facilities at nearby Petropavlovsk would enable Russian merchants to withhold Russian goods until the price was right. Russian trade with Hakodate could be strengthened further if the government would permit Mr. Dobbel, a citizen of the United States, to realize the plans which he had proposed.[4] In view of Golovnin's experience, he alone should be given command of another Russian expedition and related negotiations; if this was impossible Rikord should be appointed. The embassy ought to include assistants and advisers from among civilians, scholars, or merchants, but not too many as the experience of Rezanov had shown that the greater in number of personnel and class distinction such embassies are, the more disorders and unpleasantnesses they entail. Command of the vessel and powers of negotiation should be in the hands of the same person. He must not be labeled an "envoy" as Japan is inclined never to enter into political relations with anybody; for purposes of trade, the Japanese regard a "chargé" sufficient. Treskin advised that Japanese claims to Etorofu and the islands to the south be respected and that no projects be undertaken on Sakhalin lest they precipitate a complete break with Japan and complications with the Manchu government that might endanger Russo-Chinese trade. He recom-

---

[4] Mr. Dobbel (Novakovskii gives the name as Dobella), an American citizen, presented to the Russian government plans for the economic development of the Russian Far East, including, among other steps, the inauguration of whaling and fishery in the waters of Russia's Pacific colonies, the occupation of the Liu Ch'iu (Ryukyu) Islands, the improvement of communications in Siberia, and the establishment of trade relations between Kamchatka and China, Japan, and other countries of the Pacific. But though the American arrived in Petropavlovsk with the necessary vessels in 1812, his farsighted plans failed to meet with the approval of the imperial government which apparently feared foreign competition. Apprehension lest foreign capital, foreign merchants, and above all foreign colonists penetrate into Siberia inhibited also the development of the northern sea route. (Constantin Krypton, *The Northern Sea Route*, v-vi.)

mended that the Russian-American Company be prohibited from penetrating beyond Uruppu. Recalling the activities of the priest Vereshchagin, who under the guise of spreading Christianity had distributed among the natives of the Kuril Islands religious images and so forth in exchange for fur, Treskin asked that the Christianization of the Ainu be halted until more trustworthy priests were found. Some of these images had eventually found their way into Japanese hands and the Japanese had been greatly perturbed by the threat of missionary activity, classing it in one category with the raids of Khvostov. Had such a priest or such images been found by the Japanese on the Kuril Islands, while Golovnin was being held captive, the fate of both priest and countrymen would have been dreadful as it would not have been possible to persuade the Japanese that such priests traveled about without authority.[5]

On November 22, 1813, Assistant Navigator Novitskii was ordered to sail to northern Etorofu to bring back the expected reply from the governor of Matsumae. On July 15, 1814, he led the transport *Boris i Gleb* out of Tigilsk, where he had spent the winter, and approached northern Etorofu. From August 1 until August 10, he cruised along the shore of the island at a distance of five to six miles. Though his vessel was no doubt clearly visible from shore no one came out to meet him, and he turned back to Russia without ever landing. Had Novitskii gone ashore, he might have succeeded in clarifying the relative extent of Japanese and Russsian authority on the Kuril Archipelago, for appropriate instructions had been sent to the island from Matsumae. The capture of Golovnin had brought home the need for a frontier agreement to both Russians and Japanese. The governor of Irkutsk had instructed Rikord to broach this matter to the Japanese, but both Golovnin and Rikord had found it inopportune to do so during the negotiations for the release of the captives. Only at their very departure did they mention the boundary problem as a topic for future consideration, the second letter of the governor of Irkutsk containing reference to it. At the time, the Japanese had mentioned that their sway extended down to (and including) Etorofu, and Golovnin interpreted this to mean that they recognized Uruppu as Russian. The instructions sent to Etorofu, where the Russians were to come for a reply, however, described Etorofu and the islands to the south as Japanese, Shimu-

[5] Polonskii, 565-571.

shiru and the islands to the north as Russian, with Uruppu as a buffer zone between.[6]

Treskin was displeased that Novitskii had not proceeded with more determination, but he did not request another voyage and recommended to Pestel that the crew of the *Diana* be released to return to St. Petersburg. This Pestel authorized, but, in accordance with a suggestion from Rikord, he instructed Treskin to send a vessel at the first convenient opportunity to the shores of Japan in quest of the reply. In 1815 the transport *Pavel* under the command of Navigator's Apprentice Srednii left Okhotsk with six Japanese castaways, three of whom had been shipwrecked off the Kuril Islands, the others having been swept to California and brought from there by an English merchantman. On August 8, the Russians were almost within reach of Hokkaido, but unfavorable winds, fog, and fear of capture by the Japanese prompted them to turn back. At Etorofu they let the castaways ashore on a leather *bidarka*, amply supplied with provisions, and returned to Okhotsk without further delay.[7] In 1816 a letter, addressed to the Japanese government in the name of the commandant of Okhotsk and requesting the expected communication, was sent by Lieutenant Rudakov, the commandant of Kamchatka, to the fourteenth island (Ushishiru) from which natives were to take it to Uruppu and there attach it to a post, erected for such purposes. The following year, in 1817, the elder Usov and five Ainu were sent to the same place for an answer. They were not heard from again. In 1821 their canoe was found overturned near the sixteenth island. Meanwhile the letter posted on Uruppu had been found by a Japanese official in the summer of 1818, but it was badly damaged by snow and rain and conveyed no more than, that in 1814 the Russians had cruised along the shores of Etorofu in expectation of a Japanese reply, and receiving none, had sailed back to Okhotsk.

Convinced of the futility of further solicitation and eager to cut its expenditures, the Irkutsk command ordered the discontinuance of attempts to establish official relations with Japan. It announced that in the future shipwrecked Japanese were to be sent only to the Kuril Islands; from there they would have to make their own way

---

[6] Nakamura, 91; *Hokkaido-shi*, II, 490-491.

[7] Polonskii asserts that Srednii did not succeed in putting the castaways ashore at Etorofu, and that they departed on the *bidarka* in 1817 from Kamchatka. This is disputed by a Japanese source, quoted by Novakovskii, which relates that the castaways—though only five of them—were questioned in the Japanese capital in 1816.

home. In accordance with this policy a number of Japanese, cast-away in Russian waters in 1836 and again in 1840, were taken to Etorofu in 1843. The doors of Japan, closed to the Western Barbarians, remained closed also to the Red Devils.

Russian disillusionment in establishing relations with the Japanese was reflected in a loss of interest in the Kuril Islands as well. Only a few officials and missionaries would visit the four islands nearest Kamchatka; rarely did they penetrate farther south and even then not beyond Ushishiru. This lack of interest extended even to Sakhalin and the whole maritime region. The cause for such a frame of mind cannot be attributed solely to Japanese reticence. It was furthered by the growing belief that Sakhalin Island was a peninsula and that the Amur Estuary was so blocked with sand as to deny access to the sea; without an outlet to the sea the development of the Far Eastern regions seemed hopeless. The Russian government furthermore derived great profit (from fifty thousand to a million rubles a year) from trade with China and was most anxious not to do anything that might antagonize the Manchus and endanger this income. At the same time developments in Europe demanded attention, for the spread of revolution was of primary concern to the Russian monarchy. The temporary discontinuance of Russia's traditional eastward expansion—the first step in the liquidation of her interests in the Western hemisphere—is vividly illustrated by her withdrawal from California. By the 1840's she was so weak in the Pacific that various Russian possessions, including the very shores of Kamchatka and fortified Petropavlovsk itself, were exposed to the forages of audacious whalers.

While the Russian government was preoccupied with the suppression of liberalism and nationalism in Europe, criticism of Russian policy in the east repeatedly penetrated through the curtain of censorship. The findings of Professor Aleksandr Middendorf, who in 1842 headed an expedition sponsored by the Academy of Sciences to northern and eastern Siberia, caught the interest of Nicholas I, for the young zoologist had supplanted his scientific investigations of the fauna and flora of Siberia with observations on the political status of the region. After traversing the Amur region, questioning natives about their relations with China and seeking out border posts and boundary lines, Middendorf had concluded that the natives in the basin of the lower reaches of the Amur were in feeling and fact completely independent from China, that the Chinese delineated their frontier with Russia considerably more to the east and south than had been realized in Russia, and that nomadic tribes frequently violated these boundaries. These findings, backed by exhortations in the press, the tradition of his forefathers, and ambitions of his own, impelled Nicholas I to order the review of reports about the Amur Estuary and Sakhalin, especially because Britain's victory over the Manchus in the so-called Opium War of 1839 to 1842 had resulted in concessions, which marked the beginning of a new phase in Chinese-European relations, that were bound to affect, sooner or later, the commercial dealings between China and Russia. As one of the members of a committee set up to recommend measures for the strengthening of the Russian trade with China at Kiakhta, Rear Admiral Evfimii Putiatin observed in a report that, although it was as yet impossible to foresee the outcome of the recent events in China, it would be advisable for Russia to explore more thoroughly her eastern border. It was known that there was no reliable port anywhere along the coast from Sakhalin Island down to the mouth of the Uda, but the region below had not been explored. The very bay between the mainland and the Sakhalin Peninsula, which was said to receive the mouth of the Amur was yet unknown. And though Krusenstern had surveyed the northern part of the island it too deserved closer scrutiny. Putiatin recommended that these regions be explored and an effort be made to find a port more convenient than Okhotsk for dealing with Kamchatka and the Russian colonies in America. At the same time, he proposed to take advantage of this opportunity to attempt anew to establish relations with Japan. Nicholas I accepted Putiatin's recommendations and ordered in 1843 that an expedition be dispatched to China and Japan to negotiate concerning commercial relations, investigating at the same time the estuary and mouth of the Amur River to determine whether the Amur was inaccessible from the sea and whether the entrance was guarded by the Chinese.[8]

Count Karl Robert Nesselrode, Chancellor and Minister of Foreign Affairs, objected to the expedition, for fear it precipitate a break with China or England, but Nicholas I persisted in his plans, commanding that Putiatin himself outfit the expedition in the Black Sea. The expedition would have no doubt taken place, had Nesselrode not succeeded in gaining over the support of Count Egor Kankrin,

[8] Sgibnev, "Popytki," 71-72; Segawa, 264; Novakovskii, 143-152; Polonskii, 571-572.

the Minister of Finance, who dreaded the thought of "wasting" 250,000 rubles on such a venture. Dwelling on the uselessness of such an expedition he remarked in his memorial to the Emperor: "In view of the undevelopment, or to put it better the non-existence of our trade in the Pacific Ocean and the lack of prospects that this trade might ever even exist without our consolidation in the Amur region, the only useful purpose of the dispatch of E. V. Putiatin would be, I suppose, the mission to ascertain, among other things, the veracity of the conviction that the mouth of the Amur River is inaccessible, a circumstance, which conditions the extent to which this river and the region that it waters are of importance to Russia." But to learn this, Kankrin observed, no such costly expedition was required. For financial and political reasons, he recommended that the government refrain from sending a large expedition of its own, but act more discreetly through the Russian-American Company. Nicholas I duly cancelled the expedition to China and Japan, and in 1844 the Russian-American Company was asked to explore the mouth of the Amur River at government expense.

On May 17, 1846, the small brig *Konstantin* set sail. In his instructions to Gavrilov, the commander of the vessel, Mikhail Tebenkov, the director of the North American colonies, had noted:

It is reported that there are at the mouth of the Amur a settlement of Russian fugitives from beyond the Baikal and a large Chinese military force. You must, therefore, take all measures of precaution to avoid hostile clashes with the Chinese and to hide from them that your vessel is Russian. Secretly enter into dealings with the Russian fugitives and promise them an amnesty. Should you encounter shallow water at the entrance to the estuary you must not subject the vessel to danger, as it is positively known, that the mouth of the river is inaccessible.[9]

Gavrilov found neither Russian fugitives nor a Manchu force; but neither did he find a satisfactory fairway into the river. Ordered to take supplies to fur-hunters on the Kuril Islands and to return to the colonies the same season, he did not have time to explore the mouth more thoroughly, and was forced to report that it could be approached only by vessels with a shallow draft. His findings were incomplete rather than negative—he stated that it was not possible to conclude from his findings whether or not the mouth of the Amur was really accessible from the sea. In the absence of anything

9 Novakovskii, 152-153.

more positive, however, Nesselrode saw no reason to question conclusions of earlier explorers and ordered that henceforth the matter
of the Amur River be considered for ever closed and that all relating
correspondence be held secret.[10]

Although concerned primarily with exploration of the Amur
Estuary, Gavrilov had visited Etorofu twice with a letter from Rikord
in the attempt to establish commercial relations with the Japanese.
In this he had not been successful, but six years later his company
once more approached the Japanese.

Russian interest in Japan declined from time to time, but never
completely died out. There were always men to revive it. The captivity of Golovnin and the mediation of Takadaya were not an
isolated and forgotten chapter in history. It had aroused in Rikord
a permanent interest in Japan, and in 1850, when Rikord was an
admiral and a person of influence, he sent a memorandum to Grand
Duke Konstantin Nikolaevich, the Lord High Admiral. As others
before him, Rikord saw in Japan a desirable source of supplies for
"the distant regions of Kamchatka and the whole of eastern Siberia."
He reviewed in the memorandum his informative conversations with
Takadaya Kahei and Murakami Teisuke at the time of his liberation
of Golovnin and told of his unremitting concern with Japanese
affairs in the thirty-seven years since then. Having established his
position as an expert—"not only in Russia but in all of Europe
there is hardly anyone who can vie with me in information about
Japan"—he proceeded to suggest ways and means of overcoming
Japanese opposition to relations with Russia. A Russian warship
was about to be dispatched to the Pacific, and he assured the Lord
High Admiral that his plan, regarding the opening of Japan, required
no special outlay on the part of the government "because all that
concerns the fulfillment of this will consist of my person alone." He
stressed the importance of rank in dealing with the Japanese and
recommended the appointment of as high a personage as possible in
name if not in fact. When he had negotiated with the Japanese in
the past, he had inflated his position to that of Military Governor
of Kamchatka. He was prepared for "extraordinary exaggeration"
of the significance of his present status, but suggested that in the
absence of a navy of their own, the Japanese would pay greater heed
to one (himself?) holding the rank of Military Governor General of

[10] Tikhmenev, II, 53; Novakovskii, 153-154.

Siberia. Relating that he had learned in England of the interception of a letter in which the Dutch factor boasted of having dissuaded the Japanese from coming to terms with Rezanov, Rikord proposed the conclusion of a preliminary understanding with the Dutch, in which Russia would agree to exclusive Dutch operation in all parts of Japan other than the northern regions. With Dutch cooperation Rikord thought it likely that Japanese consent to dealings with Russia could at last be attained. If the Japanese again refused, Rikord continued, there was justification in their treacherous seizure of Golovnin to take resolute action against them. He realized that the size and self-sacrifice of the Japanese population precluded an invasion of their country.

But there is another way, which demands neither outlay nor actions directly hostile, yet which at the same time can undoubtedly make it necessary for the Japanese to agree to friendly relations with us, and to show them how many harmful consequences may otherwise follow from their stubbornness, consequences for which they will not have the right to reproach us, keeping in mind their treatment of Golovnin, which by their own concepts and admission deserves revenge on our part, and thus justifies our actions.

In Japan there are no overland roads for the delivery of provisions as well as other necessities from one point of their extensive country to another, and therefore all transportation is made by means of coasting vessels (1850). The presence of a warship of ours in the Strait of Matsumae will suffice to keep them in constant fear and from time to time to carry out attacks, greatly removed from direct hostility, on their coasting vessels, which come and leave with provisions, stopping them and taking from them the cargoes, leaving untouched the vessels themselves and the persons on board: we have need neither of their vessels nor their men. Here there will also be the advantage for us, that we shall be obtaining without any expense the freshest and best provisions, which they will have to lose solely because of their stubbornness.[11]

On June 10, 1852, on orders from the director of the colonies, the *Kniaz Menshikov*, under the command of Shipmaster Lindenberg, departed from Novo-Arkhangelsk, and, clearing Sitka Bay, set course for Shimoda Harbor, with seven Japanese castaways on board. Slowed down by weather, the *Kniaz Menshikov* did not reach Izu Peninsula, on the southwestern part of which Shimoda is situated, until August 9. As the Russians approached a little island in the center of the bay, Japanese on several boats hurried out to them

[11] Admiral Petr Ivanovich Rikord, "Zapiska, predstavlennaia im general-admiralu E. I. V. Velikomu Kniaziu Konstantinu Nikolaevichu v 1850 g.," 177-182.

to persuade them not to go further, but Lindenberg ignored them and penetrated deeper into the bay, past the roadstead, into the harbor itself, before the Japanese could stop him, and cast anchor at a depth of about forty-two feet. No sooner had the *Kniaz Menshikov* cast anchor in the picturesque, but open bay, than she was overrun by hundreds of curious visitors, who refused to take turns, since they would not be able to board the vessel once the governor arrived. Before long the governor of Shimoda came out with a large retinue to question the castaways and inspect the ship, noting down everything carefully.

Lindenberg invited the Japanese officials to his cabin and there explained to them the purpose of his arrival, adding that he had a paper from the chairman of the board of the company to the governor of the city, that he wished to present it and to receive a reply. The governor thanked the Russians in the name of the Japanese nation for having brought to their homeland his shipwrecked compatriots and for many things done for them during their stay in Russia, indicating through gestures that such behavior on the part of the Russians moved him to the verge of tears. He added, however, that, without special permission from Edo, he could accept neither the paper nor the castaways. After much persuasion on the part of Lindenberg, the Japanese finally agreed to look at the paper, but, after scanning it, declared, with due respect, that, although the writing was like that of his country, he could not understand the meaning, and that, as he was not allowed to accept the paper, he be permitted to copy it; the paper was in Chinese and he supposed, if he might copy, it could be understood by the Chinese interpreters. Lindenberg agreed to this to expedite matters—the history of Russo-Japanese relations having proved that the Japanese refused to accept any document, whose content they did not know beforehand—and the governor himself took out brush and ink and immediately copied the paper. Having done so, he asked if the Russians needed anything. Lindenberg told him that they would like to have fresh provisions, fish or meat, and that of course he would pay for them. The governor readily agreed, and water, chickens, eggs, and fresh fish (but not meat) were later supplied. Before leaving, he announced that he would post guard boats alongside the ship and that Lindenberg was to send no one ashore. Should he himself wish to go ashore, he should first notify the governor, who would then accompany him. Lindenberg would have liked to go ashore then and there, but it was already dark and he was afraid that the inappropriate display of curiosity would arouse Japanese suspicion. And so six guard boats were posted.

The next day the governor came again. Once more he interrogated the castaways in detail about their experiences—their shipwreck, their stay in Russia, the treatment and food they had received—and asked questions about Kamchatka, Okhotsk, Sitka, the Kuril Islands and other areas close to Japan. Then he inspected the *Kniaz Menshikov* again, directing his attention particularly to the weapons of ship and crew, and asked whether additional arms and ammunition were stored in the hold of the ship. Japanese artists meanwhile sketched various parts of the vessel. When Lindenberg, having invited the officials to his cabin, expressed the intention of going ashore, however, the governor refused him on the ground that he did not have the authority to permit this without special sanction from the government. Lindenberg reminded him of the promise he had made just the day before, but the governor, though embarrassed, remained adamant in his refusal. Nevertheless relations continued to be amicable for several days. The Japanese visited the *Kniaz Menshikov* on business only and categorically refused to accept gifts or to buy anything (saying that trade with foreigners was confined by law to Nagasaki), yet they enjoyed visiting and gave the impression of being generally well-disposed toward the Russians. But with every day the strictness of Japanese surveillance increased. The number of guard boats grew and the soldiers, who manned them, isolated the Russians from the population. Behind the façade of friendliness and gratitude for the repatriation of the castaways, there was concern about the arrival of the strangers and their violation of the seclusion laws. From all sides, heavily armed troops began converging on Shimoda.[12]

. . . whole caravans with laden buffaloes and horses stretched past our ship along the seashore which was traversed by a road from the interior of the country to the city of Shimoda, and although, because of the darkness of twilight, we were not able to behold what they were conveying, one must suppose, however, that it was cannons, inasmuch as soon there appeared among the trees on shore opposite the ship at a distance of one and a half cable's lengths flag-topped tents, that looked very much like concealed batteries.[13]

[12] Shipmaster Lindenberg, "O plavanii v Iaponiiu korablia Rossiisko-Amerikanskoi kompanii 'Kniaz Menshikov' v 1852 g.," 131-135; Novakovskii, 155-157.
[13] Lindenberg, 135.

The governor and his officials still continued to visit the vessel and to thank the Russians with every mark of sincerity for having been so gracious to their compatriots, and take note of Lindenberg's assurance that the repeated repatriation of Japanese castaways was proof of Russian friendship.

On August 12, the vice-governor of Odawara came aboard. He too examined the ship and interrogated the castaways. When Lindenberg asked when the castaways could be handed over, the vice-governor replied that they were awaiting instructions from the capital, and that the governor of Odawara would arrive together with these instructions. Lindenberg offered to pay for the provisions, which he had received, but the official refused to accept compensation on the pretext that Japanese assistance had amounted to nothing compared with what the Russians had done for the castaways and brushed aside Lindenberg's argument, that to accept anything without charge was inconsistent with Russian honor.

On the evening of August 13, the governor of Odawara was seen to arrive in Shimoda with a large military retinue. The following day, on August 14, the vice-governor of Odawara came aboard again and asked that the castaways be called together. When they had gathered on deck, he addressed them. Bent over low, they listened with respect, but suddenly the immobile expression of respectful submission, which had masked their faces, was distorted into grimaces of sorrow, and loud sobs gave vent to their utter despair. When Lindenberg asked what was the matter, one of the castaways explained that the governor had announced to them that they could not return to their fatherland, but must remain with the Russians. The refusal was even more painful, because the castaways had never doubted that they would be permitted to land. Lindenberg did not wish to remonstrate with the vice-governor in public and asked him to step down to his cabin. In the cabin the vice-governor informed Lindenberg that the orders, which had arrived from the capital, forbade him to accept either the castaways or any documents. They stated unequivocally that Shimoda was not open to foreigners and that he must not enter into any dealings with the Russians. Under the circumstances, the vice-governor noted, he must ask Lindenberg to depart at once. In vain Lindenberg pleaded that this decision was cruel and absurd; it had been the sole purpose of his arrival to return these unfortunate people to their homeland and families. He even threatened that, if the Japanese did not accept them now, another vessel would bring them again the following year and that, eventually, they would have to accept them anyway. But the vice-governor replied that the answer of the Japanese would always be the same, that it was the will of their government and that there was nothing that Lindenberg could accomplish in Shimoda. The official spoke with determination, yet it was clear that he himself found no joy in the reply. It was evident to Lindenberg, as he looked into the faces of the vice-governor and all the other Japanese, "that inside them they did not approve of this decision, though they had to comply with it." He asked, therefore, to speak with the governor of Odawara, but the vice-governor retorted that this was not possible and begged him to hasten away while the wind was favorable. As it was, the vice-governor remarked, Lindenberg had been extended unusual consideration in not having been asked to surrender his arms and ammunition during his stay. He suggested, furthermore, that Lindenberg might try to hand the castaways over at Nagasaki. But Lindenberg regarded this merely as a means of expediting his departure and stated, therefore, that he could not go to Nagasaki without orders from his government. He had been instructed to deliver the castaways to Shimoda, and, if the vice-governor would not receive them, he would simply put them in a boat and send them ashore. At the thought that Lindenberg might do so in this harbor, the vice-governor jumped up in panic and was about to hurry away, when Lindenberg calmed him with the assurance that, though he had come to repatriate the castaways, he had no intention of damaging relations between the Japanese and Russia by flaunting their decrees. Yet, he too had orders to obey, and if he could not land the castaways here, he would have to do so elsewhere. To this the governor did not object. What Lindenberg did elsewhere was none of his concern. But now, he repeated, the vessel must leave without delay.

In his report to the governor of the colonies, Lindenberg explained his next step:

Deeming it unwise, if not impossible, to put the Japanese ashore here by force, and not seeing means of compelling the governor to accept the paper of Your Excellency against his will and being sure that in the event that I persisted the Japanese would resort to hostile measures, in view of the preparations they had made for this, and though the accuracy of Japanese shots is not dangerous, not wishing to expose the flag to humiliation having neither the permission of Your Excellency nor the means successfully to meet force with force, I decided not to let it come to this, and seeing no other way out of the difficult situation, I was forced to give in, and therefore declared to the vice-governor, that inasmuch as he did not accept his compatriots and did not wish to enter into any dealings with me, there was nothing left for me to do here, and that in line with his request I was ready to go out to sea, but that nonetheless I would put the Japanese ashore right here in the vicinity.[14]

Towed out by twenty large barges, the *Kniaz Menshikov* left Shimoda. The castaways were heartbroken. They told Lindenberg that they did not wish to proceed any further, but wanted to be put ashore where they were, even though this meant certain death. Heading for China, where every foot of space would be needed for tea, Lindenberg readily considered the plea, and in a small bay some five miles from Shimoda Harbor, in the vicinity of Nakagi village, he let the Japanese head ashore in two boats brought along for the purpose. Once again the Russian-American Company had failed to make a visible dent in the seclusion policy of the Shogunate. But every expedition was another blow at the wall of isolation, which the Japanese had erected. By itself, no single blow had a telling effect. But together they slowly weakened the foundation, until, only two years after Lindenberg's failure, increased pressure from different sides brought a large part of the wall of isolation tumbling down. Before Lindenberg had returned to Russia, another expedition, sponsored on a much larger scale by the government itself, was already on its way to Japan, and, though it was to call at Nagasaki, where the Japanese had directed the Russians so persistently, it would be at Shimoda that the first treaty between Russia and Japan would be signed.[15]

THE OCCUPATION OF SAKHALIN

One of the major stepping-stones from Russia to Japan was Sakhalin Island. The Russians had landed there repeatedly. Shelting had partly surveyed its shores in 1742, and Khvostov and Davydov had done so more thoroughly in 1806-1807.[16] Khvostov and Davydov

---

[14] *Ibid.*, 136-138; Novakovskii, 157-158.

[15] Lindenberg, 138-139; Novakovskii, 158-159; Heki, *Koku-shi*, v, 38.

[16] Rezanov had heard of a Russian settlement on Sakhalin in the eighteenth century. Nothing is known about it, but when Mogami Tokunai arrived on the island in 1792, he found a Russian by the name of Ivan, who had been living on the island for a long time. (Numata Iichiro, *Nichi-Ro gaiko-shi*, 7; Minakawa, 117-119.) According to Japanese sources the Russians first set foot on Sakhalin in 1783 (Ota, 349) and during the

had even left five sailors on the island to announce its annexation by Russia to the vessels of other nations. But, though some imperialists in later years were to lay claim to Sakhalin on the ground that the stay of these sailors constituted prior Russian settlement, the Russian government had disassociated itself from the aggression of Khvostov and Davydov.[17] The Japanese had visited Sakhalin as early as the seventeenth century, when fishermen had established posts in the southern half of the island. Sato Kamozaemon and Kakizaki Kurando are said to have been ordered to inspect Sakhalin in 1635; the explorer Oishi Ippei went across in 1786. Since Hokkaido itself was not seriously colonized until the nineteenth century, relatively little attention was paid by the Japanese to Sakhalin until the raids of Khvostov and Davydov. Then, in 1806, the noted explorer Mamiya Rinzo charted and described the island and focused attention on its defense against Russian encroachment.[18]

Sakhalin was important as a stepping-stone from Russia to Japan only if the Amur River were in Russian hands. Yet, an attempt, in the late seventeenth century, to acquire the Amur region by diplomatic negotiation with Manchu China had failed, and the misconception that Sakhalin was a peninsula blocking the mouth of the river deflected the attention of the Russian government toward Europe, and Nicholas I, on Nesselrode's recommendation, decreed that the Amur question be dropped. But not everyone agreed.

Most notable among those, who persisted in the conviction that the Amur was accessible from the sea and that Sakhalin was an island, was Captain Gennadii Nevelskoi, a naval officer of independent character and fervor, not readily bridled by instructions from above. Fanatically devoted to the cause of Russian expansion, he had studied with care the various expeditions to the Amur. When he concluded that the explorations had not been thorough enough, he refused to accept as final the verdict that the Amur must be explored no further. In this he won the sympathetic support of the governor general of Siberia, Nikolai Muravev (later known as

Temmei period (1781-1788). (Otomo, *Hokumon sosho*, III, 466-467.) It is not clear whether or not these observations refer to the expedition of Petr, son of Rihachiro, all members of which purportedly had been slain by the natives.

[17] Golovnin considered the southern part of Sakhalin as Japanese, the northern part as Chinese. (Golovnin, *Zapiski*, III, 109-110, 119-120.)

[18] Mamiya Rinzo had been preceded by Mogami Tokunai in 1792. Even Russian sources date the first Japanese visits to Sakhalin back to 1613. (Anton Chekhov, *Ostrov Sakhalin*, 16.)

Muravev-Amurskii), when he expounded his views to him.[19] But the chief of the naval staff, Prince Aleksandr Menshikov, rejected, in 1848, Nevelskoi's request for permission to explore the mouth and the estuary of the Amur. He explained that the vessel would be completed too late in the season; that the funds, allotted for its voyage to the Siberian ports, with much needed supplies, were inadequate for continuing it beyond the present year; that it had been proven positively that the mouth of the Amur was blocked by sandbanks; and that Nesselrode would never approve, because such a venture might bring about complications with China. Nevelskoi's ambition was not quenched that easily, however. All that these objections meant, he reflected, was that he would have to work rapidly enough, so that time and funds did suffice, and that he would have to engineer the project in such a way that the exploration of the Amur could be executed as if by chance, incidental to the description of the southwestern shores of the Sea of Okhotsk. Industriously Nevelskoi succeeded in speeding up the construction of the transport *Baikal* and obtained Menshikov's permission for a different method of loading the vessel, which dispensed with much time-consuming red tape. Menshikov did not authorize the exploration of the southwestern shores of the Sea of Okhotsk, noting that, important as he himself also thought it, Nesselrode regarded the territory as Chinese, and that though Muravev had pointed out that the treaty with China left this region undelineated, Nesselrode wished to avoid complications with the Chinese. But neither did Menshikov explicitly forbid the exploration of the Okhotsk shores, and Nevelskoi rushed preparations for an early departure. At the same time, he wrote a letter to Muravev requesting his support. He expected to reach Kamchatka in May of 1849. It would take him a fortnight to unload his cargo; the rest of the summer he could devote to the exploration of the Okhotsk shores down to the Amur River, of the Amur itself and its estuary, and of the northeastern shore of Sakhalin Island. In view of the importance of these regions to eastern Siberia, of which Muravev was governor general, he asked whether Muravev could not get him the necessary permission and outlined the type of instructions that he required. In July Nevelskoi received a reply, in which Muravev praised him highly for his patriotic ardor and said that instructions had been drawn up for him on the basis of those he had proposed himself, that Prince Menshikov

[19] Tikhmenev, II, 39-61; Nevelskoi, 74-75.

and Minister of the Interior Lev Perovskii were sympathetic, and that there was reason to hope that the Emperor would approve the instructions.

On February 10, 1849, there was appointed by order of Nicholas I a committee in which the Amur question was discussed. On the recommendation of this committee, the Emperor sanctioned, on February 20, the exploration of the mouth of the Amur River. The committee expressed it desirable that neither the left bank of the Amur nor the part of Sakhalin Island opposite it be occupied by any foreign power. It warned, however, against alarming the Chinese, and Nesselrode proposed that the Amur be approached from the sea under some innocent looking pretext by a small expedition under a commander noted for caution. He added that in the event that England or another foreign power should make any attempt to encroach on the Amur River or Sakhalin Island, the Chinese should be informed thereof in order to dispel whatever suspicions they might harbor against Russia. Nevelskoi was not noted for caution, but, since he had already departed for the shores of the Okhotsk Sea in the beginning of September 1848, Nesselrode, eager to carry out the matter quietly, felt it best to use him, and Nevelskoi was ordered to survey the shores of the Sea of Okhotsk from the Shantar Islands to the mouth of the Amur, as well as the northern shores of Sakhalin. In this region, preferably near the mouth of the Amur, he was to earmark an advantageous point for possible occupation at a later time.

Nevelskoi meanwhile was already en route from Kronstadt to Kamchatka by way of Cape Horn. At Rio de Janeiro, he mailed a letter to Muravev in which he wrote that he expected to reach Petropavlovsk in May and planned, after unloading his cargo, to embark directly on the description of the eastern shores of Sakhalin and the Amur Estuary and requested Muravev's help in the event that imperial permission for such action had not been granted by that time. In Petropavlovsk, Nevelskoi received a secret note from Muravev in which he communicated the instructions submitted for imperial approval. They ordered Nevelskoi to proceed to northern Sakhalin in order to look for a roadstead or sheltered harbor there and to explore the Amur River from this direction. He was to investigate the approaches to the river and the river itself, locate suitable defense positions, and determine whether Sakhalin was a peninsula. Should he find that it was an island, he was to explore the strait, which separated it from the mainland, and seek out a place from where the southern approaches of the Amur could be guarded. He was instructed also to chart the southwestern shore of the Sea of Okhotsk and Konstantin Bay. These explorations Nevelskoi was to carry out unobtrusively, without flying a Russian flag, naval or commercial, and in rowboats, leaving the transport behind at Cape Golovachev. The importance of keeping this expedition and its findings secret was emphasized and Nevelskoi was instructed to make a secret report of everything as soon as possible to Menshikov and to Muravev. It was hoped that, before the end of September, he could be back in Okhotsk and start out with all his officers for St. Petersburg. Muravev expressed the belief that the instructions would be approved, but Nevelskoi did not await confirmation. In mid-June 1849, he weighed anchor, informing Muravev in another letter that he was setting sail for Sakhalin and the Amur Estuary, in the northern part of which he hoped to be before the middle of July.[20]

On June 24, the *Baikal* reached the eastern shores of Sakhalin, and turning northward proceeded to examine the coastline from about latitude 51°37′ N. Rounding the northern projection of the island, the *Baikal* continued southwestward, down the western shore of Sakhalin. The exploration of these waters and the search for the Amur Estuary were a slow and hazardous process. The transport was repeatedly caught on sandbanks. On July 9,[21] the Russians entered the estuary. In the face of mounting dangers, Nevelskoi doggedly persisted in his investigations. Accompanied by three officers, the doctor, and fourteen seamen in three boats, and supplied with provisions for three weeks, he explored the lower reaches of the Amur River and found them navigable. Resuming his southward penetration, he discovered at last, on August 3, 1849, a navigable strait about four miles in width, that separated Sakhalin from the mainland, and proved thereby that Sakhalin was an island and that the Amur could be entered by ships both from the Sea of Okhotsk in the north and Tatar Strait in the south.[22]

The discovery proved that eastern Siberia was effectively connected with the Sea of Japan and the Pacific Ocean by the Amur River and

[20] I. P. Barsukov, *Graf Nikolai Nikolaevich Muravev-Amurskii*, I, 195-198; Nevelskoi, 88-91.

[21] Barsukov gives the dates one day ahead.

[22] The "Bay" or "Gulf" of Tatary thus was a strait, and though "Tatar Strait" is used here, Nevelskoi himself by force of habit continued to refer to the strait as the Bay or Gulf of Tatary, a name it has retained on most maps.

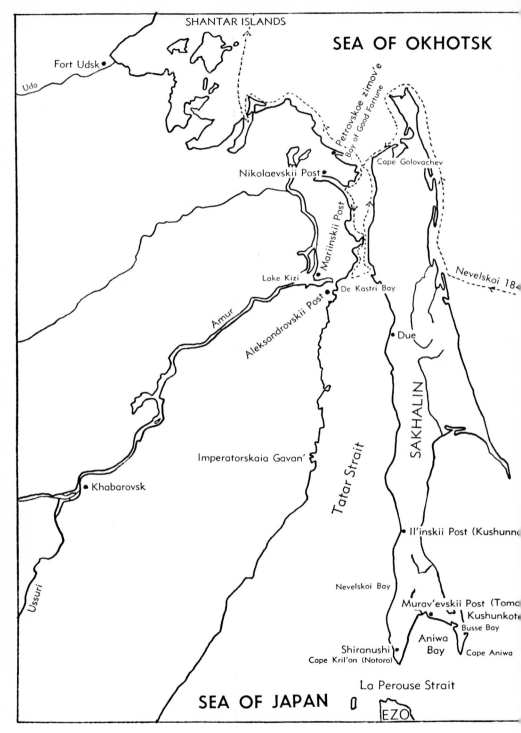

The Occupation of Sakhalin

that consequently possession of the Amur region would be of utmost importance to Russia. For this reason Nevelskoi recommended to Muravev, shortly after his return to Irkutsk, that Russia establish herself without delay on the lower Amur for fear that she forfeit to another power control of the entrance into the river. Muravev shared this view, and, in February of 1850, Nevelskoi repeated the proposal to Menshikov in St. Petersburg, backed by a report of Muravev, urging the occupation of the mouth of the Amur by a force of seventy men that very season. Menshikov was sympathetic to the proposal and so was Perovskii, but the majority of the Special Committee under the chairmanship of Nesselrode distrusted Nevelskoi's findings and resented that he had acted without awaiting authorization, not to mention the fact that the Emperor had granted permission for the survey of the Amur and its estuary without consulting them, and they dreaded complications with China. When it was decreed, therefore, on February 15, 1850, that Nevelskoi be dispatched again to the southwestern shore of the Sea of Okhotsk to establish a wintering station, needed by the Russian-American Company for trade with the Gilyaks, he was specifically forbidden to establish the station either at the Amur Estuary or along the river itself, and it was stipulated that under no circumstances was the Russian-American Company to have any contact whatsoever with the Amur River and its estuary.

In the Bay of Good Fortune, to the north of the Amur Estuary, Nevelskoi established the wintering station Petrovskoe Zimov'e, commonly called simply Petrovskoe. Undaunted, he then proceeded into the Amur River, and brazenly announced to a group of Manchus and to native tribesmen that this whole region—the river, the maritime area, and Sakhalin Island—had always been regarded as Russian by his countrymen and that he had been sent to inform them that the great Emperor of Russia was taking them under his protection, fortified posts being established to safeguard them from the aggression of foreign vessels. He commanded that all foreigners be shown the following proclamation:

In the name of the Russian Government all foreign vessels sailing in the Gulf of Tatary are hereby notified that inasmuch as the shore of this gulf and the whole Amur region down to the Korean frontier as well as Sakhalin Island constitute Russian possessions, neither unauthorized dispositions nor injuries to the inhabitants can be tolerated here. For this purpose Russian military posts have now been established in the Bay of

Iskai [Good Fortune] and in the mouth of the Amur River. The under-signed, who has been sent by the government as plenipotentiary, suggests that one turn to the commanders of these posts in case of any needs or of a clash with the local inhabitants.[23]

On August 13, 1850, Nevelskoi on his own responsibility established the six-man Nikolaevskii Post and boldly hoisted the Russian flag over the Amur.

When Nesselrode and Minister of War Prince Aleksandr Cherny-shev learned of this, they were outraged and wished to cashier Nevelskoi and remove the post on the Amur. It was then that Nicholas I made the ringing declaration that "where once the Russian flag has flown, it must not be lowered again," and, instead of punishing Nevelskoi, praised his action as courageous, noble, and patriotic, and decorated him with the Cross of Vladimir, Fourth Class. At the same time the Tsar took the chairmanship of the Special Committee out of the hands of Nesselrode, and appointed, in his stead, Crown Prince Aleksandr Nikolaevich (later Alexander II).[24] Nevelskoi was to remain in direct command of the posts and related activities—the whole venture being named the Amur Expedition. Encouraged by imperial patronage, Nevelskoi continued to extend the sway of the Russian Empire. Jubilantly, he recorded that, after a lapse of two centuries, Russians had advanced once more into the wastes of the Amur region, praying to the Almighty for courage and fortitude. Again Russian shots were fired, but not to murder or subjugate, only to salute the Russian banner. "These shots greeted the victory of truth over century-old error! They greeted in the wastes of the Amur region the victory of civilization over ignorance and the dawn of the near realization of the ideas of Peter I and Catherine II in our remote East."[25]

Toward the end of 1851, four Gilyaks from Sakhalin Island arrived in Petrovskoe. On one of them the Russians noticed a button made of coal. On inquiring, they learned that there was coal on Sakhalin. They heard also that five Russians (no doubt those left by Khvostov) had lived on the island and that the last of the five had just recently died; these Russians, the Gilyaks stated, had arrived much earlier than any Japanese. Greatly interested, Nevelskoi dispatched Lieu-

---

[23] Nevelskoi, 92-121; Novakovskii, 160.

[24] On February 27, 1851 Russia informed the government of China that it intended to watch over the mouth of the Amur. (Konstantin Apollonovich Skalkovskii, *Vneshniaia politika Rossii i polozhenie inostranykh derzhav*, 451-452.)

[25] Nevelskoi, 122-125, 142.

tenant Boshniak and two men[26] across the ice to Sakhalin in February of 1852, ordering them to locate the coal deposits and to determine their accessibility, to determine the most populous and important point of the island, the relationship of the inhabitants to China and Japan, the arrival of foreign vessels, and to ascertain whether Russians had really lived there. When Boshniak returned a month later, he brought back not only the desired information about the coal fields and their accessibility and evidence that Russians had lived on Sakhalin, but also an alleged plea by the natives that the Russians come and protect them against the forays of foreign vessels. In the summer of the same year, Nevelskoi sent Second Lieutenant Voronin to Sakhalin on a sloop-of-war in order to investigate the territory and waters near the settlement Düe, to determine whether a Russian settlement could favorably be established there and whether ships could come up to take on cargoes of coal. At the same time Voronin was to announce to the inhabitants that, since the island was Russian territory, they were being taken under Russian protection. Should foreign vessels appear, he was to observe them closely and, hoisting the Russian flag on the sloop, inform them, in the name of the Russian government, that Sakhalin Island and the continental shore of Tatar Strait down to the Korean frontier were Russian territory, and that no unauthorized acts on their part would be tolerated.

In the early months of 1853, Nevelskoi extended Russian occupation along the Amur River and the maritime region to the settlement Kizi and to De-Kastri Bay, pleading constantly in letters to Muravev for more men, more vessels, and more supplies to ensure Russian domination of the Amur and Ussuri regions and of Sakhalin. He was much concerned about foreign encroachment and, when he learned toward the end of May about the possible appearance of the vessels of the American expeditions of Commodore Matthew C. Perry (who hoped to establish diplomatic and commercial relations with Japan) and of Commander Cadwalader Ringgold (who was to make a scientific investigation of the Pacific shores up to Bering Strait), he immediately sent word to Nikolaevsk that, should the Americans come to De-Kastri, they be welcomed amicably and politely, but told that navigation in the Amur Estuary was not only difficult, but extremely dangerous for low-lying vessels and completely impossible for vessels of medium class, that this whole region was waste, mountainous, and

[26] The Gilyak Pozvein who spoke Tungusic and Ainu and the Cossack Parfentev who also spoke Tungusic.

without means of communication, and that all of it down to the Korean frontier and including Sakhalin had always belonged to Russia. This claim was to be justified on the basis of the Treaty of Nerchinsk with China (1689), the occupation of Sakhalin by Russian Tungus in the seventeenth century, the description of the island in 1742 (by Shelting), and the occupation of its southern part in 1806 (by Khvostov).[27]

While Nevelskoi thrust deeper into the Far East, Muravev was kept busy wringing the necessary authorizations from the government *post factum*. Advanced as Nevelskoi usually was in his actions, Muravev was not far behind in making zealous plans for the Amur region. On March 3, 1852, in a report about conditions in Siberia, he expressed the fear that China and Japan were falling into English and American hands. "In accordance with the project of Palmer,"[28] American steamships would soon hasten to Japan, "armed and ready for battle," and, though Golovnin had pointed to Japan some forty years ago, "now, of course, she is already lost for us." But there was still the opportunity for Russia to reach "at least secondary importance in these seas," he argued, if she acted promptly to open navigation on the Amur River, whose upper reaches she possessed.[29]

The outfitting of an American expedition to Japan smoothed the path for Muravev in St. Petersburg in selling Nevelskoi's plans for the occupation of points on Sakhalin, and on July 23, 1853, Nevelskoi received the long awaited imperial instructions (dated April 23):

(1) The Russian-American Company is to occupy Sakhalin Island and to hold it on the same basis as it holds other lands mentioned in its privileges.

(2) To promise the Company that officers and men will be put at its full disposal for the occupation of Sakhalin and for the defense of Company establishments thereon. These men will be considered in the service of the Company and will be fully maintained by it.

(3) To occupy on Sakhalin those points, which according to local considerations will be found most important; this is to be begun without fail during the navigation of this year 1853, and from the year 1854 the Company must have there its own special governor who from a political standpoint will be under the command of the Governor General of

[27] Nevelskoi, 141-182, 194-198, 201-204.

[28] The intrepid businessman Aaron Haight Palmer of New York. For a discussion of his role in the outfitting of an American expedition to Japan, see Claude S. Phillips, Jr., "Some Forces Behind the Opening of Japan."

[29] Barsukov, I, 308-309.

Eastern Siberia or another governmental chief commander, who will be indicated by the Emperor.

(4) The Company must not allow on Sakhalin any foreign settlements, either arbitrary or by mutual agreement, and can transfer this island only to the government.

(5) The government makes use on Sakhalin Island of coal for governmental needs without compensation, but mines it at its own expense.

(6) For the protection of the shores of the island and the harbors against the intrusion of foreigners, the Company commits itself to maintain a sufficient number of vessels, but in case of a military attack demands troops for defense from the government.

(7) During the initial occupation of Sakhalin Island this year, there can be used with permission of the Governor General military personnel and resources of the Amur expedition under the command of the commander of that Amur expedition; however, it must be completely separate from the Sakhalin expedition and remain as before under the direct command of the government.

(8) The Company authorities must direct their demands concerning the assignment to them of officers and men to the Governor General of Eastern Siberia, and the latter is obliged to carry out this demand without delay; however, the governing board of the Company may in case of need turn with questions concerning this subject also to the higher government should it be necessary and convenient to send officers and soldiers from Baltic ports to Sakhalin on vessels making round-the-world cruises.

(9) Officers and men, headed for Sakhalin, must be sent there on vessels and at the maintenance of the Company from the very place of their former service.

(10) To appoint this year no less than 100 men from Kamchatka and to obligate the Company to maintain them.

(11) For expenses in connection with this undertaking to release to the Company now irrevocably and without any later accounting 50,000 rubles in silver from the sum, allocated at the disposal of the Governor General of Eastern Siberia for the setting up of a special fund for undertakings concerning the Gilyaks.

Forwarding the imperial instructions to Nevelskoi and commanding their immediate execution, Muravev reiterated in a note of his own that Nevelskoi was to be in charge of all establishments founded by him that year and of all members of the Sakhalin expedition in all respects, until the arrival of a special governor on the island in 1854, and outlined the steps which he deemed necessary to carry out the intentions of the government:

a) To occupy on Sakhalin Island this year two or three points on the eastern or western shore, but as far south as possible.

b) Not to harass the Japanese fishermen who are on the southern extremity of Sakhalin and to show them a friendly disposition, assuring them that we are occupying Sakhalin Island in order to guard it against the encroachment of foreigners and that under our protection they can continue in safety their fishery and trade there.

c) For the occupation of Sakhalin Island there have been appointed now from Kamchatka 100 men with two officers. For the selection of these men and their delivery to you, I have assigned Major [Nikolai] Busse, who is attached to me. I have ordered [Aleksandr] Kashevarov [commandant of the port of Aian] to send to the harbor of Good Fortune—Petrovskoe—the timber prepared in Aian for the wintering of the men on Sakhalin and one vessel for your disposition; it must remain there to winter; concerning the personnel I sent instructions to Zavoiko and consider it necessary to notify you that Major Busse must deliver to you the designated detachment, with the two officers and with all provision supplies, arms, and everything necessary for the building, as well as goods to Petrovskoe toward the end of July [first half of August], but in no case later than August 1 [13] or 4 [16].

d) In the event that you should consider it necessary immediately upon receipt of this to occupy some points on Sakhalin prior to the arrival of the designated men, this is left to be done at your discretion with those means, which you have in the expedition entrusted to you.

e) In the beginning [middle] of July a 16-power steamer, bought by the Company in England, is to come to you in Petrovskoe; you will probably get it at the same time as the present instructions; I ask you to make use of it in the occupation of Sakhalin; it would be very useful if, with the help of this steamer, you would lead the vessel, on which Major Busse will come to you, into Tatar Strait by way of the Amur Estuary. You may leave this vessel to winter on Sakhalin.

f) At the places, which you will occupy on Sakhalin, it is necessary to place guns and to construct fences or fortifications, and

g) When N. V. Busse will deliver to you everything, mentioned above, you will immediately send him to me with reports.[30]

On May 5, Muravev supplemented these instructions with the demand that in the summer Nevelskoi occupy De-Kastri Bay and, leaving there a guard of not less than one officer and ten men, establish at the neighboring settlement of Kizi a military post for the reinforcement and supplying of De-Kastri. But he warned that "in accordance with the Imperial instructions concerning our boundary with China, it is not permitted to go beyond De-Kastri and Kizi" and ordered Nevelskoi to direct his main attention to Sakhalin.

Nevelskoi, who had anticipated the occupation of De-Kastri and Kizi, was delighted and reassured that the orders covered what he

30 Nevelskoi, 216-218.

had already done. He was pleased that the government had declared Sakhalin a Russian possession, and that he was now free to concentrate on the occupation of the island. But, he was disgruntled that the government had focused its attention on Sakhalin to the exclusion of the Amur region, content to draw the border with China along the left bank of the Amur, and decided to occupy Imperatorskaia Gavan' and the shore to the south in defiance of instructions.

Nevelskoi was unable to understand how an officer could hesitate to violate orders, if the situation seemed to demand it. When Major Busse informed him by letter that he was in Aian, but would not be able to deliver to him the required men and supplies by mid-August, as stipulated, because his instructions did not authorize the use of government vessels and no company ships were in port, Nevelskoi was infuriated and complained to Muravev about Busse's apparent "inexperience and ignorance of those important consequences, which may result from his indecision," adding venomously that "there is nothing more that one can expect from an officer, taken directly from the parade ground." Arguing that further delays could well be fatal, since to leave men on the barren eastern or western shore of Sakhalin in September would be tantamount to abandoning them to inevitable sickness or death, and pointing to the fact that the imperial instructions regarded the whole of Sakhalin as Russian territory, Nevelskoi wrote that he felt it necessary to occupy its main point, Tomari,[31] where the troops could readily be landed and quartered for the winter. He asserted that to occupy any minor point on the eastern or western shore of the island, without first gaining control over Tomari, might make Russian action appear timid and undecided, and would not only be unworthy of Russian dignity, but invite trouble with the Japanese government. As if to clinch his case for acting again without due authority, Nevelskoi concluded that it was essential to be able to prove to the American squadron, which was expected to visit Sakhalin, that the island was Russian. Upon Busse's arrival with the landing party, therefore, he would proceed to establish himself in Aniwa Bay.

Meanwhile, on July 26, 1853, Nevelskoi departed on the transport *Baikal* for Sakhalin, leaving word that, should Busse arrive during his absence, he be instructed not to unload men or supplies, but await his return. With D. I. Orlov and fifteen men Nevelskoi sailed

[31] Tomari was located in Aniwa Bay. Nevelskoi referred to it as Tamari-Aniva.

down the eastern shore of Sakhalin, rounded Capes Aniwa and Kril'on, then worked his way northward along the western shore. Crossing over to the mainland, he established Konstantinovskii Post in Imperatorskaia Gavan' (August 18) and further north, in De-Kastri Bay, Aleksandrovskii Post (August 21). Here he went ashore, ordering the transport to return to the western coast of Sakhalin to land Orlov and several men in a bay near 50° lat. N., and there, Orlov was instructed to establish Il'inskii Post, call together the inhabitants, and announce to them, that the island was a Russian possession and that they were now under Russian protection. All foreign vessels, which Orlov and the commander of the *Baikal* might meet, were also to be informed, in the name of the Russian government, that the entire Amur and Ussuri regions as well as Sakhalin were Russian territory. Orlov was to explore the southwestern shore of the island and by September 27, await Nevelskoi on the east side of Cape Kril'on; should the *Baikal* fail to arrive there by October 2, he was to proceed to Tomari, which by then would be in Russian hands. The *Baikal*, meanwhile, having assisted Orlov in the establishment of Il'inskii Post, was to cruise about in Tatar Strait, keeping a lookout for the American squadron; by September 17, she was to return to Petrovskoe.[32]

Nevelskoi himself returned to Petrovskoe on August 29, having visited Lake Kizi and having established Mariinskii Post. A company vessel, meanwhile, had brought supplies and new personnel (Lieutenant Commander A. V. Bachmanov and the priest Gavriil and their wives) as well as dispatches from the board of directors of the company and from Aleksandr Kashevarov, commandant of the Port of Aian. The company papers, in conformity with an imperial ukase of April 23 and in agreement with Muravev, invested Nevelskoi with full authority over the Sakhalin expedition, until the expected arrival of Lieutenant Commander Furugelm, who had been appointed governor of the island, some time in 1854. Nevelskoi was informed that in addition to the main point, where the government of the island

---

[32] According to Barsukov, Nevelskoi established Il'inskii Post, manned by six men with a Gilyak boat, at the mouth of Kusunai River, at the narrowest part of the island on August 8, before crossing over to the mainland coast. This is not corroborated by Nevelskoi's narrative, but Nevelskoi's own version may be incorrect. Tikhmenev asserts that although Nevelskoi reported to the company that he had established the Il'inskii Post, other documents show that he did not in fact have time to do so because of the lateness of the season. Barsukov gives slightly different dates for the establishment of the other posts: Konstantinovskii (August 13), Aleksandrovskii (August 17).

would be centered, the company desired no more than two or three enclosed Russian outposts, and that he confine himself to the company brig *Konstantin* in transporting his men. Kashevarov communicated that Busse had set out for Petropavlovsk on the company vessel *Imperator Nikolai*[33] to get the landing party, but had been unable to take along a large part of the designated supplies, which had only just been received in Aian and had not yet been sorted out, much less properly prepared for dispatch to Sakhalin. Although no other vessels were expected in Aian, Furugelm warned Nevelskoi not to detain the *Imperator Nikolai*, which had orders to continue directly to the colonies.[34]

The *Imperator Nikolai* arrived in the Bay of Good Fortune on September 6. The sea was very rough and the captain hesitated to send a boat ashore, but impatiently Nevelskoi dispatched a *bidarka* to the ship and Busse had to negotiate the raging waters on the fidgety little leather craft. As he set foot on land, he was met by Nevelskoi, who led him to his small wooden residence, from which his young wife came out to greet them. Having heard a great many conflicting appraisals of Nevelskoi, Busse was pleased to make his acquaintance, and, as they sat down at a table, he examined him with curiosity. Busse did not find Nevelskoi handsome. "The small stature, the thin, wrinkled face, covered with little pockmarks, the large bald pate surrounded by dishevelled grizzled hair and the small grey eyes, which he constantly screws, give him an elderly and decrepit appearance. But the wide forehead and the liveliness of the eyes show in him energy and fieriness of character."[35]

If Busse lacked more tangible evidence of Nevelskoi's impetuosity, it was soon forthcoming. He was reporting about the seventy men and one officer, whom he had brought, when Nevelskoi criticized him for not having brought also the necessary supplies and, asserting

[33] Tikhmenev gives the name of the vessel as *Imperator Nikolai*; Nevelskoi gives it as *Nikolai I*; Soviet historians refer to it simply as *Nikolai*.

[34] Nevelskoi, 218-226; Barsukov, I, 328-329; Tikhmenev, II, 103-106; N. V. Busse, *Ostrov Sakhalin: Ekspeditsiia 1853-54 gg.* 3. Tikhmenev asserts that Busse had orders from the commandant of Aian to winter on Sakhalin and to be at the complete disposal of Nevelskoi. Only if the lateness of the season or ill health among the crew made this impossible, should the vessel seek permission to continue to the Sandwich (Hawaiian) Islands and from there in spring to Novo-Arkhangelsk. Busse himself noted as follows: "In virtue of the instructions given to me, I should properly have returned to Aian, to go to the river Mago to inspect the new settlements, and from there to Yakutsk, where I had been instructed to inspect the Cossack regiment, and then by the first winter way to appear in Irkutsk for a personal report to the governor about everything that I had seen."

[35] Busse, 4-5.

that the vessel could not be unloaded at Petrovskoe, refused to let him go back. Neither the little steam cutter, which Nevelskoi had, nor the *Konstantin*, which might come later in the year, were adequate to transporting a well equipped force to Sakhalin. He needed the *Imperator Nikolai*. Arguing that Russia must lose no time in occupying Imperatorskaia Gavan' and Tomari in order to forestall foreign encroachment in Tatar Strait, Nevelskoi philosophized that circumstances and not instructions must guide the deeds of a commander in a distant region and insisted on resolute action, unrestrained by any "Petersburg considerations and orders." To Busse's chagrin, Nevelskoi brushed aside the command that he draw additional officers for the Sakhalin landing party from the Amur expedition, and over his protests impressed him into service as commandant of Sakhalin Island.[36]

The diary record, which Busse has left, of the events that followed is one of the most intriguing documents of Russian expansion. Unlike most accounts, which took pride in noble deeds and courted public praise and recognition, it glorified neither imperialism nor empire builders and showed refreshing candor in its critique of Russian activities in the Far East. To date Busse's military experience had been limited largely to service in a guard regiment in St. Petersburg. Busse could not adjust himself to the informality and nervous impatience of Nevelskoi, who got so worked up in his plans that "he tore the hair on his head" and hated the Russian-American Company (under whose auspices Sakhalin was to be occupied) with such passion that the mere mention of the word "company" would bring forth "a collection of the strongest imprecations and sometimes also swearwords." He admitted that Nevelskoi was the right man for spreading Russian influence in the Amur region, but thought it necessary to put a "prudent, cool, and well-intentioned" person at his side to subdue his "too stormy character."

On the evening of September 8, the *Imperator Nikolai* weighed anchor. Slowed down by lack of wind, she did not reach the bay of Aian until the evening of the twelfth, and then was becalmed at the very entrance. Nevelskoi sent Busse ashore to ask Commandant Kashevarov to come aboard. Busse set out with misgivings, for he knew well that Nevelskoi and Kashevarov were enemies, but he resolved to act as peace-maker and had hopes of mediating a prompt and amicable agreement regarding the immediate freighting of the

36 Nevelskoi, 227-230.

Imperator Nikolai. In this he was unsuccessful, however, since Kashevarov did not agree either to leave the vessel with the Sakhalin expedition or to come aboard to confer with Nevelskoi, and blamed Busse for not having landed the contingent at Petrovskoe as planned. When Busse reported this to Nevelskoi, they decided to go ashore together and demand a conference with Kashevarov and the recent commander of Petropavlovsk, Commander Freigang, "a tenderhearted and sensitive German" who was passing through Aian on his way to the capital.

At the ensuing meeting Nevelskoi and Kashevarov had a bitter exchange, and barely skirting open insult, accused each other of rudeness and dereliction of duty. Nevertheless Kashevarov's insistence that the *Imperator Nikolai* go directly to America was finally overwhelmed by Nevelskoi with orders, pleadings, and embraces, as Freigang, an old friend of both, intervened just when the two seemed to have worked themselves up to a point of no return. "It was unpleasant to watch these embraces," Busse noted with distaste. "Their fervor was a mask, particularly unbecoming in relation to Kashevarov. Embracing such a man as Kashevarov, Nevelskoi made a great and generous sacrifice for the good of the cause." Sincere or not, the embraces provided a harmless release for the pent-up emotions of the disputants and, after a tasty supper and a good night's sleep, the whole matter was settled amicably aboard ship. Kashevarov agreed to let the *Imperator Nikolai* go to Sakhalin and thence to Tatary Strait for the winter, unless another company vessel arrived to replace it.

On September 15, the heavily laden *Imperator Nikolai* left Aian. Three days later, she reached the roadstead of Petrovskoe, where a sudden storm threatened to send her to the bottom of the sea. The inexperienced sailors of the landing party proved almost as dangerous as the mountainous seas, disorder becoming chaos as Captain Klinkofstrem barked orders in Swedish, Nevelskoi and Rudanovskii in Russian. Somehow the *Imperator Nikolai* weathered the storm, but a new rift developed among the officers. On the way to shore, Rudanovskii began cursing the sailors and threatened to whip the noncommissioned officer, ignoring the presence of Busse, his senior in rank and future superior. Offended, Busse afterwards took him to task for this rudeness, and in his diary stated that Rudanovskii was "difficult as a subordinate, and intolerable as a comrade."[37]

[37] Busse, 5-18.

The following day, on September 19, the naval transports *Baikal* and *Irtysh* arrived in Petrovskoe. It was decided that the *Imperator Nikolai* should depart for Aniwa that evening, the *Irtysh* to follow there after unloading the cargo of the Amur expedition. The *Irtysh* was to stay at the place of landing as long as her protection was needed, then sail to Imperatorskaia Gavan' for the winter. The *Baikal* meanwhile was to proceed directly to Aian and Kamchatka with cargo transferred from the *Irtysh*.

The *Imperator Nikolai* weighed anchor as scheduled. Sailing around the northern part of Sakhalin, she continued down the eastern shore, rounded Cape Aniwa on the 29th, and headed for Cape Kril'on (Notoro) where Orlov, who had been put ashore by the *Baikal* on the east coast in the vicinity of latitude 51° N. at the end of August, was to be waiting. As the *Imperator Nikolai* traversed Aniwa Bay, she was accompanied by whales and shoals of a variety of fishes. Busse realized that it was this abundance of fish that attracted the Japanese to this region.

Throughout the voyage, conversation revolved around the occupation of Sakhalin, around the Amur region, and around the activities of the Russian-American Company. As to the occupation of Sakhalin, Nevelskoi stated at first that, since it was already later in the season than planned, he would put ashore in Aniwa, away from the Japanese settlements, merely a post of ten men, as token of the occupation of the island, letting the rest of the landing party spend the winter in Imperatorskaia Gavan'; in early spring Busse could return to Aniwa and occupy a point which he would judge most suitable. But the wonderful weather, which greeted the expedition at Cape Aniwa, changed Nevelskoi's plans. It was necessary, he now said, to occupy Aniwa without delay, and announced that since the post should be as close as possible to the Japanese, the venture could not be entrusted to Rudanovskii alone and that Busse must winter on the island too. Busse agreed, but remonstrated that a final decision should await more definite information about the Japanese. "I regretted afterwards," he recalled, "that I had argued about this with Nevelskoi, but it vexed me to hear superficial and not very serious considerations of the business, the unsuccessful execution of which could have a very unfavorable influence on our relations with Japan and China as well as on the very possession of Sakhalin and its inhabitants."[38]

[38] *Ibid.*, 19-21.

On the evening of September 30, the *Imperator Nikolai* approached Cape Kril'on and discharged nine shots, a signal prearranged with Orlov. There was no reply. The following day, on October 1, the vessel began to maneuver toward land. It was already dark when the Russians cast anchor. The noise of the anchor chain awakened the Japanese, and lights appeared on shore. In the morning, on October 2, the *Imperator Nikolai*, her naval flag proudly displayed, took up position vis-à-vis the settlement of Usunnoi. At about 11 a.m. Busse and Nevelskoi set out for shore with two boats and a *bidarka*, having instructed Klinkofstrem to rush reinforcements to them, if they raised a flag, and to draw closer to shore and open up with broadsides against the settlement if a shot was fired. To minimize the alarm that their appearance was bound to cause, they hid their weapons on the bottom of the boats and took along various trifles as gifts. Some seven hundred feet from shore the boats ran onto sandbanks. "Savages" darted into the water and quickly surrounded them, exclaiming "Amerika, Amerika!" Not knowing that "Amerika" was a term applied to foreigners in general,[39] the Russians took great pains to explain that they were not Americans, but Russians, and Nevelskoi sought to convey through gestures that it was in order to protect the inhabitants from the Americans, that the Russians had come to settle on the island. It seemed to the Russians that the natives had understood. Whether they had or not, they gladly accepted the gifts that the Russians offered them.

After some time several Japanese came up also. Markedly different in physiognomy from the Ainu, they reminded Busse of the caricatures, which he had seen on posters of Russian tea shops, "only their eyes are not slanted upward so much, and they do not wear mustaches." Disparagingly he added: "Their movements and manners are ridiculous, similar to those of women." Informed by the Japanese of the whereabouts of their superiors, the Russians got off the sandbank and headed for a large settlement, where they were able to ride all the way up to shore. A Japanese came out to meet them, and gestured that they follow him into the settlement. Seeing neither fortifications nor troops, the Russians felt safe and, accompanied by a crowd of Ainu, went with the Japanese to a fairly large building of Japanese design. Here they met seven Japanese, seated around a square fireplace. To these they tried to explain why they had come.

[39] Ivan Makhov, letter from Hakodate, dated January 31 (February 12), 1862 (?), 82; Koshizaki Soichi, *Hokkaido shashin bunka-shi*, 29.

They could not have been very convincing, for as Busse noted, "it was ridiculous to watch how Nevelskoi tried to explain to the Japanese that the Russians wanted to live in friendship with them and the Ainu, and that they were occupying Sakhalin to defend it from the Americans." The Japanese accepted Russian gifts and treated the strangers to cooked fish, teaching them how to use chopsticks. But though they drank Russian wine with evident pleasure, they remained stone cold when Nevelskoi began to embrace and kiss them in emphasis of his gestured assertion that the Russians wished to live in friendship with the Japanese and that their cannons were intended merely to keep Americans away from the island.

Following the meeting with the Japanese, the Russians set out to find a suitable location for their post. Had Nevelskoi, who was in charge of operations, proceeded more systematically it is likely that the fine Bay of Puruan-Tomari would not have escaped their attention. But for a man with great plans for the extension of Russia's frontiers, Nevelskoi was surprisingly casual about the selection of an advantageous place on the island, and, anxious to leave the open bay as soon as possible and reach Petrovskoe before the freeze, limited Russian exploration to less than a day. Busse, who would have the responsibility of maintaining the position selected by Nevelskoi, bitterly resented this, and when Nevelskoi decreed that the men be landed at the main Japanese settlement, protested.

Determinately I told Nevelskoi that we should not establish ourselves in the settlement of the Japanese, among their dwellings, because this would be a forcible act; that it will be difficult at such close quarters to prevent some kind of insignificant, yet in our condition important, clashes of our men with the Japanese; that finally this is contrary to the instructions of the governor, who ordered us to settle away from the Japanese settlements, as well as contrary to the very words of the instructions, which he, Nevelskoi, himself, had given me concerning the handling of the Japanese and the natives; in these instructions it stated that I was to deal with the Japanese peacefully, impressing on them that the Russians had come to Sakhalin to defend them from the foreigners, and by no means to alarm and restrain them. Finally, in these instructions I have been ordered not to violate the interests of the Japanese in trade with the natives. Having noted all this to Nevelskoi I asked him how to act to bring into harmony these peaceful and careful relations and the occupation of the Japanese settlement, settling, so to speak, in their home, and consequently restraining them.[40]

40 Busse, 23-27.

When Nevelskoi replied that he did not think it possible to disembark elsewhere, Busse had to comply, but remarked that the spirit of the expedition had changed since henceforth cannons and cannon balls would be more in view than goods, and warned that this might well have an adverse bearing on Russo-Japanese relations, particularly on the negotiations of Vice-Admiral Evfimii Putiatin in Nagasaki.

On October 3, the Russians went ashore on two row boats, flying white flags, and on the long boat, on which two tarpaulin-covered cannons and muskets had been concealed, flying the naval flag. They landed at Tomari or, as Japanese sources put it, at Kushunkotan, which Khvostov had raided in 1807. To the Ainu and Japanese, who had gathered at the water, Nevelskoi tried to convey the peacefulness of Russian intentions, while Busse gave orders to the contingent.

The sailors lined up in two ranks. I raised the flag, and stood in front of them. I commanded: "Uncover!" Nevelskoi ordered to sing a prayer. The crew sang the prayer "Our Father," then sang "God save the Tsar"; there resounded a Russian hurrah, echoed aboard the vessel, and Sakhalin became a Russian possession.[41]

The Japanese and Ainu watched in astonishment. The Russians hoisted their flag to a post on the pier, and mounted a guard next to it. In back of the flag they put up two tents. Then Nevelskoi followed the Japanese to their commander, while Busse and Rudanovskii explored the neighborhood in search of a suitable place for their settlement. It did not take Busse and Rudanovskii long to find out that all desirable locations had been occupied by the Japanese. This they reported to Nevelskoi. Busse considered the northern cape as the only spot suitable for the establishment of a Russian post. Within easy access, it was militarily ideal, as batteries placed there would command the bay and the Japanese settlements. But the northern cape was already occupied by Japanese magazines, which would have to be taken over or removed, and this would mean coercion. Nevelskoi did not follow Japanese suggestions to withdraw to the neighboring settlement, but chose to establish the Russian post on the northern cape, though not on the highest spot, which Busse favored. It was decided to place the batteries in two rows, taking over the Japanese sheds between them. Two of the sheds the Japanese readily sold, but three others they could not surrender, because they were filled with various necessities.

[41] *Ibid.*, 27-28; *Hokkaido-shi*, II, 585-586.

On October 4, the Russians began to unload the supplies and furnishings for their post. With the help of native crafts and labor, the task was completed on the 7th. Not the full complement of the Sakhalin expedition was landed, only fifty-nine sailors and eight laborers, to be reinforced by the five cossacks and one sailor, who had been put ashore with Orlov. The remainder of the landing party was to help man the ship during the arduous autumn sailing and winter with it in Imperatorskaia Gavan', where eleven more cossacks of the Sakhalin expedition were to join them.

When Busse went ashore on October 7, he discovered that his apprehensions had been justified. Frightened by the Russian invasion, the Japanese had deserted the settlement during the night and had fled into the interior. Nevelskoi grabbed an Ainu elder by the beard and demanded that he bring the Japanese back. With some difficulty Busse persuaded Nevelskoi that it would be best to leave the Ainu and Japanese alone and that force would only make matters worse.

After breakfast the men were lined up in two ranks and Nevelskoi officially surrendered the command of the Murav'evskii Post to Busse. Then he went aboard ship, as the batteries on shore thundered a farewell. Busse visited the vessel once more for a festive dinner. When he and Rudanovskii returned to the island, the *Imperator Nikolai* fired a salute. Russian cannon shots pierced the silence and Russian cheers echoed from the boats and from shore. Toward evening the *Imperator Nikolai* was becalmed and could not weigh anchor; but by morning she was gone.

Busily the landing party set to work. With timber, purchased from the Ainu, the Russians started building the stronghold planned by Busse: on the top of the cape, two barracks for forty men, an officer's wing (brought ready-made from Aian) and a bake-house connected by a loopholed wall, with two guns each mounted on towers at two corners, and a barrack for twenty men, with a wall and tower of its own, near the lower battery. At the same time they continued the exploration of the island and were in constant search of fresh supplies. Many were their surprises. One Sunday morning, for example, the St. Petersburg guard officer visited a little mountain shrine in the woods. When he pulled back the curtains behind which he expected to see the usual idol, he was shocked to find himself staring at an erect gilded phallus, flanked by a phallus of stone and a phallus of wood, pointing at the sky. Another time he was startled to have an

Ainu offer him the use of his beautiful wife and though the lady herself, breasts practically uncovered, seemed eager to oblige, he nervously feigned that he did not understand the proposition.

As so often, the Russians had less trouble getting along with the Japanese and the Ainu than with themselves. Busse had assigned Rudanovskii to work on the lower barracks, to remove physically "his quarrelsome and difficult character." But he still found it necessary to curb his independence several times and to remind him "that there cannot be two masters in the home." Meanwhile Samarin, the keeper of company property, had taken to the bottle. "With sorrow thought I," Busse recalled, "that I would have to spend the whole winter with such people—one well-born, but quarrelsome and somewhat rude, the other a drunkard." Again and again the reluctant commander of Sakhalin bemoaned the fate that had cast him from the midst of kind relatives in St. Petersburg to an island, where his sole companions were people "who only add to the unpleasantness of the life." "Samarin with his politeness, laziness, and strangeness of ideas, if he does not bore me, cannot, of course, interest or amuse me. Rudanovskii, however, constitutes real bane. His continuous sharp outbursts and a particularly insulting manner of speaking, often lead me to the thought of entirely relieving him from duty. I feel that thereby I shall damage the well-being of the expedition greatly, as I would take away the only person who is able to make maps of shores and interior places of the island, as yet unknown to anyone. But, it seems, my patience will not hold out."

On October 11, the *Irtysh* appeared at the shores of Sakhalin. Unfavorable winds made it difficult for her to reach the Russian post, and Busse ordered her to head directly for the place of winterage. Just then, however, Orlov arrived with his six men and Busse, considering the plain-looking person of about fifty unsuitable company for the winter, turned back the vessel with three cannon shots. The *Irtysh* cast anchor late on the 14th. When she left again during the night, she carried with her reports to Muravev and Nevelskoi as well as personal correspondence.[42]

Orlov had explored only part of the western shore of Sakhalin. Warned by the Ainu that the Japanese along the western shore planned to capture him and his men, he had traversed the island and continued down the east coast. In the mountains he had encoun-

[42] Busse, 28-36, 40-41, 50-51.

tered groups of Japanese, but they had seemed more afraid of the Russians than the Russians of them. Visiting Busse daily, the Ainu gave similar warnings of Japanese hostility, but though they brought "wooden brooms"[43] as a sign of respect and accepted Russian presents without the least inhibition, Busse gained the impression that "in general the Ainu love to deceive one, and therefore it is difficult to learn anything reliable from them about the country." He believed that it was fear of the Japanese that made the Ainu hide so much, and was more and more convinced that the Ainu chief of the settlement was sly as well as devoted to the Japanese.

One Ainu had secretly joined Busse and stayed in his attic. Busse wrote:

I wanted to attach some Ainu to myself in order to find out from him about the country and to teach him Russian; but the influence of the Japanese over the Ainu is so great, that none of them, it seemed, would have dared to show open adherence to the Russians. In secret, almost all the Ainu who came to visit me inveighed against the Japanese, saying . . . the Japanese is bad, the Japanese beats the Ainu, the Russian is kind and good.

They often repeated these words, hoping that for this they would receive gifts from us. My position, I confess, is very embarrassing—if I join the Ainu in inveighing against the Japanese, the latter will inevitably learn about this from the Ainu who are loyal to them (and there are enough of those), and then their trust in us will be completely destroyed. On the other hand, I cannot praise the Japanese and take their side before the Ainu, without frightening the Ainu thereby into believing that we shall mistreat them at one with the Japanese. I usually laughed and did not answer when the Ainu who came to me began to inveigh against the Japanese. The Ainu who dared to sleep at my place had come to us from the settlement Shiretoku, situated some 150 miles from us. He seemed to me a tramp and therefore probably also agreed to be almost a servant in my house. I once noticed that our Ainu elder inveighed against him, probably for working for Russians; I threatened the chief and he went away.

When the Ainu who stayed with him asserted that the village chief had persuaded the Japanese to massacre the Russians, Busse laughed in order to show him that Russians were not afraid of such conspiracies and threatened that if one of his men were touched, he would have all settlements destroyed and all Japanese and "bad" Ainu killed. The Ainu joined in the laughter, yet from time to time

---

[43] Actually pieces of whittled willow wood, with the shavings left attached to the top; known as *inao*, these were sacred offerings to the gods.

repeated his warnings against the native chief and against the Japanese who, he asserted, only awaited the arrival of Japanese reinforcements in spring before launching an attack.

On October 24, three Japanese returned to the settlement. One of them was very talkative and fond of strong drink. Busse treated him to tea and rum in the hope of learning a great deal. But though the Japanese obligingly wrote the "alphabet," he got the better of the bargain in the exchange of information, for Busse told him that in the spring four Russian vessels would come to Tomari from Imperatorskaia Gavan' and Kamchatka and drew a map of Sakhalin and the Amur region, which the Japanese took with him.

Gradually more Japanese returned to the settlement. On November 1, an official and a number of followers called on Busse. They enjoyed the Russian refreshments and seemed reassured that they had nothing to fear from these Russians and chatted with them freely and amicably. The talkative Japanese, whom Busse had entertained earlier with tea and rum, invited Busse to his own house and having imbibed too much sake became embarrassingly familiar. The other Japanese and Busse continued to visit each other, however, and barter developed, the Japanese being particularly fond of game.[44]

These social visits were a welcome break in the monotony of Sakhalin life, but the Russians, the Japanese and the Ainu remained on guard against each other's intentions and capabilities. The Ainu were often useful channels of information. But their constant presence exasperated Busse.

The visits of the Ainu have brought me absolutely to the end of my patience; from early morning till evening, one after another they come to me, and what for—in order to sit down on the floor and gape at me and the room. Not knowing how to use doors, they leave them open, not understanding, that to chill the room is some kind of inconvenience. The doors at the partition are made with handles and bolts. Unable to open them, they work on them for a long time; finally, whether one wants to or not, one must get up to open the door. I ask them humbly to occupy themselves with something. At this very time two fools sit on the floor and gape. I, of course, pay no attention to them, because there is not enough strength, nor patience to talk to everyone. The only way of shunning them is to go out of the house and to ramble about the yard without aim. One needs a house of several rooms, one of which is set aside specifically for these intolerable guests, with chimneys to draw out the inferior

[44] Busse, 39, 40-50.

tobacco. . . . Will God help me soon to leave the fatherland of the most unbearable Ainu?[45]

The Japanese did not confine their questions to Russian activities on Sakhalin. They examined Russian maps and sketched the locations of Japan, China, and Russia. Never certain how honest the Japanese were in their replies, Busse could not help departing from the truth himself. As he admitted in his diary, "I exaggerated a little our possessions contiguous with China, having annexed to us the Amur River and the coast of Tatar Strait till latitude 47° N." The Japanese also inquired whether the Russians planned to go to Nagasaki. One day they thumbed through Golovnin's narrative, a copy of which Busse had with him, and were startled to find that the Russians had sketches of Japanese harbors.

Occasionally the apparent harmony in Russo-Japanese relations was interrupted. Rumors had reached Busse that the Japanese toured the Ainu settlements and forbade the natives to work for the Russians or to sell them anything. His own observations tended to support this. When the Ainu, who lived with the Russians, complained that he had been beaten by the Japanese for serving the Russians, Busse angrily scolded two of the Japanese elders. The latter denied everything, but Busse felt it necessary to show his displeasure and, if necessary, to threaten the Japanese, for fear they might show "excessive boldness or insolence."

The Ainu continued to warn Busse that in spring well-armed Japanese would descend on the island at different points, surround the Russians, and kill them. There were stories also that the Japanese on Sakhalin were planning to invite the Russians to a great banquet, get them drunk, and then dispatch them with the aid of the Ainu. Busse was not distressed. Proudly he wrote:

All these stories originate, of course, in conversations of the Japanese with the Ainu, and although the Japanese would be capable of such hostile actions, they are too cowardly to carry out their threats. As regards the coming of vessels in spring, the number of Japanese and their actions against us, nothing can be said—all this will depend on their emperor. If he will deem Sakhalin necessary for himself, he will either decide to change the law forbidding relations with foreigners . . . or else he will decide to chase us from Sakhalin, and then, of course, in accordance with Japanese bravery, he will send no less than a thousand Japanese against sixty Russians. I think that neither one nor the other will be, and that the Japanese will simply leave Sakhalin.

[45] *Ibid.,* 109.

Busse confronted the Japanese with stories of their intentions to kill the Russians and threatened that, in the event of hostilities on their part, Russian vessels would not permit a single Japanese to leave the island. Of course, the Japanese denied any animosity, and sought to allay Russian suspicions. They declared that not only were the Ainu allegations untrue, but that the Ainu had told them the same thing about Russian intentions toward them. When the Cossack Diachkov, who spoke Ainu quite well, repeated to the Japanese that Russia had no territorial designs on Sakhalin, but merely wished to keep it out of foreign hands, that Russian vessels and troops would come in force, but would not remain over the winter, that the Russian Emperor had written about all this to the sovereign of Japan, and that Busse's ill disposition was due to Japanese attempts to hinder Russian dealings with the Ainu, the Japanese declared themselves willing to exchange necessities with the Russians until the arrival of their superior in the spring, who would determine further relations. They expressed the hope that the reply of their ruler would be amicable, for the Russians, they said, had demonstrated their goodness by the kind treatment of Japanese castaways, shipwrecked off Kamchatka. Later the Japanese entertained the Russians at a feast and telling them that they were going to another part of the island to call together Ainu for spring work, asked Busse that the Russians keep an eye on the Japanese magazines, during their absence, to prevent the Ainu from pilfering the stores.

Busse realized that, should the Japanese decide to attack, the Russian position would be precarious. With his sixty men, of whom up to twenty were constantly sick, he could not possibly patrol the extended coastline nor prevent a Japanese landing. The entire contingent was inadequate for the defense of the Russian stronghold. There was not enough timber to connect the little fort and the lower battery with walls, and if there had been, there would not have been enough men to defend them effectively. The protection of both the upper and lower fortifications required a fatal division in personnel. On the other hand, the lower battery was too exposed from the top to concentrate all efforts there, while withdrawal into the little fort above would mean to be left without water. But perhaps the greatest problem in the event of a Japanese attack would have been the fact that the Russian troops had no notion of soldiering. Busse recorded that only about eight of his men had had any military training. The others were merely worker-peasants. When he had ordered gun drill during their sea voyage to the island, "a large number of the men did not know how to hold the gun and with fear drew back the cock." Busse planned to provide the necessary training, limiting himself to "the lightest demands and rules," but he could not do so until spring, and that was when the Japanese were expected.

Busse understood that the Russian invasion of Sakhalin meant different things to the Japanese and to the Ainu.

The Japanese saw in it the destruction of their mastery on the island and perhaps the loss of rich industries. Our assertions that we have come to protect them from the Americans, they do not believe, of course. They did not have the forces to hinder our landing; all that they could do, was to inform their government, for which purpose they sent a junk with thirteen Japanese sailors to Matsumae. But the Ainu were glad of our coming, since they hoped that we would chase away the Japanese or kill them, and thereby free them from the yoke which they hated. . . . The Ainu, uncertain about their future fate, are waiting to see who will prevail in spring—the Russians or the Japanese. They wish success to the Russians because they hope that they are after all better than the Japanese and will not beat them. There are of course also those who wish success to the Japanese—these are those Ainu who live in their house as servants and mistresses of the Japanese. But one must not even expect help or attack from the Ainu; their role is strictly passive. Of course, if the Russians were to begin to fight with the Japanese and were to overpower them, the Ainu would be glad to come in time to take vengeance, to throw themselves on the defeated Japanese, and to kill them. Meanwhile they fear both us and the Japanese. . . .

With Japanese, Ainu, and Russian interests in conflict, the task of alienating neither the Japanese nor the Ainu and establish trade relations with both was not an easy one. The fact that goods brought by the Russians were so ill-suited to native needs that by Busse's admission "if there were no Japanese on the island, we could not satisfy the demands of the inhabitants" only complicated matters. If the Russians wished to prove to the Japanese that their presence would not aversely affect Japanese fishery, they would have to recognize Sakhalin as Japanese territory, and the Japanese as complete masters over the inhabitants. Yet leaving the Ainu in Japanese bondage, would arouse the hatred of the Ainu. On the other hand, if the Russians proclaimed the island their own and prohibited the Japanese to use force toward the Ainu, they would ruin Japanese fishery, because the Ainu would not voluntarily work for the Japanese and because the Japanese, according to the laws of their country, could not visit foreign territory. Busse chose a middle path, warning the Japanese not to mistreat the Ainu publicly, yet refraining from interfering in their private relations, unless Ainu, who worked for the Russians, were involved. This was a half-way measure that pleased no one. "Our so-called armed neutrality," Busse observed, "has produced a good effect on the Japanese only in the respect that they have stopped thinking that we have come with the intention of chasing them off the island and to seize it. Yet they see in the future their inevitable expulsion, notwithstanding our exhortations and assurances." To take the side of the Ainu meant to alienate the Japanese; to take the side of the Japanese meant to alienate the Ainu; to impose a rule of one's own over Ainu and Japanese, meant to alienate them both. Clearly the road to empire provided little opportunity for making friends.

At the heart of the problem was a basic contradiction in Russian policy. On one hand the Russians wished to remain on the best of terms with the Japanese, with whom they were trying to conclude a commercial treaty, and anxious to get accustomed to living side by side with the Japanese, urged them to remain in Tomari; on the other hand they established themselves at a place, where they were bound to disrupt Japanese enterprise and to arouse Japanese hostility. All this could have been avoided, had the Russians chosen a point to the north of the Japanese settlements, especially as domination of the island depended primarily on naval supremacy. The occupation of Aniwa Bay had broader implications—or so at least it would appear to the Japanese, for Busse recognized, "the idea that in order to command Sakhalin, one must be in control of Aniwa—this idea can apply only in case of a military plan of action against Japan."

What had been the major objectives of the Russian government in dispatching the Sakhalin expedition? The commander himself was not sure. "The purpose of the occupation of Sakhalin was not expressed in the orders of the government; it was announced only, that the right of governing the island is given to the Russian-American Company." Analyzing the various possible objectives in the light of what Golovnin had written about Japan and what he himself had learned about conditions on Sakhalin, he reflected: "At the present time . . . Admiral Putiatin has been sent to Japan to negotiate with its government, while the Americans want to open the ports by force. It is clear that the thought of occupying Sakhalin is related to these circumstances, because its occupation is useful in establishing trade with the Japanese and is essential to anticipate the establishment of foreigners at this point, which is situated on the border of the possessions of the Japanese and of ourselves. Furthermore, this island because of its location serves as a supplement to the Amur region, the annexation of which is so necessary for Russia.[46]

Mounting Russian preoccupation with the ambitions of rival Western powers in the Far East—an element, which was to transform the simple relationship between Russia and Japan into a triangular relationship between Russia, Japan, and the United States and into a fragment of Far Eastern power politics—was expressed by Muravev in a memorandum to Alexander II in March of 1853.

Twenty-five years ago the Russian-American Company requested from the government the occupation of California, which at that time was still hardly controlled by anyone, expressing on this occasion its apprehension that soon this region would become an acquisition of the United States of America. In Petersburg this apprehension was not shared and it was asserted that this could happen only in one hundred years. The Company maintained, that this would happen in twenty-five years, and now it has been already over a year, that California constitutes one of the North American States. One could not but foresee the rapid spread of the sway of the North American States in North America, nor could one but foresee, that these States, once they had established themselves on the Pacific Ocean, would soon take precedence over all other naval powers there, and would require the whole northwestern shore of America. The sovereignty of the North American States in all of North America is so natural, that we should not regret very much that we did not consolidate our position in California twenty-five years ago—sooner or later we would have had to yield it; but yielding it *peacefully*, we could have received from the Americans other benefits in exchange. Besides now, with the invention and development of railroads, one must become convinced, even more than before, that the North American States will without fail spread over all of North America, and *we cannot but bear in mind that sooner or later we shall have to yield to them our North American possessions*. However, neither could one but bear in mind something else in connection with this consideration, namely, that it is highly natural also for Russia, if not to possess all of Eastern Asia, so to rule over the whole Asian littoral of the Pacific Ocean. Due to various circumstances we allowed the intrusion of this part of Asia by the English, who very naturally to the detriment and reproach of all of Europe, disturbing the peace and well-being of other nations, prescribe from their little island their own laws in all parts of the world, excluding America, laws not in the least aimed at the benefit of mankind, but only at the satisfaction

46 *Ibid.*, 40-52, 60-66, 74-79, 88-98.

of the commercial interests of Great Britain—but the matter can still be mended *by a close tie on our part with the North American States.* England exerts all efforts not to permit this bond; her agents try everywhere and with all means to estrange America from Russia. In this respect England's most essential conditions must include: to gain possession of Kamchatka or to leave it waste and to rule over the Pacific shores of China and Japan and thus, so to speak, to cut *Russia off from the Pacific Ocean.* There is no doubt that this system must include also the acquisition of Sakhalin and the Amur estuary. In order to prepare, in view of the above-mentioned considerations, a firm and convenient domain for our American Company in place of the North American shore on one hand, and on the other hand in order to develop quicker and truer our sway over the shore of the Pacific Ocean belonging to us, it is essential to permit the Russian-American Company right now to establish itself on Sakhalin, whence her trade will inevitably develop with Japan and Korea. . . .[47]

Sakhalin was not yet considered important in its own right. Its occupation was conceived as staking a claim to the island to forestall its use against Russia and as a step toward the opening of Japan. The peaceful character that was given the occupation, when it was carried out under the flag of the Russian-American Company, was not merely a subterfuge. "The number of people allotted to the expedition," Busse noted, "shows that the possibility of military action and the necessity of defending the island against the Japanese or any other country had not been planned. These one hundred men were intended, of course, for the defense of our commercial settlement against the native savages or the Japanese fishermen, and this number is more than enough for the attainment of this purpose." On the other hand, the significance of the Russian landing party greatly exceeded its size or strategic strength. As Busse remarked, "regardless of what we occupy, no force of sixty men will defend the inhabitants of the island against other nations, but the flag, which is under the protection of our government." Busse noted that the occupation of Tomari on Sakhalin was quite different in significance from the Russian expansion into the Amur region. In the Amur region Russian competition was a detriment to a mere handful of Manchu traders; the population in general profited from Russian commerce. The losses of a few minor traders could not be expected to arouse the tottering Manchu government to action. On Sakhalin, however, the Russians had deprived Japan of one of her major sources of nourish-

[47] Muravev to Alexander II, March 1853. (Barsukov, I, 322-323.)

ment for her entire population, "and therefore the loss of the shores of Aniwa is more important for Japan, than the loss of the whole Amur region adjoining the Amur is for China." Furthermore, the military occupation of Sakhalin posed a direct threat to the Japanese on Etorofu and Kunashiri, and it was obvious to Busse that, however amicable personal relations with the Japanese might remain, their government was bound to react with serious measures.

In the light of the importance of the Russian occupation of Sakhalin to Japan and of Busse's realization that his force would not be able to cope with the Japanese, if the latter received substantial reinforcements in the spring, it is of interest to note that the Russians made no attempt to prevent communication with Matsumae. Shortly after the Russian landing, the Japanese had secretly informed their government about it, but toward the end of March they first inquired whether Busse would object, before sending out a large boat with papers and letters. Busse approved, for it was not his purpose to isolate Sakhalin from Japan, yet when the Japanese departed on April 4, he recorded in his diary concern at the growing weakness of the Russian position.

> Scurvy has increased again. There are nineteen ill with scurvy, who do not go out to work; there are three who are considered healthy, but who are also subject to scurvy. The total number sick, including other illnesses, is 37 men; of these nine men are severely ill, unable to rise from bed. Twenty men go out to work.
>
> The second tower is not yet completed, the straw roofs have not yet been taken down, boards have not been sawn. If the Japanese want to find us unprepared, this will not be difficult for them to do.

Two weeks later, on April 19, the Japanese informed Busse that five of their vessels had arrived at Shiranushi. The following day a Japanese official, senior to Maruyama, arrived in Tomari. He called the Ainu together and exhorted them to work for the Japanese as before, declaring that the arrival of the Russians did not concern them. The Japanese, he said, did not know why the Russians had come; they had nothing in common with either the Japanese or the Ainu. Such talk was disquieting and though this official called on Busse, the latter had to conclude that Japanese intentions were "not completely friendly." The arrival of Japanese boats and news that large quantities of officers and troops were being massed on Matsumae Island, called for continuous vigilance on the part of the Russians. Two squads were ordered to sleep in the fortress, while the guard was strengthened, Busse and Rudanovskii taking turn at night duty in the fortress. The Cossack Berezkin and the sailor Alekseev were sent to Cape Shiranushi to keep a lookout for Japanese and Russian ships.

En route to Shiranushi, Berezkin and Alekseev came upon Maruyama, who told them to return to Tomari. When they refused to withdraw, he took them to the officials, who had newly arrived. These asked Berezkin and Alekseev to ride with them on their boats to Tomari so that the Russians would not open fire with their "angry" guns, and sent an Ainu to inform the Russians that Berezkin and Alekseev were with them. The Japanese were quite concerned about the Russian cannons, for not only were they mounted in such a way as to point at one from whatever direction approached, but it was said that they were so angry that whenever the Russians fired them, they made a backward somersault—a notion not entirely without foundation, since, during the winter, the Russians had loaded one of their cannons with too strong a charge of gunpowder and the piece had actually overturned.

Busse studied the four Japanese boats through his telescope, as they approached Tomari. In his estimation they could not hold more than two hundred and fifty men. Confident that "it could not even occur to the Japanese with such a number to attack sixty Russian sailors with eight cannons," he concluded that their intentions were not hostile, and ordered the choir to assemble on the lower tower and receive the Japanese with a gay song. The Japanese were truly puzzled as the strains of the Russian tune drifted across the bay. Staring at the tower, they could see an armed guard, surrounded by a number of Red Devils shouting at the top of their lungs. But, when Berezkin explained that his countrymen were singing to show how happy they were at their arrival, the Japanese were delighted and immediately began to sing, clapping their hands in rhythm. Busse thought of Golovnin's narrative. How much guidance one could find in its pages for the successful establishment of friendly relations with the Japanese!

The Japanese officials, headed by Miwa, called on Busse. The usual pleasantries passed between them. Busse realized that it was neither his diplomatic skill nor the desire of the Japanese to continue their industries undisturbed that had averted a military clash. The Russian post may have been sufficiently organized by now to withstand an attack by the Japanese already on the island, but the Japanese government could easily send whatever reinforcements would be necessary to wipe out the Russian stronghold. Busse comprehended that the course of events on Sakhalin was being determined elsewhere. The Japanese mentioned the negotiations of Vice-Admiral Putiatin. Busse wrote: "The influence of Putiatin is clear—but it is difficult to guess how he came to terms with the Japanese concerning the occupation of Sakhalin by the Russians; at any rate we owe it to Putiatin that it did not come to the use of cannons at our place. Should this have happened, I cannot say, that the chances of success would have been on our side." Aware that the occupation of Tomari must have affected Putiatin's negotiations with the Japanese, Busse wondered what orders Putiatin would give to the Sakhalin expedition. "I think all the time that there is nothing good here, and that we shall have to leave Aniwa."

Meanwhile more and more Japanese officials began to arrive. They made no show of hostility, but their increasing number was in itself a threat to both the Russians and the Ainu. To reassure them, one of the Japanese made this speech to the Ainu:

The past autumn a Russian vessel came to this land, put ashore officers, soldiers and cannons. The Russians began to build houses. The Japanese scattered from fear, half of them going away to Matsumae to report about what had happened and to bemoan the Japanese who had remained, who had scattered to the different Japanese settlements on Sakhalin; at this time the Ainu bore themselves badly, pilfered barley from the granaries and got drunk. But this is still excusable; what is bad, is that in winter too the Ainu conducted themselves badly. The Japanese, who had run away, luckily met the Russians, who were coming from the land of the Gilyaks. These Russians calmed them, having told them, that the Russians wanted to live with them in friendship, and asked that they return to Tomari. The Japanese returned, were kindly received by the Russian commander and his soldiers. They began to live amicably, but here the Ainu began to try to set them at variance. To the Russians you came to say, that the Japanese wanted to knife the Russians to death, when they would be asleep. To the Japanese you said, that the Russians wanted to kill the Japanese. In spite of this the Russians have lived with the Japanese in peace and friendship. Whether the Russians will remain here to live or will go away, I cannot tell you, because I do not know. From their great commander, who has been in Nagasaki, a paper will come, and then it will be known about this. Meanwhile you work, as you worked before, for which as before you will receive payment. In past years few soldiers came to this place, this year many have come,—but do not think that this is for fighting with the Russians, this is only for the protection of our officers.

In more informal statements the Japanese repeated that the many officers were the retinue of senior officials, and that Putiatin had expressed the intention of sending two vessels to Sakhalin. Unpleasantly surprised as Busse was at the high proportion of officials, who were arriving on the island, he tended to believe "that the Japanese officers have really arrived as a formal retinue for the senior commander, who has been charged to negotiate with those sent by Putiatin, and perhaps with him in person."[48] As it happened, Putiatin did not visit Sakhalin, but he had intended at one time to continue his negotiations on Sakhalin, and had instructed the Japanese to send officials there.[49] Busse was right when he suspected that the future of the Sakhalin expedition would be molded by Putiatin rather than by Nevelskoi or Muravev.

On May 11, 1854 two Russian vessels arrived at Tomari: the corvet *Olivutsa,* under the command of Captain Nikolai Nazimov, and a whale-boat with Orlov on board. During the winter Busse had sent some reports across the ice to Petrovskoe and had received in the same manner a brief message from Nevelskoi. Now he received a whole batch of official papers and personal letters. Muravev and Nevelskoi did not disclose their future plans. Muravev merely confirmed Busse in his position as commandant of Sakhalin, until such time as a company replacement arrived, and patted him on the back for doing a fine job. Nevelskoi expressed the hope that Busse would avoid any brush with the Japanese. But there was an item of news that foreshadowed the termination of the expedition. Russia and Turkey had broken off diplomatic relations and a Russian break with England and France was likely. This, Busse realized, complicated his position, "should the Japanese learn about our break with strong naval powers, with whom it will be difficult for us to fight in the Pacific Ocean." To make matters worse, a deadly outbreak of scurvy could be expected to detain the *Irtysh* and *Imperator Nikolai* in Imperatorskaia Gavan' until June, while the *Olivutsa* had orders to hasten to Petropavlovsk for the defense of Kamchatka.[50]

Muravev was pleased with Russian activities on Sakhalin, delighted that both Japanese and Ainu, as he put it in a letter of March 1854,

[48] Busse, 79-84, 110-124, 127, 133.
[49] See Lensen, *Russia's Japan Expedition,* 66.
[50] Busse, 141.

"plan to sleep peacefully under the protection of our battery and crew."[51] But by summer the curtain had fallen on this dramatic interlude in Russo-Japanese relations. The details of the Russsian withdrawal are not clear. Busse's diary peters out with these brief entries:

> May 15 [27]. The *Baikal* came.
> May 17 [29]. Forty-six Japanese arrived.
> May 18 [30]. Dinner in the forest with the Japanese.
> May 19 [31]. The *Baikal* weighed anchor.
>
> .   .   .   .
> .   .   .   .[52]

If Busse ever intended to fill in these entries, he did not do so. Nevelskoi, who had engineered the whole venture, notes merely that he dispatched the *Irtysh* and *Kniaz Menshikov* to Aniwa Bay, where they joined the *Baikal*, which had also proceeded there on his orders, and that "the commandant of Murav'evskii Post, N. V. Busse, on the suggestion of Admiral E. V. Putiatin . . . removed the Murav'-evskii Post, and K. N. Poset, having distributed the detachment and the property of the post on the vessels mentioned, departed from Aniwa to Imperatorskaia Gavan'." According to Japanese sources the Russian departure took place on June 13, 1854.

The reasons for the sudden Russian withdrawal seem to have been: the outbreak of the Crimean War and the course of Putiatin's negotiations in Japan. Putiatin's objections antedated the commencement of hostilities. When Nevelskoi returned to Petrovskoe in the winter of 1853, he learned that one of Putiatin's officers (Voin Rimskii-Korsakov, captain of the *Vostok*), had left word, during his absence, that Putiatin opposed annexation of any territory along the Amur, which he considered Chinese, and protested especially the occupation of Sakhalin, as this would hinder his negotiations with the Japanese. The outbreak of the Crimean War enabled Putiatin to order the immediate evacuation of the island on the grounds that the Russian post could be neither supplied nor defended and that every man was needed to protect the shores of Siberia itself from attack by the British and French. A letter in Dutch, left by the Russians on their departure from Sakhalin, referred to their role in the defense of their homeland. But, though Japanese sources admit that the Russian withdrawal was forced by the outbreak of

---

[51] Letter of Muravev to Grand Duke Konstantin Nikolaevich, dated March 2 (14), 1854. (Barsukov, I, 349-350.)
[52] Busse, 145.

the Crimean War rather than by the arrival of Japanese troops, the mounting number of reinforcements from Matsumae no doubt made the Russian evacuation seem entirely logical.[53]

Whatever the reasons for the Russian withdrawal, it is significant that it was effected without bloodshed. This permitted Putiatin to turn it to advantage and exploit it as a demonstration of Russian good will and peaceful intentions toward Japan. The treaty, which he succeeded in concluding with the Japanese in 1855, left Sakhalin for the time being in joint possession of Russia and Japan. But the explorations of Rudanovskii, Busse, and other members of the Sakhalin expedition had prepared the way for the eventual acquisition of the island by Russia.

[53] Nevelskoi, 292; Barsukov, I, 330-331; *Hokkaido-shi,* II, 589-590.

CHAPTER NINE · THE OPENING
OF JAPAN

THE FIRST PUTIATIN EXPEDITION,

1852-1855

VICE-ADMIRAL Evfimii Putiatin's interference in the annexation of Sakhalin and his opposition to Russian expansion in the Amur region angered Muravev.[1] "Putiatin is really not a bad man, but it is a pity that he has meddled in the Amur affairs, which he may damage," Muravev wrote in a letter. "Now we prepare for the [Easter] sacrament and keep the fast, therefore any unrelated arguments will be inappropriate, but when one will kiss each other on Easter day in commemoration of Christ's resurrection I shall be many-worded."[2] Yet, ironically, it had been Muravev himself who had put Putiatin into the position, which had prompted him to interfere, when he had prevailed upon the Emperor to dispatch the long-planned expedition to Japan.[3] In 1843, Nicholas I had almost sent Putiatin to Japan, but opposition from the chancellor and especially from the minister of finance had persuaded him to substitute a "private" expedition on a small scale. This and another private attempt to establish relations with the Japanese were futile—nowhere is the maxim "penny wise, pound foolish" more applicable than in international relations.

By mid-century important changes were afoot in the Far East. Like Japan, China had found it necessary to restrict intercourse with Westerners, though not as completely. Closing the interior to all Westerners, except the Russians, the Chinese had continued to admit European merchants to the port city of Canton during the trading season. This they did out of the goodness of their heart, believing that the Westerners would perish without the invaluable products of the Middle Kingdom. An attitude of blatant superiority

---

[1] As noted already, Putiatin was anxious not to alienate either the Japanese or the Chinese. His relations with the Japanese will be discussed below. It must be kept in mind that he was delegated to negotiate with the Chinese as well and was ever conscious, therefore, of any Russian policies that might complicate the already difficult task of seeking closer relations with China and Japan.

[2] Letter to Mikhail Korsakov, dated April 2 (14), 1857, in Barsukov, I, 493.

[3] As early as 1843 the expedition to Japan was envisaged as part of Russian activities in the Amur region and China. (Baron F. P. Osten-Saken, "Vospominanie o Grafe E. V. Putiatine," 386.)

on the part of the Chinese may have been justified in the eighteenth century. By the middle of the nineteenth century the industrial revolution had propelled the West ahead of China in military power, and Europeans, especially the English, would no longer tolerate the iniquities of the Canton trade, the humiliating restrictions of which sprang from the Chinese view that the trade was a privilege graciously granted by China to the foreign "barbarians." It was the conflict of this belief, nurtured by centuries of Chinese superiority in the Far East and the consequent inability of the Chinese and their Manchu rulers to envisage the political equality of nations, with the nineteenth century dogma of the West that trade was a natural right, rather than the issue of opium that really precipitated the so-called Opium War of 1839-1842 between Great Britain and China. By the treaty of Nanking (1842) Great Britain obtained the island of Hong Kong and commercial concessions, including the opening of additional ports to trade and the establishment of a "fair and regular" tariff on imports and exports (a restriction which was to plague China until 1930). In 1843, when the Putiatin expedition was first discussed, England had begun to encroach on the privileged position, which Russia had enjoyed in China on the basis of the treaties of Nerchinsk (1689) and Kiakhta (1727), which provided for overland trade between the two empires and authorized the establishment of a Russian Orthodox mission in Peking. By midcentury, this rift in Chinese seclusion had been widened by the conclusion of the Sino-American Treaty of Wanghia (1844) with its amplification of extraterritoriality and its most-favored-nation clause, by the Sino-French Treaty of Whampoa (1844) and treaties with Sweden and Norway (1847) and by other concessions to the Westerners proclaimed by imperial decrees.

Events in China bore a direct relationship to Japanese security. King William II of the Netherlands vainly tried, in 1844, to arouse the Japanese from their dream of peaceful isolation, by expounding to them on the lesson of China in an unprecedented letter to the Shogun, "our Friend, the very noble, most serene, and allpowerful sovereign of the great Empire of Japan, who has his seat in the Imperial Palace of Yedo, the abode of peace." Though the Shogunate rejected King William's advice to ameliorate the laws against foreigners "lest happy Japan be destroyed by war," his dramatic portrayal of "the superior power of European military tactics" remained a warning of the mounting danger to the independence of Japan.[4]

It was the appearance of the United States on the Far Eastern scene that most affected Russian interests. To some Russian statesmen the United States appeared as a potential ally against Great Britain; Muravev expressed this view in the memorandum quoted above. To others the United States presented a potential challenge, greater even than that of England.

As early as 1791, Americans had approached Japan in a futile attempt to sell sea-otter peltries. The development of the Pacific Northwest fur trade, and the spread of steam navigation brought to the shores of Japan an ever growing number of Americans, cloaked in the mantle of trade, evangelization, and Manifest Destiny. In 1837, the Americans had attempted to repatriate Japanese castaways, taking advantage of the opportunity to try to open Japan to trade and missionary work. The Japanese had responded to this amicable mission with cannon fire, after her officials had visited the *Morrison* and had assured themselves that she was unarmed. Undaunted, the Americans had renewed their efforts in 1846. But Commodore James Biddle, though he arrived with two men-of-war, was literally pushed aside by a common Japanese soldier. When the commodore did not hack him to pieces forthwith, but accepted the assurances of Japanese officials that the man would be punished in accordance with Japanese law, Americans became the laughing stock of Japan. Yet the martial spirit of Manifest Destiny was by now rampant in the United States. Going to war with Mexico (1846-1848), the young nation wrested from her New Mexico and California in addition to the recently acquired Texas. When a new and powerful expedition to Japan was outfitted in 1852, it was clear to everyone that no further insults would be brooked by the Americans, least of all by Commodore Matthew Calbraith Perry.

The advance of Americans into the Pacific antedates the establishment of the United States as a country. The Revolutionary War and the displacement of the British East India Company monopoly opened the flood gates of American interest in the Far East. The westward expansion of the United States (in many ways similar to the eastward drive of Russia) was intimately connected with its desire for Asian markets. The potentials of the young nation were dazzling. "We should not be surprised that the English colonists

[4] D. C. Greene, "Correspondence between William II of Holland and the Shogun of Japan," 110-113.

of America, republican and independent, are putting into practice the design of discovering a safe port in the South Sea and trying to hold it by travelling across the immense territory of this continent above our possessions in Texas, New Mexico and California," the Viceroy of Peru wrote to the Spanish minister of foreign affairs toward the end of the eighteenth century: "Much more wandering about may be expected from an active nation, which bases all its hopes on navigation and trade; and in truth it could hold the riches of Great China and of India, if it succeeds in establishing a colony on the western coasts of America." Americans themselves had magnificent visions. They saw in the United States, as it pushed westward, a source of "science, liberal principles in government, and the true religion" for the peoples of the Far East, and thought of the Columbia Valley as "the granary of China and Japan, and an outlet to their imprisoned and exuberant population." A Senate committee report in 1846 viewed the occupation of Oregon as a commercial link with Asia, Polynesia, and South America and predicted that "all this mighty laboratory whence the world has supplied itself for fifty centuries with articles of luxury, comfort and common use, will pour itself forth in exchange for the produce of the Mississippi Valley."[5]

In our own day Winston Churchill has referred to China as "the great American illusion." A century ago the illusion was not so apparent, and in 1851, on the eve of Commodore Perry's expedition an English historian predicted the conquest of China and Japan by the United States.

Opposite to San Francisco, on the coast of that ocean, lie the wealthy but decrepit empires of China and Japan. Numerous groups of islets stud the larger part of the intervening sea, and form convenient stepping-stones for the progress of commerce or ambition. The intercourse of traffic between these ancient Asiatic monarchies and the young Anglo-American republic must be rapid and extensive. Any attempt of the Chinese or Japanese rulers to check it will only accelerate an armed collision. The American will either buy or force his way. Between such populations as that of China and Japan on the one side, and that of the United States on the other—the former haughty, formal, and insolent; the latter bold, intrusive, and unscrupulous—causes of quarrel must sooner or later arise. The results of such a quarrel cannot be doubted. America will scarcely imitate the forbearance shown by England at the end of our late war with the Celestial Empire; and the conquests of

[5] Foster Rhea Dulles, *America in the Pacific*, 14, 31, 39.

China and Japan, by the fleets and armies of the United States, are events which many now living are likely to witness.[6]

It was the expectancy of American expansion, topped by news of the imminence of an American expedition to Japan, and British gun boat diplomacy in China that made valid Muravev's warning, early in 1852, that if Russia wished to retain a strong position in the Far East she must establish good relations with Japan and could not let the Americans and the British gain there the extent of influence they had achieved in China, and persuaded Nicholas I to cast aside financial considerations and to get underway the long-proposed Russian-Japanese expedition of Vice-Admiral Putiatin without further delay.[7]

On October 19, 1852 the frigate *Pallada*, flagship of the expedition, departed from Kronstadt and headed for Portsmouth, England, where Putiatin had hurried ahead to purchase an iron screw-schooner. On January 18, 1853 the *Pallada* and the newly acquired schooner *Vostok* left Portsmouth and proceeded separately to the Madeira and the Cape Verde Islands and to Simon's Bay at the Cape of Good Hope. In April the vessels parted company again and, after a brief reunion at Hong Kong, followed their separate ways to the Bonin Islands, where two more vessels, the corvet *Olivutsa* and the transport *Kniaz Menshikov* awaited them. Together they set sail for Japan, urged on by the knowledge that Commodore Perry was a step ahead.[8]

On August 21, 1853 the Russian squadron arrived off Nagasaki, and the following morning entered the outer roadstead. The Dutch had written to the Japanese government of the imminence of a Russian expedition "to follow the movements of the American fleet," but the warning had not yet reached the capital, and the unexpected appearance of the Russian men-of-war caused considerable consternation. No attempt was made by the Nagasaki authorities, however, to interdict the Russian approach. Before the vessels had even dropped anchor, Osawa Shitetsu, Lord of Bungo, the governor of Nagasaki, sent permission for them to draw closer to the city. This was the first of many signs that the wall of seclusion was beginning

---

[6] E.S.Creasy, *The Fifteen Decisive Battles of the World*, 329.

[7] Krupinski, 21; Osten-Saken, 388.

[8] Evfimii Vasilevich Putiatin, "Vsepoddaneishii otchet general-adiutanta grafa Putiatina," 22-40; Russia, Ministry of the Navy, Naval Scientific Section, "Otchet o plavanii fregata *Pallada*, shkuny *Vostok*, korveta *Olivutsa* i transporta *Kniaz Menshikov*" (hereinafter cited as Russia, "Otchet"), 132-149; Lensen, *Russia's Japan Expedition*, 1-6.

to crumble. As Putiatin observed, at the very beginning of his dealings with the Japanese, "the Japanese are no longer what they were forty or fifty years ago."[9]

The raids of Khvostov and Davydov, not to mention the highhanded conduct of the skipper of the English frigate *Phaeton*, who

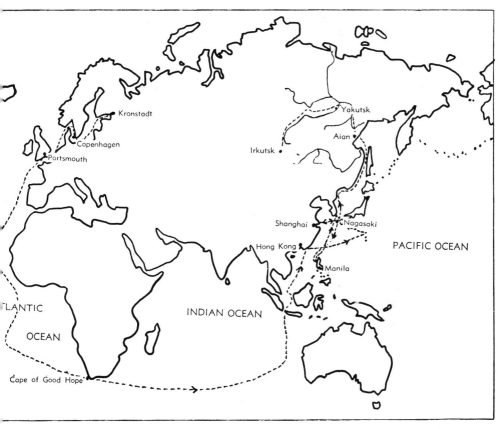

Route of the Frigate *Pallada*

in 1808 had exacted provisions in Nagasaki Harbor at gunpoint, had finally spurred the Shogunate into taking resolute steps to strengthen Japan's coastal defenses. But the determination of the officialdom was short-lived, and, before many years, foreign vessels were again able to approach the shores of Japan in quest of supplies without fear of the defense forces. New British violence had caused the Japanese government to issue, in 1825, the *Ni-nen-naku* (No-second-

9 Putiatin, "Vsepoddaneishii otchet," 35.

thought) Expulsion Order, which had commanded the local authorities to initiate without hesitation or further deliberation hostilities against any foreign vessel that arrived in their territory. But, though the *Morrison* had been duly shelled at Uraga in 1837, half a decade later Japanese vigilance had relaxed again. The disastrous destruction of Chinese warships by British men-of-war without loss to the latter, during the Opium War (1839-1842), had shocked Japanese officialdom, their apprehensions multiplied by wild rumors, which had magnified the size of British forces in the Far East and credited the British fleet with over twenty-five thousand vessels in number. Japanese resolution had become softened by caution, and in 1842 official orders had been issued modifying the *Ni-nen-naku* edict; henceforth foodstuffs and fuel were to be provided for foreign ships, which would then be "advised" to go away.[10] When Commodore Perry arrived at the very gates of the capital in July of 1853, the Japanese batteries did not open fire, and the Shogunate, whose *raison d'être* was the defense of the country against barbarians and which had issued decree after decree ordering the repulsion of the foreigners, failed to act, without first seeking the advice of all the daimyo and officials of importance. As Lord Tokugawa Nariaki, one of the most noted statesmen of the day, summarized the procrastination of the government and the vacillation of the officialdom in defense measures:

There have already been clashes in Ezo during the Kansei [1789-1801] and Bunka [1804-18] periods, but despite the Shogunate's efforts to effect military preparations they have not yet been completed. Again, relaxation of the expulsion laws was ordered in 1842, with the apparent object of first placating the foreigners and then using the respite to complete military preparations, but here, too, I do not think the various lords have made any particular progress in rearming in the twelve years that have since elapsed. On the arrival of the foreign ships recently, all fell into panic. Some take matters very seriously while foreign ships are actually at anchor here, but once the ships leave and orders are given for them to revert to normal, they all relax once more into idleness and immediately disperse the military equipment which they had hurriedly assembled. It is just as if, regardless of a fire burning beneath the floor of one's house, one neglected all fire-fighting precautions. Indeed, it shows a shameful spirit.[11]

The Opium War, like the raids of Khvostov and Davydov, had

10 Sansom, *The Western World and Japan*, 245-246.
11 W. G. Beasley, *Select Documents on Japanese Foreign Policy*, 106.

given new momentum to individual demands for coastal defense. Takashima Shuhan, for example, urged Japanese adoption of Western gunnery and drill and himself trained a military unit, clad in new uniforms and responding to commands in Dutch. But his modern methods of warfare did not arouse as much approval among the ruling samurai as might have been expected, because the Shogunate had lost much of its early military complexion, Confucian sentiment was powerful, and because Takashima had alienated some by his insistence on the opening of Japan in order to bolster her economy and rejuvenate her culture. Officials, like Egawa Tarozaemon were favorably impressed by the Takashima-style drill and for a while Takashima was free to teach his methods. Reactionary opposition was plotting his ruin, however, and he was imprisoned and then confined under house arrest on charges of treason, espionage, and embezzlement. Only in 1853, when the arrival of Perry shook the more traditional officials out of their complacency, were Takashima's services sought again.[12]

Aizawa Seishisai and Fujita Toko challenged the assertion of those who favored the opening of Japan on the ground that foreign trade would benefit Japan, pointing out that in the past commercial relations had led to the exchange of valuable Japanese metals for valueless foreign luxuries. They agreed that trade with the West might help Japan acquire the modern weapons, which she needed, but feared that this advantage would be outweighed by the impact of Western culture on Japanese society, which was already threatened with disintegration. War, or the threat of war, on the other hand, would serve to unite the Japanese people; after unity had been achieved, then Japan could reenter world affairs, adopting only those aspects of Western civilization, which it truly needed. Tokugawa Nariaki, most prominent advocate of the expulsion of the barbarians though he was, also recognized the value of Western learning. As early as 1846, he urged the Shogunate to import Western books on such subjects as gunnery, and in later years, opposed as he was to the general study of Western culture, recommended the adoption of Western military training and even the use of foreign instructors. He wrote in 1854: "My view is, that without abandoning Japanese ways we should adopt the best of foreign methods and join them to the best of our own.[13] Attributing Western victory over China not

---

[12] Sansom, *The Western World and Japan*, 251-253.
[13] Beasley, *Select Documents*, 10-12.

merely to military superiority, but to the scientific achievements underlying this superiority, Sakuma Shozan strove for the application of modern methods to ancient traditions—"Western science and Eastern morals," as he put it. Unlike Tokugawa Nariaki, he favored a "qualified internationalism," believing it necessary that Japan should open her doors in order to let in Western knowledge, and, making use of that Western knowledge to strengthen her army, take a ranking position in world affairs.[14]

As in years past, a number of fiery patriots saw the answer to the foreign threat in counter-expansion on the part of Japan. Aizawa Hakumin, in 1825, viewed the defense of China and Japan against Russia as a single strategic problem.[15] Conscious of Japan's weakness, some hoped to facilitate Japanese expansion by alliances with one or two of the Western powers. Advocating Japanese expansion into Manchuria, Korea, India, and America, Hashimoto Sanai proposed, in the wake of the Opium War, friendly relations with the United States ("we must regard America as our national defense in the East") and an alliance with either England or Russia, whose conflicting interests and steadily increasing enmity precluded their coexistence as powers in the Far East. "I am strongly inclined toward Russia," Hashimoto wrote. "Great Britain is both tricky and more aggressive and takes unjustifiable steps. Moreover, she is self-centered. Russia is more trustworthy, and she is our neighbor, her borders adjoining those of Japan. If we should show a readiness to coöperate in a military way with Russia, she would recognize our friendship as being of great value and would make ample return by giving us needed assistance in international affairs."[16]

The arrival of Commodore Perry's "black ships" forced the shogunate to speed up its search for a suitable foreign policy. The edicts of repulsion seemed no longer practicable. The choice had narrowed down to two alternatives: permitting a limited amount of trade immediately or permitting it later. The coastal defense officers Tsutsui Masanori and Kawaji Toshiakira would have pre-

14 Sansom, *The Western World and Japan*, 256-258.

15 W. G. Beasley, *Great Britain and the Opening of Japan*, 36.

16 Kuno, II, 355-357. See also Nakajima Shunzo, *Hokuho bummei shiwa* (Tokyo, 1942). Like Yoshida Shoin and other nationalists whose outspokenness had been a thorn in the flesh of the shogunate, Hashimoto was beheaded in 1859, ironically *after* the opening of Japan. Discussing Hashimoto's advocacy of a Russo-Japanese alliance, as well as similar views in the twentieth century, Nakajima likens the history of Russo-Japanese relations to *shukumei kankei*—relations preordained by fate from a former life.

ferred the former, and recommended that commercial relations be established with the United States, trade with the Dutch being cut in half. When Tokugawa Nariaki, to whom they made this recommendation, disagreed they backtracked on their proposal and set forth a policy of procrastination, hoping to avoid giving a definite reply for a period of five to ten years; by that time Japan should be able to have made the necessary military preparations and reject the foreign demands. The speedy departure of Perry gave support to the second alternative, and pressure removed, the shogunate slowed down the pace of deliberations. Then Putiatin arrived and the whole matter assumed new urgency. The question of an alliance with a foreign nation had already been broached earlier. Hashimoto had recommended relying on both Russia and the United States for assistance against all other countries; with Perry and Putiatin competing in the opening of Japan, substance was now given to the idea of relying on Russia and the United States as protection against each other. A number of junior officials, notably Tsutsui and Kawaji as well as Inoue Kiyonao, Iwase Tadanari, and Nagai Naomune conceived of using the Russians as a shield against the Americans. Arguing that in recent years powerful Russia had shown herself less dangerous than England, France, or America, they proposed that Japan make concessions to Russia in return for Russian help against all other countries.[17]

In a letter to Governor Osawa of Nagasaki, Oi Saburosuke, Baba Gorozaemon, and Shiraishi Tozaburo, his aides, wrote that the Russians had come to assist the Japanese after learning of secret American plans to invade Japan. They argued that there was consequently nothing disturbing in the arrival of the Russians, but that suspicion might arouse their resentment; thus they pleaded for the establishment of trade relations with Russia. Osawa agreed with this point of view and forwarded the letter to Abe Masahiro of the Supreme Council. Coastal Defense Officer Ishikawa Masahei also believed in giving preference to Russia. He went so far as to advocate an exclusive commercial agreement with Russia, in return for which the latter would have to protect Japan against all other nations. Abe, on whose military staff these coastal defense officers were, no doubt considered their views. At any rate, he himself told Tokugawa Nariaki that he favored making an agreement with Russia and warding off America. It does not follow from this that the Japanese

[17] Beasley, *Select Documents*, 24; Ishin Shiryo Hensan Jimusho, *Ishin-shi*, II, 122-123.

317

officials were Russophile, but simply that Russia at the time seemed the lesser of two evils, Russia having apologized for the actions of Khvostov and Davydov, and Putiatin speaking somewhat more softly than Perry, who was back at the shores of Japan with as many as nine men-of-war (carrying almost one-fourth of the entire personnel of the United States Navy) and threatened to multiply them tenfold within twenty days in case of hostilities. The outbreak of the Crimean War, however, weakened Russia's position as a potential protector of Japan, and Abe and other Shogunate officials decided to extend the same policy to all foreigners.

To ascertain what policy would be most advisable, the government sought the views of all the notables. Some lords replied that harbors should be opened to supply vessels with coal and foodstuffs only. Some felt that trade should be permitted for a fixed period of time; some that it should be halted, if not profitable. Some insisted that, harmful as friendship and commerce might be, war must be avoided. Some proposed that trade be tolerated only until the defenses were sufficiently strengthened to drive the foreigners away. Others demanded outright rejection of Western demands and immediate preparations for war. Of the sixty-one clans whose answers have been handed down, twenty-two may be said to have favored opening the country, eighteen to avert war, nineteen to rebuff the Westerns, while two remained undecided. Some of the opinions wavered from one policy to another. Nevertheless it is clear that the majority of the lords came out in favor of opening the country and averting war.

Similar views were expressed by most other officials. Coastal defense officers spoke of the eventual repulsion of the Westerners, but they too did not demand immediate hostilities. Only a very few samurai insisted on an uncompromising rejection of Western demands. Japanese publicists similarly fell into three categories: those who advocated the opening of the country, those who stressed the avoidance of war, and those who favored outright opposition—the latter were outnumbered at least two to one. The moderate tone of the policy to be followed, if and when the Americans returned again, as finally proclaimed by the councillors of state, reflected the anti-war trend of the replies:

We have all carefully examined every proposal received concerning the letters from the United States of America and upon thorough consideration have presented them to the Shogun. His opinion is that there are differences in the various statements, but that in general they boil down to the two words "war" and "peace." Since in your estimation the defense lines etc. are not adequate today, we shall avoid a definite answer when they come next year, as stated in their letter. Although we on our part shall proceed as peacefully as possible, it is difficult to tell whether or not there will be violent conduct on their part. If so, we shall disgrace our country, unless spiritually prepared for it. We must, therefore, on one hand, try as hard as possible to make preparations for the practical use of the defenses and, on the other hand, must bear our indignation with patience and save up our heroism and carefully observe their movements. Should hostilities be opened on their part, we must in unison exhaust our strength and diligently show our loyalty so as not to defile our country even a little bit.[18]

The fact that most officials sought to avoid war did not mean that they were anxious to deal with the West. As in years past the views of those advocating the opening of the country (*kaikoku*) and of those favoring the expulsion of the foreigners (*joi*) were not strictly opposed to each other. "The policy of *joi*, like that of *kaikoku*, had its roots in the warnings about Russian expansion sounded at the end of the eighteenth century and it accordingly shared the general preoccupation with coastal defense." Both *kaikoku* and *joi* advocates regarded Western activities as a threat to Japan. They differed essentially only in the means of defending their country. Following the arrival of Commodore Perry those, who favored the opening of the country, argued with renewed vigor that Japan was not capable of resisting the Westerners, who now seemed prepared to resort to arms, if rebuffed again, and that temporary concessions would gain for Japan time to arm; while those, who opposed any concessions, even at the risk of war, argued that Japan was too unprepared for the introduction of foreign ideas and that reforms at home must precede the opening of the country. In a lengthy memorial on coastal defense in August of 1853, Tokugawa Nariaki clearly stated the case of those who wished the Westerners repelled by force of arms: War was a means of uniting the Japanese people and "if the people of Japan stand firmly united, if we complete our military preparations and return to the state of society that existed before the Middle Ages, then we will even be able to go out against foreign countries and spread abroad our fame and prestige." A policy of appeasement would endanger Japan not only from abroad but also from within. "I hear that all, even though they be commoners, who have witnessed the recent actions of the foreigners, think them abomi-

[18] Inobe, 495-513.

nable; and if the Shogunate does not expel these insolent foreigners root and branch there may be some who will complain in secret, asking to what purpose have been all the preparations of gun-emplacements," Tokugawa wrote and warned that "since even ignorant commoners are talking in this way, I fear that if the Shogunate does not decide to carry out expulsion . . . the lower orders may fail to understand its ideas and hence opposition might arise from evil men who had lost their respect for Shogunate authority. It might even be that Shogunate control of the great lords would itself be endangered."[19]

Yoshida Shoin expressed the same sentiment in poems which were remembered by his countrymen in World War II.

Abokuto ga	Even if the Americans
Yora wo yaku shi	With the Europeans as allies
Kitaru tomo	Come to invade us,
Sonae no araba	If our defence is strong,
Nadoko osoren.	There is nothing to fear.

* * *

Sonae to wa	Our defence
Kan to ho to no	Is not the warship and the cannon,
Iinarazu	But it is
Waga shikishima no	Our Japanese spirit.
Yamato damashii.	

* * *

Nana tabi mo	Even if I return
Ikikaeri tsutsu	Seven times from the dead.
Ebisu wo zo	I shall never forget
Harawan kokoro	To drive away
Ware wasureme ya.	The foreigner.[20]

Like Honda Toshiaki and Sanai Hashimoto, Yoshida went beyond the mere repulsion of the foreigners, and advocated Japanese expansion on the Asiatic continent. He envisaged a defensive alliance with Russia and, at one time, Japanese conquest of territory in India, South America, and even in Europe. His line of argument ran as follows:

The sun rises or otherwise sets. The moon likewise waxes or otherwise wanes. The nation is destined to decline unless it advances and flourishes. Therefore, those who know how to look after the welfare of their country should not be satisfied with maintaining and protecting that which their

---

[19] Beasley, *Select Documents*, 8, 15, 102-107.
[20] H. van Straelen, *Yoshida Shoin*, 115-117.

country already has, but at the same time should aim to reform and improve upon that which their country already possesses. They should also strive to gain and add that which their country has not, thereby extending the power and glory of the nation beyond its borders. Present-day Japan should first of all complete her military preparations, by building the necessary battleships and by providing herself with all sorts of military weapons and ammunition. Then she should develop and colonize Yezo and entrust its rule to worthy feudal lords. At her earliest opportunity, Japan should occupy Kamchatka with an army and place the Sea of Okhotsk under her sole control. Liu Chiu [otherwise known as Lu Choo or as Ryu Kyu] should be instructed to make her king come in person to pay homage to Japan as do all the feudal lords in the homeland. Japan should upbraid Korea for her long negligence in the observation of her duty to Japan, and have her send tribute-bearing envoys, and Japan should also instruct Korea to give hostages to Japan for her good behavior, as she did during the glorious imperial period of ancient Japan. In the north, Manchuria should be sliced off [from China for the benefit of Japan]. In the south, Japan should receive [take under her control] Formosa and the Philippines. In this way, Japan should demonstrate her policy of expansion to the outside world. We should always look after the welfare of our people. At the same time, we should raise and train fighting men to meet the needs of the nation. Then our country and the far-off lands in our possession will be well guarded and protected. By pursuing these policies, Japan may go forth into the world and proclaim that she is able to maintain her national standing. If a nation in this struggling world should be surrounded by nations of aggressive inclination and should remain inactive, she would certainly be destined to decline and become obscure.[21]

Blatant as the call to arms of the *joi* spokesmen sounded, it was to a certain extent for home consumption—to unite the people behind the government—the actual policy of these militarists toward the foreigners often being a more conciliatory, sort of "war at home, peace abroad" policy.[22] The political implications embodied in practically every argument for or against the opening of Japan—the request for advice on the part of the government being in itself a sign of its indecision and weakness—help to explain why the Shogunate viewed without enthusiasm pronouncements, however patriotic, that emphasized its lack of military preparedness. The Shogunate's uneasiness was not without foundation for it outlasted the opening of the country by only about fourteen years. The ambition of young samurai was a prime factor in the ultimate downfall of the Tokugawa, and the Dutch Studies (with the accompanying demands for coastal

---

[21] Kuno, II, 352-353.   [22] Beasley, *Select Documents*, 13.

defense and the opening of the country) were a means for the young samurai's personal and political ends. Personal rivalry was therefore an inevitable factor in the strategic and political considerations of the officialdom. Significantly, once the Shogunate had decided to acquiesce in the opening of the country, the *joi* arguments assumed political significance as "a stick to beat the Bakufu."[23] The consequent fear of its own officials on the part of the shogunate and vice versa often seemed to crowd out the apprehension of Western designs. The ultimate fate of Yoshida is a case in point. An ardent patriot and essentially anti-western, he tried to leave Japan with Putiatin and, when he missed the Russian ships, with Perry, in order to learn Western military methods. He was caught and, following his involvement in a plot against the Shogunate, sentenced to death. His sentence read:

Item: He tried to go to America.
Item: He advised the government on coastal defense while in jail.
Item: He opposed hereditary succession to office and favored the selection of able men by popular vote.
Item: He planned to give his opinion concerning foreigners to the Bakufu.
Item: He did such things while in domiciliary confinement, thus showing great disrespect for high officials.[24]

The expressed desire for peace on the part of most Japanese had not been a declaration of sympathy for America or Russia, but a confession of weakness. Disagreeing with the contention of Tokugawa Nariaki that "if we do not drive them [the Americans] away now, we shall never have another opportunity," most officials followed the line of thought of Abe Masahiro, president of the Supreme Council:

. . . as we are not the equals of foreigners in the mechanical arts, let us have intercourse with foreign countries, learn their drill and tactics and when we have made the nation as united as one family, we shall be able to go abroad and give lands in foreign countries to those who have distinguished themselves in battle; the soldiers will vie with one another in displaying their intrepidity, and it will not be too late then to declare war. Now we shall have to defend ourselves against these foreign enemies skilled in the use of mechanical appliances, with our soldiers whose mili-

[23] Sansom, *The Western World and Japan*, 254-255; Beasley, *Select Documents*, 16.
[24] Sansom, *The Western World and Japan*, 274; van Straelen, 44. Perry refused to take along Yoshida. Inasmuch as Putiatin carried away another Japanese, it is quite possible that Yoshida, had he reached Nagasaki in time, might have succeeded in his plan.

tary skill has considerably diminished during a long peace of three hundred years, and we certainly could not feel sure of victory, especially in a naval war.[25]

To the interpreters, who brought the permission to enter the inner roadstead, the Russians announced that they had a letter for the governor, in which the reasons for their arrival were explained. The following day, on August 23, Putiatin explained to two city elders, who had come aboard with their retinue and interpreters, that he had brought letters from Chancellor Nesselrode to the governor of Nagasaki and to Japan's Supreme Council and wished to transmit them personally to the governor. But Osawa would not and could not meet Putiatin without permission from the Shogunate. He agreed to accept the letter addressed to himself, if the Russians would hand it to his subordinates. The paper to the Supreme Council, on the other hand, he refused to accept under any conditions without instructions from Edo. Putiatin agreed to wait as long as a month for some reply from the Japanese government, but if no answer was received by then, he would take his squadron to the very capital and there negotiate directly with the government.

The thirty days were not up, when the Japanese informed Putiatin on September 18, that the governor had been granted permission to receive the admiral and to accept the paper. All that remained to be done before the meeting was to determine the proper ceremonial formalities. For over two days Japanese and Russians haggled over details, determined not to humiliate their country in the eyes of the other. No longer were the Russians willing, as Rezanov had been, to ride ashore in Japanese boats, to remove their boots when entering a Japanese building, or to squat on the matted floor. Nor were they satisfied to limit the size of the landing party to that of Rezanov's retinue. The Japanese pointed to Rezanov's embassy as a restricting precedent, but unswayed, Putiatin remarked that the present embassy had been undertaken on a larger scale.[26]

On September 21, Putiatin went ashore with his fellow officers and orderlies, guard of honor, band and banners. Without the slightest fear of meeting the type of reception accorded to Golovnin, Putiatin

[25] Ernest Satow, *Japan 1853-1864*, 5-8.

[26] Ivan Goncharov, *Fregat Pallada*, 2-38; Koga Kinichiro, "Roshia osetsu-kakari Koga Kinichiro (Masaru) seishi nikki," 197, 238; *Bakumatsu*, I, 539-541; Putiatin, "Vsepoddaneishii otchet," 41-48; Tokutomi, XXXI, 327-328; Martin Ramming, "Über den Anteil der Russen und der Eröffnung Japans für den Verkehr mit den Westlichen Mächten," 18; Russia, "Otchet," 150-151.

entered the government office with only a dozen companions, and boldly walked past row after row of Japanese retainers. In the audience hall the Russians seated themselves on chairs brought from the ship, while the Japanese settled on a small platform of similar height.[27] After the usual refreshments and "rest" from the negotiations not yet begun, Governor Osawa accepted Nesselrode's letter to the Supreme Council, but announced that a speedy reply was not possible. Putiatin, who had catered to Japanese good will by coming to Nagasaki, renewed his threat of moving to the capital, if the Japanese procrastinated, a threat, which visibly impressed Osawa.

The Japanese would not permit the Russians to live on shore, but they suggested that they draw closer to land. This the Russians did, examining life on shore through their telescopes. But they retained their freedom of operations, scattering the vessels over the roadstead and brooking no interference with the movement of their boats.

Time passed. The first anniversary of the expedition was celebrated on October 7. The arrival of a new governor, Mizuno Tadanori, Lord of Chikugo, in late September had not accelerated matters. On October 21, the Japanese announced that their shogun, Tokugawa Ieyoshi, had died shortly after the arrival of the vessels and that a further delay in answer was inevitable. Putiatin sympathized with the Japanese loss, but argued that no circumstances could be permitted to halt the affairs of a great state and noted that the death had not prevented the Supreme Council from accepting the Russian letter and from determining the formalities of his meeting with Osawa. Again he threatened to move to Edo Bay and was about to do so, when the Japanese, on November 18, hastily produced a letter from Abe Masahiro to the effect that four plenipotentiaries were on their way from the capital to negotiate with him. Putiatin agreed to wait, but, as the letter did not specify when the plenipotentiaries would reach Nagasaki and since it seemed unlikely that they would arrive for at least another month, decided to make a quick trip to Shanghai in order to stock up on fresh supplies, change some of his letters of credit, repair some damages on the *Vostok*, and gather news about the latest developments in Europe. The *Kniaz Menshikov* had reported in September, after a visit to China, that a break between Russia on one hand, and Turkey, France, and England on the other was imminent. Putiatin sent ashore papers for the

---

[27] For pictures of the negotiations, see Lensen, *Russia's Japan Expedition*, between pages 34 and 35.

plenipotentiaries, and, warning the Japanese that, if upon his return to Nagasaki he found neither the plenipotentiaries nor a reply to the Russian state paper, he would continue directly to the capital, he departed with his squadron on November 23.

On January 3, 1854, the Russians returned to Nagasaki. The plenipotentiaries had not come yet, but Putiatin was persuaded to wait until the twelfth. On the seventh, the plenipotentiaries duly arrived and two days later Putiatin was informed of it. On the twelfth, Putiatin went ashore to meet with the plenipotentiaries. The Russian landing was executed with greater ceremony and pomp than ever. As the boats pushed off from the flag-bedecked vessels, the band struck up "God Save the Tsar"; the sailors cheered lustily, and cannons thundered in salute. On land the Russians fell into military formation and, to the merry tunes of the band, marched briskly to the meeting place.

In the western government office the plenipotentiaries of both countries faced each other. Japan was represented by the amiable, aged Tsutsui Masanori, Lord of Hizen, and the younger, but more important Kawaji Toshiakira, an intelligent and energetic samurai in the early fifties, as well as by Arao Narimasa, Lord of Tosa, and Koga Masaru, a Confucian scholar. Putiatin was assisted by an equal number of countrymen: by Lieutenant Commander Ivan Unkovskii, commander of the *Pallada*, by Lieutenant Commander Konstantin Poset, and by Ivan Goncharov, the celebrated writer of later years, who had joined the expedition as secretary to Putiatin. The Japanese plenipotentiaries were all politeness, and so were the Russians. The apparent genuineness of their greetings and compliments belied the fact that there was a vital conflict between the policies of their countries. Tsutsui seemed perfectly sincere, when he told the Russians at the banquet, which was shortly spread out: "We have come from beyond many hundreds, you from many thousands of miles. We had never seen each other, were so far apart, and now have become acquainted, sit, chat and dine together. How strange and pleasant this is!"

The first meeting was confined to pleasantries, the Japanese refusing to mar the etiquette of introduction by launching into business talk. It was followed three days later, on the fifteenth, by a meeting on the *Pallada*, but now the Russians entertained and the Japanese still refused to consider matters of state. It was a meeting of mutual merrymaking, initiated by the exchange of splendid gifts, including an exquisite Japanese sword presented by Kawaji as "a gesture of friendship."

The spirits of the Japanese seemed the gayer for all the trepidation with which they had anticipated the meeting. Tsutsui had warned his colleagues that if they went aboard the Russian ship, the Russians might press upon them and try to force them to determine Japan's boundaries. Others had expressed the fear, remembering perhaps what had happened to Takadaya Kahei, that the Russians would kidnap the plenipotentiaries, and made various proposals for setting fire to the frigate. But Kawaji reflected the impact of mounting foreign pressure on Japan, when he argued that Japan could not afford to arouse the hostility of Russia and that it would be best, were he captured aboard ship, for him to proceed to Russia and to confer with its ruler. Now that it was evident that the Russians had no such designs, the Japanese were greatly relieved. But they did not take every compliment at its face value and inwardly watched the "barbarians" with a mixture of mistrust and patronage.

On January 16, the plenipotentiaries finally transmitted their government's reply, artistically written on thick gilded paper, and wrapped in several layers of silk, boxed in a delicate lacquered box, the innermost of a shell of six boxes. Even more ornate in style than in appearance, the Russians could not decipher it and requested a Dutch translation. This caused some embarrassment, for the Japanese interpreters themselves could not understand it and Koga, one of the plenipotentiaries, had to translate the difficult Chinese text into Japanese, so that it could be rendered into Dutch and ultimately into Russian. Both sides agreed that henceforth all notes must be in Japanese, Chinese, and Dutch.[28]

The state paper which Putiatin had brought, demanded the clarification of the boundaries between Russia and Japan and the opening of Japanese ports to Russian vessels. Nesselrode had written that the boundary question could be postponed no longer, that its solution was "the basis of mutual peace." He assured the Japanese government that Russia was vast in extent and had no further territorial ambitions, and that the Tsar merely wished to safeguard profits justly belonging to his subjects. He had requested, therefore, that it

[28] Goncharov, *Fregat Pallada*, 104, 110, 180-210; Putiatin, "Vsepoddaneishii otchet," 49-56; Tokutomi, XXXI, 358; Russia, Ministry of the Navy, Naval Scientific Section, "Izvlechenie iz pisem morskikh ofitserov: Zarubina, Peshchurova i Boltina" (hereafter cited as Russia, "Izvlechenie"), 324-325; Kawaji Saemon-no-jo "Roshia osetsu-kakari Kawaji Saemon-no-jo (Toshiakira) nikki," 35-39, 49, 134; Koga, 198, 236-246.

be determined at a joint conference, conducted "for the benefit of both countries," which islands constituted the northern and southern boundaries of Japan and Russia respectively and who owned the southern coast of Sakhalin. As to the opening of Japanese ports to Russian vessels, Nesselrode had conveyed the wish of the Tsar to see Japanese ports opened to Russian merchantmen for commercial relations and to Russian warships, on their way to America, for replenishing supplies in case of emergency. Nesselrode denied any intentions of depriving the Japanese of profit, and pointing out the proximity of the two countries argued that it was only natural for them to have friendly intercourse. He emphasized the peculiarity of Russia's position, insisting that establishing relations with Russia would be different from having relations with distant countries.[29]

The Japanese in their reply agreed in principle to the clarification of the boundaries between Japan and Russia and declared that border fiefs had been already ordered to make a careful investigation and that envoys would be sent to confer with Russian officials. At the same time, they remonstrated that reliable maps and documents were needed and that the problem required most scrupulous examination; "such an investigation cannot be done today." As to trade, the Supreme Council reiterated that it was strictly prohibited by laws handed down from their ancestors, and reminded the Russians that they had frequently been so informed. In the same breath the government retreated from the unequivocal stand of former years, and alluded to an ultimate change in policy, conceding that the world situation was changing rapidly and that trade was developing steadily. "We definitely cannot take the old tradition and laws to regulate present day affairs." The Supreme Council admitted that the Americans had demanded commercial relations and that others would no doubt follow suit. Nesselrode had asserted that the proximity of Russia put her in a special position vis-à-vis Japan, but the Supreme Council replied that, "if we trade, we shall trade with all countries, if we refuse, we shall refuse all. If we sign a treaty with your country, we cannot but sign with all nations." This line of argument shows not only the realization on the part of Japanese statesmen that the rivalry of Western powers could be turned to the advantage of Japan, but it permitted the Supreme Council to develop a logical plea for delay. "Considering that we have only the strength of one nation to supply the demands of ten thousand nations scat-

[29] *Bakumatsu*, II, 141; Tokutomi, XXXI, 341-342.

tered like stars, we do not know whether our resources will suffice."
A study would have to be made of Japan's potentialities and of her
needs. "There are numerous and complicated problems that cannot
be decided in a day or a night." Furthermore the new sovereign had
not yet familiarized himself with everything, the whole problem
would have to be reported to Kyoto, and the feudal lords would have
to be consulted. "From the looks of things, it will take at least three
to five years." The Japanese realized that this might look like mere
procrastination, but asked the Russians to have patience. They
promised to inform them as soon as they reached a decision. To come
again before that would be a waste of time. "What advantage would
you gain from this endless running around?" Meanwhile the Russians
could obtain firewood, food, and water at Nagasaki. "We are ashamed
that it has to be this way," the leaders of Japan concluded, "but we
cannot keep quiet, therefore answer you like this."[30]

Putiatin was not satisfied with the reply, and during the negotiations that followed on shore almost daily between himself, Poset,
Iosif Goshkevich (the Russian Chinese language specialist), Goncharov and one or two other Russian officers on one hand and the Japanese officials on the other, from January 18 to February 1, pressed
for the immediate opening of Japan, alluding now to the inadequacy
of the defenses of Nagasaki, now to the advantages of foreign trade
and tempting the Japanese not only with offers of foodstuffs and
domestic necessities, but of steamers and big guns. Yet the Japanese
demurred. "Trade in our place is new. It has not yet matured; one
must deliberate how to trade, where and with what. . . . You give a
maiden into marriage when she grows up; our trade has not yet
grown up."[31]

Negotiations reached an impasse and, finally, the Japanese plenipotentiaries announced that they must return to the capital, where
the Russian demands would be studied further. When they visited
the frigate, on February 1, to attend a farewell banquet and exchange
more gifts with the Russians, a highly interesting conversation ensued between Putiatin and Kawaji, during which the latter acknowledged that Russia as a neighboring country, with boundaries adjacent

---

[30] *Bakumatsu*, III, 53-54; Tokutomi, XXXI, 411-413. Signed by: Abe Masahiro (Lord of
Ise), Makino Tadamasa (Lord of Bizen), Matsudaira Noriyasu (Lord of Izumi), Matsudaira Tadayoshi (Lord of Iga), Kuze Hiroshika (Lord of Yamato), Naito Nobuchika
(Lord of Kii).
[31] Goncharov, *Fregat Pallada*, 233; Kyozawa Kiyoshi, *Gaiko-shi*, 59.

to those of Japan, deserved special consideration, and promised that "should communication and trade be permitted to foreign countries, they will of course be permitted to Russia," and that "if trade will be permitted, the things permitted to foreigners will also be permitted to Russia." Most important of all, in view of Commodore Perry's negotiations in Edo Bay and his rejection of an offer by Putiatin to make common cause, was Kawaji's probing declaration that "even when in the future we open amicable relations, because your country is a great country with boundaries adjacent to ours, we consider you as a defense against other countries," and Putiatin's ready assurance that " in the event that people from other countries cause violent disturbances, we are prepared to give you any assistance."[32] Two days later, on February 3, Putiatin received a note from the plenipotentiaries in which they promised Russia preferential treatment. "Should our country finally permit trade," they wrote, "it will be first to your country."[33]

There was little sense in remaining in Nagasaki while the plenipotentiaries returned to the capital. It was too early in the season to attempt passage to the northern territories of Russia, and the waste shores of Tatar Strait and the Sea of Okhotsk lacked the supplies which the expedition needed. Putiatin decided, therefore, to sail to the Philippines, some Russian letters of credit having been addressed to Manila. He planned to resume the negotiations with the plenipotentiaries in the spring, but by then, it appeared, Russia would be at war with England and France and he did not know whether he could risk returning to Japan itself. At the last moment, therefore, on February 5, when he had weighed anchor and the Japanese had no time to object, he sent word that the plenipotentiaries meet him in the spring in Aniwa Bay. It was no doubt this decision that brought the great influx of Japanese officialdom to Sakhalin, which had so concerned Busse. But Putiatin did not come to the place, which he himself had selected, even though he repeated his intention to do so, when he stopped at Nagasaki, from April 18 to 26, on his way back from the Philippines.

Meanwhile Tsarist occupation of the decadent Ottoman Empire's Danubian principalities in an attempt to pressure the "Sick Man of Europe" into granting Russia a protectorate over Orthodox churches in Constantinople "and elsewhere" had aroused much

[32] *Bakumatsu*, IV, 38-40; Koga, 259.
[33] *Bakumatsu*, IV, 54.

opposition. The Turks had declared war on Russia in October 1853, and the English and French had followed suit on March 28, 1854. As a consequence Russian efforts to establish regular relations with Japan had to be cut down.

When Putiatin reached the eastern shore of Siberia, orders awaited him to take his vessels into De-Kastri Bay. On July 4, 1854, Governor General Muravev came aboard the *Pallada*. The corvet *Olivutsa* had separated from the expedition, even before the April visit to Nagasaki, in order to assist in the defense of Kamchatka. Muravev now released the transport *Kniaz Menshikov* to the local authorities of the Russian-American Company, and gave a special assignment to the schooner *Vostok*. As for the flagship, the frigate *Pallada*, Muravev ordered her to seek shelter from ice and enemies in the confines of the Amur River. It had been obvious from the very beginning that the *Pallada* was no longer sturdy enough to withstand the rigors of the protracted Japan expedition, and Putiatin had requested as early as spring of 1853, that the newly constructed frigate *Diana* of the Baltic Fleet be sent in replacement. When the *Diana* now reached De-Kastri Bay, Putiatin moved aboard (August 16, 1854), keeping at his side all the officers (except Unkovskii) and many of the sailors of the *Pallada*. On October 15, 1854 Putiatin departed once more for the shores of Japan.

It had been Putiatin's original intention to continue negotiations in Aniwa Bay. But the contingent of Major Busse had already been removed from the island, partly because its presence might have invited British attack. Whether Putiatin considered the neutral harbors of Japan proper more secure, whether the speed of his new frigate made the long crossing less dangerous, or whether temporary American occupation of the Liu Ch'iu Islands "in reclamation for some demands that had not been satisfied by the Japanese government" had spurred him on to more forthright action—whatever the reason—Putiatin had taken advantage of the lifting of the Russian post on Sakhalin to send word to Tsutsui and Kawaji that he had decided to resume the negotiations in a harbor near the Japanese capital.[34] He sailed directly to Hakodate, from where he sent a letter to the Japanese government, giving notice that he was on his way to Osaka and requesting that the plenipotentiaries be sent there to conclude the negotiations.

[34] Putiatin, "Vsepoddaneishii otchet," 60-70; Russia, "Otchet," 163-173; *Hokkaido-shi*, II, 589.

Much had happened since Putiatin's last visit. His expedition had shrunk from four vessels to one and the one was restricted in its movements, for fear that it be tracked down by superior Anglo-French forces. Most important of all, despite the promise of priority of treatment that Kawaji had made to Putiatin, the Japanese government had concluded a Treaty of Amity and Friendship with the United States (March 31, 1854) and with Great Britain (October 14). The Treaty of Kanagawa between Japan and the United States provided for (1) "a perfect, permanent, and universal peace, and a sincere and cordial amity between the two countries"; (2) the opening of the ports of Shimoda and Hakodate "as ports for the reception of American ships, where they can be supplied with wood, water, provisions, and coal, and other articles their necessities may require, as far as the Japanese have them"; (3) reciprocal assistance to vessels in distress, American crews cast to the shores of Japan to be delivered into the hands of their fellow countrymen at Shimoda or Hakodate; (4) freedom from confinement and freedom of movement of castaways and other temporary inhabitants within designated limits in Shimoda and Hakodate; (5) exchange of gold and silver coins and various goods by American vessels according to Japanese regulations; (6) procurement of wood, water, provisions, coal and other necessities through the agency of special Japanese officers only; (7) most-favored-nation treatment (the automatic extension to the United States of privileges and advantages granted to other countries); (8) the appointment of American consuls or agents to reside in Shimoda a year and a half after signature of the treaty "provided that either of the two governments deem such arrangement necessary."[35]

Perry's success paved the way for a Russo-Japanese agreement, but not, it must be added, because Perry had wished to open Japan to all countries. On the contrary, Perry had tried repeatedly to thwart Russian plans and would have been delighted to exclude Russia from Japan. Nor was Perry's success an asset to Russian diplomacy in that it multiplied foreign pressure. Prior to the signing of the Japanese-American treaty this had been true, but now it was not the fear of combined foreign pressure, but the hope of manipulating rival foreign pressures so that they cancel each other out—the time-honored Chinese strategy of "fighting barbarians with barbarians"—that made the Japanese almost eager to conclude an agreement with

[35] William M. Malloy, *Treaties*, I, 996-998.

Russia. Kawaji and Tsutsui had not knowingly deceived Putiatin with their promises. Liaison between Edo and Nagasaki had been inadequate and communications slow. When, on their way back to the capital, they had learned of the conclusion of the Japanese-American treaty, they had offered their resignations in protest and had agreed to continue in their positions as plenipotentiaries only after the Shogunate had authorized them to grant the Russians upon their return the same concessions that had been made to the Americans.[36] When Putiatin arrived in Hakodate (October 21), he was informed that the Japanese government had already written to his government through the Dutch, suggesting that someone be sent to conclude the negotiations begun by him. He was not able, however, to resume the negotiations in Osaka. When he arrived there, on November 7, the Japanese insisted that the harbor was not open to Westerners. A courier was sent to Edo and word was brought back that the plenipotentiaries would meet with Putiatin at Shimoda, one of the ports opened by the American treaty. Putiatin reached Shimoda on December 4. He was displeased with the unprotected anchorage, but stayed where he was in order to avoid further delay. The plenipotentiaries had not yet arrived and the Russians went ashore to explore the countryside, roving about town, blowing bugles, and singing songs, while the inevitable crowd of children followed noisily in their footsteps. At the same time the Russians kept a close look-out for the English. In Yura Strait one of the castaways, repatriated by Lindenberg near Shimoda in 1852, had managed to get aboard the frigate to warn the Russians that the British squadron of Sir James Sterling had been in Nagasaki waters as late as October. The *Diana* was kept ready for all eventualities, and the seamen were exhorted "to fight to the last drop of blood" and "not to surrender alive."[37]

The Japanese plenipotentiaries arrived by the middle of December and, after the usual exchange of formal visits on shore and aboard ship (December 20-21), negotiations were resumed in earnest, on December 22, at the Fukusen Temple. Since Kawaji and Tsutsui had come prepared to extend to Putiatin whatever concessions Perry had obtained, Putiatin could have concluded a treaty in no time had he satisfied himself with the provisions of the American agreement.

[36] Ramming, "Über den Anteil der Russen," 25.

[37] Vasilii Makhov, *Fregat Diana*, 35-37; Putiatin, "Vsepoddaneishii otchet," 72-78; Nikolai G. Schilling, II, "Iz vospominanii starago moriaka," 146-149; Illustrated London News, "British Expedition at Japan," 94-99; Putiatin, "Raport General-Adiutanta Putiatina Velikomu Kniaziu General-Admiralu," 231.

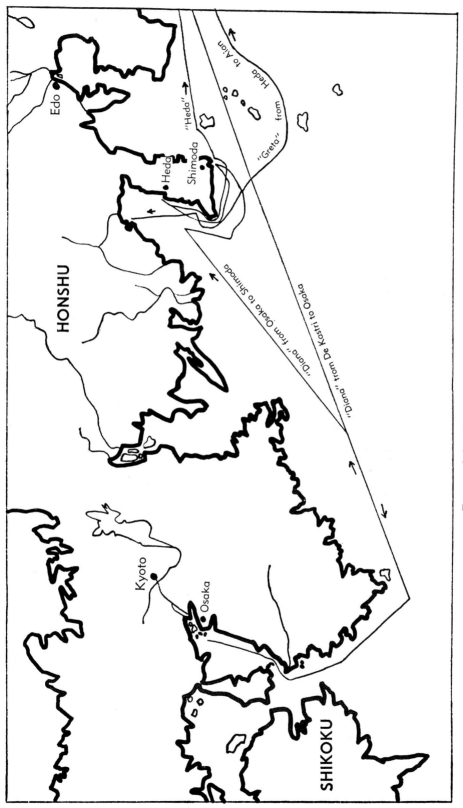

Routes of the *Diana*, *Greta*, and *Heda*

But Perry had concluded little more than a shipwreck convention and the ports opened by the Japanese were most disadvantageous—isolated from the heart of Japan by distance or natural barriers, and were in themselves a partial negation of the unwilling concession. Putiatin wished to substitute better and more harbors; above all he wanted to determine the Russo-Japanese frontier.

The negotiations had barely been resumed, when sudden disaster overtook both sides. In the forenoon of December 23, an earthquake shook the area and a great tidal wave deluged the coast. Billows of water, some twenty-one feet above normal sea level, washed the entire town of Shimoda into the Pacific, while the *Diana* was caught in a furious whirlpool between an island at sea and the shore, and was spun around and around for forty-two complete rotations in half an hour. She tilted precariously, developed a serious leak and lost her sternpost and rudder; but she was not smashed against any of the rocks.

When the ocean subsided, an inspection of the *Diana* showed that she required major repairs. The ship's artillery pieces with gun carriages were taken ashore to lighten the vessel, while Russian and Japanese officers examined nearby bays to find a suitable place for the urgent repairs. On January 12, the *Diana* weighed anchor and began to limp toward the Bay of Heda, in the company of a Russian-manned junk. The frigate safely rounded the southern promontory of Izu peninsula and slowly pushed northward. But with every day the battle became more hopeless—wind and swell continued to weaken the frigate; pump after pump kept breaking down; and her leaking increased steadily. On January 16 and 17, all hands were taken ashore with the aid of the Japanese. The following day their personal belongings were taken off the vessel. On January 19, the *Diana* was taken in tow by over a hundred Japanese boats in an attempt to pull her to sheltered Heda Harbor, and there run her aground, pump out the water, and make a new keel. For a while all went well and success seemed close at hand, when a sudden storm forced the boats to desert the frigate. The wind swung the *Diana* around and drove her back. Soon she began to list, rolled over, and sank. The Russian-Japanese expedition, which had been reduced already from four vessels to one, now had none. Putiatin and his whole crew were completely at the mercy of the Japanese.[38]

[38] Putiatin, "Vsepoddaneishii otchet," 79-90; Putiatin, "Raport," 232-242; Schilling, 151-159, 247-263; Koga, 356-357; Makhov, *Fregat Diana*, 43-48.

The shipwreck of the *Diana* (not unlike the captivity of Golovnin) proved to be a blessing in disguise. Though it was Western pressure that precipitated the opening of Japan, it was paradoxically Western pressure that the Japanese resisted most. The tragedy of Shimoda brought both sides together in a bond of mutual commiseration, and insured a protracted contact between Russians and Japanese. Above all, it deprived the Russians of the show of power. As Kawaji noted in his diary, "The Russians were repeatedly humble in speech . . . their words tamed us greatly."[39] Always anxious lest it lose face in the eyes of its own subjects by yielding to foreign threats, the Japanese government was now in a position, where it could well afford to be generous. It would have been easy for the Japanese to have wiped out the Russian expedition, as Tokugawa Nariaki indeed recommended.[40] All they really would have had to do would have been to turn their back on the Russian disaster. Instead, they exerted every effort to help the Russians. They assisted in attempts to keep the *Diana* afloat, and when this proved impossible helped to bring the crew ashore safely, and supported the Russians in spite of the great privations they themselves were suffering at the time. As Putiatin reported to his government, "one cannot praise enough their philanthropic care for us."[41] Nor was gratitude one-sided. The Japanese deeply appreciated the fact that the Russians, as they were being battered themselves by the tidal wave, valiantly rescued some Japanese, who had been swept into the sea and that the following day the admiral himself had gone ashore with Poset and the doctor to offer their help. Had the vessel sunk and had all the Russians drowned during the tidal wave, the Japanese would not have been particularly distressed; some indeed would have been pleased. Once the Japanese had begun towing the frigate and otherwise assisting the Russians, however, they had incurred a moral obligation for their welfare, which they could not dismiss now, even if they had wished to do so. Sighed Koga: "The will of Heaven really cannot be understood."[42] Inherent generosity, gratitude, or moral obligation—whatever the motivation of Japanese solicitude—the Japanese appeared in a new light to the Russians. They appeared as "the kindest of people." The priest Vasilii Makhov wrote:

The compassion of the Japanese government promptly expressed itself in sincere goodness of heart, particular consideration, and manifest phi-

[39] Kawaji, 148. [40] Beasley, *Select Documents*, 11.
[41] Putiatin, "Raport," 242. [42] Koga, 356.

lanthropy. The officials specially sent from the capital city, bemoaned the misfortune that had befallen us, were anxious to console us, and took much trouble to find means of drying, warming, and feeding us. The Japanese people, who arrived daily from the cities and settlements in a crowd, and especially the inhabitants of Miyashima, showed us whatever assistance they could: some hastily erected boarded sheds and fence-roofs to shelter us from the bad weather; others carried matting, mats, carpets, wadded blankets, robes and various footwear; some brought teapots with boiling water and tea, others rice, sake, oranges, fish, and eggs; it was remarkable that some of the Japanese would take off their kimono and right away give them to our quite frozen and shivering sailors. . . . Assistance indeed was expressed on the face of the Japanese; a tender, comforting smile, sighs, bows of greeting, a sorrowful bearing and other acts lightened our grief.[43]

The tidal wave had washed away the restraints of ceremonial propriety and of traditional prohibitions. Despite the belligerent seclusion policy, the Japanese were not naturally xenophobic. In the days of Laxman, Rezanov, and Golovnin personal kindness had constantly shown itself through the façade of official bigotry. But now the restrictions on fraternization came off like a mask and, as there was no longer any question that the Russians could live on Japanese land, free reign was given to Japanese hospitality. The Russians were moved to Heda, where barracks had been erected for the crew. The officers were housed in a temple, where, in the words of Baron Nikolai Schilling, "the idols had been placed facing the wall, probably so that they would not be embarrassed by the sight of Christians in their holy places."[44] The Japanese government proclaimed the uninvited intruders to be its guests and, though Putiatin insisted that a record be kept of Japanese expenditures for ultimate reimbursement, proceeded to treat the Russians with heretofore unexpressed courtesy. This new spirit was carried over into the negotiations, which Putiatin resumed after the shipwreck, and both sides were more cooperative and conciliatory in approach.

Once the American treaty had been signed, Putiatin could have obtained the identical concessions without effort. The Japanese plenipotentiaries did not disclose the terms of the treaty, of course, but the Russians obtained a copy by bribing one of the Japanese interpreters.[45] It was Putiatin's attempt to open different ports and the need for the delineation of the Russo-Japanese frontier that pro-

[43] Makhov, *Fregat Diana*, 48-49.   [44] Schilling, 265.
[45] *Ibid.*, 158.

tracted his negotiations with Kawaji and Tsutsui. As to the opening of other ports, the Japanese willingly added Nagasaki to the list, but, though the shipwreck of the *Diana* dramatized the unprotectedness of Shimoda Harbor, Putiatin failed to obtain the opening of Osaka, Uraga, or any other port near a political or commercial center of the main island. Concerning the boundaries between Russia and Japan there was considerable debate, Kawaji insisting at first that all the Kuril Islands were Japanese. Finally it was decided to divide the Kuril Archipelago between them, but to leave Sakhalin Island in common possession, until its disposition could be studied more thoroughly. On February 7, 1855, Putiatin, Kawaji, and Tsutsui finally signed the first treaty between Japan and Russia at the Choraku Temple in Shimoda. Prepared in Japanese, Chinese, and Dutch, the treaty provided for: (1) continuous peace and friendship between the two countries and reciprocal protection of their subjects, (2) the recognition of Etorofu and the Kuril Islands to the south as Japanese, of Uruppu and the islands to the north as Russian, Sakhalin remaining in common possession, (3) the opening of Shimoda, Hakodate, and Nagasaki to Russian vessels for making repairs and taking on supplies, (4) reciprocal aid to and nonconfinement of shipwrecked people, (5) barter and purchase of goods in Shimoda and Hakodate, (6) the appointment of a Russian consul at Shimoda or Hakodate, when thought "indispensable" by the Russian government, (7) reciprocal extraterritoriality, and (8) most-favored-nation treatment of Russia.[46]

The treaty of Shimoda was similar to the American treaty in its provisions for the protection of shipwrecked persons and of vessels in distress, the opening of certain ports to ships and permission to purchase supplies, the appointment of consular agents and most-favored-nation treatment. It went beyond the American treaty in opening three Japanese ports instead of two and in providing for consuls at either Hakodate or Shimoda, in delineating the Russo-Japanese boundary, and in providing for reciprocal extraterritoriality. Putiatin had not prevented the planting of American and English influence in Japan, but he had assured Russia of a position of at least equal importance.

Now that a treaty between Russia and Japan had been signed at last, and copies of it had been exchanged by Putiatin and the pleni-

---

[46] For the complete text of the treaty and explanatory articles, see Appendix I.

potentiaries, all that remained to be done was to present the Russian copies to the Russian government and to make a full report of the negotiation. This was no minor task, for the expedition was stranded in Japan and English men-of-war were prowling the seas. The Japanese had turned down Sir James Sterling's request for permission to engage the Russian vessels in Japanese waters, for fear that Japan's relations with Russia be compromised, and had heeded Putiatin's plea, after the Shimoda disaster, to hide the cannons, which had been saved from the *Diana*. But there was always the danger that British and French men-of-war were lying in wait for Putiatin beyond the territorial waters of Japan or that they would violate the neutrality of Japan, despite Japanese protests.[47]

Resentful as the Russians would have been of British violation of Japanese neutrality, it was apparently only American interference that thwarted a similar transgression by themselves. The occasion had been the arrival of the French three-master *Napoleon III* in Shimoda toward the end of January, 1855. Putiatin, who had been on his way from Heda to Shimoda, when he had learned of it, had sent back orders for a surprise night attack on the French whaler. Two Russian boats manned by over eighty men armed with cutlasses, hatchets, and bayonets hurried to Shimoda, but the vessel had already left port, warned, it was said, by the Americans.[48]

The American action was designed to protect the neutral rights of Japan; it was not anti-Russian in nature. Commodore Perry himself had been anti-Russian to the extent of turning down an offer by Putiatin to join forces in their attempt to open Japan and even went so far as to predict the inevitability "sooner or later" of war between the United States and Russia over eastern Asia. Other Americans did not share Perry's outlook, however, and Commander H. A. Adams, and Captain W. J. McCluney, who had returned to Shimoda toward the end of January 1855 with the ratified Japanese-American treaty, extended to the Russians every aid. McCluney even offered to take the Russians to Shanghai. This the Russians declined, for fear that they would be captured there by the English or French, but they

---

[47] W. G. Beasley notes that Sterling's letter to the governor of Nagasaki was really in the nature of an inquiry rather than of a demand, but that its character was changed by the Dutch and Japanese translators. Sterling did desire access to Japanese ports "in order to prevent the Russian ships of war and their prizes from making use of those ports, to the detriment of the interests of Great Britain and her allies." (*Great Britain*, 117-119.)

[48] Putiatin, "Vsepoddaneishii otchet," 78, 91-92; Putiatin, "Raport," 231; Schilling, 266; Koga, 314, 318, 349, 367-368; Tokutomi, xxxiii, 162-167.

asked whether the commander of the American squadron in the Pacific could not send a steamer in April to transport them directly to Petropavlovsk. It was through Adams also that Putiatin sent to St. Petersburg, via Washington and Vienna, copies of the important treaty with Japan, which he had concluded, and various reports. The American government did not find it possible to send a warship to repatriate the Russians; aside from this, however, it promised to give every assistance to the Russians at Shimoda. In mid-May of 1855, two vessels of Captain John Rodgers' United States Surveying Expedition entered Shimoda. When the Japanese, eager to keep Americans and Russians apart, tried to prevent the *John Hancock* from proceeding to Heda, Rodgers rebuffed the Japanese objections and, pointing to the propriety of helping shipwrecked persons in general, made it clear that Russia and the United States were on friendly terms with each other: "The Russian Emperor is the friend of our President, and our President is his friend. The two countries are at peace, and in friendship."[49]

While Putiatin was negotiating with the plenipotentiaries, the crew of the *Diana* had begun the construction of a schooner in Heda. Putiatin had drawn up the plans for the schooner from the detailed description of a yacht in one of the issues of a journal saved from the frigate. The Japanese did not object. On the contrary, they put Japanese workers at the disposal of the Russians, realizing that this was an opportunity for them to learn the techniques of modern shipbuilding. Japanese officials and artisans carefully sketched and recorded every step of the operation. For both the Russians and the Japanese the loss of the *Diana* proved a blessing in disguise. As Captain Mizuno Hironori was to write in later years, "these workmen were the first to learn the art of occidental shipbuilding"; attached eventually to the Shogun's navy they became "the fathers of the shipbuilding industry in modern Japan."[50]

[49] Allan B. Cole, *Yankee Surveyors in the Shogun's Seas*, 65-66; Lensen, *Russia's Japan Expedition*, 127-134; Putiatin, "Vsepoddaneishii otchet," 93.

[50] Mizuno Hironori, "The Japanese Navy," 417. Oaki Kakichi and his son Kikusaburo were among these workers. After the Restoration of imperial authority in 1868, they moved to Tokyo (the "Eastern Capital," new name for Edo), and established themselves as shipwrights at Kyobashi. The foreign-style vessels built by them gave rise to the so-called Kimizawa-style of construction, named after the district in the province of Izu from which they hailed and in which the town of Heda lay. A branch workshop which they opened at Ishikawajima in 1880 was the origin of the important Ishikawajima Shipbuilding Yard of later years. (Ki Kimura, "Dawn of Modern Industry in Japan," 491-492; see also *Hokkaido-shi*, II, 787-788.)

When Putiatin returned to Shimoda on February 14, considerable progress had been made in the construction of the schooner. Instruments, building materials, and workmen had been brought into Heda and a Russian blacksmith's shop had been constructed. But the schooner, named *Heda* in honor of the place of construction, was designed primarily to bring back news to Russia of the events which had transpired. It was too small to carry all the crew of the *Diana*; it had space for less than one-eleventh of the complement. Other arrangements had to be made for the return of the remaining seamen. Putiatin tried to negotiate with the skippers of other ships. The giant American clipper *Young America* could have repatriated everyone, but at one point the American crew mutinied against transporting the Russians for fear that they themselves be taken prisoner by the English or French; and the "crafty Yankee" skipper Mr. Babcock took advantage of this to tear up the contract he had already signed with Putiatin and to hold out for an exorbitant price. On April 11, 1855, the first group of Russians—Lieutenant Commander Stepan Lesovskii, commander of the *Diana*, eight officers, and one hundred and fifty men—departed for Kamchatka on the American schooner *Caroline E. Foote*. They arrived safely in Petropavlovsk and continued from there on another American vessel, the merchantman *William Penn*, to De-Kastri Bay. About a month later, on May 8, Putiatin followed with Poset and thirty-nine others on the *Heda*. Ten days before their departure the French steamer *Colbert* arrived at Shimoda, and the Russians were in constant danger of capture. They stole into Petropavlovsk on May 22, as the English and French vessels were already gathering at the mouth of the bay. When they learned that all Russian ships had been ordered to evacuate the port and to seek refuge in De-Kastri Bay, they sailed out again and, under the cover of darkness, slipped past the English squadron. Constantly on the verge of capture, Putiatin and his shipmates finally reached the mouth of the Amur (June 20). At Nikolaevsk they transferred to the cutter *Nadezhda*, leaving instructions that the *Heda* return to Hakodate or Shimoda at the earliest opportunity. After a long and tedious trip Putiatin arrived safely in Moscow on November 10, 1855.

The remainder of the *Diana's* complement, in fact the majority—Lieutenants Aleksandr Musin-Pushkin and Schilling, five fellow officers, the doctor, the linguist, the priest and two hundred and seventy-five men of lower rank—were not so fortunate. They succeeded in chartering the German brig *Greta* from the supercargo Mr. Lühdorf of the Bremen Free State, and set out from Shimoda for Port Aian on July 14, 1855, but on August 1, at the northern extremity of Sakhalin, the dense fog, which had hidden them from the eyes of their enemies, suddenly lifted and they found themselves within reach of an English warship, the man-of-war *Barracouta*. The Russians hid in the hold of the brig, and the German captain raised the American flag, but the British were not that easily fooled. They came aboard and discovered the Russians, given away by some of the Chinese members of the brig's crew. In vain the Russians argued that they were unarmed persons not participating in military operations and that as such, according to international law, they could not be regarded as prisoners of war. The *Greta* was declared a prize and its crew and the Russian seamen distributed on English men-of-war. Aboard these vessels the Russians saw Hakodate and Nagasaki again, but only at a distance because the Japanese did not permit the British to enter the inner roadstead. The priest, the doctor, and the wounded were put ashore at Aian, which had been occupied by the British; the majority of the prisoners were kept aboard the men-of-war, however, and finally taken to England, and did not return to Russia until after the end of war (1856).[51]

Among this unfortunate group of seamen, whose privations during the shipwreck of their frigate had been only a prelude to further suffering, there was a Japanese adventurer by the name of Tachibana Kosai. A man with a checkered past (running the gamut from experiences as a warrior and a Nichiren priest to adventures in gambling, swindling, imprisonment, murder, and women), he had furtively entered into dealings with Goshkevich, teaching him Japanese

[51] A. K. (Aleksandr Kolokoltsov?), "Postroenie shkuny *Kheda* v Iaponii," 279-298; Putiatin, "Vsepoddaneishii otchet," 94-95; Schilling, 266-276, 288-318; Russia, Ministry of the Navy, Naval Scientific Section, "O plavanii v vostochnom okeane general-adiutanta Putiatina i kontr-admirala Zavoiki" (hereinafter cited as Russia, "O plavanii"), 174-187. Schilling, Musin-Pushkin, Goshkevich, Tachibana and one hundred and five men remained at first on the *Barracouta*, two officers and forty men being placed aboard the *Spartan*, the remaining officers and men on board the *Sybille*. At Nagasaki H. M. S. *Nankin* was called upon for transportation to Hong Kong. (J. M. Tronson, *Personal Narrative of a Voyage to Japan*, 139-141) Schilling and some of the captives then proceeded to England on the *Rotler* (?). At Portsmouth they were transferred onto the *Victory* on which Nelson had been killed at the battle of Trafalgar and then onto the huge transport *Emperatrice*, on which they found many other Russian prisoners—some forty officers and over fifteen hundred men—among them Goshkevich. (Schilling, 309-317; Makhov, *Fregat Diana*, 62-63; Mario Emelio Cosenza, *The Complete Journal of Townsend Harris*, 267 note 325.) For a report by Musin-Pushkin, senior officer, to the agent of the Russian-American Company and for the text of the imperial ukase of December 18, 1855 making Putiatin a count, see Lensen, *Russia's Japan Expedition*, 139-141.

and selling him books and even a map of Japan. This was treason by Japanese standards, and when his activities came to light, he sought refuge with the Russians. There is some divergence in Russian sources as to when Tachibana actually did so. Putiatin reported that he came aboard the *Diana* at Hakodate in October of 1854; Schilling and Japanese authorities state that he joined the Russians only at Heda, where he had been living. It is beyond doubt, however, that Putiatin in contrast to Commodore Perry, who refused to take along Yoshida Shoin, permitted Tachibana to remain with him. It was not an easy task to smuggle Tachibana out of Japan, especially after the ship-wreck of the *Diana* forced the Russians to live on shore, in the midst of the inquisitive officialdom. But they disguised him in a black hemp wig and a Russian sailor suit and kept him surrounded by members of the crew. When Japanese officials posted a guard at the well-illuminated wharf and shone a lantern into everyone's face at the time of embarkation, the Russians slipped Tachibana aboard in a crate.

A refugee, rather than a castaway or a prisoner, Tachibana was still a direct successor to the line of Japanese who, since the end of the seventeenth century, had been cast or carried to Russia to play a supporting role in the drama of Russian relations with Japan. During their British captivity Goshkevich worked with Tachibana on the compilation of the first real Japanese-Russian dictionary.[52] Goshkevich had spent nine years in China with the Orthodox Mission in Peking (1839-1848); his study of Chinese no doubt facilitated his efforts in Japanese. With Tachibana's tutoring in captivity and after-wards, Goshkevich had attained a fair degree of proficiency in the language by the time he returned to Hakodate in 1858 as first Russian consul to Japan. Tachibana, meanwhile, changed his name to Vladimir Iosifovich Yamatov, acquired a Russian family, and served variously as official of the Russian Ministry of Foreign Affairs, professor of Japanese at the Imperial University of St. Petersburg, and interpreter on Russian men-of-war.[53]

[52] Entitled *Iaponsko-Russkii slovar'* and *Wa-Ro tsugen hiko*, the dictionary was published by the Asian Department of the Russian Ministry of Foreign Affairs in 1857. For further detail, see Lensen, *Report from Hokkaido*, 65-67, 70-72.

[53] Putiatin, "Vsepoddaneishii otchet," 74; Suzuki Rüchiro, "Tachibana Kosai," undated, unpublished manuscript; Bartold, *Materialy*, 80-95; *Biograficheskii slovar' professorov i prepodavatelei imperatorskago S.-Peterburgskago Universiteta*, II, 362-363; Ramming, "Über den Anteil der Russen," 28-29; Watanabe Shujiro, *Sekai ni okeru Nihonjin*, 350-360; Schilling, 272; F. A. Brokgauz and I. A. Efron, *Entsiklopedicheskii Slovar'*, XLI, 651; Osatake Takeki, *Kokusai-ho yori mitaru Bakumatsu gaiko monogatari*, 476-478. For photographs of Tachibana see Lensen, *Report from Hokkaido*, 68-69. Tachibana returned to Japan in 1874.

The Russian government was well-pleased with the conduct of the Russian Japan Expedition. The officers were decorated, and officers and men received generous financial compensation for personal losses and for "service beyond the line of duty," and Alexander II, who had succeeded Nicholas I to the throne, bestowed on Putiatin and his descendants the title of count to preserve the memory of his services.

More effective in preserving the memory of Putiatin's dealings with the Japanese than such an official pronouncement, were the personal recollections of members of the expedition. Among these the best known are the writings of Goncharov (*Fregat Pallada*) and of Schilling (*Vospominaniia Starago Moriaka*). Goncharov's work became a highly popular book, read especially by the young people of Russia; the fame and style of the author insured it a permanent place in Russian literature. In view of subsequent Russo-Japanese relations this was unfortunate, because *Fregat Pallada* overshadowed, if it did not displace, the less readable, less heroic, but far more penetrating narrative of Golovnin. The fact that Goncharov described only the first half of the expedition is not crucial in itself, though perhaps his participation in the final phase with its closer contact with the Japanese might have modified his views. Goncharov's sketches of the Japanese are masterful and the characters vivid and alive. But unfortunately it was with mockery and ridicule that Goncharov most frequently achieved his effect. He portrayed the Japanese as generally stupid, ludicrous, ugly, childish, and feminine, and though he sympathized with the Japanese desire to be left in peace he did so patronizingly. His comment on the imminent breakdown of Japan's seclusion policy was typical:

They see that their system of locking themselves in and alienation in which alone they sought safety has taught them nothing and only stopped their growth. Like a school plot, it has collapsed instantly with the appearance of the teacher. They are alone, without help. There is nothing for them to do but break out in tears and say: "we are guilty, we are children," and like children put themselves under the guidance of elders.

But who will these elders be? Here are the crafty indefatigable manufacturers, the Americans, and here a handful of Russians: the Russian bayonet, although still peaceful and inoffensive, still a guest, has already sparkled in the rays of the Japanese sun, and on the Japanese shore the command "Forward!" has been heard. *Avis au Japon!*

If not we, then the Americans, if not the Americans, then those who follow them—whoever it might be, is soon fated to pour into the veins of Japan those healthy juices which she has suicidally excreted from her body together with her own blood so that she has grown decrepit in weakness and the gloom of a pitiful childhood.[54]

Golovnin had seen beneath the surface of exoticism; Goncharov had exploited the quaintness of Japanese manners. This is significant because the popularity of Goncharov's writings contributed no doubt to the unfortunate failure of the Russians in later years to take the Japanese seriously.

THE SECOND PUTIATIN EXPEDITION, 1858-1859

The Treaty of Amity between Russia and Japan, concluded by Putiatin on February 7, 1855, provided that ratifications thereof be exchanged in Shimoda "not sooner than in nine months or as circumstances will permit." On November 8, 1856, Captain Poset returned to Shimoda with the ratified copy of the treaty. He came on the corvet *Olivutsa*, by now "a poor affair, old in age and older in model," accompanied by a pretty schooner, built at the Amur River as a gift for the Japanese.

Shortly after his arrival Poset was welcomed by a fellow-Westerner—Townsend Harris, the first American consul general and minister to Japan. A New York businessman and one-time president of the Board of Education, Harris had transferred his commercial activities to Southeast Asia and China in the late 1840's and in 1854 had been appointed consul in Ningpo. Dissatisfied with this position, he had actively sought and finally received, through influential political friends, appointment as consul general to Japan. Though aware of the social banishment and mental isolation, which awaited him in Japan, and resolved to meet it, Harris had not been prepared for the objections that the Japanese were to raise to his very arrival in the autumn of 1856.[55] This Japanese opposition was a reflection of internal political problems and also a difference in interpretation of Article XI of the treaty with the United States. The treaty stipulated the appointment of American consuls or agents to reside in Shimoda "provided that either of the two governments deem such arrangement necessary"; in the Japanese text this clause remained without a subject and the decision, as to whether or not such appoint-

[54] Goncharov, *Fregat Pallada*, 56-57.
[55] Tyler Dennett, *Americans in Eastern Asia*, 348-352.

ment was necessary, could be interpreted variously as being the prerogative of both the United States and Japan or of only the United States or of only Japan.[56] It was with the anticipation of companionship and support rather than with fear of competition that Harris welcomed Poset. Anglophobic in upbringing—his grandmother had raised him "to tell the truth, fear God, and hate the British"—Harris was "much pleased" with the officers on his first visit, and remained well-disposed toward them. After entertaining several of them for dinner, he recorded in his diary: "I never passed a more agreeable evening. The Russians behaved like polished men of the world, and at my table they did not merit the charge so often brought against them of being hard drinkers. They ate with good appetites (and my dinner was both good and abundant), and took their wine in moderation. I do think the same number of American and English officers would have drunk twice the quantity of wine the Russians did." Another time he wrote: "The more I see of the Russian officers the more I am pleased with them. They are polished in manner and exceedingly well informed. There is scarcely one of them that does not speak two or more languages."[57]

Harris was an ailing and lonely man, ostracized by the Japanese, and scandalously neglected by his own government, which only a few years before had seemed so interested in Japan. "I am a prey of unceasing anxiety," he confided to his diary (May 5, 1857). "I have not heard from Washington since I left the United States, say October 1855." The companionship of Western gentlemen thus meant a great deal to Harris, and, unlike Perry, he did not turn down Russian assistance. The Russians loaned Harris barometers and other instruments, presented him with a thermometer, offered him as a gift one of the boats of the *Diana* (Harris declined the offer as the boats were too heavy for his use), set up the rigging and stays of the American flagstaff, sent him Hakodate potatoes and spirits of turpentine, and, last but not least, offered him the services of the ship's surgeon. When Harris and his secretary, Henry C. J. Heusken dined aboard the corvet, Poset honored Harris with a salute of thirteen guns—rules of the Russian service entitled him to a salute of eleven guns only—so that he would not receive less than the governor of Shimoda.

Harris in turn gave the Russians some coffee, a Siamese sarong, and Siamese coins, lent them over eighteen hundred Mexican dol-

---

[56] Borton, 45 note 10.   [57] Cosenza, 260-270.

lars, offered the two captains the services of his washman "as the Japanese do not know how to wash," sent them valuable books about Japan, and, when they were about to leave, gave them letters of introduction to persons in Macao and Hong Kong and sent his "rascally" tailor on board the corvette.

More important than this exchange of gifts and favors was the cooperation between Harris and the Russians in their dealings with the Japanese. They shared information about past developments, the Russians giving Harris a Dutch copy of their treaty with Japan, telling him that within the past eighteen months nearly fifty letters had been sent to Russia by the Japanese, and providing him with a copy of the letter Poset had written to the Japanese authorities concerning Shimoda after the shipwreck of the *Diana*; while Harris gave them copies of the American and Dutch treaties with Japan, and the treaty with Siam, which he had concluded at Bangkok. They kept each other informed also of their current negotiations with the Japanese and often collaborated in the determination of a certain policy. For example, Poset agreed to pay the Japanese no more than the currency exchange ratio proposed by Harris; if the Japanese were not satisfied he would place the difference in Harris' hands, until the final settlement of the matter. "I am much pleased with this," Harris recorded, "as it will greatly strengthen my demands for the adjustment of the question."

Neither Perry nor Putiatin had truly opened Japan. It was Townsend Harris who did so, with dogged patience and unarmed tenacity, occasional threats of the danger to Japan of the impatience of other powers, in case she delayed further, being his only weapon. The negotiations of Poset with the Japanese contributed to Harris' ultimate success. "Constant conversations are held by Captain Possiet with the Japanese on the subject of finally and fully opening Japan to the commerce of the world," Harris wrote on November 14, 1856. "All agree that it is only a question of time, and Moriyama Yenosuke [Einosuke] goes so far as to place it less than three years distant. All these things will help prepare the way for me in my attempt to make a treaty which shall at once open Japan (at different dates for different ports) to our commerce." When the Japanese tried to renege on some of the concessions already made, and asked Poset to order that none of his officers sleep on shore, he held his ground and firmly claimed the right, within the agreed circumference, "to sleep on shore as often as it suited their convenience." When an official began to shadow Poset and the secretary of the American legation on a walk, Poset ordered the Japanese away and, when he returned, seized him and gave him a thorough shaking, so that the official, when he was released, "started off running like a deer and no more appeared."[58]

Putiatin had recommended to his government that the cannons saved from the *Diana* be given to Japan as a gift in token of Russian friendship and of appreciation of Japanese help. On November 22, 1856 Poset formally transferred these guns to the Japanese and helped them in setting up all the necessary fittings for mounting the weapons.[59] On December 5, Poset invited Harris to "assist" on the occasion of the exchange of ratifications of the Russo-Japanese treaty. But as the ceremony was scheduled for a Sunday (December 7), Harris, who had consistently refused to attend any kind of business on that day, could not participate without contradicting all his previous acts and losing his reputation for consistency, "a point that cannot be too carefully watched in dealing with people like the Japanese." As Poset landed on December 7 at about 11 a. m., the *Olivutsa* fired a salute and two hours later another salute of twenty-one guns was fired in honor of the exchange of ratifications, with the Russian, American, and Japanese flags flying from the vessel's masts. After the exchange of ratifications, the *Diana's* neatly-furbished guns, over which a double honor guard of Russians and Japanese had been mounted, were formally presented to the Japanese. "The commissioners then attended the Commodore to the corvette, where they received a salute and a dinner, and thus completed the ceremonies of the day."

On December 13, Harris went aboard the *Olivutsa* to see the Russians off, but the wind was unfavorable and they could not clear the harbor. Not feeling well, he bid adieu to all and went on shore. Again Harris was alone. "I am only nine days distant from Hongkong, yet I am more isolated than any American official in any part of the world." He looked forward to the arrival of the Russian consul, having been told that he was very friendly toward Americans and spoke English fluently. On May 5, 1857 he recorded: "What can be the cause of this prolonged absence of an American man-of-war? Where

[58] *Ibid.*, 262-270, 274, 278-281, 288-290, 357-358.

[59] Putiatin, "Vsepoddaneishii otchet," 94; Cosenza, 276. Harris lists the guns as eighteen short 24-pounders, thirty long 24-pounders, and four Paixhan 68-pounders, shell guns. For a photograph of some of these guns and an account of their disposition in later years, see Lensen, *Report from Hokkaido*, 59-60; a different photograph may be found in Osatake, *Kokusai-ho yori*, 272-273.

are the English? Where the French? And, above all, where is the Russian consul? He should have been here before this."[60]

Iosif Goshkevich, to whom Harris referred, did not reach Japan until the autumn of 1858, and then did not settle in Shimoda, but closer to Russia, in Hakodate. Before this, however, Putiatin revisited Japan, including Shimoda. First on September 21, 1857, he arrived in Nagasaki. There the Dutch had been negotiating throughout the summer in an attempt to open Japan to trade. As the Dutch seemed willing to content themselves with limited commerce somewhat reminiscent of the Deshima trade, conducted through local officials and confined to Nagasaki and Hakodate only, Mizuno Tadanori and other Japanese negotiators urged on their government the speedy conclusion of a treaty on such lines, to create a precedent and a model for treaties demanded by Great Britain and the United States. The arrival of Putiatin brought Japanese deliberations to a head, and Mizuno, Arao Narimasa, and Iwase Tadanari, who in 1854 had been among those who had favored an alliance with Russia, hastily recommended to the Supreme Council the conclusion of a treaty with Putiatin also, in the belief that a treaty signed by both Holland and Russia would be a more persuasive model in their negotiations with other powers. "If an agreement is concluded with Russia as well as with Holland and the pattern of trade is thus established by two models [rather than one], then even if the English, French, and others come subsequently and conduct separate discussions, it is not easy to see how they could with propiety find occasion for the use of force." The officials did not fail to remind the Supreme Council furthermore that Putiatin had been promised during his earlier negotiations with Tsutsui and Kawaji that "should Japan ever decide to permit trade with foreign countries, Russia would be granted it before the other powers." To negotiate with the Dutch without negotiating with the Russians would be impolitic, especially as once a treaty with the Dutch was concluded, Japan would have to notify the Russians anyway. It seemed to the officials, therefore, that the arrival of the Russian warship was "in some degree fortunate."

Even if Putiatin does not bring up the question of trade, we should, by broaching the subject ourselves, be keeping our word in accordance with the promise previously made to him, which would be both proper and advisable. And though we realize that we must never open discussion

[60] Cosenza, 264, 285-286, 290, 357-358.

of the subject ourselves while still not in receipt of your instructions, yet if by the nature of Putiatin's demands we are left no choice but to discuss it, then we shall handle the negotiations in the manner that seems best calculated to serve the Shogunate's future interests.

Soon after the dispatch of this note, with the content of which he was unacquainted, Putiatin departed for China. When he returned to Nagasaki on October 11 of the same year, the Japanese officials had as yet received no reply from the Shogunate, but they ventured to assume that silence meant approval, and on their own signed the agreement with the Dutch and a similar one with Putiatin. In a letter to Kawaji, who had concluded the first treaty with Putiatin, Mizuno promised to negotiate an agreement which "will preserve the Shogunate's dignity, cause no difficulties when applied to other countries, and avoid inconvenience for the future."

Nevertheless, as we have said in our official report, it is an act of the greatest temerity on our part to decide a matter of such immense importance on our own responsibility and before receiving the Shogunate's instructions. Yet nothing could be worse than to cause the Shogunate further difficulties and we have therefore all resolved to take this step even though it cost us our lives. If, however, what we have done should prove contrary in substance to present government policy, even the sacrifice of our lives could not justify us. Since this step is our responsibility alone you can, when next you send us orders, send us where you will, regardless of our personal fate, whether it be to Putiatin or to the Russian monarch, to explain this and to withdraw the agreement. And yet I fear that once matters have been mismanaged, though only here in this distant province, all else would be of no avail.

Since we have formed our resolution on these lines and are acting upon it, we ask that if our action seems wrong and contrary to the present ideas of the Shogunate, you may accord us the severest treatment, that we may serve as a warning to others. We do not ask for any leniency. There is but this. Although we said, in the reports sent by previous mail concerning the expected arrival of the English and the attitude of Putiatin, that we would take no decisive action before receiving Shogunate orders, the fact that to this day we have still received no orders might mean that the views of the Shogunate do not greatly differ from our own in substance. Moreover, before I was sent here, [Kawaji] Saemon-no-jo allowed me to see a report from which I understood that he has no immediate objections to such a course. And recently I had word from [Toki] Lord of Tamba to the same effect. It is these indications alone that encourage me to hope that we may have a chance of escaping punishment.[61]

---

[61] Beasley, *Select Documents*, 28-30, 144-149.

The new treaty between Russia and Japan was concluded on October 24, 1857. It was not yet a full-fledged commercial agreement but a "supplementary treaty" to the Treaty of Shimoda. Signed by Putiatin, Mizuno, Arao and Iwase, it enacted "for the promotion of trade and of relations between Russia and Japan on more durable foundations" a set of new regulations by which relations between Russians and Japanese were to be governed in Hakodate and Nagasaki, leaving relations in Shimoda on the same basis as before, until it was determined whether Shimoda would or would not be replaced by a more sheltered harbor.

Less than a year later, on July 29, 1858, Townsend Harris succeeded in concluding a commercial treaty with Japan that went beyond the "model" that the plenipotentiaries had hoped the supplementary treaty to be. Putiatin, who was at the time in China, where he had concluded a treaty of peace, friendship, commerce, and navigation (June 13, 1858), hurried to Japan when he learned of Harris's accomplishment. Although Russia, by virtue of the most-favored-nation clause of the Treaty of Shimoda, was entitled to the same concessions without further negotiation, Putiatin hastened to formalize the establishment of commercial relations, spurred on by reports that the English and the French were about to come to Japan also.

The competition of Russia, the United States, and other powers to be first in coming to various agreements with the Japanese was motivated less by the desire to be first as such, or by fear that the first to conclude a treaty would gain inordinate concessions, than by the wish to be the one to determine the direction in which future relations with Japan would be channeled. As one Russian naval officer put it (though not quite accurately):

> In dealing with eastern peoples in general and with the Chinese and the Japanese in particular, it is of importance to come earlier than the others, and make use of all the advantages or freedom in the negotiations, unimpeded by treaties of other nations previously concluded, because the people of the East, concluding treaties against their will, making no distinction between nations, not understanding as yet the advantages and not seeing the purpose of relations with foreigners, do not agree in any way to the slightest deviation from the original conclusion of a treaty, though this deviation be in their own interest.[62]

Stopping in Nagasaki for only three days to replenish the coal supply, Putiatin headed for Kanagawa Harbor at the gates of the

---

[62] Lieutenant Litke, "Fregat 'Askold' v Iaponii," 11:331.

capital. Three years earlier his arrival in Nagasaki, not to mention the expressed intention of continuing to Edo Bay, would have caused alarm and consternation. But now the visit of the frigate *Askold*, his flagship, created no excitement whatsoever. At Shimoda, where the vessel cast anchor, on July 26, 1858, side by side with the American men-of-war *Mississsippi* and *Powhatan*, Governor Nakamura Tameya, with whom Putiatin had become acquainted during his previous negotiations in the city, came aboard and welcomed the admiral with extended arms, shouting "Putiatin! Putiatin!" in his hoarse voice. When Putiatin made him a present of a group photograph of the officers of the frigate *Pallada* (who, with the exception of Unkovskii had also officered the *Diana*) his joy was boundless. Other Japanese inquired with great interest after those mariners who had not returned, remembered them all by name, repeated Russian words, and eagerly learned new ones. Many of them had written Russian alphabets which they knew well.[63]

Nakamura did not protest Putiatin's intention to proceed to the capital, but he asked Putiatin to wait in Shimoda three or four days to give him time to send word ahead of his coming. To this Putiatin agreed, if only to spare Nakamura from trouble with his own government. On July 30 the *Askold* sailed across to Kanagawa with several Japanese aboard. The same day Japanese plenipotentiaries also arrived in Kanagawa from Edo on the side-wheeler *Kanko Maru*, the first Japanese warship of modern times.[64] For almost two weeks Putiatin engaged in preliminary talks with the plenipotentiaries on board the *Askold*. When everything was ready for his reception in the capital itself, Putiatin joined the procession overland with his two secretaries, the commanders of the *Askold* and of the corvet *Strelok*, which had joined the frigate at Kanagawa, and five officers.

This was not the first Japanese procession in which the Russians had traveled, but it was the first time that they were permitted to enter the capital. The Japanese had provided Putiatin and his entourage with *norimono*—that of the admiral carried by eight bearers, the others by four—but the Russians were too big and too un-

---

[63] Russia, Ministry of the Navy, Naval Scientific Section, "Pis'mo s fregata 'Askold,'" 164; Litke, 11: 332. Nakamura Tameya (called incorrectly Nakashura-Dewano-kami in the letter) had conferred both with the Russians and the Americans. In 1857 he had been promoted from financial examiner to governor of Shimoda.

[64] Litke, 11: 333-334; Mizuno, "The Japanese Navy," 418. The *Kanko Maru* had been obtained by the Japanese from Holland. It was the former Dutch man-of-war *Soembing*. The Shogunate had three other warships of European construction by this time.

accustomed to this mode of transportation to ride in comfort and walked most of the way. The Dutch, who had visited the capital periodically, had not been permitted to look out of the litters, much less to walk outside in open view of everyone. As the Russians now approached Edo, therefore, the populace was even more interested in them than they in the populace. Mounting crowds of Japanese lined the road on which they passed, touched their clothing, and examined their boots, wondering no doubt whether there was truth to the rumor that Westerners had no heels. Eventually the crowds became so dense and their curiosity so intense that the Russians sought refuge in the uncomfortable *norimono*. On August 12 the Russians at last entered the Japanese capital "with that feeling of pride and strength which comes from the realization of one's moral superiority before ignorance."[65]

The Russians were housed in the Shiba Shimbuku Temple where the negotiations, begun on the frigate, were resumed shortly with Nagai Naomune, Lord of Gemba, a highly intelligent Japanese statesman, who spoke Dutch and English and was familiar with the structure of European governments and the habits and customs of "civilized" nations. On August 19, 1858, the Russo-Japanese Treaty of Friendship and Commerce (variously known as the Ansei Treaty or the Edo Alliance) was concluded. Signed by Putiatin and Nagai, as well as Inoue, Lord of Shinano, Hori, Lord of Oribe, Iwase, Lord of Higo, and Tsuda Hanzaburo, its provisions included: the exchange and permanent residence of diplomatic and consular agents, the opening of Kanagawa, Hyogo, and one other, unspecified, port in western Honshu (the first two in addition to Hakodate and Nagasaki, the third in place of Shimoda) in 1859, 1863, and 1860 respectively; the admittance of families; permanent residence in the open ports; freedom of movement within specified geographical limits; the leasing of land; the renting, buying, or building of houses, stores, and churches; residence in Edo and Osaka for commercial purposes only, as of 1862 and 1863 respectively; trade without government interference; the determination of import and export tariffs; the prohibition of traffic in opium; the sale of arms to no one but the Japanese government and foreigners; the prohibition of rice, wheat, and copper exportation; the acceptance of foreign cur-

---

[65] Inazo Nitobe mentions how even in later years Japanese speculated still whether Westerners had heels and whether they needed boots to stand erect. (*Reminiscences of Childhood*, 11-12.)

rency; extraterritoriality; and reciprocal most-favored-nation treatment.[66] It was stipulated that the treaty could be revised after 1872, but, though the appended tariff was superseded by the convention of 1867 and the treaty as a whole was modified by new commercial agreements in 1889 and 1895, the main body of the treaty of 1858 governed relations between Russia and Japan until 1904.

The negotiation of this basic treaty was crowned by a meeting of the Russian envoy with the members of the Supreme Council, his reception by Tokugawa Keifuku (later known as Iemochi), the young heir apparent of Shogun Tokugawa Iesada, and a farewell dinner. On August 20 Putiatin returned to Kanagawa, escorted by a colorful paper-lantern procession.

During Putiatin's stay in Edo, those officers, who had accompanied him, had seen some exciting sights. They had even obtained printed Japanese maps, and, guided by these, had toured the capital and had ridden into the surrounding countryside. But those who had stayed on the vessels were not permitted by the Japanese to visit Kanagawa and had been restricted to Yokohama, a picturesque, but as yet practically uninhabited area, separated from Kanagawa by a broad plain and a small river. Though treated to tea and fruit by the Japanese officials, they had no contact with the inhabitants of Japan and found diversion primarily in riding about the Kanagawa roadstead in their boats. It was with impatience, therefore, that the men of the *Askold* and the *Strelok* awaited Putiatin's return and were anxious for the termination of their dull month-long anchorage.[67]

On August 22 Putiatin departed for Shanghai on the clipper *Strelok*, while the frigate *Askold* made preparations to leave for Hakodate. The *Strelok* got only as far as Shimoda, however. Boiler damage and the inability to continue to China solely by sail in the face of rough seas and strong unfavorable winds, forced her to turn back. On his return to Kanagawa on August 24, Putiatin moved aboard the

---

[66] For the complete text of the treaty, see Appendix III. The treaty follows the pattern of the American treaty of the same year. There are minor divergences, such as American preference for July 4 as opening date for most of the harbors. Article II of the American treaty is of particular interest. It states that "the President of the United States, at the request of the Japanese Government, will act as a friendly mediator in such matters of difference as may arise between the Government of Japan and any European power" and that "the ships of war of the United States shall render friendly aid and assistance to such Japanese vessels as they may meet on high seas, so far as can be done without a breach of neutrality." (Malloy, I, 1001.)

[67] Litke, II: 334-338.

Askold, and the following day, on August 25, set out for Shanghai again. The high seas and stormy weather spelled trouble for the frigate as well. A raging typhoon almost sent her to the bottom and she limped into Wusung Harbor seriously crippled. An early return of the frigate to Russia was now out of the question, and as soon as Putiatin had departed on a mail steamer, the *Askold* sailed back to Japan for repairs, driven from the Chinese coast by its high prices and bad climate.[68]

As Putiatin headed back to Russia, having himself negotiated the original Treaty of Amity, the Supplementary Treaty, and the Treaty of Commerce and Navigation, he left behind a good and lasting impression; the esteem in which he was held in Japan exceeding his reputation in China, if not in his own country. It was no doubt a reflection of Japanese confidence in Putiatin himself that, particular as the Japanese always had been in the verification of credentials, they concluded the commercial treaty with Putiatin without his being formally empowered to negotiate with them. As one of the Russian officers put it, evaluating Putiatin's accomplishments in the Far East:

In such a short time he has brought Russia here so much benefit! Japan may perhaps not see him again, but it will not soon forget the name of Count Putiatin. The treaty, concluded without formal plenipotence to the Japanese government, demonstrates to what extent the admiral had been able to inspire the trust and respect of the Japanese toward himself during his first stay in this country.[69]

[68] Pompe van Meerdervoort estimated that repairs in Shanghai would have cost ten times as much as in Nagasaki. (J. L. C. Pompe van Meerdervoort, *Vijf Jaren in Japan*, II, 129.)

[69] Litke, II: 338.

CHAPTER TEN · IN OPENED JAPAN

IN NAGASAKI

THE first Russians to live in Japan after the treaty of 1858 were the men of the *Askold*, who returned from China to repair the frigate. They ran into bad weather with heavy seas and when they finally reached Nagasaki were ill and exhausted. The vessel was badly in need of repair and the outbreak of a severe epidemic of malignant malaria and dysentery threatened to destroy the crew. Had it not been for the rest and recuperation which the climate, hospitality, and facilities of Nagasaki offered, more than half of the Russians, Dr. Vitovskii estimates, would have died and the rest might never have succeeded in returning to Russia. As it was, the number of men, who died in Nagasaki during the following eight months, was so large that "the graveyard there was transformed from a Dutch one into a Russian one."[1]

The men of the *Askold* were well received in Nagasaki and there was no delay in permitting the captain to see the governor. The successful rehabilitation of the vessel and crew depended on the cooperation of the Japanese authorities. It was a great relief, therefore, when the governor showed himself well-disposed toward the Russians.

Here we experienced again and could fully appreciate that tremendous influence of Russians in Japan, which was spread and left for us as heritage by Count Putiatin, during his twofold stay in Japan [wrote Lieutenant Litke]. By his wise orders, just demands and courteous, modest, but at the same time firm and persistent conduct, the count won the confidence and goodwill of the Japanese; all his subordinates tried to imitate him in this, in so far as possible. There is no doubt, that the governor has received orders to treat us as well as possible, because we could not even have expected from him more amiableness and desire to help us, not to mention the fact, that right after the visit of the captain, he came aboard the frigate and even agreed to have dinner with the captain. Immediately after the first meeting there was assigned to us one of the highest officials of the city, through whom all our demands had to be carried out, and from that day on, one can say, there was no delay in anything, except for the inherent Japanese slowness in whatever they do.[2]

Urgent as the repair of the frigate was, it was obvious that it could

[1] Russia, Ministry of the Navy, Naval Scientific Section, "Russkii beregovoi lazaret v Nagasaki," 91-93.
[2] Litke, 11: 343-344.

not be begun until a majority of the mariners had recovered their strength. This was impossible in the cramped living conditions aboard ship and the governor assigned a place on land to the sick, ideally situated above the noise and dirt of the city, and wide open to the healing rays of the sun. Nor were accommodations on land confined to the sick. The officers were quartered in the monks' dormitory of Goshin Temple (the bonzes being moved to the temple proper) and the crew was housed in two barracks, constructed nearby. A level plot of land facing the moorage was sold to the Russians to provide them with space for a small "admiralty" and a supply dump. In contrast to Putiatin's futile efforts to obtain such a place before the opening of the country, the Japanese had made a proposition even more remarkable in the light of their traditional efforts to isolate all foreigners from intercourse with the populace. They had suggested that the officers be put up in private houses in the city itself. But the Russians declined this unusual offer, for fear that the separation of officers and sailors be inconvenient to the officers if not demoralizing to the men.[3]

At the entrance to the temple grounds the Russians erected a tall flagpole, mounted an armed guard, and hoisted the Russian flag, which was visible from everywhere on the roadstead. Nothing so accentuated the change in Russo-Japanese relations effected by the treaties of 1858, as the unopposed landing of Russian artillery—two mountain howitzers and a longboat gun. Litke remarked: "The cannons which had been landed, as well as the guns and the carbines—without, of course, any hostile objective—gave a more military appearance and independent position to our small colony in the eyes both of the Japanese and of the foreigners; these cannons were the first yet to be brought ashore by foreigners without the least protest on the part of the city authorities and even without their notification." Nor did the Japanese object when the Russians, having posted the howitzers before the entrance to the captain's quarters and the longboat gun on the large square behind the low stone enclosure which surrounded the temple grounds, proceeded to fire the longboat gun daily at noon and at sunset. Japanese law still forbade the slaughter of cattle, but when the Russians pleaded that "it is extremely difficult for Europeans to live without meat," the Japanese consented to sell them cattle and let it graze and fatten in one part of the compound, pro-

---

[3] *Ibid.*, 11: 344-346; Russia, "Russkii beregovoi lazaret," 91.

vided the Russians themselves would do the butchering. Gradually the police official, who was posted within the compound to keep Russian actions within the limits of Japanese laws, dropped his role of overseer and became more of an assistant to the captain. "In a word," Litke wrote, "the whole place belonging to the temple and surrounded by the enclosure became totally a Russian settlement; here there were Russian ways and customs, and the inhabitants were governed by Russian laws." When the Russians celebrated the official opening of their "colony" with a banquet for the Japanese city authorities and the Dutch (the only other Westerners then living in Nagasaki), the governor and his replacement joined in the festivities—the first time, since the seclusion of the country, that a Japanese governor had visited foreigners on shore.

And so two Japanese governors and twenty senior officials of the city dined in European style at the place of the Russian captain. When a toast was given to the health of the Russian and Japanese emperors, salutes were fired from the mountain howitzers, which stood in the small courtyard. The dinner lasted for a long time. The guests were gay and parted late in the evening, having forgotten, at least outwardly, their old habits and customs. Rockets and bengal lights accompanied them all the way to the wharf.[4]

The hospitable reception of the men of the *Askold* in Nagasaki was the result of Japan's new policy, stemming from the confidence created by the Putiatin expeditions. It was an important step in the history of foreign relations, offering Westerners a freedom of action to an extent unknown before in modern Japan. Needless to say other Westerners watched the Russian activities with attention and not without misgivings. The impression received by Sir Rutherford Alcock, the British consul general, upon a visit to the Russian settlement in Nagasaki in June of 1859 is interesting:

If the Russians, as some have surmised, intended a permanent settlement, it could not have been better chosen; but I saw nothing to indicate more than what it professed to be—a temporary location for the crew of the frigate 'Aschol,' requiring a thorough repair and refit; for which this retired and snug bay was admirably adapted. They had been here some months, and this had evidently been made the rendezvous for a Commodore's squadron, consisting of the frigate and half a dozen corvettes and gunboats—supposed to be on their way to the Amoor. I dare say, being here in force, the Russian had had it pretty much his own way—and obtained what supplies he wanted,—with fair words or the strong hand,

4 Litke, 11: 345-348.

as the case might require. But, under similar circumstances, the same thing would probably have been done by the senior officer of any other foreign squadron.[5]

The favorable location of the lazaret, the healthy climate, and rest gradually restored the health of the seamen, so that a month and a half after their arrival "even the memory of the epidemic had disappeared."[6] Not all aspects of Japanese hospitality were propitious, however, and soon an alarming number of sailors were bedridden with a new disease, "the causes of which were no longer conditions aboard ship, but conditions of the very life on shore." More than one quarter of the men, who had survived the epidemic unscathed, had contracted syphilis. The treatment of this disease with mercury proved "quite satisfactory," but it was difficult to effect cures because "the sick were running away from the hospital into a near-by brothel, and bonzes and other Japanese were bringing alcoholic beverages to the hospital."[7]

In November of 1858 repairs were finally begun. There were three major projects on which the Russians labored simultaneously: carpenter-work aboard the frigate itself, mastwork done near the "admiralty," and sloop work executed near the temple. It was an enormous task, hindered by the shortage of shipwrights (carpenters having to be trained by the few experts from among the crew at large), slowness in the delivery of the necessary materials, and the discovery of further rot. The Japanese and the Dutch considered the task impossible. Yet by dint of hard work and high morale the men of the *Askold* overcame all the obstacles, and by June of 1859 the frigate could be reloaded and rearmed. On June 26, the *Askold* pulled out into the roadstead, fully prepared to undertake any kind of voyage.[8]

The Russians, like the Japanese, enjoy singing, and the seamen returned from the day's labors, singing gay sea chanteys. There was a great celebration when the clippers *Dzhigit* and *Strelok* arrived at New Year and for four days the Russians made merry with their countrymen. There were those among the new arrivals, who had been in Japan before, and marvelled at the change. They visited the Japanese corvet *Edo* and several hours later her captain returned the call. "The commander of the *Edo*," wrote one of the men from the *Dzhigit*, "came in patent leather shoes, chamois-leather gloves

---

[5] Sir Rutherford Alcock, *The Capital of the Tycoon*, I, 84.
[6] Litke, 11: 344.   [7] Russia, "Russkii beregovoi lazaret," 92-95.
[8] Litke, 12: 156-161; 13: 391.

and, not finding the captain at home, left his card with one corner folded. Recognize here the former Japanese!"[9] On their first visit to Japan with Putiatin, the men of the *Askold* had neither time nor opportunity to mingle with the people. But now, as in 1855, when the shipwreck of the *Diana* and the construction of the schooner had thrown the Russians and Japanese together, there was an opportunity for extensive personal contacts. Nagasaki was large, the legal prohibitions on intercourse with foreigners had been lifted, and the Russians found the Japanese generally well-disposed toward them.

As their oldest acquaintances, the first who had settled on shore for a longer period of time and had entered into the closest relations with them, we enjoyed the utmost confidence and respect of the private inhabitants of Nagasaki as well as of government personnel. In regard to the former we could notice this from the good and polite reception which we constantly met in whatever private home we happened to enter. In stores we bought various things better and cheaper than other foreigners; several objects which the Japanese were not permitted to sell to foreigners they secretly brought to the temple at our request, and we had occasion thus to obtain different things [such as swords] for foreign acquaintances who had tried in vain to get them in stores. As regards officials, the preference which they gave us before all other nations which visited Nagasaki was obvious. In all their difficulties with foreigners they usually turned to us for advice before reaching a decision. Often, merely to oblige us, they satisfied demands which were not in accordance with their laws and customs, and in general, by all their actions, showed respect and trust [toward us].[10]

The Japanese acceptance of the Russians and fraternization with them was furthered by the noncommercial attitude of the Russians in Japan and by general conditions in opened Japan at that time. Japanese arguments against the immediate opening of the country may or may not have been sincere, but the apprehension that unrestricted foreign trade would not be to the advantage of Japan was proved justified. In the decade following the establishment of commercial relations, foreign merchants, especially the British, drew most of the profits, leaving the Japanese viewing with alarm the scarcity of goods, rising prices, and the disturbing outflow of gold—a million gold pieces being exported from Japan during the last six months of 1859 alone.[11] As a result, foreign merchants were not popular, although most of the foreigners, who visited Nagasaki, were merchants. In contrast, the Russians were represented exclusively by naval

[9] N. K. "Iz Iaponii," 14.   [10] Litke, 13: 394.   [11] Borton, 59-60.

personnel and bureaucratic officials. The misconception, which spread among the Japanese, that there was no merchant class in Russia elevated the Russians in Japanese esteem. Nor was this merely a matter of Japanese ignorance, for there was a definite meeting of minds in regard to private commerce, Russian naval officers and bureaucrats sharing in full the well-known disdain of the samurai for merchants, and inveighing frequently against English and American "shopkeepers."[12] In this they were supported by the fact that among the traders, who came to Japan in these years, there were many adventurous characters concerned with nothing but personal gain. It is commonly believed that the failure of Russian merchantmen to follow up the opening of the country had made the Japanese suspect that Russian pleas for trade had been merely a pretext for more sinister designs. This was not the case in the late 1850's. The Japanese had their fill of foreign merchants and were glad rather than fearful that the Russian vessels, which frequented Japanese ports, were warships rather than merchantmen.

Russian popularity was enhanced by the unfortunate character of the transient foreign community. In the words of Sir Rutherford Alcock, "nothing could have been worse than the conduct of the body [of foreigners] generally; and the acts of many individuals are altogether disgraceful."[13] American sailors who had represented the United States in the Far East in the early days of the republic had been, according to an American historian, "good, average American-born citizens, recruited either from the sea-faring population or from the farms," and thus had been "quite unlike the crews of the British Indiamen, recruited from the dregs of English cities, which at Canton spread terror in their path, creating no end of trouble for the British authorities and even imperilling the continuance of trade itself," but "the American sailor of the early fifties in China had all the vices of the English sailor, plus initiative and liberty."[14] It is not surprising, therefore, that the good name of the United States should have been compromised by the wanton destruction of property and by assaults on shopkeepers on the part of sailors from the men-of-war *Mississippi* and *Powhatan*; that of Great Britain by the attempt of an Englishman to smuggle opium into Japan, the passing of forged assignments in payment for Japanese goods by another Englishman and the wound-

---

[12] See for example K. Skalkovskii, *Russkaia torgovlia v Tikhom okeane*, 358.

[13] P. J. Treat, *Diplomatic Relations between the United States and Japan*, I, 102 note 64.

[14] Dennett, 15.

ing of a Japanese guide during a hunt by a third Englishman; and that of France by a French merchant's transportation of his Japanese maid to Shanghai.

Not all Japanese were sophisticated enough to differentiate between the Russians and other "barbarians." Thus a Russian ensign, who had trespassed into the courtyard of one of the noble houses, was promptly ejected by officials within. The Russian was in the wrong, such intrusion being expressly prohibited by treaty. Nevertheless his captain was aroused by the Japanese action and decided on "swift and strict punishment." Normally he made it a point of seeking redress through the Japanese authorities, but now he commanded the officials, who had ejected the midshipman, to report to him without delay and threatened to level their house with gunfire, if they did not appear at once. When they came, he deprived them of their swords and held them prisoner, until a representative of their master, the lord of Chikuzen, had made a public apology in the lord's name and had promised that the officials would be punished in accordance with Japanese law. Highhanded as this action of the Russian captain may have been, it would have been far less provoking had the captain not felt called upon to advise the Japanese in another matter soon afterward. The secretary of the Dutch commissioner had slapped the face of a Japanese official. When the Japanese authorities planned to punish this insult in a manner corresponding to the Russian example, the captain informed them that such measures were not taken among European nations, that a foreigner could not be confined unless his government had been notified beforehand, and that every member of an embassay or commissariat was further protected by diplomatic immunity, the violation of which would rupture friendly relations between the states concerned. When the Japanese referred to the measures the captain himself had taken recently, he brushed aside their objections and warned that Russia had an alliance with the Dutch, that the rulers of the two countries were even related, and that, if the Japanese dared so much as touch a single hair of the secretary's head, the Russians would demand satisfaction, if need be, by open force. The reason for the captain's behavior is reflected in the words of Litke: "Here there were neither Hollanders, nor Russians, nor Englishmen, in a word, there was not a separate nation; there were Europeans who found themselves all without exception in alliance with each other for the attainment of a common purpose." The double standard applied by the captain was not peculiar; it was characteristic of the international law of the West in the age of imperialism. Nevertheless there was more unintentional encouragement to the Japanese pride than the captain could have imagined, when he remarked to the Japanese ironically that they could proceed as they wished, without concern for the laws and customs of "civilized" nations, once their shores were studded with guns and protected by a powerful fleet, but that until then, such action would be "careless."

Whatever resentment the captain's double standard had aroused was dramatically wiped away by the heroic conduct of the Russian crew in helping to save Nagasaki from a sudden conflagration, which destroyed most of the Dutch buildings on Deshima. Awakened in the middle of the night by the frantic shouts of the monks, the Russians rushed to the great fire, which they could see on the other side of the bay, bringing their own buckets, mats, axes, and fire pumps. Within half an hour the first Russian boat arrived at Deshima. Litke recalled:

The picture, which we found, was both terrible and funny. Several houses had already burned down; the fire was spreading with invincible speed. The poor Dutchmen had lost their heads, rushed from one end to the other, having neither men nor instruments and thus means of containing the fire. The Japanese, on the other hand, who had come running in masses from the city, were afraid to come near. Their fire brigades in distinguished many colored costumes with lanterns on long poles and with huge boat-hooks stood lined up along the street, without moving from their place, and only made noise and shouted.

Seeing such disorder the captain took charge. The seamen rushed into the burning houses and began tossing out of the windows goods and belongings which were still intact. As boxes and furniture began to pile up outside and block the work, the Russians turned to the Japanese, who stood rooted to the ground looking on with amazement, and prevailed on them to move the things to the bay shore. Meanwhile the Russians tried to wet down the house which had caught fire last, but it was low tide and the distance from which water had to be carried was too great and their pumps were inadequate. It was only then that the Japanese firemen admitted that they had larger and more powerful pumps and offered to send for them. Meantime the Russians managed to halt the further spread of the flames by leveling completely the house burning next to the untouched buildings. While the Russians were risking their lives in saving the property of the Dutch and the Japanese—there were Japanese warehouses among the buildings of the Dutch—and in warding off danger to the city of Nagasaki itself, and while the Japanese dutifully carried the things to the shore and even began to assist in putting out the remnants of the fire, less scrupulous Europeans tried to take advantage of the tragedy and plunder the goods piled up near the water. Boats from the merchantmen on the roadstead pulled up to Deshima and began helping themselves to Dutch and Japanese possessions. When the Russians were informed of this by the Japanese they hurried to the scene. Quickly the laden boats pushed off from shore, but the Russians plunged into the water and, reaching the boats, forced them to return the property which, as Litke put it, "had been plundered to our shame by Europeans before the eyes of almost the whole population of Nagasaki."

Embarrassed as the Russians may have been that fellow Europeans should thus disgrace the West, they made good use of the transgressions of others to project Russian assistance to the foreground again.

The gratitude of the Japanese was boundless. The city authorities correctly appraised the full importance of the service of our men; they understood, that without us the fire could easily have spread to the city and with the least wind from the sea not one house would have been spared. The populace was enraptured by the daring of the Russians, by their resolution and speed of action, and marvelled at the disinterested self-denial of the men. Soon there appeared pictures, depicting the fire in Deshima, with enthusiastic descriptions. On all corners there were sung different songs, celebrating the struggle of the Russians with the fire and their victory over it; in some of them, in those parts of the city where we were better known, one could even hear the family names of the officers, who had most contributed to the extinction of the fire. On the streets not one person, one can say, passed us without saying something nice, and in private houses we were received with joy and honor.

There was more than gratitude that this event evoked in the Japanese. They admired the spirit and daring with which the Russians had thrown themselves into the fire, their energy and efficiency, and "they realized the superiority of moral power and education." "This realization together with the feeling of gratitude conclusively reconciled us with the Japanese, and the harmony and friendly relations remained unbroken until the very departure of the frigate." The Japanese did not differentiate very much between foreigners, yet for the time being in Nagasaki the balance had swung in favor of the Russians, and even foreigners sought their advice and catered to their needs. The Deshima tragedy had dramatically improved the status of the Russians, but the exemplary daily conduct of the crew, strictly held in check by the ship's officers, contributed also to winning the confidence of the people, who had viewed with alarm the original settlement of the four hundred foreign seamen on shore. Last but not least the close individual contacts, which the Russians established with the Japanese during the eight months that they lived among them, were bound to undermine traditional prejudices and develop a friendly relationship. In the words of Litke:

When we moved ashore, there was only a tiny little village near our temple, then there began to appear sheds in which Japanese merchants, coming from the city, traded different kinds of goods and foodstuffs; some set up kitchens, so that our sailors, returning in the evening from work, found here a ready supper of cooked fish, chicken, eggs, with the indispensable addition of sake (Japanese vodka). These sheds gradually were transformed into houses, so quickly erected in Japan, and toward the end of our stay in Japan the whole area between the temple and the shore, a distance of about six tenth of a mile, was built up with houses, and thus in a period of eight months the dead little village grew into a huge live settlement. Frequently one could see in the evenings a sailor, sitting on the threshold of a Japanese house and nursing in his coarse arms an infant, while the mother prepared for him tea, or some other kind of refreshment. The attachment of the inhabitants to our sailors reached such a point toward the end, that there were cases when they tried to hide and justify a man, who deserved punishment for having brought injury to themselves, though it must be added that they would first deal with him in their own way, and the sailor, of course, conscious of his guilt, would in these cases not even think of complaining about their having taken the law into their own hands.

Our rapprochement with the Japanese became ever easier and easier with each day, in consequence of the further fact that not only the officers, but very many of the sailors too began to understand and even to speak Japanese quite adequately; and as a result of this also misunderstandings, which in the beginning so frequently had been the cause of unpleasantnesses and quarrels, never occurred toward the end. The Japanese on their part studied Russian and began to understand our language quicker than we Japanese. We supported, of course, their desire to study Russian with all our might and in so far as possible satisfied it, as one of the best means of increasing the goodwill toward the Russians, which they showed perhaps most of all by this desire. Dutch and English several Japanese studied on order of the government, which was preparing them for the position of interpreters, for the study of Russian on the other hand very many young people from the merchant class and even from among the officialdom came to us voluntarily to take lessons, so that some of our officers, who could be spared from repair duties, sometimes spent whole mornings in study with them. . . .[15]

Among the officials who thus learned Russian and "listened to the affairs of the West," there was, for example, Shiga Shimpo, who was to become one of Japan's foremost experts on Russia.[16]

The good will of the people of Nagasaki for the men of the *Askold* was demonstrated most clearly at the time of separation, when expressions of friendship could not have been motivated by hopes for patronage and business. Litke wrote:

Several days yet before the embarkation of the crew on the frigate there began in the village a general entertainment and leave-taking; the inhabitants, both men and women without distinction, embraced with our sailors, kissed each other and cried; during the embarkation, in spite of the fact that the sailors were being led in formation, they found means of separating, and it cost great pains to seek them out in the houses where the Japanese literally hid them from the officers; at the same time the majority of the villagers sobbed as they accompanied the formation to the very wharf; meanwhile the officers received incessantly farewell calls from city acquaintances, officials and merchants, who most sincerely expressed their regret, that they had to part with us, brought gifts in remembrance and begged not to forget them. The official assigned to the affairs of the Russians, Nakayama, one of the most important . . . in the city, though for several weeks already he had been confined to bed by illness, learning that the frigate had pulled into the roadstead, had himself carried onto a boat in a sedan chair and came to bid us farewell. Finally, on the day of the frigate's departure, the whole roadstead was strewn with boats from early morning, while the inhabitants of our village on three tremendous boats moved round and round near the frigate, exchanging shouts with the sailors, and when the frigate got under way, began to shout in one voice and in Russian: "farewell, farewell, we won't see you again, don't forget us." Our contractors, with whom we had been in daily contact, accompanied us on the frigate till the very outlet to the sea and cried like little children.[17]

This and some of the other descriptions of Litke sound exaggerated, if not incredible. But the triple embrace and kiss were traditional among Russians, and anyone, who has lived among the Japanese for as long as the men of the *Askold*, can testify to the overwhelming warmheartedness and ceremony of Japanese farewells. Japanese

[15] Litke, 13: 394-408.

[16] Shiga Shimpo was sent to Russia both by the Shogunate (1867) and by the imperial government (1873-1875). When Grand Duke Aleksei visited Japan in 1872, Shiga acted as interpreter at the imperial reception. (Heibonsha, *Shinsen dai-jimmei jiten*, IV, 393.)

[17] Litke, 13: 408-409.

sources furthermore corroborate Japanese interest in Russian civilization,[18] and an English eye-witness account of Russian life in Nagasaki bears out Litke's portrayal of Russian conduct and of the Japanese reaction to it.

They seemed to live, all of them, a very jolly life in this old temple. Plentifully supplied with all the necessaries and luxuries of life from Shanghai, they had formed quite a little farm about them, and oxen, sheep, and pigs, were slaughtered: much to the disgust, no doubt, of their shaven hosts. They had made themselves quite at home; many had formed liaisons with some pretty Japanese women, and had their own menage in town. Nearly all spoke Japanese sufficient to make themselves understood; a few had made such progress as to speak with facility, and even to write and read.

To this they were, in a measure, indebted for their popularity among the people, but especially because they were very observant of their customs, and careful not to offend their little scruples. I saw one or two instances of men speaking the English language, entering the clean, mat-spread rooms of the Japanese, in their dirty boots, in spite of the protestations by words and signs, and the looks of despair of the owners. To shout at and abuse the people, tiresome and procrastinating though they be, is ill calculated on the part of foreigners to gain their willing services; yet I witnessed many instances of such violations of civility during my stay in Nangasaki. I wish my countrymen and Americans would remember, that to treat the people of Japan, with whom they may have to do, as they would a Hindoo servant or a Chinese cooley, will be the very worst manner of having their wants or wishes attended to. On the other hand, kindness and attention not to violate their prejudices, and, if possible, to enter into their social life, will be the best method of having everything that may be required. This was the way in which the Russians, during their stay of nine months in Nangasaki, contrived to gain the affections, not only of the people, but of the higher authorities. Captain Unkofsky, and through him, his officers, had only to express a wish to have it satisfied, where it was possible; his name was known for miles around, and called aloud to us in the streets as we passed. The officers in their walks through the town, were surrounded by laughing children, backed by a circle of pretty girls, with the men peering over their shoulders. One officer especially, Prince Ouktomsky, the grand duke's aide-de-camp, knew, I think, all the children of Nangasaki, for they would crowd round him, shake him by the hand, and in their gentle, pretty little way, talk to him till he arrived at his destination.

All the trading classes in Japan are considered contemptible by the higher authorities, government employés, and feudal retainers. Formerly

[18] Dr. Naito, for example, notes that at the "wintering place of the Russian Far Eastern naval unit" enterprising merchants displayed Russian signboards, and, it is said, "even a mere child also understood Russian." (Naito Kano, *Ken-Ro denshusei shimatsu*, 5-6.)

few or no Russian traders had ever come to Japan, while numbers of English, American, and Dutch had at different times touched at their ports. This circumstance has given the Japanese a high idea of Russia, and a great respect for its officers; which prestige, of course, the latter endeavour to support. Such was the explanation given me by an intelligent Japanese, an officer of the Government at Nangasaki.[19]

The Englishman, Henry Arthur Tilley, who served as language tutor on the *Rynda*, testified further that in Kanagawa and Hakodate "many of the shopkeepers had learned so much Russian as to make themselves intelligible to the Russian sailors." No strenuous linguistic efforts were required, when it came to relations with the women. In one of the teahouses, of which they had taken exclusive possession, the Russian naval officers consorted with the dancing and singing girls, taking their photographs, and changing costumes. The girls came out in uniform, "with pantaloons and swords girded on"; the officers in kimono and obi, "their hair dressed out *à la Japonaise* with coloured crape, and flowers, as well as in more elementary fashion."[20]

The effectiveness of the Russian policy is also described by J. L. C. Pompe van Meerdervoort, a Dutch physician, who treated the crew of the *Askold* during their stay in Nagasaki and who, when their own doctor was ill, was a daily witness of their relations with the Japanese:

From the beginning they have conducted a sturdy and consequential policy of state; it is true that they do not bother with trade, as a result of which they never have commercial possibilities, and even assume the appearance of unselfishness. They have stationed in Hakodate a very competent diplomat as political agent and maybe just there, because the island Ezo is of the utmost importance to them; on top of that for several years they have had a powerful fleet in these waters, on an average of about twenty ships, which, it is very interesting, all are being commanded by naval officers of renown; these men-of-war are dispersed all right, but when necessary they can be assembled in a few days, since there is always a despatch steam-yacht of very great horsepower with the flag, which rounds up the ships with great speed. Russia has insisted from the beginning upon strict compliance with the treaty (except on the commercial part); if one refuses to comply, then she emerges as her own judge, taking great care not to take more than she is entitled to, and to pay well for everything; for the implementation of this policy one finds the necessary support in the fleet. The Japanese know already for a long time

[19] Henry Arthur Tilley, *Japan, the Amoor and the Pacific*, 59-62.
[20] *Ibid.*, 63, 67-69.

that they cannot play around with Russia, and that they cannot renege on their obligations with banalities. For the rest Russia is very obliging and very courteous, and on the latter the Japanese put great value; they leave the Russian popes and some officers free to give instruction, through which the Russian language is propagated. In Hakodate everybody understands Russian; the Japanese learn that language with great speed.[21]

Pompe van Meerdervoort attributed Unkovskii's success to polite firmness and determination, and to the fact that he made it perfectly clear that it was "not easy to play fool with the Russian captain." When the Japanese seemed unable to find suitable accommodations on shore, Unkovskii himself found the temple at Inasa; when the Japanese deliberated at length about the sale of cattle, he went ahead and had bought up all that was needed, paying whatever price the Japanese asked; when the Japanese tried to delay on the delivery of timber, he showed them that he knew where to find it—and got it. Once the Russians had obtained what they needed—without force or threats of force—they got along very well with the Japanese and there was complete harmony. Unkovskii and the governor dined together; the priest gave instructions in the Russian language and arithmetic to forty Japanese youths; while some other officers also taught. Pompe van Meerdervoort was impressed by the excellent conduct of the crew. But courteous as the Russian officers always were in their relationship with the Japanese officials, they made it plain that they would not stand for any infringement of their treaty rights. For the first time the Japanese government learned that the Russians refused to regard the treaty as a dead letter. Commenting on their arrest of the drunken samurai, who had insulted a Russian midshipman, the Dutchman wrote: "One has tried to defame these forceful and prompt measures of the Russians by saying: yes, they do whatever enters their head regardless as to whether it is right or wrong; but I must contradict that very strongly: the Russians, at least in the case of the *Askold*, have claimed nothing to which they did not have the fullest right under the treaty; but they did not let themselves be intimidated by anything, nor did they let themselves be turned down with banal replies, and the envy of the less happily successful will in vain try to wrench the crown from their work."

Pompe van Meerdervoort did not think it wise to try to coerce the Japanese by threats or rough boasts; *Zachtheid* was a far better

---

[21] Pompe van Meerdervoort, II, 127-128. I am indebted to the late Professor Andre L. Van Assenderp for assistance in the translation of this Dutch text.

policy. By *Zachtheid* he did not mean so much "softness" or "leniency," as precisely the type of approach that Unkovskii had used. Noting that the Russians had insisted on strict compliance with the treaties, that they had instructed Japanese youths, and had refused to be intimidated, he declared that Russian policy was worthy of imitation.

Describing the influence of the Russian stay in Nagasaki, Pompe van Meerdervoort observed: "The Russians left also many souvenirs of their sojourn at Inasa of which one should obtain telling evidence, if several years later one would observe with intent the playing youths in that village."[22] Without doubt the Russians were overwhelmed by Japanese hospitality as they left Nagasaki. "How can one fail to acknowledge after this the sincerity of the disposition and friendship of the Japanese?" asked Litke. "How can one fail to acknowledge that our winterage in Nagasaki brought beneficial results and laid a firm beginning for the influence, of which the Russians must make use in Japan?"[23]

IN KANAGAWA

Nagasaki was more or less used to foreigners; not so other regions. Occasionally the Russians would penetrate into areas still closed. The populace, always inquisitive, would throng together to stare at the strangers, but promptly the Japanese police would interfere and, unable to prevail upon the visitors to leave, would try to keep the people and especially the women away from them. Japanese curiosity is not easily thwarted and, as in years past, hundreds of eyes followed every movement of the foreigners. As one of the Russians wrote concerning the futile efforts of the police to block the view of their countrymen during an unauthorized visit of the *Dzhigit* to Niigata:

From behind raised or slid open screens there could be seen bold, black eyes, which, it seemed, did not really have to move the screens, they would have seen through paper. But then we would not have seen! Some of the women, and as I noticed, all of them pretty, even climbed onto the roofs. It is a pity that treaties were made not with the fair sex. Then all the ports of Japan would have been opened.[24]

Near the capital the situation was different. There the curiosity and potential friendliness of the populace quickly turned into mounting resentment at the high-handed conduct of the Western residents

22 Pompe van Meerdervoort, 128-133.   23 Litke, 13: 409.
24 N. K., "Iz Iaponii," 23.

and ultimately erupted in a series of incidents. It is unlikely that the presence of Putiatin himself, whose restraint had smoothed the ruffled feelings of the Japanese, would have safeguarded his men from the hostility of some of the more diehard seclusionists. Fresh from China, where his diplomatic victories, embodied in the Treaty of Aigun (May 28, 1858) had won for Russia the left bank of the Amur River and for himself the title "Graf Amurskii" (Count of Amur) and the name Muravev-Amurskii, Muravev's threatening approach invited the attention of would-be-assassins.

Muravev-Amurskii had shared Nevelskoi's view of an "active" policy in the Far East and had been annoyed at Putiatin's interference in the annexation of Sakhalin. He now arrived to claim the island, the occupation of which Putiatin had considered less important than Japanese good will, and came close to wrecking everything that Putiatin had built up. Throughout, Muravev-Amurskii and Putiatin reflected a very different attitude in their negotiations with the Chinese and the Japanese. Both naked threats and patient perseverance seemed equally effective in hard-pressed China, the backbone of whose resistance to Western demands appeared to have been broken. But in Japan, successful though the strong stand of Perry had been and effective though naval actions against the Choshu and Satsuma clans were to prove in later years, Western arrogance and swaggering were likely to call forth a violent reaction on the part of her proud and militant ruling class. The difference in Chinese and Japanese response and the slowness of Westerners to recognize it, is well illustrated in the celebrated Richardson incident of 1862. Instead of showing his respect by dismounting, as was the Japanese custom, when he came upon the train of an imperial envoy, Charles L. Richardson, an Englishman, who for many years had lived in China as a merchant, gave the impression of wanting to force his way through the procession, and was mortally wounded by one of the swordsmen. Richardson's companions had tried to avoid trouble, but Richardson had brushed aside their pleas for caution with the famous last words: "Let me alone; I have lived in China fourteen years, and know how to manage this people."[25] When Muravev-Amurskii arrived in the summer of 1859, the representatives of foreign naval powers had already met with insults in the streets of Edo,

---

[25] David Murray, *Japan*, 343.

though they had studiously ignored them in order to avoid incidents with which they were not yet strong enough to deal.[26]

Muravev-Amurskii first touched Japan at Hakodate in the far north, where he stopped from July 6 to July 27, 1859, on his way from Nikolaevsk to the Gulf of Pechili. The steamer *Amerika*, on which he travelled, had outrun his other vessels, and he waited in Hakodate for the remainder of the expedition: the corvettes *Voevoda*, *Boiarin*, and *Novik* and the transport *Iaponets* ("The Japanese"). He met Goshkevich, who was residing there as the Russian consul since the autumn of 1858, and found him in good spirits. In a report to Grand Duke Konstantin Nikolaevich, dated May 14, 1859, Muravev-Amurskii had listed the main objectives of his voyage as: (1) to present in Hakodate the credentials empowering him to negotiate with the Japanese; (2) to meet in Suifun Bay with Chief Quartermaster Budogosskii, who was demarcating an overland boundary line between the upper reaches of the Ussuri River and the sea; (3) to deliver maps of the new Russian boundaries to the Gulf of Pechili for transmission to Peking through the Russian plenipotentiary; and (4) to return to Japan for negotiations with the government. He agreed with Goshkevich that he would return from the shores of China in about a month, pick him up, and with him continue to the capital, Goshkevich meanwhile informing the Japanese government of this by letter.[27]

The disposition of Sakhalin was constantly on Muravev-Amurskii's mind. He had favored the annexation of the island in the early 1850's, and had not been pleased when Putiatin had found it necessary to leave the boundary in this region undelineated. But he himself had advised Putiatin from Port Aian in August of 1854, "that it is better to leave the boundary question undecided as before, than to confirm them in even the tiniest part of Sakhalin." He had expressed confidence that if circumstances made the immediate occupation of Aniwa inadvisable, the government would in time, "perhaps even next year," permit him to establish himself there with the necessary forces, and hoped that jurisdiction over the island would pass from the Company to the government itself. For that reason he counseled Putiatin to tell the Japanese, "that they can continue as before to engage in fishery there and to have their shops, but that the defense of these places belongs to us, as to the strongest, and that the temporary removal of

---

[26] A. Kornilov II, "Izvestiia iz Iaponii," 99.
[27] Barsukov, I, 556-558; II, 226-227.

the post was merely a hygienic measure, to preserve the health of our men, who were seriously falling sick because of their fewness in number and the consequent difficult service in maintaining guards." He had warned that the Japanese must be given no indication that the Russians feared the English and the French; "on the contrary, they must be told, that we have now shipped down the Amur to this place tremendous forces against these enemies; one must not hide this fact, as they know it already, and, on the contrary, one ought to ascribe to it even greater importance and power, than is actually the case. . . ."[28] In November of 1858 Muravev-Amurskii stressed the urgency of settling the Sakhalin question in a letter to the director of the Asiatic Department. "If Count Putiatin has decided nothing about Sakhalin after the Treaty of Tientsin,[29] and if the imperial government desires to entrust this matter to me," he wrote, "send plenipotentiary credentials, in which, however, *demarcation on Sakhalin should not* be mentioned, because according to all considerations it is essential for us to have this entire island in our possession, otherwise we shall meet there the English, who will take from the Japanese whatever they wish."[30]

When he returned from China on August 2, 1859, he was optimistic. His first visit with four vessels had only foreshadowed the size of his expedition. In May he had reported to Grand Duke Konstantin Nikolaevich that he planned to collect as large a squadron as possible "so that the Japanese and the Chinese could see our naval forces too." When he returned to Hakodate on the steamer *Amerika* to call for Goshkevich, he found the *Askold*, which had entered the harbor on its way back to Russia in order to take home gifts which the consul had received from the Japanese for his government, and required her services. He had not been too happy aboard the *Amerika*, complaining at the time of his earlier visit to Hakodate that "frequently I am being driven mad by the seamen, whom I scold accordingly, and soon I shall also begin to change commanders." The enlistment of the frigate provided him with the opportunity to do so gracefully. "Here I move aboard the frigate *Askold* to Unkovskii, where I shall also raise my flag," he wrote in a letter to Count M. S.

[28] *Ibid.*, II, 115-116.

[29] Concluded by Putiatin on June 13, 1858, sixteen days after Muravev's signature of the Treaty of Aigun. The Treaty of Tientsin guaranteed Russia most-favored-nation treatment; unaware of Muravev's success, Putiatin demanded also clarification of the frontier.

[30] Barsukov, II, 217.

Korsakov, "and in Edo I shall have a pretty good squadron gather; this will, of course, help to conclude the Sakhalin matters, but I fear the slowness of the Japanese, and that I shall have to return to the Amur very late."[31] In addition to the *Askold*, the corvettes *Rynda* and *Griden* were "caught" in Hakodate, having found orders to await Muravev-Amurskii's return, when they had entered Hakodate en route from Nagasaki to the Amur. The gunboat *Plastun* was added to the Russian squadron in similar fashion.[32]

On August 5, the *Rynda*, *Griden*, and *Plastun* departed for the Bay of Kanagawa, general rendezvous of the expedition. The *Askold* and the *Amerika* followed suit somewhat later, the *Amerika* overtaking the corvettes at the entrance to Kanagawa Bay on August 13. Kanagawa Harbor had been opened to Westerners in place of Shimoda since the summer of 1859. Situated twelve miles from Edo, and far more convenient than the roadstead of the capital itself, which was too distant from the shore, it seemed to have a good future ahead of it. Actually the roadstead of Kanagawa was rather far from shore also and the Westerners found it necessary to land not at Kanagawa but two miles distant. The Japanese were pleased, and promptly built for the Westerners at a chosen site warehouses and consular residences and shops for their own people. When they demanded, however, that Westerners stay out of Kanagawa completely, the Westerners did not agree and frustrated the Japanese, the consuls taking up residence in Kanagawa as originally agreed, the other foreigners settling in the new area, known as Yokohama. It is interesting that when Alcock was first shown Yokohama, he compared what he saw to "a scene which could hardly have been enacted anywhere except in Russia, where whole villages appeared as if by magic at the mandate of Potemkin, to greet the Empress Catherine in her progress through her dominions, with evidence of a flourishing and populous empire, where ten days before there was only desert."[33]

Without awaiting the arrival of Muravev-Amurskii, some of the Russians went ashore and looked around. Kornilov marveled at the dainty Japanese lacquer ware in the stores of Yokohama, but to transport it back to Russia on a man-of-war would have been, as he put it, like taking a watermelon by post from Kharkov to Moscow. As for the European goods that were displayed in many of the stores, Kornilov remarked that the Japanese did not touch them. "The Japanese not only do not buy them, they do not even want to look at

---

[31] *Ibid.*, I, 555-558.   [32] Tilley, 70, 102-103, 136.   [33] Alcock, I, 145.

them. The government tries to explain this standstill by the shortage of money and the unaccustomedness of the people to trade, but the merchants say something different: they assert that the government secretly forbids its subjects to trade with foreigners." This seemed more likely, because elsewhere the Japanese had been eager to barter with the Russians. The apparent interference with trade plus delays and difficulties made in the delivery of coal to the Russian vessels prompted Kornilov to observe, "No, say what you may, you will yet come to the opinion, expressed still at the very beginning of the conclusion of the treaties, that the matter will not do without cannons. . . ."[34]

On August 16 the *Askold* also reached the Bay of Kanagawa. Joined here by two more corvettes, Muravev-Amurskii steamed up to the gates of the capital at Shinagawa on August 17 with the formidable squadron of seven warships—the frigate *Askold*, the steamer yacht *Amerika*, the corvettes *Rynda, Griden, Novik,* and *Voevoda,* and the gunboat *Plastun*—mounting altogether one hundred and five guns, joined before long by the clipper *Dzhigit* and two more vessels. Facing this array of steam-powered Russian men-of-war, the Japanese had only two screw-corvettes, a screw-yacht, and "the skeleton of an antediluvian merchant ship, purchased, like the former three from the Dutch, but only God knows when," and these were so obviously inadequate to the task of defense, that the Japanese soon withdrew most of them "just in case." Japanese land forces were no more impressive; Japanese troops were armed with bows and spears and fortifications were limited mostly to a few mounds, "which the first broadside of a frigate would have demolished or a handful of marines taken at bayonet point."

Informed of the presence of so noted a personage as Muravev-Amurskii, the governor of Edo came aboard the flagship the day after the expedition's arrival. Muravev-Amurskii declined to receive him officially; except for this, the governor was treated with due respect and attention. Other officials also visited the frigate, among them, on August 20, Endo, Lord of Tajima, and Sakai Ukyonosuke, the Japanese plenipotentiaries, and arrangements were made for the resumption of diplomatic negotiations.[35] It was not difficult to imag-

---

[34] Kornilov, "Izvestiia," 101-103, 105.

[35] Kornilov, "Izvestiia," 100-101, 106-113; Tilley, 144-148; Russia, Ministry of the Navy, *Obzor zagranichnykh plavanii sudov russkogo voennago flota,* 601-602; Litke, 13: 411; Tokutomi, XLIV, 259-260; Tanaka Bunichiro, *Nichi-Ro kosho-shi,* 83.

ine the personal anxiety which was hidden behind the calm and dignified countenance of the samurai. Tilley wrote:

I cannot help pitying the state of these unfortunate officials, and the perplexity they must have felt at each new arrival of fleets to make treaties, or re-make them; for negotiating with foreign powers, a new kind of diplomacy to the Japanese, had been proved to be most disastrous to the ministers engaged in it. With the best intentions, perhaps, they have to cede to the force of circumstances and the power of the stranger from without, to combat the opposition of a powerful anti-progressive and anti-reform party within, and run the risk of meeting destruction whichever way they act. Both are most hard alternatives; and a Japanese statesman must have an extraordinary quantity and quality of the duplicity which is characteristic of his race and profession if he can steer clear and turn to his profit the difficulties which attend all diplomacy with the foreigners. If he refuse to grant their demands he knows not how soon their cannon may be thundering around the shores of his country; if he grant too freely, or grant at all, he is never certain of the day when a small sword, presented to him with the greatest respect, is to be the symbol of his downfall, and the signal that he must use it on his own person, to save his family from being involved in the same disgrace. It is not, therefore, to be wondered at that procrastination and all sorts of excuses should attend the making of a treaty, and that all sorts of difficulties and falsehoods should be made use of afterwards to nullify it.[36]

On August 22 Muravev-Amurskii went ashore with a most impressive retinue—a suite of about forty officers, an honor guard of three hundred armed sailors, and a drum and bugle corps—and proceeded in colorful formation to the temple set aside for his stay on land. After the usual greetings, a festive dinner, and preliminary small talk, Muravev-Amurskii opened the negotiations with a most remarkable statement:

In the friendly treaties, concluded between our two great states, one important matter has not been completed. Since remote times Japanese fishermen have engaged in their industry in Aniwa, on the southern tip of the island Sakhalin or Karafuto; both these ancient names bear witness to the fact that this island is homogeneous with the river, which is called Sakhalin-Ula or, in Russian, Amur, and that for the past one hundred and seventy years it was considered Chinese, i.e., much before the time when Japanese fishermen founded their business there; but before that time the river Sakhalin-Ula, and therefore also the island Sakhalin, belonged to Russia. Following the voice of justice and desiring to preserve friendly relations, both states—the Russian and the Chinese—agreed between themselves that the Russians occupy Sakhalin-Ula (Amur) as before, and

[36] Tilley, 147-148.

consequently six years ago a Russian guard was placed on the southern tip of Sakhalin, in Aniwa Bay; but our people falling sick because of their fewness in number, and Admiral Putiatin, fearing that they would all die, ordered the guard temporarily removed from Aniwa, having left the building in the care of the Japanese who were there.

But now, when the number of land and sea forces under my command in Eastern Siberia has increased considerably and when these forces have moved up to the mouth of the Amur, I can send a sizable unit to Aniwa, and construct good buildings; then there will be no danger that our people will get sick from the difficult service, as was the case in 1854. But as my great Ruler ordered me in all border matters first to talk things over with the bordering friendly states—Japan and China—and to this purpose provided me with the necessary authorization, I hasten to come here to confer with the wise Japanese statesmen in order to put an end in writing to all doubts concerning Sakhalin.

The interest of both our states demands that this matter be decided definitively as quickly as possible, because foreigners may take advantage of the uncertainty of its condition and occupy for themselves a place on the island Sakhalin, something which, of course, can no longer happen when the whole island will be acknowledged in writing as in Russian territory, and will be under the protection of the forces entrusted to me. The Japanese government itself sees now what significant naval forces are already at the disposal of Russia here; but the building up of these forces was begun only five years ago, and they will increase each year. For the above mentioned reasons it is essential for mutual security that the whole island be under our protection.[37]

The Japanese themselves were anxious to settle the boundary issue. The governor of Hakodate had vainly tried to broach the subject to Muravev-Amurskii, who had insisted, however, on dealing directly with the central authorities. But eager though the plenipotentiaries were for a solution, they failed to see the validity or honesty of Muravev-Amurskii's arguments. Pointing to Article II of the Treaty of Shimoda, which provided that Sakhalin "remains unpartitioned between Russia and Japan, as has been the case to this time," they refused to draw a line of demarcation to the south of the island. Muravev-Amurskii advanced the startling argument that Putiatin had not been empowered to discuss Sakhalin, as Sakhalin was within his own jurisdiction as governor-general of eastern Siberia, and rejected their compromise offer to divide the island at latitude 50° N. He would not settle for less than the entire island of Sakhalin.[38]

---

[37] Barsukov, II, 278-279.

[38] Muravev-Amurskii to Prince Aleksandr Gorchakov, dated October 17 (29), 1859 and marked "very urgent," Barsukov, II, 276-277. For a more detailed verbal exchange between Muravev and Endo, see Ota Saburo, *Nichi-Ro Karafuto gaiko-sen*, 96-105.

In a letter to Prince Aleksandr Gorchakov, the minister of foreign affairs, he explained his stand: "Considering that the rights of the Japanese are just as indeterminate as ours . . . I could not agree to any division of it between Japan and us, and particularly in consideration of the fact that, because of Japan's weakness, any foreign state can easily take possession of that part which will be recognized Japanese, consolidate its position there, and inflict on us thereby considerable damage for all times to come, especially in relation to La Perouse Strait, which constitutes the nearest and only exit for our vessels from Tatar Strait into the Pacific Ocean."[39] Unable to sway the Japanese, Muravev-Amurskii still did not weaken in his own determination. He wrote to the Tsar: "The occupation of a point on the southern tip of Sakhalin is essential for us, and does not contradict the treaty of 1855. Of course, this will not please the Japanese government, yet it will not break up our peaceful relations with it and will further strengthen that influence which we have on it as the closest and strong neighbors."[40]

Muravev-Amurskii's clumsy attempt to trick and frighten the Japanese into the cession of Sakhalin Island aroused great resentment in Japan. It is easier to understand why the Japanese should have been antagonized by Muravev-Amurskii's crude deception, than why he should have stooped to such tactics, for he fully appreciated the efficacy of Putiatin's friendly and sincere approach, the relatively good disposition of the Japanese toward Russia, and their inherent acumen and astuteness. From Hakodate he wrote:

Having been in Japan I agree with the opinion of Putiatin [and Muravev-Amurskii did not often agree with Putiatin] that it is much pleasanter to have dealings with this people than with the Chinese; I must also give him credit that the relations which he began with this people have left them with a good impression of the Russians: they like us more than the Americans; but here, too, I do not understand the passion of Putiatin to *teach*! They will learn everything without us, particularly navigation; we had better learn ourselves than teach people who will soon surpass us.[41]

He expressed the same idea in a letter to Egor Kovalevskii, Director of the Asiatic Department:

I do not understand the Russian people who wish to teach everything to the Japanese and Chinese, and arm them; they will be taught without

[39] Barsukov, II, 276-277.
[40] Muravev-Amurskii to Alexander II, October 18 (30), 1859. Barsukov, II, 279-280.
[41] Barsukov, I, 558-559.

us, and we had better study ourselves in order not to fall behind at least the former, who are very enterprising and capable. In all fairness to the Japanese in general one must say that they are well disposed toward us, particularly the common people, a fact which, it is said, is not very pleasing to their government, but pleases me greatly.[42]

Why, then, did Muravev-Amurskii blunder in his approach? Perhaps the simplest, and kindest, explanation can be found in Litke's observation: "Unfortunately the time at the disposal of Count Muravev was too short, particularly in view of prevalent conditions."[43] Pressed for time—he was anxious to return to the Amur—Muravev-Amurskii had tried a bluff and had lost; "lost," for the stakes included not only Sakhalin but confidence in the sincerity of the Russian government. The expedition did accomplish one objective: Goshkevich exchanged "without obstacle" the ratification of the Treaty of Edo, which Putiatin had negotiated the previous year. But this could have been done without warships or trickery. For some time foreigners had been molested by the increasingly restless population of the capital; now the Russians too became targets for affront and injury. They had felt with reason, that the assaults on the other foreigners were partly the fault of the foreigners themselves, but, as the English noted with glee: "They have been mobbed at Jeddo [Edo] since . . . with a perfectly impartial rudeness."[44]

One day, for example, three unarmed Russian officers went sight-seeing in Edo, unmindful of the fact that others had been stoned in town the day before. When they left the main streets, an unruly crowd gathered behind them and began pelting them with little stones. Unable to shake off their pursuers, though they zigzagged "like a rabbit chased by dogs," the Russians sought refuge in a small hotel. The locked-out rabble threatened to break through the flimsy doors and walls, but fortunately police, summoned by the reluctant host, arrived in time to escort the "tourists" out of the district unharmed. Similar protection was required several more times in other districts until the vicinity of the palace grounds was reached. Turning into a familiar street, the Russians swaggered "like dandies from Nevskii Avenue" into a restaurant frequented by Westerners. Here they were surrounded "with all possible respect and comfort . . . including a fifteen-year-old beauty who [would come up to them] on her knees

[42] *Ibid.*, ii, 266-267.   [43] Litke, 13: 411.
[44] Report dated Tokyo, August 28, in the *London Times* of November 17, 1859, p. 5.

offering [them] sweet cake."[45] When Muravev-Amurskii learned of the way his officers had been molested, he complained to the Japanese authorities, and the officials responsible for the district in question were apparently degraded. This did not endear the Russians to the samurai.

The sights of Edo were too alluring for the Russians to remain in the safety of the temple. There were colorful processions, such as the cortege of one of the ministers who visited the frigate. In the words of Tilley, who came upon this procession, as he and Goshkevich rode into the city, themselves followed by palanquins after the fashion of Japanese noblemen:

First come lictors with gilded spears and pikes, then men with great black boxes slung on poles, resembling the milliners' boxes one sometimes sees borne about London to the abodes of fashion, but in Japan they contain papers, documents, and such like. Then comes the great man's horse, richly caparisoned in red and blue, with silken bridle and gay trappings, led by two grooms; more lictors, more black boxes, and at last the palanquin of bamboo with bamboo blinds, through which the great man peeps, if there happen to be anything unusual in the road, such for instance as a pair of barbarians on horseback; more black boxes and more lictors bring up the rear. When the great man issues from his abode, the lictors rush out first, brandishing their pikes, and cry, *Suaro! Suaro!* (Sit down! Sit down!) Immediately the people, hearing the well-known cry, squat down on the ground, bringing their hams and thighs together, and throwing all the weight of the body on the toes. The ordinary mode of sitting is nearly the same, only the soles of the feet support that part of the body which Europeans deposit upon a chair. The same mark of respect is shown the great man all along the road, and on his leaving the palanquin.

There were magnificent stores. "One, a silk and stuff warehouse, was twice the size of the large draper's shop in Waterloo Place, London. A large mat-covered platform, on which were piles of goods, shopmen seated and clerks making up accounts, occupied the centre. On the edge of the platform sat the purchasers, among them a two-sworded gentleman here and there, but, as in other lands, the ladies were the most interested in examining silks, crapes, and embroidery." And the city itself, though disappointing in its lack of grandeur, was notable at once for its simplicity and police state control.

The generality of houses in the capital are little superior to those in other parts; they are mostly of pine wood, of only one story, and unpainted;

---

[45] Kornilov, "Izvestiia," 115-117.

many, however, in Yedo, as in Nangasaki, are built of harder wood, have an upper story to hold goods, and a few can boast of some little external decorations. The tea and other large houses of public entertainment are exceptions, having generally capacious apartments above. Earthquakes and fires are of such constant occurrence that great stability, decoration, or loftiness is not considered. The streets are divided into wards enclosed by gates, on either side of which are little wooden guard-houses, with openings so contrived that the inmates have a clear view of all that passes in the street on either side. All is under strict municipal law. Besides the regular officers of each district, every inhabitant must take his turn of duty as a watchman, and each ward is responsible for all unlawful acts committed within its boundaries. This is so throughout every town and village in Japan, and it is very seldom that crimes are committed without instant detection. In the street through which we rode, these wards extended only about one hundred yards from gate to gate, and the side streets seemed partitioned off in the same manner.

Goskevich and Tilley visited many stores. Tilley wrote:

In most of the shops we were taken up into an upper chamber, and after some fruit, tea, and sweetmeats were set before us, and we were fanned cool by attendant boys and maidens, we proceeded to view the wares. Anything purchased was sent after us to the temple, and in every transaction there always seemed to be some combination between the merchant and an officer who made his appearance at the moment. The compact, as I afterwards heard, concerned how much of the profits the latter should receive. We found all manufactures much dearer in Yedo than in Yokohama, but there were many curiosities to be found in the former place which the Japanese no doubt thought could not be of any interest to Europeans, compared with silks, lacquer boxes, porcelain, and such like. Among these were ivory and wood carvings, objects made of rock crystal, and numerous articles of virtu.

But wherever Goshkevich and Tilley went, they themselves inevitably became the center of attraction. Tilley reported:

We rode too fast to permit of a crowd thronging us; nevertheless our presence caused an unusual excitement. The shop doors were crowded, grave two-sworders stopped and even turned round to gaze after us; a few old women hobbled away slightly alarmed, and many young ones looked on with curious eyes. But on our dismounting and entering a shop, a crowd of some hundreds immediately collected round the door, and as there were none of the officials present whose ostensible duty it was to protect us, it became at last very disagreeable. The shopkeeper, on one occasion, made a barrier of rope around his house to keep off the multitude; on another, at a china shop, the master set two of his men to take our horses and clear the crowd with their heels, which was done quite efficiently. But at last a band of "gamins," like mischievous little imps as they are in all countries, began to hoot and cry, and throw little pieces of mud at us. The gesticulations of the shopmen were in vain; the fun seemed to spread from the boys to the grown-up people; there was nobody near of sufficient rank to influence the people, and we began to be threatened with serious annoyance. But a little champion soon rescued us. This was a little fellow about fourteen years old; but his two swords, one of which was almost as big as himself, and his silk and crape dress, must have informed the mob of his rank, for when he took up a stick and laid it about the persons in the foreground, the whole mass fell back without a murmur. They were as submissive to that two-sworded child, as a flock of sheep to a shepherd. He followed us into one or two other shops and protected us from any further annoyance.[46]

The danger of such incidents soon discouraged individual strolls about town, and the Russians ventured ashore in larger groups and saw sights in the company of Japanese officials, but they still went where they pleased, ignoring warnings about angry crowds and conservatives. "Sometimes," Ensign Kornilov wrote, "we did indeed chance upon relatively large throngs of people, who looked at us in the same way as in our country peasants look at a bear on a chain, that is, they met us largely with shouts and laughter, but in these shouts and laughter there could be heard much more astonishment and curiosity than enmity and ridicule.[47]

But the misgivings of the officials were justified, and tragedy was to mar the rest of the expedition's stay. Having found it inconvenient to obtain provisions through government authorities, the Russians did their own shopping in Yokohama, which had rapidly been transformed from an "empty dale" into a "rather significant little city where foreigners settled."[48] One evening, on August 25, Ensign Roman Mofet and two sailors, Sokolov and Korolkov, had completed their purchases and were on their way back from the shops to the longboat—Sokolov, carrying a box with unspent money, walked with Mofet, with Korolkov some distance ahead—when suddenly several Japanese with drawn swords set upon them from a side street. Sokolov was killed on the spot. Mofet fled some distance but collapsed mortally injured.[49] "The wounds inflicted on them were most ghastly; the sailor's skull was cleft in two places; both his shoulder-blades cut through deep into the back; the joints of the elbows severed; the thigh cut through to the bone; and, not content with this, the miscreants

[46] Tilley, 154-159.   [47] Kornilov, "Izvestiia," 119-120.

[48] Litke, 13: 412.

[49] Kornilov, "Izvestiia," 120; Zhukov, 133-134; Heki Shoichi, *Kokushi dai-nempyo,* v, 108.

must have pierced him through the back when down. The poor young officer . . . who was universally loved for his amiable disposition, was little less severely wounded, and it is astonishing with what tenacity he clung to life. His brain was protruding from a skull wound: he had received the same sort of cuts in the shoulder-blades as the sailor, so that the lung and (lower down) the entrails were laid bare; and there were other cuts, not mortal. He was, of course, unable to give any particulars of the attack; all his thoughts, poor fellow, seemed centered in his mother and his home."[50] Korolkov had been warned by shouts from Mofet and managed to escape alive, though not without wounds, by rushing into a Japanese shop. When Ensign Avinov, who had stayed with the longboat, reached Mofet, he found him surrounded by Americans, "but in spite of the help immeditely given by a Japanese doctor and later on also by an American one, all attempts to prolong Mr. Mofet's life were doomed to failure."[51] Two hours after receiving the wounds Mofet was dead.

Reconstructing the crime—the first murder of foreigners in opened Japan—on the basis of Korolkov's disposition, Tilley wrote:

The steward affirmed that there were several persons, six or eight, concerned in the murder; but he was so terrified that he may have been deceived in the number. That at least there were three, was evident from the fact of our men being all attacked at the same moment. The bag containing the silver was carried off, and was found a few days afterwards in the neighbourhood; the Japanese money only had been taken, the dollars were left. A piece of a sword, about four inches in length, a fragment of the over-robe worn by officers, no doubt torn off by one of the unfortunate men in his struggles, and a straw sandal, were found near the spot. Unfortunately there was no badge or distinguishing mark of clan upon the fragment of dress which could give a clue to the wearer. On our visiting the place a few hours afterwards, two pools of blood, barely covered with gravel, showed that the unfortunate men must have been struck down on the spot, and lain there as they fell. Near where the sailor fell, the post of a stall was daubed with blood, and had a piece struck out of it by a descending weapon; this was probably the way in which the sword was broken.[52]

As soon as the governor of Kanagawa learned of the incident, he informed the consuls of Great Britain, Holland, and the United States of it, and asked them to meet him in Yokohama. Dutch and English representatives came at once, the American consul several

---

[50] Tilley, 164.   [51] Kornilov, "Izvestiia," 120-121.
[52] Tilley, 165.

hours later. The Europeans demanded that the murderers be apprehended, and advised the governor to close all shops, detain all junks, and search all roads. This he promised to do, but in effect his measures were only halfhearted. The Western position was weakened by the moderation of the American consul who, when he arrived, objected to any measures that might hinder the continuous flow of trade.

Who were the killers? What had been the motive for their attack? Sir Rutherford Alcock dismissed the possibility of banditry. He recalls that "no one believed that it was a mere case of highway robbery and murder." There was evidence that samurai had participated in the attack, and the wounds were not merely death blows. "There was something savage and vindictive, indicating personal or political feeling, in the number and nature of the wounds."[53] It is possible that the officials, degraded as a result of Muravev-Amurskii's complaint, had had a hand in this attack. Others speculated that Muravev-Amurskii's designs on Sakhalin had become known and that the murder was patriotic in motivation; others rose to romantic heights in attributing the whole matter to love, jealousy, and revenge.[54] It appeared to the consuls that the governor treated the question with "brutal levity." Tilley believed that the consuls must have been mistaken in this, "as that peculiar contortion of the mouth, and inhalation of the breath, which is peculiar to a Japanese when he listens attentively and has understood you, sounds and seems very much like a giggle," and noted that the "gravity and good breeding" of the governor "would have prevented . . . [him] from showing any sign of pleasure, even if he felt it." But Tilley agreed that the governor failed to pursue the investigation energetically. This failure gives support to the theory that the governor's hands were tied; that men of higher rank than himself were involved. Improbable as it might have been that an official high in the councils of the Shogunate should have chosen to intimidate foreigners at the moment when, as Alcock pointed out, "by a rare chance, there was a powerful foreign squadron in the bay of the nation to which the victims belonged, and a chief in Count Mouravieff, who could land an army on their territory from the neighbouring coast if he pleased, in a shorter period than any other foreign representative or government," popular rumors had it that it was precisely because of this that the Russians had been

---

[53] Alcock, I, 242-243. [54] Tilley, 172-173.

singled out by enemies of the Shogunate, probably by adherents of the lord of Mito, who wished to further their own political ends by embarrassing the government.[55] Whoever the instigators may have been, "the general opinion [of the Westerners] was that the murderers must have been recognized by some of the bystanders, but that the Governor either would not or could not have them arrested, and that they were permitted to escape." Nevertheless the Japanese were uneasy.

During the whole of the day, and till late at night, interpreters were constantly arriving with letters or messages of condolence from the Governor, and polite inquiries as to the state of our feelings and health, which the interpreter expressed in most droll but execrable English, literally translated from his own flowery language. Baskets of fruit and sweetmeats were also sent to us, and the same to the guard which had been placed over the corpses. . . .

During the night the Governor of Yedo arrived. He had been dispatched by the Council immediately on the news of the murder being known in Yedo. The greatest alarm was manifested by all the Ministers as to what steps the Russian Governor would take. Two of the Japanese steam corvettes before mentioned went off for a voyage during the night, as though the government thought they were not unlikely to be seized. Double attention was paid by all ranks of officials; matters which were difficulties before were now rendered quite easy; things were supplied which had before been refused.

Japanese misgivings were not without basis. When Tilley had hastened ashore with the doctor upon hearing of the attack, he had found the foreign community in a state of great excitement. "On landing, we were met by the officer who survived, and by nearly all the European inhabitants, armed with revolvers," he reported. "Gloom and horror pervaded every countenance; business was not thought of; all the shops were closed; and even the groups of natives in the streets seemed mournful and horrified, as they held aloof."

Most of the European merchants were aghast at this murder: they declared that none of their lives were safe, and few went abroad without a revolver. Each had his own plan of what ought to be done: some were for burning the town down, others for attacking Yedo; one or two sensible ones proposed that the authorities should forbid their officials to wear their swords within the districts opened to foreigners. All expected that some severe act of retribution would, of course, be inflicted on the murderers if caught, but if not, on the Government, by the large Russian squadron in the neighbourhood, as a warning and a lesson that it would

[55] Alcock, I, 242; Tilley, 166.

be called to account for the life of every foreigner by all European governments combined. All were anxious, therefore, to know what the Russians would do, to punish this, the first murder committed on one of their subjects, an unoffending officer in his uniform, peaceably walking along the street.[56]

The situation was not without irony. "It is, perhaps, so far fortunate that such a tragedy should not have happened before the arrival of the Russian squadron, as it is some six weeks since any British man-of-war has been seen here, nor is there any on the Japan station, unless one has recently arrived in the south," wrote an English correspondent to the London *Times*. "An American man-of-war has not been seen for a still longer period, nor is it likely any will appear frequently, since it is seldom that more than one or two are ever stationed in the China Seas. . . . In the present state of affairs in Europe it would certainly be a strange eventuality if England, France, and America all should owe to the intention of a Governor-General of Siberia, and the unforeseen presence of a powerful Russian squadron, the personal safety of their diplomatic agents in Japan, as well as the possibility of maintaining their position."[57]

The burial of the Russian mariners—the first funeral in Yokohama—was performed with great ceremony, the governors of Kanagawa (Mizuno Tadanori, and Sakai, Lord of Oki) and their retinue being required to attend.[58] In the words of Tilley:

The funeral took place in the afternoon. The authorities had only provided cumbersome deal boxes for coffins, and the whole morning we had been occupied in covering them with silk, to make them as decent as possible. Two priests of the Greek Church were present; one hundred and thirty men were landed, with all the officers from the corvette. The Consuls or their representatives, the officers of the wrecked U.S. schooner [*Fenimore Cooper*], and the sailors, as well as nearly all the foreign residents, were present. The ceremony of the Greek Church is impressive. The priests chanted the service, and the sailors outside chanted the responses; each mourner held a lighted wax taper in his hand. The mass being finished, the Commodore [Popov] entered the room, knelt for a moment by the corpses, and kissed the cold lips of each; all the late officers' comrades followed this example. They then bore the coffins themselves, the Commodore supporting one side, and the mournful procession took its way through the pretty village amid crowds of squatting Japanese, who had been ordered to attend. Many of the *moosoome* I saw

---

[56] Tilley, 163-170.
[57] Report dated Tokyo, August 28, in the *London Times*, November 17, 1859, p. 5.
[58] Joseph Heco, *The Narrative of a Japanese*, I, 222-224.

were much affected, wiping their eyes and cheeks on their little pieces
of paper, taken from the sleeve of their robes. All were very grave and
seemed much impressed by the ceremony. At the gates of a temple which
we passed, the corps of holy men, dressed out in their best raiment,
lifted their joint hands as we passed. The Governor of Yedo and Kanagawa, and many of the chief officers in palanquins, were present. On
the side of a little mount covered with trees, two shallow graves had
been dug. The rest of the funeral service was here chanted, one last look
given at the dead, the coffins were nailed down, and the unfortunate
victims were soon covered up by the numerous Japanese who had till
now been concealed behind the brushwood. Three volleys of musketry
were then fired in the air by the sailors who were stationed a few paces
off; minute guns had been all along fired from the corvette.[59]

Meanwhile no progress was made in the tracing of the killers. The
foreign community clamored for strong measures, but Muravev-
Amurskii exercised remarkable restraint. He accepted the findings
of a committee of inquiry, which he had appointed, that the murders
must be considered a simple act of brigandage, and satisfied himself
with an official Japanese expression of regret, the dismissal of the
local governors, the promise that everything would be done to catch
the assassins and execute them in the presence of Russian witnesses
at the scene of the crime, and the pledge that a Japanese guard would
be kept in perpetuity at the mortuary chapel, the construction of
which was financed by the officers and midshipmen of the Russian
squadron. On September 5, 1859, having moved once more aboard
the *Amerika*, Muravev-Amurskii departed with his squadron, leaving
only the *Askold* behind until the twenty-ninth to conclude the settlement of the incident.[60]

And so ended the first of a long series of tragedies, with something
very like a solemn farce [Alcock asserted years later]; the apology and the
promise were made, the chapel has been built, but of course nothing
has ever been heard of the perpetrators, and the very Governor so disgraced was actually named, two years later, to proceed as one of the
Tycoon's Envoys on a mission to the Treaty Powers in Europe—the court
of Russia among the rest: and it was only on my remonstrance that he
was removed from the mission and another appointed in his place. The

[59] Tilley, 171-172. In November of 1860 the bodies of the Russian seamen were
moved to a new cemetery in Kanagawa. No Russians were then in that area, but on
the call of Mr. Howard Vyse, the British Vice-Consul in Kanagawa, all the representatives of the other European powers in the capital attended the reburial and "honored
the memory of the deceased with the warmest and brotherly commiseration. . . ."
(Russia, Ministry of the Navy, Naval Scientific Section, Letter from Hakodate, undated, unsigned, 163-164.)
[60] Kornilov, "Izvestiia," 121; Litke, 13: 412; Heki, 109.

struggle had now commenced in earnest, and first blood had been shed—the struggle between European diplomacy with protocols and the appliances of modern warfare in the background;—and Japanese policy, animated by a fierce spirit of national fanaticism and hostilities to all innovation, backed by the assassin's steel and all the weapons of oriental treachery and ruthless cruelty.[61]

The reasons for Muravev-Amurskii's moderation were various. By necessity, his considerations were "both of expediency and practicability." Alcock, with whom he had conferred, admitted: "To blockade the port and bombard the city, assuming it were in the Count's power to do either, gave little promise of better result. The first would have the immediate effect of making both the Capital and port of Kanagawa untenable to Foreigners;—and the last was an extreme measure, likely to cost the lives of thousands of innocent and harmless people, without doing the least injury to those really concerned in the wrong."[62] But the fact remains that Muravev-Amurskii, had he wished to do so, could easily have exploited the murder of his men as a pretext for advancing his otherwise "active" Far Eastern policy. In the light of European reprisals in later years, it would not have been extraordinary had Muravev-Amurskii at this time annexed Sakhalin; as a matter of fact there were rumors current in Japan that one of his officers had presented the Shogunate with a demand for the cession of the Japanese half of the island. It is to the everlasting credit of Muravev-Amurskii that he did not resort to such measures and did not even demand a financial indemnity, brushing aside the arguments of those who suggested it, with the proud statement that "Russia does not sell the blood of her subjects."[63] At the same time there is proof in this moderation that Russia did not harbor any aggressive designs against Japan at that time. Muravev-Amurskii summed up the situation neatly on the eve of his departure in a letter to General Nikolai Ignatev, Russian Ambassador in China: "Of course, I shall depart from here with due satisfaction from the Japanese government; at the same time I shall leave them with the thought that I took great pity on them when I did not resort to bombardment. But the Sakhalin question, unfortunately, will not be finished, and the English newspapers will take advantage of this incident to proclaim to the whole world *comme*

[61] Alcock, I, 245.   [62] *Ibid.*, I, 244.
[63] Treat, I, 91-92; Kornilov, "Izvestiia," 121.

on traite les Russes au Japon, malgré la présence de leur nombreuse escadre."[64]

IN HAKODATE

It was in Hakodate, where the Russian consul resided, far from the turbulence of the capital city with its mounting number of assassinations and incidents, that Russo-Japanese relations developed most regularly in the years following the opening of the country. Iosif Goshkevich, who had become acquainted with Japan at the time of the first Putiatin expedition and who had continued his study of the Japanese language in later years with the assistance of Tachibana Kosai alias Vladimir Iosifovich Yamatov, arrived in Hakodate as first Russian consul on the clipper *Dzhigit* on November 5, 1858, and established himself at the Jitsugyo-ji, a temple set aside for him by the authorities as temporary consulate. He came accompanied by Mrs. Goshkevich and their son, by a naval agent attached to the consulate (Lieutenant Pavel Nazimov), a physician and his wife (Dr. and Mrs. Mikhail Albrecht), a priest (Vasilii Makhov), a secretary, and male and female servants.[65]

Goshkevich was not the first Western representative to settle in this region, Mr. Elisha E. Rice, the U.S. Commercial Agent at Hakodate, who represented himself as being a consul, having taken up residence already, but Goshkevich was of greater stature, of a caliber more like that of Townsend Harris, and was to impress both the Japanese and the foreigners. It was said of Goshkevich that he was "a man speaking or writing most European tongues," while Rice's correspondence in his own language was at best "a curiosity in composition and orthography."[66] Goshkevich was worthy of respect also, because like a samurai of Japan, he had duties that were purely official, while Rice and his successors were involved in private commercial transactions. The appointment of merchants as diplomatic representatives, economical as it may have been in the short run, brought little prestige to the United States, least of all in China and

[64] *Materialy otnosiashchiesia do prebyvaniia v Kitae N. P. Ignateva v 1859-60 godakh*, 79-80.

[65] Russia, *Obzor*, 627; Abe Masami, "Hakodate chusatsu Rokoku ryoji Gosukeuichi," 2: 141-142; Hakodate Kyoiku-kai, *Hakodate kyoiku nempyo*, 18; Russia, "Russkii beregovoi lazaret," 96.

[66] Tilley, 119; Cosenza, 376; K. Zelenoi, "Iz zapisok o krugosvetnom plavanii," 92. In the early 1860's the foreign colony in Hakodate included also the British consul C. Pemberton Hodgson, who represented at the same time the interests of France, Portugal, and the Netherlands, as well as the Jesuit Mermet, who acted as secretary for the French consulate.

Japan, where merchants were regarded as the lowest of the traditional four classes of society. To make matters worse, Rice had a talent for alienating others—Japanese, Russians, Englishmen, and even his own countrymen. "If anything ought to prevent governments intrusting political business to trading men, especially in such a country as Japan," wrote Tilley, "the disgraceful scenes in this town of Hakodadi ought to be a lesson." One day, for example, Rice engaged in fisticuffs with the commander of a clipper-schooner. "Whatever may have been the disputes between these two men, who accused each other (and the whole was an affair of dollars, or the means of getting them)," observed Tilley, "the fact of a representative of a great people like that of the United States, so far forgetting himself as to come to blows with his opponent, and even to fight a maudlin kind of duel with him, and then their both running to complain to the consul of another nation of each other's proceedings, is to make a consulship a laughing-stock to all lookers-on; and a pretty picture it was to set before a people like the Japanese and their officers, whose satirical nature, though their words may not be understood, can be unmistakably read in the nervous twitching of their mouths, and the droll twinkling of their eyes."[67] As so often in those days, the frontier-type rowdyism of a number of mid-nineteenth century Americans in Japan struck blows that shook Japanese resistance to Russian penetration.

One of the first tasks that confronted Goshkevich was the clarification of the monetary rate of exchange, a problem on which Poset and Townsend Harris had collaborated in the capital, and which was to remain a source of friction between the foreigners and the Japanese for some time to come. The relative current value of gold, silver, and copper in Japan and other countries was so ill-adjusted that Japan was threatened by the outflow of her gold and copper in exchange for silver. To alleviate the situation, Westerners proposed that the Japanese raise the relative value of their gold coinage; the Japanese on the other hand preferred to depreciate their silver by two thirds in relation to the copper coin. But this pushed up the cost of Japanese products excessively and the Westerners accused the Japanese of scheming to thwart foreign trade, while the Japanese accused the Westerners of seeking to rob her of her metallic wealth.[68] Goshkevich was faced with the additional problem of establishing the relative value of Russian currency. Concerning the situation in

---

[67] Tilley, 119-120. See also letter from Lieutenant Nazimov, dated November 1 (13), 1860, 229.

[68] Alcock, I, 146-149.

Hakodate Kornilov wrote: "The exchange rate of foreign currency has not yet been fully established until now. American and English silver the Japanese know already, but ours was seen here probably for the first time in autumn. At first our silver ruble was taken for a dollar, and a quarter of a ruble for a shilling, but then the consulate succeeded in establishing the relative value of our silver."[69]

A student of Chinese and Japanese language and culture, Goshkevich was truly interested in life about him and well able to exert considerable influence. Nothing so flatters the Japanese as a foreigner's observance of their ways, and the Russians (though by no means all of them) were generally far more inclined to do in Japan as the Japanese did than were their English and American counterparts. At the same time, paradoxical as this may seem, their respect for Japanese customs attracted the Japanese to Russian ways in an atmosphere of give-and-take. Goshkevich, who was popularly known as "the white haired consul," personally acquainted the people of Hakodate with miscellaneous contributions of the West, including the art of photography.[70] Most significant perhaps was his role in introducing Russian medical practice and Russian learning. One of his first official acts was to obtain permission for the naval physician attached to the consulate to give free medical treatment to the populace. A letter from Dr. Albrecht, dated July 31, 1859, gives a revealing side light of contemporary Hakodate:

Since April of this year, when I received permission from Edo to practice medicine, I am frequently visited by sick Japanese. I have succeeded in gaining their confidence by the fortunate healing of dropsy in two patients who had been treated without success by Japanese doctors. We do not yet have a hospital for the reception of sick Japanese; we ourselves remain as yet lodged in one temple of very limited space, and there is little hope to move by winter into the houses, which are being built by the consulate. Nor do I have a medical assistant, of whom I am in great need, because till this day I must prepare the medicine myself.

My practice now consists partly in treating those who come to my lodgings; partly it is that of a polyclinic. With the first arrival of the Japanese, there came to me also a Japanese doctor on the desire of the governor to observe my ambulatory and polyclinic practice; later he was joined by two more Japanese doctors, who visit with me daily. As the number of patients who come to me is large, and as it is impossible

---

[69] A. Kornilov II, "Zimovka v Khakodate," 98. In 1860 one American dollar was worth one ruble and thirty-three kopecks. (Letter from Ivan Makhov, dated Hakodate, November 26 [December 8], 1860, 84.)

[70] Koshizaki, *Hokkaido shashin bunka-shi*, 29-31; Koshizaki, *Ezo byobu*, 39-42.

for me alone to examine so many sick, and moreover to prepare medicine for them, I let the Japanese doctors treat part of the sick under my direction. When they are in want of necessary medicaments, I let them have them from my pharmacy. Of the three Japanese doctors only one speaks a little Dutch and knows a considerable number of generally used medicaments, even has a small supply of them. With him I occupy myself specially. Among other things, he learns from me Russian, and I in turn study Japanese. Calomel is much misused here; it is given internally even for itch without any external remedies. So far I have not tested Japanese medicaments, but will not delay doing so. In the Japanese herb shops there are many herbs and roots and of course each herb has in Japan its special medical designation. The patients who come to me, unfortunately, represent for the greater part the most inveterate, neglected maladies, where the skill of the Japanese doctors has failed already. . . . Diseases which are exhibited more frequently are eye diseases and syphilis. Both are so amazingly wide-spread here, as I have not seen anywhere; the profligacy of women is very wide-spread, yet there is no trace of medical police. . . .[71]

In 1859 a temporary naval lazaret was established at nearby Kameda-mura, supplanted before long by a regular hospital at Moto-machi, adjacent to the consular building. Here about a hundred Japanese were treated each year. As the number of Japanese patients increased, the authorities became concerned for fear that political complications might develop, especially since the doctors of Hakodate resented the competition and alien methods of Dr. Albrecht and, after his demise, of Dr. Zalesskii, his successor, and proscribed Russian treatment of the populace. But those Japanese, who were studying medicine with the Russian doctor, were permitted to continue their training, and Russian practice was kept alive under the guise of medical instruction.[72]

Meanwhile the construction of the consulate and subsidiary buildings was seen through to completion by Goshkevich. Erected after much debate and delay at Kamishiomi-cho (now known as Moto-machi), the consular building, though made of wood, was large and impressive, so much so that the rumor spread in Hakodate that it was intended not for the Russian consul but for the future Russian governor of Hokkaido, a rumor which Nazimov attributed to the representatives of Great Britain and the United States.[73] From

---

[71] Letter from Dr. Albrecht, dated Hakodate, July 19 (31), 1859, 26-29.

[72] Russia, "Russkii beregovoi lazaret," 96-97; Okada Kenzo, *Roshia bunka to Hako-date*, 9.

[73] Letter from Nazimov, dated November 1 (13), 1860, 227-230.

the consular settlement Russian influence emanated through the consulate itself, the hospital, a language school, personal contacts, and the church.

Dr. Albrecht had noted in his letter that he taught Russian to one of the doctors. Most of the Russians taught their language to a number of Japanese at one time or another, but though a Russian language school had been established by a naval officer in Nagasaki by 1860, language instruction developed more slowly in Hakodate.[74] There the most constructive step in the teaching of Russian was the compilation of a little children's primer by Ivan Makhov. Published in 1861 under the double title *Russkaia azbuka* and *Roshiya no iroha,* it acquainted students with the Russian alphabet and its *kana* transliteration as well as with a number of useful phrases.[75] Repeated Japanese requests for a teacher of Russian had gone unheeded,[76] and it was for this reason that Makhov undertook the task, and because he had little else to do. For some time he had been wondering how to turn his idleness to a constructive purpose: "To collect plants—there are many botanists among us; insects—there are amateurs in this field too; shells—there are also experts; to stuff animals—I can't, it turns my stomach . . . moreover, for all this one needs knowledge and skill, and finally there must be an objective— where to get rid of what. . . ." The compilation of a Russo-Japanese primer appeared more attractive. "I began to draw printed and written letters in four forms; it is difficult, and dull, but comes out not bad." With much effort and loss of patience Makhov saw the little book through the wood-block printing process. But at last it was finished. "By the Japanese New Year one hundred alphabet books had been completed, among them two on Russian stationery in silken binding and one on many-colored stationery in a binding of the best silk material; all three with pictures. The first two I presented as a gift to the Hakodate governor and vice-governor on New Year's Day (January 29 [February 10]), the third one was given to the governor for transmittal to the Shogun." One hundred copies were offered to the governor as gifts for the children of Edo, Kyoto, and Nagasaki. Others were distributed freely to children and adults.

Preparations were made also for regular classroom instruction, but

74 Ivan Makhov, letter of November 26 (December 8), 1860, 87.
75 For an illustrated description of the primer, see Lensen, *Report from Hokkaido,* 89-94.
76 Letter from Ivan Makhov, dated June 24 (July 6), 1861, 81.

it is not clear when it was first begun. In his letter of February 12, 1862, Ivan Makhov wrote that he had moved into his regular quarters in a newly built little house in the courtyard of the consulate. His four-room apartment occupied only half of the house; the other half was to be a school for Japanese boys. "The boy students, as has been heard, have already been appointed by the governor, but the cleanly finished rooms of the school are occupied meanwhile by soldiers' sons and carpenters—by Japanese, who make furniture, green-houses or hotbeds, and all kinds of trifles, so that school has been postponed for an indefinite time. . . ."[77] By 1872 there were five Japanese instructors of Russian at the government school Hakodate Gakko and in the summer of 1873 the psalmist Vissarion Sartov became an instructor of Russian language, mathematics, geography, and history there. Before long the school was renamed Ro-Gakko (Russian School) and the curriculum was confined increasingly to language instruction. The Russian Missionary School founded in 1873 offered courses in Russian; so did more and more Japanese schools in Hakodate and elsewhere.[78] Perhaps the most dramatic step in acquainting Japanese pupils with Russia was the despatch of a group of Japanese students to Russia in 1865. This was done on the suggestion of Goshkevich, who was then returning to Russia. But though Goshkevich gave them occasional instruction during their stay in St. Petersburg (1867-1868), and though one of them stayed on in Putiatin's house, detained by a love affair with a Russian girl and did not return to Japan until November of 1873, the educational venture proved disappointing as neither government had worked out a program of study for the students and they themselves were not yet sure of their own interests. As things worked out, their major source of information and their only true friend and companion in the Russian capital turned out to be Tachibana Kosai, who told them a great deal about Russian customs. A significant precedent had been set, however, and a number of Japanese who in their later years were to be prominent in the development of Hokkaido received training in Russia.[79]

[77] Letter from Ivan Makhov, dated Hakodate, January 31 (February 12), 1862, 81-86.

[78] For further detail, see Lensen, *Report from Hokkaido*, 111-120. A brief but useful description of the development of foreign language schools in other parts of Japan will be found in Peter Berton, Paul Langer, and Rodger Swearingen, *Japanese Training and Research in the Russian Field*, 12-16.

[79] Naito, *Ken-Ro denshusei shimatsu*; Okada, *Roshia bunka*, 14-15. For photographs of the students, see Lensen, *Report from Hokkaido*, 128-145.

The ice-free roadstead, the Russian hospital, and fresh provisions made Hakodate a welcome stopping place for Russian vessels.[80] Returning from less hospitable regions in the Far East, Russian mariners referred to Hakodate as "home" and looked forward to the amateur plays, masquerades, and ladies' picnics that awaited them there.[81] In later years the state of Hakodate's foreign society was to appear "peculiar" to a prominent Western traveler.

A limited number of residents, with little or no business to occupy them, induces a state to which all small communities are liable. A most healthy climate permits of no disease in the body, but the mind broods over its own cares, and it must be added—the cares of others. The latter begets scandal, the first insobriety. People who should live as one family—two dozen foreigners in the midst of thirty-seven thousand natives—exist as cats and dogs, some cats together and some dogs together. Some wear brass collars, such as consuls, some wear black coats, such as missionaries: some would be industrious dogs if they had enough to do, some would be sleepy, quiet cats, if their tails were not trodden upon.[82]

With longing he recalled life in Hakodate in the early 1860's:

There was generally a Russian vessel of war lying in the harbour, which added its officers to the society of the place, and its drunken sailors to the streets of the town. Naturally, in so small a community, all nationality was dropped, and the residents were more like the members of one family, such etiquette as formal invitations and calls being discarded, for the more open and cordial hospitality induced by a common feeling of being strangers amongst a treacherous and deceitful race; and all seemed to look to one another for mutual protection.[83]

The Japanese were exposed to Russian ways. To be sure contact was restricted even now. Dr. Albrecht reported that Russian relations with the Japanese were solely of an official and business nature, and though there was probably more sincerity and spontaneity in Japanese reluctance to invite the Westerners into their humble homes than Albrecht realized, his assertion that the authorities did not want the populace to fraternize with the foreigners was essentially correct.[84] Every attempt was made meanwhile by the Russians

[80] Dr. Albrecht reported on April 28, 1862 that Hakodate had been visited "in the past ten years" by fourteen Russian warships, as well as by one whaler of the Finland Company, two English warships and nine merchantmen, eight American merchantmen en route to Nikolaevsk, eleven American whalers, three Oldenburg whalers and one whaler flying the flag of the Sandwich (Hawaiian) Islands. (80-86.) For an account of the first winterage of a Russian vessel in Hakodate Bay, see Kornilov, "Zimovka," 87-106.

[81] N. K., "Iz Iaponii," 15.   [82] T. W. B. [Blakestone], *Japan in Yezo*, 15.

[83] *Ibid.*, 5.

[84] Letter from Albrecht, dated April 16 (28), 1862, 84.

to win the good will of the ruling class. One Christmas Eve, 1858, for example, a Christmas tree had been put up in the consulate for the children of the officialdom, and not only the children but their elders joined in the festivities in a room, thoughtfully decorated with Russian and Japanese flags. On New Year's Eve a masquerade was staged, and on New Year's Day the governor and fifteen important officials were wined and dined and shown a great many things of interest, including a map of the Amur River and the eastern shores of Siberia.[85] But in general the Russians were less successful in undermining the resistance of the samurai, who, as Albrecht put it, "under the influence of Japanese politics, do not show us much sympathy and look at us askance, as at uninvited guests, who by their presence defile the sacred soil of Japan," than in winning the tolerance, if not the good will, of the common people, "who do not harbor toward us the deep prejudice of the Japanese officialdom; on the contrary always meet us with good-natured and smiling faces, and the most hearty reception awaits us always in Japanese inns when we travel out of town."[86]

This does not mean that Russo-Japanese relations were completely devoid of friction in the north. In the summer of 1861, the officers of the Russian warship *Naezdnik*, having heard that the crew of their vessel had had a glorious time with "pleasure women" at one of the houses in Hakodate went ashore to share the experiences of their subordinates, but were refused admission. Frustrated, they began to molest a lady who happened to pass through the neighborhood. This annoyed the townspeople and they gave the Russian officers a sound thrashing. The officers thereupon dragged the proprietor of the establishment to the local authorities and filed a complaint. The following day Japanese officials called on Goshkevich to inquire after the health of the officers and to request that they appear as witnesses. Anxious to hush up the whole matter, Goshkevich refused to produce the witnesses and the case was dropped, although not without further embarrassment as officers and crew of the same vessel went ashore at what is now Muroran Harbor and climbed a volcano, despite the Japanese protest that the area had not been opened to foreigners.[87]

The year before, in December of 1860, the Goshkeviches had gone

[85] Letter from Goshkevich, published in *Severnaia Pchela* on October 27, 1859, as cited in Zhukov, 126-127.
[86] Letter from Albrecht, dated April 16 (28), 1862, 84.
[87] Abe Masami, 3: 308-309.

to Nagasaki together with Mrs. Albrecht and Mrs. Fletcher, wife of an American merchant. On their way back to Hakodate, they had decided to continue from Edo overland. Although travel on land was permitted only to consul generals, Goshkevich, as the only Russian consul in Japan, enjoyed similar privileges. The Japanese authorized the voyage and in March of 1861, Consul and Mrs. Goshkevich and their son, Mrs. Albrecht, Mrs. Fletcher, and a maid set out for Hakodate, carried in palanquins. They traveled in a long procession, with officials and servants of all sorts and a following of up to a thousand, whose oil-paper lanterns gave a magic touch to the mountain trails. The Japanese government had sent ahead word of the procession and everywhere everything had been prepared so that the tired travelers could rest in rooms, wall-papered and furnished in Western style. Yet the trip was not without danger, for the mountain slopes of northern Japan which the fleetfooted bearers traversed were steep and covered with snow. But most dangerous of all, disgruntled Sendai clansmen are said to have plotted the assassination of the Russians. They did not find the necessary cut-throats, however, and had to watch the procession pass by, "gnashing their teeth with deep regret." On the twenty-fourth day of their voyage, the Russians reached Sai, where they were carried aboard a clipper. Four hours later they arrived safely in Hakodate, unaware of the danger which had lurked along the road.[88]

The friendliness that existed between the Russians and Americans in Japan in the late 1850's and early 1860's, based to a large extent on a common animosity toward the British, was bound to arouse British misgivings. The American public had sympathized with Russia during the Crimean War and the Tsar Liberator supported the Union during the American Civil War and sent a Russian squadron to New York and another one to San Francisco to forestall British and French intervention. Linking the importance of Hakodate with his suspicion of Russians and Americans—suspicions not so startling if one keeps in mind that in 1863 the average American citizen believed that there was a secret alliance between his country and Russia[89]—Consul C. Pemberton Hodgson wrote a vivid summation of the British view of Russia's progression toward Japan. Tracing Russian activities in Siberia, the Amur region, China and

---

[88] Letter from Mrs. Albrecht, 70-72; letter from Ivan Makhov of November 26 (December 8), 1860, 87.

[89] Edward H. Zabriskie, *American-Russian Rivalry in the Far East*, 13.

Tatar Strait and Russian penetration and Russianization of the larger part of Sakhalin and of the Kuril Islands, he commented: "Her polar bears had walked across from land to land, and exchanged cards with their 'confrères' of Sagahlien. The invitation was accepted, and the visit returned. The volcanic isles rose up like spirits from the frozen deep, to afford these rude visitors a stepping-stone, and in 1855 we first hear that the flag of Russia is waving in Japan, and that the Okhotsk Sea has a natural and, in case of need, an artificial barrier." Hodgson spoke of the Russian push across the Asian continent and of the freezing climate which affected it, of the difficulty of overland transportation.

A harbour must be found, say the Russians. Sagahlien is reached. Tonquien Bay is found, but no safe anchorage. A little lower, coal—ah! warm your hands, you are getting hotter on the scent. Where are Shanghae, Hongkong, and India?

Sagahlien is a pretty place, but no port. Let us cross over. Castries Bay is very good, but only open for four months; but then the ice! Barracouta Harbour, or Port Imperial? What splendid pines, what glorious timber! but during eight months of the year we can never see your foliage, and the ice is very thick. Port Seymour? this is better: let us advance. Hornet Bay? a convenient place to come out and leave our sting behind us. Victoria Bay? well, this might do; down yet a little lower. Such is fate. Broughton Bay is occupied, and from Nicolaiesk to Broughton Bay, if not to Tsusima Island, all the coast of Mantchouria and the Corea is Russianised.

But to the east we must have a port; there is only one poor roadstead in all Sagahlien. Up to Port Seymour we are frozen in nearly three-fourths of the year. Let us cross over. Hakodate is close to Shanghae, Hongkong, India, and all those choice spots we love so well, not to colonize, but only to visit from time to time. Hakodate will do. . . .

Steamers have not yet steamed across the vast Pacific; they *may* soon do so; but until this fact is realised, we must have a shelter in that grand breakwater to the Japanese sea. Let us make offers to the Princes of Nambu, Matsmai, and others. Let us offer them the protection of our double-headed eagle, and as there is no doubt that all Japan was once Russian or Mongolian (for have we not exhumed plates and other relics[90] with Russian hieroglyphs?), we shall find that the old links will easily be rejoined, though centuries of ice and distance have separated us so long.

Hodgson had no quarrel with Russians as individuals. He regarded the Russian officers as "gentlemen and charming companions" and

---

[90] Hodgson comments in a footnote that "it was never ascertained how long these plates and relics *had been* under ground."

admitted that he did not know how he would have passed his first summer in Hakodate without their help. But he felt it his duty to expose Russian influence in Hakodate, "the turnpike-gate between America and the Pacific on the one side, and the Japanese Sea and Russia on the other—for it is useless longer to disguise the fact that all Mantchourie and Corea is today Russian." Fearing that the Russians had plans of making the lord of Matsumae "nominal monarch, *pro tem.*, of the island, until a convenient season," he warned that Hakodate, though as yet not impregnable by land on the east side, might become a Gibraltar or Aden in the hands of a European power. He felt it necessary to awaken his countrymen to the great strides the Russians were making in the Far East as a whole.

They do *all* so well, so thoroughly, and with such "franchise," they disguise nothing. No, they tell you, "We have taken this point and fortified it: it was necessary. We have found coal there, and claim the mines. We have ships at Nicolaiesk, but they are all frozen in; so many buildings at Kamschatka, where there is beautiful timber; and then the few we are graciously permitted to bring round the Cape. These altogether will make a nice little squadron; and should the happy day arrive that we could make a descent on the devoted Elysian shores, our thirty-two and sixty-eight little houris would thunder back the Bomarsund bullets, and make little "Eknesses" of Hongkong and Singapore.

At the same time Hodgson wrote that the Japanese were defying the Russians on Sakhalin—"ten thousand men dispute their right to it, and do not recognize the link in the chain which they pretend connects their modern Romanoff with the descendants of the sun-born goddess"—and that with foreign support the Japanese could readily assure the territorial integrity of their country. Certain that "the United States had silently encouraged the Russian Government in her designs against devoted Hakodate," he believed that American preoccupation with the Civil War would simplify matters.[91]

Yezo was to have been a Russian appendage to the Kuril Isles, but now, thank Heaven! it is still Japanese: and I trust the Treaty powers, if not from love of these kind friends, will, even from selfish motives, coalesce and maintain its inviolability and its integrity as part of the Tycoon's dominions. If not, although they may beat them at their ports, where of course they will stop trade and commerce, they will find a brave and hardy race ready to defend their shores, burn their villages, set loose their waters, and retire where all Europe will quake to follow them.[92]

[91] No American warships visited Hakodate during Hodgson's stay there.
[92] C. Pemberton Hodgson, *A Residence at Nagasaki and Hakodate*, 300-308.

Hostile though some Japanese remained to "foreign barbarians" in general, and much as officials tried to isolate the populace from the Westerners, more and more inhabitants of Hakodate succumbed to the influence of the small foreign community. In the summer of 1861 Ivan Makhov related:

The Europeans either walk in pairs (husband and wife) along the streets, or, in large company, ride on horseback at great speed, gallop, hastening somewhere on a distant outing, a sportive picnic, to a hot pie. And the Japanese marvel at European sumptuousness, and come running out of their little houses to look at the cavalcade, at our amazons, Mrs. Fletcher and Mrs. Albrecht, marvel and surreptitiously appropriate a little at a time. There, you see, a little house has been renovated, and there, there has grown, as if by magic, not a little house, but a whole house with entresols, a gallery and a large open shop of Japanese and partly even European goods. Not paper windows only does one see in the houses of new construction, but Japanese persons are visible from the street through windows of glass, large and small, square and triangular in size. In another house one can find an easy chair or a stool, a European wine-glass, a drinking glass, a plate. . . . And then, some other Japanese, with pretensions already to a certain amount of culture of a European, will nonchalantly take out of his bosom a watch on a chain and ask to check it with yours; on the nose of another you will see glasses, perhaps of green color; in a word, quietly, a little at a time, European customs incite the Japanese, who have sat immovably in seclusion for about two and a half thousand [sic] years.[93]

Perhaps the most notable role in the propagation of the Russian language, Russian concepts, and beliefs in Hakodate and eventually in other parts of Japan was played by the Russian Orthodox Church. Backed by the diplomatic support of Goshkevich, it was to leave a lasting imprint, symbolized to this day by such outstanding landmarks as the Russian church overlooking Hakodate and the magnificent Russian cathedral in the heart of Tokyo.

[93] Letter from Ivan Makhov of June 24 (July 6), 1861, 80-81.

CHAPTER ELEVEN · WITH CROSS AND ABACUS

THE ORTHODOX CHURCH IN JAPAN

THE first Russian priest to reside in Japan was Vasilii Makhov, who had arrived in Hakodate together with Consul Goshkevich on November 5, 1858.[1] Like Goshkevich he was not new to Japan, but had visited it already aboard the frigate *Diana* with Putiatin. He too had been shipwrecked at Shimoda, and heading for home on the brig *Greta* had been taken prisoner by the British, though thanks to his priestly calling he was released three days later. But, when Makhov arrived in Hakodate, he was already in his sixties, and experienced and capable a man though he may have been—one compatriot described him as "a kind-hearted old man, a person not at all stupid, but without much education"[2]—the long voyages and the change in climate had undermined his health and he was forced to return to Russia in 1860.[3] By this time a modest place of worship had been completed. An eyewitness recalled its construction and consecration in 1859:

A church was being built in conjunction with the consulate. The ladies decorated it, and our artists painted religious images. All participated spiritually in the building of the first Christian temple in Japan after two hundred and twenty-one years following the banishment of Christians. . . .

[1] Abe Masami, 2: 141-142. According to the biographical sketch in *Fregat Diana*, Vasilii Makhov arrived in Japan on June 25, 1859, thus later than Goshkevich.

[2] Schilling, 7: 290.

[3] "Iv. M-v" in preface to Vasilii Makhov, *Fregat Diana*, p. vi. Japanese sources give the name of the chaplain in Hakodate simply as Makhov, without any given name. No doubt it was for this reason that Okada Kenzo in his excellent survey of Russian cultural influence on life in Hakodate and Abe Masami in his story of Goshkevich's activities in the same city assumed that Makhov the priest and Makhov the author of the Russian primer published in 1861 were one and the same person. With no further data at my disposal during my research in Hakodate in 1953-1954, I fell into the same mistake, identifying in my *Report from Hokkaido* Ivan Makhov, the author, as also the chaplain. Only later did I find in Tokyo, among stacks of books stored away underneath the dome of the Orthodox cathedral, *Fregat Diana*, an account of the sailings and shipwreck of Putiatin's flagship, written by the archpriest Vasilii Emelianovich Makhov, with a preface by "Iv. M-v" (Ivan Makhov?). In the preface it was stated that Vasilii Makhov stayed in Japan only from June, 1859 to July, 1860. This plus the discovery of a series of letters from Hakodate by Ivan Makhov in 1861 and 1862, including the above mentioned account of his compilation of the primer, establish beyond doubt that Vasilii Makhov, the chaplain, and Ivan Makhov, the author, were two different persons.

And after somewhat more than two centuries, this trampled cross has risen again. We, who only recently had seen [Mt.] Papenberg, from which Catholic monks had been thrown into the sea, succeeded in being present at the consecration of the Christian temple, erected in the name of the Resurrection, and on the following day I saw in this temple a Portuguese (a sailor from a whaling ship) who prayed amongst us. A strange chance.[4]

It was Makhov's successor, the monk Nikolai (Ioan Kasatkin), who was to build up the Russian Orthodox Church in Japan and, in over fifty years of service in that country, contribute significantly to the spread of Japanese knowledge about Russia. Born in 1836, the son of a deacon, Ioan Kasatkin had lost his mother when he was only five. The difficulties and hardships of his youth had developed in him that will power and strength of character for which he became so noted in later years. Upon completion in 1856 of seminary studies in Smolensk, he had been sent at government expense to the theological academy in St. Petersburg, from which he had graduated in 1860. It had been there that he had come upon an announcement seeking a graduate of the academy for the consular church in Hakodate. His interest in Japan already aroused by the memoirs of Golovnin, which he had read, he was overcome by the urge to go to Japan and had expressed the desire to do so, not as a married priest, however, but as a monk. In the summer of 1860 he had been ordained as the monk Nikolai.[5]

From the capital, Nikolai made his way to the Pacific across Siberia, wintering in Nikolaevsk, where he became acquainted with the great missionary Innokentii, receiving useful advice from him. In later years Nikolai recalled the youthful enthusiasm and optimism with which he had set out for Japan: "When I was going there, I dreamed much of my Japan. It was painted in my imagination as a bride, awaiting my arrival with a bouquet in her hands." The Japanese were just waiting for him, he thought. He would bring the good news, and everything would change. But when Nikolai arrived in Hakodate on June 14, 1861 on the man-of-war *Amur*, he found that "his bride slept most prosaically and did not even think of him." Aside from the fact that the spreading of Christianity was as yet forbidden by law, missionary activity would not have been fruitful. In the words of Nikolai, "the Japanese of that day looked on foreigners as on

[4] N. K., "Iz Iaponii," 15.
[5] A. Platonova, *Apostol Iaponii*, 6-9; Hiyane Yasusada, *Shukyo-shi*, 149; Nihon Sei-kyokai Somu Kyoku, *Dai-shukyo Nikorai-shi jiseki*, 14-18.

animals, and on Christianity as on a wicked sect, to which only arrant evil-doers and sorcerers can belong."

Realizing that the mastery of Japanese was a prerequisite to successful missionary work, Nikolai devoted all his energies to this task, though the difficulties were especially great for lack of dictionaries and textbooks, and he had to tackle the "barbaric" tongue more by instinct than reason. For over seven years he slaved. "Somehow I learned at last to speak Japanese and mastered the same simple and easy means of writing, which is used in original and translated scholarly essays." With time his Japanese improved, and Nikolai became noted for his knowledge and forceful use of the language. His effectiveness was greatly augmented by the fact that he had devoted serious study also to Japanese literature, history, philosophy, religion, and customs. This the Japanese have always appreciated. He had waded through the Confucian classics, Hinayana and Mahayana Buddhist scriptures, and Japanese literature ranging from the *Kojiki* and *Nihon-shoki*, Japan's earliest extant histories, to various fictitious novels. One day when a Hakodate bookstore was about to go out of business he bought its entire collection for the church library. Soon his comments and notes graced the margins of Japanese books on diverse topics, from foreign relations to travel diaries and novels. Without question he was "one of the most scholarly and eloquent speakers (of Japanese) among the foreign residents of Japan."[6]

The anti-foreign, anti-Christian feeling was still very strong. At the house of Consul Goshkevich, Nikolai frequently met a Japanese who eyed him with bitter hatred, so much so that one day he could not resist asking him, "Why are you so angry at me?" This Japanese was Sawabe Takuma, a samurai from Tosa, one of the four clans most vociferous in their demand for "reverence to the Emperor, and expulsion of the barbarians." Married to the daughter of a Shinto priest, he had fallen heir to the Shinto duties; but it was as a former fencing instructor that he had been invited to teach the consul's son. Confronted by Nikolai he replied with heat: "You foreigners must all be killed. You have come here to spy on our country. And you with your preaching will hurt Japan most of all." It looked as if he himself would have killed Nikolai without the slightest hesitation and indeed some accounts assert that he had sought out Nikolai to

[6] Platonova, 10-20; Nihon Sei-kyokai, 22-23; Ernest W. Clement, *Christianity in Modern Japan*, 52; Cary, *History*, I, 20-21.

402

engage him in argument, and, if it proved impossible to defeat him in words, to kill him.

"Are you acquainted with my teaching then?" Nikolai asked.

"No," Sawabe replied truthfully.

Nikolai then asked him how he could judge what he did not know, and Sawabe agreed to listen. He listened and he heard. He had come to humiliate, if not kill Nikolai; instead he left imbued with new thoughts. He was to return again and again and be transformed from a fiery xenophobe into an ardent advocate of Christianity. Needless to say his countrymen were amazed, and some of his friends considered him insane.[7] "There comes to me a priest of the ancient religion to study our faith," Nikolai soon reported home. "If he does not cool, or does not perish [by execution for adopting Christianity], much can be expected from him." And before long he added that Sawabe planned to translate the Bible into Japanese from Chinese, and that they were only awaiting the necessary books from Peking. Sawabe was well educated, intelligent, and an excellent speaker. He was eager to be christened and as anxious to spread the Christian faith as he had once been to stamp it out. It was Nikolai who had to bridle his enthusiasm "lest he loses his head, before he succeeds to do anything for this end." So strict were the laws of the country, that there was no question of a Japanese studying Christianity openly. Sawabe had to read the Gospel surreptitiously while performing the Shinto services in his shrine. "I would put before me the Gospel instead of the heathen missal and read it, beating the usual drum. No one would think, that I am reading a foreign heresy."[8] But so eager and sincere was Sawabe in his desire for conversion, that Nikolai gave in at last, and accepting him into the Church, christened him Pavel.

It was a thorny path that Sawabe had chosen. His beloved wife went insane and during one of her attacks of madness burned down their home. His formal conversion had cost him whatever income he had received from the Shinto shrine. Now he had nothing. Nor could he count on the support of relatives and friends. They turned on him with the same bitterness with which he had once attacked Nikolai. But Sawabe was not the man to shun a fight and, the more hostility he encountered, the more forceful he became in his stand.

[7] Platonova, 21-22; Cary, I, 378-379; Kishimoto Hideo, *Shukyo-hen*, 266; Nihon Seikyokai, 27-28.

[8] Platonova, 22-23.

He debated the merits of the Christian faith at length with his friend Dr. Sakai Tokurei and emerged victorious. Sakai went to Nikolai himself for further instruction and was christened ultimately Ioan Sakai. Such zealous activity could not go unnoticed, and it was evident that his former friends, not to mention his mother-in-law, might well report Sawabe to the authorities.[9] Together with Dr. Sakai and another Christian, Iakov Urano, Mrs. Sakai and her daughter, and his own servant, Sawabe quitted Hakodate. After a while they felt it safer to separate, and Sawabe continued alone. This was not a wise decision for Sawabe was soon arrested as a spy. His clan had risen against the government and he was given away by his dialect as a man from Tosa. Proving that he was on his way from Hakodate, he was released, but the shelter he found in the home of Mrs. Sakai's parents in one of the villages proved short-lived, for as word got around that he was a Christian, the relatives, though they did not ask him to leave, began to discharge rifles before the house. They did this, they said, to frighten away evil spirits, but Sawabe took the hint and set out for Tokyo, where he hoped to find refuge. He had not gotten far, however, before he was arrested again as a spy. The officials who interrogated him this time were not as readily convinced of his harmlessness, and, though they did not detain him, they would not permit him to proceed to the capital, but insisted that he return to Hakodate. Hearing that Christians were being ferreted out there by the authorities, Sawabe hid for a while in a neighboring village, but at last he returned to Hakodate and called on Nikolai. There it was futile to hide, yet to his surprise no one arrested him. The die-hard adherents of the Shogunate had gathered in the city to make a last stand against the imperial forces, and military and political problems so absorbed the attention of officialdom that they could not concern themselves with the enforcement of the anti-Christian laws.[10]

Nikolai meanwhile had continued laying the groundwork for his missionary work. He did not tramp about the countryside with a sermon at the tip of his tongue, but concentrated at first in becoming acquainted with the ways of the Japanese and in making friends. "At the beginning to conquer love, then to spread the word"—such was his approach. He did not attack the adherents of other religions.

[9] According to Platonova they did and Sawabe was incarcerated, but though his health was undermined, his faith remained unbroken and in 1875 he was ordained into the priesthood. (25-26)

[10] Cary, *History*, I, 380-382.

He did not cross swords with the Buddhist clergy, but visited their temples and was well received. Once, for example, when Nikolai had entered a Buddhist temple to listen to a sermon, the Buddhist chief priest, in the absence of any chairs, cleared the altar and invited him to his amazement to use it as a seat. So respected was Nikolai by the Japanese!

The restoration of the Emperor in 1868 brought endless restrictions on missionary activities. As a government decree proclaimed: "The heretical religion of Christianity is strictly prohibited. A reward will be given to those who report any suspicious person to the nearest public office." Only the strong protests from Western diplomatic representatives dissuaded the Japanese from scattering converts in the Nagasaki area to regions where they could be de-Christianized effectively. Yet Nikolai was satisfied with his labors. Writing in 1869, he attributed his success in spreading the gospel to two factors: that Japan was ripe to accept Christianity in general, and that Christianity was presented by him in the Orthodox form, not in the Roman Catholic or Protestant forms.[11] He might have added that his success lay also in the upheaval of Japan in general during the years of transition to imperial government, and of Hakodate in particular. In the wake of the reopening of Japan the minds of the Japanese had been exposed to foreign influences. As those who had sought to maintain the seclusion policy had feared, an increasing number of Japanese were attracted to foreign methods and ideologies. This does not mean that the Japanese suddenly became pro-Western. Often foreign ways were regarded as sort of shortcut to military power. Buddhism is a great religion, but its original introduction into Japan was not religious in motivation, and its influence was not confined to the religious sphere. Buddhism was a vehicle for the introduction of Chinese learning and ideas—political and scientific as well as philosophical and artistic. No doubt Christianity was approached by many in the same light, and not without reason; Christianity like Buddhism—if not even more than Buddhism—proved a means through which foreign ideas were brought into Japan.

Nikolai found the Japanese increasingly receptive. When he taught Russian to several officials he could get on the subject of Christianity without apparent embarrassment to them. The time had come for

11 Platonova, 28-30.

the commencement of full-scale missionary activity, which was be-yond the resources of a consular chaplain. Nikolai entrusted his work in Hakodate to Pavel Sawabe and Ioan Sakai, while he himself, in late 1869, hastened to Russia to plead before the Holy Synod for the establishment of a Russian spiritual mission in Japan. When Nikolai arrived in Russia in March of 1870 the Holy Synod was considering the establishment of a bishopric in China and offered it to him. But he declined it, choosing to return to Japan, and on April 18, 1870, obtained approval for the establishment of a Russian mission in Japan. The mission was put under the jurisdiction of the Bishop of Kamchatka, and it was to consist, in addition to Nikolai himself, of three regular priests—two missionaries and one church-man—with posts in Tokyo, Kyoto, Nagasaki, and Hakodate. But, although financial support for the mission was promised by the gov-ernment and by many private persons,[12] Nikolai returned to Japan with only one new co-worker, Father Grigorii Vorontsov, and the latter fell ill and had to return to Russia after only two months.[13]

Father Nikolai, now elevated as head of the mission to the position of archimandrite, had made careful plans for the spreading of the gospel. The Orthodox missionaries, he believed, must not confine their work to oral preaching in Japanese and to personal contact with the people, but must set about translating the Holy Scriptures into Japanese and to compose religious textbooks for the children. Before going to Russia he had embodied his evangelistic approach in a set of rules, which are one of the keys to the success of the Orthodox mission in Japan.

The evangelists shall be organised as a deliberative body.

These evangelists shall teach Christian truth to other people while still continuing to study it for themselves.

There shall be two kinds of meetings. In the first, the evangelists, to-gether with others who know the essential doctrines but desire further study, shall meet to read and explain the New Testament. Such meetings shall be held twice a week, the evangelists taking turns in conducting them. None of the number should fail to attend; if any person is un-avoidably prevented from coming, he ought before the next meeting to learn from someone else what was said. The second meeting is for

---

[12] The government gave but little support. The Ministry of Finance assigned to the Mission an immediate payment of five thousand rubles, followed by three thousand rubles a year. One merchant alone, on the other hand, contributed ten thousand rubles anonymously.

[13] Platonova, 30-37; *Polnoe sobranie zakonov*, XLV, pt. 1, no. 48232; Cary, *History*, I, 390.

the benefit of those—whether men, women, or children—who are commencing to study Christian doctrines. The evangelists shall explain to them the Creed, the Lord's Prayer, and the Ten Commandments. This meeting shall be held twice a week. The evangelists shall divide the people into classes for instruction. If for any reason a person is not present at a meeting, the evangelist shall ask some one of the absentee's family to inform him of what was said or shall go himself to the person's house for that purpose.

In neither kind of meeting shall there be discussion until after the explanation is finished, although the meaning may be asked of anything that has not been understood.

Besides conducting the two kinds of meetings already mentioned, the evangelists shall go about the city every day trying to win new enquirers. If among those interested are persons unable to attend the meetings, the evangelists shall go to their houses in order to explain the Creed, the Lord's Prayer, and the Ten Commandments. This is to be regarded as of prime importance and should be done even if, for lack of time, the evangelist is obliged to omit the meeting for reading the New Testament.

When persons have thoroughly learned the Creed, the Lord's Prayer, and the Ten Commandments, and are established in the faith, they shall be presented to the priest for baptism.

Whenever any point of doctrine is not understood, it shall be brought to the priest for explanation, and, if it is a matter of importance, the explanation shall be written down in a notebook.

On Sundays the Association of Evangelists shall meet at the house of the priest to report what has been done during the previous week, as well as to consult together and decide on what shall be done in the week to come. These decisions shall be recorded by the evangelists in their notebooks.

A record shall be kept of baptisms, births, marriages, and deaths.

A book for recording receipts and expenditures shall be prepared and put in the care of a person to be chosen by the Association.

The money first collected shall be used for the propagation of Christianity.

When sufficient money has been gathered, a young man shall be taught the Russian language and sent to a theological school in Russia. On the completion of his education, he shall return to Japan and there establish a school for teaching Christian doctrine and the sciences. He shall also translate religious books. Another young man shall be sent to a medical school in Russia and on completing his studies shall return to found a hospital and a medical school.

When the number of baptised believers reaches five hundred, one of the evangelists shall be chosen for sending to Russia that he may be ordained to the priesthood. Afterwards, one person shall be ordained for every additional five hundred converts. When there are five thousand believers, a request shall be made for the appointment of a bishop.

The evangelists who go to teach Christianity in the different provinces shall strictly observe the above rules.[14]

On his return from Russia in the early months of 1871 Nikolai resumed his missionary activity in Hakodate. During his absence Arai had invited some of his Sendai clansmen to study Christianity and they had come to Hakodate, where Arai and Sawabe did their best to expound what they knew of the faith. But their money gave out—though Sawabe sold his sword and offered to sell his wife— and all but two of them returned to Sendai without awaiting Nikolai. When Nikolai arrived in Hakodate he invited those who were interested in Christianity to come again. In a building connected with the consulate he instructed them in the Russian language and the Christian faith. For many of the Sendai clansmen and other students, Russian was the main attraction. But teaching Russian was in itself an important task. Nikolai's students helped him in the translation of religious writings and in the preparation of a Russo-Japanese dictionary.[15] Toward the end of 1871 several of the Sendai clansmen were baptized and three of them—Ioan Ono, Petr Sasagawa, and Iakov Takaya—returned to Sendai as evangelists. In 1872 an Orthodox church was completed at Moto-machi. Officially called Hakodate Fukkatsu Seido (Hakodate Resurrection Church), it was popularly known as Gangan-dera (Gangan Temple) after the un-Japanese sound of its bells. The construction of this church, together with that of the consulate and hospital, provided local workmen with their first experience in European architecture.[16]

The remoteness of Hakodate had been an advantage in the early stages of Nikolai's activities for they were beyond the close scrutiny of the government. But the remoteness of Hakodate was at the same time a barrier to the spread of his teachings to the heart of Japan. When Father Anatolii, a regular priest, arrived in 1872, therefore, Nikolai left the work in Hakodate in his hands, and himself proceeded to the capital. American and French missionaries were already in Yokohama and Tokyo, but Christianity was still illegal. After

14 Cary, *History*, I, 383-384.

15 The Lord's Prayer and doctrinal manuals were printed by lithographic press; the dictionary was reproduced by hand until the publication of a dictionary by the Education Department in 1881. Among the works published by Nikolai were *Nissho kyomon* (Everyday scriptures), *Kyori mondo* (Religious questions and answers), *Seisho nyumon* (Introduction to the Bible), *Saijitsu kyokuroku* (Index for religious holidays) and *Seikyo jisseki roku* (Record of the accomplishments of religious doctrine).

16 Okada, *Roshia bunka*, 11; Hiyane, 150; Cary, *History*, I, 390-392.

preaching for a while at Tsukiji, Nikolai secured in the name of the Russian legation a lease on a piece of ground on Surugadai, a hill in a central part of the city. In the dingy buildings on that ground Nikolai gathered about him a number of students. In the daytime he taught them Russian; only in the evening did he discuss the Christian faith with those who cared to listen. Lecture rooms were established also in other parts of the city—in Kanda, Nihombashi, Yatsuya, Shitaya, Asakusa, and Honjo—and his teaching of Russian and preaching brought increasing attendance. In the autumn of 1872 he baptized ten Japanese. But he did so with the greatest secrecy and was appalled to learn several days later that the ceremony had been attended by a spy who had submitted a complete report to the government.

There was cause for anxiety, since earlier that year many converts had been arrested in the north. The evangelists, whom Nikolai had sent back to Sendai, had been successful in attracting many listeners —more than a hundred each day—but as rumors of their mounting following spread through the city with stories of Christian magic, the Japanese officials were forced to take action. On February 25, 1872 police surrounded Ono's house and arrested Sawabe, who had come down to Sendai to preach. They confiscated Ono's books and trampled on the icons. Sasagawa and Takaya and some of those who had attended the meetings were also thrown into prison. Others—about a hundred and fifty—were questioned, then released in the care and surveillance of relatives. Though Sawabe was scolded for trying to dispute the accusation that he was teaching an evil doctrine, none of the prisoners were physically mistreated.

In Hakodate meanwhile the excitement of the Easter services had precipitated the arrest of Dr. Sakai, and of Pavel Tsuda and Danil Kageda. In the Orthodox faith Easter is the greatest holiday. For a week the church bells ring every day. When bells of the consular church thus rang and rang, crowds of curious Japanese began to gather. To these crowds the Japanese catechists preached with mounting ardor, and soon everyone seemed to be arguing about Christianity. So often in Japan (as elsewhere) it matters less what one does than how one does it. This was too public a flouting of official prohibitions to pass unnoticed, and the governor had the catechists arrested. Christian officials were deprived of their positions; Christians were driven out of the city and the printing facilities of the Church were closed down.

It must be realized that the Japanese antagonism was not produced by bigotry. As in the seventeenth century national security and public peace were the foundation of Japanese government. The motives of Nikolai were not imperialistic; nor did he try to manipulate the political loyalty of Orthodox converts; but there is evidence that many of the converts on their part—even Sawabe himself—had chosen Christianity for motives that were more political than religious. There is no doubt that among them there were opponents of the government. Kannari and Arai, for example, were Sendai clansmen who plotted to rally the remaining shogunate forces in Ezo to resist the restoration of imperial authority. They spread their teachings among fellow clansmen and though resistance to the imperial troops proved futile, some hoped that the new religion might prove a vehicle for the political and spiritual renovation of their country. When Arai had urged his clansmen to come to Hakodate to study the Christian faith he had held it up as the best instrument for uniting the hearts of those who wished to improve the political condition of Japan in general and the position of Sendai in particular. Kageda, one of those who visited Hakodate and listened to the Christian teachings, was a prominent Sendai samurai and in hiding as a rebel. Sawabe himself is said to have looked more like a rough and ready swordsman than a peaceful evangelist. The interrogation of Tsuda in Hakodate reflects the political preoccupation of both converts and officials. Asked why he had come to Hakodate, Tsuda replied that he had come to study the Russian language. When asked why he was also studying Christianity he replied that the teachings of Jesus had brought the countries of Europe and America to their present state of civilization. The officials were willing to concede that as a student it might be all right for him to investigate Christianity; their main objection was to his evangelism. "The people of Hakodate are unintelligent," they argued. "Hitherto they have been satisfied with Buddhism. To teach them something new, even though it may be good in itself, will only confuse them."

Understandable or not, the arrests in Sendai and Hakodate were cause enough for Nikolai to view with alarm the discovery that a government spy had been present at the secret baptism in Tokyo. But when nothing further happened, it became apparent that the government had relaxed its position, and Nikolai continued his conversions with renewed confidence. Meanwhile the Christians in Sendai and Hakodate were released from confinement. Ono, who had been in Tokyo when the police had raided his house in Sendai, had pleaded with government officials for the release of his clansmen and had obtained the support of the noted figure Fukuzawa Yukichi, who remonstrated that the persecution of Christians would shame Japan in the eyes of the world. At the same time Western diplomats made representations. It was the exigency of international relations that prevailed over domestic considerations, but, though Nikolai tried to dispel the fear of some that he was a spy or political agent and assured the Foreign Ministry in a memorial that Christian doctrines were not subversive to the state, the Japanese authorities did not relax their vigilance and continued to plant agents among the flock of faithful. The fact that the powerful Russian Emperor was the head of the Orthodox Church exposed Russian missionaries to more suspicion than their Protestant or even Catholic counterparts.

In 1873 the centuries-old prohibitions against Christianity were lifted. In his rules for the Association of Evangelists Nikolai had stipulated that a priest should be ordained from among the evangelists when the number of baptized followers reached five hundred. In 1875, when the bishop of Kamchatka visited Hakodate, Pavel Sawabe was ordained. Three years later, in 1878, five more evangelists were ordained in Vladivostok. The Orthodox church now had six native priests, twenty-seven catechists and fifty catechist assistants. Construction was begun on a house chapel and mission buildings. With only limited funds provided by the Russian government, the realization of this project was greatly advanced through the efforts of Count Putiatin, who had negotiated the first treaties between Russia and Japan, and of his daughter, Countess Olga Putiatin. Together they collected 32,000 rubles for the construction of the main building. When completed, it was a fine two story structure of many rooms. Soon Nikolai set upon the development of the Russian language school into a theological seminary. In 1881, it was established in several Japanese houses near the mission buildings. The students lived together, and studied the same seven-year course as in a seminary in Russia, except that the classical languages were omitted. Instruction was in Japanese, but as no suitable textbooks were as yet available in Japanese, Russian books had to be used. As a result the first years of seminary work were still devoted to a large extent to the study of Russian. For many years Nikolai himself taught theology. When he surrendered this task to the rector of the seminary, he left it in the hands a Japanese who had received his higher theological education in Russia. Like the rector, others of superior ability were sent from the seminary to Russia for higher theological instruction.

In addition to the seminary there was established a school for catechists, in which the evangelists of the Orthodox faith were trained, and a theological school for women with a dormitory, built at the expense of the Countess Putiatin and of the Countess Orlov-Davydov. In this school the girls received serious religious instruction as well as training in housekeeping and handicraft. Often these girls would marry future preachers and assist them in spreading the faith, especially among women.[17]

Nikolai was a man of strong character. "Bishop Nikolai, a tall, lean, robust person, gives the impression of an unusually hale and hearty, energetic promoter, precisely a promoter, and appears much younger than his years (he is way past fifty), notwithstanding his deep wrinkles, which thirty years of ceaseless labor have furrowed on his face," wrote a lady doctor who visited him in his later years. "It seems to me somehow that two Nikolais could not get along in one Tokyo. He is just that type of talented Russian persons, who are strong only alone and who, with all their great merits, have always a considerable dose of despotic autocracy as well as perhaps the inability to measure others except by their own high standard. . . ."[18] It was to the perseverance of Nikolai that the Orthodox Church of Japan, which was poor in comparison not only with Christian missions of other sects but with Orthodox missions in other countries, owed its existence and development. The awe in which he was held by his admirers may be seen from this Japanese description of his life:

Father Nicolai sympathizes profoundly with the evangelists in their hard life and grants all the aid in his power, at the same time earnestly urging upon the churches the importance of helping their evangelists and pastors. And these nearly two hundred pastors and evangelists who preach the gospel while enduring hardness have a worthy example in the bishop himself. Being, of course, unmarried, he has no house of his own. This man, who in Russia would be fit for a minister of State, has not only no home of his own, he has no property, hardly anything at all. In a corner of the cathedral at Surugadai, a room of eight mats (twelve feet square) serves as office, bedroom, and dining room. The furniture consists of a table, a bed, two chairs, a small bureau, bookshelf, and bookrack. There is not a simple article of ornament. He has also a small reception room where he receives every one, student or minister of State

17 Platonova, 32-39; Cary, *History*, I, 384-404; Kishimoto, 266-267; Hiyane, 150-151.
18 A. A. Cherevkova, *Ocherki sovremennoi Iaponii*, 150-51.

alike. As for clothes, he has one or two suits for special occasions and two or three ordinary suits for summer and winter. Bishop though he is, he has a scantier wardrobe than some of us. In his room no clock is seen. The plain silver watch he carries was given him by relatives. He has no finger rings or other such ornaments, of course. His best pair of spectacles is framed in silver. I have friends, evangelists, who have finer watches and spectacles than the bishop.

As to daily habits: He rises at six a. m. and breakfasts at half-past six on a bit of bread and a cup of tea. Butter and the like he does not use at all. At half-past seven, the year round, he goes to his translation. The New Testament, prayer books, and other important literature used in the *Sei Kyokwai* [Orthodox Church] were all prepared by the bishop and his helpers. He works till noon, with an intermission of ten minutes. At noon he takes luncheon, consisting of two or three very plain articles. He then takes a siesta till about two p.m. From two p.m. he transacts business with his secretaries and managers for several hours. From six to nine p.m. he works as in the forenoon. As he takes no evening meal, he has really but one meal a day.

The whole business of the church is in the hands of this one man, Father Nicolai, with his sixty-eight or sixty-nine years. On this account he never takes a summer vacation. We usually go away for a month in summer, but he remains summer and winter working away in the little room described above. Here he works without relaxation the year through. In my opinion Father Nicolai does more work than the eight ministers of State in Japan put together.[19]

It does not appear that Nikolai was loved by everyone. Though Foreign Minister Soejima sent his own son and two nephews to Nikolai's school,[20] there were many Japanese who suspected his activities and opposed the spread of the foreign faith.

In 1880, Nikolai visited Russia and on March 30 was elevated to the dignity of Bishop of Japan. Returning to Japan with sizable donations for the mission, Nikolai was able to begin work on the Cathedral of Resurrection (Sobor Voskreseniia Khristova) in 1884. Such was the suspicion of the man in the street that rumors circulated that the Russians were building a fortress with cannons in the belfry, and suggestions were made that the building on the hill be surrounded with so high a wall that the imperial palace could not be seen from it or better still that the building be purchased and presented to the Emperor as a gift.[21] When completed seven years later, the Cathedral of Resurrection was the finest and most elaborate Christian house of worship in Japan. Indeed its size and Byzantine

[19] Clement, 54-55.
[20] Berton, 12.
[21] Platonova, 39-48.

magnificence made it the largest and most beautiful of all Orthodox churches in the Far East and on the Pacific shores, and to this day a noted landmark in Tokyo.[22] Covering an area of over eleven thousand feet with a cathedral dome one hundred and fifteen feet high and a bell tower one hundred and twenty-five feet high, it could accommodate fifteen hundred persons. The formal dedication on March 8, 1891 attracted much public attention. Together with Nikolai, there officiated nineteen priests and four deacons with the assistance of a choir of one hundred and fifty voices of male and female students. It was through the Orthodox church that Western choral music was introduced to Japan. Even Europeans marveled at the choir of the Orthodox cathedral in Tokyo.

One may hear the finest choral music in the empire. Those who believe it to be impossible to train well Japanese voices have but to attend a service at this cathedral to have their ideas changed. A choir of several hundred voices has been trained to sing in perfect harmony and the music is inspiring. Travelers who have heard the music of the most famous cathedrals and churches of Europe and America say that this will compare favorably with the best. The development of music in the Greek Church of Japan has been marvelous.[23]

By 1884, when the construction of the cathedral was begun, there were within the jurisdiction of the Orthodox mission one hundred and sixteen church buildings and sixty-five parishes, and the personnel of the mission, in addition to two bishops, numbered one hundred and nine persons: twelve priests (nine of them Japanese), two deacons (Japanese) and ninety-five preachers (Japanese). In the autumn of 1884, the Countess Putiatin arrived to serve as a deaconess. The total number of Orthodox believers had reached almost ten thousand. The Orthodox Church of Japan was unusually patriarchal in organization, almost completely independent from the Russian mother church. Every summer a synod met in Tokyo to consider the requests and petitions of the Japanese from every corner of the land, to elect catechists, designate candidates for the priesthood, and determine matters concerning church administration.[24] Meanwhile

[22] Report of Archbishop Benjamin of Japan to the eighth all-American Synod of the Russian Orthodox Church in New York, December 6-8, 1950. MS. During the tragic earthquake of 1923 the cathedral was severely damaged by fire, but was restored eventually through the efforts of Nikolai's successor, the Archbishop—later Metropolitan—Sergius.

[23] Clement, 57; Platonova, 49-50.

[24] Platonova, 53-54. For further data, see Josef Glazik, *Die russisch-orthodoxe Heidenmission seit Peter dem Grossen,* 178-196.

Anatolii had moved from Hakodate to Tokyo (1879) as chaplain of the legation. Other Russian priests were to visit Hakodate, but not for long. There as elsewhere, the work of the church was to be increasingly in Japanese hands. Indeed it was a characteristic of the Orthodox Church of Japan that it depended so little on the work of foreign missionaries. In the words of *Fukuin Shimpo* (The Japanese Evangelist):

> In methods no attempt is made at external show. The one method of the *Sei Kyokwai* is a method of the utmost quiet and mental concentration, viz., expounder and hearers sitting together in a quiet room tasting the gospel. Instead of noisy "lecture meetings," like the blare of trumpets in the ears of hundreds of auditors, one method is to sit in the secret room urging sinners to repentance by the light of the gospel. The Kingdom of Christ is not to be organized from students seeking novelty nor from people who are amused with the striking terms of the so-called "New Theology," but it is to be made up of repentant and converted sinners.[25]

The figure of Nikolai dominated the scene so much that the Resurrection Cathedral became popularly known as Nikolai-do and "Nikolai" became a synonym for Orthodox Christianity. But occupied though Nikolai was with the many functions of the bishopric, he did not neglect the task begun in Hakodate. Almost daily from six until ten p.m. he continued to work on the translation of holy scriptures and service books with his assistant, Nakae. Eventually he directed a whole staff of translators, having founded the Aiai-sha or Love-love Company for the translation and printing of religious literature. He personally edited four church journals, among them the *Orthodox Report* (*Seikyō-shoshō*) and an admirable library, entering each book in his own hand in the catalogue.[26] In the years that followed the Orthodox Church continued to grow, but its influence remained confined primarily to northeastern Hondo. Its Achilles' heel was its connection with the Russian government. Mounting imperialistic rivalry between Russia and Japan over Korea and Manchuria turned the Japanese against the Russian Church for patriotic reasons, though the Japanese Orthodox Church was not essentially Russian. The attitude of the Orthodox Church of Japan was well illustrated in a speech by Nikolai on the outbreak of the Russo-Japanese War in 1904. He announced that he himself would refrain during the war from public prayer because he could not pray for

25 Clement, 57.
26 Hiyane, 150-151; Platonova, 59-61.

the victory of the Japanese Emperor over his own country. But he urged the Japanese to continue with their worship as before:

I hope there will be no change in our Church through the outbreak of the war. Evangelists must propagate the Master's Gospel, students must attend the Mission School as usual, and I will devote myself to the translation of the Prayer-book with my assistant Mr. Nakae. And if an Imperial Proclamation of war is issued, your members must pray for the triumph of Japan, and when the Japanese army has conquered the Russian forces you must offer to God a prayer of thankfulness. This is the obligation laid on the Orthodox Christian in his native country. Our Lord Jesus Christ teaches us patriotism and loyalty. Christ Himself shed tears for Jerusalem. That was because of His patriotism, and you must follow in your Master's steps.[27]

Nikolai's mission had received less material help from the Orthodox Missionary Society than had Russian missions elsewhere, yet thanks mainly to his devotion and ability the Orthodox Mission of Japan won over a larger number of converts to Russian Christianity from among non-Christians outside of Russian territory than had any Orthodox mission elsewhere.[28] When Nikolai's ministry came to an end years later, in 1912, after over half a century of service in Japan, he had won the respect of high and low. The funeral services at the Resurrection Cathedral were attended not only by ambassadors of Christian nations, but by ministers of the Japanese government, and flowers were sent by the Prime Minister and even the Imperial family.[29]

[27] Cary, *History*, I, 414-418.

[28] Kenneth Scott Latourette, *A History of the Expansion of Christianity*, 379; Donald Attwater, *The Christian Churches of the East*, II, 147.

[29] Hiyane, 152-153. A word about the Orthodox Church in Kyoto. In 1954 the author caught the reflection of the characteristic, onion-shaped top of a Russian church in his viewfinder as he was taking a panoramic photograph from one of the top floors of the Kyoto Hotel. Japanese and Westerners alike denied the existence of a Russian church in the ancient imperial capital, yet after hours of systematic search on foot the author discovered (and photographed) the church. Surrounded by Japanese dwellings on four sides, it is hidden from sight until one reaches an adjacent yard. Then the name of Nikolai at the gates to the church land leaves no doubt that another fruit of his labors has been found. The following brief account of the history of the Russian church in Kyoto, communicated to the author by A. Bakulevskii, secretary of the Archbishop Irinei of Tokyo and Japan, in a letter dated January 21, 1958, may be of general interest:

The preaching of the Russian Orthodox faith in Kyoto, the center of Buddhism, began in 1893. Orthodox Japanese converts gathered for prayer in an upstairs room of a private house.

The steadily increasing Orthodox community decided to build a temple. Part of the money for the construction of the temple was collected among the Orthodox Christians of the city of Kyoto, but there was not enough money for the equipping of the temple. (*footnote continues on p. 417*)

COMMERCIAL RELATIONS

The desire for trade had been the primary driving force behind the persistent Russian attempts in the eighteenth and early nineteenth centuries to establish relations with the Japanese. Even in the 1850's, when political considerations prompted the dispatch of the first Putiatin expedition, to prevent Great Britain and the United States from attaining preponderant influence in Japan, trade remained a major Russian objective, and when the first Russian consul left for Japan, there was the general expectation that brisk commercial relations between the two countries would follow suit. Russian optimism was not justified, however, and Japanese trade with Russia developed very slowly.

There were a number of reasons for this. In the first place, Russian expectations of supplying Siberia with foodstuffs from Japan were frustrated by prohibitions in the commercial treaty of 1858 against the exportation of rice and wheat, while the promises of great Russian contributions to the economy and military strength of

---

The archbishop (then still bishop) Nikolai decided to turn for help to Moscow. He wrote a letter to his former school-fellow, archpriest Nikolai Blagorazumov, who did come to the aid of bishop Nikolai. On the request of archpriest Blagorazumov, one of his parishioners, Vasilii Dodiskin, donated the ikons for the future temple. A generous response to his request was obtained also from Lev Tikhomirov, editor of *Moskovskie Vedomosti* [the Moscow News], who published in the paper an appeal for help for the temple in Kyoto. Obtaining the bells was connected with great difficulty, as it was very expensive to order them in Japan. Through the efforts of archpriest Blagorazumov and Lev Tikhomirov there was opened a collection and the bells were purchased with the money which was donated. The employees of the *Moskovskie Vedomosti* donated the candlesticks and church-chandelier. The society of gonfaloniers of the Moscow Kremlin cathedral donated gonfalons and church vessels. With joint efforts there was built and outfitted the temple in memory of the Annunciation of the Most Holy Virgin, which was consecrated by bishop Nikolai on May 10 [23?] 1903, assisted by the priest Simeon Miya, superior of the temple, the future archpriest of the Tokyo cathedral church, a man of exceptional spiritual qualities, the priest Ioan Ono, the future first and till this time [January, 1958] only [native] Japanese bishop, who died at an old age last year [1957], the priest Sergii Suzuki, the priest Petr Shibayama, the deacon Stefan Kugimiya and twenty catechists. The consecration was attended by the governor of Kyoto, the teacher and the pupils of the church school for females, opened not long before this, journalists and 126 parishioners. Congratulations were received from the other parishes in Japan. The temple was built by the Japanese architect Matsumura.

At the present time, after the death last year of archpriest Vissarion Takahashi, who for a long time had been the superior of the temple, Grigorii Naito is the superior of the temple. Through the efforts of Archbishop Irinei, present head of the Japanese Orthodox Church, there were opened about two years ago at the church in Kyoto courses in Russian language for the Japanese, taught by the priest Naito, Valentina Hayashi (a Russian [lady] married to a Japanese) and Mrs. Meiers, who comes twice a week from the city of Kobe.

The church has also courses in cutting out and sewing.

Japan were dispelled by the belated realization that, though Japan and Russia were neighboring countries, European Russia, which alone was more advanced than Japan in modern ways, was for all practical purposes at the other end of the world; as far as relations between Japan and Siberia were concerned, it was Japan that could do more for Russia than Russia for Japan. A Russian letter from Hakodate, published in the official nautical journal *Morskoi Sbornik* in 1863, pointed to the role which Japanese labor could play in the development of Russia's far eastern regions, and envisaged the fishery concessions, which became an important reality in later years.

The density of the population of Japan presents an amazing contrast with the sparse population of our shores. The cheapness of labor, which is a natural concomitant, is of utmost importance to us in the establishment of new ports and cities in the Amur region. If it were possible to attain a supplement to the treaty regarding the free absentment of Japanese to our neighboring harbors, we could have an immense number of excellent artisans for a very cheap price. Stone-masons and excavators can be especially useful to the naval authorities in the construction of docks, wharfs, rocks, embankments and like structures. It would be beneficial to adopt their method of stoning coastal and other earthen walls. There is no doubt that the Japanese will enter our employ with pleasure, thinking of the good earnings and the freer life than in their fatherland, the more so because in view of the short distance they can always return home in case of failure and we could hire workers for a certain number of days, as needed, and thus, without having a population of our own, we would have at our disposal an immense labor force. . . .

Fishery may be developed at our shores through the intermediacy of the Japanese, giving to the Japanese leasehold use of coastal lands. Of particular importance is the obtainment of sea plants and animals, very highly valued in China and Japan. . . .[30]

In the second place, foreign trade in general had not developed in Japan as Westerners had predicted. The difficulties, which confronted the Japanese in the wake of the commercial treaties, were graphically relayed toward the end of the nineteenth century by a Russian observer, who had toured the Far East on a commercial survey in the 1880's.

When merely seven cities—Nagasaki, Kobe, Osaka, Yokohama, Hakodate, Tokyo and Niigata—had been opened to Europeans, it was already easy to appreciate the harm brought to the country by revived relations with Europe. To this one may say: but Japan has recognized the good of European civilization. Indeed, there have been created among the

[30] Russia, letter from Hakodate, unsigned, undated, 76-77.

Japanese some artificial needs; many Japanese wear pince-nez, top hats, starched shirts, narrow lacquered shoes and ties, drink some sour French wine and bad American alcohol, take photographs of their actresses and courtesans; but the question arises for what the Japanese need all this, when they had lived gaily and without poverty, having no proletariat, while Europe does not know how to calm her working people and where to stick the superfluity of her population and her productiveness. But to acquire from Europe some machines and physical instruments, none had prevented the Japanese from doing formerly also. . . .

In concluding the diplomatic-commercial treaties the Japanese did not suspect, and could not have suspected, the meaning which, especially after the construction of the Suez canal, steam navigation would acquire; therefore, they admitted into their country goods with an insignificant customs duty and moreover carelessly tied their hands in this respect for the future. The consequences did not keep one waiting long. The country, whose outward sufficiency obliged one to consider her rich, was brought in ten, fifteen years to bankruptcy. Even foreign trade, which was profitable in the first years after the opening of the ports, has begun to bring losses; the warehouses have been filled up with European odds and ends, while importation of European products has been maintained exclusively by orders of the government, especially due to the desire to have, it is not known for what need, an army, organized in the European manner, i.e., costing very much.

He reported that the Westerners had purchased few Japanese products. They had begun by draining the country of gold and copper and art treasures. When the European silk industry had been plagued by disease, they had purchased silk and silk-worm eggs for a while. Now they were interested only in tea, the sale of which did not suffice to balance the foreign trade of Japan.

In consequence of European competition, prices have gone up five or six times: foodstuffs have become especially expensive, and the common people are in need. In 1873 the government, on the proposal of Minister of Finance Okuma [Shigenobu], lowered the land tax by 1/6, but this decrease came out as an increase, because at the same time there was made a new cadastre, which extended the tax to new lands. Buying cannons and ammunition abroad, the government can no longer collect taxes in rice; it demands money, but in Japan there was never enough currency. It is true, she had gold and silver, but these metals were obtained from the poorest beds, since a day's labor did not cost more than six kopecks, while now a worker in a day eats up twenty kopecks of rice alone, thus there is no profit in exploiting sands and mines of poor content. The shortage of precious metals made it necessary to issue paper money. In consequence of this issue, all hard money was either carried out of the country or hidden in banks and in the hands of changers, the agio went as high as sixty per cent, and what is still worse, there were formed special exchanges for playing on this agio, which fluctuated as much as thirty per cent, and on the price of rice, which fluctuated just as rapidly due to the instability of the paper monetary unit. In April of 1880 the government closed down the exchanges by force.

With the increase in taxes there appeared at once political dissatisfaction also in the mass of the people, which until then had been completely indifferent concerning politics. In such a way, dissatisfaction below has joined the natural dissatisfaction above, which had been brought about by the revolution of 1868, and the subsequent reforms.[31]

The Japanese government had not desired foreign trade. The officials had opened the country against their will. It is not surprising that they should have sabotaged the natural development of commercial relations, especially when it appeared that their fears had been justified and that the stability of their country was threatened by foreign intercourse. Dr. Albrecht reported from Hakodate that the authorities did not permit every merchant to deal in foreign goods. In 1862, there were only three stores in the city that carried any European products whatsoever. Among the various measures to which the Japanese government resorted to limit foreign trade, one of the most vexing was its strict prohibition against Japanese merchants accepting earnest-money from foreigners, "which completely contravenes freedom of trade and mutual confidence of merchants, and is not in accordance with the treaty, which permits free commerce in any commodity except military stores, without any interference on the part of the Japanese government."[32] Ivan Makhov described the tedious machinations which accompanied any exchange of currency, and related the difficulties which the Japanese officials made for their own merchants. Regarding the red tape to which the foreign residents of Hakodate were subjected, whenever they wished to obtain Japanese currency he wrote: "Firstly, one must have a note from the consul for the exchange of a specific and very limited amount of money; secondly, one must wait in the office for an hour or more, while the report is transmitted with Japanese ceremony from the lower class of officialdom to the higher one, and the permission back the same way; and thirdly, to pay interest for the exchange of silver for silver." Reflectively he added: "It happens also, that the office will flatly refuse to change [money]. . . ."[33]

31 Skalkovskii, *Vneshniaia*, 476-477.
32 Letter from Albrecht, dated April 16 (28), 1862, 81.
33 Letter from Ivan Makhov of November 26 (December 8), 1860, 85.

The most dramatic attempt of the Japanese government to alleviate the unfavorable balance of trade was the issuance of a new, devaluated coin, which would have tripled the cost of the Japanese goods to foreigners. This the Westerners would not tolerate, and though the Japanese step was not unjustified in view of the maladjusted ratio of gold to silver in Japan, they forced the Japanese into withdrawing the new coin. The result was detrimental in two ways: outflow of gold continued unabated, and the ability to make quick and easy money in this fashion spelled the neglect of the tea and silk trade, from which Japan would have derived some profit and which might have laid the foundations for more stable relations.[34] Aside from all high level considerations, however, there was a variety of basic factors which prevented the rapid development of foreign trade: settled in their way of life, the Japanese people did not feel the need for foreign products; most important of all, even if they had wished to acquire them, the cost of European wares was far too high by Japanese standards.[35] Moreover, isolated from the rest of the world for centuries, Japanese merchants needed time to figure out the proper relationship of prices; for the time being they priced their own goods exceedingly high, afraid that by charging too little they would set a dangerous precedent.[36]

If foreign trade in general had not developed as expected, Japanese trade with Russia was even more disappointing, lagging behind trade with German, French, and Dutch merchants, not to mention commercial relations with the United States and Great Britain. Not the least of the reasons was Russia's industrial backwardness. In the words of one historian:

The tsar [Peter the Great]'s ardent desire to make Russia into a country exporting manufactured goods in Russian bottoms was never realized, and until the fall of the empire some two hundred years later she continued to export chiefly agricultural produce, raw materials, and semi-manufactured goods. . . . Technical backwardness, lack of capital, absence of credit and banking facilities, and the inborn aversion of an essentially continental people to the sea defeated all government efforts for the promotion of a merchant marine. . . . The land-bound nation, and especially its trading classes, never understood or shared its first emperor's enthusiasm for the sea.[37]

[34] Bruno Siemers, *Japans Eingliederung in den Weltverkehr*, 42.
[35] Letter from Albrecht, dated April 16 (28), 1862, 81.
[36] Kornilov, "Zimovka," 97.
[37] Michael T. Florinsky, *Russia*, I, 393.

There was also the usual problem of price; despite the writings of various Russians, who had visited Japan, Russian merchants proved insufficiently informed about true Japanese needs and about the condition of the Japanese market. There was much goodwill toward the Russians, and the Japanese seemed inclined to think that Russian traders were less likely to deceive them than the other foreigners, but whatever illusions they may have had on this account were soon dispelled when they discovered that the goods on Russian vessels were several times more expensive than those brought from China. This was due to the lack of suitable Russian merchantships, which could deliver the cargo from Nikolaevsk to Hakodate, and to the period of navigation in the northern waters, requiring from one and a half to two years for the transportation of goods from Siberia to Japan. But the fact that there were honest reasons for the cost of Russian goods did not alter the situation. Nor was high cost the only weak-point in the Russian position. Fur, timber, and skins—the main objects of Siberian trade—were not required by the Japanese, while the various products which they purchased from the Americans and the Europeans were not yet available in Siberia. A variety of manufactures from European Russia, especially stearine candles, did reach Japan, but indirectly by way of Hamburg, Shanghai, or Nikolaevsk. The Russians in turn bought a number of minor Japanese articles. The export of the one commodity, which the Russians had wanted and which they might have purchased in large quantity—rice—was prohibited by law. The largest item of trade was the provisioning of Russian warships at Hakodate.[38]

The dissolution of the Russian-American Company, which had shown such an active interest in trade with Japan, in 1860, and the sale of the Russian colonies in North America to the United States in 1867, also slowed down the development of commercial relations. It was not until after the opening of the Suez Canal and particularly, several decades later, after the building of the Trans-Siberian Railroad that Russian trade with Japan gained momentum. As late as 1879 the total of Russo-Japanese trade (exports plus imports) amounted to less than 60,000 yen,[39] and in 1883 Konstantin Skalkov-

---

[38] Novakovskii, 205-209.

[39] Exports: 49,177 yen; imports: 10,280 yen. According to the same customs data, exports from Japan consisted of an insignificant amount of the following taxed items: coal and charcoal, fish, glue, beans, potatoes, victuals, spirit, salt, sulphur, tea, wood, tobacco, turtle ware, and vermicelli; and the following duty-free items: clothing, tex-

skii could report: "In spite of the privileges received [by the commercial treaty of 1858 as supplemented by the tariff convention of 1867] our commercial relations with Japan have been utterly insignificant until recently, when Nagasaki became a port of call for vessels of the Volunteer Fleet and was joined with Vladivostok by quick communication with the help of Japanese steam navigation. There is nothing resembling relations with China here, and one can talk only of the future."[40]

Not only the Russians but Japanese merchants and colonizers in the north were disappointed. When the expected onrush of Russian merchants had failed to develop, the authorities in Hokkaido had taken the initiative themselves and sent out commercial missions to Siberia. The *Kameda Maru*, the first Western-style ship constructed in Hakodate and built by craftsmen trained under Takadaya Kahei, visited De-Kastri and Nikolaevsk in 1861, returning safely with useful nautical and geographical data, interesting observations on the life and history of the regions visited, and some bartered goods. In 1878, Kuroda Kiyotaka, a leading figure in the development of Hokkaido, sent a group of merchants and officials to Vladivostok on the *Hakodate Maru* with samples of Hokkaido products, following himself with more officials on the man-of-war *Kongo Kan* in order to give added weight to whatever observations, recommendations, or agreements the merchants might make. But though Russian buyers expressed interest in the importation of various Hokkaido commodities, especially foodstuffs, the Japanese saw that the small population of Vladivostok—then less than forty-five hundred—precluded any profitable commercial relations.[41]

The Japanese were disappointed. More than that, they were beginning to wonder. At first, when Russian merchants had failed to appear, the Japanese, who had not desired trade, had been well pleased; in time, as commerce became less objectionable, the Japanese began to ask themselves why the Russians, who more persistently than all others had clamored for trade, failed to take advantage of the opening of the country, and in some circles the suspicion was

---

tiles, porcelain and earthenware, flour, rye, paper and lacquerware. Imports to Japan consisted of insignificant quantities of rope, furs, glass, horns, iron goods, musk, victuals, salted fish, mammoth teeth, wood, tobacco, and flour, the latter being brought in duty-free.

[40] K. A. Shalkovskii, *Russkaia torgovlia v Tikhom okeane*, 367.

[41] Okada, *Roshia bunka*, 13, 15-16; Honjo Eijiro, *Bakumatsu no shin-seisaku*, 442-447.

voiced that Russian requests for trade had been no more than a pretext for more sinister designs. But above all, the inability of Russia to develop the much-vaunted commercial relations revealed to the Japanese Russia's economic backwardness and vulnerability in the Far East.

CHAPTER TWELVE · DELINEATION OF THE FRONTIER

THE SAKHALIN QUESTION

HE Treaty of Shimoda (1855) divided the Kuril Archipelago between Russia and Japan—Uruppu and the islands to the north were recognized as Russian, Etorofu and the islands to the south as Japanese. No decision could be reached, however, concerning Sakhalin, and the large island (larger than Hokkaido or Kyushu and Shikoku combined) remained in joint possession. From a purely historical point of view, Russian claims were not impressive. Golovnin had not considered the island Russian, regarding the southern half as Japanese, the northern as a dependency of China; a Russian officer, writing in the early 1870's, though he himself desired Russian possession of Sakhalin, admitted that in the process of freeing Golovnin, Russia had formally renounced whatever rights to the island she had.[1] Following this renunciation, the strongest historical argument that Russian protagonists could muster was that, despite the continued portrayal of Sakhalin as part Chinese and part Japanese on European maps, *de jure* the island belonged to nobody, the relations of China and Japan to Sakhalin resembling in many points the contemporary relations of Russia, Norway, and Holland with regard to Spitzbergen. In 1853, Nevelskoi and Busse side-stepped the arguments of historical priority and boldly annexed Sakhalin to the Russian Empire, but this action was nullified by Putiatin, less from Japanese military pressure than from Putiatin's fear that Russian occupation of Sakhalin might block his attempt to establish friendly relations with Japan and, once the Crimean War had broken out, might invite an Anglo-French attack. The treaty which Putiatin succeeded in concluding at Shimoda did not demarcate the specific extent of Japanese and Russian influence on Sakhalin, yet it is significant that it recognized the right of both Japan and Russia (and no one else) to the island, and thus left the door open for Russian expansion.

The Crimean War is viewed generally in its Near Eastern and European setting. Its direct effect on Russian Far Eastern policy is often overlooked. At first it would appear that Russia's defeat in that

[1] Golownin, *Memoirs*, III, 2-3; Colonel Veniukof, "On the Island of Saghalin," 373.

425

war would have weakened her position throughout the world. But Russia's victorious repulsion of an Anglo-French amphibious assault on Kamchatka at Petropavlovsk strengthened Russian prestige in the Far East, and the closing of the Black Sea to her ships of war and the frustration of her ambitions in central Europe, deflected and accelerated her efforts in the direction of the Far East, there to find compensation for the losses she had suffered in the west.[2]

The Crimean War had scarcely ended when the Russians resumed their activities on Sakhalin. Step by step they extended their influence over the island, establishing posts at points of strategic importance as well as wherever coal had been discovered. The original object in occupying Sakhalin for the protection of the Amur Estuary was supplanted, due to the lack of government foundries in Eastern Siberia, by plans for the exploitation of the island's coal resources by forced labor and the eventual transfer of the penal system from Siberia to Sakhalin. The true geographical relationship of Sakhalin Island to the Amur Estuary (including the question whether Russian possession of the whole island was absolutely necessary to insure freedom of navigation) was aptly summarized by Colonel Mikhail Veniukov:

The straits between Saghalin and the shores of the Amoor country deserve particular attention in the sense that, by their nature, the character of the intercourse between this island and the continent of Asia is decided. In the first place, these straits are frozen for three or four months in the year, and, consequently, the possibility of direct communication between the shores is opened, even if the sea were not generally commanded by us. Secondly, it is known that the channel of the river Amoor, near its mouth, is divided into three branches. One runs to the north-east, i.e. towards the Sea of Okhotsk, but, not reaching it, is lost in shallows; the second goes straight to Saghalin, but also does not reach the Channel of Tatary; and the third alone, stretching toward the south to Cape Lazareff, leads to the Sea of North Japan. Therefore, strictly speaking, the straits of Mamio Rinzo, 5 miles broad, must be possessed to attack from Saghalin ships issuing from the Amoor. From the Sea of Okhotsk and from the north-west shores of Saghalin it would then be impossible to penetrate directly to the Amoor, but it would be necessary to descend to latitude 52°25′, i.e. to arrive again in sight of Cape Lazareff and then tack round to the north-north-west. Thus, if there is a point in Saghalin which may be called the key of the Amoor, it is in the close neighbourhood of Pogobi, but by no means the whole island, which

2 Lobanov-Rostovsky, 142; E. V. Tarle, *Krymskaia voina*, II, 212-227; Pierre Fistié, *Le réveil de l'Extrême-Orient*, 42.

only commands the Amoor as England commands the mouths of the Seine, Scheldt, and Rhine. On this account the Straits of Mamio Rinzo have a double importance, because it is possible to pass through them to the Amoor, and also to the north-west shore of Saghalin itself; inasmuch as northward from these straits goes a direct channel from the Sea of Japan into the Sea of Okhotsk, a little south of Cape Golovacheff, touching the Saghalin shore.

Many of the Russian posts were symbolic reservations for later occupation, rather than actual military strongholds or bases of operations. As late as the early 1870's Russian military power on Sakhalin was insignificant. In the words of Veniukov:

> We have at present in Saghalin one battalion of infantry, two mountain guns, one local command (at Dooi), which are disposed in the following manner: two companies and a section of artillery at Mooravieff, one company at Korsakoff and Naiboochi, one at Mauka Bay, one at Koossoonai and Manuyeh, the chief command at Dooi and Taraika. But the companies, in their turn, are scattered in small detachments of seven or nine; and there are posts where there are not more than two soldiers, merely to prove to the Japanese the presence of the Russians in a given locality.[3]

This force could not have defended the island against any major attack. But the Japanese who frequented Sakhalin, concentrated on fishery and on trade with the Ainu. They lived along the shores in the summer, returning to Hakodate and other parts of Japan for the winter. In time they awakened to the danger of Russian expansion and began to match Russian posts with corresponding posts of their own in the same areas (occasionally even in the same barracks), but even then only in the southern part of the island.[4] "The Japanese settlements in Saghalin are confined to the South and South East of the island," the Englishman John O'Driscoll reported after a visit in 1869. "The settlers whose total number may be estimated at from 200 to 300 are scattered in small parties through villages, the communication between which is always irregular and often entirely discontinued. These villages are all situated to the South of a line drawn about the 48th parallel of North latitude from Kushunnai on the West to Manoi on the East side of the island." Small and inadequate as the Russian footholds were on Sakhalin, the Japanese settlements were even more inferior. The English observer wrote:

[3] Veniukof, 376-377, 387.
[4] Skalkovskii, *Vneshniaia*, 600-601.

None of them can be said to be in a prosperous condition. The listless unbusinesslike air of the Japanese villages, which H.M.S. Cormorant visited, contrasted very unfavourably with the bustle and animation of the Russian settlements. It is worthy of remark too that the Japanese settlements are declining in importance year by year, and their population is diminishing in numbers whilst the Russian settlements are rapidly increasing in size and importance. If a line be drawn above the 48th parallel of North latitude it will divide Saghalin into two parts, the Northern portion inhabited only by Russians and the native tribes, the Southern by Russians, Japanese, and Ainos. It will be seen from this that the Russians hold possession of three fourths of the whole island and in the remaining fourth their settlements are far larger and more important than the rude villages occupied by the Japanese.[5]

O'Driscoll found the Japanese quite uninformed about the country beyond the surroundings of Aniwa Bay; they seldom stirred out of the vicinity of their villages. At the same time he found them concerned about Russian designs and reported that many Japanese officers communicated to him the opinion, "that at no very distant date some decisive steps on the part of the Russians might be looked for in the South of the island which it would be equally imprudent and impossible for the Japanese to attempt to resist."[6] The Russians, on the other hand, though they had little intercourse with the Japanese and knew little about them, had explored the island thoroughly and were confident in their position. Though Lieutenant Colonel de Preradovich, commander of the Russian forces on Sakhalin, assured Okamoto Kansuke, the official in charge of the Japanese settlements, that the Russian government had no intention of disturbing the friendly relations with Japan and that rumors of an impending war between the two countries were an American fabrication, that he had neither the right nor the intention of interfering with the settlement of Japanese peasants on the island, and would be happy to cooperate with the Japanese commander in settling all minor misunderstandings,[7] clashes did occur,[8] and de Preradovich himself was described by O'Driscoll as believing that Russia would soon annex the whole island.

He seemed rather anxious to discuss the question of the occupation of Saghalin, and during the course of a long conversation frequently recurred

[5] "Report on Saghalin by J. O'Driscoll," 201-202, 207.
[6] *Ibid.*, 216.
[7] Letter from de Preradovich, 25-26.
[8] "Report of the Brig 'Jolly,'" 486-489.

to the same topic. He dwelt at some length on the failure of the Japanese to develop the great natural resources of the island and endeavored to show that its occupation by Russia would be advantageous for everybody. He frankly acknowledged that the Russians were forming new settlements over the whole island but he reminded us that they were only taking advantage of their Treaty rights and then he went on to point out that in the opinion of Russians the whole of Saghalin belonged to them and that the straits of La Perouse formed the only real boundary between Russia and Japan. No line of boundary, he said, could be drawn within the island itself, and joint possession was an impossibility.[9]

The occupation of the whole island, as Veniukov admitted, was not really a strategic necessity; nor would an equitable division of the island have been impossible. But whatever the theoretical possibilities may have been, there was ample evidence that "joint" possession would eventually become tantamount to Russian possession and Japanese statesmen, who in 1859 had been startled by Muravev-Amurskii's blustering bid for the whole island, at last took the initiative to try to stem the Russian tide by diplomatic negotiation, and, if it proved impossible to retain possession of Sakhalin, at least to receive appropriate compensation for it. They were spurred on by the additional fear that incidents issuing from the joint occupation of the island might result not only in the uncompensated loss of the island itself, but provide the Russians with an excuse for annexing Hakodate if not the whole of Hokkaido.[10] The Russians had already made an attempt to take over Tsushima, an island between the Korea Strait and Tsushima Strait, some sixty miles northwest of Kyushu.

The first opportunity for the reopening of the Sakhalin question presented itself to the Japanese government in 1862 with the dispatch of a mission to the European treaty nations to plead for a postponement in the opening of additional ports in the face of mounting anti-foreign incidents. Takenouchi Yasunori, Lord of Shimotsuke, superintendent of the treasury and at the same time commissioner of foreign affairs, was named Envoy Extraordinary and Minister Plenipotentiary; Matsudaira Yasunao, Lord of Iwami, state councilor, governor of Kanagawa and commissioner of foreign affairs, was named Second Minister Plenipotentiary, and Censor Kyogoku Takaaki, Lord of Noto, Third Minister Plenipotentiary.[11] This was not

---

[9] O'Driscoll, 213-214.

[10] The British warned the Japanese that the Russians had such designs ("Report of the Brig 'Jolly,'" 486-489; Harrison, *Japan's Northern Frontier*, 51).

[11] Alcock, II, 381; Ishin-shi Gakkai, *Bakumatsu ishin gaiko shiryo shusei*, I, 285-286.

the first Japanese mission to go abroad, Japanese dignitaries having been dispatched to the United States in 1860 to exchange ratifications of the commercial treaty concluded by Townsend Harris.[12] But that had been another group, and these plenipotentiaries and their retinue of thirty-two subordinate officers and servants were as yet unfamiliar with western modes of travel. Sir Rutherford Alcock, who was personally involved in launching this "Great Eastern" mission since the first leg of the voyage was to be on a British ship, has left an account of the accommodations that had been prepared for the Japanese on board H.M.S. *Odin*.

A whole suite of cabins had been prepared for them by Lord John Hay with sliding panels, papered with Japanese patterns, and as innocent of furniture as their own reception rooms. Our advice to them was, to sleep either on a matted floor, as was their custom, or in cots, that could be removed by day, without lumbering their cabins. But they finally decided on having bunks put up. Nothing could have been more liberal or considerate than the arrangements as to space, &c., made for their comfort by the Commodore. The whole of the main deck had been given up to their use. The Ministers and superior officers were provided for abaft the main-mast, and the subordinates and servants forward. To each set of cabins there were two or three bath-rooms, with moveable heating apparatus, on the Italian plan of a double tube and central heater. A pantry also, and place for the storage of all their crockery and stores for daily consumption were attached to each class of cabins; for I should say they began by sending on board fifty crockery teapots, an immense supply of soy in five hundred champagne bottles; then a service of five porcelain cups for every individual, with saucers innumerable to answer for plates. There were also some fifty *Hebachis*, or vessels for burning charcoal and warming the rooms, corresponding with the Spanish *Brazeiro*. But I heard something about these being all stowed down below in utterly inaccessible places—a needful precaution if the Commodore ever intended to convey them as far as Suez, or arrive there himself, without a conflagration;—which, bye the bye, he did not succeed in doing, though from no fault of the passengers.[13]

On January 23, 1862 the Takenouchi mission departed from Yokohama.[14] After visiting England, France, Holland, and Prussia, they

---

[12] Treat, I, 99-100; Borton, 51-52.

[13] Alcock, II, 378-379.

[14] Writers who refer to the departure of the Takenouchi mission by year only, tend to misdate it as having occurred in 1861. This is due to the fact that the mission left in the first year of Bunkyu, which chronological tables list as 1861. But the first day of the twelfth lunar month of Bunkyu 1, is already December 31, 1861. Any event occurring after that day—Takenouchi boarded the ship at Shinagawa on the twenty-second day of the twelfth lunar month—must be dated as falling into 1862.

arrived in St. Petersburg on August 9, 1862. On the balcony of a hotel in Birmingham one of the members of the embassy had been approached in Japanese by a Russian "barbarian," who had participated in the fateful voyage of Putiatin's *Diana*. "I was at that time in the service of my former master, and remembered what had happened then quite clearly," recorded the Japanese in his diary; "so we talked a little about bygone times, which somewhat amused the mind of the wanderer. It was rather an extraordinary thing."[15] At the London Convention (June 6, 1862) the Japanese had succeeded in postponing the opening of Niigata and Hyogo and the residence of British subjects in the capital and in Osaka until 1868; the other European treaty powers had concurred with this, and now the plenipotentiaries were free to devote their full attention to the Sakhalin question. Their arrival was heralded by the Russian press. "At last we too are visited by the Japanese envoys, who have lived in Paris, where the novelty of the inhabitants of islands, neighboring unto the celestial empire, was the primary cause for the reception of these overseas guests." The weekly *Illiustratsiia* was favorably impressed by the Japanese. It carried a picture of the delegates, and, identifying them, reported that Takenouchi was notable for his taciturnity, but that his colleague was talkative, and that the secretaries were friendly and of noble character.[16]

The Japanese plenipotentiaries were received in an audience by Alexander II, and met with Gorchakov, who was both Prime Minister and Foreign Minister. Though the Japanese government had been led to believe by Goshkevich and others that St. Petersburg would welcome a solution of the Sakhalin question, the Russians appeared not at all eager to resume negotiations, pointing to the failure of both Putiatin and Muravev-Amurskii to come to a satisfactory agreement with the Japanese. Inasmuch as the Japanese plenipotentiaries had come all the way to the Russian capital, however, Gorchakov agreed to have the matter reopened and appointed as negotiator Count Nikolai Ignatev, the Director of the Asian Department of the Ministry of Foreign Affairs, who in 1860, as minister to China, had brought the territory east of the Ussuri River into the Russian realm by some very shrewd bargaining.

Six times the plenipotentiaries met. The Japanese government had instructed Takenouchi to seek the Russian withdrawal from the

---

[15] Ernest M. Satow, "Diary of a Member of the Japanese Embassy to Europe," 576.
[16] *Illiustratsiia*, 70.

portion of Sakhalin south of latitude 50° N. or, if unsuccessful in this, to press for a rental agreement, which would, at least indirectly, acknowledge Japanese suzerainty over that territory. He laid claim to the region south of the fiftieth parallel, arguing that both Japanese documents and European maps (including a map aboard Putiatin's flagship during his first visit and one in the Russian Astronomical Observatory) designated it as Japanese, that it was within the limits of Japanese administration, and that it was frequented by Ainu hunters as far north as Porokotan. But Ignatev declared that the whole of Sakhalin was Russian. He dismissed maps as unreliable—no more than hearsay of travelers or theories of scientists—pointed to the absence of Japanese administrators on the island, and denied the existence of Ainu penetration north of Kushunnai, the site of a Russian camp along the forty-eighth parallel. Russian withdrawals from Sakhalin had occurred as the result of climatic conditions and not because of any agreement made by Putiatin, who, Ignatev alleged as Muravev-Amurskii had earlier, had not been empowered to deal with the boundary issue. He accused the Japanese of obstructing native association with his countrymen and asked whether, in their recent activities on Sakhalin, the Japanese were not in complicity with another power. The Japanese replied that if there was any foreign inspiration to their policy, it was Russia's contention that Japanese defenses on Sakhalin were inadequate.[17] Modifying his original position that Sakhalin in its entirety must be Russian, Ignatev finally suggested that the forty-eighth parallel might make an acceptable dividing line. This was contrary to the instructions of the Japanese government, but Takenouchi and Matsudaira realized that if they rejected this proposal there might never be another opportunity to settle the question on this favorable a basis. In conference with the third minister plenipotentiary they spoke up in favor of an immediate agreement, promising to disembowel themselves should their action be censored upon their return home. Kyogoku, however, vetoed acceptance of the Russian proposal, noting indignantly that, although he too was prepared to sacrifice his life for his country, a hundred seppuku would not make up for national disgrace. He warned that should Takenouchi and Matsudaira conclude an agreement, which was in excess of their instructions, he would not only withhold his name from the document, but seek to

[17] Tanaka, 84-90; Kyozawa, 182; Shimada Saburo, "Japan's Introduction to the Comity of Nations," 85-86; Ota, 109-112.

dissolve the treaty by virtue of the authority vested in him as super-intendent. In September the Japanese and Russian plenipotentiaries officially decided to postpone a decision, agreeing only that Admiral Kazakevich, governor of the Maritime Province, should represent Russia in subsequent negotiations.[18]

Unsuccessful as the Japanese were in settling the Sakhalin ques-tion, they had succeeded in postponing the opening of additional ports, and the European tour had been an educational experience, impressing them with the military and industrial backwardness of Japan. The many new and unaccustomed sights and experiences must have bewildered them. "A confused account of a trip to Europe, like a fly on a horse's tail," one of the Japanese entitled his diary of the expedition.[19] But the Japanese were careful not to display their feelings, affecting the same combination of well-mannered re-straint and sophistication that had amazed Russians in earlier years. "It is remarkable," the Russian press noted, "that the Japanese who have come show extremely little attentiveness and curiosity in re-gards to the European way of life, and are completely unwilling to leave the quarters set aside for them to view interesting collections of the works of industry, science, and art."[20] In part this attitude of the Japanese may have been due to the fact that the Russians had succeeded in providing them with a home away from home, for un-like the European accommodations that had been made available to the visiting plenipotentiaries elsewhere, it was a Japanese setting that the Japanese found to their delight in the Russian capital. Fukuzawa Yukichi, the noted educator and journalist of later years, who was among the retinue of this mission wrote: "In our rooms there were sword racks such as we used at home; on the beds were Japanese pillows with wooden bases; in the bathrooms we found bags of rice bran instead of soap; even our food was cooked some-what in our style; and the rice bowls and chopsticks were entirely too Japanese to have been thought of by the Russians. There was no doubt at all in my mind that a fellow-Japanese had attended us somehow." Fukuzawa's assumption was correct, Tachibana Kosai, who worked for the Russian Ministry of Foreign Affairs, having taken charge of the arrangements. Wondering about the mysterious person

[18] Kyozawa, 183; Asahi Shimbun-sha, *Meiji Taisho-shi*, II, 102-103; Tanaka, 90; Ota, 112-115; Osatake Takeki, *Iteki no kuni e*, 263-271.
[19] Satow, 305.
[20] *Illiustratsiia*, 70.

behind the scenes, Fukuzawa had jotted down a Chinese-style poem
in his diary:

> Upon rising I come to the table, eat
> my fill, and fall asleep again.
> So, eating and sleeping, I spend the year
> that comes and goes away.
> If ever I should meet a man you know,
> I will tell him
> "The sky of Europe and the sky of Japan
> are not at all unlike."[21]

To a certain extent Japanese curiosity may have been restrained
by an innate feeling of superiority; an account of this mission together with narratives of other missions abroad in the same decade
were published in Japan under the title *Iteki no kuni e* (To the
countries of the barbarians). The greatest inhibition to any outward
display of interest, however, was the totalitarian system of the
Tokugawa police state which preoccupied every official with the dread
of being suspected of disloyal tendencies. Evidence of this may be
found in another observation of Fukuzawa. He was approached by
one of the Russians about remaining in Russia, implying that Japan
was no place for an ambitious youth. Though he flatly rejected the
overture, saying, "I am in the service of the embassy. I cannot withdraw and stay here as you suggest," he did not dare repeat this conversation to his associates. "I could not tell this little incident to any
of my colleagues," he wrote years later in his autobiography. "For
any suggestion of private communication might be taken as suspicious. So I kept it secret even after I returned to Japan. Indeed, it
is not improbable that other members of our party had the same
experience and, likewise fearing suspicion, had also kept silent." The
tendency of the Japanese plenipotentiaries and their entourage to
stay together and close to their quarters was due also to the feeling
which Fukuzawa expressed when he recalled that "I decided that
Russia was a country in which we could not safely unburden our
minds."[22]

In August 1863, after the Takenouchi mission had returned to
Japan, the Russian government sought to reopen negotiations and
proposed through Goshkevich that Japanese plenipotentiaries accompany him on a Russian man-of-war to Nikolaevsk, where Kazakevich would confer with them. But the Japanese government made no

---

[21] Eiichi Kiyooka, *The Autobiography of Fukuzawa Yukichi*, 145-146.
[22] *Ibid.*, 148.

answer, because the Russian proposal revived the claim that the whole of Sakhalin was Russian, and because it was preoccupied at that time with internal affairs. After several months Kazakevich communicated to the Japanese government that he concluded from its silence that it did not care to determine a boundary line. When in 1865, spurred on by renewed incidents on the island, the government finally decided to move, Kazakevich had left Nikolaevsk.[23]

Late in 1866 the Japanese government sent Koide Hidesane,[24] Lord of Yamato, and Ishikawa Kanzaburo, Lord of Suruga, to St. Petersburg. Koide, who was governor of Hakodate, had urged his government in a memorial the previous year to hasten the determination of a definite frontier on Sakhalin, advising that Japan agree to the forty-eighth parallel proposed by Ignatev; he had even suggested that consideration be given, as a last resort, to the exchange of Japanese rights to Sakhalin for the northern Kuril Islands. The Japanese government had appointed him plenipotentiary, but had exhorted him to do all he could to try to delineate the frontier along the forty-ninth parallel. In February and March of 1867, Koide and Ishikawa conferred with Petr Stremoukhov, who was now director of the Asian Department of the Ministry of Foreign Affairs.

Stremoukhov revived the claim that Sakhalin was Russian in toto. When Koide and Ishikawa referred to the status quo provision of the Treaty of Shimoda and to the Russian agreement to a joint local investigation to determine the proper location of the frontier line, Stremoukhov asserted that having failed to send a mission, Japan had forfeited any rights to the island. He spoke of his country's friendship toward Japan and expressed sympathy with the latter's internal problems, but insisted that international obligations take precedence over internal considerations. Then he raised the old argument that Sakhalin would fall prey to a third power unless owned and protected by Russia. It was his proposal that the entire island be acknowledged as Russian, with La Perouse Strait as the "natural" frontier; in return Russia would safeguard Japanese fishing rights and would cede to Japan the islands Uruppu, Broton, Chirpoi, and Brother of Chirpoi. The Japanese plenipotentiaries objected. As proof of Japanese suzerainty over at least the southern part of Sa-

[23] Tanaka, 91-93; Hiroteru Yamamoto, "History of the Kuriles, Shikotan and the Habomai Islands," 481; Ota, 118-121.

[24] The recently published biographical dictionary of Hokkaido history gives the reading of Koide's given name as Hidesane. (Kitsu Bunshichi, *Hokkaido-shi jimmei jiten*, II, 50.) It could be read also Hidemi.

khalin they cited the punishment of Khvostov for his raids on the island, and also comments in the writings of a member of Rezanov's mission, possibly Krusenstern, and the text of a document left by Putiatin. They declared that the Japanese people would not tolerate the cession of Sakhalin to Russia and even warned of foreign repercussions in the event of such a transaction. But Stremoukhov remained adamant, even after Koide offered to accept the delineation of the frontier along the forty-eighth parallel as proposed by Ignatev in 1862. Unable to agree on a boundary line, the negotiators perpetuated their dilemma in a set of "temporary regulations relative to the island of Sakhalin," signed at St. Petersburg on March 30, 1867. Leaving the island in common possession, the regulations provided for: (1) the settlement of disputes by local authorities or, in the event that these could not agree, by the nearest Russian and Japanese governors, (2) the free movement of Russians and Japanese throughout the whole island and the unrestrained settlement and erection of buildings at unoccupied places, (3) the protection and employment of the Ainu, and (4) the negotiation of a final treaty, if "in the course of time" the Japanese government agreed to exchange its territorial rights to Sakhalin for Uruppu and three neighboring islets,[25] Japanese fishing rights remaining intact.[26]

Upon the return of the Koide mission to Japan (June 12, 1867), the Shogunate reaffirmed its stand on the Sakhalin issue. In a message to Evgenii Biutsov, Russian consul in Hakodate, it reiterated the Japanese rejection of the Sakhalin-Kuril Islands exchange proposal, expressing preference for the continuation of the joint occupancy of Sakhalin. At the same time it set about strengthening Japan's position on the island by removing previous restrictions on immigration. One writer commented on the inevitable effect of stipulating the common right of Russians and Japanese to occupy any unoccupied places on Sakhalin:

This strange definition gave rise to a colonising steeplechase, in which the Russians were no match for the alert Japanese, who, in their usual systematic way, began organizing the settlement of the country. The populous Japanese islands were near, and readily furnished colonists, while the Russians had to draw settlers from Europe with the inducement of great privileges, or to found settlements of unmarried soldiers, utterly valueless for peopling the country. The Russians crossed the Kusunai

[25] Uruppu, Broton (Broughton), Chirpoi (Kita-jima and Minami-jima) or Black Brothers.
[26] For the full text of the agreement, see Appendix IV.

and went south to found a port at Aniwa, and the Japanese in their turn went north of the Kusunai, hunting for unoccupied places. As the Russians had not sufficient soldiers to occupy all desirable places, they erected posts with inscriptions to denote that an occupation had taken place. This ingenious scheme was quickly adopted by the Japanese.

This keen competition occasioned many disputes between the local officials of the two countries, but it is remarkable that the confusion caused by the extraordinary diplomatic definition gave rise to no collision between rival detachments. This mutual forbearance was probably due to the good temper of both races. The good relations of the two peoples went further than mere politeness, as on two occasions outlying Russian posts were saved from starvation by the assistance of the Japanese. . . .[27]

In 1868 the Emperor of Japan was restored to power. For years it had become increasingly apparent that the Tokugawa Shogunate had outlived its usefulness. The failure of the barbarian-subduing generalissimo to turn away the foreigners—prima facie evidence of the dictatorship's impotence—was the culmination of a rapidly accelerating process of military, economic, moral, and political disintegration. The death of Shogun Iemochi in August of 1866, followed less than a year later by the death of the extremely isolationist and reactionary Emperor Komei, set the stage for a dramatic transfer of authority. By November of 1867, the young and reluctant successor to the Shogun was persuaded to resign by the advocates of imperial rule—a coalition of young samurai and merchants from the more modernized western clans, who saw in "imperial rule," the rule of their own clans through the Emperor. In January of 1868, after a brief civil war, young Emperor Meiji assumed the reins of government and the capital city of the Shogunate was renamed Tokyo, "the Eastern Capital."

The new imperial government pledged adherence to the treaties concluded by the Shogunate with the Western powers, but announced that it would seek a revision of all inequitable provisions. Although Article XV of the treaty of 1858 provided that, "if subsequently it will be found necessary to alter or supplement the existing Treaties between the two Empires, either of the Governments may demand their revision, but not before July 1 (new style) eighteen hundred and seventy-two and upon notice thereof one year in advance," Japan requested an earlier revision in a letter of February 23, 1869 to S. Trakhtenberg, Russian representative in Japan, on the grounds that the abolition of the Shogunate left some of the statements "no longer

---

[27] Vladimir (Zenone Volpicelli), *Russia on the Pacific and the Siberian Railway*, 323-324.

true to name and reality," and two weeks later, on March 22, in another letter refused to join Russia in confirmation of the tariff convention of December 23, 1867. But Trakhtenberg saw no justification for treaty revision prior to the agreed date, particularly as the
Japanese had not specified what changes they desired, and warned
that Japanese rejection of the convention might hinder rather than
further the conclusion of new treaties. The Japanese therefore agreed
to wait until July 1, 1872, and promised to communicate suggestions
for revisions beforehand.[28] Meanwhile the imperial government continued the Shogunate's policy of colonizing Sakhalin, and considered
the planned migration of carpenters and "persons useless in Japan,
such as surrendered [Shogunate] troops, beggars, worthless ruffians,
and priests." But Russian activity, including the destruction of a
Japanese post in 1868 and the arrival of the first exiles, a group
of about eight hundred prisoners (men and women), not to mention
guard reinforcements, overshadowed the Japanese efforts, and the
new government decided to seek the assistance of a third power in
settling the potentially explosive Sakhalin question.[29]

Japan turned to the United States as the "most impartial friend of
both parties." The Japanese were confident that the United States
would welcome the role of arbiter, for Sakhalin was close to her own
possessions, and American fishermen frequented these waters. Moreover the American treaty of 1858 contained a standing arbitration

[28] Roy Hidemichi Akagi, *Japan's Foreign Relations*, 85; Tanaka, 167-169. In December of 1871 the Japanese government dispatched Iwakura Tomomi, Kido Takayoshi,
Okubo Toshimichi, Ito Hirobumi, Yamaguchi Yoshika and forty-four officials to the
United States and Europe to lay the groundwork for later treaty revision. After conferring with top officials in the United States, England, France, Belgium, the Netherlands, and Germany (where Otto von Bismarck lectured to them on the facts of *Real-
politik* and *Machtpolitik*), the ambassadors arrived in St. Petersburg on April 25, 1873,
and were received in audience by Alexander II on April 29. The Japanese transmitted
to the Russian Foreign Minister a written summation of the current state of foreign
privileges and of their government's basic objectives: the recovery by Japan of the
right to determine independently import and export duties as well as residence and
port regulations, and the subjection of foreigners to Japanese laws and courts. The
Russian government promised to reply to this note through its representative in Japan
and on September 3, two months before Iwakura returned to Japan, Biutsov reported
to the Japanese government that he had been authorized to discuss treaty revision.
But preoccupation with territorial problems and domestic politics forced the Japanese
government to postpone such negotiations, and although the question of treaty revision was reopened in 1875, it was not until 1894 that the first revised treaty was attained and June 8, 1895 before such a treaty was signed with Russia. (Tanaka, 169-
173; Chitoshi Yanaga, *Japan since Perry*, 177-179.)

[29] Tanaka, 101-102, 120-121; Harrison, *Japan's Northern Frontier*, 51; Brokgauz and
Efron, LVI, 484; Veniukof, 374. For further detail concerning Japanese counter-measures
on Sakhalin, see Ota, 147-166.

offer, and the relations between the United States and Russia in those days had been very friendly.[30] In October of 1869, when William H. Seward, the former American secretary of state, visited Japan, the Japanese sounded him out about possible American mediation and asked his advice. Having himself negotiated the purchase of Alaska from Russia only two years before, Seward recommended to the Japanese that they seek to buy northern Sakhalin.[31] On March 15, 1870, the Japanese government officially approached Charles E. De Long, the United States minister to Japan, and filed a request for American mediation in the Sakhalin dispute.

De Long had demanded a detailed account of the boundary problem and related negotiations, with proof of all Japanese claims, as basis for his report to Washington. The documents conveyed to him on March 15 (including the proposal that Sakhalin be divided along the fiftieth parallel) did not satisfy him, and he requested further data. The memorandum which the Japanese offered in substitution on March 23 did not differ in substance. The plea for presidential mediation, for example, had been withdrawn, but it was replaced by the request that the American government transmit Japan's proposals "and kindly negotiate the matter with the Russian government." Upon De Long's insistence on further proof, members of the Japanese Foreign Office went over their records with A. L. C. Portman, American chargé d'affaires. Portman then drew up a list of questions, the documented answers to which finally provided him with a history of the controversy. On September 20, De Long dispatched this survey, together with a Japanese certification that it included all the facts at their disposal, to the U.S. State Department, expressing the hope that successful American mediation would "go very far to advance American influence and promote American interests" in Japan, in spite of Portman's objection that the Japanese had "imperfectly stated and partly misrepresented" the case.

Hamilton Fish, President Ulysses S. Grant's secretary of state, duly approached the Russian government through the American ambassador in St. Petersburg in December of 1870, but the Russians declined the American proffer of mediation for fear that a precedent be established for further intervention. They added, however, that if the United States could induce Japan to accept the Russian claims, Japan would get not only her *intérêts réels* but a satisfactory guar-

30 Treat, I, 363-364, 369.
31 William H. Seward, *Travels Around the World* (New York, 1873), 58.

antee that no Russian aggression would ensue from such a settlement. To his chagrin, De Long was now instructed by his government to inquire whether the Russian proposition suited the Japanese government, and if it did, to offer the President's assistance in resolving the issue. Embarrassed by his inability to answer Japanese questions concerning the details of the correspondence between his government and that of Russia, De Long floundered into offering the services of the President to secure a compromise, intimating that "material interests" might be obtained. When he learned that the Japanese had reopened direct talks with the Russians, he was happy to be able to wash his hands of the whole affair.[32]

It was Evgenii Biutsov, one-time Russian consul at Hakodate and then minister to China, who on a visit to Tokyo, late in 1870, had prevailed upon the Japanese government to send an envoy to Nikolaevsk rather than to Washington. Soejima Taneomi was appointed plenipotentiary and was preparing to leave for Russia, when word was received, in August of 1871, through the consul in Hakodate that a change of governors, not yet completed, precluded negotiations in Siberia, but that Biutsov had been appointed Russian minister to Japan and was on his way to confer with the Japanese in their own country.[33] By this time the rumors of war between Russia and Japan had spread among the foreign community in Yokohama and it was apparent that an answer to the boundary question must be found before the unrestrained force of events gave substance to the rumors. In 1870, Lieutenant Staritskii had urged his countrymen to reach a speedy agreement with the Japanese in order to deprive "newspapers and ill-meaning advisers" of any pretext for arousing public opinion against Russia. He insisted that all of Sakhalin must be Russian, but did not regard this as a source of Japanese resentment, if an agreement were made at that time. "For the sake of unchangeable permanent friendship with Russia, for the sake of her own peace of mind," he wrote, "Japan must drop all her pretensions to the southern part of Sakhalin, and it is very easy for her to do this, because as yet she has no serious interests on that island."[34]

The talks which took place in Tokyo, in June and July of 1872, brought the Japanese and the Russians no closer to agreement. Though Biutsov insisted that any division of Sakhalin would be im-

32 Treat, I, 363-368.
33 Tanaka, 124-126.
34 Letter from Lieutenant Staritskii, dated Hakodate April 4 (16), 1870, 17-19.

practical, he was not prepared to purchase the Japanese share of the island; on the other hand he was not willing to sell the Russian part to the Japanese. There was a great deal of recrimination, the pleni-potentiaries of both sides accusing each other of acting against the interests of their own governments. Biutsov had information that the Japanese wished to sell their share of Sakhalin as a means of protecting Hokkaido, while Soejima had heard that the Russians wished to sell their share to cut expenses. In the end negotiations came to a halt when Soejima departed for China to congratulate the young Emperor T'ung Chih (Mu Tsung) on the end of the regency and his assumption of the direct rule of the empire, and to discuss the problem which had arisen over the murder of some shipwrecked sailors from the Liu Ch'iu Islands by aborigines on Formosa. Nor were the talks resumed upon Soejima's return, for the Japanese did not favor Biutsov's proposal of trading several northern Kuril Islands for southern Sakhalin and they insisted that precedence must be given to a local investigation and settlement of renewed incidents on Sakhalin over the delineation of the frontier. Thus Biutsov left Japan without having contributed to the solution of the boundary problem.[35]

The Russians thought the Japanese unwillingness to sell Sakhalin was due to British and American influence. There is no doubt that by this time the United States looked with apprehension at Russian expansion. As Kurd von Schlözer, German minister in Washington, reported to Chancellor Prince Otto von Bismarck in 1874, after a long talk with Secretary of State Fish, touching on the relations of the different foreign nations with Japan: "Only one power was passed over in silence: the Secretary of State never speaks of Russia, when one talks concerning Japan. Because the United States regards Japan as an appendage of America. And although the Yankee feels strongly enough to be able to hope that sooner or later he will be in a posi-tion to paralyze the influence of all European powers in Japan, the Asiatic proximity of Russia yet fills him with a secret fear, and the colonization of the Amur region as well as the Russian settlements on

35 Tanaka, 126-128; Ota, 181-185; Hosea Ballou Morse, *The International Relations of the Chinese Empire*, II, 266-271. Biutsov, his wife, Rear Admiral Fedorovskii and others had been received in audience by the Emperor on June 23. (Russia, *Obzor* [1868-1877], 518-521) The Russian refusal to sell their part of the island is noteworthy, because some Japanese historians place the whole blame for Japan's failure to purchase Northern Sakhalin on Kuroda's opposition to such a move.

Sakhalin island are well suited to darken for every American politician of the future the heaven of his Japanese hopes."[36] But there is no evidence that either the United States or any other power had interfered in the boundary negotiations. In a confidential report to von Bismarck, Max August Scipio von Brandt, the German minister to Japan, specifically asserted that the Russians were probably mistaken in attributing the Japanese opposition to foreign influence, and suggested a more plausible reason for the Japanese deferment: "One is aware in Edo that the Sakhalin Question must be followed by the Ezo Question, and one is perhaps not wrong, therefore, in postponing a settlement of the first question as long as possible in order to find time and means to populate Ezo and thus make it less susceptible to attack."[37]

By 1874, the Japanese government decided that it was not wise to prolong the dispute with Russia. The previous year, in 1873, General Kuroda Kiyotaka, the colonization commissioner of the northern territories, had warned sternly that the incidents which were an inevitable result of the joint occupation of Sakhalin were a threat to the security of Hokkaido. In 1874 a large part of the Japanese colonists were actually pulled back from Sakhalin to Hokkaido, to decrease the chances of dangerous incidents, and to cut down government expenses. Although many Japanese had different ideas regarding the boundary question, by 1874 the government, which could examine the problem from the vantage point of overall policy and national development, had reached the decision of giving up the island. Fear of a possible collision with Russia was only one of the reasons for this switch in position. The expense of colonizing Sakhalin was another, and a factor of importance, because Japan had to scrape together all her resources to carry through the ambitious program of industrialization and modernization of the Meiji period. At the same time serious questions were being raised by Kuroda and others concerning the economic value of Sakhalin. Furthermore, the Japanese people turned out to be poor colonizers of northern regions. The abandonment of Sakhalin reflected the feeling of the government that Japanese ener-

[36] Report dated Washington March 16, 1874, in microfilm collection of German Archival Materials before 1918 of the Florida State University Library (hereafter cited as F.S.U. Film 189), reel 130, Japan I.B., 16.

[37] Report dated Tokyo, April 17, 1874, F.S.U. Film 189, reel 130, Japan I.B., 16, 1.

gies might better be expended elsewhere, not only in Hokkaido but in the warmer regions of Korea and Formosa.[38]

The Japanese decision to come to terms with Russia was not yet known to the Russians, nor to any other Westerners. As late as July of 1874, a German report from St. Petersburg described the equanimity with which the Russians regarded the settlement of the Sakhalin question, convinced that the Japanese were not serious in seeking a solution. When Enomoto Takeaki, one-time commander of the anti-imperial remnant forces of the Shogunate on Hokkaido, was appointed Japanese plenipotentiary and imperial minister to Russia and arrived in St. Petersburg, in August of 1874, eager to discuss the boundary issue, the Russians were astonished. Stremoukhov had taken for granted that negotiations would be continued in Tokyo and had already provided Kiril Struve, the new Russian ambassador to Japan, with the appropriate credentials. It was decided eventually to work out the principles of agreement in St. Petersburg, leaving details for elaboration in Japan, and the negotiations were finally resumed in the beginning of 1875.[39]

Following a preliminary of the usual arguments, and after the subject of territorial exchange had been broached by Gorchakov, Enomoto disclosed the proposals embodied in his instructions.[40] On May 7, 1875, the Karafuto-Chishima or Sakhalin-Kuril Islands Exchange Treaty was signed in St. Petersburg. It provided for: (1) the exchange of Japanese rights to Sakhalin for Russian rights to the northern Kuril Islands, recognizing, in other words, the entire island of Sakhalin as Russian and the entire Kuril Archipelago as Japanese, (2) compensation for buildings and movable properties ceded, (3) repatriation of those in the exchanged territories who wished to leave, protection of those who chose to remain, (4) use by Japanese vessels of Korsakov (Kushun-kotan) Harbor and their exemption from harbor dues and custom duties for at least ten years, (5) the stationing of a Japanese consul or consular agent at Korsakov, (6) Japanese trade and navigation at the ports of the Sea of Okhotsk and at two ports in Kamchatka, (7) Japanese fishery in these regions,

---

38 Report from von Brandt to von Bismarck, dated Edo (Tokyo), September 5, 1874, F.S.U. Film 189, reel 130, Japan I.B., I6, 3; Tanaka, 121-129; Funaoka, II, 450-451; Ota, 186-197.

39 Report dated St. Petersburg, July 3, 1874, F.S.U. Film 189, reel 130, Japan I.B., I6, 2; Tanaka, 128-129.

40 For the text of the preliminary instructions given to the Japanese plenipotentiaries by their government, see Yamamoto, 485-487.

and (8) most-favored-nation treatment of Japanese vessels and merchants in Russia.[41]

The treaty was supplemented by a joint declaration, signed the same day, elaborating on some of the provisions. When ratifications were duly exchanged in the Japanese capital, on August 22, 1875, a "Supplementary Article" was added. Signed by Struve and Terashima Munenori, the Japanese foreign minister, it dwelled on the new status of the inhabitants of Sakhalin and the Kuril Islands, stipulating, for example, that the aborigines, unlike Russian or Japanese inhabitants, had to choose between domicile and allegiance: those who did not move to the other territory—Sakhalin or the Kuril Islands, as the case might be—became subjects of the new possessor after three years.[42]

News of the successful completion of the Russo-Japanese exchange agreement came as a complete surprise to the foreign diplomats in Tokyo. Baron von Holleben, the German minister, reported on May 28, 1875:

A few days ago the local diplomatic world was surprised by a London telegram, according to which the part of Sakhalin island hitherto belonging to Japan is said now to have been ceded definitely to Russia. After this question had been aired here for years and the negotiations had consistently gotten nowhere, one was very astounded to hear that apparently the matter had been disposed of rapidly in St. Petersburg without anyone here seeming to know about it. The English envoy, who is in the habit of following with particular care the detail of Japan's relations with Russia, was most open in expressing his surprise, that the matter had been settled so quietly; he consoled himself, however, that the agreement in question had supposedly been reached, as he gave the appearance of believing, behind the back of the local Russian representative also.[43]

There was much speculation among the foreign community in Tokyo about the true meaning and implications of the agreement. Was this a first step toward renewed Russian expansion? Had there been some additional secret understanding? Was it a fair exchange, or did the Japanese get the short end of the bargain? In later years Japanese historians condemned the exchange and accused Russia of having robbed Japan of the valuable mineral resources of the island, giving the impression that the exchange agreement was responsible

---

[41] For the full text of the treaty and of a supplementary declaration, see Appendix VI.

[42] For the full text of the Supplementary Articles, see Appendix VII.

[43] Holleben to von Bismarck, dated Yedo, May 28, 1875, F.S.U. Film 189, reel 130, Japan I.B., 16, 5.

for a decline in Russo-Japanese relations.[44] This was not the case. On the contrary, the treaty of 1875 removed the major source of irritation and in the words of the noted Japanese statesman Okuma Shigenobu, "the relations of Japan and Russia became very friendly after the exchange of the Kuril Islands and Sakhalin."[45] On the occasion of the ratification of the treaty the Japanese Emperor bestowed on Struve a decoration, higher than that held by any other foreign envoy at that time.[46]

An evaluation of the exchange agreement and its effect on the Japanese attitude toward Russia in the late nineteenth century must not be based on present conditions; instead it should take into consideration the views and opinions expressed by competent observers at the time. The German reports, relatively disinterested in the matter, are very helpful. On receiving the London telegram in Tokyo, Holleben sought out Struve. Though Struve himself did not have details of the agreement, he believed that the Russian government must have decided "to cede all the Kurils, thus by an exchange favorable to Japan to resolve the question at last." Von Holleben observed: "According to Mr. von Struve's deposition, Russian interest in the acquisition of Sakhalin is confined to establishing a penal colony there and to relieve Siberia in this respect. This may be related to a number of civilizing projects which are being entertained in regards to Siberia, but in any case it will not be possible to leave a penal colony without strong military protection, whereby in turn the whole military power position of Russia in eastern Asia, especially the defense of the Amur territory, would gain considerably. For Japan the exchange is probably in fact not unprofitable, as no revenues at all flowed in from Sakhalin, while the Kurils through their excellent seal hunting could permit a rich financial exploitation.[47] In a later report, von Holleben wrote to von Bismarck: "There is much dispute in the local diplomatic circles as well as in the foreign papers published here about the value of the mutual relinquishments. One wonders on one hand that Japan has given up the Sakhalin coal-beds, but must admit on the other hand that

[44] Ota, for example, objects to calling the territorial agreement an "exchange." It is his contention that Japan was confirmed in the possession of Kuril Islands, already in her influence, in compensation for the cession of the whole island of Sakhalin, that there was left in Japanese bosoms the feeling that Japan had been "robbed" of Karafuto. (Ota, 221-222)

[45] Okuma Shigenobu, *Kaikoku taisei-shi*, 1211.

[46] Report from the German minister resident in Japan to von Bülow, dated Tokyo, December 1, 1877, F.S.U. Film 189, reel 130, Japan I.B., 16, 2.

[47] Holleben to von Bismarck, May 28, 1875.

these have to date given not the least profit and without extremely costly harbor installations would hardly have given any ever."[48]

In the light of the third quarter of the nineteenth century, the Chishima-Karafuto Exchange Treaty of 1875 was far from discreditable. Japan's legal claims to Sakhalin were not beyond question. She had been outdistanced in colonization and her military position on the island had become untenable. Russia could not be expected to pull out of northwestern Sakhalin, which dominated the Amur Estuary, while incidents arising from the joint occupation of the island made Sakhalin the Achilles' heel of Japan, endangering the security of the whole empire. The fact that the Russians had permitted negotiations to drag on for over twenty years without resorting to arms spoke in their favor. Nor had the Russians acquired something for nothing. At the time the economic value of the islands may have been relatively insignificant per se, but not when viewed in their relationship to the Russian coast, for the Kuril Archipelago enclosed the Sea of Okhotsk, and possession of the entire chain of islands would have gained for Russia economic and strategical advantages by making of the Sea of Okhotsk a *mare clausum* and excluding all foreigners.[49] In the opinion of Soviet historians the Tsarist government was guilty of "extreme shortsightedness" when it ceded the Kuril Islands, to which, they argue, Russia had first claim, in exchange for southern Sakhalin, to which, they insist, the Japanese had no valid pretensions.[50] This view is, of course, as unbalanced as its chauvinistic modern Japanese counterpart.

Time was on the side of the Russians and Sakhalin eventually would have become Russian, treaty or no treaty. The exchange agreement assured the Japanese of at least some compensation; and to many the compensation seemed not unfair. It was with justification that the Japanese legal delegate to the Hague Conference wrote a generation later: "If the loss of Sakhalin were regrettable, we have at least this consolation, that the treaty of 1875 was drawn up in a spirit of perfect equality, and in terms quite honourable to Japan, whose position then differed much from the position she now occupies."[51]

[48] Holleben to von Bismarck, dated Tokyo, August 10, 1875. F.S.U. Film 189, reel 130, Japan I.B., I6,5.
[49] Skalkovskii, *Vneshniaia*, 601-602.
[50] E. M. Zhukov, *Mezhdunarodnye otnosheniia na dal'nem vostoke*, 39.
[51] Nagao Ariga, "Diplomacy," 175.

CHAPTER THIRTEEN · END OF AN ERA

TURNING POINT IN RUSSO-JAPANESE RELATIONS

AKHALIN Island proved inadequate for Russian needs. The prediction of a British traveler in 1860 that Sakhalin Island would soon be added to the Russian Empire and would give it "splendid harbors in the Pacific, and leave her fleets free for operations throughout every part of the year,"[1] was only partially fulfilled. The island was acquired by Russia, but important though its possession was in many ways, its maritime usefulness was limited. As Colonel Veniukov reported, "Saghalin has not a single port which may be termed a safe place of refuge." He noted that "Saghalin, on account of its climate, is incapable of supplying the necessaries of life to the troops and the exiles, i.e. to the settlers; and even the agriculturists living there can scarcely have their corn regularly," and pointed out that "the possession of Saghalin will be expensive in proportion to the number of the extraneous population introduced into it, who do not live on the corn raised there." He warned:

The land defence of Saghalin, in case of an enemy invading it in force, and consequently able to disembark simultaneously at different points, is, in the present condition of our forces in the East, impossible, and will probably continue so for long. To the insufficiency of our forces in such a case is added the elongated conformation of the island, which permits an enemy to disembark, say at Koossoonai, and cut off completely our South Saghalin posts from reinforcement from the north.

Poor in natural production, and not possessing a single fort, Saghalin could not serve us as a base for offensive operations against a foreign enemy, not only in the event of preparing a descent, but as a starting-point for our cruisers. Even in the interior of the island, in case of the appearance there of an enemy, under the present circumstances it would be impossible for us to think of offensive warfare, on account of (1) the want of roads; (2) the extreme dispersion of our forces, and (3) on account of their incomplete tactical education.

From this it is plain that the possession of Saghalin does not offer us supreme economic advantages, or present strategic importance. . . .[2]

---

[1] Thomas Witlam Atkinson, *Travels in the Regions of the Upper and Lower Amoor*, 395.
[2] Veniukof, 387-388.

Sooner or later, therefore, the harmony that had been gained by the exchange of the northern Kuril Islands for southern Sakhalin was bound to be shattered by renewed Russian attempts to secure an ice-free outlet to the Pacific. This was indicated in 1861 by the Tsushima affair.

Tsushima, an island two hundred and seventy-one square miles in size, is situated about midway between Korea and Kyushu. It is a convenient stepping-stone from one to the other, and guards the gateway from the East China Sea to the Sea of Japan. It was near Tsushima that Admiral Togo Nakagoro was to win in later years his celebrated victory over the Russian fleet. In the hands of any naval power the island would offer a convenient base of operations against either China or Japan. It was only natural, therefore, that Great Britain, France, and Russia in their rivalry for control of the Far East should have been interested in this Japanese possession and have done everything possible to prevent each other from establishing themselves there.

The surveying of the Tsushima coast by an English warship in 1861 strengthened the Russian conviction that the British, who had been prevented by the Russo-Chinese treaties of 1858 and 1860 from gaining a naval station on the Asian continent between the Amur River and Korea, might try to annex Tsushima and ultimately bottle up Russian expansion at this point.[3] Consul Goshkevich informed the Shogunate that the British had designs on the island, and urged the Japanese to make adequate defense preparations, offering Russian assistance in supplying Tsushima with cannons and in constructing suitable gun emplacements. The Japanese declined his offer. Nevertheless a Russian man-of-war soon arrived at Tsushima and the Russians appeared to be about to take over the island.[4]

The Russian vessel was the corvet *Posadnik* under Captain Birilev. On March 13, 1861, it cast anchor in Osaki Bay.[5] The Russians briefly surveyed the surrounding waters, then landed and announced that they had come to make repairs on their vessel. They informed the officials who met them and tried to turn them away to Nagasaki, that they had been en route from Hakodate to the Kanto region

---

[3] During the Crimean War French forces had landed on Uruppu Island, had destroyed the storehouse of the Russian-American Company, and had proclaimed the island an Allied possession. (Ravenstein, 135)

[4] Hiraoka, *Nichi-Ro*, 367-368; Takada Rikichi, "Bakumatsu Ro-kan no Tsushima senkyu," 21-22; Harrison, *Japan's Northern Frontier*, 46.

[5] Russia, *Obzor*, 646; Tanaka, 34; A. W. Ward, *The Cambridge Modern History*, XI, 843.

when damage to the body of the vessel had forced them to call at this place. Insisting that it would be too risky for them to continue, they estimated that they would have to stay for two or three weeks and requested a supply of timber and carpenters. Tsushima had not been opened to the West by any of the treaties, but at the same time the treaties did stipulate that ships in distress be offered assistance at any place, whether a treaty port or not, and the Tsushima officials finally agreed to help the Russians, if only to expedite their departure.[6]

It was true that the vessel was in need of some repairs. The foremast, for example, had been damaged on the eve of their arrival.[7] But there is evidence that repairs were not the sole cause of the visit. Using repairs as an excuse, the Russians requested not only foodstuffs and timber, but the leasing of a favorable site and gave every appearance of planning to stay indefinitely. They even engaged in gunnery practice. The *Posadnik* changed anchorage several times, and Russian barracks were finally constructed at Imozaki Bay. The local authorities reported everything to the Shogunate and to the governor of Nagasaki, pleading that steps be taken to make the Russians leave. Birilev meanwhile demanded an interview with the local clan chief, warning against British designs on Tsushima and declaring that he had been sent as a safeguard against British aggression, and that he had a letter from the Tsar to the clan chief. He urged Japan to seek security by allying herself with Russia and offered the clan chief a gift of fifty cannons for the desired lease of land. The local officials were in no position to make any commitments, even if they had wanted. They supplied the Russians with whatever goods were demanded and putting on a peaceful front waited for help from the outside.

Both sides were suspicious of each other's intentions and sooner or later incidents were bound to occur. At one point Japanese guards tried to block the advance of Russian boats engaged in surveying. When the Russians failed to stop, the guards began throwing rocks and pieces of wood. The Russians replied with gunfire, killing several Japanese and wounding others. They also took several prisoners, adding to them, the following day, three officials whom they captured in their office.

6 Takada Rikichi, 22.
7 Russia, *Obzor*, 646.

A letter from the governor of Nagasaki, rebuking Birilev for his arbitrary conduct and telling him to undertake repairs in an opened port, was of no effect. Birilev refused even to accept it on the ground that it bore the Shogun's seal, despite Japanese assurances that the seal was not the Shogun's but that of the governor of Nagasaki. Birilev continued to act as he pleased, letting the cattle graze on shore and, when some of them died, demanded that the Japanese sell him more, intimidating them with various threats. Commissioner of Foreign Affairs Oguri Tadanori and Censor Mizoguchi Hachiju-goro, emissaries sent from the capital, were no more successful in expediting Birilev's departure. Indeed, a second Russian warship arrived and its commander, Captain Peshchurov, added his voice in seeking the right to "defend" the island.[8] The Japanese government complained to Consul Goshkevich through Governor Muragaki Norimasa of Hakodate, and at the same time requested British mediation.

Goshkevich protested that he knew nothing about Russian activities on Tsushima and promised to demand an explanation from the local naval commander, Commodore Likhachev. Though it has been said that Goshkevich was himself the channel through which Likhachev had received his instructions,[9] there is evidence that Likhachev had tried to keep from Goshkevich the plans to occupy Tsushima.[10] The British meanwhile acted with promptness. Having advised the Japanese government to direct a protest to the Russian government itself, Sir Rutherford Alcock dispatched Sir James Hope, commander of the British Asia squadron, and the chief secretary of the embassy to Tsushima with two warships. Arriving on August 27, the British found "a very complete naval depot including a hospital and workshop with the Russian flag flying on the hill above." Asked if his orders called for his leaving the island, if the Japanese government so requested, Birilev replied evasively, though one Russian source alleges that Hope succeeded in drawing considerable information out of the captain after thoroughly wetting down his throat with sherry. Leaving a strong note of protest to be transmitted to Likhachev, Hope departed to look for the latter in Olga Bay. Not finding

8 Tanaka, 22-25; Hiraoka, *Nichi-Ro*, 368-369; Tokutomi, XLIV, 367-369; Takada Riki-chi, 26.

9 Ward, 843-844.

10 Konstantin Pavlovich Pilkin, "Zaniatie v 1862 g. russkimi sudami ostrova Tsu-Sima," 2.

him there, he left another note in uncommonly strong language, demanding to know when the establishment begun by Birilev would be removed.[11]

In response to British pressure, as well as a protest of the Japanese government transmitted through Goshkevich and to the personal remonstrances of the latter, who wished to preserve Japanese goodwill, Likhachev dispatched the clipper *Oprichnik* to Tsushima with orders for Birilev to depart. The *Posadnik* left on September 19, but the *Oprichnik* remained behind. When Likhachev visited Hakodate on September 21, Governor Muragaki called on him to make sure that the *Oprichnik* would leave also. As a result Likhachev ordered still another vessel, the clipper *Abrek* under Commander Konstantin Pilkin, to proceed to Tsushima with orders for all Russians to evacuate the island. This was done, but Pilkin voiced the bewilderment of those associated with the Tsushima affair when he confided to his diary:

In other words, we had given serious thought to the annexation of Tsushima, but in that case is it possible that a mere letter of Hope could disarrange everything? Is it possible, that occupying Tsushima, we did not foresee objections? Japanese officials are to accompany me to make sure that we are really leaving Tsushima. How we have disgraced ourselves! This means that we had not looked before leaping. It seems to me, that having once begun the matter, it was wrong to give in, as Likhachev did.[12]

But the Russian withdrawal was to the advantage of Russia, for friendly relations were reestablished with Japan and the way prepared for an understanding concerning Sakhalin. The Russian government disclaimed any complicity in the affair and not only Birilev but Likhachev too was recalled, being replaced by Admiral Andrei Popov, whose squadron inherited, however, the detailed maps compiled by Birilev, with suitable fortifications sketched in.[13] Is is natural to assume that the Tsushima affair must have turned the Japanese against Russia, but relations between Japan and the other Western powers became far more critical when an English squadron leveled the city of Kagoshima in 1863 and a joint expeditionary force of American, British, French, and Dutch vessels attacked Shimonoseki

11 *Ibid.*, 3; Ward, 843-844.
12 Pilkin, 3; Ishin Shiryo Hensan Jimusho, *Ishin-shi*, II, 932.
13 V. de Mars, "La diplomatie russe dans l'extrême Orient," 714-715.

in 1864, while the Russians scrupulously avoided becoming involved.[14]

That Japan should have ever felt friendly toward Russia is not comprehended by many Western writers; that she should have relied on Russian assistance even after Russia's defeat in the Crimean War seems illogical. But the fact remains that the Crimean War did not shatter Russian prestige in Japan, depite English efforts to undermine it. C. Pemberton Hodgson, British consul in Nagasaki and Hakodate from 1858 to 1860, describes the Japanese respect for Russia:

It was at a private meeting of great men: the highest functionary asked me which is the greatest nation in the world (after Japan, it was understood)? I said that in my opinion there were five great nations, viz. France, the Germanic Confederation, Great Britain, Russia, and the United States, and that Turkey, Sardinia, Spain, and Portugal were secondary powers.
Q. Russia is a first-rate power?
R. Certainly.
Q. France and Great Britain first-rate powers?
R. Certainly.
Q. Very good: Sardinia and Turkey are second-rate powers?
R. Yes, but of great political importance.
Q. Are they great powers?
R. Yes, very useful ones.
Result. Then, by your own confession, you admit that two first-rate powers and two second-rate powers, fought for two years against Russia, and you were obliged to go away—at any rate, that you were glad to go away; so Russia, who could conquer four great powers, must be a grand nation.
It was useless to discuss the question. I did my best; but the Japanese have still an idea that the Emperor of Russia is second only to the Tycoon of Yedo.[15]

To the French and the English the Russian friendship for Japan was a pretext; but the tsarist government was skillful in disentangling itself from incidents which reflected adversely on the sincerity of Russian intentions and at least, until about 1875, Russian policy succeeded in gaining a position of relative respect and popularity for its countrymen. The observations of V. de Mars, an astute contemporary French observer, are of interest. He reported that Rus-

---

[14] Funaoka, II, 449. The fact that Russian absorption in the so-called Second Polish Revolution precluded full Russian participation did not alter the beneficial effect of Russian abstention on Japanese public opinion.
[15] Hodgson, 308-309.

sian vessels, though they visited the two Indies, Australia, and other distant regions regularly, had a special predilection for Japan. "There they feel at home, they know the bays and channels of this country much better than their own coasts and their ports in Manchuria." Indeed the principal station of the Russians in these seas was not a harbor of their own but Hakodate. The Russians stayed away from Edo, where friction and disputes dominated Japanese relations with the West. In this de Mars saw a "calculated absence" to befriend the Japanese.

Farsighted Russians, and they are not rare, have told themselves that, since for a long time yet one could not dream of extending direct domination over Japan, it was best to gain the friendship of this country, to hold oneself well toward it, to enchain it by a close alliance, by rapidly multiplied relations. From that time, the program of Russian policy was about found and could be summed up like this: to employ all means for gaining the friendship of the Japanese, never to oppose them, even in their most inadmissible demands, and at the propitious moment always to give good counsel concerning the relations and disputes with the European powers—to demonstrate to them the difference between the disinterested amity of the tsar and the behavior of the sovereigns of other countries, to incite them directly to resistance, to involve them even in troubles and push them into acts of hostility against the Occidental nations, which could place into relief the eminently pacific character of their relations with the government of Petersburg, then one day to render themselves indispensable and make the Japanese feel at that time that they cannot be saved except by the all-powerful protection of the tsars.[16]

Such a policy, de Mars continued, could not have been carried out if the Russian representative had resided among the other diplomats—"it would have been impossible for him to remain neutral in the presence of their frequent protestations, which were made habitually in the form of collective notes." For this reason Putiatin had negotiated the opening of Hakodate, the isolation of which gave the Russian representative a freedom which he could not have enjoyed in Edo and "assures Russian propaganda facilities which it would not have elsewhere." De Mars sketched the unique position of the Russians in Hakodate:

The residence of the Muscovite envoy, placed at the summit of a mountain, dominates the village which extends in the shape of an amphitheater at its feet and, compared with the very simple habitations of the other European agents, it looks like the place of some governor of the country. Enclosed by a high wall and by a vast esplanade, it has the appearance

16 DeMars, 710-711.

and the advantages of a retrenched encampment. The enclosure finally contains the office, the lodgings of the employees, a hospital of thirty or forty beds for the sick persons of the Russian squadron, a school for the young Japanese, and all the appendages with which the Muscovite diplomats like to surround themselves abroad. The Russian flag thus floats above all the others and seems to be there perfectly at home. On the other side of the bay, there are furthermore baths for the crews, bakeries, stores and other establishments indispensable for a maritime station, solidly constructed. It is in the neighboring villages and at the merchants of Hakodate that the staff and the crews proceed to spend their money; it is in Hakodate that the cruisers are being repaired, and all this, in the final analysis, profits the inhabitants, who cannot but desire the presence of such guests and form a high idea of the tsar, the more so as they have never seen until now any power represented in such grand fashion. Of all the foreign languages which one hears in Hakodate, it is already the Russian language which is most widespread. Young Japanese, taught at the consulate, speak it with extreme facility, even write it, and become in a way natural missionaries in aid of Muscovite policy. It is also Russian books that one reads most, and remarkable thing, the book which one circulates with the greatest of care is a history of the campaign of 1812.

De Mars described the policy of Russia toward Japan, initiated by Putiatin, "in not disdaining any means, in progressing slowly, but progressing always." It was a policy of infiltration which, at a moment of crisis, he feared, would show the Japanese people "already more than half subjugated." Foreign ideas and influences were bound to precipitate a civil war between rival political forces in Japan.

That day, be it distant or nearby, is the rôle of Russia not all traced out in advance? Why would she not extend her protection to her nearest neighbor, the prince of Matsumae, the lord of that island where she creates for herself today partisans and means of action? In closing the straits of La Perouse and Sangar, she would make on that side out of the Sea of Japan a closed sea. Hakodate would easily become another Sevastopol in these seas, and the small Japanese princes could prepare themselves from that time to go get their education in the military schools and in the regiments of the imperial guard at St. Petersburg.[17]

The picture of Russian life in Hakodate was quite accurate, but as time proved, French fears of Russian designs on Hokkaido were not then justified. When the civil war did break out in 1868, the French were more involved than the Russians in Japanese affairs. In the nineteenth century, when Western imperialism in the Far East was at its peak and when Russia pursued a strong policy toward

[17] *Ibid.*, 711-713.

China, Russia exercised restraint and consideration in her relations with Japan.

The Tsushima affair was a harbinger of conflicts to come. Not only had Britain run interference in Russia's attempt to gain a foothold on the island, speaking in terms so strong as to endanger relations between the two countries and prepared to demand the opening of Tsushima and the neighboring coast of Korea, if the Russians did not leave, but the United States was prepared to ask Russia for an official explanation.[18] In the words of a German historian: "At Tsushima, for the first time since the inauguration of treaty relations with the Far Eastern island empire, there had clearly appeared the contradiction of the objectives and aims of the individual Western powers. On the one side stood Russia, on the other stood England and France, between the two groups the United States, whose representative suspiciously kept guard that the European powers not extend their policy of conquest to the land opened by himself and Perry."[19] The Tsushima affair forecast the persistence of the Russian search for an ice-free outlet to the Pacific, the English backing of Japanese interests, and the American mediation of Russo-Japanese differences should the balance of power in the Far East be disturbed in one way or another.[20]

In about 1875, the year in which the Kuril Islands-Sakhalin exchange had seemed to resolve the major source of controversy, a new era was begun in the history of Russo-Japanese relations. Prior to that time, from the appearance of the first Japanese castaway on the shores of Russia in 1697, the stream of Russo-Japanese relations had flowed primarily in one direction: from Russia toward Japan. The Russian efforts to open up Japan, to establish commercial relations, and to delineate the frontier in the face of Japanese isolationism had made this a period of Russian initiative and Japanese withdrawal. The treaties of 1855, 1858, and 1875 had realized the Russian objectives with a minimum of ill will and resentment. But with the renunciation of her rights to southern Sakhalin in exchange for the northern Kuril Islands, Japan had arrived at a turning point in her relations with Russia. Henceforth the stream of Russo-Japanese relations was to flow in crosscurrents of purpose, direction, and initiative. The limited Russian objectives of trade and frontiers and the Jap-

18 Treat, I, 125 footnote 59.
19 Siemers, 59.
20 G. F. Hudson, *The Far East in World Politics*, 64.

anese policy of isolationism and appeasement had run their course. Stronger and more vital interests were developing in the international relations of the Far East. The dispatching of the first Putiatin expedition to Japan was prompted by American attempts to open the country and the Tsushima affair had been climaxed by British intervention, but in general, prior to 1875, Russo-Japanese relations were confined to dealings between the individuals of the two countries. With the extension of Russo-Japanese relations to the Asian continent after 1875, the romantic pageant of individual adventurers faded into the background and the impersonal forces of national and international power began to dominate the scene.

In the twenty years since the Treaty of Shimoda (1855), Japan had made remarkable strides on the road to modernization, emulating Western methods and techniques in the pursuit of military power and national prosperity. Another generation was to pass before Japan could successfully challenge Russia, but by 1875 she was willing and able to initiate an active policy toward the Manchu Empire and its coastal possessions, Formosa and Korea. Meanwhile agreements with China in 1858 and 1860 had brought Russia new territory and the right of navigation on the Amur River, furthering Russsian expansion into Manchu territory. The great Russian push into Manchuria, connected with the extension of the Trans-Siberian Railroad across northern Manchuria to Vladivostok, was still in the future, but in 1875, a scheme had been proposed for a railway from Nizhnii Novgorod on the Volga River to the Pacific Ocean, and the direction of Russian expansion, climaxed by the sale of Alaska to the United States in 1867, had swung from east to south, and the historic search for an ice-free Pacific base continued unabated.

The blocking of Russian ambitions in the Balkan region in the mid-fifties contributed directly to the renewed vigor of the Russian advance into the Far East. In the middle of the nineteenth century (as in the middle of the twentieth) Russian policy at opposite ends of the globe possessed a unity and interrelationship that was as obvious as it was ignored by most observers due to the regional compartmentalization of their training and interest. In the words of de Mars:

Russian policy more than any other is remarkable for its manifold and intricate effort, which embraces so many countries at the same time in Europe and in Asia. At the moment when it seems stopped and defeated on one side, it rises up again and extends on the other; under the blow of a defeat it ties anew all the threads of its vast and persevering designs. The immensity of its sphere of action, the diversity of its territories, readily give it a mystery favorable to its intentions. . . .

Thus Muravev had turned the Russian retreat, from Petropavlovsk into the Amur River, to advantage by occupying Chinese territory under the pretext of having to supply the blockaded fleet with vital provisions, and had retained and expanded this territory upon termination of the Crimean War. "In this wise, having scarcely emerged from a struggle which had menaced its ascendancy in Europe and its domination in the Caucasus, Russia had established at the other end of the globe the base of a new system of conquests."[21]

Analyzing the success of Russian tactics and its meaning for the future, a contemporary French critic wrote:

It is not since today that Russia plays her rôle in that part of the Orient. She has preceded Europe there, she remains there stronger than Europe by virtue of proximity, of the practice of things and men, of a system of ruse enhanced at a pinch by audacity and based on the knowledge of all the resorts of the Japanese character. Her whole art consists in making her way without explosion and without noise insofar as possible, in distinguishing herself in everything from the other countries, in enveloping the Japanese, in their passing if necessary many evils, without however permitting the conception of an exceptional power to weaken in their mind, in their carefully inculcating on the contrary the idea that these condescensions are nothing but the moderation of a friendly power, benevolent and naturally protective. . . . The other countries torment Japan for the murders or violences of which their nationals are the victims: Russia throws a veil over these deeds, she represents them as incidents unfortunately too common of the life of the peoples, which have nothing to do with politics, which above all cannot become an occasion for hostilities, and while England, France, and the United States use force, she contents herself with satisfactions which would be mediocre, if she did not pursue a greater end. . . .

These tactics, if one examines them there well, have been singularly deceitful for the Japanese. On one hand, they have made the Russian policy appear in their eyes as a model of disinterestedness, on the other they have put them on the road of resistance to the other countries with whom they have business. They have told themselves quite naturally that inasmuch as the tsar, a sovereign so powerful, abstains from employing arms, they should not let themselves be intimidated by European demonstrations. . . . This is how Russia is today [1866] more than ever in a position of arriving at her ends. She does not retrograde, she advances.

The day when the Russian policy will have arrived at taking the position to which it aspires in the seas of the Far East, the only force which could

[21] De Mars, 693-694.

easily and seriously thwart its designs is that other power bordering on the Pacific Ocean, which also tends to dominate over the continent where she plays such a great rôle: we mean the United States of America. . . .[22]

The Russians and the Japanese, in spite of mounting rivalry after 1875, were by no means hereditary or inevitable opponents. In the years before and after the Russo-Japanese War (and every great war since then) consideration was given in both capitals to the idea of Japan and Russia achieving their objectives in the Far East by joining forces. During the boundary negotiations in 1873, the Japanese minister of foreign affairs hinted that the Sakhalin question could be easily solved, if the Russians would support Japanese claims to Korea,[23] and, though the Russians refused to do so lest they endanger their own interests in China, the final conclusion of the Kuril Islands-Sakhalin exchange aroused speculation among Western diplomats in Tokyo "that Russia had come to an understanding with Japan concerning possible joint action against China, an understanding which might find expression perhaps very soon already in connection with a clash between Japan and Korea."[24] The rising imperialistic ambitions of both Russia and Japan did not, in the nineteenth century, point to the inevitability of war. This is brought out clearly in the writings of such contemporaries as A. Ia. Maksimov, who wrote in 1894: "A close alliance with Japan is not only desirable but actually necessary [for Russia], once we want to establish ourselves firmly on the shores of the Pacific Ocean and force England and China to treat us with due respect and conscientiousness. The Japanese government itself, almost the whole press, and the reasonable Japanese society stand for a close alliance with Russia. It is easy to find ground for political understandings of Russia and Japan, having [once] abolished the only possible bone of contention— Korea."[25] Maksimov believed that, despite the mistakes made by the Russian government, there continued to exist a sympathy of the Japanese for the Russian people, and that this sympathy would provide the necessary foundation for a firm alliance between the two countries and would help to overcome whatever political difficulties lay ahead. There is reason to believe that, as late as 1901, a *modus*

[22] *Ibid.*, 715-716.

[23] Von Brandt to von Bismarck, dated Tokyo, April 11, 1874, F.S.U. Film 189, reel 130, Japan I.B., 16, 1.

[24] Holleben to von Bismarck, dated Tokyo, August 10, 1875, F.S.U. Film 189, reel 130, Japan I.B., 16, 5.

[25] A. Ia. Maksimov, *Nashi zadàchi na Tikhom Okeane*, 58.

vivendi might have been found (as indeed it was found in the years immediately following the Russo-Japanese war)[26] had there not developed in the meantime a fatal degeneration in Russian diplomacy.

The sense of continuity and cautiousness, which had characterized Russia's Far Eastern policy during the nineteenth century, gave way to "a period of waywardness and reckless gambling," as the imperial court of young Nicholas II became "a happy hunting ground for all kinds of adventurers from occultists and cranks . . . to . . . dangerous speculators and promoters such as those who were responsible for the Yalu affair."[27] This problem is beyond the scope of the present volume, but there is one aspect of the fateful change in Russian attitude which deserves attention here, because it stemmed directly from the observations and opinions of those who had dealings with the Japanese in the nineteenth century—the gradual ascendancy of the views of those who had nothing but contempt for the Japanese. That such views prevailed was surprising in the light of the repeated Russian expressions of affinity with the Japanese.

With time the Russians and the Japanese discovered that they shared many values and prejudices not common to the nationals of other countries, and that consequently they could understand each other, though not always agree with each other. The Russians and the Japanese were both imbued with respect for autocracy and government regulation, for rank and protocol, and were equally disdainful of merchants and money-makers. Both were troubled by a pull in opposite cultural directions; both dreamed of becoming the bridge between East and West, the catalyst of a new and universal civilization.

The confrontation of Japanese culture with Russian culture in the nineteenth century has as its counterpart the confrontation of Russian culture with Western European culture in the days since Peter the Great; and the debate by Japanese statesmen of the pros and cons of Western culture compared to Japanese culture sounded like an extension of the contemporary controversy in Russia between

[26] As Ernest Batson Price observes, "it seems fairly clear that, although their efforts proved ineffective at the time, and it took the Russo-Japanese War to show that they were right, leading statesmen of both Russia and Japan even before the war had become convinced that, as the two nations must needs live together in Northeastern Asia, they might as well live in peace; and that the only way in which this could be accomplished was by a friendly understanding, cemented by treaty, with respect to their mutual rights and interests in the area." (*The Russo-Japanese Treaties of 1907-1916 Concerning Manchuria and Mongolia*, 21.)

[27] Lobanov-Rostovsky, 214-215.

the so-called Westerners and Slavophils. Because of military necessity both Russia and Japan adopted Western methods and the outward trappings of Western culture rapidly, selectively, and by government decree. Both employed foreigners in positions of importance. The reigns of Peter the Great and Emperor Meiji had much in common, and the societies that evolved resembled each other—the old traditions existing side by side with the new.

An American author has written of Russia in our own day: "In few countries will a traveler find greater divergence between the old and the new civilization than in Russia. Two civilizations have been contesting each other, one stubbornly refusing to pass into history, while the other with equal stubbornness persisting in establishing itself. Amidst this conflict a traveler can find much to suit his taste or strengthen his preconceived picture of the country. There is much that some like to label 'Asiatic,' and there is just as much to fit the designation of 'European.' "[28] Almost the same could be said of contemporary Japan. The Russian preoccupation with the question to follow a unique destiny of their own or to join with the nations of Europe in a common cause gave them an appreciation of the problems facing Japan, and some of their conclusions were almost Japanese in outlook. Toward the end of the nineteenth century Skalkovskii wrote:

Passionate Westerners in Japan, as in Russia, say that by means of living together there is broadened the intellectual and moral sphere of the activity of a nation, which has stood apart, the development becomes more diverse and stronger, richer in results. Theoretically, of course, one cannot argue against this, but "living together" is a conditional concept. Japan cannot skim the cream of European civilization; like Russia of pre-reform times, she contents herself with mere imitation, which borders unto apishness; under the name of civilizers there have come to her a lot of sharpers, Englishmen, Americans, Jews—the foremost swindlers in the world. These are representatives not of European science, but of the trash of the European colonies of the Far East. The Japanese people had excelled in sincerity and honesty, Japanese jails with their paper walls had contained until recently the most insignificant number of criminals, no one had suspected the existence of locks in doors. And now not only in the store but even in the treaty the Japanese frequently does not wish to take from you all the money due him, out of delicateness it seems to him somehow that he has demanded too much. One can imagine what a convenient field of profit such a people offers.[29]

[28] Anatole G. Mazour, *Russia Past and Present*, 23.
[29] Skalkovskii, *Vneshniaia*, 478.

The Russians frequently remarked how much closer they felt to the Japanese than to other Asian nations, in some respects closer even than to fellow-Europeans. Kanagawa reminded them of a large Little Russian village, and the retinue of Edo officials of the retinue of Russian squires.[30] One of the clearest expressions of this feeling was the statement made several years later by Prince E. E. Ukhtomskii in the official account of Crown Prince Nikolai's tour of the Far East, despite the fact that one of the Japanese police officers had nearly succeeded in assassinating the future (and last) emperor of Russia. He wrote:

There is nothing simpler for Russians, it appears, than to get on together with Asians. Between them and ourselves there is such a complete harmony of thought concerning the essential problems of life that some sort of kinship of souls is always determined quickly and in the closest way. Notwithstanding the deep, almost fundamental, differences in psycho-physical features, the Japanese and the common Russian are still somehow brotherly closer to each other than to Europeans.[31]

Other Westerners were aware of the advantage held by the Russians in dealing with Asians, though they expressed it in somewhat less flattering terms. As one observer put it: "The Russian diplomat has all the softness and suavity of his Asiatic congeners; he can glide through their closest net of diplomacy without displaying an angle in his body; he conforms to their customs, and allows them to delay and prevaricate to their hearts' content. But his point once gained he is unyielding. He is an adept in the art of bribery; has emissaries everywhere; in fact, thoroughly understands how to deal with Asia, and is too strongly imbued with this Asiatic spirit for European patience."[32]

The ultimate ascendancy of contempt for the Japanese was no less surprising in view of a whole series of reports by Russians stressing the great possibilities of Japan and her people. Golovnin had been of a very high opinion of the Japanese. Putiatin had treated them with respect and even Muravev-Amurskii, despite his futile policy of bluster, had expressed his appreciation of their discrimination and astuteness. Tilley had illustrated in his writings how the Japanese had begun to modernize their forces. From the supercargo of the brig *Greta* which had taken on a large part of the *Diana's* crew at

[30] Kornilov, "Izvestiia," 109, 111.
[31] *Puteshestvie Gosudaria Imperatora Nikolaia II na Vostok*, 5:10.
[32] Frederic William Unger, *Russia and Japan*, 78.

Shimoda in 1855, the Japanese had purchased ten thousand muskets at five dollars a piece. "The bayonets which were a dollar extra, they would not take, and they are still at Shimoda. They took one, indeed, as a model, and soon afterwards manufactured themselves as many as they required." In 1855 there had been few adequate points of fortification along the coast of Japan, but only four years later a considerable change could be noticed:

Four large forts, before mentioned, are in front of Yedo; one still larger, capable of holding several thousand men, and mounting some hundred cannon, is now on the point of completion at Hakodadi. Heavy batteries were in course of construction to defend the entrance of the bay of Nangasaki. Cannon have been largely purchased, and companies of men instructed in their use; the roar of these guns, and the continued rattle of small arms, could be distinctly heard during our stay in Yedo, the small arms practice being in close vicinity to the temple where we resided.

It had been evident to Tilley that the ruling men of Japan "seek to strengthen their own forces after the manner of those they would have to oppose, in case of necessity," and that "when they consider themselves capable of coping with their adversary, they will resist all further encroachments by force."[33] Kornilov had reported in 1859 that Western-style ships, obtained by the Japanese, were manned and commanded by Japanese exclusively and that even Japanese machinists measured up to European demands.[34] Lieutenant Nazimov had made a similar observation two years later, and, surveying Japanese naval forces in 1860, had not only listed an increasing number of ships, but had underlined that Japan could readily recruit "tens of thousands" of courageous and experienced seamen from among her numerous and highly patriotic fishing population.[35] A similar note had been sounded about a decade later by another Russian naval officer, Lieutenant Staritskii, after an account of Japan's merchant and naval vessels:

Thus, if we add the merchant vessels to the warships, those that have gone down to those in existence, and add further the numerous purchases of Japan in machinery, artillery, and armament, as well as the huge expenditures in connection with the building of the Yokosuka arsenal and another similar naval establishment in Akunara [Akunoura] near Nagasaki, we shall get a very respectable figure, the expenditure of which on the part of little Japan points to her serious intention to establish a naval might, corresponding to the insular position of the country.

33 Tilley, 148.   34 Kornilov, "Izvestiia," 106-107.
35 Lieutenant Nazimov, "Iz vospominanii ob Iaponii," 328.

The question remained whether these changes were to be welcomed or not. "Can we Russians be pleased with such a course of naval affairs in Japan?" Staritskii asked, and at once replied himself: "Certainly, we should be pleased and even help, because from a humanitarian and even from a political standpoint, it is much better for us to have a neighbor who is independent, strong and self-reliant than a mass of slaves, submitting to foreign influence, which any day might become hostile to us because of interests that have nothing to do with the east." Staritskii went on to say that the Russians had been the first practical teachers of the Japanese in European naval construction; that the *Heda* had been the "grandmother" of the Japanese fleet; that the Russians had furthermore been their first teachers in the construction of European fortifications and in the handling of European weapons, at least the first in northern Japan, where the Hakodate city fortress had been built according to the plans of the late Lieutenant Commander Kostyrev, who over a period of several years had guided the Japanese in the construction of this fortress, had taught them how to shoot the cannons of the *Diana*, which had been given to them as gift, and how to handle sails and navigate ships. "Is it possible," he asked, "that now when the seeds, sown ten to fifteen years ago, are beginning to bear rich fruit, we shall start to fear the too rapid growth of our former foster child, and instead of further assistance, shall start to keep him back?"[36] But there were others no less sympathetic to Japan, who questioned the wisdom of hastening the modernization of the country. In 1894, after years of study of Japanese history as well as of first hand observation, V. Cherevkov wrote:

Should one desire that Japan break as soon as possible with the old patriarchal methods of production and introduce everywhere machine-work, which will crush millions of small handicraftsmen and will make it possible for a capitalist regime with all its charms to grow up on their remains?

For us Russians, who more than all other nations, are interested in Japan's preservation of her political and economical independence, there can be no answer to these questions, but a negative one. And from this there must obviously follow also our special relationship to the question of treaty revision in Japan, giving us the opportunity to take here a position, such as would ensure for us for ever the friendship of this beautiful, attractive country, no matter what regime would hold sway in her.[37]

36 Letter from Staritskii, 16-17.
37 V. Cherevkov, "Iz noveishei istorii Iaponii," 524.

The average Russian visitor to Japan found it more entertaining to ridicule the Japanese, than to take them seriously. Thus such books as the invaluable narrative of Golovnin were soon replaced in popularity by Goncharov's *Fregat Pallada* and other contributions of lesser value, contributions which, however accurate historically, managed to mislead their readers by dwelling on unimportant aspects of Japanese life, those most different from their own. Nor were some of the serious appraisals of growing Japanese naval power free of slighting remarks. Staritskii wrote that the complements of Japanese men-of-war looked so much like children, "that one wonders unconsciously how such a serious toy has fallen into their hands and how they have not broken it till this time?"[38] Kornilov expressed similar thoughts in regard to the Japanese pilots who had boarded his vessel. "The gravity and serious countenance with which they guided the clipper, which without them knew the route well by the map, amused us," he recalled. "So much childishness was noticeable in all their movements, that one was reminded unwittingly of the joy of a twelve-year old boy, when he is allowed, for example, to hold the reins, and of the impatience if anyone of the adults wants to warn or teach him." Mocking the Japanese men-of-war, he said "of course there is on them no sign of what we are accustomed to call a warship, unless it be only the fairly accurate raising of the flag." Nor was he impressed by Japanese gunnery practice on shore. "One must see how caricature-like the crews stepped out in their Japanese costumes, with inexpressibly sad faces, to the monotonous sounds of a drum and a shell, under the command of an officer, who tried with all his might that his subordinates would fall into step and not forget to turn in a previously practiced manner; one must see how they distorted European military exercise unmercifully—in order to understand how difficult it was not to burst out laughing when looking on these wailsome processions. A Japanese and a soldier—they absolutely are two incompatible concepts."[39]

At the beginning of the twentieth century the Russian public knew less of the true character of the Japanese than the Japanese of the true character of the Russians. At the outbreak of the Russo-Japanese War one Russian writer complained that Russia had "not a single book about Japan," but only books about such marginal topics as geisha, teahouses, hairdos, and legends. "Be they Japan-

[38] Letter from Staritskii, 13.
[39] Kornilov, "Zimovka," 88-96, 106.

464

ophile or Japanophobe, these books look upon Japan merely as upon a *partie de plaisir*. And now, when we had to look upon Japan as upon a *partie de guerre*, our knowledge of the geisha and jinriksha proved inapplicable. And in some questions we stand wrapped in a yellow fog of ignorance."[40] At the end of the book the author mentioned his discovery of Golovnin's narrative with which he had not been acquainted when he had started writing his account and remarked that there were very few people who knew of Golovnin's work.[41] The distorted image of Japan in Russia at the end of the nineteenth century was well illustrated by T. Bogdanovich, who had this to say in 1905, with tongue in cheek, about the exotic appearance of Japanese customs:

That appearance differs so much from everything to which we have become accustomed in Europe, seems so exotic, so Asiatic, that unwittingly it arouses in the observer a distrustful attitude toward the culture.

And it is not surprising. For a very long time it was difficult for us to believe that a man, dressed in a smock-frock or a peasant's overcoat or who had just replaced them by German dress, could think and feel like we, who almost from the cradle had grown together with cultured dress. It is not strange at all that we could not take serious people, who walked along the streets in long silken robes or, still worse, in European uniforms and wooden clogs, which they took off when entering a house. How can we consider as equal to ourselves people who cannot eat with our forks and who sit crossleggedly on mats! Those are not people—those are yellowfaced barbarians or simply reborn macacos![42]

LOOKING BACK

The discovery of the Japanese castaway Dembei by a Russian explorer on Kamchatka in 1697 marks the beginning of Russo-Japanese relations. It stirred the interest of Peter the Great in trade with Japan and started the first Russian attempts to reach Japan. These early efforts, undertaken on government initiative and by private adventurers, who sought to ingratiate themselves with the Emperor, were primitive and unsuccessful. Only in 1739, more than a generation after Dembei's discovery and over a decade after Peter's death, did the Russians succeed in making their way to Japan. This time the expedition had been conceived on a much larger scale and had

[40] N. Shebuev, *Iaponskie vechera*, 3.
[41] *Ibid.*, 201-203.
[42] T. Bogdanovich, *Ocherki iz proshlago i nastoiashchago Iaponii*, 198.

required years of planning and preparation. Four Russian ships penetrated down to the Japanese main island and some of the Russians actually set foot on Japanese soil, but though they were well received, they made no attempt to negotiate with the Japanese, and the records of their sailing were so faulty that upon their return to Russia the authorities did not believe that they had actually visited Japan. An attempt by the same mariners to retrace their voyage ended in failure, and for the next half century Russian activities in this region were confined primarily to the Kuril Islands. Initiative passed into the hands of private individuals and of local officials, who saw in the arable southern islands a source of agriculture and a potential channel of trade with Japan. In 1778 and again in 1779, members of a secret expedition followed the archipelago all the way down to Hokkaido, but though they managed to confer amicably with Japanese officials, they were informed that the foreign trade of Japan was limited to Nagasaki exclusively. In 1792, an expedition dispatched by Catherine the Great proceeded once more to Hokkaido. Again the Russians were directed to Nagasaki, and were given a special permit. Not until 1804 did they make use of this permit. It was no more than a permit of entry, however, and negotiations in Nagasaki proved as fruitless as ever. Then the Russian envoy Nikolai Rezanov resorted to military pressure and instructed two naval officers in the service of the Russian-American Company to raid the territories of Japan. This they did, in 1806 and 1807, incurring the enmity of the Japanese and laying the basis for the capture of another Russian officer, who years later, in 1811, strayed into a Japanese trap on one of the Kuril Islands. Following the release of Lieutenant Commander Golovnin, who had been taken to Hokkaido, Russo-Japanese relations shrank to isolated messages left on the Kuril Islands, until 1852, when another futile private attempt at opening Japan was made by a vessel of the Russian-American Company at the Japanese main island. Only in 1855, after American and other foreign pressure had been brought to bear on Japan, did the Russians succeed in signing a treaty of amity with the Japanese and partially delineate the frontier between them. In 1858, again in the wake of foreign success, they concluded a commercial agreement and in 1875 made a "final" disposition of their respective rights to Sakhalin and the Kuril Islands.

The Russian push toward Japan was part of the Russian push east, across Siberia, across the Pacific Ocean, to the American continent. It did not command the full and unabated attention of the tsarist government, which did not wish to endanger commercial relations with China and which was more concerned with events in Europe than expansion in the Far East. The major force of the Russian thrust east was generated by individuals—adventurers, merchants, Siberian officials, mariners, scholars. The central government, until the second half of the nineteenth century, lacked interest in Russian imperialism in the Far East. Territorial ambitions in Europe, the spread of American and French revolutionary ideas, and Dutch and English commercial competition held its attention in the west. Prodded though it was by proposals for action against China and Japan, the tsarist government remained conservative, cautious, and apathetic, doing more to restrain than to encourage its enterprising subjects in the Pacific. As the American Press recalled, in 1958, on the day after the United States Senate voted to admit Alaska to statehood: "Russia's pioneers were in Alaska more than thirty years before the thirteen American colonies rebelled against the rule of England's King George III. They were hunting sea otters off the California coast when no white man had ventured west of the Missouri River. They were in the Hawaiian Islands while the United States was still licking the wounds of the War of 1812." Yet the Russians "merely marked time" in Alaska and California while Americans "pushed relentlessly westward" until Russia could do little more than withdraw gracefully and recognize "the manifest destiny of America." Recalling the dreams and schemes of Rezanov and his associates, the American Press commented: "These men were empire builders denied their tools, architects of expansion whose plans died on the drawing board. Had their visions and energies been shared in the courts of the tsars in St. Petersburg, Alaska might yet belong to Russia; Northern California, Oregon, and Washington might today be under the hammer and sickle."[43] But, if the Russian push toward Japan also received this half-hearted support from the government and was frequently thwarted by the priority of other considerations, its role in the overall expansion of the Russian Empire and in the development of Siberia assured it of continued momentum. In time the sapping of Russian energy in the Far East by the demands of Russian policy in Europe was compensated by the renewed vigor of Russian expansion eastward, when frustrated

[43] *Tallahassee Democrat*, July 1, 1958, 7.

in the west, and by the middle of the nineteenth century a definite pattern of Russian policy at the opposite ends of the globe became apparent.

In terms of centuries one can talk of a Russian push toward Japan—a gradual, inexorable drive to find Japan and to establish relations with her. It was not a military conquest. At first Russian aims in Japan were essentially economic: to obtain a source of vital supplies for the far flung territories of the Russian Far East. Characteristically the instructions of envoy Rezanov had been drafted not by the Minister of Foreign Affairs but by the Minister of Commerce. Later, by the middle of the nineteenth century, the pressure of rival powers on the tottering Manchu Empire gave a more strategic character to the Russian interests in Japan, and the tsarist government assumed a more active role. Japan was important to Russia as a source of supplies, as an ice-free naval base for operations against China and patrolling the Russian shores, and as a coaling station on the way to Alaska. Japan was only one of many regions of Russian interest; she was not the major concern of the Russian policy makers.

In terms of decades Russian policy appears erratic and to lack a definite course. The drive that is apparent over a period of centuries is overshadowed by conflicting policies, which tend to change with every change in personnel at home and abroad. The Russian general public showed little interest in Japan, accounts of Russians in Japan, for example of Mrs. Goshkevich, wife of the consul, usually finding their way into French newspapers first.[44] Like their American counterparts, Russian representatives in Japan were left to shift for themselves by their government. Lieutenant Nazimov complained in 1860 that in the two years that he had been in Hakodate, he had not received a single journal and consequently was deprived "of the pleasure and necessity of knowing news from the fatherland," and that when letters did occasionally reach him and his countrymen, they were from twelve to eighteen months old.[45]

On the whole, the policy of the tsarist government toward Japan was one of indifference. If the Japanese were willing to come to an agreement with Russia, well and good; if not, that was their prerogative. In the period from 1697 to 1875 force was not a measure of Russia government policy toward Japan. With the exception of the unauthorized and ultimately condemned raids of Khvostov and

[44] Letter from Ivan Makhov of November 26 (December 8), 1860, 87.
[45] Letter from Nazimov of November 1 (13), 1860, 228.

Davydov, the actions of individuals were restrained. Inexplicably clumsy and offensive as Muravev-Amurskii's attempt to talk the Japanese out of Sakhalin may have been, he took "no" for an answer and refrained from exploiting the wanton murder of two of his subordinates by the Japanese, despite the presence of his fleet and the clamor for punitive action on the part of his fellow Europeans. Even the occupation of Sakhalin in 1853 and the Tsushima affair of 1861 were settled amicably by Russian withdrawal without recourse to arms.

It is possible that Russia could have opened Japan at an earlier date, had she acted with greater energy and persistence. The reluctance of the tsarist government to exert military pressure encouraged the Shogunate in its policy of deferment. Yet when relations were established at last, they were established without force. Though it was Western pressure that ultimately led to the opening of Japan, it was Western pressure that the Japanese resisted most. Russian restraint was not confined to military pressure alone. Like the Dutch, the Russians avoided any public display of their religion, until after the opening of Japan. Even then they made every effort to adapt the Orthodox Church in tone and loyalty to Japanese tradition. Without humbling themselves, like the Dutch, the Russians made a point of respecting Oriental customs.

Japanese interest in Russia was total, constant, occasionally verging on hysteria, and shaped by an overestimation of actual Russian interest in Japan. In the words of Sir George Sansom, "it is not far out to say that much of the anxiety displayed by the party that was urging military preparation on the Bakufu was inspired by fears of imperialistic policies on the part of England and Russia that did not then exist."[46] Not all Japanese reacted in the same manner to the Russian push toward Japan. It is a characteristic of Russo-Japanese relations that even at moments of extreme irritation with Russia, there were spokesmen in or near the Japanese government, who sought to deflect Russian pressure on their country by alliance with Russia rather than by direct opposition. The generally amicable personal relations between the Russians and the Japanese strengthened this attitude.[47] The conditions of trade in Japan and the tradi-

[46] Sansom, *The Western World*, 250.

[47] Among the more distinguished Russian visitors who were received with particular warmth by the Japanese, there was Grand Duke Aleksei Aleksandrovich. In October and November of 1872 he visited, Nagasaki, Kobe, Osaka, Yokohama, Tokyo, and Hakodate. In the capital he had been received by the Emperor, and the Emperor himself had repaid the visit at the Grand Duke's hotel. There had been much enter-

tional contempt of samurai for merchants, prompted the Japanese to accept with less suspicion the preponderance of Russian naval officers in their country. Russian popularity was enhanced by Russian willingness—whenever the prestige of their country was not directly at stake—to conform with Japanese customs. It was on the Russian Emperor, Alexander II, that the Japanese called in 1872 "with boundless confidence" to arbitrate a dispute with the government of Peru.[48] The Russian officers and officials were in a peculiarly advantageous position to understand Japanese problems. They shared with the Japanese many values and prejudices, notably respect for autocracy and disdain for capitalism. Above all they had a similar background of Westernization and could draw on their own experiences concerning such common problems as the clash of cultures and the employment of foreigners.

Tempting as it may be to project modern conflict into the past and to claim to be able to discern the seeds of permanent Russo-Japanese discord in such incidents as the raids of Khvostov and Davydov, the incidents had neither fatal nor lasting meaning and cannot justly be offered as evidence of an "historical enmity" between Russia and Japan. On the Russian side, the writings of Golovnin, Rikord, and Maksimov are examples of the persistence of Russian faith in the feasibility, if not the necessity, of friendly relations with Japan.

Japan's reluctant entry into the arena of world affairs was bound to alter the character of Russo-Japanese relations. Japanese reaction to the demands of Russia, the United States, and the other Western powers was cumulative. The opening of the country was only the

---

tainment, and military and naval parades had been held in honor of the Russian visitor. The Russian government formally expressed appreciation for the warm hospitality extended to Aleksei Aleksandrovich, and later Alexander II personally told the Japanese vice-minister Hanabusa in Russia that the way in which his son had been welcomed in Japan had done much to strengthen further the friendly relations between Russia and Japan. (Tanaka, 147-148.)

[48] In July of 1872 the Peruvian vessel *Maria Luz* entered Yokohama for repairs with two hundred and thirty-two Chinese coolies, purchased in Macao, on board. Japanese law forbade traffic in human beings and when the nature of the ship's cargo became known—one of the coolies jumped overboard and sought refuge on a British man-of-war—Minister of Foreign Affairs Soejima had the case taken before the district court of Kanagawa prefecture. There the coolies were freed, and fed and clothed by the local authorities until aid came from the Chinese government, which had been informed of the matter. The Peruvian captain, Ricardo Herero, meanwhile, had abandoned the *Maria Luz* and had fled to San Francisco whence he wired his government for help. The case was finally submitted to the arbitration of Alexander II, who decided in favor of Japan (June 14, 1875). (Ariga, 175) For the English text of the Japanese argument in the Maria Luz Case, see *Dai-Nihon gaiko monjo*, viii, 395-419.

beginning of a journey that was to take Japan along the very road envisaged by such men as Honda Toshiaki and Yoshida Shoin. Japan's preoccupation with military matters—partly forced upon her by the threat of Western imperialism, partly rooted in her own militaristic past—and her rapid modernization brought Russian expansion on the Asiatic continent face to face with renewed Japanese expansion in Korea and beyond. Even then open conflict was not inevitable, enmity was not hereditary, and the policies of Russia and Japan need not have ended in war. After 1875 the bilateral nature of early Russo-Japanese relations gave way to the more complex interplay of political and economic forces on an international scale and the influence of individual Russian and Japanese adventurers faded into the background.

In the years following the opening of Japan great political upheavals were to shake Japan, Korea, China, and Russia herself, upheavals that were to affect basically the whole course of Far Eastern international relations. Japan's loss of her empire, as the result of defeat in World War II, has turned the clock of Russo-Japanese relations back to the nineteenth century. Not only does the frontier question of today revert directly to the period before 1875, but the absence of normal diplomatic and commercial relations between Russia and Japan, delay in the repatriation of prisoners of war, and the arrest of Japanese fishermen are reminiscent of the days of the Seclusion Period, even though the roles of Japan and Russia may have been somewhat reversed. A booklet recently published by the Japanese Ministry of Foreign Affairs in support of Japan's position in the territorial dispute with the Soviet Union goes back all the way to the activities of Ivan Kozyrevskii in 1711.[49] To the Japanese of today the era of the opening of their country is no more remote than is the "War between the States" to the average Southerner in the United States. The Japanese preoccupation with the Tokugawa era is similar to the American idolization of the Wild West, and adventures of castaways like Kodayu still find a ready audience. The leading figures of the Russian push toward Japan may be unfamiliar to Americans (if not to modern Russians), but they are well known to Japanese students of foreign relations, and the visitor to Hakodate and Nagasaki will find the name of many a ship, mentioned in this book, engraved on the tombstones of Russian seamen, who failed to return from Japan.

---

[49] Japan, Ministry of Foreign Affairs, Public Information Bureau, *The Northern Islands*, 18.

APPENDICES

TREATIES AND AGREEMENTS

I. TREATY OF PEACE AND FRIENDSHIP (1855): THE TREATY OF SHIMODA.*

In order to establish peace and friendship between Russia and Japan and to affirm them by treaty, His Majesty the Emperor, Autocrat of all the Russias,† has appointed as Plenipotentiary His Vice-Admiral and Aide-de-Camp, General Evfimii Putiatin, and His Majesty the Great Sovereign of all Japan has appointed as Plenipotentiaries His eminent subjects: Tsutsui Hizen-no-kami and Kawaji Saemon-no-jo.

The above-mentioned Plenipotentiaries have laid down the following articles:

ARTICLE I

Henceforth let there be continuous peace and sincere friendship between Russia and Japan. In the possession of both Empires, Russians and Japanese enjoy protection and defense in regards to their personal safety as well as to the inviolability of their property.

ARTICLE II

Henceforth the boundaries between Russia and Japan will pass between the islands Etorofu and Uruppu. The whole island of Etorofu belongs to Japan and the whole island Uruppu and the other Kuril Islands to the north constitute possessions of Russia. As regards the island Karafuto (Sakhalin), it remains unpartitioned between Russia and Japan, as has been the case up to this time.

ARTICLE III

The Japanese Government opens for Russian vessels three ports: Shimoda in the principality Izu, Hakodate in the district Hakodate, and Nagasaki in the principality Hizen. In these three ports, Russian vessels can henceforth repair their damages, supply themselves with water, firewood, victuals, and other necessities, even coal, where it can be obtained, and pay for all this with gold or silver specie, and in case of lack of money substitute for it goods from their store.

With the exception of the above-mentioned harbors, Russian vessels will not visit other ports, except in cases when because of extreme exigency the vessel will not be able to continue the voyage. Outlays made in such cases will be reimbursed in one of the opened ports.

ARTICLE IV

Shipwrecked vessels and people in both Empires will be shown all kinds of assistance and all survivors will be delivered to open ports.

* Japan, Foreign Office, *Treaties and Conventions*, 585-592. Treaty ratifications were exchanged at Shimoda on December 7, 1856. The above is a translation of the Russian text, checked against the Dutch text, with Japanese names spelled according to the Japanese original. The suffix *"no kami"* means "Lord of." Tsutsui Hizen-no-kami, thus is equivalent to Tsutsui, Lord of Hizen.

† Great Russia, Little Russia, White Russia.

Throughout all of their stay in the foreign land they shall enjoy freedom, but submit to the just laws of the country.

Article V

In the first two of the opened ports, the Russians are allowed to exchange desired goods and property for goods, property, and money brought.

Article VI

The Russian Government will, when it finds it indispensable, appoint a consul to one of the two first mentioned ports.

Article VII

If some question or matter demanding consideration or decision should arise, it will be considered in detail and set in order by the Japanese Government.

Article VIII

A Russian in Japan, as well as a Japanese in Russia, are always free and are not subject to any constraints. A person who has committed a crime can be arrested, but is tried in no other way than according to the laws of his own country.

Article IX

In consideration of the proximity of both Empires, all rights and privileges which Japan has granted at present or will give in the future to other nations extend at the same time also to Russian subjects.

This treaty will be ratified by His Highness the Emperor and Autocrat of all the Russias and His Majesty the Great Sovereign of all Japan, or as stated in the attached special agreement, and the ratifications will be exchanged in Shimoda not sooner than in nine months or as circumstances will permit. As for the present, copies of the treaty bearing the signatures and seals of the Plenipotentiaries of both Empires are exchanged, and all its articles come into force from the day of signature and will be observed by both negotiating parties faithfully and inviolably.

Concluded and signed in the city of Shimoda in the 1855th year from the birth of Christ, on the 26th day of January (7th day of February), or in the first year of Ansei on the 21st day of the twelfth month.

Signed:
Evfimii Putiatin
Tsutsui Hizen-no-kami
Kawaji Saemon-no-jo

EXPLANATORY ARTICLES OF THE TREATY BETWEEN RUSSIA AND JAPAN

Corroborated by the Russian Plenipotentiary Vice-Admiral and Aide-de-Camp, General Evfimii Putiatin and the Japanese Plenipotentiaries Tsutsui Hizen-no-kami and Kawaji Saemon-no-jo.

To Article III

A. In the first two of the designated ports, the Russians can go about freely; in the city of Shimoda and its environs for a distance of seven miles counting from Inubashiri Island, and in Hakodate for a distance of five Japanese miles. They can also visit shops, shrines, and, until the arrangement of inns, designated houses for resting. As for private houses, they must not enter them, except by invitation. In Nagasaki—as will be determined later for the others.

B. For the burial of the deceased, a place will be set aside in each port and these cemeteries must be inviolable.

To Article V

The release of goods will take place in a specially designated government building, whither the goods and gold and silver specie brought will also be delivered. The Russians, having selected in the shops goods or property and having agreed with the vendor on the price, pay for them or exchange them for the goods brought on the vessel in the designated house through the mediation of Japanese officials.

To Article VI

A. Russian consuls will be appointed from the year 1856.

B. Places and houses for the consulate will be determined by the Japanese Government, and the Russians will live in them according to their own customs and laws.

To Article IX

The rights and privileges mentioned in Article IX, of whatever sort they might be, given to other nations, are similarly extended to Russia without further negotiations.

These explanatory articles have all the force of the treaty and are equally binding on both negotiating parties, in proof whereof they are countersigned by the signature and seals of the Plenipotentiaries of both Empires.

Concluded and signed in the city of Shimoda in the 1855th year from the birth of Christ, on the 26th day of January (7th day of February), or in the first year of Ansei on the 21st day of the 12th month.

Signed:

Evfimii Putiatin
Tsutsui Hizen-no-kami
Kawaji Saemon-no-jo

II. SUPPLEMENTARY TREATY BETWEEN JAPAN AND RUSSIA (1857): THE TREATY OF NAGASAKI*

In supplement to the Treaty concluded between Russia and Japan in Shimoda on January 26 (February 7), 1855, or the 21st day of the 12th month of the first year of Ansei, their Excellencies Mizuno Chikugo-no-kami, Controller and [First] Governor of the city of Nagasaki, Arao Iwami-no-kami, [Second] Governor of the city of Nagasaki, and Iwase Iga-no-kami, Governmental Commissioner, and Count Evfimii Putiatin, Vice-Admiral and Aide-de-Camp, General of His Majesty the Emperor of all the Russias, came to an agreement and have stipulated the following articles:

ARTICLE I

In order to establish commerce and friendly intercourse between Russia and Japan on more solid foundations, new regulations are enacted for the guidance of Russians and Japanese in the ports of Hakodate and Nagasaki.

As to the port of Shimoda, however, which does not offer safe shelter to vessels, there shall be observed in it at the present time only the former regulations confirmed by the Treaty of 26 January (7 February), 1855, or the 21st day of the 12th month of Ansei 1. The new regulations shall not be applied to it until it will not have been finally decided whether Shimoda will remain an opened port or whether another port more convenient for trade will be opened for foreign vessels.

ARTICLE II

Henceforth the number of vessels and the amount of money employed in trade shall not be limited by anything and all commercial transactions shall be effected by the mutual consent of Russian and Japanese merchants.

ARTICLE III

Upon the arrival of a Russian merchant vessel into one of the above-named ports, the Captain or Supercargo of the vessel is bound to present through the Russian Consulate, and where there is none, directly to the local authorities a declaration about the name of the vessel and the number of its tons, about the name of the Captain or the Supercargo and about the kind and quantity of wares brought. Such an announcement must be made during the first day and under no circumstances later than after two days, or forty-eight hours. During this time the Captain is bound to pay the anchorage fee, amounting to five maas or forty-two kopecks silver per ton for vessels above fifteen hundred tons and to

---

* Japan, Foreign Office, *Treaties and Conventions*, 593-606; Great Britain, Foreign Office, *British and Foreign State Papers*, LVII, 1057-1061. The above is a translation of the Russian text, correlated with the meaning of the Dutch, Japanese, and English versions.

one maas or nine kopecks per ton for vessels of one hundred and fifty tons or smaller. This money is paid also when a merchant vessel, having entered port not for trade, will stay in it for longer than two days. In the event that a vessel enters port for repairs, the anchorage fee will not be levied, provided it will not unload all or part of its merchandise onto shore or onto another vessel. Having received the anchorage fee, the Customhouse is bound to give a receipt for it and at the same time to permit an immediate unloading of the goods.

Article IV

If the Captain of a merchantman does not present a declaration during the first forty-eight hours after arrival in port, he shall have to pay a fine of sixty-five rubles and fifty kopecks for each day; but this fine cannot exceed in total two hundred and sixty-six rubles. In case of a false declaration, however, the Captain must enter a six hundred and sixty-five rubles fine, and for unauthorized unloading, the wares are confiscated and a fine of six hundred and sixty-five rubles is paid in addition.

Article V

Russian vessels coming to Japan, having paid the anchorage fee in the first port visited by them, may cross over to other Japanese ports without paying there this money for a second time, but presenting only the receipt given to them in the first port. It is understood that this does not relate to vessels which during their voyage enter and take new cargoes in ports of other countries.

Article VI

Boats needed for towing, the unloading and loading of goods, as well as workers, must be hired only from among the number designated for that object by the local Japanese authorities. The above-mentioned boats and all the row boats in general must put to shore at specified wharfs.

Article VII

Goods purchased by the Japanese are transmitted to them from the Russian vessel through the Customhouse and conversely payment for these with goods is done by the Japanese also through the Customhouse. Except for such transmission, the Customhouse is not to interfere in any commercial transactions of Japanese merchants with Russians.

Article VIII

In default of Japanese goods to be exchanged for the Russian ones sold, the Japanese Customhouse shall pay for them in foreign silver or gold coin according to the fixed rate of exchange.

Article IX

Until the compilation of a tariff, the existing tariff of 35% shall be levied on the sum realized for goods sold by public sale or by private transactions. For this purpose the Consul or the Captain of the merchant vessel is bound to signify at the Customhouse the payments agreed upon for the goods sold. This duty does not apply to goods purchased by the Customhouse. The exposition of the goods and public sale may be repeated as often as the Russian merchant desires and the Customhouse cannot limit the number of Japanese merchants coming to that sale.

ARTICLE X

If the goods are sold at public sale, the Customhouse is answerable for the payment. In private transactions it does not take this responsibility upon itself, but shall examine and decide together with the Consul any complaints which may arise concerning such transactions. Once the goods have been accepted by one side or the other, no complaints will be accepted concerning quality or value of the goods sold.

ARTICLE XI

Goods purchased by Russians in Japanese stores will be paid for in paper money obtainable from the Customhouse, for which it is bound to give real coin to the Japanese merchants immediately on the presentation of the paper money received by them. The same manner of payment is made by Russians for the renting of boats, the purchase of provisions and other objects, but the payment in Russian and other coin must always be made through the Customhouse.

ARTICLE XII

In settling accounts for goods and all kinds of purchases, the value of the money shall be determined by the comparative weight and quality of the Russian or foreign gold and silver with the Japanese gold or silver ichibu, viz., gold with gold and silver with silver, and after the exact appreciation of their value, there shall be added to the calculated value of the Russian or foreign coin a further sum of 6% in favor of the Japanese Government for the expense of recoinage. The settlement of accounts may be done also by equating one Spanish taler to two and a half Dutch florins, or to one ruble and thirty-three kopecks of Russian money; and the Mexican taler—to two florins and fifty-five cents, or to one ruble and thirty-five kopecks of silver.

The weights, the measures of capacity and length shall be compared and fixed in each of the opened ports by persons appointed by both Governments.

ARTICLE XIII

All articles of war cannot be sold to private persons but to the Government alone.

Should the Japanese government find it necessary in the future to halt the sale into private hands of some goods unknown to it, newly brought by Russian merchants, these goods shall be purchased in this case by the Customhouse.

Article XIV

In case Russian vessels should import opium into Japan, the cargo of the vessel shall be confiscated and the guilty shall be dealt with according to the Russian laws, which strictly prohibit this pernicious trade.

Article XV

The exportation from Japan of gold and silver in coin or bars is prohibited, with the exception of gilt objects and gold and silver manufactured wares.

Copper, all sorts of arms, horse harness, silken stuff called Yamato-nishiki can be obtained only for goods purchased or ordered by the Japanese Government.

Article XVI

Rice, barley, wheat, red and white beans, coal, writing paper called Mino and Hanshi, books, charts and copper wares can be purchased in no other way than through the Customhouse; but this prohibition does not apply to those who purchase these objects for personal use, with the exception of proscribed charts and books. Furthermore, in the event of bad harvests, the exportation of articles of food, wax and paper may be halted for a time.

Article XVII

To prevent smuggling, guard-boats may be stationed near the commercial vessels by the local authorities; but expenses on this account are not to be levied on Russian trade.

Article XVIII

To prevent smuggling the crew of a merchant vessel and boats laden with goods may be subjected to inspection when entering and leaving the Customhouse or the place designated for the storage of goods.

Article XIX

If any loss of goods or other objects belonging to the Russians should ensue during the transportation in hired boats, a strict examination about such loss shall be made at once and all means taken to recover what was lost; but in this case as in all similar difficulties, the Customhouse, except for making inquiries, shall not be responsible for any losses.

Article XX

The transshipment of goods from one Russian vessel to another Russian one, or to a foreign one, can be done in no other way than by prior declaration to the Customhouse by the Russian Consul or the Captain of the vessel about the kind and quality of goods intended for transfer, and in such a case the Customhouse has the right to send its official onto the vessel to insure that no contraband should take place during the dischargement. If the transshipment is done without license, the Customhouse shall make it known to the Consul or, where there is none, shall itself stop and confiscate the discharged goods.

Article XXI

When a Russian vessel engages in smuggling in opened ports, the goods alone shall be confiscated, but if in other ports of Japan, the vessel itself shall be confiscated also, but only after prior consideration of such a case by the Japanese authorities jointly with the Russian Consul.

Article XXII

If the Captain of a merchantman or anybody belonging to the vessel desire to make a gift to some Japanese, they are to hand over with it a note certifying the gift made.

Article XXIII

During the stay of a vessel in port all the ship's papers are to be kept by the Russian Consul, and where there is none, they are to be handed over to the local authorities. The Russian Consul or the local authorities must not give up the ship's papers at the departure of the vessel without first ascertaining that all accounts are settled with the Customhouse and the merchants.

Article XXIV

Russians, desiring to study the Japanese language, or any of the Japanese arts, must report this through their Consul or the Captain to the local authorities, which in such a case shall appoint qualified persons for the teaching of the desired subjects.

Article XXV

All communications made by the Russian Government to the Japanese one must be delivered to the highest person, representing Russian authority in Japan and shall be transmitted by him to the local Governor. If, however, due to some circumstances, this paper is brought into a port where there is no Russian Consul, it shall be handed to those entrusted by the Governor of the port and shall be sent out by him immediately to its destination. The answer may be delivered to that port, in which the paper has been transmitted, if the vessel, which had brought it, awaits it there, or it can be sent to the Consul to be forwarded by him at the first opportunity to Russia.

Article XXVI

The rights of neutrality, acknowledged by all civilized nations, oblige two belligerent states not to attack the ships of their adversaries in neutral ports and it is understood that in case of war of Russia and another nation, Russian vessels shall not attack their enemies lying in Japanese ports.

Article XXVII

Russians staying in Japan permanently or temporarily, have the right to bring their wives and families thither for residence.

Article XXVIII

If in the future it will be found necessary to alter or add some of the articles of this Treaty, each of the Governments has the right to demand their revision.

The ratification of this supplementary Treaty shall follow not earlier than in eight months or as circumstances will permit. Now, however, copies of it in Russian, Japanese, Dutch, and Chinese languages, under the signature and seals of the negotiating persons, are exchanged. All articles of this supplementary Treaty are binding from the day of the present signature and shall be observed by both parties faithfully and without violation.

Concluded and signed in the city of Nagasaki in the 1857th year from the birth of Christ or the third year of the reign of His Majesty the Emperor and Autocrat of all the Russias Alexander II, on October 12/24, or the 7th day of the 9th month of the fourth year of Ansei.

M. P.
Signed:

Count Evfimii Putiatin
Mizuno Chikugo-no-kami
Arao Iwami-no-kami
Iwase Iga-no-kami

III. TREATY OF FRIENDSHIP AND COMMERCE (1858):
THE TREATY OF EDO*

His Majesty the Emperor of all the Russias and His Majesty the Taikun, the Supreme Ruler of Japan, desiring to broaden the friendly relations between their Empires and to establish trade on firmer foundations, have considered it good to conclude a new Treaty with this object, and for that purpose have empowered:

His Majesty the Emperor of all the Russias, His General Aide-de-Camp and Vice-Admiral Count Evfimii Putiatin, and

His Majesty the Taikun of Japan, His High Officers of State: Nagai Gemba-no-kami, Inoue Shinano-no-kami, Hori Oribe-no-kami, Iwase Higo-no-kami and Tsuda Hanzaburo.

The said plenipotentiaries have, by common agreement, confirmed the following articles:

ARTICLE 1

Such articles of the Treaty concluded between Russia and Japan at Shimoda on January 26/February 7, 1855 (by Japanese reckoning on the 21st day of the 12th month of Ansei 1) as are not at variance with the stipulations of the present Treaty shall remain in force. The explanatory articles to the Shimoda Treaty, however, together with the supplementary Treaty, signed at Nagasaki on October 12/24, 1857 (according to Japanese reckoning on the 7th day of the 9th month of Ansei 4) are hereby annulled.

ARTICLE 2

Henceforth His Majesty the Emperor of all the Russias shall have the right to appoint a Diplomatic Agent to the Court of His Majesty the Taikun of Japan and reciprocally His Majesty the Taikun of Japan may appoint a Diplomatic Agent to the Court of His Majesty the Emperor of all the Russias. The Diplomatic Agent may hold the rank of Ambassador, Envoy, Minister, or Chargé d'Affaires.

The Russian Diplomatic Agent shall have the right of permanent residence in Edo and on entering upon his duty may freely visit all other parts of the Japanese Empire. The Russian Consul General may also enjoy the latter right.

The Japanese Diplomatic Agent and Consul General in Russia shall enjoy the same rights as those accorded in Japan to the Russian Diplomatic Agent and Consul General.

ARTICLE 3

In addition to the ports of Hakodate and Nagasaki already opened and in place of the port of Shimoda, the Japanese Government shall further open the following ports:

* Japan, Foreign Office, *Treaties and Conventions*, 607-632; Great Britain, Foreign Office, *British and Foreign State Papers*, LVII, 751-760. Ratifications were exchanged in Edo on August 8/20, 1859 (10th day of the 7th month of Ansei 6).

Kanagawa from July 1st (new style) eighteen hundred and fifty-nine.

Hyogo from January 1st (new style) eighteen hundred and sixty-three.

In addition to these two ports, the Japanese Government shall further open from January 1st (new style) eighteen hundred and sixty, a convenient port on the western coast of the island Nippon [Honshu] and shall notify the Russian Government thereof prior to the designated time, as soon as the port will have been chosen.

The port of Shimoda shall be closed six months after the opening of the port of Kanagawa.

ARTICLE 4

The Russian Government may have Consuls or Consular Agents in all or some of the Japanese ports opened to Russian trade.

The Japanese Government shall, when necessary, assign suitable spots for the houses of the Consul and persons attached to him, as well as for schools, hospitals, etc.

ARTICLE 5

At the above-mentioned five ports the Russians may reside temporarily and permanently; they shall have the right of renting land and of buying or renting houses and other buildings on this land; likewise of building their own churches, houses, and storehouses. No military fortifications whatsoever shall be erected under the guise of dwellings and other buildings, and the Japanese authorities may with this view exercise a supervision over the construction and alteration of buildings.

The places, where Russians may build and the local regulations to be observed in each port, shall be fixed by the Russian Consul jointly with the local Japanese authorities. Matters in dispute shall be settled by the Russian Diplomatic Agent and the Japanese Government.

ARTICLE 6

In the cities of Edo and Osaka the Russians may reside only for the purposes of trade, in the former from January first (new style) eighteen hundred and sixty-two, and in the latter from January first eighteen hundred and sixty-three.

By agreement of the Russian Diplomatic Agent and the Japanese Government, a suitable place shall be set apart in each of these two cities, where the Russians may erect houses, and an area shall be determined beyond the lines of which they must not take off.

ARTICLE 7

Russians staying in Japan permanently or temporarily, may live there with their families, following their own laws and customs. They shall enjoy the right of free and open worship, and the Japanese Government shall stop the practice of trampling on objects serving as symbols of their religion.

ARTICLE 8

In the opened ports of Japan, Russians may go wherever they may wish within the following limits:

in Hakodate,—in all directions whatsoever for ten ri;

in Nagasaki,—in all adjacent territories of the Supreme Ruler of Japan;

in Kanagawa,—towards Edo as far as the river Rokugo which flows into Edo Bay between Kawasaki and Shinagawa, and in all other directions for ten ri;

in Hyogo,—also for ten ri in all directions, not approaching, however, the city of Kyoto within a distance of ten ri. The crews of vessels which come to Hyogo shall not cross the river Inagawa, which runs into Sesshu Bay, between the cities of Hyogo and Osaka.

The City Halls in each port shall serve as starting point of all the shown distances, which must be measured along the ground, one ri being considered as equal to three versts and three hundred and thirty-two sagenes or fourteen thousand and one hundred and seventy-five Russian feet.

The boundaries at the port, which shall be opened on the western shore of the island of Nippon shall be fixed by mutual agreement between the Russian Diplomatic Agent in Japan and the Japanese Government.

The right of penetrating into the interior from the above ports for the distances above specified shall not be enjoyed by Russians who may have been convicted of a felony, or twice convicted of misdemeanors. They shall not proceed from their place of residence toward the interior for more than one mile. The Japanese authorities may also demand the deportation of such persons from the country, but in this case the Russian Consul has the right to set a suitable period, not to exceed one year, for the settlement of their affairs.

Forts, Government houses and all fenced-in places may be visited by invitation only; temples, hotels, and the like are open to all.

ARTICLE 9

Trade between Russians and Japanese shall be carried out freely, according to mutual agreements, without any interference on the part of the authorities of either country.

Russians may hire Japanese for commercial transactions, as servants and for other employments.

Japanese of all classes may freely buy, resell, have in their possession and use objects brought by the Russians.

These enactments shall be promulgated by the Japanese Government throughout the whole Empire at the same time that the present Treaty comes into force.

The trade regulations attached to this Treaty shall have the same force and effect, as if they had been embodied in the Treaty itself.

ARTICLE 10

Custom duties on imported and exported goods shall be levied for the benefit of the Japanese Government, according to the Tariff attached to this Treaty, based on an *ad valorem* percentage.

Should the Japanese Customs officials disagree with the owner concerning the value of the goods declared by him, they may set their own value for the goods and propose to the owner that he surrender his merchandise to them for it. If the owner does not agree to this proposal, he shall pay duty on the value determined by the Customhouse; but if he accepts it, he shall forthwith receive the whole sum in full.

Russian goods, on which duty has been paid at the opened ports and cities of Japan, may be transshipped from there by Japanese to all other parts of the country, without further imposts whatsoever being levied on them.

If the duties fixed by the Tariff shall be reduced by the Japanese Government for Japanese vessels or those of other nations, this advantage shall be extended at the same time to Russian vessels.

No duties shall be levied on the naval stores of the Russian Government, which may have depots of them in the ports of Hakodate, Kanagawa and Nagasaki. These stores must be kept in special storehouses in charge of a person entrusted by the Russian Government, and should anything from among them be sold, the established duty shall be paid to the Japanese authorities by the purchaser.

ARTICLE 11

The importation of opium into Japan is prohibited and if a greater quantity than three catties, or four pounds and thirty-six zolotniks of opium be found on any Russian vessel, which may have arrived for purposes of trade, the Japanese authorities may seize and destroy the quantity in excess.

Russians found guilty of trading in opium in Japan shall, in addition to its confiscation and the payment of a fine of twenty rubles silver per catty to the Japanese Government, also be liable to punishment under the laws of Russia, which are very stringent with respect to this harmful trade.

ARTICLE 12

Arms of every kind may be sold in Japan only to the Government and to foreigners.

The exportation of cargoes of rice and wheat from Japan is not permitted; but they may be sold in sufficient quantity both to Russians residing in Japan for their consumption as well as to Russian vessels arriving there, for the requirements of their crews and passengers.

In the event, when the Japanese Government shall judge the quantity of copper produced to be sufficient to admit of sale, it shall sell the same by public auction.

ARTICLE 13

All foreign coins may circulate in Japan according to their weight and value as compared with Japanese coins of similar character.

All payments between Russians and Japanese may be made without distinction with foreign or Japanese money.

For a period of a year after the opening of each of the above-mentioned ports, the Japanese Government shall furnish to the Russians Japanese coins in exchange for foreign ones without any discount whatsoever.

Coins of every kind, excepting Japanese copper coins, as well as foreign gold or silver may be exported from Japan.

ARTICLE 14

The investigation of all matters at issue between Russians and Japanese shall be conducted by the Russian Consul in conjunction with the Japanese authorities, and in the event that Russians will be incriminated, they shall be prosecuted according to Russian laws, while Japanese who are guilty, shall be punished according to the laws of their own country, as stipulated in the Treaty, concluded at Shimoda.

On the demand of the Russian Consul, the Japanese authorities shall render him every assistance in regard to Russians, who have committed some crime. Any expenses incurred in such matter shall be defrayed by the Consul.

In ports where there is no Russian Consul, a guilty Russian may be detained by the Japanese authorities; but this must at once be reported to the Russian Consul of the nearest of the other ports in order that he may make appropriate arrangements.

All demands relating to confiscations and payment of fines for the violation of the enactments of this Treaty or of the trade regulations attached to it, shall be lodged at the Consulate, and everything that will be exacted in such a manner shall be transmitted to the Japanese Government.

ARTICLE 15

If subsequently it will be found necessary to alter or supplement the existing Treaties between the two Empires, either of the Governments may demand their revision, but not before July 1 (new style) eighteen hundred and seventy-two and upon notice thereof one year in advance.

ARTICLE 16

All rights and privileges, which may subsequently be accorded to other nations, shall at the same time be extended to the Russians, without further negotiations.

In Russia Japanese shall enjoy the same rights and privileges, as are granted in it to all other foreigners.

ARTICLE 17

This Treaty shall acquire force and effect from July first (new style) eighteen hundred and fifty-nine.

The present Treaty shall be ratified:

on the part of Russia—by the Personal signature of His Majesty the Emperor, countersigned by His Minister of Foreign Affairs, with the State Seal attached;

and on the part of Japan—by the Signature and Seal of His Majesty the Taikun, countersigned by His Minister of Foreign Affairs.

Ratifications shall be exchanged in St. Petersburg or in Edo by July first (new style) eighteen hundred and fifty-nine, or as circumstances will permit; at present, however, copies of the Treaty in Russian, Japanese, and Dutch are exchanged. The Russian and Japanese texts shall be signed and sealed by the Plenipotentiaries of both Empires; but the Dutch text shall be certified by the signatures of the persons composing it, and shall serve to clarify the meaning of all the articles of the Treaty.

Concluded and signed at Edo in the eighteen hundred and fifty-eighth year since the birth of Christ, or the fourth year of the reign of His Imperial Majesty and Autocrat of all the Russias Alexander II, on August 7/19, or on the eleventh day of the seventh lunar month of the fifth year of Ansei according to Japanese reckoning.

M. P.
Signed:

Count Evfimii Putiatin
Nagai Gemba-no-kami
Inoue Shinano-no-kami
Hori Oribe Masashi
Iwase Higo-no-kami
Tsuda Hanzaburo

A. REGULATIONS

under which the trade of the Russians may be carried on in Japan.

1st Regulation

Within two days, or 48 hours, after the arrival of a Russian merchant vessel in a Japanese port, the Captain or Supercargo of the vessel shall present to the Customs authorities a certificate from the Russian Consul to the effect that all the ship's papers are in perfect order and have been deposited at the Consulate.

They shall at the same time present a written and certified declaration showing: the name of the vessel and the port from which it has come; the number of crew members and the tonnage of the vessel; the names of the Captain or Supercargo and of the passengers, when there are such. They shall also, at the same time, present to the Customhouse an invoice or manifest of the cargo brought, listing in this invoice or manifest the number of the packages of goods, their marks and contents, in conformity with what shall be shown under these several heads in the certificates of goods received on board, and showing also the names of the persons to whom the goods shall have been consigned. To such an invoice shall be attached a list of the ship's stores. The Captain or Supercargo of the vessel shall certify by their signatures that the declaration submitted by them respecting the cargo and ship's stores is entirely correct.

Should any error be discovered in the invoice or manifest, the mistake may be corrected within twenty-four hours after the declaration shall have been submitted without payment of any fine; but for every change or addition made in the manifest after this period there shall be exacted twenty rubles in silver.

All goods not shown in the invoice or manifest shall be subject to double the usual rate of duty on being landed.

Should the Captain or Supercargo not present the said declaration and invoice within forty-eight hours after the arrival of the vessel in port, the Customs shall levy a fine of eighty-one rubles in silver for each subsequent day of delay.

In ports where there is no Russian Consul, all matters pertaining to Consular duties may be executed either through the Consul of any other Power friendly to Russia or through the Japanese Customs authorities.

2ND REGULATION

The Customs authorities of Japan may place their officers on board Russian vessels arriving in Japanese ports, but only on board commercial ones and not naval ones. Such officials shall be politely received and shall have such convenient accommodation allotted to them as the vessel may possibly afford.

Goods shall not be unloaded from the vessel during the interval of time between sunset and sunrise, except by special permission of the Customhouse. During that time Japanese Customs officers may seal, fasten with locks, or otherwise, all the hatches and entrances in those parts of the vessel where the goods shall be kept.

Should anyone open the hatches and entrances thus locked or break a seal, lock, and in general any fastenings applied by the Japanese officials, the guilty party shall be liable to a fine of eighty-one rubles silver for every such act.

Goods, unloaded, or which somebody attempts to unload from the vessel without making an entry thereof at the Customhouse, as stipulated below, shall be detained and confiscated by it.

Similarly any packed parcels of goods in which there shall be found objects not indicated in the invoice and for which duties ought to be paid shall be subject to confiscation.

Russian merchant vessels which shall commit contraband or shall attempt such in one of the unopened ports of Japan, shall lose the goods which shall be seized on such occasion, and the vessel shall be liable to a fine of one thousand three hundred and fifty rubles in silver for each such act.

Vessels, requiring repairs, may unload their cargoes without payment of duties under the charge of Japanese authorities, and paying all just expenses which may be incurred thereby, such as: for storehouses, laborers, and inspectors. The established duties shall be paid on any part of such goods as shall be sold.

The transshipment of goods from one vessel to another in the same port, may be executed without payment of duties on the goods. Every such transshipment shall be conducted under the supervision of Japanese officers and with the permission of the Customs authorities, which may demand sufficient proofs that the transfer is being made with a legitimate object (*bona fide*).

3RD REGULATION

The owner or receiver of goods, desirous of landing the same, shall inform the Customs thereof and present a written declaration, indicating in it: the name of the person making the declaration, of the vessel on which the goods shall have been brought, the marks and numbers of the packages of goods, the quantity, nature and value of the goods contained therein. At the end of the declaration shall be shown the total value of all the goods specified therein and the owner or receiver shall certify in such entry that the value of the goods has been declared justly and that nothing has been concealed to the detriment of the Customs revenues.

The original invoices of the goods, thus entered at the Customhouse, shall likewise be presented to it and shall be kept there until the above-mentioned declaration from the owner or receiver of the goods shall have been checked against it.

The Japanese Customs officers may open packages of goods and may take them for such purpose also to the Customhouse; but, in so doing, they shall not subject the owner to any expenses or cause any damage to the goods.

After examination, which shall be effected without any unnecessary delays, the goods shall be repacked by the Japanese and as far as possible shall be restored to the conditions in which they were before the opening by the Customs.

Should the owner or receiver discover that the goods were damaged on the way, they may inform the Customs authorities thereof before they shall have been delivered to them and may demand that the damaged goods be impartially appraised by two or more competent persons. These persons shall issue a certificate of the depreciated value of the goods from damage, and shall indicate such decrease for every package of goods separately, stating the number of such packages and the marks which they bear. This certificate shall be signed by the appraisers in the presence of the Customs authorities and the owner may present it, together with the declaration for the goods to be unloaded, and denote the deductions to be made from the original value thereof. This shall not prevent the Customs authorities from making their own appraisal of the goods, as stipulated in the tenth article of the Treaty, to which these regulations are appended.

On payment of the duties, permission shall be given to the owner to receive the goods either from the vessel or from the Customhouse, depending on where they may be.

All goods, destined for exportation, shall be declared at the Customhouse prior to loading onto the ship. The declaration must be in writing and shall contain: the name of the vessel onto which the goods are to be loaded, the number of packages of goods with their signs or marks, the quantity, nature, and value of the objects which they contain. The exporter shall certify by his signature that everything has been indicated truthfully in the declaration.

All goods loaded on board the vessel without notification having been made thereof at the Customhouse, and all packages containing articles which it is not permitted to export, shall be confiscated for the benefit of the Japanese Government.

No declaration is made of supplies for the vessel, her crew and passengers, nor of the clothes and other such things belonging to the passengers.

4TH REGULATION

Vessels leaving the port shall notify the Customs thereof twenty-four hours in advance and at the expiration of this period shall receive permission to go out; but should they be refused in this, the Customs authorities shall at once notify the Captain or the person to whom the vessel shall have been addressed of the reasons why the vessel is not permitted to leave the port, and at the same time the Russian Consulate, if one is in that port, is informed thereof.

Warships shall not be registered at the Customhouse, either when entering the port, or when leaving it. Similarly they shall not be subject to inspections by Customs or police officers.

Mail steamers may clear at the Customs on the same day both for entering the port and for leaving it; they do not have to make a declaration of cargo and passengers that do not remain in the port. Mail steamers shall, however, always register at the Customs.

Merchant vessels which shall have entered a harbor due to disaster at sea or in order to take on board the vessel fresh provisions and other stores, shall not be bound to present manifests or a declaration of cargoes which they have, as long as they do not engage in trade. Then, they shall have to present a manifest of their wares, as specified in the 1st regulation.

5TH REGULATION

Anyone who shall have signed an incorrect declaration or certificate with the intention of inflicting a loss on the Japanese Customs revenues, shall pay for every such act the sum of one hundred and sixty-eight rubles.

6TH REGULATION

Russian merchant vessels arriving in Japanese ports, shall not be liable to any charges on the tonnage of the vessel.

They shall be liable only to the following Customhouse fees:—

Twenty rubles and twenty kopecks silver for clearing the vessel on arrival; ten rubles of silver for clearance on sailing; two rubles and two kopecks silver for every permit or other document issued by the Customs authorities in various circumstances.

M. P.
Signed:

Count Evfimii Putiatin
Nagai Gemba-no-kami
Inoue Shinano-no-kami
Hori Oribe Masashi
Iwase Higo-no-kami
Tsuda Hanzaburo

B. TARIFF

Duties shall be paid to the Japanese Government on goods brought by Russians into Japan and unloaded there according to the following Tariff:

1st Section

Not liable to duty:
Gold and silver, coined or uncoined.
Clothing ordinarily used.
All household appurtenances and printed books, when those goods shall be imported not for sale, but for personal use.

2nd Section

Liable to an *ad valorem* duty of five per cent:
Articles necessary for the building, rigging, repairing and outfitting of vessels.
Whaling gear.
Timber for the construction of buildings.
Steam machinery.
Coal.
Zinc.
Lead.
Tin.
Silk and raw silk.
Rice, cleaned and uncleaned.
Biscuits and baked breadstuffs generally.
Salted provisions of any kind.
Live animals.

3rd Section

Liable to duty of thirty-five per cent:
All strong liquors, in whatever manner produced.

4TH SECTION

All goods not mentioned above shall be liable to a duty of twenty per cent.

All Japanese products exported as cargo shall be liable to a duty of five per cent; with the exception of gold and silver coins and copper.

At the expiration of five years from the first of July (new style) eighteen hundred and fifty-nine this Tariff may at the desire of the Japanese Government, be subject to revision.

M. P.
Signed:

Count Evfimii Putiatin
Nagai Gemba-no-kami
Inoue Shinano-no-kami
Hori Oribe Masashi
Iwase Higo-no-kami
Tsuda Hanzaburo

IV. TEMPORARY REGULATIONS RELATIVE TO THE ISLAND OF SAKHALIN OR KARAFUTO (1867): THE CONVENTION OF ST. PETERSBURG*

The Envoys of His Majesty the Tycoon of Japan, arrived at St. Petersburg, communicated to the Ministry of the Foreign Affairs that their Government fearing misunderstandings, which may arise on the island of Sakhalin in consequence of the common possession of this island and in order to strengthen friendship now existing between Russia and Japan, desires† to determine the frontier line, admitting as such any natural boundary, mountain or river.

In the conferences which took place on this subject, the Private Counsellor Stremoouhow [Stremoukhov], Director of the Asiatic Department, declared that the Russian Government could not accept the proposals to draw the frontier line on the island itself for the reasons which were fully explained to the Envoy of His Majesty the Tycoon. At the same time the Russian Government desirous of mutual and friendly understanding on Sakhalin question made the following proposals:

1) To consider the maritime straits bearing the name of Laperouse [La Perouse] as the frontier between Japan and Russia, these straits being the natural boundary between the two states, under the condition of appropriating the whole island of Sakhalin to Russia.

2) All the fisheries now belonging to the Japanese on the island of Sakhalin will in the future remain in their enjoyment.

3) To concede to Japan complete and indisputable possession of the island of Uroop, now belonging to Russia with three neighboring small islets, called Tcherpoy, brother of Tcherpoy and Broten.

4) In case an understanding concerning the former articles should prove impossible, the island of Sakhalin will remain as before in common possession.

Both parties not having come to an understanding on this subject, the island of Sakhalin is left as before in common possession, and the following temporary regulations are agreed upon in order to promote peace and good intelligence between the subjects of both states;

ARTICLE I

The Russians and Japanese on the island of Sakhalin shall maintain peaceful and friendly relations. The settlement of any disputes and misunderstanding arising is intrusted to the local authorities. If these

---

* The text given here is that of the official English translation. The Japanese and Russian originals end before the statement "For copy true." They are signed by Stremoukhov, Koide Yamato-no-kami and Ishikawa Suruga-no-kami. Japan, Foreign Office, *Treaties*, 633-637; Ota, 123-132.

† The original Russian text also gives the plural "envoys" and singular "desires"; the Japanese text, of course, does not distinguish between plural and singular.

local authorities can not settle the dispute, it shall be submitted to the nearest Russian and Japanese Governors.

ARTICLE II

In consequence of common possession, the Russians and Japanese are at liberty to circulate upon the whole island, to make settlement and erect buildings in all localities not yet occupied by buildings, industrial establishments or gardens.

ARTICLE III

The indigenes of the island have full and free enjoyment of their personal rights as well as of their properties. They can by their own agreement be hired by the Russians or Japanese. The indigenes having contracted debts, in cash or goods, or being in debt the present moment towards the Russians or Japanese, are allowed to cancel them by work or services for any term previously determined, if they are willing.

ARTICLE IV

If the Japanese Government should in the course of time agree with above-mentioned proposals of the Russian Government, the nearest local governors will be appointed to negotiate a final treaty.

ARTICLE V

The above-mentioned regulations are to be applied from the moment of their reception on the island of Sakhalin by the local authorities, i.e. no later than six months after their signature. All other less important questions shall be resolved by the local authorities of both states in the same manner as before.

In witness whereof the Plenipotentiaries of both parties signed these temporary regulations and caused the seals to be affixed.

An English translation is joined to the present duly signed by the interpreters of both parties.

St. Petersburg, March eighteenth [30], one thousand eight hundred and sixty-seven.

For copy true. The chief of the Section of Asiatic Department, Counsellor of College.

(Signed) W. Waletsky.
(Signed) Namoora Gohatsiro.

V. SUPPLEMENTARY AGREEMENT OF COMMERCE AND NAVIGATION (1867): THE CONVENTION OF EDO*

The Governments of Russia and Japan, deeming it necessary to effect in the Treaty concluded between them in Edo on August 7, 1858 (the 11th day of the 7th month of Ansei 5) as well as in the Tariff attached thereto alterations and additions, which may serve to facilitate commercial relations between the two Empires, have empowered for the conclusion of a convention regarding this matter:

The Russian Government,—the Russian consul in Hakodate, the Collegiate Councilor Evgenii Biutsov,

and the Japanese Government,—the member of the Ministry of Foreign Affairs, Edzure Kaga-no-kami.

The aforesaid plenipotentiaries, upon mutual agreement, have laid down the following articles:

First Article

The tariff of customs duties on imports and exports, attached to the present convention, shall be binding as of the day of the signing of the present convention.

The tariff, attached to the treaty, concluded in the year 1858 (Ansei 5), and all alterations and additions made in it subsequently are abrogated.

Second Article

The new tariff shall have the same force and effect, as if it were imbodied in the treaty itself, concluded in the year 1858 (Ansei 5), and shall be subject to revision from July 1 (new style), 1872.

However, either of the contracting parties shall have the right upon the expiration of six months after the signing of the present convention, to demand a change in duties on tea and silk, taking as the basis five per cent of the value of these goods over the period of the three preceding years.

Third Article

The fees for permits issued by the Customhouses, fixed in the sixth article of the regulations, appended to the Treaty, concluded in the year 1858 (Ansei 5), are hereby abrogated. Permits for unloading and loading of goods will be issued as before, but free of charge.

Fourth Article

The Japanese Government shall establish in each of the opened ports of Japan storehouses which, upon the request of the merchants, shall

* Japan, Foreign Office, *Treaties and Conventions*, 638-645. For a lengthy table of import and export tariffs and additional trade regulations, see Great Britain, Foreign Office, *British and Foreign State Papers*, LXII, 312-317.

receive imported goods for storage without the levy of duties thereon. The Japanese Government shall guarantee the safekeeping of the goods throughout their storage, but it shall not be held responsible in the event of their destruction by fire; nonetheless the storehouses shall be constructed in such a way, that they can be insured by foreign insurance companies against fire.

When a merchant who has brought the goods or their owner desires to draw them out of storage, he shall pay the duties, provided by the tariff; but he shall have the right to carry the goods back out of the harbor without the payment of import duties on them. In either case, payment for the safekeeping of the goods shall be collected on their release from the storehouses, the amount of payment as well as the manner of acceptance, storage, and release of the goods shall be determined upon mutual agreement of the contracting parties.

Fifth Article

Any Japanese products may be transported from all parts of Japan into the opened ports, without being liable to the payment of any kind of transit or other duties whatsoever, other than the usual road fees, levied equally on all merchants for the maintenance of roads and water ways.

Sixth Article

Desirous of doing away with the still existing impediments to the free circulation of foreign coins in Japan due to article thirteen of the Treaty, concluded between Russia and Japan in the year 1858, the Japanese Government shall introduce without delay necessary changes and improvements in the production of Japanese coins; thereafter all foreign coins, as well as gold and silver bars shall be accepted at the Japanese mint and at special places which will be designated in each of the opened ports and cities of Japan from foreigners and Japanese of all classes in exchange for Japanese coins, equivalent according to relative weight and value, except for the retention of a certain recoinage fee; the amount of this fee shall be determined by common agreement between both Governments.

The Government of Japan shall effect this measure not later than a year after the signing of the present convention, or earlier, if circumstances permit, and at the proper time shall make announcement thereof throughout Japan.

Seventh Article

In view of the necessity of doing away with the abuses and constraints existing in the opened ports relative to the execution of business in the Customhouses, the loading and unloading of goods, the hiring of row boats, laborers, servants, and the like, the Governors of the opened ports shall be instructed without delay to come to terms with the Consuls concerning the measures, necessary for the termination of these abuses and constraints, and for the procuring of the desirable facilities and safety for the commercial and private relations between foreigners and Japanese.

Provision shall be made also in the rules, which shall be drawn up to this end, for the construction at the wharfs in each of the opened ports of one or more hangars for the sheltering of the goods from damage during their transshipment onto vessels or onto shore.

EIGHTH ARTICLE

Japanese subjects are permitted to buy in the opened ports of Japan and abroad any kind of vessels, sail or steam, transport or passenger, with the exception of warships, which they may obtain only with permission of the Government.

Patents for the raising of the Japanese flag on Russian vessels, purchased by Japanese subjects, shall be issued against payment of a duty of three *bu* per ton for steam vessels and one *bu* per ton for sailing vessels. The number of tons of the purchased vessel shall be determined on the basis of the Russian ship's papers, which, upon the request of the Japanese authorities, shall be delivered to them by the Consul, with their authenticity certified.

NINTH ARTICLE

Japanese merchants of all classes may trade directly with Russian merchants, without the intervention of any officials of the Government, not only in the opened ports of Japan, but also in Russia, upon having received the necessary permission for leaving Japan in accordance with the enactment on this subject in the tenth article of the present convention. In their commercial dealings with Russian subjects, Japanese shall not be liable to the payment of duties higher than those which are imposed on them in their ordinary transactions among each other.

Likewise Japanese princes and persons in their service may, under the same condition, proceed to Russia and similarly to the opened ports of Japan, and there trade with Russians freely and without the intervention of Japanese authorities, provided, however, that they shall conform to existing police regulations and the payment of established duties.

TENTH ARTICLE

Japanese subjects may dispatch goods from the opened Japanese ports, or from the Russian ports, on any vessel, belonging to a Japanese or a Russian subject.

Furthermore, they are permitted to proceed to Russia for scientific or commercial purposes, upon the receipt of a passport from the proper authorities, in accordance with that which has been determined concerning this subject in the declaration of the Japanese Government of May 11, 1866. They can also hire themselves out onto Russian vessels for all kind of employment.

Japanese in the service of Russians may receive a passport for travel abroad from the Governor of any open port.

Eleventh Article

For the safety of navigation in the vicinity of the open ports of Japan, the Japanese Government shall set up the necessary lighthouses, buoys, and beacons.

Twelfth Article

The present convention shall acquire force and effect from the day of its signature.

When this convention will have been confirmed by both Governments, the contracting parties shall notify each other thereof; this written exchange shall take the place of a formal exchange of ratifications. As for the present, there are being exchanged two out of a total of four copies of the convention, composed in Russian and Japanese, and signed and sealed by both plenipotentiaries.

Concluded and signed at Edo, in the eighteen hundred and sixty-seventh year from the birth of Christ, on the eleventh/twenty-third day of December, or, according to Japanese reckoning, in the third year of Keio, on the twenty-eighth day of the eleventh month.

Biutsov
Edzure Kaga-no-kami

VI. SAKHALIN-KURIL ISLANDS (KARAFUTO-CHISHIMA) EXCHANGE TREATY (1875): THE TREATY OF ST. PETERSBURG*

His Majesty the Emperor of all the Russias and His Majesty the Emperor of Japan, desiring to end the numerous inconveniences resulting from the common possession of the island of Sakhalin and to consolidate the good understanding which exists between them, have agreed to conclude a treaty of the reciprocal cession by His Majesty the Emperor of all the Russias of the group of Kuril Islands and by His Majesty the Emperor of Japan of His rights on the island of Sakhalin, and have appointed for this purpose as their plenipotentiaries the following:

His Majesty the Emperor of all the Russias:

Prince Aleksandr Gorchakov, His Chancellor of the Empire, who has [been honored with] a diamond bejewelled portrait of His Majesty the Emperor, [and is] Knight of the Russian Orders of St. Andrew in diamonds, of St. Vladimir First Class, of St. Aleksandr Nevskii, of the White Eagle, of St. Anna First Class and of St. Stanislas First Class, Knight of the Great Cross of the Legion of Honor of France, of the Golden Fleece of Spain, of Annonciade of Italy, of St. Etienne of Austria, of the Black Eagle of Prussia in diamonds and of many other foreign orders;

and His Majesty the Emperor of Japan:

Vice-Admiral Enomoto Takeaki, His Majesty's Envoy Extraordinary and Minister Plenipotentiary to the Court of His Majesty the Emperor of all the Russias, who have concluded and signed the following Articles:

ARTICLE I

His Majesty the Emperor of Japan, for Himself and His descendants, cedes to His Majesty the Emperor of all the Russias, the part of territory of the island of Sakhalin (Karafuto) which he possesses at present together with all the rights of sovereignty appertaining to this possession, so that henceforth the said island of Sakhalin (Karafuto) in its entirety shall form an integral part of the Russian Empire, and that the boundary between the Empires of Russia and Japan in these areas shall pass through La Perouse Strait.

ARTICLE II

In exchange for the cession to Russia of the rights on the island of Sakhalin, stipulated in the first article, His Majesty the Emperor of all the Russias, for Himself and His descendants, cedes to His Majesty the Emperor of Japan the group of the Kuril islands which he possesses at present, together with all the rights of sovereignty appertaining to this

* Japan, Foreign Office, *Dai-Nihon gaiko monjo*, VIII, 216-226. The treaty and declaration were written in French and in Japanese. The above is a translation of the French text, with names converted to the proper Japanese and Russian transliteration.

possesssion, so that henceforth the said group of Kuril islands shall belong to the Empire of Japan. This group comprises the following eighteen islands: (1) Shimushu, (2) Araido, (3) Paramushiru, (4) Makanrushi, (5) Onekotan, (6) Harumukotan, (7) Ekaruma, (8) Shasukotan, (9) Mushiru, (10) Raikoke, (11) Matsuwa, (12) Rashuwa, (13) Suride and Ushishiru, (14) Ketoi, (15) Shimushiru, (16) Buroton, (17) Cherupoi and Buratto Cherupoefu [Chirihoi and Brother Chirihoi, or Black Brothers], (18) Uruppu, so that the boundary between the Empires of Russia and Japan in these areas shall pass through the Strait between Cape Lopatka of the peninsula of Kamchatka and the islands of Shimushu.

ARTICLE III

The reciprocal transfer of the territories designated in the preceding two Articles shall take place immediately after the exchange of ratifications of the present Treaty, and the said territories shall pass to their new possessors with the revenues from the day of taking possession; the reciprocal cession with the right of immediate possession, however, must be considered complete and absolute from the day of the exchange of ratifications.

The formal transfer shall be carried out by a mixed Commission composed of one or several representatives appointed by each of the High Contracting Parties.

ARTICLE IV

The territories reciprocally ceded under the preceding articles include the right of ownership to all public lands, unoccupied grounds, all the public buildings, fortifications, barracks and other buildings which are not private property. But the buildings and movable properties now belonging to the respective Governments shall be ascertained, and their appraisal shall be verified by the Commission mentioned in the third article; the amount of the appraisal shall be paid by the Government which comes into possession of the territory.

ARTICLE V

The residents of the territories ceded from one and the other, the Russian and Japanese subjects, may retain their nationality and return to their respective countries; but if they prefer to remain in the ceded territories, they shall be allowed to stay and shall receive protection in the full exercise of their industry, their right of property and religion, on the same footing as the nationals, provided that they submit to the laws and jurisdiction of the country to which the possession of the respective territories passes.

ARTICLE VI

In consideration of the benefits accruing from the cession of the island of Sakhalin, His Majesty the Emperor of all the Russias accords:

1) to Japanese vessels the right to frequent Korsakov harbor (Ku-

shunkotan), exempted from all harbor dues and customs duties for the period of ten years from the date of the exchange of ratifications. Upon the expiration of that term it will depend on His Majesty the Emperor of all the Russias whether to continue this exemption or to suspend it. His Majesty the Emperor of all the Russias furthermore grants to the Japanese Government the right to station a Consul or Consular Agent in the port of Korsakov.

2) to Japanese vessels and merchants the same rights and privileges as those enjoyed in the Empire of Russia by the vessels and merchants of the most favored nations in regards to navigation and commerce in the ports of the Sea of Okhotsk and of Kamchatka, as well as fishery in those waters and along the shores.

Article VII

In consideration of the fact that, although the credentials of Vice-Admiral Enomoto Takeaki have not yet arrived at the destination, their dispatch from Japan has been confirmed by telegraph, it has been agreed not to delay any further the signing of the present Treaty, with the stipulation that the formality of the exchange of credentials shall take place as soon as the Japanese plenipotentiary will receive his, and that a special protocol shall be drawn up to certify the accomplishment of this formality.

Article VIII

The present Treaty shall be approved and ratified by His Majesty the Emperor of all the Russias and by His Majesty the Emperor of Japan, and the ratifications thereof shall be exchanged in Tokyo (Edo) within six months from the date of signing, or earlier if possible.

In faith whereof the respective plenipotentiaries have signed and affixed their seals to the present Treaty.

Done in duplicate original at St. Petersburg, the twenty-fifth of April/ May seventh, eighteen hundred and seventy-five, corresponding to the seventh day of the fifth month of the eighth year of Meiji.

(Signed) Gorchakov
(Signed) Enomoto Takeaki

DECLARATION

The Government of His Majesty the Emperor of Russia and the Government of His Majesty the Emperor of Japan, desiring to complete the stipulations of Article IV of the treaty signed on this very day between the Empires of Russia and Japan, the undersigned duly authorized for this purpose have agreed upon the following dispositions:

Article I

The Imperial Government of Russia accepts as basis of evaluation for payment to the Japanese Government for the buildings and movable properties which must be transferred to the former in conformity with the treaty of this very day, the figures communicated by the Government of Japan, namely for 194 buildings, seventy-four thousand sixty three yen (dollars of Japan) and for the movable properties, nineteen thousand eight hundred fourteen yen.

ARTICLE II

The mixed Commission established under Article III of the Treaty of this very day shall proceed jointly to confirm and verify the buildings and the movable properties before they become respectively the property of the Russian and Japanese Governments. After the receipt of the report of the commission concerning the respective transmission of the territories, buildings and movable properties, as well as confirmation of the amount finally agreed upon as indemnity due to the Government of Japan, this amount, with the deduction made from the amount due to the Government of Russia, shall be paid at St. Petersburg either to the diplomatic Representative of the Emperor of Japan or to another agent of His Majesty duly authorized for this purpose, not later than six months counting from the official transfer of the territories, buildings, and movable properties mutually ceded.

ARTICLE III

In order to complete and expand Article V of the Treaty signed this very day concerning the rights and status of the respective subjects remaining in the territories reciprocally ceded, as well as relating to the aborigines of these territories, a supplementary article shall be negotiated and concluded between the Government of Japan and the Minister Resident of Russia in Tokyo (Edo) who shall be provided with full authority for this purpose.

ARTICLE IV

The arrangements contained in the three preceding articles shall have the same force and authority as if they had been inserted in the text of the Treaty signed this very day.

In faith whereof the respective Plenipotentiaries have drawn up the present declaration and have affixed their seals thereto.

Done in duplicate copies at St. Petersburg, the twenty-fifth of April/ seventh of May eighteen hundred seventy-five corresponding to the seventh day of the fifth month of the eighth year of Meiji.

(Signed) Gorchakov
(Signed) Enomoto Takeaki

VII. SUPPLEMENTARY ARTICLE TO THE SAKHALIN-KURIL ISLANDS EXCHANGE (1875): THE TREATY OF TOKYO*

In conformity with Article III of the declaration signed at St. Petersburg on 25 April/7 May 1875, corresponding to the seventh day of the fifth month of the eighth year of Meiji, and in order to complete and expand Article V of the treaty signed on the same day, relating to the rights and the status of the respective subjects remaining in the territories reciprocally ceded, as well as relating to the aborigines of these territories, His Majesty the Emperor of all the Russias and His Majesty the Emperor of Japan have appointed as their plenipotentiaries the following:

His Majesty the Emperor of all the Russias: His Chamberlain and Counsellor of State Charles Struve, His Minister Resident in Japan;

and His Majesty the Emperor of Japan: His Minister of Foreign Affairs Terashima Munenori;

who, after having exchanged credentials and having found them in good and proper form, have agreed upon the following:

a. The inhabitants of the territories ceded from one and the other, the Russian and Japanese subjects, who desire to remain domiciled in the localities which they occupy at present, shall be maintained in the full exercise of their industries. They shall retain the right of fishery and hunting within the limits belonging to them and shall be exempted from any tax on their respective industries for the rest of their life.

b. The Japanese subjects who will remain on the island of Sakhalin and the Russian subjects who will remain on the Kuril Islands shall be maintained and protected in the full exercise of their present right of property. Certificates shall be given to them, confirming their right of usufruct and ownership of the immovable properties in their possession.

c. A full and perfect freedom of religion is accorded to the Japanese subjects residing on the island of Sakhalin, as well as to the Russian subjects residing on the Kuril Islands. The Churches, temples and cemeteries shall be respected.

d. The aborigines of Sakhalin as well as of the Kurils shall not enjoy the right to remain domiciled in the localities which they now occupy and at the same time to keep their present subjection. If they desire to remain subject to their present Government, they must leave their domicile and go to the territory belonging to their Sovereign; if they wish to remain domiciled in the localities which they occupy at present, they must change their subjection. They shall be given, however, a period of three years from the date of their notification of this supplementary treaty for making a decision on this matter. During these three years,

* Japan, Foreign Office, *Dai-Nihon gaiko monjo*, VIII, 259-263. The above is a translation of the original French text.

505

they shall maintain the right of fishery, hunting and any other industry which they have been engaged in until this day, on the same conditions as regards privileges and obligations which have existed for them until now on the island of Sakhalin and on the Kuril islands, but during all this time they shall be subject to local laws and regulations. At the expiration of this term, the aborigines who are domiciled in the territories reciprocally ceded, shall become the subjects of the Government, to which the ownership of the territory will pass.

e. A full and perfect freedom of religion is accorded to all the aborigines of the island of Sakhalin and of the Kuril Islands. The temples and the cemeteries shall be respected.

f. The stipulations contained in the preceding five paragraphs shall have the same force and effect as if they had been inserted in the text of the treaty signed at St. Petersburg on 25 April/7 May, 1875.

In faith whereof the respective Plenipotentiaries have signed the present supplementary article and affixed their seal thereto.

Done in duplicate copies at Tokyo on the twenty-second/tenth of August of the year of Grace eighteen hundred seventy-five, corresponding to the twenty-fifth day of the eighth month of the eighth year of Meiji.

(Signed) C. Struve
(Signed) Terashima Munenori

BIBLIOGRAPHY

BIBLIOGRAPHY

Abe, Masami. "Hakodate chusatsu Rokoku ryoji Gosukeuichi" (Goshke-vich, Russian resident Consul in Hakodate), *Rekishi chiri*, vol. xxxvi (Tokyo 1920), no. 2, pp. 141-146; no. 3, pp. 249-254; no. 4, pp. 308-316.

Abe, Tatsuo. *Hakodate no iji to ijin* (Medicine and doctors of Hako-date). Hakodate 1951.

———. *Nakagawa Goroji to shuto denrai* (Nakagawa Goroji and the transmission of vaccination). Hakodate 1943.

Adamov, A. *G. I. Shelikhov.* Moscow 1952.

Akaba, Sozo. "Gorouin seikin no jokyo" (Circumstances of Golovnin's capture), *Tenseki*, no. 18 (Tokyo 1955), pp. 25-30; no. 21 (1956), pp. 39-43; no. 22 (1957), pp. 38-42.

———. "Gorouin to Ishizaka Buhei" (Golovnin and Ishizaka Buhei), *Tenseki*, no. 8 (Tokyo 1953), pp. 15-17; no. 9, pp. 18-22.

———. "Mamiya Rinzo no jimbutsu" (Mamiya Rinzo), *Denki*, vol. x, no. 3 (Tokyo 1943), pp. 1-8.

———. "Takahashi Sampei no Kunashiri toko" (Takahashi Sampei's Kunashiri voyage), *Tenseki*, no. 11 (Tokyo 1954), pp. 9 (410)-12 (413); no. 12, pp. 18 (441)-20 (443); no. 14, pp. 28 (503)-33 (508); no. 15 (1955), pp. 19 (496)-22 (496 [sic; pages misnumbered in journal]); no. 16, pp. 16-20.

———. "Tsushi Kiserefu (Ishi-no-maki no Zenroku)" (The interpreter Kisselev [Zenroku of Ishi-no-maki]), *Edo Nagasaki dangi*, vol. iii, no. 2 (Tokyo 1956), pp. 44-47; vol. iii, no. 3 (1957), pp. 42-46.

Akagi, Roy Hidemichi. *Japan's Foreign Relations.* Tokyo 1936.

Albrekht (Albrecht), M(ikhail). "Izvestie iz Iaponii (Izvlechenie iz pis'ma vracha morskogo vedomstva, pri russkom konsul'stve v Iaponii, nadvornago Sovetnika Albrekhta, iz Khakodate, ot 19 Iulia 1859)" (News from Japan [Excerpt from the letter of Aulic Councilor Albrekht, Navy doctor attached to the Russian consulate in Japan, from Hakodate, dated July 19 (31), 1859]), *Morskoi Sbornik*, vol. xlv, no. 1 (January 1860), part 4, pp. 26-29.

———. Letter, dated Hakodate, April 16 (28), 1862, *Morskoi Sbornik*, vol. lxii, no. 9 (September 1862), part 4, pp. 80-86.

Albrekht, Mrs. Excerpt from letter, *Morskoi Sbornik*, vol. liv, no. 7 (July 1861), pp. 70-77.

Alcock, Sir Rutherford. *The Capital of the Tycoon: A Narrative of a Three Years Residence in Japan.* 2 vols., London 1863.

Amidon, William C. "The Issue of Sakhalin in Russo-Japanese Rela-tions," Center of Japanese Studies, *Occasional Papers*, no. 7 (Ann Arbor 1957), pp. 60-69.

Ariga, Nagao. "Diplomacy," in Alfred Stead ed., *Japan by the Japanese: A Survey by Its Highest Authorities.* New York 1904.

Asahi Shimbun-sha (comp.). *Meiji Taisho-shi* (History of the Meiji and Taisho eras). 5 vols., Tokyo 1930.

Aston, W. G. "Russian descents into Saghalien and Itorup," *Transactions of the Asiatic Society of Japan*. Ser. 1, vol. 1 (Tokyo 1882), pp. 78-86.

Atherton, Gertrude. "Nikolai Petrovich Rezanov," *The North American Review*, vol. CLXXXIX (New York 1909), pp. 651-661.

Atkinson, Thomas Witlam. *Travels in the Regions of the Upper and Lower Amoor and the Russian Acquisitions on the Confines of India and China*. New York 1860.

Attwater, Donald. *The Christian Churches of the East*, vol. II (Milwaukee 1947).

Avarin, V. *Bor'ba za Tikhii Okean* (Struggle for the Pacific Ocean). Leningrad 1947.

Ayuzawa, Shintaro. "Bakumatsu Roshia shisetsu no shorai shita ,chizu to sono Nihon e no eikyo" (The maps left behind by the Russian ambassador in the Bakumatsu period and their influence on Japan), in Kaikoku Hyakunen Kinen Bunka Jigyo Kai (comp.), *Kaikoku hyakunen kinen Meiji bunka-shi ronshu* (Tokyo 1952), pp. 419-449.

B. (Blakestone), T. W. *Japan in Yezo: A Series of Papers Descriptive of Journeys Undertaken in the Islands of Yezo at Intervals Between 1862 and 1882* (Originally published in the *Japan Gazette* in February to October 1883) Yokohama 1883.

Baer, K. E. *Die Verdienste Peter des Grossen um die Erweiterung der geographischen Kenntnisse* (Peter the Great's part in the widening of geographical knowledge), vol. XVI of *Beiträge zur Kenntnis des russischen Reiches*. St. Petersburg 1872.

Barsukov, Ivan. *Graf Nikolai Nikolaevich Murav'ev-Amurskii po ego pis'mam, offitsial'nym dokumentam, razskazam sovremennikov i pechatnym istochnikam* (Count Nikolai Nikolaevich Muravev-Amurskii [as seen] through his letters, official documents, accounts of contemporaries and printed sources). 2 vols. in 1, Moscow 1891.

Barthold, Wilhelm (Bartol'd, Vasilii Vladimirovich). *Die geographische und historische Erforschung des Orientes mit besonderer Berücksichtigung der russischen Arbeiten* (The geographical and historical investigation of the Orient with special reference to Russian works), vol. VIII of *Quellen und Forschungen zur Erd- und Kulturkunde*. Leipzig 1913.

Barthold, V. V. *La Découverte de l'Asie; Histoire de l'Orientalisme en Europe et en Russe* (The discovery of Asia; History of Orientalism in Europe and in Russia), translated from the Russian and annotated by B. Nikitine. Paris 1947.

Bartol'd, V. V. (ed.). *Materialy dlia istorii fakulteta vostochnykh iazykov* (Material for the history of the faculty of eastern languages). 4 vols., St. Petersburg 1905-1909.

Beasley, W. G. *Great Britain and the Opening of Japan. 1834-1858*. London 1951.

———. *Select Documents on Japanese Foreign Policy 1853-1868*. London 1955.

Berg, L. S. *Ocherki po istorii russkikh geograficheskikh otkrytii* (Essays concerning the history of Russian geographical discoveries), Moscow 1946.

Berkh, V. N. "Pobeg gr. Beniovskago" (The flight of Count Benyovszky), *Syn Otechestva*, vols. xxvii-xxviii (St. Petersburg 1821).

Berton, Peter, Paul Langer, and Rodger Swearingen. *Japanese Training and Research in the Russian Field*, No. 1 of Far Eastern and Russian Research Series of the School of International Relations, the University of Southern California. Los Angeles 1956.

Bezobrazov, V. (publ.). *Entsiklopediia voennykh i morskikh nauk* (Encyclopedia of military and naval sciences). St. Petersburg 1893.

Biograficheskii slovar' professorov i prepodovatelei imperatorskago S.-Peterburgskago universiteta za istekshuiu tret'iu chetvert' veka ego sushchestvovaniia. 1869-1894 (Biographical dictionary of professors and instructors of the imperial St. Petersburg university for the past third quarter of a century of its existence. 1869-1894), 2 vols., St. Petersburg 1896-98.

Bludov, D. N. "Bunt Beniovskago v Bol'sheretskom ostroge" (Benyovszky's insurrection in fort Bol'sheretsk) in Egor Petrovich Kovalevskii, *Graf Bludov i ego vremia* (St. Petersburg 1866), pp. 200-218.

Bogdanovich, T. *Ocherki iz proshlago i nastoiashchago Iaponii* (Sketches from the past and present of Japan). St. Petersburg 1905.

Boguslavskii, Colonel Nikolai Dmitrievich. *Iaponiia; voenno-geograficheskoe i statisticheskoe obozrenie* (Japan; a military-geographical and statistical survey). St. Petersburg 1904.

Boltin, Aleksandr. "Shtorm v vostochnom okeane vyderszhennyi fr. Pallada" (The storm in the Pacific Ocean weathered by the frigate *Pallada*), *Morskoi Sbornik*, vol. xvii, no. 7 (July 1855), part 5, pp. 7-10.

Borton, Hugh. *Japan's Modern Century*. New York 1955.

Boxer, C. R. *The Christian Century in Japan, 1549-1650*. Berkeley 1951.

Brandt, M. von. *Dreiunddreiszig Jahre in Ostasien. Erinnerungen eines deutschen Diplomaten* (Thirty-three years in East Asia: Reminiscences of a German diplomat) 3 vols., Leipzig 1901.

Brokgauz (Brockhaus), F. A. and I. A. Efron (publ.). *Entsiklopedicheskii slovar'* (Encyclopedic dictionary). 41 vols., St. Petersburg 1890-1904.

Buinitskii, A. "Istoricheskii obzor snoshenii obrazovannago mira s Iaponieiu" (Historical survey of the relations of the civilized world with Japan), *Morskoi Sbornik*, vol. xlviii, no. 9 (August 1860), part 3, pp. 460-482; vol. xlix, no. 10 (September 1860), part 3, pp. 57-87.

Burney, Captain James. *A Chronological History of North-eastern Voyages of Discovery; and of the Early Navigations of the Russians*. London 1819.

Busse, N. V. *Ostrov Sakhalin: Ekspeditsiia 1853-54 gg.* (Sakhalin Island: the expedition of 1853-54). St. Petersburg 1872.

Cahen, Gaston. *Some Early Russo-Chinese Relations*. Translated from the French (*Histoire des Relations de la Russie avec la Chine sous Pierre le Grand [1689-1730]*) and annotated by W. Shelton Ridge. Peking 1940 (reprint of original edition, Shanghai 1912).

Cary, Otis. *A History of Christianity in Japan*. 2 vols., New York, 1909.

———. *Loose Leaves from Japanese History*. Compiled by Frank Cary. Kobe 1935.

Chekhov, Anton Pavlovich. *Ostrov Sakhalin* (Sakhalin Island). Moscow 1895.

Cherevkov, V. "Iz noveishei istorii Iaponii 1854-1894" (From the modern history of Japan 1854-1895), *Vestnik Evropy. Zhurnal istorii-politiki-literatury*, vol. 170, twenty-ninth year, no. VI (St. Petersburg, November-December 1894), pp. 227-272; 478-524.

Cherevkova, A. A. *Ocherki sovremennoi Iaponii* (Sketches of contemporary Japan). St. Petersburg 1898.

Clement, Ernest W. *Christianity in Modern Japan*. Philadelphia 1905.

Cole, Allen B. (ed.), *Yankee Surveyors in the Shogun's Seas*. Princeton 1947.

Cosenza, Mario Emelio (ed.), *The Complete Journal of Townsend Harris, First American Consul General and Minister to Japan*. Garden City 1930.

Coxe, William. *Account of the Russian Discoveries between Asia and America, to which are added, the Conquest of Siberia and the History of the Transactions and Commerce between Russia and China*. London 1803.

Creasy, E. S. *The Fifteen Decisive Battles of the World from Marathon to Waterloo*. New York 1851.

Dallin, David. *The Rise of Russia in Asia*. New Haven 1949.

Davydov, Gavrilo Ivanovich. *Dvukratnoe puteshestvie v Ameriku morskikh ofitserov Khvostova i Davydova, pisannoe sim poslednim* (Twofold voyage to America of the naval officers Khvostov and Davydov, written by the latter), with a biographical preface by Vice-Admiral Shishkov. 2 vols., St. Petersburg 1810.

De Mars, V. "La diplomatie russe dans l'extrême Orient" (Russian diplomacy in the Far East), *Revue des Deux Mondes*, vol. LXI (Paris 1866), pp. 693-718.

De Preradovich, Lieutenant Colonel. Letter to Okamoto Kansuke, *Dai-Nihon gaiko monjo*, vol. II, part 3 (Tokyo 1938), pp. 25-26.

Dennett, Tyler. *Americans in Eastern Asia*. New York 1941.

Divin, V. A. *Velikii russkii moreplavatel' A. I. Chirikov* (The great Russian seafarer A. I. Chirikov). Moscow 1953.

Douteau, Robert. "La croisière extraordinaire de la galiote 'St. Pierre et St. Paul'" (The extraordinary cruise of the galiot *St. Peter and St. Paul*), *Monumenta Nipponica*, vol. I (July 1938), pp. 146-158.

Dulles, Foster Rhea. *America in the Pacific*. Boston 1932.

Ebina, Kazuo. "Kaikoku-ron no bokko to Tanuma jidai" (The sudden rise of open-the-country arguments and the Tanuma period), *Rekishi chiri*, vol. xxxi (Tokyo 1918), no. 2, pp. 49 (159)-55 (165).

————. "Kaikoku-ron no ransho" (The beginning of open-the-country arguments), *Rekishi chiri*, vol. xvi (Tokyo 1910), no. 2, pp. 32 (148)-35 (151); no. 4, pp. 61 (373)-74 (386).

Eckel, Paul E. "The Crimean War and Japan," *The Far Eastern Quarterly*, vol. iii, no. 2 (Menasha, February 1944), pp. 109-118.

Efimov, A. V. *Iz istorii russkikh ekspeditsii na Tikhom Okeane. (Pervaia polovina XVIII veka)* (From the history of Russian expeditions on the Pacific Ocean. [First half of the 18th century]). Moscow 1948.

————. *Iz istorii velikikh russkikh geograficheskikh otkrytii v Severnom Ledovitom i Tikhom Okeanakh XVII—pervaia polovina XVIII v.* (From the history of great Russian geographical discoveries in the Northern Arctic and Pacific Oceans in the 17th and first half of the 18th cent.). Moscow 1950.

Efremov, Iu. K. *Kuril'skoe ozherel'e* (The Kuril Necklace). Moscow 1951.

Engelgardt, B. (ed.). "Putevye pis'ma I. A. Goncharova iz Krugosvetnago plavaniia" (Travel letters of I. A. Goncharov from a voyage around the world), *Literaturnoe Nasledstvo*, vol. xxii-xxiv (Moscow 1935), pp. 309-426.

Fisher, Raymond H. *The Russian Fur Trade 1550-1700*, Berkeley 1943.

————. "Semen Dezhnev and Professor Golder," *Pacific Historical Review*, vol. xxv, no. 3 (August 1956), pp. 281-292.

Fistié, Pierre. *Le réveil de l'Extrême-Orient. Guerres et révolutions 1832-1954* (The awakening of the Far East. Wars and revolutions 1832-1954). Paris 1956.

Franke, O(tto). *Die Groszmächte in Ostasien von 1894 bis 1914. Ein Beitrag zur Vorgeschichte des Krieges* (The great powers in East Asia from 1894 to 1914. A contribution to the history anteceding the war). Braunschweig 1923.

Fujita, Koun (comp.). *Takadaya Kahei-o shoden* (Excerpt biography of Takadaya Kahei). Hyogo 1933.

Fukase, Shunichi. "Bunka Roko jiken to rakushu" (The incident of Russian aggression in the Bunka period and satirical poems), *Rekishi chiri*, vol. lxii (Tokyo 1933), no. 2, pp. 157 (53)-162 (58); no. 3, pp. 255 (53)-262 (60).

————. "Gaikoku to shite Takadaya Kahei" (Takadaya Kahei as a diplomat), *Rekishi chiri*, vol. xlviii (Tokyo 1926), no. 2, pp. 62 (278)-73 (298).

Fukuchi, Genichiro. *Nagasaki sambyaku nen-kan. Gaiko hensen jijo* (Nagasaki during three hundred years. Circumstances of the changes in foreign relations). Tokyo 1902.

Fukuoka, Takejiro. *Hakodate enkaku-shi* (History of the development of Hakodate). Hakodate 1899.

Funaoka, Seigo. *Japan im Sternbild Ostasiens. Darbietung einer geschichtlichen Grundlage für die Aussenpolitik Japans in der Neuzeit* (Japan in the constellation of East Asia. Presentation of a historical basis for the foreign policy of Japan in modern times). 2 vols., Tokyo 1942.

Gentleman's Magazine, vol. IX (London, August 1790).

Germany. *German Foreign Ministry Archives, 1867-1920*. Microfilms at Florida State University of documents kept in Whaddon Hall, England.

Glazik, Josef. *Die russisch-orthodoxe Heidenmission seit Peter dem Grossen* (The Russian Orthodox heathen mission since Peter the Great), vol. 19 of *Missionswissenschaftliche Abhandlungen und Texte*, Münster 1954.

Golder, F. A. *Bering's Voyages. An Account of the Efforts of the Russians to Determine the Relation of Asia and America*. 2 vols., New York 1922-1925.

————. *Russian Expansion on the Pacific 1641-1850*. Cleveland 1914.

Golovnin, Vasilii Mikhailovich. *Sochineniia* (Writings). Edited by I. P. Magidovich. Moscow 1949.

————. "Zapiska Kapitana 2 ranga Golovnina o sostoianii Rossiisko-Amerikanskoi Kompanii v 1818 godu" (Report of Commander Golovnin about the condition of the Russian-American Company in the year 1818), *Materialy dlia istorii russkikh zaselenii po beregam Vostochnago okeana* (St. Petersburg 1861), supplement to *Morskoi Sbornik*, no. 1, 1861, pp. 48-115.

————. *Zapiski Vasiliia Mikhailovicha Golovnina v plenu u iapontsev v 1811, 1812 i 1813 godakh* (Memoirs of Vasilii Mikhailovich Golovnin, who was prisoner of the Japanese in 1811, 1812, and 1813). St. Petersburg 1851.

Golownin (Golovnin), Captain. *Memoirs of a Captivity in Japan, During the Years 1811, 1812, and 1813; With Observations of the Country and the People*. 3 vols., London 1824.

Goncharov, Ivan Aleksandrovich. *Fregat Pallada* (The Frigate *Pallada*), vol. VII of *Polnoe Sobranie Sochinenii* (Complete Works). St. Petersburg 1884.

————. *Fregat Pallada*, abr. ed., with introduction and commentary by S. D. Muraveiskii, Moscow: Gosudarstvennoe Izdatel'stvo Geograficheskoi Literatury, 1949.

————. "Russkie v Iaponii v kontse 1853 i v nachale 1854 goda (Ekspeditsiia grafa Putiatina)" (Russians in Japan at the end of 1853 and the beginning of 1854 [The expedition of Count Putiatin]), *Morskoi Sbornik*, vol. XVIII, no. 9 (September 1855), part 1, section 4, pp. 14-84; part 2, section 4, pp. 127-162; no. 10 (October 1855), part 1, section 4, pp 299-327; part 2, section 4, pp. 417-453; no. 11 (November 1855), section 4, pp. 63-128.

Goshkevich, Iosif Antonovich and Tachibana Kosai. *Iaponsko-Russkii slovar' (Wa-Ro tsugen hiko)* (Japanese-Russian dictionary). St. Petersburg 1857.

Great Britain, Foreign Office. *British and Foreign State Papers*, vols. LVII (London 1871), LXI (1877), LXII.

Greene, D. C. "Correspondence between William II of Holland and the Shogun of Japan. A.D. 1844," *Transactions of the Asiatic Society of Japan*, ser. 1, vol. XXXIV, part 4 (Tokyo, June 1907), pp. 99-132.

——. (transl. and ed.). "Osada's Life of Takano Nagahide," *Transactions of the Asiatic Society of Japan*, ser. 1, vol. XLI (Tokyo 1913), part 3, pp. 379-492.

Griffis, William Elliot. *The Mikado's Empire*. 2 vols., New York 1906.

Grimm, E. D. ed., *Sbornik dogovorov i drugikh dokumentov po istorii mezhdunarodnykh otnoshenii na Dal'nem Vostoke (1842-1925)* (Collection of treaties and other documents pertaining to the history of international relations in the Far East [1842-1925]). Moscow 1927.

Gubbins, John Harrington. *The Progress of Japan, 1853-1871*. Oxford 1911.

Hakodate koen ni chinretsu no Rokoku monsho-zuki kaho no yurai (Origin of the exhibition of the Russian guns in Hakodate). MS (author and date unknown) in Hakodate Municipal Library.

Hakodate Kuyakusho (comp.). *Hakodate kushi* (History of Hakodate-ku). Hakodate 1911.

Hakodate Kyoiku-kai (comp.). *Hakodate kyoiku nempyo* (Chronology of education in Hakodate). Hakodate 1937.

Hakodate-shi Kyoiku Iin-kai (comp.). *Hakodate oyobi shiseki* (Hakodate and historical remains). Hakodate 1954.

Hall, John Whitney. *Tanuma Okitsugu, 1719-1788: Forerunner of Modern Japan*. Cambridge 1955.

Hamada, Yoshizumi. *Nichi-Ro gaiko nenshi* (Chronological history of Russo-Japanese foreign relations). Tokyo 1904.

Hani, Goro (transl.). *Kuruzenshuterun Nihon kiko* (Krusenstern's Japan expedition). 2 vols., Tokyo 1931.

Harima, Narayoshi. "Rokoku ni okeru Nihongo gakko no enkaku" (History of the Japanese language school in Russia), *Shigaku Zasshi*, vol. XXXIII, no. 10 (October 1922), pp. 45 (791)-54 (800).

Harrison, E. J. *Peace or War East of Baikal*. Yokohama 1910.

Harrison, John A. *Japan's Northern Frontier. A Preliminary Study in Colonization and Expansion with Special Reference to the Relations of Japan and Russia*. Gainesville 1953.

——. "Kita Yezo Zusetsu or a description of the island of Northern Yezo by Mamiya Rinso," *Proceedings of the American Philosophical Society*, vol. 99, no. 2 (Philadelphia, April 1955), pp. 93-117.

——. "The Saghalien trade: a contribution to Ainu studies," *Southwestern Journal of Anthropology*, vol. X, no. 3 (Albuquerque, Autumn 1954), pp. 278-293.

Hawks, Francis L. (comp.). *Narrative of the Expedition of an American Squadron to the China Seas and Japan, Performed in the Years 1852, 1853, and 1854 under the Command of Commodore M. C. Perry,*

United States Navy, by Order of the Government of the United States. New York 1856.

Hayashi, D. (unsigned). "Diary of an Official of the Bakufu," *Transactions of the Asiatic Society of Japan,* ser. 2, vol. VII (Tokyo 1930), pp. 98-120.

Hayashi, Kingo (transl.). *Roshiajin Nihon empo-ki* (Record of visits of Russians to Japan), translation of A. Polonskii's "Kurily." Tokyo 1953.

Heco, Joseph. *The Narrative of a Japanese; What He Has Seen and the People He Has Met in the Course of the Last Forty Years.* Edited by James Murdoch. 2 vols. in 1, San Francisco 1895 (?).

Heibonsha (publ.). *Shinsen dai-jimmei jiten* (Revised large biographical encyclopedia). 9 vols., Toyko 1937-1941.

Heine, Wilhelm. *Reise um die Erde nach Japan an Bord der Expeditions-Escadre unter Commodore M. C. Perry in den Jahren 1853, 1854, und 1855, unternommen im Auftrage der Regierung der Vereinigten Staaten* (Voyage around the world to Japan aboard the Expeditionary Squadron under the command of Commodore M. C. Perry in the years 1853, 1854, and 1855, undertaken by orders of the government of the United States). 2 vols., Leipzig 1856.

Heki, Shoichi (comp.). *Kokushi dai-nempyo* (Large chronology of Japanese history). 6 vols., Tokyo 1935.

———. *Nihon rekishi jimmei jiten* (Biographical dictionary of Japanese history), Tokyo 1938.

Hildreth, Richard. *Japan as It Was and Is.* 2 vols., Boston 1855.

Hiraoka, Masahide. *Ishin zengo no Nihon to Roshiya* (Russia and Japan before and after the Restoration). Tokyo 1934.

———. *Nichi-Ro kosho shiwa* (History of Russo-Japanese Relations), revision of *Ishin zengo no Nihon to Roshiya.* Tokyo 1944.

———. "Nihon Roshiagaku-shi ko" (Thoughts concerning the history of Russian studies in Japan), *Toyo,* vol. XXXI (Tokyo 1928), no. 4, pp. 50-66; no. 5, pp. 31-38; no. 6, pp. 36-45; no. 8, pp. 19-27; no. 9, pp. 27-33.

Hirabayashi, Hirondo, "The Discovery of Japan from the North," *Japan Quarterly,* vol. IV, no. 3 (Tokyo, July-September 1957), pp. 318-328.

Hirose, Hikota (ed.). *Enomoto Buyo Shiberia nikki* (The Siberian diary of Enomoto Buyo). Tokyo 1941.

Hiyane, Yasusada. *Shukyo-shi* (History of religion). Revised by Anesaki Masaharu. Tokyo 1941.

Hodgson, C. Pemberton. *A Residence at Nagasaki and Hakodate in 1859-1860.* London 1861.

Hokkaido-cho (comp.). *Shinsen Hokkaido-shi* (Revised History of Hokkaido). 7 vols., Tokyo 1937.

Honjo, Eijiro. *A Social and Economic History of Japan.* Kyoto 1935.

———. *Bakumatsu no shin-seisaku* (New policy of the Bakumatsu [period]), rev. ed. Tokyo 1940.

Horikawa, Ryujin. *Shiberi odan-sha Saga Juan* (Saga Juan, the person who crossed Siberia). Tokyo 1936.

Hosoda, Tamiki. "Zeniya Gohei," in Hosoda Tamiki and others, *Zoku itsuwaranu Nihon-shi*, Tokyo 1952, pp. 123-164.

Hudson, G. F. *The Far East in World Politics*. Oxford 1937.

Hyakka zuihitsu (Collection of miscellaneous writings), vol. ii. Tokyo 1917-1918.

Ibara, Nori. *Tokugawa jidai tsushi* (History of the Tokugawa period). rev. ed., Tokyo 1928.

Ichinohe, Takajiro. *Enomoto Buyo-shi* (Enomoto Buyo). Tokyo 1909.

Ides, E. Ysbrants. *Three Years Travels from Moscow over-land to China: Thro' Great Ustiga, Siriania, Permia, Sibiria, Daour, Great Tartary, &C. to Peking*. London 1706.

Ikokujin no e (Picture scroll of foreigners). ms (author unknown), 1804, in the Hakodate Municipal Library.

Illiustratsiia. Ezhenedel'noe Obozrenie, no. 230 (St. Petersburg, August 2 [14], 1862).

Illustrated London News, "British Expedition at Japan," *The Nautical Magazine and Naval Chronicle for 1855*. London 1855.

Inobe, Shigeo. *Ishin zenshi no kenkyu* (Historical study of the pre-Restoration period). Tokyo 1935.

Iohara, Michimaro. *Tekikan jiryaku* (Enemy ship incident). ms (author unknown) ca. 1804-1817.

Iolkin, Petr. "Zametki o gidrograficheskikh zaniatiiakh, vo vremia krugo-svetnago plavanii na fregate *Diana* s 1853 po 1855 god" (Notes about hydrographical exercises during the round-the-world voyage aboard the frigate *Diana* from 1853 to 1855), *Morskoi Sbornik*, vol. xxiv, no. 10 (August 1856), part 2, pp. 105-131.

Ishii, Kendo (comp.). *Ikoku hyoryu kidan-shu* (Collection of strange stories of drifting to foreign countries). Tokyo 1927.

Ishin Shiryo Hensan Jimusho (publ.) *Ishin-shi* (History of the Restoration). 6 vols., Tokyo 1939-1943.

Ishin Shiryo Hensan-kai (comp.). *Dai-Nihon ishin shiryo* (Historical Material Concerning the Meiji Restoration). 18 vols., Tokyo 1938-1943.

Ishin-shi Gakkai (comp.). *Bakumatsu ishin gaiko shiryo shusei* (Collected material in diplomatic history toward the end of the Shogunate and during the Restoration). 6 vols., Tokyo 1942-1944.

Ishizaka, Buhei. *Too hensu iji* (The remains [of an incident] in the distant East Oshu regions). ms ca. 1811, in Hakodate Municipal Library.

Istomin, V. K. "Admiral I. S. Unkovskoi. Razskazy iz ego zhizni" (Admiral I. S. Unkovskoi. Stories out of his life), *Russkii Arkhiv* (1887), part 1, pp. 129-145; part 2, pp. 280-288; part 5, pp. 117-129.

Iwakura-ku Kyuseki Hozon-kai (comp.). *Iwakura-ko jikki* (True record of Prince Iwakura), vol. ii, Tokyo 1927.

Japan, Foreign Office. *Treaties and Conventions between the Empire of*

Japan and other Powers together with Universal Conventions, Regulations and Communications since March 1854. Rev. ed. Tokyo 1884.

Japan, Foreign Office. Chosa-bu (comp.). *Dai-Nihon gaiko monjo* (Diplomatic documents of Japan). Tokyo 1936-

Japan, Ministry of Foreign Affairs, Public Information Bureau. *The Northern Islands. Background of Territorial Problems in the Japanese-Soviet Negotiations.* Tokyo 1955.

Japan, Navy. *Nihon yushu jitsuki* (True report of my captivity in Japan), Japanese version of Captain Golovnin's memoirs of his captivity. Tokyo 1894.

Jiji Shimpo Kabukushi Kaisha ed., *Fukuzawa zenshu* (The collected works of Kukuzawa). 3 vols., Tokyo 1926.

K., A. (Kolokoltsov, Aleksandr?). "Postroenie shkuny *Kheda* v Iaponii" (Construction of the schooner *Heda* in Japan), *Morskoi Sbornik,* vol. XXIII, no. 8 (June 1856), part 3, pp. 270-299.

K., N. "Iz Iaponii" (From Japan), letter dated Clipper *Dzhigit,* 1859, *Morskoi Sbornik,* vol. XLV, no. 1 (January 1860), part 4, pp. 13-26.

Kaempfer [Kämpfer], Engelbert. *The History of Japan. Together with a Description of the Kingdom of Siam. 1690-92.* 3 vols., Glasgow 1906.

Kaikoku Hyakunen Kinen Bunka Jigyo-kai (comp.). *Sakoku jidai Nihonjin no kaigai chishiki* (Knowledge of the Japanese about overseas during the Seclusion period). Tokyo 1953.

Kaitakushi (comp.). *Gaikokujin jisho kashiwatashi sono ta kisoku kankeisho tsuzuri* (Material concerning places leased to foreigners and related regulations). MS Hakodate 1869, in Hakodate Municipal Library.

———. *Rokoku shinno Hakodate raiko nisshi* (Record of the visit of the Russian Imperial Prince to Hakodate harbor). MS Hakodate 1872, in Hakodate Municipal Library.

Kamanin, L. G. *Pervye issledovateli Dal'nego Vostoka* (First explorers of the Far East). Moscow 1946.

Kameda, Jiro. "Rokoku sokan Nichi-Ro jiten oyobi sono hensan mono" (The first Japanese-Russian dictionary published in Russia and its compilers), *Kokugaku-in zasshi,* vol. XXIX, no. 11, pp. 1-25.

Kamei, Takataka. *Hokusa monryaku* (Brief notes on the northern regions). Tokyo 1937.

Kato, K. and P. D. *Putevoditel' po g. Khakodate Iaponii* (Guide to the city of Hakodate, Japan). Tokyo 1912.

Katsu, Yasuyoshi. *Kaikoku kigen* (How Japan was Opened up). 3 vols., Tokyo 1893.

Katsuragawa, Hoshu. *Roshia-shi* (Russia's intentions). MS Edo 1793, in Hakodate Municipal Library.

Kawaji, Saemon-no-jo (Toshiakira). "Roshia osetsu-kakari Kawaji Saemon-no-jo (Toshiakira) nikki" (Diaries of Kawaji Saemon-no-jo [Toshiakira], charged with the reception of [the] Russia[ns]), *Bakumatsu* (see *Tokyo teikoku daigaku*), sup. 1 (1913), pp. 1-193.

Keene, Donald. *The Japanese Discovery of Europe. Honda Toshiaki and other Discoverers 1720-1798.* New York 1954.

Kemuyama, S. "Nichiro no gaiko" (Russo-Japanese diplomatic relations), in Japan, Department of Education, *Rokoku kenkyu* (A study of Russia) (Tokyo 1917), 399-443.

Kerner, Robert J. "The Russian Eastward Movement: Some Observations on Its Historical Significance," *Pacific Historical Review*, vol. XVII (May 1948), pp. 135-148.

———. *The Urge to the Sea. The Course of Russian History. The role of rivers, portages, ostrogs, monasteries, and furs.* Berkeley 1942.

Kimura, Ki. "Dawn of Modern Industry in Japan," *Contemporary Japan*, vol. XXIII (1955), nos. 7-9, pp. 483-494.

Kishimoto Hideo (comp.). *Shukyo-hen* (Compilation on Religion), Tokyo 1954.

Kitsu Bunshichi (comp.). *Hokkaido-shi jimmei jiten* (Biographical dictionary of Hokkaido history), 4 vols., Sapporo 1953-1957.

Kiuner, N. V. *Snosheniia Rossii s Dal'nim Vostokom na protiazhenii tsarstvovaniia Doma Romanovykh* (Relations of Russia with the Far East during the reign of the House of Romanov), reprinted from issues of *Dalekaia Okraina*. Vladivostok 1913.

Kiyooka, Eiichi (transl.) *The Autobiography of Fukuzawa Yukichi.* Tokyo 1948.

Kobayashi, Shojiro. *Bakumatsu* (End of Shogunate period), vol. XI of *Nihon jidai-shi.* Tokyo 1927.

Koga, Kinichiro (Masaru). "Roshia osetsu-kakari Koga Kinichiro (Masaru) seishi nikki" (Diaries of the western mission of Koga Kinichiro [Masaru], charged with the reception of [the] Russia[ns]), *Bakumatsu*, sup. 1, pp. 194-413.

Kohira, Kinjiro, ed. *Hokkaido gakuji shimpo* (Hokkaido education news), nos. 1-15 (Hakodate 1881-1882).

Kokubo, Saito. "Zeniya Gohei zen" (Complete [account] of Zeniya Gohei), *Ijin shiso*, no. 14 (Tokyo 1897).

Konda, Keiichi. "Hokkaido ni okeru yoga no shinko" (The furtherance of Western painting in Hokkaido), in Sapporo Chuo Hoso Kyoku (comp.), *Hokkaido bunka-shi ko* (Tokyo 1944), pp. 236-251.

Kondo, Juzo. *Ihaku raiko nempyo* (Chronology of visits of foreign vessels). Hakodate 1953.

Kondo, Morishige. *Henyo bunkai zuko* (Maps and thoughts concerning the important outlying frontier). Tokyo 1804.

Königliche Akademie der Wissenschaften, Historische Commission, *Allgemeine Deutsche Biographie* (Universal German Biography). 56 vols., Leipzig 1875-1912.

Kono, Tsunekichi. "Anei izen Matsumae-han to Rojin to no kankei" (Relations between the Matsumae clan and the Russians prior to the Anei period), *Shigaku zasshi*, vol. XXVII (Tokyo 1916), no. 6, pp. 18 (662)-33 (677).

Konstantinov, V. M. "Svidetel'stva Iapontsev o Rossii XVIII veka" (Testimonies of Japanese about Russia of the 18th century), *Sovetskoe Vostokovedenie*, no. 2 (Moscow 1958), pp. 76-81.

Kornilov, Ensign A. II. "Izvestiia iz Iaponii" (News from Japan), letter dated San Francisco, December 17 (29), 1859, *Morskoi Sbornik*, vol. XLVI, no. 4 (April 1860), part 4, pp. 99-122.

———. "Zimovka v Khakodate" (Winterage in Hakodate), *Morskoi Sbornik*, vol. XLIV, no. 12 (December 1859), part 4, pp. 87-106.

Koshizaki, Soichi. *Hokkaido shashin bunka-shi* (History of photography culture in Hokkaido). Tokyo 1946.

———. *Ezo byobu* (Ezo folding screen). Tokyo 1953.

Kotzebue, Augustus von. "Count Benyowsky; or the Conspiracy of Kamchatka. A drama, in five acts." Translated from German by Benjamin Thompson. *German Theater*, vol. II (London 1800).

Koyama, Shigeru (comp.). *Hakodate Kyoiku-kai enkaku-shi* (History of the development of the Hakodate Education Society). Hakodate 1944.

Krasheninnikov, Stepan Petrovich. *Opisanie zemli Kamchatki, s prilozheniem raportov, donesenii i drugikh neopublikovannykh materialov* (Description of the land Kamchatka, supplemented by reports, statements and other unpublished material). Moscow 1949.

Krupinski, Kurt. *Japan und Russland. Ihre Beziehungen bis zum Frieden von Portsmouth* (Japan and Russia. Their relations till the Peace of Portsmouth). Königsberg 1940.

Krusenstern, Capitain (Adam Johann von). *Atlas zur Reise um die Welt unternommen auf Befehl Seiner Kaiserlichen Majestät Alexander des Ersten auf den Schiffen Nadeshda und Neva unter dem Commando des Capitains von der kaiserlichen Marine A. J. von Krusenstern* (Atlas for the voyage round the world undertaken on order of His Imperial Majesty Alexander the First on the vessels *Nadezhda* and *Neva* under the command of Captain A. J. von Krusenstern of the Imperial Navy). St. Petersburg 1814.

Kruzenshtern, Ivan Fedorovich (Adam Johann von Krusenstern). *Puteshestvie vokrug sveta v 1803, 4, 5 i 1806 godakh. Po poveleniiu Ego Imperatorskago Velichestva Aleksandra Pervago, na korabliakh Nadezhde i Neve, pod nachal'stvom flota Kapitan-leitenanta, nyne Kapitana vtorogo ranga, Kruzenshterna* (Voyage round the world in the years 1803, 4, 5, and 1806. On orders of His Imperial Majesty Alexander the First, on the vessels *Nadezhda* and *Neva*, under the command of Lieutenant Commander, now Commander, Krusenstern). 2 vols., St. Petersburg 1809-1813.

Krypton, Constantin. *The Northern Sea Route. Its Place in Russian Economic History before 1917*. New York 1953.

Kudo, Heisuke. *Aka-Ezo fusetsu-ki narabi ni Oshu Matsumae-ryo sannin kojogaki no utsushi* (Account of reports about Red-Ezo [Russia] and a copy of what three Oshu and Matsumae castaways reported). MS ca. 1781-1788, in Hakodate Municipal Library.

Kuiper, J. Feenstra. "Some Notes on the Foreign Relations of Japan in the Early Napoleonic Period (1798-1805)," *Transactions of the Asiatic Society of Japan*, ser. 2, vol. 1 (Tokyo, December 1923), pp. 55-82.

Kuno, Yoshi S. *Japanese Expansion on the Asiatic Continent. A Study in the History of Japan with Special Reference to Her International Relations with China, Korea, and Russia*, vol. 11 (Berkeley 1940).

Kurita, Mototsugu. *Sogo kokushi kenkyu* (Synthetic study of Japanese history). 3 vols., Tokyo 1935-1936.

Kuroda, Kiyotaka. *Kanyu nikki* (Travel diary). 3 vols., Tokyo 1887.

Kuroiwa, Yoshitsugu. "Nagasaki 'Karasune doma' kangae" (Opinion concerning the 'Karasune doma' [Red House] of Nagasaki), *Koten kenkyu*, vol. IV (Tokyo 1939), no. 8, pp. 33-41.

———. "Rensen-shi to Roshiya bunka kenkyu" (Mr. Lensen and the study of Russian culture), *Edo Nagasaki dangi*, no. 1 (Tokyo 1954), p. 32.

Kyoiku Gakujutsu Kenkyu-kai (comp.). *Rokoku kenkyu* (Russian Studies). Tokyo 1916.

Kyozawa, Kiyoshi. *Gaiko-shi* (History of diplomatic relations), vol. III of *Gendai Nihon bummei-shi*. Tokyo 1941.

Lagus, Vilgelm. *Erik Laksman, Ego zhizn', puteshestviia, issledovaniia i perepiska* (Eric Laxman, His life, travels, investigations, and correspondence). St. Petersburg 1890.

Lagus, M. W. *Quelques remarques et une proposition au sujet de la première expedition Russe au Japon* (Some remarks and a proposal on the subject of the first Russian expedition to Japan). No date or place of publication indicated.

Langsdorff, Georg Heinrich von. *Bemerkungen auf einer Reise um die Welt in den Jahren 1803 bis 1807* (Observations on a voyage around the world in the years 1803 to 1807). Frankfort-on-the-Main 1812.

———. *Voyages and Travels in Various Parts of the World, During the Years 1803, 1804, 1805, 1806, and 1807*. London 1817.

Latourette, Kenneth Scott. *A History of the Expansion of Christianity*. vol. VI (New York 1944).

Lensen, George Alexander. "Early Russo-Japanese Relations," *The Far Eastern Quarterly*, vol. x, no. 1 (November 1950), pp. 2-37.

———. "The Historicity of *Fregat Pallada*," *Modern Language Notes* (November 1953), pp. 462-466.

———. "One Hundred Years Ago: Commodore Perry in Japan," *Florida State University Studies*, vol. x (1953), pp. 41-47.

———. "The Importance of Tsarist Russia to Japan," *Contemporary Japan*, vol. xxiv, nos. 10-12 (April 1957), pp. 626-639.

———. *Report from Hokkaido: The Remains of Russian Culture in Northern Japan*. Hakodate 1954.

———. "Russians in Japan, 1858-1859," *The Journal of Modern History*, vol. xxvi (June 1954), pp. 162-173.

———. *Russia's Japan Expedition of 1852 to 1855*. Gainesville 1955.

Lensen, George Alexander. "The Russo-Japanese Frontier," *Florida State University Studies*, vol. XIV (1954), pp. 23-40.

Lesovskii, Stepan Stepanovich. "Vypiska iz shkanechnago zhurnala fregata *Diana* (Extract from the logbook of the frigate *Diana*), *Morskoi Sbornik*, vol. XVII, no. 7 (July 1855), part 2, pp. 244-257.

Lindenberg, Shipmaster. "O plavanii v Iaponiiu korablia Rossiisko-Amerikanskoi kompanii 'Kniaz' Menshikov' v 1852 g. Vypiska iz raporta komandira etogo korablia rossisskago shkipera Lindenberga k g. glavnomu pravitel'iu kolonii, or 17 oktiabria 1852 goda" (Concerning the voyaging to Japan of the Russian-American Company ship *Kniaz Menshikov* in the year 1852. Extract from the report of the commander of this vessel the Russian skipper Lindenberg to the governor of the colonies, dated October 17 [29], 1852), *Vestnik Imperatorskago Russkago Geograficheskago Obshchestva*, vol. VIII (St. Petersburg 1853), no. 7, pp. 131-139.

Litke, Lieutenant. "Fregat 'Askol'd' v Iaponii" (The frigate *Askold* in Japan), *Morskoi Sbornik*, vol. XLIX, no. 11 (October 1860), part 3, pp. 330-348; vol. L, no. 12 (November 1860), part 3, pp. 146-162; vol. L, no. 13 (December 1860), part 3, pp. 387-413.

Lobanov-Rostovsky, Prince A. *Russia and Asia*. New York 1933.

Losev, Konstantin. "O Nagasakskikh ukrepleniiakh" (Concerning the Nagasaki fortifications), *Morskoi Sbornik*, vol. XXIII, no. 8 (June 1856), part 3, pp. 300-306.

Mainov, V. "Uspekhi geograficheskikh znanii v Rossii (1855-1880)" (Progress of geographical knowledge in Russia [1855-1880]), *Istoricheskii Vestnik*, vol. III (1880), pp. 70-96.

Makhov, Ivan. Letters from Hakodate. Letter of November 26 (December 8), 1860, *Morskoi Sbornik*, vol. LII, no. 3 (March 1861), part 4, pp. 84-87; letter of June 24 (July 6), 1861, *Morskoi Sbornik*, vol. LVI, no. 11 (November 1861), part 5, pp. 80-83; letter dated January 31 (February 12), 1862(?), *Morskoi Sbornik*, vol. LVII, no. 1 (January 1862), part 4, pp. 81-86.

———. *Russkaia azbuka* (Russian alphabet). Hakodate 1861.

Makhov, Vasilii. *Fregat Diana* (The frigate *Diana*). St. Petersburg 1867.

Maksimov, A. Ia. *Nashi zadachi na Tikhom Okeane. Politicheskie etiudy* (Our tasks in the Pacific Ocean. Political studies). St. Petersburg 1894.

Malloy, William M. (comp.). *Treaties, Conventions, International Acts, Protocols and Agreements, Between the United States of America and Other Powers 1776-1909*, vol. I (Washington 1910).

Malone, Dumas (ed.). *Dictionary of American Biography*, vol. XV, New York 1935.

Maruyama, Kunio. *Nihon hokuho hatten-shi* (History of developments in Japan's northern regions). Tokyo 1942.

Materialy otnosiashchiesia do prebyvaniia v Kitae N. P. Ignat'eva v 1859-

60 godakh (Material relating to N. P. Ignatev's stay in China in the years 1859-60). St. Petersburg 1895.

Matsukaze, Yoshisada. *Zeniya Gohei shinden* (True biography of Zeniya Gohei). Tokyo 1930.

Mazour, Anatole G. *Russia Past and Present.* New York 1951.

McCracken, Harold. *Hunters of the Stormy Sea.* Garden City 1957.

Minakawa, Shinsaku. *Mogami Tokunai.* Tokyo 1943.

Mitchell, Mairin. *The Maritime History of Russia, 1848-1948.* London 1949.

Mitsukuri, Gempo (Kenju). "Roshia osetsu-kakari tsuke Tsuyama hanshi Mitsukuri Gempo (Kenju) seisei kiko" (Journal of the western travel of the Tsuyama clansman Mitsukuri Gempo [Kenju], attached [to those charged with the] Russian reception), *Bakumatsu,* sup. 1, pp. 414-527.

Mizuno, Hironori. "The Japanese Navy," in Inazo Nitobe and others, *Western influences in modern Japan,* Chicago 1931, pp. 408-446.

Mizuno, Shodayu and others (comp.). *Kokuryu-ko shi* (Record of the Amur river). No date or place of publication indicated.

Morse, Hosea Ballou. *Chronicles of the East India Company trading to China, 1635-1834.* 5 vols., Cambridge 1926-1929.

———. *The International Relations of the Chinese Empire.* 3 vols., Shanghai 1910-1918.

Motoyama, Keisen. *Mamiya Rinzo tairiku kiko* (Mamiya Rinzo's record of traveling on the continent). Tokyo 1942.

Müller, Gerhard Friedrich (Miller, Fedor Ivanovich). *Sammlung russischer Geschichte* (Collection of Russian history). 9 vols., St. Petersburg 1732-1764.

Murakami, Teisuke. *Hyoryaku ibun* (Strange stories about castaways). MS, 1805.

———. *Roshiajin Moru zonki-sho* (Account left by the Russian Mur). MS, 1812.

Murdoch, James. *A History of Japan.* 3 vols., London 1926.

Murray, David. *Japan.* New York 1904.

Musin-Pushkin, Aleksandr. "Pis'mo Leit. Musina-Pushkina" (Letter of Lt. Musin-Pushkin), *Morskoi Sbornik,* vol. XIX, no. 11 (November 1855), part 2, pp. 8-10.

Naberfeld, P. Emil. *Grundriss der Japanischen Geschichte zum Memorieren, Orientieren und Repetieren* (Outline of Japanese history for memorizing, orienting, and repeating). Tokyo 1940.

Nachod, Oskar. *Die Beziehungen der Niederländischen ostindischen Kompagnie zu Japan im siebzehnten Jahrhundert.* (Relations of the Dutch East India Company with Japan in the seventeenth century). Berlin 1897.

Naito, Kano. *Ken-Ro denshusei shimatsu* (Record of Japanese students sent to Russia). Tokyo 1943.

Nakagawa, Goroji. *Goroji moshiageru aramashi* (Gist of what Goroji said). MS, 1812.

Nakagawa, Goroji. *Ikyo zatsuwa* (Idle talk about foreign lands). MS, 1816.

Nakajima, Shunzo. *Hokuho bummei shiwa* (Historical account of culture in the northern region). Tokyo 1942.

Nakamura, Zentaro. *Chishima Karafuto shinryaku-shi* (History of aggression on the Kuril Islands and Sakhalin). Tokyo 1943.

Nasa, Sezaemon. *Ikokujin toriosae soro shimatsu saicho* (Thorough report about the capture of foreigners). MS, 1811.

Nazimov, Lieutenant P. "Iz vospominanii ob Iaponii" (From recollections about Japan), *Morskoi Sbornik*, vol. LV, no. 10 (October 1861), part 3, pp. 328-347.

———. Letters from Hakodate. Letter dated March 17 (29), 1860, *Morskoi Sbornik*, vol. XLVIII, no. 9 (August 1860), part 4, pp. 140-151; letter dated November 1 (13), 1860, *Morskoi Sbornik*, vol. LI, no. 2 (February 1861), part 4, pp. 227-230.

Nevelskoi, Admiral G. I. *Podvigi russkikh morskikh ofitserov na krainem vostoke Rossii 1849-1855* (Exploits of Russian naval officers in the far east of Russia 1849-1855), posthumous memoirs edited by his wife, Ekaterina Ivanovna Nevelskoi, repr. ed., Moscow 1947.

Nevskii, V. *Vokrug sveta pod russkim flagom. Pervoe krugosvetnoe puteshestvie russkikh na korabliakh "Nadezhda" i "Neva" pod nachal'stvom Flota Kapitan-Leitenantov Ivana Kruzenshterna i Iuriia Lisianskogo v 1803-1806 godakh* (Around the world under the Russian flag. First round the world voyage of the Russians on the vessels *Nadezhda* and *Neva* under the command of Lieutenant Commanders Ivan Krusenstern and Iurii Lisianskii in the years 1803-1806). Moscow 1953.

Nicholson, William. *The Memoirs and Travels of Mauritius Augustus Count de Benyowsky in Siberia, Kamchatka, Japan, the Liukiu Islands and Formosa from the translation of his original manuscript (1741-1771)*, edited by Captain Pasfield Oliver. London 1893.

Nihon Harisuto Seikyokai Somu Kyoku (comp.). *Dai-shukyo Nikorai-shi jiseki* (The story of Archbishop Nikolai). Tokyo 1937.

Nitobe, Inazo, and others. *Western Influences in Modern Japan.* Chicago 1931.

———. *Reminiscences of Childhood.* Tokyo 1934.

Novakovskii, S. I. *Iaponiia i Rossiia* (Japan and Russia). Tokyo 1918.

Nozikov, N. *Russian voyages round the world.* Edited by M. A. Sergeiev; translated by Ernst and Mira Lesser. Hutchinson 1945.

Numata, Ichiro. *Nichi-Ro gaiko-shi* (History of Japanese-Russian diplomatic relations). Tokyo 1943.

O'Driscoll, J. "Report on Saghalin by J. O'Driscoll," *Dai-Nihon gaiko monjo*, vol. II, part 3 (Tokyo 1938), pp. 197-222.

Ogloblin, N. N. "Pervyi Iaponets v Rossii 1701-1705" (The first Japanese in Russia 1701-1705), *Russkaia Starina*, vol. LXXII (St. Petersburg, October 1891), pp. 11-24.

Okada, Kenzo. *Hakodate kaiko shiwa* (Historical talk about the opening of Hakodate harbor). Hakodate 1946.

———. *Roshia bunka to Hakodate* (Russian culture and Hakodate). Hakodate 1926.

———. (ed.), *Shodai Watanabe Kohei den* (Biography of Watanabe Kohei the First). Tokyo 1939.

Okamoto, Ryunosuke. *Nichi-Ro kosho Hokkaido shiko* (Hokkaido historical documents concerning Russo-Japanese relations). Tokyo 1898.

Okudaira, T. "Kurimiya senso to kyokuto" (The Crimean War and the Far East), *Kokusai-ho gaiko zasshi*. Tokyo 1936.

Okuma, Shigenobu. *Kaikoku taisei-shi* (History of the opening of Japan). Tokyo 1913.

Okun, S. B. *The Russian-American Company*. Edited by B. D. Grekov; translated by Carl Ginsburg. Cambridge 1951.

Oma, Tateaki (comp.). *Bakumatsu ken-O shisetsu dampan shiki* (Personal records of the negotiations of the envoys sent to Europe during the Bakumatsu period). Tokyo 1919.

Osatake, Takeki. *Iteki no kuni e. Bakumatsu kengai shisetsu monogatari* (To the countries of the barbarians. Tales of envoys sent abroad in the closing years of the Shogunate). Tokyo 1929. Republished in 1948 as vol. 7 of the collected works of Osatake under the abbreviated title *Bakumatsu kengai shisetsu monogatari*.

———. *Kokusai-ho yori mitaru bakumatsu gaiko monogatari* (Account of foreign relations in the closing years of the Shogunate, seen from [the standpoint of] international law). Tokyo 1930.

Ose, Keishi. *Nichi-Ro bunka sodan* (Collected talk about Japanese-Russian culture). Tokyo 1941.

Osten-Saken, Baron F. R. "Vospominanie o Grafe E. V. Putiatine" (Remembrance of Count E. V. Putiatin), *Izvestiia Imperatorskago Russkago Geograficheskago Obshchestva*, vol. XIX (St. Petersburg 1883), pp. 383-397.

Ota, Saburo. *Nichi-Ro Karafuto gaiko-sen* (Russo-Japanese diplomacy and war over Sakhalin). Tokyo 1941.

Otomo, Kisaku (comp.). *Hokumon sosho* (Northern gate series). vols. 1-6 (Tokyo 1943-1944).

———. *Tai-Ro kokubo no ransho. Akaezo fusetsu ko.* (Origin of Japanese defense against Russia. The *Akaezo fusetsu ko* [Kudo Heisuke's "Reflections about Rumors concerning Red-Ezo"]). Tokyo 1935.

Otsuki, Gentaku, *Kankai ibun* (Seagirt Tales). 4 vols., MS, no date.

Ozawa, Toshio. *Nagasaki nempyo* (Chronology of Nagasaki). Nagasaki 1935.

Ozawa, Yonezo (comp.). *Kaikoku hachiju nenshi* (History of the eighty years since the opening of Japan). Tokyo 1931.

Papinot, E. (comp.) *Historical and Geographical Dictionary of Japan*. Yokohama 1910.

Pavlovsky, Michel N. *Chinese-Russian Relations*. New York 1949.

Peshchurov, A. "Shkuna Kheda v Tatarskom prolive" (The schooner *Heda* in the Strait of Tatary), *Morskoi Sbornik*, vol. xxii, no. 6 (April 1856), part 4, pp. 1-4.

——— (? unsigned). "Opisanie Nagasakskago Porta" (Description of Nagasaki harbor), *Morskoi Sbornik*, vol. xx, no. 1 (January 1856), part 1, pp. 202-215.

Petrov, Arkadii N. *Politicheskaia zhizn' Iaponii* (The political life of Japan). Place of publication not indicated, 1910.

Petrova, O. P. "Admiral E. V. Putiatin v bukhte Kheda" (Admiral E. V. Putiatin in Heda Bay), *Sovetskoe Vostokovedenie*, vol. vi (Moscow 1949), pp. 368-382.

Phillips, Claude S. "Some Forces Behind the Opening of Japan," *Contemporary Japan*, vol. xxiv (1956), nos. 7-9, pp. 431-459.

Pilkin, Konstantin Pavlovich. "Zaniatie v 1862 g. russkimi sudami ostrova Tsu-sima" (The occupation of Tsushima Island by Russian vessels in 1862), extract from the journal of the commander of the clipper *Abrek*, Commander Konstantin Pavlovich Pilkin, *Morskiia Zapiski: The Naval Records*, vol. viii, no. 1 (New York, March 1950), pp. 2-7.

Pis'ma i bumagi Imperatora Petra Velikogo (Letters and papers of Emperor Peter the Great). St. Petersburg 1887-1918.

Platonova, A. *Apostol Iaponii Arkhiepiskop Nikolai* (Archbishop Nikolai, Apostle of Japan) St. Petersburg 1916.

Polnoe sobranie zakonov rossiskoi imperii s 1649 goda (Complete collection of the laws of the Russian Empire since 1649). 240 vols., St. Petersburg 1830-1916.

Polonskii, A. "Kurily" (The Kurils), *Zapiski imperatorskago russkago geograficheskago obshchestva. Po otdeleniiu etnografii*, vol. iv (St. Petersburg 1871), pp. 367-576.

Polovtsov, A. A. (ed.). *Russkii Biograficheskii Slovar'*. 25 vols., St. Petersburg 1896-1918.

Pompe van Meerdervoort, J. L. C. *Vijf Jaren in Japan (1857-1863)* (Five years in Japan [1857-1863]). 2 vols., Leiden 1867-1868.

Popov, A. "Tsarskaia diplomatiia v epokhu Taipinskogo vosstaniia" (Tsarist diplomacy at the time of the T'ai-p'ing rebellion), *Krasnyi Arkhiv. Istoricheskii zhurnal*, vol. ii (21) (Moscow 1927), pp. 182-199.

Poset, Konstantin Nikolaevich. "O plavanii iz Anglii na mys Dobroi Nadezhdy i v Zondskii proliv v 1853 godu" (Concerning the sailing from England to the Cape of Good Hope and Sunda Strait in the year 1853), *Morskoi Sbornik*, vol. x, no. 9 (1853).

——— (here given as Capitaine Ponsset). "Opisanie zemletriaseniia v Simode i krusheniia fregata *Diana*" (Description of the earthquake in Shimoda and the shipwreck of the frigate *Diana*), *Morskoi Sbornik*, vol. xv, no. 4 (April 1855), part 4, pp. 293-296.

Pozdneev, Dimitrii M. *Materialy po istorii severnoi Iaponii i eia otnoshenii k materiku Azii i Rossii* (Material concerning the history of northern

Japan and her relations to the Asiatic mainland of Russia). 2 vols., Tokyo 1909.

Price, Ernest Batson. *The Russo-Japanese Treaties of 1907-1916 concerning Manchuria and Mongolia.* Baltimore 1933.

Putiatin, Evfimii Vasilevich. "Raport General-Adiutanta Putiatina Veli-komu Kniaziu General-Admiralu (O zemletriasenii i krushenii fregata *Diana*)" (Report of Aide-de-Camp [to the Emperor] Putiatin to the Grand Duke Lord High Admiral [concerning the earthquake and shipwreck of the frigate *Diana*]), *Morskoi Sbornik,* vol. xvii, no. 7 (July 1855), part 2, pp. 231-243.

————. "Vsepoddaneishii otchet general-adiutanta grafa Putiatina, o plavanii otriada voennykh sudov nashikh v Iaponiiu i Kitai, 1852-1855 god" (Most devoted report of Aide-de-Camp, General Count Putiatin about the sailing of a detachment of our warships to Japan and China, 1852-1855), *Morskoi Sbornik,* vol. xxiv, no. 10 (August 1856), part i, pp. 22-104.

Ramming, Martin. *Reisen schiffbrüchiger Japaner im XVIII. Jahrhundert* (Voyages of shipwrecked Japanese in the 18th century). Berlin 1931.

————. Über den Anteil der Russen an der Eröffnung Japans für den Verkehr mit den Westlichen Mächten" (Concerning the role of the Russians in the opening of Japan to intercourse with the Western Powers), *Mitteilungen der Deutschen Gesellschaft für Natur- und Völkerkunde Ostasiens,* vol. xxi, part B (Tokyo 1926).

Ravenstein, E. G. *The Russians on the Amur; Its Discovery, Conquest, and Colonisation, with a Description of the Country, Its Inhabitants, Productions, and Commercial Capabilities; and Personal Accounts of Russian Travellers.* London 1861.

Reisner, I. M. and B. K. Rubtsov. *Novaia istoriia stran zarubezhnago vostoka* (New history of the lands of the east beyond the boundary). 2 vols., Moscow 1952.

"Report of the Brig 'Jolly' of Leith from the Port of 'Boussie' in Lat. 46.29, N. and Long. 143.18, E. in Aniwa Bay," *Dai-Nihon gaiko monjo,* vol. ii, part 2 (Tokyo 1938), pp. 486-489.

Rezanov, Nikolai Petrovich. Letter to Ivan Ivanovich Dmitriev, dated St. Petersburg, April 1803, *Russkii Arkhiv,* vol. iv (Moscow 1866), pp. 1331-1332.

————. "Pervoe puteshestvie Rossian vokrug sveta, opisannoe N. Riaza-novym, Polnomochnym Posslannikom ko Dvoru Iaponskomu" (First voyage of the Russians around the world, described by N. Rezanov, plenipotentiary envoy to the Japanese court), *Otechestvennyia za-piski,* vol. x (St. Petersburg 1882), pp. 194-219; vol. xi, pp. 90-144; vol. xii, pp. 196-211; 359-374; vol. xiv (1823), pp. 25-37; 328-350; vol. xv, pp. 248-274; vol. xx (1824), pp. 131-163, 204-223; vol. xxiii (1825), pp. 173-188, 366-396; vol. xxiv, pp. 73-96, 242-253.

Rikord, Petr Ivanovich. *Zapiski Flota Kapitana Rikorda o plavanii ego k iaponskim beregam v 1812 i 1813 godakh i o snosheniiakh s iapon-*

tsami (Report of Captain Rikord about his sailing to the Japanese shores in the years 1812 and 1813 and about dealings with the Japanese). St. Petersburg 1875.

————. "Zapiska, predstavlennaia im general-admiralu E. I. V. Velikomu Kniaziu Konstantinu Nikolaevichu v 1850 g. (o. snosheniiakh s Iaponieiu)" (Memorandum, submitted by him to the Lord High Admiral H.I.H. Grand Duke Konstantin Nikolaevich in 1850 [concerning relations with Japan]), *Russkaia Starina,* vol. LXIII (July-August-September 1889), pp. 177-182.

Riumin, Ivan. *Zapiski kantseliarista Riumina o prikliucheniiakh ego s Beniovskim* (Memoirs of the chancery clerk Riumin concerning his adventures with Benyovszky). St. Petersburg 1822. (Reprinted from *Severnyi Arkhiv,* 1822, nos. 5-7.)

Rosen, Baron (Roman Romanovich). *Forty years of Diplomacy.* 2 vols., London 1922.

Roryo Gyogyo Godo Kinenshi Kanko-kai (comp.). *Roryo gyogyo godo kinenshi* (Commemorative account of the Roryo Gyogyo Godo [Fisheries]). Tokyo 1932.

Roshia furyo-ki (Record of Russian prisoners). MS Author and date unknown; in Hakodate Municipal Library.

Russell, Thomas C. (transl. and ed.). *Langsdorff's Narrative of the Rezanov Voyage to Nueva California in 1806; Being that Division of Doctor Georg H. von Langsdorff's Bemerkungen auf einer Reise um die Welt, when, as personal physician, he accompanied Rezanov to Nueva California from Sitka, Alaska, and back; an English translation, revised, with the Teutonisms of the original Hispaniolized, Russianized, or Anglicized.* San Francisco 1927.

Russia, Inspector's Department. Circular No. 318 (January 1, 1857), *Morskoi Sbornik,* vol. XXXIII, no. 1 (January 1858), part 1, pp. xxv-xxvi.

Russia, Ministry of the Navy. *Kratkii otchet po morskomu ministerstvu za 1853 i 1854 god* (Brief account of [the activities of] the Ministry of the Navy during the years 1853 and 1854). St. Petersburg 1860.

————. *Letopis' krushenii i drugikh bedstvennykh sluchaev voennykh sudov russkago flota* (Annals of shipwrecks and other calamities [suffered] by warships of the Russian Navy). St. Petersburg 1874.

————. *Morskoi Atlas* (Nautical Atlas). Edited by I. S. Isakov and L. A. Demin. Moscow 1950-1953.

————. *Obzor zagranichnykh plavanii sudov russkago voennago flota s 1850 po 1868 god* (Survey of foreign voyages of vessels of the Russian Navy from 1850 to 1868). 2 vols., St. Petersburg 1871.

————. *Pervoe prodolzhenie obzora zagranichnykh plavanii sudov russkago voennago flota s 1868 po 1877 god* (First continuation of the survey of foreign voyages of vessels of the Russian Navy from 1868 to 1877). 2 vols., St. Petersburg 1878.

————. Naval Scientific Section, Technical Committee. "Dopolnitel'nye svedeniia ob ekipazhe fregata *Diana*" (Supplementary news about the crew of the frigate *Diana*), *Morskoi Sbornik*, vol. XVII, no. 8 (August 1855), pp. 282-285.

———. "Izvlechenie is pisem morskikh ofitserov: Zarubina, Peshchurova i Boltina, nakhodiashchikhsia na eskadre Vitse-Admirala Putiatina" (Extracts from letters of the naval officers Zarubin, Peshchurov, and Boltin, serving with the squadron of Vice-Admiral Putiatin), *Morskoi Sbornik*, vol. XII, no. 7 (July 1854), part 3, pp. 319-332.

———. "Komand fregatov: *Pallada, Diana, Avrora*, shkuny *Vostok* i dr., nakhodivshikhsia vo vremia krymskoi voiny u beregov Sibiri" (The crew of the frigates *Pallada, Diana, Avrora*, the schooner *Vostok* and others, which were at the shores of Siberia during the Crimean war), *Morskoi Sbornik*, vol. XXIII, no. 1 (January 1858), part 1, pp. xxv-xxvi.

———. Letter from Hakodate, unsigned, undated, *Morskoi Sbornik*, vol. LIII, no. 6 (June 1861), part 4, pp. 163-164.

———. Letter from Hakodate, unsigned, undated, *Morskoi Sbornik*, vol. LXVII, no. 8 (August 1863), part 4, pp. 76-77.

———. "O plavanii fregata *Pallada* iz Anglii k mysu Dobroi Nadezhdy (Iz doneseniia general-adiutanta Putiatina)" (Concerning the sailing of the frigate *Pallada* from England to the Cape of Good Hope [From a report of Aide-de-Camp, General Putiatin]), *Morskoi Sbornik*, vol. IX, no. 6 (1853), pp. 494-499.

———. "O plavanii v vostochnom okeane general-adiutanta Putiatina i kontr-admirala Zavoiki" (About the sailing of Aide-de-Camp, General Putiatin and Rear-Admiral Zavoiko on the Pacific Ocean), *Morskoi Sbornik*, vol. XX, no. 1 (January 1856), part 3, pp. 174-187.

———. "Otchet o plavanii fregata *Pallada*, shkuny *Vostok*, korveta *Olivutsa* i transporta *Kniaz Menshikov*, pod komandoiu General-Adiutanta Putiatina, v 1852, 53 i 54 godakh, s prilozheniem otcheta o plavanii fregata *Diana*, v 1853, 54 i 55 godakh" (Account of the sailing of the frigate *Pallada*, the schooner *Vostok*, the corvet *Olivutsa*, and the transport *Kniaz Menshikov*, under the command of Aide-de-Camp, General Putiatin, in the years 1852, 1853, and 1854, with a supplementary account of the sailing of the frigate *Diana*, in the years 1853, 1854, and 1855), *Morskoi Sbornik*, vol. XX, no. 1 (January 1856), part 3, pp. 132-173.

———. "Pis'mo s fregata 'Askol'd'" (Letter from the frigate *Askold*), unsigned, dated Shanghai, September 6 (18), 1858, *Morskoi Sbornik*, vol. XXXIX, no. 1 (1859), part 3, pp. 161-176.

———. "Plavanie eskadry general-adiutanta Putiatina, sostoiashchei iz fregata *Pallada*, korveta *Olivutsa*, shkuny *Vostok*, i transporta Amer. kompanii *Kniaz Menshikov*" (Sailing of Aide-de-Camp, General Putiatin's squadron, consisting of the frigate *Pallada*, the corvet *Olivutsa*, the schooner *Vostok*, and the Transport of the American Company *Kniaz Menshikov*), *Morskoi Sbornik*, vol. X, no. 12 (1853), pp. 168-171; vol. XI, no. 3 (1854), pp. 150-152; no. 4 (1854), pp. 265-267; vol. XIII, no. 9 (1854), pp. 55 ff.

Russia, Ministry of the Navy. "Russkii beregovoi lazaret v Nagasaki dlia komand plavaiushchikh v Tikhom okeane sudov" (The Russian shore lazaret in Nagasaki for the crews of vessels voyaging in the Pacific Ocean), *Morskoi Sbornik*, vol. ccxx, no. 5 (May 1887), pp. 91-154.

———. "Vysochaishii ukaz o pozhalovanii vitse-admiralu Putiatinu grafskago dostoinstva" (Imperial ukase about conferring the dignity of a count on Vice-Admiral Putiatin), *Morskoi Sbornik*, vol. xx, no. 1 (January 1856), part 1, pp. lxiv-lxv.

———. "Zamechaniia o shtorme, vyderzhannom fregatom *Pallada* v 1853 godu" (Observations concerning the storm weathered by the frigate *Pallada* in the year 1853), *Morskoi Sbornik*, vol. xx, no. 2 (February 1856), part 3, pp. 459-468.

Russia, Procurator-General of the Holy Synod. *Vsepoddaneishii otchet oberprokurora sveteishago sinoda K. Pobedonostseva po vedomstvu pravoslavnago ispovedaniia* (Most devoted report of the Procurator-General of the Most Holy Synod K. Pobedonostsev concerning the Department of Orthodox Faith). St. Petersburg 1886-1898 (vols. for the years 1884-1895).

Sadler, A. L. *The Maker of Modern Japan: The Life of Tokugawa Ieyasu.* London 1937.

Sakamaki, Shunzo. *Japan and the United States, 1790-1853* (vol. xiii of Second Series of Transactions of the Asiatic Society of Japan). Tokyo 1939.

Samoilov, V. A. *Semen Dezhnev i ego vremia* (Semen Dezhnev and his time). Moscow 1945.

Sansom, G. B. *Japan. A Short Cultural History.* rev. ed. New York 1943.

———. *The Western World and Japan.* New York 1950.

Sapporo Hosso Kyoku (comp.). *Hokkaido kyodoshi kenkyu* (Study of the local history of Hokkaido). Sapporo 1932.

Satow, Ernest M. (transl.). "Diary of a Member of the Japanese Embassy to Europe in 1862-63," *The Chinese and Japanese Repository of Facts and Events in Science, History, and Art, relating to Eastern Asia*, vol. iii (London 1865), pp. 305-312, 361-380, 425-437, 465-472, 521-528, 569-576.

———. *Japan 1853-1864 (Genji yume monogatari).* Tokyo 1905.

Scheinpflug, Alfons. *Die Japanische Kolonisation in Hokkaido* (Japanese Colonisation in Hokkaido). Leipzig 1935.

Schilling, Nikolai G. II. "Iz vospominanii starago moriaka" (Memoirs of an old mariner), *Russkii Arkhiv*, vol. ii (Moscow 1892), no. 5, pp. 126-159; no. 6, pp. 247-276; no. 7, pp. 287-318. Reprinted also as *Vospominaniia Starago Moriaka* (Moscow 1892).

Schischkoff [Shishkov], Vice-Admiral. "Account of the Voyages of Messrs. Chwostoff and Dawidoff," in Golownin, *Memoirs*, vol. iii, pp. 253-302.

Segawa, Hisashi and Okahisa Ijo. *Takadaya Kahei.* Tokyo 1942.

Seward, William H. *Travels Around the World.* New York 1873.

Sgibnev, A. "Bunt Ben'evskago v Kamchatke v 1771 g." "The uprising of Benevszky in Kamchatka in 1771), *Russkaia Starina*, vol. xv (St. Petersburg 1876), pp. 526-542, 757-769.

―――. "Istoricheskii ocherk glavneishikh sobytii v Kamchatke" (Historical sketch of the most important events in Kamchatka), *Morskoi Sbornik*, vol. ci, no. 4 (April 1869), part 2, pp. 65-142; vol. cii, no. 5 (May), part 2, pp. 52-84; no. 6 (June), part 2, pp. 37-69.

―――. "Popytki russkikh k zavedeniiu torgovykh snoshenii s Iaponieiu (v xviii i nachale xix stoletii)" (Attempts of the Russians to establish trade relations with Japan [in the eighteenth and in the beginning of the nineteenth centuries]), *Morskoi Sbornik*, vol. c, no. 1 (January 1869), part 2, pp. 37-72.

Shanghai Mercury (comp.). *The Story of Russia and the Far East. Being a Series of Papers Contributed to the "Shanghai Mercury" During the Latter Part of the Year 1899*. Shanghai 1899.

Shebuev. N. *Iaponskie vechera* (Japanese evenings). St. Petersburg 1905.

Shibusawa, Eiichi. *Tokugawa Yoshinobu-ko den* (Biography of Prince Tokugawa Yoshinobu). 8 vols. Tokyo 1918.

Shimada, Saburo. "Japan's Introduction to the Comity of Nations," in Okuma Shigenobu (comp.), *Fifty Years of New Japan*, vol. 1 (London 1910), pp. 93-121.

―――. *Nihon to Roshia* (Japan and Russia). Tokyo 1900.

Shiritsu Toshokan Takashima Bunko (comp.). *Fukui kenjin Karafuto keiei shi* (History of the development of Karafuto by natives of Fukui-*ken*). Tokyo 1912.

Shtein, V. I. "Samozvannyi imperator madagarskii (M. A. Ben'ovskii)" (The false emperor of Madagascar [M. A. Benevszky]), *Istoricheskii Vestnik*, vol. cxiii (St. Petersburg, July 1908), pp. 176-197; (August), pp. 597-618.

Siebold, Philipp Franz von. "Deistviia Rossii i Niderlandov k otkrytiiu Iaponii dlia torgovli vsekh narodov" (Actions of Russia and the Netherlands toward the opening of Japan for the trade of all nations), translated from the German (*Urkundliche Darstellung der Bestrebungen von Niederland und Russland zur Eröffnung Japans für die Schiffahrt und den Seehandel aller Nationen* [Bonn 1854]), *Morskoi Sbornik*, vol. xv, no. 3 (March 1855), part 4, pp. 1-41.

―――. *Nippon. Archiv zur Beschreibung von Japan* (Nippon. Records for the description of Japan). Republication of original (1832) edition. 5 vols., Berlin 1930.

Siemers, Bruno. *Japans Eingliederung in den Weltverkehr 1853-1869* (Japan's inclusion into international intercourse 1853-1869) (monograph 316 of *Historische Studien*). Berlin 1937.

Skalkovskii K(onstantin Apollonovich). *Russkaia torgovlia v Tikhom Okeane* (Russian trade in the Pacific Ocean). St. Petersburg 1883.

―――. *Vneshniaia politika Rossii i polozhenie inostranykh derzhav* (The foreign policy of Russia and the position of the foreign powers). St. Petersburg 1897.

Smith, Neil Skene. *Materials on Japanese Social and Economic History: Tokugawa Japan (1)*. Tokyo 1937.

Spalding, J. W. *Japan and Around the World*. New York 1855.

Staritskii, Lieutenant. "Pis'ma leitenanta Staritskago" (Letters of Lieutenant Staritskii), letters dated Hakodate, clipper *Vsadnik*, April 4 (16), 1870, *Morskoi Sbornik*, vol. CIX, no. 8 (1870), part 4, pp. 8-42.

Strahlenberg, Philipp Johann von. *Das Nord- und Östliche Theil von Europa und Asia, in so weit solches das gantze Ruszische Reich mit Siberien und der grossen Tartarey in Sich begreiffet, in einer Historisch-geographischen der alten und neuen Zeiten, und vielen andern unbekannten Nachrichten vorgestellet* ([Published in English under the title] *An historico-geographical description of the north and eastern parts of Europe and Asia; but more particularly of Russia, Siberia, and Great Tartary; both in their ancient and modern state: together with an entire new polyglot-table of the dialects of 32 Tartarian nations* [London 1738]). Stockholm 1730.

Suematsu, Yasukazu. *Kinsei ni okeru hokuho mondai no shinten* (Development of the northern region problem in modern times). Tokyo 1928.

Sumi, Goro. *Nihonjin hyoryu monogatari* (Stories of Japanese floating about). Tokyo 1954.

Sumida, Masaichi, ed. *Kaiji shiryo sosho* (Collectanea of historical material on maritime affairs). 20 vols., Tokyo 1929-1931.

Sutton, Joseph L. "Territorial Claims of Russia and Japan in the Kurile Islands," Center of Japanese Studies, *Occasional Papers*, no. 7 (Ann Arbor 1957), pp. 60-99.

Suzuki, Daisuke. *Urajiosutoku kiko* (Voyage to Vladivostok). Sapporo 1879.

Suzuki, Riichiro. "Tachibana Kosai," sixteen-page MS by mayor of Kakegawa-*machi* in Ogasa-*gun*, Shizuoka-*ken*; undated.

Swischer, Earl. "Commodore Perry's Imperialism in Relation to America's Present-Day Position in the Pacific," *Pacific Historical Review*, vol. XVI, no. 1 (February 1947), pp. 30-40.

Szcześniak, B. "Russian Knowledge of Japanese Geography During the Reign of Peter the Great. A Bibliographical Note," *Monumenta Nipponica*, vol. XII (Tokyo 1956), nos. 3-4, pp. 131-140.

Tabohashi, Kiyoshi. "Junana-hachi seki ni watareru Rokoku no Taiheiyo hatten to tai-Nichi kankei" (Russian expansion in the Pacific Ocean in the seventeenth and eighteenth centuries and its relation to Japan), *Rekishi chiri*, vol. 34 (Tokyo 1924), no. 5, pp. 1 (391)-24 (414); no. 6, pp. 19 (501)-34 (516).

———. *Kindai Nihon gaikoku kankei-shi* (History of Japan's foreign relations in recent times). Tokyo 1930.

———. "Kyokuto ni okeru Roshia kaigun no hattatsu" (Growth of the Russian navy in the Far East), *Rekishi chiri*, vol. 63 (Tokyo 1934), no. 5, pp. 589 (183)-608 (202).

Takada, Atsutaro (comp.). *Takadaya Kahei Rokoku yuki ikken shimatsu* (Circumstances of the affair of Takadaya Kahei's going to Russia). MS undated.

Takada, Rikichi. "Bakumatsu Rokan no Tsushima senkyo" (The occupation of Tsushima by a Russian warship during the Bakumatsu period). *Rekishi chiri*, vol. XLIII (Tokyo, January 1924), pp. 21-40.

Takadaya, Kahei. *Bunka kyunen Takadaya Kahei Roshia-sen ni toraerare do junen kikoku gokogi Matsumae go-bugyo e joshin shimatsu-sho utsushi* (Copy of the report to the Shogunate official governor of Matsumae about Takadaya Kahei's seizure by a Russian vessel in 1812 and his return to Japan in 1813). MS 1814.

———. "Takadaya Kahei Roshia jijo hokoku" (Account of Takadaya Kahei's Russian affair), *Hokuto*, vol. II (Toyohara 1911).

Takano, Akira. "Gonchyarofu no 'Fregat Pallada' ni miru bakumatsu Nihon" (Japan in the closing years of the Shogunate as seen in Goncharov's *Fregat Pallada*), *Nihon rekishi*, no. 49 (Tokyo 1952), pp. 46-53.

———. " 'Oroshiya no gen' to 'Kanchyattka kotoba' " ("Russian speech" and "Kamchatka dialect"), *Nihon Rekishi*, no. 71 (Tokyo 1954), pp. 16-20.

Takeda, Ayasaburo. "Kokuryo-ko kiji" (Description of the Amur River), in Mizuno Yukitoshi, *Chikuto Takeda sensei den* (Tokyo 1897), pp. 26-37.

Takemura, Kokichi. *Gyogyo Nihon hokuyo monogatari* (Fishery Japan: Tales of the Northern Waters). Tokyo 1944.

Takeuchi, Yasunori. *Bunkyu ninen Karafuto kyokai dampan shimatsu* (The Sakhalin boundary negotiations of 1862). MS 1864; in Hakodate Municipal Library.

Tanaka, Bunichiro (comp.). *Nichi-Ro kosho-shi* (History of Russo-Japanese relations). Publication of the Japanese Ministry of Foreign Affairs, classified "secret"; available on microfilm from the U.S. Library of Congress as reel SP 3 of the Japanese Archives Project. Tokyo 1944.

Tarle, E. V. *Krymskaia voina* (The Crimean War). 2 vols., Moscow 1950.

Tarsaidze, Alexandre. *Czars and Presidents. The Story of a Forgotten Friendship.* New York 1958.

Thomas, Benjamin Platt. *Russo-American Relations, 1815-1867.* Baltimore 1930.

Tikhmenev, P. *Istoricheskoe obozrenie obrazovaniia Rossiisko-Amerikanskoi Kompanii i deistvii eia do nastoiashchago vremeni* (Historical survey of the founding of the Russian-American Company and its activities till the present time). St. Petersburg 1861.

Tilley, Henry Arthur. *Japan, the Amoor and the Pacific; with Notices of other Places Comprised in a Voyage of Circumnavigation in the Imperial Russian corvette "Rynda," in 1858-60.* London 1861.

Tochinai, Sojiro. *Yojin Nihon tanken nempyo* (Chronology of Western voyages of discovery to Japan). Tokyo 1929.

Tokutomi, Iichiro. *Kinsei Nihon kokumin-shi* (History of the Japanese People in Modern Times).

    vol. XXIII. *Tanuma Jidai* (The Tanuma Period). Tokyo 1936.

    vol. XXIV. *Matsudaira Sadanobu Jidai* (The Matsudaira Sadanobu Period). Tokyo 1936.

    vol. XXV. *Bakufu bunkai sekkin jidai* (Period of the approach of the dissolution of the Shogunate). Tokyo 1936.

    vol. XXX. *Peri raiko izen no keisei* (State of affairs before the arrival of Perry). Tokyo 1936.

    vol. XXXI. *Peri raiko oyobi sono toji* (Perry's visit to the shores of Japan and those times). Tokyo 1936.

    vol. XXXII. *Kanagawa joyaku teiketsu-hen* (Conclusion of the Treaty of Kanagawa). Tokyo 1936.

    vol. XXXIII. *Nichi-Ro Ei-Ran joyaku teiketsu-hen* (Conclusion of treaties between Japan and Russia, England, and Holland). Tokyo 1929-1930.

    vol. XLIV. *Kaikoku shoki-hen* (The early years of Opened Japan). Tokyo 1936.

Tokyo Teikoku Daigaku (comp.). *Bakumatsu gaikoku kankei monjo* (Documents [pertaining to] foreign relations [during] the closing years of the Shogunate), series C of *Dai-Nihon ko-monjo* (Ancient documents of Japan). Tokyo 1901-

Treat, Payson J. *Diplomatic Relations between the United States and Japan, 1853-1895.* 2 vols., Stanford University 1932.

Tronson, J(ohn) M(ortlock), M.D. *Personal Narrative of a Voyage to Japan, Kamschatka, Siberia, Tartary, and various parts of coast of China; in H.M.S. Barracouta.* London 1859.

Tsuji, Zennosuke. *Kaigai kotsu shiwa* (History of Japanese intercourse with foreign countries). Tokyo 1930.

Turkovskii, V. "Krugosvetnoe puteshestvie neskol'kikh iapontsev cherez Sibir' sto let nazad" (Round the world voyage of several Japanese through Siberia a hundred years ago) (translation of "Weltreise mehrerer Japaner über Sibirien vor 100 Jahren," a survey by the Japanese "Kisak Tamai," appended to his own German diary *Karavanen-Reise in Sibirien*), *Istoricheskii vestnik*, vol. LXXIII (1898), pp. 193-210.

Uehara, Kumajiro (comp.). *Ezo-go senzen* (Complete Ezo language documents). Edo 1854.

Ukhtomskii, E. E. *Puteshestvie Gosudaria Imperatora Nikolaia II na Vostok (v 1890-1891)* (Journey of His Majesty the Emperor Nicholas II to the East [in 1890-1891]). 6 parts in 3 vols., St. Petersburg 1897.

Umemori, Saburo (comp.). *Nichi-Ro kokko shiryo* (Materials for the history of Russo-Japanese relations). Tokyo 1915.

Unger, Frederic William. *Russia and Japan and a Complete History of the War in the Far East.* Philadelphia 1905.

Van Straelen, H. *Yoshida Shoin, Forerunner of the Meiji Restoration. A Biographical Study.* Leiden 1952.

Veniukof (Veniukov), Colonel (Mikhail). "On the island of Saghalin" (translated from the Russian by Captain Spalding), *The Journal of the Royal Geographical Society*, vol. XLII (London 1872), pp. 373-388.

Veniukova, M. *Ocherki Iaponii* (Sketches of Japan). St. Petersburg 1869.

Vinacke, Harold M. *A History of the Far East in Modern Times.* 5 ed. New York 1950.

Vladimir (Volpicelli, Zenone). *Russia on the Pacific and the Siberian Railway.* London 1899.

Voeikov, Aleksandr Ivanovich. "Iz puteshestviia po Iaponii" (From a voyage across Japan), *Izvestiia Imperatorskago geograficheskago obshchestva*, vol. XIII (St. Petersburg 1877), part 2, pp. 195-240; vol. XIV (1878), part 2, pp. 142-204.

Voenskii, K. "Russkoe posol'stvo v Iaponiiu v nachale XIX veka. (Posol'stvo Rezanova v Iaponiiu v 1803-1805 gg.)" (A Russian embassy to Japan at the beginning of the 19th century. [The embassy of Rezanov to Japan in the years 1803-1805]), *Russkaia starina*, vol. LXXXIV (July 1895), pp. 123-141 (October), pp. 201-235.

Wada, Bunjiro. "Shiberia odan daiichi ninsha Saga Juan" (Saga Juan, the first [Japanese] to cross Siberia). Newspaper clippings in eight parts covering fifteen pages of a scrapbook in the Hakodate Municipal Library. Source and date unknown.

Walworth, Arthur. *Black Ships Off Japan.* New York 1949.

Ward, A. W. and G. W. Prothero and Stanley Leathes (ed.). *The Cambridge Modern History*, vol. XI (New York 1909).

Watanabe, Ikujiro. *Nihon kinsei gaiko-shi* (History of Japanese foreign relations in modern times). Tokyo 1938.

Watanabe, Shintaro (comp.). *Nichi-Ro kosho iho* (Collected information about Russo-Japanese relations). Tokyo 1896.

Watanabe, Shujiro. *Nichi-Ro kosho Takadaya Kahei* (Takadaya Kahei [who was connected with] Russo-Japanese relations. Tokyo 1900.

―――. *Sekai ni okeru Nihonjin* (Japanese in the world). Tokyo 1942.

Waxell, Sven. *The American Expedition.* Translated with an introduction and note by M. A. Michael. London 1952.

Weigh, K. S. *Russo-Chinese Diplomacy.* Shanghai 1928.

Whittingham, Capt. Bernard. *Notes on the Late Expedition against the Russian Settlements in Eastern Siberia; and of a Visit to Japan and to the Shores of Tartary, and of the Sea of Okhotsk.* London 1856.

Whyte, A. F. *China and Foreign Powers.* London 1927.

Wildes, Harry Emerson. *Aliens in the East. A New History of Japan's Foreign Intercourse.* Philadelphia 1937.

―――. "Russia Meets the Japanese," *The Russian Review*, vol. III, no. 1 (Autumn 1943), pp. 55-63.

―――. "Russia's Attempts to Open Japan," *The Russian Review*, vol. V, no. 1 (Autumn 1945), pp. 70-79.

Williams, Samuel Wells. "A Journal of the Perry Expedition to Japan (1853-1854)," *Transactions of the Asiatic Society of Japan*, ser. 1, vol. XXXVII, part 2 (Tokyo 1910), pp. 1-259.

Wroth, Lawrence C. *The Early Cartography of the Pacific*, vol. 38 of *The Papers of the Bibliographical Society of America*, no. 2, pp. 87-268, New York 1944.

Wu, Aitchen K. *China and the Soviet Union. A Study of Sino-Soviet Relations*. New York 1950.

Yakhontoff, Victor A. *Russia and the Soviet Union in the Far East*. London 1932.

Yamamoto, Hiroteru. "History of the Kuriles, Shikotan and the Habomai Islands," *Contemporary Japan*, vol. XX, nos. 10-12 (Tokyo, October-December 1951), pp. 459-495.

Yamasaki, Naozo. *L'action de la civilization européenne sur la vie japonaise avant l'arrivée du Commodore Perry* (The action of European civilisation on Japanese life before the arrival of Commodore Perry). Paris 1910.

Yamashita, Saichiro (comp.). *Takadaya Kahei den* (Biography of Takadaya Kahei). Tokyo 1884.

Yamazaki, Keizo. *Kodayu hyoryu monogatari (Roshiya jotei ni atta sento no hanashi)* (Account of Kodayu's being cast away [The story of the ship captain who met the Russian empress]). Tokyo 1949.

Yanaga, Chitoshi. *Japan since Perry*. New York 1949.

Yano, Niichi (ed.). *Roshia no toho seisaku* (Russia's Far Eastern policy) (vol. VI of *Ajia rekishi sosho* [History of Asia series]). Tokyo 1942.

Yarmolinsky, Avrahm. "A rambling note on the 'Russian Columbus' Nikolai Petrovich Rezanov," *Bulletin of the New York Public Library*, vol. XXXI, no. 9 (September 1927), pp. 707-713.

Yashiro, Kuniji, Hayakawa Junzaburo and Inobe Shigeo (ed.). *Kokushi dai-jiten* (Large dictionary of Japanese history). 6 vols., Tokyo 1927.

Yoshida, Togo (ed.). *Dai Nihon chimei jisho* (Encyclopedia of Japanese geographical names). 7 vols., Tokyo 1911-1913.

Yoshino, Sakuzo. *Rokoku kikan no hyoryu-min Kodayu* (The castaway Kodayu who returned from Russia). Tokyo 1924.

Yushu Matsumae Gorouin kojutsu Rogo hikae (Notes of Russian language dictated by Golovnin, prisoner in Matsumae). MS in Hakodate Municipal Library.

Zabriskie, Edward H. *American-Russian Rivalry in the Far East. A Study in Diplomacy and Power Politics 1895-1914*. Philadelphia 1946.

Zelenoi, K. "Iz zapisok o krugosvetnom plavanii (1861-1864 godu)" (From notes about an around the world voyage [in 1861-1864], *Morskoi Sbornik*, vol. LXXIX, no. 7 (July 1865), part 3, pp. 73-94.

Zepelin, General C. von. *Der Ferne Osten. Seine Geschichte, seine Entwicklung in der neuesten Zeit und seine Lage nach dem russisch-japanischen Kriege* (The Far East. Its history, its development in modern times and its position after the Russo-Japanese war) (vol. VIII of *Russland in Asien*). Berlin 1907.

Zhukov, E. M. (ed.). *Mezhdunarodnye otnosheniia na dal'nem vostoke (1870-1945 gg.)* (International relations in the Far East [1870-1945]). Moscow 1951.

Zhukov, Iurii. *Russkie i Iaponiia* (The Russians and Japan). Moscow 1945.

Znamenskii, S. *V poiskakh Iaponii, Iz istorii russkikh geograficheskikh otkrytii i morekhodstva v Tikhom Okeane* (In search of Japan, from the history of Russian geographical discoveries and seafaring in the Pacific Ocean). Vladivostok 1929.

Zybin, Efim. Letter to General Ia. V. Brius, general in charge of artillery, as quoted by D. P. Strukov, *Russkaia Starina*, vol. XI (October 1891), p. 464.

INDEX